Sincerely,

Don Crowzon

Even with unpaved streets, Winthrop College appeared quite modern in this 1920's aerial view. Some photographs are courtesy of Winthrop College.

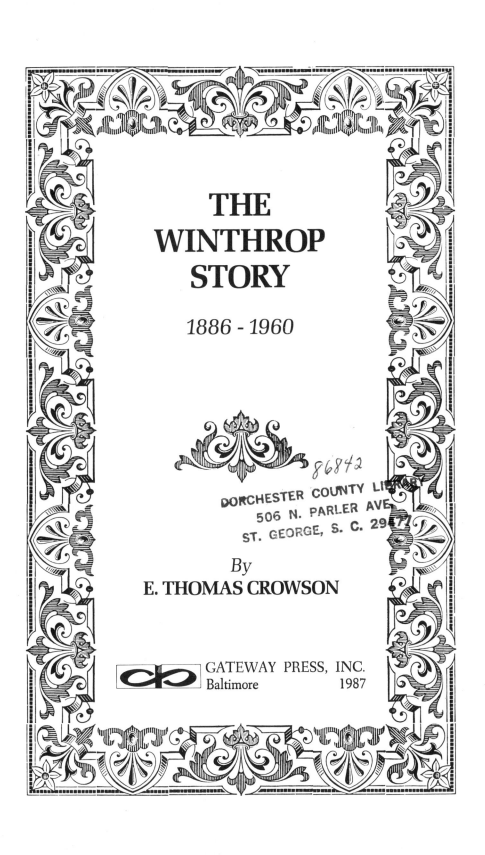

THE
WINTHROP
STORY

1886 - 1960

86842

By

E. THOMAS CROWSON

GATEWAY PRESS, INC.
Baltimore   1987

Please direct all correspondence and book orders to:

E. Thomas Crowson
657 Stratford Lane
Heritage Court
Rock Hill, SC 29730

Published for the author by
Gateway Press, Inc.
1001 N. Calvert Street
Baltimore, MD 21202

Made in the United States of America

TABLE OF CONTENTS

	Preface	i
I	The Rebirth of South Carolina Education	1
II	The Drive for Greater Economic, Political, and Educational Opportunities	8
III	A Modest Beginning	18
IV	Extending and Perfecting the Program	24
V	Ben Tillman Gives a Big Push	34
VI	Bidding for a State College	63
VII	Bringing Winthrop to Rock Hill	76
VIII	"Carolina's Crown of Glory"	97
IX	Building on a Firm Foundation, 1896–1909	120
X	Bringing Winthrop to Most South Carolina Homes, 1909–1913	172
XI	Reaching a Pinnacle of Influence and Performance, 1913–1919	223
XII	Institutionalizing D. B. Johnson, 1918–1929	316
XIII	President James Pinckney Kinard	406
XIV	Dr. Shelton Joseph Phelps Takes the Helm	462
XV	Senator Henry Radcliffe Sims Accepts the Challenge	503
	Index	590
	Epilogue	599

PREFACE

Thinking Americans are concerned today about education in the United States. Many blast the American educational system while comparing it to those in Germany, Japan, and other countries. While critics often blame weaknesses on school trustees, administrators, teachers, legislators, and others, those groups tend to point fingers at one another. And armchair experts abound. All too frequently a half-baked panacea promises to rectify the mistakes that a materialistic, single-minded populace has foisted on the nation and its unsuspecting, pleasure-oriented youth.

Over a century ago, following the Great War of 1861-1865 and political Reconstruction, education in the American South found itself in a similar situation: frequently weak, often inadequate, and sometimes nonexistent. Instead of pointing fingers, a small corps of public-spirited, educated leaders took reins in hand. With dedication, determination, and meager resources, they wrought educational miracles in several states including South Carolina.

In this rather detailed account of the Winthrop story, we see how a people were turned from despair and abject poverty, thanks to the leadership of Benjamin R. Tillman, Edward S. Joynes, David B. Johnson, John Swearingen, and many others. They developed a betterment program in South Carolina that emphasized work and learning and that met the needs of a people eager to turn their land away from despair toward hope, progress, and beauty. The documented story following is a classic example of what education means and what it can do when citizens care, will work, and will learn.

Over the past thirty years, I have observed the more modern aspects of the South's educational revolution and have researched its history, which I chronicle herein. Many people helped in the effort. Most especially, I wish to thank my daughter, Susan Crowson Hite, for her untiring efforts and expertise in shaping this manuscript. The account is also indebted to the late Miss Iva Bishop, who served Winthrop's first five presidents as either secretary, assistant, or archivist. Further, I am eternally thankful to the late Dr. and Mrs. Henry R. Sims for their help and thoughtfulness in making available invaluable information and papers. And I heartily thank Mrs. Crowson, who has encouraged my efforts for forty-three years and who read the manuscript. Also thanks go to Miss Rita Settle and Merry Secretarial Services, Inc., for their fine work in typing the material, and to Mary B. Crowson for her interest and help in expediting publication.

E. Thomas Crowson, 1986
657 Stratford Lane
Rock Hill, South Carolina
29730

CHAPTER I

THE REBIRTH OF SOUTH CAROLINA EDUCATION

The dawn of May 3, 1912, ushered in a pleasant day. Early that morning visitors began to assemble before the Main Hall of Winthrop College at Rock Hill, South Carolina. The crowd socialized. At 9:30 the roll of distinguished guests was called, and soon the procession composed of Masons, trustees, faculty, students and alumnae moved out and crossed Oakland Avenue to the new Training School, where the assembled crowd witnessed the laying of the cornerstone. After these ceremonies the procession re-formed and moved to the college Auditorium. There a scholarly old gentleman--with piercing eyes and a low-country accent--gave a proud, straight-forward account of the "Origin and Early History of Winthrop College."[1]

Speaking at this twenty-fifth anniversary celebration, Dr. Edward Southey Joynes, a living symbol of the educational progress of the New South, enjoyed distinction as the only surviving member of the original Winthrop trustee board. Speaking with authority, this gentleman of the "old school" gave a forceful description of how two diverse, yet concurrent, influences had played a large part in the development of this college. Joynes reminded his appreciative audience that the great institutions of civilization owed their origins generally to concurrent and often distinct influences, "working unconsciously together under separate leadership" and in the process "progressively educating the public mind to needed change." Such was the case with Winthrop.[2]

Although Dr. Joynes was retired on that fine May morning when he spoke to the Winthrop community, his life of service in education actually extended from 1858 to the 1920s. These years were in many respects the most barren and difficult in the annals of Southern educational history, for during that period the transition from Old to New South took place with the attendant

1

hardships of civil strife, "Reconstruction," and general economic depression. Through all difficulties Joynes persevered, building an untarnished record as gentleman scholar. And ultimately on December 19, 1907, the Carnegie Fund for the Advancement of Teaching would honor him with a life annuity for his service to Southern education.

Born at the Montpelier plantation in Accomack County, Virginia, he was the youngest of a prominent lawyer-planter's nine children. Schooled on the plantation and at the nearby Latin School in the court-house village, Joynes entered the University of Virginia at sixteen. Three years of hard work brought him a master's degree with an assistantship at his alma mater. When his father died in 1856, Edward was left a plantation, slaves, a large library, and money to complete his education.[3]

Joynes completed his formal training in modern languages at the University of Berlin in 1858. During his stay he travelled extensively in western Europe, availing himself of the cultural benefits of art galleries, concert halls, museums, and zoological and botanical gardens. While at Berlin, Joynes was elected to the Chair of Greek and German at the College of William and Mary, the second oldest institution of higher learning in the United States.[4]

Professor Joynes's sojourn at Williamsburg, Virginia, was most fruitful. Marrying a lovely and gifted young lady, Miss Eliza Waller Vest, Joynes settled down to a profitable and rewarding career. But civil conflict soon ingulfed the nation and Joynes moved to Richmond, where he was assigned as the Chief Civilian Administrative Officer of the Confederate War Department. In this capacity he became acquainted with General Robert E. Lee.[5]

Near the end of the War, Joynes left government to teach at the Hollins Institute in Virginia, one of the South's best seminaries for the higher education of women. This was the beginning of Joynes's long association with women's

2

education. After two years, he left for Washington College in Lexington to fill the chair of English under President Robert E. Lee. There Joynes was instrumental in making English a specific field of collegiate study, the first time it was so recognized in the South. To Joynes, this period was his "golden age." His attachment to General Lee was very strong; following Lee's death, Joynes became restless. Later he moved to the newly created Vanderbilt University in Nashville, Tennessee.[6]

Joynes worked hard at Vanderbilt. He was the first professor of modern languages and English. According to Edward Mims, Vanderbilt's official historian, Joynes was dismissed after three years because his drinking habits had rendered him unacceptable to this Methodist institution. Mims suggests that Joynes's drinking was confined to wine and beer, a habit acquired during his residence in Europe. Despite this, the record at Vanderbilt shows Joynes was a good teacher, an excellent scholar, and a very popular person, except with the Methodist hierarchy.[7]

From 1878 to 1882 Joynes occupied a similar chair at the new East Tennessee University. Recognizing Joynes's affinity for politics, the Tennesseans sent him to represent their institution before the General Assembly at Nashville to help in securing its recognition as the University of Tennessee. Joynes touched many lives beneficially in Nashville and at the university: Among the latter was a student, David Bancroft Johnson, who came to South Carolina and later became famous in Southern education. Joynes left Tennessee in 1882 for the South Carolina College, where he, Johnson, and Benjamin R. Tillman became a great educational triumvirate in late nineteenth-century educational advancements of South Carolina.[8]

Building anew from a base of despondency born of the rigors and dislocations of war and "Reconstruction," South Carolina had lost her once proud standing as a center for an elite and educated aristocracy. Jabez L. M. Curry, one of the foremost educational leaders in the post-bellum period suggested in 1889 that the South had been heretofore a leader in higher education. Quoting the 1860 census, Curry pointed out that the North with 19,000,000 people had fewer colleges than the South had with 8,000,000. The North boasted of 205 colleges, 1407 professors, and 29,044 students compared with 262 colleges in the South where 1488 professors taught 27,055 students. However, this emphasis had radically changed by 1880 in South Carolina, except in the fading memories of the broken aristocracy.[9]

The rigors of war and "Reconstruction" had a devastating effect on the free schools, academies, and colleges of South Carolina, most of which dated from the early decades of the nineteenth century. Even the once-proud Carolina College closed its doors during "Reconstruction" and became a casualty of The Prostrate State. As for the public schools, the Constitution of 1868 provided for a state-wide system of public education, supported by taxation, with a State Superintendent of Education popularly elected as well as local boards entrusted with local control of the system. The system was handicapped by economic and social confusion. Little had been done between 1868 and 1877, when Hugh S. Thompson, the State Superintendent, began a program designed to develop public education throughout South Carolina.[10]

In the 1870s and 1880s, Thompson's work was vital in breathing life into the newly constituted school system. Attempting to train students and teachers was no easy task in a state where the ravages of war and an impotent economy resulted in little money that could be appropriated for any services. Despite these handicaps, South Carolina could count 3,057 public-school teachers in 1881. A majority of the towns in this predominately rural state had "fairly adequate" systems, but the rural schools were substandard in most respects. Following the leadership of the Graniteville Manufacturing Company, several mills had started schools for the children of their employees. But the greatest advance at this time revolved around the teacher-training Institutes held each summer in selected areas of the state.[11]

4

The Teacher's Institutes movement spread rapidly in the South. The first general agent of the Peabody Education Board, Dr. Barnas Sears, had brought them to Virginia in 1867. Sears was a distinguished man full of years and honor, having served as the Secretary of the Massachusetts Board of Education and President of Brown University. At first general distrust met this Yankee's mission. Some felt that carpetbag educators could not be trusted, but after receiving a cordial reception from President Robert E. Lee and his faculty at Washington College, Dr. Sears and his Institutes enjoyed the support of the educational community.[12]

In 1875 Dr. Sears offered financial aid to Tennessee for teacher training. There Dr. Joynes, who had been a part of the Virginia program, worked with Sears and the state superintendent in the early teacher-training institution of that state.[13]

In like manner, Dr. Sears gave counsel and assistance to State Superintendent Thompson of South Carolina, helping in 1881 to organize the first Teacher's Institute there. Among the faculty suggested by Sears were Louis Soldan and Edward Joynes, both of whom had studied in the highly effective university system of Germany. Professor Soldan had attained a reputation in Missouri for his normal-school work, and Joynes had gained recognition as one of the South's foremost scholars.[14]

Joynes had worked closely with the Peabody Educational Board, which was dedicated to improving education, and had considerable experience with the Teacher's Institutes. He was regarded as a "zealous promoter" of public education from the primary to the university. For years he stressed the values of education, always making this simple statement: "It was the education of Germany that conquered France." Coming in 1880 from Knoxville to Spartanburg, Joynes associated himself with Thompson and Soldan. Soon the three became close friends as co-workers in the first Teacher's Institute in South Carolina.[15]

This fledgling Institute proved to be a novelty as well as a fruitful experience for 197

South Carolina teachers and many townspeople (who attended the public lectures at night). The mid-summer work was conducted during approximately four weeks in the chapel and classrooms of Wofford College. Professor Joynes was much impressed with Mr. Thompson and the whole affair. He related to a friend that each day after school was out, "we lived and conversed into the wee small hours." Since Joynes liked to talk and to meet people, he highly praised the good fellowship and witty conversations, calling the latter some of the best he had encountered. Joynes had found another mutual admiration society.[16]

The first Summer Institute's success prompted Superintendent Thompson to schedule two for the summer of 1881. Writing to Robert Means Davis, principal of the highly regarded Mount Zion Academy in Winnsboro, Thompson stated that there would be an "Institute for colored teachers" in Columbia July 5 through 29, and an "Institute for white teachers" at Greenville August 2 through August 29. Soldan would lead the Greenville Institute and Joynes would lecture the whole summer. With the state and the Peabody Fund underwriting these, Thompson agreed to pay Davis $125 for heading a department in the white Institute. The regular course included Normal instructions in methods of teaching reading, English language, geography, arithmetic, and pedagogies. Optional courses included Latin, German, French, algebra, physical geography, vocal music, and calisthenics. Dr. Joynes's lectures were eloquent, attractive, and useful for the new light they threw upon studying the mother tongue.[17]

This 1881 Institute served 335 teachers at Greenville and established the desire for more teacher training. Since Superintendent Thompson was preparing to run for Governor, the 1882 Institute was scheduled at Carolina College under the general management of Professor M. A. Newell of Baltimore. Before this began, some of the leading educators and governor-elect Thompson of South Carolina laid plans to bring Joynes and Soldan to Carolina College as permanent professors to help rejuvenate the sleeping school. Replying to Means

Davis's proposal, the flattered Joynes refused to be an active candidate for the job. Expressing pride in the proposal, Joynes declared that he would be "most happy to live and work in South Carolina." However, Joynes was concerned about the trustees, on whom, he wrote, "will depend whether or not the old college may be renewed." Much correspondence resulted. In the summer, 1882, Joynes was called to the chair of Modern Languages and English at the South Carolina College.[18] Joynes had finally found a compatible home for his talents, moving eventually into a position of strength and influence in South Carolina education.

In November, 1882, the optimistic Joynes reported to Dr. John McBryde, chairman of the faculty, that "the burden of my work is greatly lightened by the good will, zeal and facility of the students under my instruction." However, at the end of the first semester, Joynes wrote again to McBryde, saying that nearly two-thirds of his first-year students in English had fallen below passing. This, Joynes emphasized, "proves simply that these young men are not prepared for collegiate courses." Joynes still continued to work in the Teachers's Institutes, broadening the program to serve more teachers who would send better-prepared students to college. The versatility of Joynes, his facility for inspiring learning, and his practice of walking around the campus and helping students whom he found studying helped him and his students overcome many obstacles. The drive for more public education was building under a new head of steam.[19]

CHAPTER II

THE DRIVE FOR GREATER ECONOMIC, POLITICAL
AND EDUCATIONAL OPPORTUNITIES

"There is no tonic like work
and hope, except love."

Edward Joynes

The "Tragic Era" had made an indelible imprint on South Carolina which only time and prosperity could erase. Defeat, devastation, disillusionment, and political servitude were the by-products of Civil War. Armies of occupation and vengeful "Reconstruction" had applied salt to painful wounds. Disintegration of the old social order resulted in greater emphasis on the white up-country farmer, who by sheer numbers played a large part in redeeming the state from all vestiges of carpetbag, scalawag, and Negro-militia rule. All crusades and considerations were subordinated to the return to home rule and to the drive to reestablish economic solvency.[1]

After the redeemers regained control of South Carolina, they examined the damages of the previous governments, setting immediate priorities. They attempted to give some relief to the citizenry. Included in new laws were stricter regulation of railroads, the establishment of an agricultural experiment station with state inspection of fertilizer, and the passage of usury and fence laws. The state government was run largely by the Wade Hampton genre of old aristocrat and by the new, aggressive merchant and banking classes. They concentrated on honesty and economical administration. These so-called Bourbons monopolized the political offices and privileges of the state. However, the great majority of the nearly 400,000 whites were farmers who were dissatisfied with the economics and politics of aristocratic South Carolina.[2]

Typical of this dissatisfaction was a considerable up-country farmer, Benjamin Ryan Tillman of Edgefield County. Working hard during

8

"Reconstruction," Tillman had made money and had added to his land holdings. As a member of the Sweetwater Saber Club and later its captain, he had been quite active in the redemption movement, becoming a respected leader and a member of his county's Democratic-party executive committee. Beginning in 1881, his operations were beset with droughts, crop failures, "sickening" prices paid to county merchants, and foreclosures. Tillman became convinced that something was radically wrong. He analyzed his personal failures as being due to insufficient agricultural training.[3]

Concurrently there was a drive by the North's farmers to share in the country's one-sided prosperity. Their desire for greater economic justice resulted in the establishment of the Patrons of Husbandry, commonly called the Grange. The Grange spread quickly in the Middle West and the South, for its principal objectives included railroad reform through fixing uniform rates and cooperative buying to limit merchants' profits. The grangers wanted to eliminate middlemen and to buy from mail-order houses. In addition the farm-based grangers wanted cheap money, equalization of taxes, and the general improvement of rural life through education and training of both farm boys and girls.[4]

Colonel D. H. Jacques of Charleston is credited with introducing the Grange into South Carolina. With his paper The Rural South Carolinian, Jacques helped to spread the philosophy of the Grange. The organization soon became a force in the state's economic, political, and educational life. Grangers had notable success in cooperative buying and selling ventures and in applying general economic pressure on the Bourbon-oriented politicians who controlled the state. Many political leaders were outwardly sympathetic with the farmers' aspirations. Yet, with the philosophy of laissez-faire and social Darwinism uppermost in the thinking of many politicians, the farmers could not expect much relief. However, South Carolina created a Department of Agriculture and provided for a Railroad Commissioner to make the railroads more sensitive to their demands. The farmer was not placated. The Grange later declined in South Carolina, its remnants joining hands with the Agricultural and Mechanical Society to hold summer meetings in the various villages.[5]

The Grange had taught the farmers the advantages of political action. It pointed the finger at government, demanding a redress for its ills. This new approach--coupled with the 1880s decline in the value of staple crops and the 1887 forfeiture of over one-million acres in South Carolina for non-payment of taxes--created great unrest and resentment, especially among the hard-pressed farmers. The discontentment had remained general but unchanneled until 1886 when Benjamin Tillman led the dissidents in organizing the Farmers' Association.[6]

Initiating this movement before a joint meeting of the Agricultural and Mechanical Society and the remaining grangers at Bennettsville in 1885, Ben Tillman, a delegate from Edgefield, drew a gloomy picture of the state's agrarian situation. To remedy the situation, Tillman proposed using the Morrill Act (land-grant money then channeled to Carolina) for practical agricultural education by establishing a separate agricultural and mechanical college. He pointed up the value of the Farmers' Institutes in spreading agricultural knowledge and proposed a State Board of Agriculture composed of farmers. Tillman reinforced his Bennettsville speech with a series of articles in the Charleston News and Courier that elaborated on his ideas. But all these efforts failed to stir the Legislature to immediate reform.[7]

In time Tillman became agriculture's Moses: the farmers' pent-up indignation had found a voice in a man who was proud to be called a farmer. Tillman successfully organized the Farmers' Association on a statewide basis. In a state convention held in Columbia on April 19, 1886, he was elected chairman of the legislative and perma-nent executive committees. A program of reform was voted at this meeting. It contained proposals to reduce the salaries paid by the state and to separate the "agricultural annex" (the department at the Carolina College) from the liberal arts. The Farmers' Association further asked that the state establish an industrial college for women. They demanded repeal of the "Lien's Law" and a state constitutional convention to write a new constitution recognizing the aspirations of the rural democracy. The farmers determined to push their fight for republican government and justice within the framework of the Democrat party.[8]

The Farmers' Convention held in Columbia in late April, 1886, fired the opening shot for the political campaign of 1886. With this blazing gun Tillman aimed to control the Democrat State Convention in August: should he win, he would be in a favorable position to nominate the next governor. Tillman did not have the necessary votes in the Convention to hit his target. He was unable to prevent the nomination of conservative John Peter Richardson of Clarendon County and to win an endorsement for the farmers' program. In the ensuing elections, Richardson won. But the Tillmanites had gained members, especially in the House.[9]

When the new session of the Legislature opened in December, 1886, men pushed for Tillman's agriculturally oriented program. Bills were introduced to implement the program, but the Senate checked the Tillmanic surge. Only one important measure, that of creating experiment stations, cleared the Senate hurdle. Pressure for an agricultural college resulted in a "fact finding" investigation. The Commissioner of Agriculture, Colonel A. P. Butler, solicited views concerning the proposed Agricultural and Mechanical College for South Carolina. The manner in which this was handled speaks for itself.[10]

Governor Richardson--as ex-officio chairman of the Board of Agriculture--reported to the Legislature that letters had been sent out to the leading people of the state, and "We regret to say," he continued, "that the replies received were not of such character as to furnish the legislature the

11

information desired." Not explaining this, Richardson stated further that "with one exception, therefore, these replies are omitted from this report." The exception was a communication from Tillman, and Governor Richardson said it "is published herewith, because it purports to be the reply of the executive committee of the Farmers' Association, an organization which, it is understood, favors the establishment of the College." This lengthy report reads:

Roper's, S.C., October 5th, 1887

Col. A. P. Butler, Commissioner Agriculture, Columbia, S.C.

Sir: Some time ago I received a communication from you, asking on behalf of the Board of Agriculture that I furnish them with 'any facts or data in my possession bearing on the location and probable or approximate cost of an Agricultural and Mechanical College in this State,' and subsequently in another letter you include in your inquiry 'the scope of instruction and the curriculum of studies to be required at the proposed College.'

Similar inquiries, addressed to other advocates of the Agricultural College, have been referred to me, as Chairman of the Executive Committee of the Farmers' Association, by those who received them, and I will therefore make my reply officially, and as an authoritative expression of the opinions and wishes of that Association, so far as it can be done in the absence of any action thereon by the Association.

First, as to 'location':

The consideration which should govern the choice of a site for the proposed College, in our opinion, should be:

12

1st, a healthy location, free from malarial influences, so that students from all parts of the State can attend it without danger of sickness. 2d. Accessibility to a railroad, so it can be easily reached. 3d. Other things being equal, the preference should be given to that portion of the State in which no higher institution of learning supported by the State is now located. 4th. A farm of not less than one thousand acres, embracing as great variety of soil as possible, and of not too poor land, should be secured to build the College on. 5th. Competition among the different counties as to which shall have the College should be allowed by authorizing any County or private individuals to donate land or bonds or money to secure it. And the Board of Control should be governed in their choice of a site by all of these things, without, however, allowing any one of them to outweigh the rest.

As a matter of information, attention is called to the De La Howe property in Abbeville, donated for educating poor orphans, and which, if the terms of the will allow, would make a very eligible site, as it consists of a large plantation of productive land, situated on Little River, within one and one-half miles of the Savannah Valley Railroad.

Second, as to the 'probable or approximate cost':

The only information I have on this point is contained in a private letter to me from Governor Stephen D. Lee, President of the Agricultural and Mechanical College of Mississippi. Writing under date of September 28th, 1866, he said: 'The [our] building was done by a Committee of Board of Trustees

13

under contract. I think improvements can
be made on our plan. In your financial
strait, coupled with calamity at
Charleston, $50,000 will give you a fair
start in building if you have a good farm
with conveniences. We got $80,000 first
appropriation. You will need at least
$100,000 to set you up in good working
order.' Further along he adds: 'We
started too hurriedly and without proper
information. We could have saved a good
deal had we visited other Colleges of
similar character and laid all our plans
before we started to build.'

By utilizing convict labor in such
work as can be thus economically performed
in erecting the College buildings, I feel
perfectly satisfied that we can build a
College in South Carolina for a good deal
less than the Mississippi College cost and
for $100,000 obtain a better plant and
more thorough equipment than they have in
Mississippi.

Third. As to the 'course of
instruction' to be taught in the proposed
College:

I am not aware that the duty of
reporting on this subject was imposed on
the Board, but supposing the question to
be asked in good faith and for the purpose
of obtaining information which the
catalogue of the South Carolina College
does not furnish, I will cheerfully answer
it. The course of instruction should
embrace the English Language and
literature, Mathematics, Agricultural
Chemistry, Animal and Vegetable Physiology, the Veterinary Art, Entomology,
Geology, Technology, Political and Farm
Economy, Horticulture, Moral Philosophy,
History, Physics, Bookkeeping, and
especially the practice and application

14

of Science and the Mechanic Arts to agriculture in the field. 'Military Tactics' should be 'included' and possibly German and French, as those languages have become so rich in scientific agricultural literature. It would depend on how the money held out.

I have, sir, answered your questions as fully and clearly as I can, but I stand ready to give any additional explanation or information in my power.

Yours respectfully,

B. R. Tillman.

The statement to the Legislature that followed this letter and bore the Governor's name suggested that the Board of Agriculture did not consider that it was called upon for any opinion or recommendations on this subject. The foregoing report was therefore submitted without comment.[11]

The subservience and inaction of the Legislature elicited Tillman's castigation and ridicule. He scorned Richardson's act to rename South Carolina College with its 192 students the University of South Carolina. Tillman attacked the "obligarchy of lawyers" in the Senate, engaging a leading senator in public debate and (with the aid of a sympathetic audience) forcing the senator to leave the meeting unheard. Disappointed with the Legislature, Tillman contended that they had been "debauched" by free liquors and entertainment. In disgust, he went into semi-retirement, feeling that his program had been turned down partly because of negative reactions to his own personality. But the seeds of change had been well sown. Retirement for Ben Tillman was impossible.[12]

A new dimension appeared on South Carolina's agrarian scene in 1887-1888. Just when the Tillman movement seemingly began to decline, the Farmers' Alliance (a national organization) began to win the support of many South Carolina farmers. The Alliance was dedicated "to labor for the education of the agricultural classes in the science of economical government in a strictly non-Partisan spirit." Its purposes were fourfold: social, educational, economic, and political. A vital facet of their program was their official organ, The Cotton Plant, a publication which served first the Grange and later the South Carolina Agricultural and Mechanical Society. [13]

In addition, the death of Thomas G. Clemson, son-in-law of John C. Calhoun, in April 1888 had a profound influence on the agricultural picture in South Carolina. Previously, Clemson and Tillman had discussed the needs of South Carolina agriculture. Clemson had agreed to leave his estate to South Carolina for an agricultural college. The will named seven life trustees, including Tillman, to control and perpetuate the bequest. The executive committee of the Farmers' Association--meeting in Columbia in April 1888--scripted a letter demanding that all candidates support the ideas of Clemson and that all agricultural teaching be consolidated on the Fort Hill estate of Calhoun. Opposition developed because the will implied private control of a would-be state institution. The Legislature's Clemson College Bill passed in December, 1888; Governor Richardson withheld his signature pending the outcome of a lawsuit contesting the will's validity. Following favorable counteraction, Governor Richardson signed the Clemson College Act, accepting the bequest on November 27, 1889. [14]

The fight over Clemson established a firm bridge-head in South Carolina politics which eventually allowed Tillman to rise to a position of eminent power. W. A. James in his reminiscences about the affair stated:

Clemson College, which was referred to to in a debate on the floor of the Senate as 'that infernal proposition' is one of the outstanding achievements of that [Tillman] great movement, and I am convinced and I know that but for the

16

exact timely bequest of Mr. Clemson, Clemson College would not have materialized; and there being no Clemson, there would have been no Winthrop. Women have always been repressed in South Carolina, and a college for women, with its threat to diminish the support flowing to the male schools, was diametrically opposed to the principles and policies of old South Carolina, thus their opposition to its establishment was more prolonged, and sustained with more energy than they directed to Clemson. [15]

This personal testimony by a knowledgeable Tillmanite stressed the fact that "the question of a college for women and a college for agriculture can be traced through all the discussions in alliance meetings, and those two items naturally and quietly dropped into every platform and remained therein." Of equal significance was Tillman's push (for a second time in 1888) for statewide canvass. But the demand in 1890 that state candidates must be invited by all county chairmen to speak in their respective counties brought action. Now Tillman saw a chance for achieving his goals--election as governor and a reorganization of South Carolina's government, following his election. [16]

On December 4, 1890, following his decisive election, a large crowd gathered in the plaza before the state capitol to witness Tillman's inauguration as governor of South Carolina. Thereby a new regime was born that changed South Carolina completely and lasted well beyond its leader's death in 1918. [17]

17

CHAPTER III

A MODEST BEGINNING

"Teaching is the highest industry, and
offers the broadest field of work for
women in this section of the country."

David Bancroft Johnson

The South Carolina College, established in
1801 and reporting to the Honorable Senate and House
of Representatives in 1886, characterized the senior
class of 1885-1886 one of the largest and most
successful in the history of the college. Only
twice had its present number of matriculates, 213,
been exceeded. In its report, the college stressed
that not the slightest disturbance had occurred
during that year. The student body, they reported,
consisted of ten postgraduates, sixteen law
students, eighteen sub-freshmen, and 171 academic
under-graduates. These statistics describe the most
important educational endeavor in South Carolina at
that time. [1]

A few blocks removed from the Carolina College on Washington Street in Columbia, the capital
city of South Carolina, young and determined
superintendent of the city schools D.B. Johnson was
preoccupied in 1886 with another educational
program, while attempting to run the small city's
public-school system. He was very much concerned
with organizing a new school to train teachers. The
young schoolman, an attractive gentleman of medium
height, could be seen all hours of the day while
moving from his office to the classroom and while
frequently walking earnestly in the streets to
superintend the whole public-education program.
This dedicated man wore a black Van Dyke beard with
the typical black suit and the cutaway coat. To the
recalcitrant student, Johnson, with his somber
countenance and left arm severed at the elbow, must
have been an awesome figure. Some of his students
learned quickly that Superintendent Johnson had no
trouble slinging a boy across his lap, planting the

arm stub in the middle of his back, and vigorously applying the rattan cane always available on such occasions.[2]

Johnson had graduated from the University of Tennessee "with first honors" and as Valedictorian of his class. Staying on to teach and study, he earned a master's degree in mathematics. In 1880 he went to Abbeville as superintendent of schools. Moving in 1882 to New Bern, North Carolina, he reorganized their schools but soon grew unhappy because of the coastal climate. In 1883 Dr. Edward S. Joynes, one of the foremost educators of the South, invited Johnson to move to Columbia to be Superintendent of Schools. Here Johnson began an unique chapter in the history of American education.[3]

Johnson's family had been associated with Hingham, Massachusetts, and Dresden, Maine, as well as La Grange and Memphis, Tennessee, and Holly Springs, Mississippi. In the summer of 1883, Johnson went North, where he enrolled in education lectures at Martha's Vineyard. Johnson evaluated several of the progressive books he owned or was studying preparatory to returning to Columbia. Joseph Payne's Science and Art of Teaching was to Johnson the best book "for solid deep reading and study on educational matters." He felt, however, that it was "too deep for women [teachers] to master in a short time." Johnson was then studying with a Colonel Parker who was quite controversial and did not want to become too closely associated with him even though Parker was "giving some grand lectures which are being enjoyed by me very much." Parker had given to Quincy, Massachusetts, one of the foremost systems of the country and Johnson had gone North especially to study with him.[4]

The big problems Johnson faced in the Columbia city schools were money and qualified personnel. He had become acutely aware of the lack of resources, yet he was determined to improve the schools. Years later Johnson reminded Joynes that most people had not known that "we raised some money in the North in the winter of 1883-84 to keep the Columbia city schools opened, as they had promised to do. Even with some special help from the city council, the schools had to be run the last two months of the nine months session on tuition."[5]

With Joynes and other interested citizens to help him, Johnson concentrated on improving the system by employing better teachers. The task seemed almost hopeless. Finally in 1886, while in the North seeking aid for a teacher-training program, Johnson was introduced by Dr. A.D. Mayo to Mr. Robert Winthrop, President of the Peabody Fund, who after hearing the young superintendent at his home in Brookline, Massachusetts, responded to Johnson's plea and promised $2,000 to help establish a training school for teachers in Columbia.[6]

There was little money in Columbia then for public use: the city had overspent its meager budget to provide water and power by developing the old Columbia canal. Thus, when Superintendent Johnson returned home with a promise of $2,000 to help train teachers, many were impressed. Johnson, who was well established then as the head of the small public-school system, met with prospective students to explain the school's purpose. He made plans for the fall opening of the proposed training school. Johnson stated later that "the city of Columbia did not contribute a dollar to its establishment other than my time."[7]

Mr. Johnson had the good fortune of being given the exclusive use of their chapel and free run of the other buildings and the grounds by the trustees of the Columbia Theological Seminary. (Interestingly, the chapel--a former coachhouse-- would later be moved to Rock Hill where it would serve as a chapel in which he would ultimately lie entombed.) These buildings had been planned in 1823 by the South Carolina architect Robert Mills, as the home of Columbia's merchant prince, Ainsley Hall. The Theological Seminary had been located in Columbia since 1829--a small, but outstanding, school. It was there that the Book of Church Order was rewritten for the Presbyterians in 1861,

20

and among its faculty in the postbellum period was Dr. Joseph Wilson, the father of Thomas Woodrow Wilson. Visiting Columbia before becoming President of the United States in 1913, Tommy Wilson (as he was known in Columbia) remarked when he visited the chapel that "on the whole the best speaking I ever heard in my life was in this little chapel." It was to this small building that a dedicated group repaired on Monday, November 15, 1886, to conduct a public exercise that would inaugurate the most important event in Columbia that school year-- namely, the establishment of a training school for teachers. [8]

Final arrangements were perfected after the October meeting of the Peabody Board. The new Winthrop Training School was organized under the general powers conferred by law upon the board of school commissioners of Columbia, South Carolina. Under the Chairmanship of Fitz Hugh W. McMaster and his fellow trustees, R. L. Bryan, William H. Lyles, W. C. Swaffield, John P. Thomas, Jr., Dr. Edward S. Joynes, and W. J. Duffie, the school was begun in earnest. Bearing the name of the Honorable Robert Charles Winthrop of Massachusetts (whose father and uncle had lived in Charleston), this training school was a fitting tribute to a venerable statesman, orator, and philanthropist. [9]

With the seminary's move to Georgia, Winthrop had nothing to hinder its progress, and on the opening day, seventeen young ladies of good families presented themselves as applicants. Having passed an entrance examination in all those subjects of the "common school study," they enrolled in a three-term session consisting of five, sixteen, and seven weeks respectively. Pursuing courses in arithmetic, geography, music, drawing, calisthenics, practice teaching and observation, they were under the guidance of Superintendent Johnson, Miss Mary H. Leonard (the principal), Miss Annie E. Bonham (the practice teacher) and Mrs. T. C. Robertson (the drawing instructor). [10]

The teachers were an unusually talented group. Miss Leonard, for example, was a graduate of and a former teacher in the Bridgewater Normal School in Massachusetts. She rendered valuable service along with the others to this new adventure in Columbia. During the first year twenty-one pupils enrolled, fourteen of whom completed the course of study and received diplomas from the School. Twelve of the graduates were residents of Columbia; the other two hailed from Summerville and Union County. [11]

The session climaxed with the June 16 graduation at the seminary chapel. Each class member explained or demonstrated a topic from her study to the audience. "The following was the program, which was listened to by an attentive and interested audience": After the devotional, Miss Louise D. Senn demonstrated "forms of water." Next Miss Isabelle R. Monteith presented "principal parts of the verb." Then the program was enlivened by a demonstration of hand exercises. Miss M. Elizabeth Muller followed with a classroom situation in which she explained the parts of a flower. Miss Maggie P. Senn was next with a discourse on seeds and growth. Again after two more demonstrations, the pace changed with the singing of "Nymphs of the Ocean Spray." Turning to the more serious side, Miss M. Margaret Selby discussed percentage and interest, Miss Emma B. Carrington gave her project on "exercise in form," and Miss Charlotte R. Burckmyer talked about "areas of rectilinear figures." Then the graduates sang "Sweet and Low." A lesson in color by Miss Frances R. Butler, a talk by Miss Agnes K. McMaster on inductive and deductive reasoning, and exercises with dumbbells were concluded before the recess. After a short break, the graduates sang "Who Will to the Greenwood Hie?" Miss Esther M. Miller proceeded to give her project on "geographical positions." The class valedictorian, Miss Sarah Ida Knight of Union, discussed longitude and time. Miss Minnie A. Marks demonstrated drawing, Miss Florence M. Curry explained the walls of the body, and Miss Kittie C. Ballinger concluded with an explanation of the ear. [12] The final song, perhaps appropriately designated for these exercises, was "Fast the Night is Falling."

Since this first graduation was such an auspicious occasion, the next evening public exercises were held for the graduates in the Columbia Opera House. These consisted of songs by the graduates, music by an orchestra, presentation of Peabody Medals and other awards, the valedictory, and presentation of diplomas by Governor John Peter Richardson.[13]

D. B. Johnson, Secretary and Treasurer of the Board of Trustees of the Winthrop Training School, made his first fiscal report on June 17, 1887. He listed under resources a $1500 donation by the Peabody Board, $217.75 tuition fees, and a $50.00 library donation from Robert C. Winthrop. This $1,767.75 was spent for the following: $1410.00 for salaries; $126.30 for fuel, printing lectures, and wages; $41.50 for furniture and supplies; and $40.37 for the library--leaving a balance to credit of $149.58. This report climaxed one of the most monumental years in South Carolina education. With so little, so much had been wrought.[14]

CHAPTER IV

EXTENDING AND PERFECTING THE PROGRAM

"I cannot but feel that whatever
is done for public instruction,
from the Atlantic to the Pacific
is done for the whole country;
and I can hardly rejoice less in
the progress of a college at
Columbia than if it were at my
own Cambridge."

Robert Charles Winthrop

The first graduates of the Winthrop Training
School were in great demand to fill local positions.
One of the graduates went to California and there
began a teaching career. Miss Sarah Ida Knight, the
first valedictorian, was employed as an assistant at
the Training School, which in its second year
established itself at a new location on Marion
Street near the Washington Street Graded School.[1]

In planning for the second session,
Superintendent Johnson projected his needs. During
the year 1887-88, the school would be in a permanent
building which could be arranged to suit its needs
and this would be most beneficial. Pointing up the
desirability of finishing the second story of the
permanent building, Johnson was thinking aloud as to
how this might be accomplished. The school was
experiencing great difficulty in procuring a few
maps and other educational aids. Johnson reported
that they needed a good globe and a complete set of
wall maps. They needed a manikin or, failing this,
a set of paper models known as Yaggy's Anatomical
Study. Also the school had no drawing aids and no
standard weights and measures for use in the
arithmetic classes. The library was almost nonexistent. They needed reference books in history,
literature, and natural sciences. The superintendent stressed in his report that the library
would be improved as fast as funds permitted. But
he added that "if any of the friends of the School

24

have it in their power to supply any of these needs, they may feel assured that such gifts will be appreciated and put to good use." [2]

Before the second session began on September 26, 1887, Columbia's Board of School Commissioners had adopted some additional regulations to guide the infant institution. The annual session was arranged to coincide with that of the city schools and was divided into three terms lasting twelve weeks each. Tuition cost $2.00 a month or $5.00 a term in advance. The board prescribed the curriculum. Applicants had to be seventeen and, before entering, had to express their intention of faithfully observing all the regulations of the school and, afterwards, of engaging in the teaching profession. [3]

By October a good class of undergraduates from all over the state were pursuing a Normal [a popular term denoting teacher training] course which included logical reviews of all subjects necessary to produce well-prepared teachers. And if a student had defective preparation, special lessons were planned as part of her teacher training. [4]

As of October 1887 many students, unable to come earlier, had expressed the hope that a new class would be formed after Christmas. This arrangement was agreed to as an alternative to receiving students in mid-term, thereby interfering materially with the school's proper conduct. Since instruction featured lectures and demonstrations, the system precluded a student's entering late in any term. [5]

The Winthrop Training School received a wonderful present on Christmas Eve, 1887, when Governor John P. Richardson, President of the Senate W. L. Mauldin, and Speaker James Simons signed an act into law incorporating the School Commissioners of Columbia as ex-officio trustees of the Winthrop Training School, a body corporate with all rights and privileges and powers belonging to such bodies. In this capacity the trustees were

25

charged with establishing by-laws and other rules not inconsistent with the laws of the land "for the better order of this corporate entirety." These rules and regulations were binding on all those connected with the school, including trustees and students.[6] Sections three, four, and five of the law expressly stipulated that "the function and duties of the Trustees of the Winthrop Training School for Teachers shall be separate and distinct from those of the School Commissioners of the School District of Columbia." In addition the trustees were empowered to receive and to hold donations, bequests, and real and personal property to the amount of $100,000 for the benefit of the school. Most importantly, the trustees were empowered to grant diplomas to all who satisfactorily completed the course. The Legislature decreed that persons holding these diplomas were entitled "without further examination to teach in any of the public schools of the State as first grade teachers." This was a most important provision.[7]

The same legislative body also passed an act appropriating $5,100 to provide annual scholarships of $150 each, to be given to one student from each of the thirty-four counties of South Carolina. Under this arrangement, $30 of the scholarship was given to the school for tuition, textbooks, and other materials. The remaining $120 was given to the students in $40 installments at the beginning of each term to assist the student in defraying her personal expenses at Winthrop. These scholarship beneficiaries were selected by competitive written examinations in the different counties. In addition those young ladies who placed second in the county examinations won tuition from the school.[8]

The scholarship program played a vital role in developing the Training School and the state's educational system. Girls from leading families vied for them, thereby ensuring a select group of students. Typical among the young recipients was Miss Alethea Leila Russell. Miss Russell's father was a Superintendent of Education in Anderson County. She described her buggy ride through driving rain to the county seat's examination center. Arriving late, she took the examination against the advice of the examiner. Winning the scholarship, she graduated in the first class that could call themselves "daughters of the state," and she had a most illustrious career as a supervisor, an extension agent, a rural-life education specialist, and the organizer of the Winthrop Alumnae Association.[9]

During its second year, the scope of the Winthrop program broadened considerably. The course load was improved and more clearly defined. English and reading were stressed as well as methods, science, geography and practice teaching. Quite noticeable were newly introduced classes in local geography, map moulding and drawing, United States history, manual training, and vocal music.[10]

In that second year the school's aims and methods had been more clearly enunciated. Admission standards remained high, for the school was designed to prepare young ladies who already had "a good education" with the most advanced methods and techniques in teaching and school management. The pupils were given responsibility for bringing resources and learning aids into the classroom and were required to put into practice those principles studied in the Normal classes.[11]

As a cultural climax to the school year, a series of lectures was scheduled during the third term. The Reverend A. D. Mayo of Boston, a leading Christian educator, gave eight lectures in April and May 1888 on education in general and on obtaining best results in teaching. These lectures appear to have been in the best traditions of transcendental-ism. Mayo was followed by a leading South Carolina minister--the Reverend William M. Grier of Erskine College, the citadel of the Associate Reformed Presbyterian Church. Dr. Grier discussed "The Ethics of Literature." Included in the program were twelve lectures on general pedagogy delivered by Dr. Edward E. Sheib of Carolina College, who was joined by Dr. B. M. Bolton. Bolton lectured on hygiene, and Professor F. C. Woodward (also of Carolina) gave twelve lectures on English literature.

27

The series was concluded by a talk on "Education" delivered by one of South Carolina's greatest ministers, the highly respected Reverend Ellison Capers.[12]

The Winthrop Board of Trustees were much impressed by Mr. Robert C. Winthrop's great encouragement of the school. To show properly their appreciation, they resolved that May 12, the birthday of Mr. Winthrop, would be set apart as an annual school holiday, a memorial day "in commemoration of the beneficences by which the School was founded." Beginning in 1888, public exercises were held each year to commemorate the day. Mr. Winthrop was unable to attend this first celebration. However, he was asked to name an orator who would deliver the oration on the twelfth, someone to help commemorate the memory of George Peabody and his beneficence to the schools of the South as now administered by the Peabody Board and its president, Mr. Winthrop.[13]

In accordance with the arrangements for the celebration, the day was set but had to be changed to May 11 because in 1888 the twelfth was not suitable. The final plans resembled a graduation exercise and a public ceremony combined. The celebration began at the school building at eleven o'clock with the following program: After the devotional, the Winthrop girls demonstrated teaching exercises, sang songs, read papers and essays, and performed calisthenics. Of special interest were Miss Marion W. Woodrow's exercise on divisibility of numbers by nine; Miss Edith Berg's biographical sketch of George Peabody; Miss Louise Beckham's eulogy of Peabody; Miss Pauline M. James' paper on Barnas Sears; Miss Susan W. Behre's essay on Mr. Winthrop; Miss Mary H. Macfeat's extracts from Mr. Winthrop's addresses; and Miss Woodrow's second performance, a summary of the Peabody Trust.[14]

The casual observer at these exercises had many questions about Peabody and Winthrop. Why extoll the virtues of these men? Why stress the names of people from Massachusetts in this ceremony at a fledging school in Columbia patronized by

28

South Carolina girls? The answers to these and other questions are an important part of a great American dream.

Vital in the development of the United States was and is the notion of progress and the perfectibility of mankind. Through education and hard work, people believed ends could be achieved and the Republic could grow and flourish. Throughout America leaders with varying abilities interested themselves in promoting a common effort to improve the country's educational opportunities. Among these people certain educational statesmen stand out. George Peabody and Robert Winthrop are excellent examples.

Peabody was born in Essex County, Massachusetts, in a section that later bore his name, on February 18, 1795. His ancestry was good but his family was poor, and his only education took place in the district school. However, it was here that he developed a great appreciation for learning and its possibilities. Apprenticed as a clerk in a New England country store, he learned much about business and correct dealing. As a youth he moved to Georgetown in the District of Columbia and later became a "traveling man," representing a Baltimore establishment in Pennsylvania, New Jersey, Maryland, and Virginia. Eventually he migrated to London and there, as a broker and general operator in exchange, acquired an estate valued at $15,000,000. He remained an American, never placing his name in the London directory. After age fifty, he made his most notable benefactions. In 1852 he gave London $2,500,000 to help the poor, estimating that with careful handling it would aid in two-hundred years two-thirds of the industrious poor of "that vast world-receptacle of mingled splendor and misery."[15] Then he began his gifts to his native town and to his adopted town of Baltimore.

Following a long correspondence, Peabody and Robert Winthrop met in October 1866. Peabody, who had never married, gave $1,000,000 cash plus an additional $1,500,000 in securities of a Southern state to educate the children of the South, who so desperately needed help after the Great War. The key to his benefaction was the selection of sixteen life trustees to attend to its management and distribution. The original board as appointed by Mr. Peabody were Robert C. Winthrop, Hamilton Fish, Reverend Charles P. McIlvaine, General U. S. Grant, Admiral D. G. Farragut, William C. Rives, John L. Clifford, William Aiken of South Carolina, William M. Evarts, William Graham, Charles Manchester, George W. Riggs, Samuel Wetmore, Edward A. Bradford, George M. Eaton, and George P. Russell. As members died they were replaced, and eventually the board contained ex-presidents and chief justices of the Supreme Court as well as financiers of the calabre of J. P. Morgan and Anthony J. Drexel. The board always contained prominent Southern leaders, and George Peabody's public benefactions, which he constantly continued to enlarge, amounted to nearly $10,000,000, while $5,000,000 he said were used "to make everyone of his near relatives rich."[16]

One condition of the Southern gift had been that Robert C. Winthrop should be the permanent president and Hamilton Fish of New York and Bishop McIlvaine of Ohio the first vice presidents. Certainly Mr. Winthrop was one of the best qualified men in America for this position. He was born in Boston, of good family, in 1809. His father, Thomas Lindall Winthrop, and uncle had engaged in business for a time in Charleston, South Carolina. The young Mr. Winthrop studied at Harvard and in Daniel Webster's law office. Rising through state politics in Massachusetts, he was elected to Congress, became speaker, and was appointed to the United States Senate to fill the vacancy caused by the resignation of Daniel Webster in 1850. Winthrop was a Whig. After the demise of that party in the 1850s, he spent the remainder of his life engaged in literary,

30

historical, and philanthropic pursuits. No cause was dearer to his heart than free schools and free government, and he delivered many stirring orations on these and other subjects.[17]

Robert Winthrop spoke out and acted for the benefit of the whole country for the greater part of his long life. At Yorktown in 1881, he declared that "slavery is but half abolished, emancipation is but half completed, while millions of freedmen with votes in their hands are without education." Winthrop was "agreeably surprised" when, in recognition of what he had done or tried to do for Southern education, his name was given to a school training teachers in Columbia, South Carolina. Again when Mr. Winthrop delivered the funeral oration for George Peabody, he seemed to capture the spirit of the new American drive for social justice when he quoted from the benefactor Peabody in announcing a final gift of $1,000,000, "this I give to the suffering South for the good of the whole country."[18]

So it would seem appropriate that the students and trustees of the Winthrop Training School commemorated the memories of George Peabody and Robert Winthrop. Following the morning celebration of the first Memorial Day proceedings at Winthrop, a much larger evening celebration was planned for the Opera House: After the music and opening prayer by Reverend A. D. Mayo of Boston, Dr. Edward S. Joynes of the Carolina College was introduced by Superintendent D. B. Johnson. Joynes spoke in place of Superintendent of State Education Dr. James H. Rice, who was unable to attend. Joynes--a ready, able, and gifted speaker --told this audience that the Winthrop Training School was a "child of the Columbia city graded schools"; stressing the importance of such a school, Joynes reminded the assembly that after all taxation, organization and equipment can do, "the teacher is the school" and that no system could rise higher than the level of the teachers who direct and inspire it. He reminded his audience that in 1883 the Columbia City Board had

sought the Peabody Board's help for its public
schools and that Superintendent Johnson had been
well received on that mission. In time the same
generosity had been applied to the Winthrop Training
School, which added greatly to the educational
advantages of South Carolina.[19]

Joynes was also generous in his praise of
Johnson, saying: "We have good reason to believe"
that he is "one of the ablest and wisest Normal-
school pedagogists in the South." Pointing out that
the Normal courses of Carolina would be opened to
Winthrop and that the latter's training classes
would be opened to University students, Joynes saw
great promise for the future of South Carolina
education.

Although Joynes made a great speech, he was
not billed as the featured speaker. However, his
closing remarks echoed, no doubt, for some time in
the minds of his hearers when he said:

O this fair city! loveliest spot on
which fate has ever arrested my own
much wandering feet; favored by Heaven,
by climate, soil, situation, surroundings; center and capital of a
grand, proud, intelligent, chivalrous
state, with the resources of a sleeping
empire; home of a noble and gifted
people with all the traditions of a
glorious past, and the instincts of an
inspiring destiny; . . . who shall
bound her horoscope, or set the limits
of her glory and strength of her beauty
in the days that are to come?[20]

Leaving to other times and other pens the
prophecy of South Carolina's industrial development, Joynes proclaimed Columbia, the seat of the
great University and of the Winthrop Training
School, "the home of one of the most cultivated and
favored communities in the American States." As
usual Joynes had carried the day. In contrast,
Governor Richardson's introduction of Mr. Winthrop's

choice to deliver the main oration (Mr. J. P. Kennedy Bryan of Charleston) and his speech were somewhat anti-climatic to say the least. But the program was well received by a kind and polite audience.[21]

Memorial Day was followed a month later by graduation. This session had served seventeen students but only eight graduated on June 14, 1888. The exercises were similar to those the year before with Misses Mary H. Macfeat, Susan W. Behre, Louise L. Beckham, Edith Berg, Georgia Miller, Marion Woodrow and Julia E. Bonham taking an active part in the program. Miss Bonham was valedictorian; State Superintendent of Education James H. Rice presented diplomas. The annual report from the Secretary and Treasurer, D. B. Johnson, listed an operating cost of $1,684.75.[22]

The rising seniors of 1888-89 showed great promise. Fifty-one students were enrolled. The boarding house established the year before under Mrs. R. G. Lamar offered only twenty rooms accommodating the young ladies of Winthrop, who were charged $15.00 a month for board, fuel, and lights. Private accommodations were under the general control of Superintendent Johnson. County scholarships, legislative recognition, the Peabody money--these ensured the survival of the infant Training School.[23]

CHAPTER V

BEN TILLMAN GIVES A BIG PUSH

"If we educate our men, their children MAY be educated; but when we educate our women, we know their children WILL be educated."

Benjamin Ryan Tillman

With the continued growth of Winthrop Training School, the conception about the school itself expanded. Whether Superintendent D. B. Johnson first intended anything more than training teachers for his own Columbia schools is not known. One of his key associates, Miss Mary Leonard, the principal, was unsure of her role or of what Johnson was attempting to do.

Years later Dr. Joynes corresponded with Miss Leonard at her home in Rochester, Massachusetts, concerning the early days at Winthrop and their mutual interest--writing and education. Responding to Joynes in 1911, Miss Leonard wrote:

I appreciate what a good friend you were to the school in those early days, and in the years of its later development also. It would have been a help and a pleasure to me if I could have talked with you somewhat freely about school problems. But I was in a somewhat uncertain state of mind during those years (1886-1894) as to what was--and what ought to be my technical relations to the school officers and other teachers that I was working with. . . . I did not wish to complicate my relations with Mr. Johnson by entering into discussions with others on subjects which he felt should be talked over with him alone. . . . It was a new chapter of experience for me, and for the rest as well.[1]

Some newspaper accounts of Winthrop's early history brought to light a controversy about Johnson and his staff. Johnson admitted that he never made a point of Miss Leonard's title at the beginning since his chief concern was results. From the accounts and correspondence it appears that Johnson was a bit jealous of Miss Leonard, who was an experienced Normal-school teacher, and that she was afraid of him. Writing to her in 1912, Johnson emphatically stated:

> I engaged you to assist me in realizing my plans. I would never have agreed to turn the new undertaking over to an unknown and untried person. It never occurred to me . . . that you did not fully understand and agree to my plans of organization. If I had, I would have started with someone else. Different understanding of the meaning of the title 'Principal' may account for our differences. . . . At the end of the first year instead of conspiring to overturn my plans you should have resigned . . . and I forgive you for what I considered your treachery to me.

Johnson later explained his regret at losing his temper, and Miss Leonard wrote him friendly letters about his mother. She also attempted to help him with Dr. Samuel Green of the Peabody Board, whose aid Johnson earnestly solicited.[2]

But great as was the success and influence of the Winthrop Training School and its dynamic superintendent, it would (according to Dr. Joynes) "probably never - certainly not so soon - have led to the creation of Winthrop College except for another contemporaneous influence."[3]

At this time Tillman's movement, demanding justice and equality for the farmers, was gathering converts. His agitation for agricultural education and for women's industrial education would not be turned aside. Favorable reports like Samuel Green's

35

in 1888 that declared "no institution of its kind [Normal school] is doing more thorough work or filling a greater want in the community" than Winthrop served to point up what could be done by enlarging its program. With an eye to industrial training, Tillman's friend Senator R. R. Hemphill, the Abbeville editor, moved to repeal in December 1888 the law of the previous year that had granted scholarships to teachers at the Training School.[4]

In the Third Annual Report of the Winthrop trustees to Governor Richardson in 1889, they emphasized that the institution was firmly established and that it was accomplishing much for the women and schools of the state. They stressed their bright prospects for the future, emphasizing the personal inspection of the school by Dr. J. L. M. Curry, agent of the Peabody Board, who recommended a $500 increase in their appropriation. The class of 1889 boasted thirty-four graduates, with one from North Carolina. As usual, Memorial Day and graduation were high points in the festivities of the school year.[5]

After the 1888 election, Tillman's forces held a majority in the State House of Representatives and they were only two votes from a majority in the Senate. They pushed for the acceptance of Clemson as a major legislative must; Governor Richardson held them up until 1889, when the bill became law. The "new democracy," as Tillman's movement was often called, waited for their chance to elect Tillman governor of South Carolina in the fall of 1890. A bitter campaign raged in the summer and early fall of 1890.[6] Tillman carried the state and was inaugurated on December 4, 1890, in the midst of a large crowd of well-wishers.[7]

Meanwhile other events were taking shape that might change the educational picture in South Carolina. The highly regarded Dr. Edward S. Joynes --long a featured teacher at the summer Teacher's Institutes--made a plea on July 30, 1890, to the teachers at Florence, calling for the transfer of the Winthrop Training School from the Columbia

36

School Board to the state's care. Joynes expressed hope that Normal and industrial training might be united in one state college for women, adding that "there will be a crown of honor in the unending future for that Legislature which creates the South Carolina Normal and Industrial College for Women, and for the Governor who first recommends it." Joynes, ever the astute politico, sent a copy of his address to Tillman with the notation that there was "a message in it for you." Tillman approved these sentiments, but he felt that a new school being organized so soon after Clemson would present certain liabilities. Later Tillman invited Joynes to visit him in Columbia. During this meeting Joynes suggested a committee to investigate the problems involved and to consider the possibility of localities' bidding for the school since considerable interest had been expressed by leaders in several areas. Joynes offered several suggestions in writing before the governor made his inaugural address on December 4, 1890.[8]

Others were trying to push Winthrop in the opposite direction. A trustee wrote the Peabody Board in October 1890 that "our teachers are in demand everywhere" and that they hoped for increased aid by the board. Bragging that "we are the only institution now in South Carolina that has no enemies," they regarded their future as bright and attributed this partially to the tact and ability of Johnson.[9]

"Captain Tillman," as he was affectionately known to many followers, had earlier (April 1886) addressed the Farmer's Convention at Columbia on women's education. He stressed that the state owed her daughters an institution for their liberal and practical education: "a school where they can be taught not only to adorn a drawing room, but be fitted to perform the duties of life and become breadwinners if need be. A Commonwealth," Tillman observed, "which does not train its future mothers can never hope to achieve any high place in the civilization of today, and both justice and wisdom demand that our girls should have an equal chance

37

with our boys." Tillman recommended using the Citadel plant for such a school and appealed to the women of South Carolina "to aid in establishing an Industrial College for females in our State like that in Columbus, Mississippi."[10]

Public pronouncements by Joynes and Tillman apropos a state college for women brought the men together prior to Tillman's inauguration. Joynes urged that Tillman appoint a committee to study the proposed school after Tillman expressed fear that he could not organize a new school so soon after Clemson. Tillman in his December 4, 1890, inaugural proposed changes in the state, including his trial balloon for women's education, which had been suggested heretofore. After outlining his plan to open Clemson by October next, he attacked the extravagance of the Citadel, saying that it was unfortunate the school ever reopened and that the $60,000 spent on rebuilding a burned wing and repairing the plant could have been used far more profitably "in erecting an industrial and normal School for girls." Still, since the Citadel was running and since "there are too few lights [of learning] in South Carolina for us to wantonly put out any of them, I recommend," Tillman said, "that the usual appropriation be granted."[11]

Some might argue that Tillman was holding up a sop to the powerful low-country delegations, many of whom had Citadel connections, but it is more probable that he was trying to be reasonable. Returning to the imperative need for a women's industrial school, Tillman stressed the practical need that some women have to make a living. Pointing to the widowed mother and the orphaned daughter whose training in music and painting offered little hope of support, he most emphatically stressed that "the State has never done anything for its women except appropriating a small amount to the Winthrop Training School for Teachers." He quickly pointed out that it would be wrong to enter into "competition with the private female colleges by establishing an ordinary school." What he wished to establish with the Legislature's aid

38

was a school offering industrial arts and science, telegraphy, designing, stenography, bookkeeping, cookery, and housekeeping. These he felt would supply "a long felt and pressing want." To effectuate this, Tillman proposed appointing three commissioners to study the requirements and costs of such an institution and to seek inducements from persons or towns around the state wishing to provide the school's location. Up to $300 would be available from the governor's contingent fund to bear the expense incurred in collecting this information. [12]

In climaxing his plea for women's education underwritten by the state, Tillman pointed to the success and value of the Winthrop Training School as an example of a judicious and fruitful service enterprise. With the cry for more and better-trained teachers, Winthrop with a one-year course and a $150 scholarship from each county of the state was doing much more than the Citadel--which spent $300 on each beneficiary there, with two being allowed from each county. After a four-year course, the graduates of the Citadel were often relieved from their obligation to teach in the public school and many, according to Tillman, left the state as soon as graduation. Truly it would appear, he said, that "Man to man so oft unjust is always so to women." No man in government had ever made a more convincing case for state aid to educate South Carolina's women than this plea by a one-eyed farm leader from Edgefield County. [13]

The editor of South Carolina's leading newspaper appeared shaken by this new thrust from "the City on the Congaree." The News and Courier whined, proclaiming "democracy and fitness are the only test for office" under Tillman. Editorial-izing under the head "Making Women Independent," the editor reported that a bill to establish a Normal and industrial college had been continued to the General Assembly's next session. Stressing that the necessity for such an institution was presented by Governor Tillman, the editorial warned that the Legislature should consider "cast-iron" conditions upon the young ladies in regard to the marital relations which many would assume after graduation. The editor seemed to be sincere in saying that once a woman became independent, she might be prone to divorce. He even cited the case of Mary Mather, an actress, who upon attaining success moved to get rid of her husband. Suggesting careful consideration of the curriculum for a Tillman-oriented industrial college, the editor counseled "we must take care that they are not made too independent."[14]

Despite this apparent lack of faith in independent women by the manhood of Charleston, Edward Joynes drew up a resolution for Tillman to set up a study committee for the proposed college. Dr. Joynes was asked to chair the group after the enabling legislation passed. Joynes wanted D. B. Johnson to serve on the commission, but Tillman felt that he could not appoint two from Columbia. Consequently, Joynes withdrew. Ultimately, the governor selected Johnson, Miss Mary L. Yeargin, and Miss Hannah Hemphill to make this important survey and inquiry. After several months' study, the Girl's Industrial College Commission (as the Charleston paper called it) met on November 14, 1891, at the Washington Street Graded School office of Professor Johnson. There they prepared their final report, which they planned to send to Governor Tillman within a week. Their work received equal billing in the press with the football game played at the fairground between Furman and Trinity College of North Carolina. The press failed to note how long Johnson's committee met, but the game lasted four hours and resulted in a score of 96 to 0 in favor of the "tarheels," who were reported to be better kickers.[15]

Preparatory to formulating their report, Mr. Johnson's commission personally inspected the leading industrial and manual-training institutions in Washington, Philadelphia, New York, Brooklyn, and Columbus, Mississippi (site of the chief experiment in adapting industrial training to the needs of Southern women). After gathering information from

40

many sources, the commission tabulated their results, sending their report to His Excellency, Governor B. R. Tillman, who lost little time in presenting it to the General Assembly for immediate consideration. Since the Commission attempted to advance their concept of a model industrial school for women and since the Legislature adopted much of the report in establishing the new State Industrial and Normal College, a more detailed look at certain sections of the report helps one to better understand the necessity for establishing a state-supported women's college in South Carolina.

The design of such an institution should be to prepare girls:

1. To earn their own livelihood by the practice of some one or another of those arts suitable for women to follow.

2. To exert an uplifting and refining influence on family and society by means of a cultivated intellect, which can only be attained by a systematic education in the higher branches of learning.

3. To be skillful and expert in those domestic arts that lie at the foundation of all successful housekeeping and home-making.

INTELLECTUAL TRAINING

Without exception, all institutions such as the one contemplated for South Carolina emphasize the necessity of providing for thorough mental culture in connection with the training in the industrial arts.

They uniformly disclaim the intention of turning out mere machines, 'mere workwomen, ignorant of everything except the narrow craft by which they earn their living,' with a manual dexterity reduced to muscular habit, to be used without thought.

The fact that this is an age in which intelligence and judgement must guide the hand in order that the resulting labor may be properly remunerative would be a sufficient explanation of this attitude of these institutions, if there were no better reasons.

It would be a very doubtful blessing to young women to induce them to enter on a trade when they were so lacking in general intelligence that they would necessarily compete with the lowest in that line of business. Dr. MacAlister, of Philadelphia, a leading authority on manual and industrial training, writes: 'What the working-man is seeking is a larger participation in the fruits of his industry; but this can only be accomplished by the laborer putting more skill and intelligence into the work of his hands. The problem for every civilized nation to-day is how the largest amount of intellectual development can be given to its industrial population. There will be no peace between labor and capital until labor has recognized the necessity for intelligence, and capital has recognized the just rights of labor, enlightened and ennobled by knowledge. What is needed is to bring thought and labor together, to make every worker a thinker and every thinker a worker.'

But there are higher considerations than that of dollars and cents which should enter into the determination of this matter. The State, in such an undertaking as this, owes it to herself to make the best womanhood possible, and to the individual to refrain from forcing upon her, with her God-given faculties, a one-sided development. No school should lose sight of the fact that its mission is to make industrious, intelligent, noble-minded human beings, capable of making a living for themselves, and those dependent upon them, if need be, and able and willing to make the world better by having lived in it.

It is presumed that no thoughtful man desires the State to establish a mere shop-school, divorcing intelligence and manual labor, and thus bring the latter into disrepute, and defeat one of the main objects of this movement. The general desire is, no doubt, that there shall be provided an institution whose organization shall aim at joining in the student 'a cultured mind' with a 'skillful hand,' thus dignifying industrial pursuits and making our youth believe in, respect and seek work, and clearing the way for our young women, in all self-respect and womanliness, to engage in many more industrial occupations than are at present open to them for self-support.

The young women who go out from this institution are expected to win for manual labor a higher place in the esteem of men by their general intelligence as well as by their skillful hands, to impress the fact that such work is worthy the study and practice of the highest ability. They are expected to prove by example that manual training instead of deadening the intellect quickens it; that it is one of the best means of culti-vating the judgment, the executive faculty and the will; that it is most helpful to the best and fullest mental development.

To this end the educative value of all manual exercises introduced into such an institution should be ever kept in view. Their value in preparing for industrial pursuits should not absorb the attention to the exclusion of their use for mind culture. Cooking and sewing, for instance, should be taught upon the basis upon which these industries, or manual training exercises, if you will, are taught in the Philadelphia schools, where much good work has been fully demonstrated. There is not only no antagonism between manual and intellectual training, but rather is the one the necessary complement of the other in a complete education.

The famous St. Louis Manual Training School 'clearly recognizes the preeminent value and necessity for intellectual development and discipline.'

The Pratt Institution of Brooklyn holds that true 'manual training aims at the broadest, most liberal education. While developing and strengthening the physical powers, it also renders more active and acute the intellectual faculties, thus enabling the pupils to acquire with greater readiness, and to use more advantageously, the literary education which should go hand in hand with the manual.'

In a report of a strong Committee to the National Council of Education on technical education for girls the same position is taken. It reads: 'The theory that better results may be expected of specialists who have had a good, general training is recognized. It is in accordance with this theory that in technological schools the aims of general culture are constantly kept in view. To do any less for woman would be to continue her inferior chance in the world.'

44

From the unanimity of the testimony there can thus be no doubt as to the advisability of providing for thorough intellectual training, and of arranging, for the purpose of instruction in literary and scientific studies, for having a Collegiate Department in the proposed Industrial School for Women.

INDUSTRIAL AND DOMESTIC TRAINING

In the selection of the industries to be taught, reference should be had to the physical capabilities of woman, to her intellectual versatility and alertness, to the fact that she possesses delicacy of touch rather than physical force, and also that she is and will always be the homemaker.

Governed by these considerations, and by the practice of existing institutions for the industrial training of women, we would suggest for the Industrial and Domestic Departments the following industries as suitable for our young women:

Sewing, art needlework, dressmaking, millinery, cooking, housekeeping, drawing (free-hand and mechanical), design (technical and decorative) and architectural drawing, clay modeling, wood carving, engraving, stenography, typewriting, telegraphy, photography, bookkeeping, type-setting and printing.

If it is not found practicable to provide instruction in all of these industries at first (and we would advise against attempting more than can be properly undertaken at the beginning), we would recommend that those having the greatest educative value and the most direct bearing upon the better performance of home duties be first arranged for. A

45

learned and experienced educator said: 'The duties that appertain to home must be numbered among the most important acquirements of a girl's education. In the multiplicity of agencies that are being pressed into service for the betterment of society, we are beginning to revert to the home as the chief centre of the noblest as well as the most practical influences that go to the building up of all that is best in human life. With us, as with all the members of that branch of the Aryan family to which we belong, the home is the sacred place where every virtue has its birth and every social duty finds its strongest nurture.'

COURSES OF STUDY AND ORGANIZATION

The complete course of study should extend over four sessions of nine months each, and the time should be equally divided between the Literary and Industrial Departments. Yet arrangements might be made for more limited courses, within a shorter time. With practical uniformity the replies from industrial schools, in answer to our letters of inquiry, agree in the statement that the age of admission to such an institution as is contemplated for this State should be not less than fifteen years, and that at least a good knowledge of the common school branches should be required of entering students. There should be more than one course of study offered, and students who have previously passed through a college course should be allowed, if desired, to devote their whole time to work in the Industrial Department. Other students should be required to take a course for literary training in connection with at least one industrial art. In addition to her industrial studies, each student should be required to do her part in keeping her own room in order, and each boarding pupil should take her turn in the work of the dining-room. Some arrangements should be made to allow students to do voluntary work in the dining-room, the kitchen, the laundry and elsewhere, for which they would receive pay at the rate of six to eight cents an hour. This would not only provide extra practice in industrial work, but would enable some worthy girls to partly support themselves at college. It would not be wise to allow a student to do more than two hours of this voluntary work per day in addition to the required work, as it has been found that more than this interferes with the successful prosecution of the regular school work.

A uniform, plainly and neatly made, of some good material, should be prescribed for all of the students. This would prevent extravagance and distraction of attention from study by considerations of dress, and would remove all objectionable and hurtful outward distinctions between fellow students.

There should be an instructor for every twenty or twenty-five students, for the best work to be done, and it is our judgment that such an institution as this is expected to be should open with a faculty of ten or twelve instructors in addition to the President, all being experts in their special lines of work. In order to secure such a faculty adequate salaries must be paid.

COST OF EQUIPMENT AND MAINTENANCE

The estimates of the cost of the necessary plant, apart from buildings, for such an institution, made by the schoolmen with whom we have corresponded on this subject, vary from $3,000 to $100,000. We are of the opinion that the furniture, laundry, steamfitting, and other plant necessitites may be secured for $15,000 or $20,000.

The buildings for the school should be constructed with a view to accommodating comfortably from 300 to 400 students. They should be built with the modern improvements in heating, lighting and ventilating, and should be adapted in every particular to the uses to which they are to be put. The sanitary arrangements for the dormitories especially should be carefully looked after. Water should be conducted in pipes to the different floors and a complete system of sewerage provided for.

There should be a large audience hall in the main building, capable of accommodating on occasion over one thousand people. The entire cost of these buildings, including a well arranged infirmary, we estimate at not over $100,000. The grounds should be ample, certainly not less than twenty acres, elevated, well drained, and conveniently located with reference to churches, and also, if possible, railroad trains.

After a careful inquiry as to the yearly cost of maintaining similar institutions elsewhere, we are of the opinion that the annual cost for conducting such an institution as is proposed for South Carolina will be $20,000 to $25,000.

NORMAL TRAINING

In the answers to the last question of our letters of inquiry, as to the practicability of combining normal and

48

industrial training in the same institution, considerable difference of opinion and practice appears.

Some eminent Normal School men, like President Boyden of the Bridgewater School, founded in 1839, the first permanently established school for the training of teachers in this country, think that the combination could not be profitably made; while others, equally eminent and successful, like Principal Parker of the Cook County Normal School, and Dr. Payne of the Peabody Normal College at Nashville, Tenn., think that it could.

But there are more than 200 Normal Schools in this country, including those whose Presidents' opinions have been given above, established for the one purpose of training teachers and having no provision for industrial training. Whether this is so because it is best, or because Normal Schools were organized and fixed in their present work and form long before the industrial training idea was developed, is an open question. Some good Normal Schools, notably the 'New York College for the Training of Teachers,' emphasize manual training as a means of mind culture in the preparation of teachers for the public schools, expressly declaring that it is no part of their intention to prepare their students for trades, but rather to equip them to meet the already strong and rapidly growing demand for the introduction of manual training, for its educative value, into the common schools of the country. But there must be in all manual training incidental industrial training, using these terms in their most generally accepted technical sense.

Eminent leaders in the manual and industrial training movement, such as

Prof. Woodward, of St. Louis, and Mr. Pratt, of Brooklyn, can see no reason why this new education should not be profitably carried on with teacher-training at the same time and in the same institution. But then the fact remains that many industrial schools have been established without making any provision for teacher-training. This, however, may have resulted not from any incompatability or antagonism between industrial-training and teacher-training, but from the fact that teacher-training was already very generally provided for when the institutions for industrial-training were organized. Four-fifths of the replies from eminent normal school and industrial school men to our iniquity, 'Could normal and industrial training be profitably carried on together in the same institution without injury to either,' are in the affirmative. The States of Mississippi, Georgia and North Carolina have provided for normal and industrial training in the same institution, but with what success yet remains to be seen.

With all the light that we can get, we think that the ideal arrangement would be a Normal School, with manual training provided for upon a mind culture basis, and a separate and distinct Industrial College, with a good collegiate department; but where this specialization of institutions cannot be made, for lack of means, we are of the opinion that, with judicious management, the two could be combined without injury to either.

BIDS FOR LOCATION

Very great interest has been manifested throughout the State in the objects of the Commission from the time of

50

its appointment. The substantial character of this interest is shown by the responses to our circular letter calling for offers from communities for the location of the proposed school. The great advantages, educationally and materially, of such an institution to a community seemed to be clearly and quickly comprehended.

We have received and have on file the following bids:

	MONEY	SITES
St. Matthews (Mrs. J. W. Kennedy)..		3 1/3 acres
Marion.................	$15,000	..20 to 100 "
Laurens................	45,000	...20 to 75 "
Camden.................	50,000	
(Out of which a desirable site can be purchased for $5,000 to $20,000.)		
Spartanburg............	51,000	.........30 "
Chester................	40,000	...20 to 50 "
Anderson (City and County)................	125,000	
(Out of which a desirable site can be purchased for $5,000 to $10,000.)		
Greenville.............	126,500	
(Out of which a desirable site can be purchased for $10,000 to $25,000.)		

These are handsome offers, being much more liberal than those made in other States for the location of similar institutions. They indicate the earnest purpose of the people of South Carolina in this matter, and should insure the speedy establishment of the Industrial School for Women.

In accordance with the requirements of the Resolutions defining our duties, we visited these places, with the exception

51

of St. Matthews, and examined carefully the nature of their bids, and inspected the various sites offered. We found all the bids to emanate from properly constituted and representative authority, and that every place could furnish a site suitable in every way to the purposes of the proposed institution.

We refrain from recommending any one of these communities as the place for the location of the school, because we are convinced that it is to the interest of the proposed institution to leave the selection of location entirely in the hands of the Board of Trustees to be chosen by the General Assembly, who will be able to make a definite contract with a community and see that the proper guarantees are fully secured before finally acting; and we recommend that this Board, when constituted, be given the authority, finally and definitely, to determine this matter. We will file with you for the use of said Board the bids and the list and description of all sites offered, and all other data in our possession bearing upon this subject.

In thus referring the choice of a location, it is hardly necessary for us to add that the place which is so selected should be healthy, having a bracing atmosphere, a good winter climate and good water, should be easily accessible to all parts of the State, should be in hearty sympathy with the objects of the institution, and should have good moral influences entirely predominant in it. Students are always very deeply influenced by the moral tone of the community in which they spend their school days, the most impressionable of life.

SPECIAL RECOMMENDATIONS

If within the province of this Report, we would suggest that in the Act creating the Industrial School for Women there be included a section allowing any community or County in which the institution is finally located to vote an appropriation for it, in bonds or otherwise. Unless this be done, no substantial progress can be made in the establishment of the school until some particular community can secure authority by special Act, at a succeeding session of the General Assembly, to vote the money pledged in its bid. We would also suggest that the Board of Trustees to be created by this Act be composed of nine members, the Governor of the State and the State Superintendent of Education, ex-officio, and seven others to be elected by the Legislature . . . in full accord with the broadest and best ideas as to the education of woman, some of whom should be women; and that the regular term of office of each be six years; but that the first seven be elected to serve, two for two years, two for four years, and three for six years, these first terms of office to be determined by lot after election.

A number of scholarships of free tuition should be provided for in this Act, and should be apportioned to; the different Counties of the State, according to the number of white girls fifteen to twenty-five years of age, if practicable; and if not, for lack of proper returns, then according to the white population as ascertained by the United States census taken just preceding each appointment.

NEED FOR TECHNICAL TRAINING FOR WOMEN

The pressing need of special or technical education for women is now

53

being generally recognized and provided for.

This is an age of directive power rather than drudgery, and alertness of intellect rather than physical force is now needed in the industries. Woman, with her versatility and alertness, her deft fingers and quick comprehension, is specially adapted to the successful prosecution of many of the industrial pursuits of the day, which she has not yet generally entered upon for lack of opportunity and training.

The new social conditions of the present and the probable developments of the future demand, not more for woman's sake than for the sake of society, higher and technical education for woman. There have been great changes in her activities and responsibilities in the last half century everywhere; but nowhere have they been greater than in the South, where as a result of the civil war, has occurred one of the greatest social revolutions of modern times, which has brought Southern women face to face with the unfamiliar problem of self support. They are bravely grappling with it, but need special training to insure the best results for their efforts.

CONCLUSION

South Carolina has always recognized her obligation to provide ample educational facilities for her sons. For their benefit she has established and liberally maintains the South Carolina College, the Citadel and Clemson College. Nor has she forgotten her colored men and women, who are cared for at Claflin University.

But, from inadvertence rather than design, we must believe, she has neglected to make provision for her fair daughters in this respect. In loyal, uncomplaining submission they have trustfully awaited the time when this unjust discrimination against them should be removed. They are greater in number than the men, and the State's welfare is more dependent upon them, on account of their greater influence upon society and citizenship through the home, where are originated the forces which determine the character of the community, the State and the nation.

Surely they are entitled by every consideration of wisdom, good policy, and right action to equal recognition with their brothers in opportunities to properly fit themselves for life's duties. As you have so well said in your able advocacy of this cause: 'Love, patriotism, justice, all demand that they be no longer neglected.'

With the submitting of this Report our special mission is at an end. We shall feel amply repaid for all the labor and thought that we may have expended in the work of this Commission, if we shall have been instrumental in giving definite shape to this important movement, and in preparing the way for its early crystallization into a noble and enduring institution for the best education of the hand, the head and the heart of South Carolina's young womanhood.

Respectfully submitted.
D. B. JOHNSON,
MARY L. YEARGIN,
HANNAH HEMPHILL,

Commissioners

November, 1891. [16]

Governor Tillman in his message to the General Assembly on Tuesday, November 24, 1891, placed considerable emphasis on the commission report and stressed several points--especially the fact that experts favored the union of industrial and Normal training in enabling one to obtain a sound scholastic education. He pointed out that different communities had offered for the newly proposed school. Recommending an act for the founding and future liberal support of the proposed school, Tillman advised that the location be awarded after careful inspection of the offers and bids. He urged that the Legislature pass an act to adopt Winthrop Training School as its Normal college and to provide for its amalgamation with the industrial college as soon as the latter was completed. He reasoned that since the Peabody Fund was to be distributed in 1897, the fund would be given as an endowment for teacher-training schools. Tillman had reason to believe that the Peabody trustees would handsomely endow the proposed college and that the new school would be as popular as Clemson.[17]

An act was approved December 23, 1891, "to establish a Normal and Industrial College in the State of South Carolina for the Education of White Girls." This all-inclusive basic statute firmly established the new state school which would be known as "The South Carolina Industrial and Winthrop Normal College." This institution was under the care of a Board of Trustees including seven members elected by the Legislature in addition to the following ex-officio members: the governor, the state superintendent of education, and the chairman of the committees on education in the Senate and in the House of Representatives. Two additional trustees would be added by the Board to serve until the General Assembly met in 1893. These two members should reside "at or near the place where the institution was located." [18]

The secretary of state was responsible for certifying the trustees. They had thirty days to accept or decline the election. Once elected, the Board was required to meet at least twice a year and a majority would constitute a quorum. Endowed with the basic powers of a corporation, the Board of Trustees were given full powers to conduct the business of the school. They were also especially charged with the "establishment, conduct and maintenance of a first-class institution" and were empowered to appoint the president, professors, and officers, and to fix salaries and wages.[19]

This act of 1891 instructed the Board of Trustees to seek a permanent home for Winthrop, looking "to the convenience of the People of every section of the State." The Board in deciding this matter should consider the advantages and disadvantages of the different offers as well as the money and locations. All bids for same should be secured, and a thirty-day notice and advertisements in three South Carolina papers were required before finally locating the institution. Once the site was selected, the Board would provide for buildings and equipment "without expense to the State." The act also provided that a county, city or town could appropriate funds to acquire the institution, provided a majority of the voters agreed to the "subscription" of a sum to be paid in money or bonds.[20]

Tuition at the new school would be forty dollars a session with provisions to admit students free of tuition charges if they were unable to pay. One-hundred and fifty dollars would be paid by the treasurer for every such beneficiary so appointed. Thirty dollars of this would go for school expenses and one-hundred and twenty would go to cover board and other needs of the beneficiary. The trustees were granted the use of as many as one-hundred able-bodied convicts from the penitentiary to erect buildings, providing the college would bear the cost of transportation, keep, and control of these men. The offer of Winthrop Training School's trustees to merge into Winthrop Normal College under this act was accepted on provision that the school be maintained in Columbia "for the present" as the Training School had been. Conditional with this arrangement was the provision to maintain the scholarship quota program of one per county, a quota that should be continued until the opening of the South Carolina Industrial and Winthrop Normal College.[21]

On the same day that this act became effective (December 23, 1891), the Honorable Eugene B. Gary, President of the South Carolina Senate, presided over the Joint Assembly's election of seven trustees for the Normal and Industrial College. They were Messrs. W.N. Elder, H.B. Buist, D.W. McLaurin, Dr. E.S. Joynes, A.H. Patterson, Dr. A.C. Fuller, and Mr. J.E. Breazeale. Governor Tillman and the Legislature had presented South Carolina with a great Christmas present, and Tillman planned an organizational meeting with the new Board early in 1892.[22]

Governor Ben Tillman met with the new Board of Trustees at 8 p.m., January 4, 1892, in the executive chamber. The governor and the superintendent of education, Mr. W.D. Mayfield, were elected temporary chairman and temporary secretary of the group. Present with Messrs. Breazeale of Anderson, Buist of Greenville, Joynes of Columbia and McLaurin of Selkirk was Superintendent D.B. Johnson, who had been elected president of the Winthrop Normal College on February 19, 1891. Tillman had taken the liberty of inviting Johnson, who reported briefly on the condition of the Normal College and promised a fuller report at his office the next day. In this meeting, Tillman read the act that provided for establishing the college. This was followed by Dr. Joyne's resolution that the chair appoint a three-member committee to report on provisions for the temporary conduct of the college and the Training School property's transfer to the college. Tillman appointed Joynes, Breazeale, and McLaurin to carry out the resolution. Joynes proposed that a second three-member committee seek a location for the college under section seven of the Act of 1891. This committee on location and organization consisted of Messrs. Mayfield, Breazeale, and Buist. The group adjourned.[23]

Joining the members the next day, January 5, at Johnson's office were A.H. Patterson of Barnwell and Dr. A.C. Fuller of Laurens, both of whom signified their acceptance as a trustee. Johnson and the Board visited the Normal College, spoke to the young ladies, and returned to the executive chamber to complete their business. Agreeing to continue the temporary organization until permanent rules and bylaws could be drawn up, the chair appointed Joynes, Mayfield, and Breazeale to prepare the permanent organization. The Board commended the "efficient work and excellent conditions of the Winthrop Training School" and received this as a valuable gift to the state. They showed their appreciation with a resolution to the Chairman of the former Board.[24]

The Board settled several organizational and procedural matters, recommending that Acting-President Johnson and his staff continue in their same capacities and with the same salaries in the Winthrop Normal College until the close of the school year. Johnson, Joynes, and Mayfield were designated an executive committee and authorized to accept money and other property of the "late Training School," and they were empowered to employ an additional teacher at not more than sixty dollars a month. The Board also planned to seek a permanent location for the college and, as soon as "practicable" after finding this location, to elect the additional trustees and a president. March 19 became the deadline for considering location bids, which would be advertised according to law for thirty days in three newspapers. Under section eight of this law, any county or incorporated city or town could bid subject to a popular referendum on the subscription by the locality. Bids were required to be submitted to the chairman and secretary. Since this Board was without funds to advertise, it was agreed that the chairman and secretary should send out the solicitation for bids, requesting that "all papers friendly to the institution" should copy and run the announcement. Before adjourning, the members drew lots for terms of office. McLaurin, Elder, and

Buist received six-year terms, Joynes and Patterson four-year terms, and Fuller and Breazeale two-year terms. One last order of business was the acceptance of Dr. Joynes' motion whereby the regulations and government of Winthrop Training School and its board would apply to the Winthrop Normal College until changed by future Board action.[25]

Two months later as planned, the Board met (March 9, 1892) in the executive chamber with Governor Tillman and the leading trustees present. Because of pressing business with the Sinking Fund Commission, Governor Tillman asked to be excused to attend the latter meeting. Dr. Fuller took the chair. President Johnson--Chairman of the Executive Committee responsible for the management of the Normal College--made his report, which was received and placed in the minutes. Reporting that the Training School Board had transferred $1042.36 worth of school supplies and equipment to the Normal College Board, Johnson noted changes in the faculty: Professor James H. Royhill was engaged to give lessons in higher reading; Miss L.B. Faulk was teaching higher vocal music; and Miss S.I. Knight had been succeeded by Miss Marion W. Woodrow, a graduate of Winthrop Training School and a teacher in the Columbia city schools. Professor Johnson reported on several items including Mr. Winthrop's usual spring donation of $50.00 for the library, the plans for the annual memorial day celebration scheduled for May 12 and a recent donation of $1,000 from Agent Curry of the Peabody Board. The latter amount brought to $1545.76 the funds on hand of the Winthrop Normal College as of March 9, 1892.[26]

At this same meeting Dr. Joynes reported for the committee on by-laws, suggesting that the governor should be ex-officio chairman of the Board, that the state superintendent of education should act as secretary and treasurer for the present, and that the special committee charged with running the college in Columbia should continue its work. A response by William H. Lyles of the old

60

Board of Trustees was read and bids that had been received for the location of the college were opened and read. The bids from Columbia and Anderson, South Carolina, were referred to the appropriate committee for immediate action.[27]

In a late afternoon session the Board reconvened with Governor Tillman in the chair. The committee on location read first Columbia's offer of up to $12,000 payable in five equal payments and a promise to help obtain grounds for the college with the proviso that the wards of Columbia would each be represented on the college's board. This was followed by the reading of Anderson's $75,000 bid in bonds from the city and a promise of land from private individuals. It was resolved to accept Anderson's bid when the bonds were delivered, and the Board planned its next meeting on April 14 at Anderson. These bids were recorded in the minutes of the Board before adjournment.[28]

The next month passed rather rapidly and soon, on April 14, 1892, the Board found itself assembled in the parlor of the Chiquola Hotel at Anderson with Governor Tillman, Dr. Joynes, Mr. Breazeale, Mr. McLaurin, Mr. Patterson, Mr. Hemphill, Dr. Fuller and Superintendent Mayfield ready to receive the mayor and officials of Anderson to transact business relative to placing the college there. After viewing the various sites and considering them, Governor Tillman and the Board learned that the $75,000 Anderson had offered would increase her indebtedness beyond the eight-percent constitutional limit based on the value of property as returned for taxes. Town officials pointed out that other property in the town limits could be taxed and that thereby they might keep within the eight-percent debt limitation. It was agreed that a friendly suit would clear up the constitutional problem; meanwhile the location of the college would be postponed, pending the case's outcome. The meeting adjourned, subject to the recall of the chairman.[29]

Nearly eight months passed before the court rendered a final decision on the validity of Anderson's bonds and bid. Governor Tillman called the Winthrop Board of Trustees to the mansion for an eight o'clock meeting on December 2, 1892, to consider Anderson's case. The governor was joined by Representatives Frank B. Gary, D.W. McLaurin, W.N. Elder, J.E. Breazeale, Senator R.R. Hemphill, Dr. E.S. Joynes, and Superintendent W.D. Mayfield. A copy of the state supreme court's decision in the Anderson bond case circulated. In light of the adverse decision, the Board decided to give notice that they would accept new bids for the location of the college. These new bids would be opened at the next meeting--scheduled for March 8, 1893, at the governor's mansion. The group adjourned after agreeing to print the report of the executive committee then send it to the Legislature. The governor and the Board seemed determined to broaden the base of the young college.[30]

CHAPTER VI

BIDDING FOR A STATE COLLEGE

"Never before, perhaps, has so much interest
been taken in a matter of public educational
importance as in the matter of the location
of the State Industrial and Normal College."
The (Columbia) State
March 30, 1893

The college that Tillman had helped to
foster and that his adminstration offered to some
South Carolina locality by qualified bids was now a
going concern ready to bring untold values to the
area making the winning bid.

Reporting from Columbia in December 1893,
seven years after founding the Training School, D.B.
Johnson (President and ex-officio Chairman of the
Special Committee in charge of the Winthrop Normal
College) stated that the recently completed seventh
session had been the most successful in their
history. In the seven years of the teacher-training
program at Columbia, Johnson had sent out
one-hundred and fifty-seven young women. These
teachers had done well. A two-year course had just
been instituted to increase the scope and
thoroughness of the program. Every area of the
school had been improved. The reading room as
constituted during the previous session contained
leading educational journals and magazines. (Mr.
Winthrop usually sent fifty dollars each year to
help in acquiring new books.) The boarding
accommodations at 18 Plain Street were an important
feature of the school, even though there were never
enough places to satisfy the demand.[1]

Of great significance in the Training
School's growth was the scholarship program. The
"first scholarships"--full scholarships--were
actively sought as were the "second" or free-tuition
scholarships. Both types were advertised in
newspapers, circulars, and catalogues. The
examiners took their responsibilities seriously;

the careful selection process brought the school the best female talent in South Carolina. Admission standards were high. The applicant had to be of "irreproachable moral character; in good health; with no physical defects, habits, or eccentricities which would interfere with success in teaching." In addition to the age requirement of seventeen, the applicant had to declare her intentions to follow the teaching profession.[2]

With a $7,500 appropriation from the Legislature, $2,000 from the Peabody Board, and seven years of successful operation, this state institution with seven teachers and a student body from every county in South Carolina seemed to have a bright future, especially now that several cities and towns were bidding to provide it with a more suitable home.[3]

The interest of South Carolina's citizens in things material, educational, and political in 1893 can be seen in part by reading the Columbia State, which had been organized two years before under the editorship of Narciso G. Gonzales, formerly the Columbia correspondent of the News and Courier. The struggling State in January, 1893, sensed a lagging public interest in the paper's opinions, which were usually oriented to a violent anti-Tillman axis.[4] In a true showman's fashion, the State advertised that the Rock Hill Buggy Company was making a fine buggy to be offered as a premium to the person sending the largest list of paid subscriptions to their semi-weekly State on or before March 1, 1893. This fine buggy would be furnished with the best wheels supplied by the Virginia and North Carolina Wheel Company of Richmond; its high-grade steel axles would come from the Sheldon Axle Company of Wilkes Barre, Pennsylvania; King of Buffalo would supply the springs; and John Reilly of Newark, the leather. The Rock Hill Buggy Company was "composed," according to the State, "of some of the strongest businessmen in that very progressive town--men who will do all they promise to do." The prize offered

64

and its successors were later described as the buggies that made Rock Hill famous.[5]

Interspersed between stories about Tillman's defying the government, his growing aristocratic ways, and many others, one finds a large number of advertisements with which the struggling State managed no doubt to keep one jump ahead of failure. Dr. Leslie E. Keeley advertised his cures for the liquor, opium, and tobacco habits and stressed his endorsement by the United States Government. Glen Springs, South Carolina, in its advertisement proudly proclaimed the curative values of its mineral water. Ayer's confidently told of its health restorer, Sassaparilla. Also two of the state constitutional officers had purchased Smith's typewriters, and Converse College in Spartanburg was announcing certain special features of the school including steam heat, gas lights, and hot and cold baths.[6]

On February 14, the State editorialized about Winthrop's future. They admonished the Columbia City Council to bid for Winthrop because once this school was permanently located, the state of South Carolina was committed to establishing, they reasoned, "a great school." They also pointed out that the school would receive a good endowment from the Peabody Fund and that if Columbia did not secure the Industrial School, they would also lose the Training School, soon to be a four-year college. Placing the argument on a material basis, Gonzales and his paper reavowed that with this college, Columbia would attain perhaps thirty- or forty-thousand people within ten years and that the college would "put tens of thousand of dollars in circulation" at Columbia. However, the paper made no mention of the educational value of the institution.[7]

With a typical Gonzales technique, the State carried the story that Spartanburg taunted Columbia, saying that Columbia could not compete with it. Soon thereafter the State carried Chester's bid of $50,000 for the Industrial School. This brought the list of serious contenders to three and, according to Gonzales, Columbia would bid at the proper time.[8]

The first stage of Columbia's bid came in mid-March, when the local Land and Investment Company offered a good site for the Industrial School. Gonzales followed this with a strong editorial advising Columbians that should they allow the smaller communities to secure the Industrial and Normal College, it would be a blow to the prestige of Columbia and that people would assert Columbia was not able or anxious to expand. He blew hard on the theme that loss of the school would mean a loss of "millions" from the soon-to-be-divided Peabody Fund. The fund, he continued, was "so large that Winthrop will be one of the best endowed institutions in the country." Becoming trapped by his own imagination, Gonzales pressed to gain the college for Columbia, urging the city council to pay no attention to the argument that Columbia was overtaxed. His punch line became "Gentlemen of the Council, do your duty and fear not!" This dramatic line was rivaled only by the ad for a new piano which read: "Cleveland is President! Cotton is King! The Fischer Piano is Queen."[9]

On March 28, 1893, the State proclamied "Look out for Chester!" in annoucing her successful elections for subscriptions to obtain the women's Industrial College. Quoting intelligence from Chester, the State pointed out that this inland town was about sixty miles from any institution of learning and that it possessed excellent railroad facilities which made the town easily accessible. With a reputation as "the liveliest town in South Carolina," this seat "of culture and liberality" possessed of beautiful rolling hills and a good climate had much to offer Winthrop.

Chester had the resources and since she had never had in her history any "state endowment or bounty whatsoever," she felt that she was entitled to get this school.[10] Chester's aggressiveness helped to stir somewhat the Columbia council, which

66

was reluctant because of a large debt to commit the city further. A resolution to have Columbia bid $50,000 and two building sites excited certain members of the council, who moved to wait until they could see what the other bidders were going to do. Mr. John P. Thomas, Jr., of the school board made "an eloquent appeal to the Council," pointing out the cultural value of the school. Even in dollars and cents, it would be a good business deal, he reasoned. Captain John G. Capers followed with another appeal, pointing out that the people of the city would back council in their bid. But Council-man George V. Allworden scoffed at utopian promises, suggesting instead that council raise enough money to establish a factory which would bring in some real returns. Allworden strengthened his argument by pointing out that neither Charleston nor Greenville with their wealth and progress saw anything "in it and left it alone." In turn, the State stressed that the council had "flunked" in not taking a more active stand for the securing of the industrial school.[11]

Reaction in late March was forthcoming. The people of Columbia demanded that council reconsider. The mayor called an extra meeting. The citizens sent a petition demanding action and saying the city should put up at least $50,000. The seven opposing councilmen stayed away; no business was transacted. The State suggested defeating these men in the next year's election. With delegations from Spartanburg, Chester, and Rock Hill gathering at the capital and anxiously awaiting action, additional frustration marked the attitude of Columbia's citizenry. Interest in the location of the State Industrial and Normal College had grown keen and great.[12]

Excitement ran high, with delegations from Rock Hill, Chester, and Spartanburg all clamoring for a chance to press their cases with the governor and the Board. Governor Tillman convened a Board meeting at the mansion at eight o'clock, March 29. With the full complement present excepting A.H. Patterson of Barnwell, the active delegations

67

pressed for immediate consideration of their bids because it was announced that supplemental bidding would end as of eleven o'clock on March 30, 1893. [13]

Chester and Rock Hill protested this point, saying that they had come with fixed bids and that Spartanburg was there represented by wealthy men who could raise any amount. After a short executive session, the Board agreed not to allow supplementary bids. About 10:30 they allowed Chester to explain its bid. Rock Hill too later received time and finally Spartanburg. Many convincing speakers rose. Just before adjournment at midnight, the Board announced that it would visit each of the places and examine the sites offered before rendering a decision. [14]

The Board reconvened at ten o'clock the following morning (March 30, 1893) at the executive mansion. They moved to have the attorney general pass on these bids and correct any defects that existed therein. They further proposed to invite any architects who desired to travel at their own expense to accompany the Board on its inspection trip of the various sites. The secretary, W.D. Mayfield, was instructed to notify the superintendent of the penitentiary that a squad of convicts would be needed about July 1 to help with buildings. The secretary was also to apprize the localities of the Board's projected visits beginning on April 19, 1893. [15]

On April 19, as planned, the Board of Trustees viewed the sites offered by Chester. Moving on to Rock Hill the next day, they viewed what that young city had to offer. Finally on April 21, they visited Spartanburg. That night the Board met in the parlor of the Merchant's Hotel with Governor Tillman and Messrs. Hemphill, Gary, Buist, Breazeale, Fuller, McLaurin, Elder, Joynes, and Mayfield present. Following the reading of the attorney general's opinions concerning the bids of the three applicants, Dr. Joynes brought up Columbia's application. Mr. Breazeale moved that Columbia's bid could not be considered because of

68

the actions of the Board on March 29 and that Columbia should be notified of same. They finally voted eight to two to locate the South Carolina Industrial and Winthrop Normal College in Rock Hill. Thirty days' notice had to be given, according to law, before finally locating the college. The Board adjourned to meet at Rock Hill May 31 unless called together sooner by the chairman.[16]

Meanwhile Columbia had tried with renewed vigor to sell the college to its citizenry. With the State proclaiming that "Columbia still has a chance" to get the school, petitions were urged on the council and proponents argued that the previous work of locating the school was only preliminary to the final consideration. The most influential citizens of Columbia had called a meeting on April 6 to make plans for keeping the college in the name of progress. Colonel F.W. McMaster spoke for the city in seeking Winthrop's location at Columbia. The editorials of the State stressed that Winthrop Training School was born there, nurtured by the city, and "does not wish to leave its mother." Five students at Carolina College, sensing the confusion of the citizenry and wishing to be more a part of things, set a bonfire and were expelled by the faculty, which left only fifty-two students at the college.[17]

A latent mass meeting packed the Columbia Opera House on April 7. The time was at hand for the people to act. The council was petitioned to float thirty-year bonds for $50,000 at six percent. Again Colonel F.W. McMaster spoke about Columbia's losing prestige as the educational center of the state if they let Winthrop go. With Clemson located at Fort Hill and Carolina "already crippled" they must, he felt, hold Winthrop. With only $1300 in the treasury and with the canal bonds and others aggregating to $900,000, the council balked at any additional expenditure. The most convincing speech came from John P. Thomas, Jr., editor of the Columbia Register and a state representative from Richland County, who said that "the greatest advantage in having the school"

69

there was "to educate our daughters and the daughters of the state. What will it cost," he asked, "if we send them away?" It was finally proposed that the matter be submitted to the people, but time was running out for Columbia's bid.[18]

South Carolina witnessed considerable newspaper sniping and ill will in the few weeks before Winthrop's destination was decided. The News and Courier carried an article saying that the Catholics of Columbia approved the school. A spokesman on the council denied it. This story perhaps arose from the impression that the Catholics were fighting all public education. The Rock Hill Herald on April 21, the day that the decision to locate the school was to be made, announced that Chester did not have the water necessary for the school.[19] The Chester Bulletin countered that if they needed water, "we don't know of any town that could spare it better than Rock Hill, if the number of Keeley graduates [cured alcoholics] is any indication." Editorially, the State blamed the aldermen for Columbia's loss, and they "dipped their flag to the pushing city amid York's hills" and predicted that if Rock Hill got the college, "Charlotte will one day be her suburb."[20]

Following the announcement of Rock Hill's victory, a great rejoicing rocked that town. Anvils were fired, factory whistles screamed, bells rang out, and the populace danced through the streets. Residents called this "the greatest day in the history of our city." A procession, led by the band, made the rounds of the town with a serenade that lasted well into the wee hours. The band and the marching citizenry paid special attention to Mrs. Ben Tillman, who was visiting in town. According to a State reporter, "no such enthusiasm was ever before known here."[21]

In rehashing the details of how Rock Hill had won this rich prize, the State held a faint hope that somehow Columbia might still have a chance, if Rock Hill's offer was found to be faulty, They also praised Dr. E.S. Joynes for his earnest

70

appeal on Columbia's behalf. Carefully they pointed out that the attorney general had advised there were some minor flaws in the bids. However, within a few days these flaws had been resolved, and the architectural firm of Niernsee and LaMotte had asked permission to submit plans for the proposed college buildings. It was soon evident to all that Columbia had lost. The State stopped grabbing at straws and returned to its accustomed pastime--critizing Governor Tillman.[22]

On May 31, 1893, at eight o'clock the Winthrop Board of Trustees met in Rock Hill, with Governor Tillman and Mr. Breazeale absent. They transacted their most pressing business and resolved to make the final site inspections at eleven the next day. Meanwhile Mr. Tillman came in and at nine o'clock on June 1, the secretary informed the town fathers that they were ready to receive the bonds of the town "in compliance with her bid for the location of the college." The mayor and council came forward with sixty one-thousand-dollar bonds for inspection. These bonds, known as "the South Carolina Industrial and Winthrop Normal College Bonds," were issued by council after their authorization had been ratified on March 27, 1893. The secretary of the Board turned these bonds over to the First National Bank of Rock Hill for safekeeping.[23]

The next order of business for June 1, 1893, was site inspections. According to plan, the Board would walk to each site, where they wished to meet a committee of five gentlemen. There they would make their inspection and perhaps return by carriage to conclude their deliberations. The selection at Rock Hill was narrowed to two, the Steele and the Oakland sites. Following inspections of both, the Board resolved to have the interested parties put their offers into legal form preparatory to a final consideration on June 2. The results show ample evidence of collective efforts.[24]

Early on the morning of June 2, the Board entertained a proposition from J.M. Cherry,

71

chairman of a Presbyterian High School committee which offered to convey and sell their property on Oakland, consisting of eight acres and improvements, to the trustees of Winthrop for $19,058.71. No action was taken.[25]

Next the Board considered the Steele site offer--which included thirty acres of land, $3000 worth of brick at $8.00 per thousand, rough lumber at $0.70 per hundred, and a granite rock quarry in the vicinity of Rock Hill. The proponents of the Steele or "Egypt" group included Iredell Jones, D. Hutchinson, I. Simpson, William White,, and W.C. Hutchinson, who stated they had learned that certain Rock Hillians had pledged a $700 cash addition to the bid made in Columbia on March 29 to help get the school there. Jones' group concluded their offer with the presumption "that the selection of the site would not affect this offer--we have not included it in the above, deeming it unnecessary, but we guarantee to make good any portion of this amount that is not paid on account of the selections of our site." In addition they promised to back the Rock Hill bonds, thereby guaranteeing the sale at par to the extent of $75,000. Mr. A.B. White, who owned the land with the springs near the Steele site, offered to give Winthrop the franchise of his springs if allowed to use them himself. The total package proved a most attractive offer.[26]

The second site, Oakland, was also very attractive. This area, three-fourths of a mile from downtown Rock Hill, bore the name of a California town which the Blackburn Wilson family had visited in 1890. They were so impressed with Oakland, California, that upon their return home "Black" Wilson, Jr., helped organize a real-estate company to lay out and develop the village of (Little) Oakland near Rock Hill, South Carolina. A public park, with a band stand for concerts during the long summer evenings, lay in the development.[27]

The vehicle for the Oakland development was the Rock Hill Land and Townsite Company, which had been chartered in 1890 "to buy, improve, lease, and sell real estate; lay out lands into lots and streets" in Oakland. The company's capital stock consisted of one-hundred-thousand dollars divided into thousand-dollar shares. At the time of its chartering by South Carolina, fifty-eight-thousand and one-hundred dollars had been subscribed. Six directors--William A. Courtenay, John J. Hemphill, W.J. Roddey, Richard T. Fewell, James M. Cherry, and W. Blackburn Wilson, Jr.--were elected. This board in turn elected Wilson as president; Fewell, vice president; Roddey, treasurer; and Cherry, secretary. This was the group that had promised thirty and a quarter acres as a vital part of Rock Hill's Winthrop bid. But such generosity should be viewed in the light of future profits in the sale and development of the Townsite Company's real estate as Winthrop helped to guarantee Rock Hill's growth.[28]

In addition to real estate, the Oakland bid contained the offer to deliver on demand 375,000 brick to the trustees and the offer to lend the use of streetcar railroad irons for a track from the brickyard and one from the Charleston, Cincinnati, and Chicago Railroad to the building site. The bid was further complemented with a promise to lend the Rock Hill Land and Townsite Company's brick plant and to give all the clay necessary for making 2,000,000 brick--or they agreed to make and deliver all brick required at $4.75 per thousand. The Rock Hill Construction Company under W.H. Stewart offered lumber at $0.70 per hundred. Mr. Stewart also signed a pledge of $700 additional to apply to the Townsite property. He was joined in the latter gift by W.F. Strait, T.A. Crawford, W.J. Roddey, W.H. Wylie, and A.R. Banks.[29]

On June 2 the Winthrop Board accepted the Oakland proposals and elected W.J. Roddey and Dr. T.A. Crawford to their board. An executive committee consisting of Governor Tillman, W.N. Elder, Jr., E.S. Joynes, W.J. Roddey, and Dr. T.A. Crawford agreed to discharge the Board's general duties when it recessed. The trustees also heard

President Johnson's suggestions on buildings and equipment. Before the Board adjourned, they expanded the secretary's role to include the duties of temporary treasurer.[30]

The organization plan which President Johnson left with the trustees called for the following: the first building, he said, should contain six rooms for academic professors; seven for industrial, two laboratories; a large gymnasium; a chapel capable of seating 800 to 1,000 persons. In addition, Johnson planned for society halls, one anteroom, and a reception room. Johnson recommended that no dormitory building be erected in the beginning, that instead students be allowed to board in the town. The first dormitory, he recommended, was to have room for 125. This report from Johnson suggested that heating be by steam or hot water and that electricity be used for lighting.[31]

Three days after the Winthrop Board adjourned, the First National Bank of Rock Hill advertised in Charleston that they were prepared to receive bids for the $60,000 in bonds issued to attract Winthrop to Rock Hill. The State, still very much agitated about Columbia's failure, reported in a special feature that the land selected in Rock Hill for the Industrial College was "one of the most beautiful places in South Carolina . . . at the summit of a gently sloping meadow, amid a group of majestic oaks." Here, according to the State, lovely walks and drives would be laid out. Nearby would be a park and lake "with many pleasure boats floating gracefully on its water." Again no mention of education. But the State was sure that with this new institution, Rock Hill was "bound to become the metropolis of upper Carolina." The Courier in its report stated that plans had already been presented to an architect: the building would start on July 1. The Charleston paper concluded its article with this philosophical prognostication: "the influence of the institution will soon be felt in every part of

74

the State and in almost every house of the State; and we will then wonder how we could have waited so long to do what was so well worth doing!"[32]

CHAPTER VII

BRINGING WINTHROP TO ROCK HILL

By the second week of June 1893, the furor over locating Winthrop had subsided, and Editor Gonzales favored his readers with some other appealing articles on education. Attention focused on the tripartite contest being waged for the Clemson College presidency among the partisans of Professor E.B. Craighead of Wofford, President Murphy of Arkansas Agricultural College, and Professor Stonewall Tompkins of the Miller School of Virginia. Another serious report on education dealt with the recent publication of the Appleton's Cyclopaedia list of famous educators. According to this list, the College of William and Mary in Virginia boasted more famous graduates than any other school in the South. South Carolina College ranked second. The universities of Georgia, North Carolina and Virginia ranked below South Carolina.[1]

Judging by the State on Sunday, June 11, Winthrop's work had gone forward without disturbance from the spirited contest to move the school upstate. Graduation appeared as an interesting event; over the next six days the paper printed a generously detailed account of the festivities. The public was invited to all exercises. The paper made much of the fact that Professor J.H. Bhalman had completed by hand the diplomas for the graduates of the city schools-- eleven for the whites and four for the blacks--as well as eight for the graduates of the Winthrop Normal College. These diplomas were described as "specimens of beautiful penmanship."[2]

Interspersed between the commencement announcements, the State advertised the competitive examinations for vacant scholarships to Winthrop Normal College, which would be held at county seats on July 7. These scholarships, according to the

State, were "prizes that the young women can ill afford to lose."[3]

Before the final exercises of 1893, D.B. Johnson had made an earnest effort in the name of the Class of 1893 to persuade Robert Winthrop of Nahant, Massachusetts, to attend the graduation ceremonies. On the morning of June 15, following the opening prayer, Mr. Johnson read Mr. Winthrop's reply to the invitation: "There is no possibility of my witnessing the commencement exercises." Sending his sincere thanks to the class, Mr. Winthrop offered them his kindest wishes for their future careers. During the morning exercises the eight young ladies were the first to complete the college's two-year course. Their essays and projects included such subjects as "Preparations for Citzenship," "Science in the Primary Schools," and "School Problems." The latter was the valedictory of Miss Nina E. Treadwell. The final evening ceremony took place at the Opera House, with Senator R.R. Hemphill delivering the diplomas and Mr. John P. Thomas making a splendid address. The News and Courier, commenting on the program, asked a blessing on the Normal College and called it "the herald of a happier era for South Carolina . . . long may it flourish as the nursery of the young womanhood of South Carolina." One somber note sounded during the proceedings of the Alumnae Association when it was pointed out that the following June would be the last time that the graduates would meet in Columbia, a city many of the graduates had known as their school home.[4]

Meanwhile Tillman and the Winthrop Board's Executive Committee had been formulating plans for the Normal College's removal to Rock Hill. Planning for the transition consumed considerable time and thought. At last the Executive Committee's work was well enough along to necessitate a general Board meeting at Rock Hill on August 7, 1893, at eight p.m. The Executive Committee reported to the full Board, which in turn listened to several architects and builders who had submitted plans. The

plans of Bruce and Morgan of Atlanta presented the
most interesting proposals. Adjourning at midnight,
the Board reconvened at 8:30 the next day. At that
time questions about costs and specifications
continued. They voted eight to five in favor of
Bruce and Morgan. They further agreed to a nine-
hundred-dollar fee plus a thirty-five-dollar
travel allotment when either member of the firm
was requested to meet with the Board.[5]

Other matters considered included the
Oakland property's deed delivery, and they moved to
contract with David E. Finley to investigate the
title at a cost not to exceed $15.00. The by-laws
for the college were voted. W.D. Mayfield reported
on funds received and disbursed by him as treasurer.
A new secretary and treasurer, W.B. Dunlap, was
elected to hold office until November 1, 1894. The
work went forward. Thus, Governor Tillman, ex-
officio Chairman of the Board, had a very encouraging report in October 1893 for members of the
General Assembly.[6]

The governor in his report to the Senate
and the House of Representatives in Columbia
reviewed Rock Hill's bid and its natural advantages
as a location for the South Carolina Industrial and
Winthrop Normal College. Stressing its location
near the foothills of the Blue Ridge Mountains, he
praised the fine water, the healthful climate, and
the good railroad connections, predicting that with
this educational institution, Rock Hill was destined
to become one of the important cities of the state.[7]

Tillman asked the Legislature to amend the
law to make it possible to have local trustees
permanently on the Board. He also asked that the
trustees be relieved of paying the expenses for the
convicts. As of August 1, 1893, there were
already sixty convicts housed, fed, and guarded
near the college grounds. They engaged in getting
wood, burning brick quarrying granite, and digging
the buildings' foundations. According to Governor
Tillman, 265,000 cubic feet of granite and nearly
a million brick were on hand, although brickmaking
would stop over the winter.[8]

78

Tillman reported to the Legislature that Bruce and Morgan of Atlanta had presented the plans for a building two-hundred by ninety feet, with three stories above the basement and forty rooms-- none dormitory rooms. This would be adequate to house the academic, Normal and industrial work with space devoted for a gymnasium and a large library. They planned to complete the building by September, 1894, with sixty-thousand dollars given by Rock Hill. Such a facility, Tillman reasoned, would provide classrooms for six-hundred girls and he hoped that the Legislature would give $50,000 for a dormitory since it was doubtful that half of those wishing to attend the college could find suitable facilities in Rock Hill.[9]

The first or Main Building, as it was called for many years, rose out of cut stone and brick, with a slate roof and galvanized iron cornices. For this vital job, the Board employed the Thompson-Decker Construction Company of Birmingham since this company had much experience with big construction. Tillman sent an artist's rendering to give the Legislature a better idea of what he and the Board had done. Tillman also informed the Legislature that some remnants of marble and tiling left from work on the State House could be used to advantage at Winthrop if the secretary of state were authorized to turn this material over to Winthrop. In concluding he told the Legislature that if $50,000 more could be authorized, two buildings could be erected "together," and with the use of convict labor and the services of Thompson-Decker, they would open the college in October, 1894.[10]

During late 1893 work went forward on the new college building. When the full Board met in the executive mansion on December 13, 1893, they approved the report of the Executive Committee, including the purchase of a farm of one-hundred and forty-one acres at $20.00 per acre. This property was located less than a mile from the college. It was further agreed to accept recommendations to purchase the Stewart property, where the president's house now stands. Messrs. Crawford and Roddey were instructed to complete the transaction.[11]

The South Carolina Industrial and Winthrop Normal College of Columbia, which continued and enlarged the work of the Winthrop Training School and provided industrial training, underwent a name change on December 23, 1893, to the Winthrop Normal and Industrial College of South Carolina. The change represented "a complete coalescence," according to Dr. Joynes, "of two conceptions of education championed by Mr. Johnson and Governor Tillman."[12]

With the work progressing on the new building, the Board met again (on January 19, 1894) at the Carolina Hotel in Rock Hill. The abstracted title to the college property was approved. The finance committee made its first detailed report: the itemized expenditures tell in part the story of progress. The second largest expenditure of $4082.63 was for the Stewart house. Other sizeable expenditures were for the stockade, quarry number one, the convicts, the brickyard, and $5,444.77 for the building to date--January 6, 1894. At this meeting the Board set the salary of Mr. Stewart, the superintendent, at $50.00 a month to increase to $75.00 monthly when brickmaking began in the spring. Other items included engaging D. A. Tompkins of Charlotte to make recommendations regarding heating, lighting, and water as well as plans for the power house. Before concluding this meeting, the local trustees were instructed to buy 300,000 or more pressed brick, suitable for facing the college and dormitory, at no more than $10.00 per thousand.[13]

The excellent treatment which the Tillmanite Legislature gave Winthrop in 1893 is reflected in the appropriations for scholarships, convict help, expert teachers, and ($50,000) building and equipping dormitories. Furthermore, a joint resolution was approved on January 4, 1894, directing the secretary of state to:

80

turn over to the Board of Trustees of the South Carolina Industrial and Winthrop Normal College all remnants of marble and tiling left over from work on the State House that the commission on the State House designates as no longer needed for its completion if such can be used to advantage in the construction of the South Carolina Industrial and Winthrop Normal College for the education of the white girls of South Carolina.[14]

From Governor Tillman's report to the General Assembly concerning the college operating year ending October 31, 1894, we see some of the many problems confronting the trustees. Admonishing the General Assembly to remember that the college was running on a small scale in Columbia while buildings were erected in Rock Hill, he reminded the representatives that the magnitude of the Rock Hill job was such that it was behind schedule. Stressing that they had planned for six-hundred students, he admitted that he and the Board had been "woefully misled by the architect's estimates." The result was two partially completed buildings and a great need for more money. "All the brick work on both is done," Tillman reported, "and the roofs on both are complete." But the problem lay in the fact that the work on the water pipes, heating, and electrical systems was time-consuming and expensive.[15]

Inviting the General Assembly to examine their financial statement, Governor Tillman stressed the acquisition of a one-hundred and forty-one acre farm and a twelve-room house (Stewart) that was on the land donated as the college site. He justified $6,904 for both properties on the basis that the house could easily be converted into an infirmary and the farm, which he bought before land values went up around the college, would be valuable and necessary in supplying vegetables, fruits, and milk, "thus cheapening the cost of board to the pupils and adding to their comfort and health." [16]

81

The report makes it abundantly clear that Tillman--who often publicly decried his handicap, a lack of formal education--was a good manager as he demonstrated what was best for the college. Another outside investment was an acre of land about one-half mile across the tracks from which they could pump 75,000 gallons of pure spring water a day, an investment entailing another expenditure of $3,600. By October, after the first full year's work in Rock Hill, Tillman and the Board borrowed to carry on the work. They had received from all sources $110,500, and they had spent this amount in a most worthwhile manner.[17]

To complete the two buildings and furnish them properly in time for school in the fall of 1895, Tillman (speaking for the Board) estimated that Winthrop needed $69,500 to finish the power house, the dormitory, and the main building, and to buy the equipment for these. Promising to have the buildings ready by September 1 next, he reported that they had already dug and laid a foundation for a second dormitory with the brick and stone on hand. Tillman promised the Legislature "the most beautiful, commodious, and well-planned college property in the Southern States for the education of women." To partially justify what he had done, Tillman called attention to the state's spending over a million dollars for three men's colleges and to the annual appropriations exceeding $100,000 to run them. Comparing this to the $50,000 already appropriated for Winthrop plus the $70,000 he was requesting, he failed to see how the state could refuse $120,000 for its future mothers. With $5,000 to operate on, Tillman promised that they could open in September next and run the school till the first of next January.[18]

Two weeks after Tillman's report, D. B. Johnson--President, and ex-officio Chairman for the Special Committee in charge of the Winthrop Normal College--made his report to the Winthrop trustees. His eighth session closed June 15, with thirty-two graduates--the first class to complete the two-year course. Johnson stressed the large and active

82

alumnae association which had adopted the motto "Devotion to duty, fidelity to self, and allegiance to the College," sentiments that had come from the writings of Mr. Winthrop. This session's highlight was the visit on May 12, 1894, of the faculty and students to the new Rock Hill campus. Taken by special train to Rock Hill, they participated in the cornerstone laying at the Main Building and helped to commemorate Mr. Winthrop's birthday in an exercise differing from those held heretofore. Johnson also announced in his report the leave of absence granted in September "on account of home affairs to Miss Mary H. Leonard, First Instructor in the School." Johnson's financial report listed resources and expenditures for his continuing operation in Columbia at $5,178.06, small compared to what Tillman and the Board were doing at Rock Hill.[19]

The Masonic ceremonies for laying the cornerstone on May 12, 1894, in Rock Hill were heart-felt and solemn. Many witnessed "this . . . great and glorious day for South Carolina," as Governor Tillman described it. Before the main address by the Grand Master of the Order, the young ladies from the Winthrop Normal College of Columbia sang "To Thee, O Country," and Governor Tillman (Chairman of the Board of Trustees) delivered what was billed as an introductory address. Paying his respects to the local citizens "whose pluck, [and] self-reliance" had helped them win this college, Tillman left little doubt as to who would control the school. Before coming to the real essence of his message, he discoursed on the history of cornerstone laying, going back to the book of Job. This Biblical approach was a vital ingredient in a Tillmanic speech, and as always it gave the one-eyed man with a powerful voice and a keen mind an opportunity to best a rival or would-be rival.[20]

Moving next into a short history of higher education in South Carolina, Tillman described Carolina College as always deserving and receiving handsome support from the state. Tillman stressed "that until the last eight years" Carolina and the

Citadel, "which were promptly reopened as soon as the white people regained possession of the government in South Carolina in 1876, were considered ample by those who had control, to supply all the needs of our people for higher education by the State."[21]

To meet a greater need, after a long and bitter struggle, another school for boys--Clemson College--had been established by the General Assembly in 1889, opening its doors to students in July 1893. Tillman described Clemson as a new departure in education, "a bread and butter school," and reminded his audience that they had "Ocular demonstrations in the splendid corps of cadets," numbering over 500, and that these young men had paid their own way to come over to the new Winthrop to add "éclat" to the occasion. Directing the audience's attention to the body of manly looking youngsters, he asked his hearers to consider that ten months ago these boys had been "gawky, slouchy country louts or city dudes," half of whom had only one semester of training at Clemson.[22]

With the background properly laid, Tillman moved to his central theme: "What have we done for our women? Where does the state educate its future mothers?" There was a slight pause and then the clear decisive answer to question one--"Nothing!" A moment later came the answer to number two-- "Nowhere!" And then accelerating the pitch of his voice, Tillman cried out, "but thank God, this great wrong will soon be righted, and our statesmanship will no longer cause us to blush!"[23]--assuring his audience that Winthrop would be "grander in design than any or all of them [the State colleges], larger and more elaborate in architecture, more beautiful and ornamental" and that Winthrop "will ere long pierce the heavens with its stately spires, and the sky of York will be promise, that will attract the gaze of people not only of this state, but of many states." According to Tillman, when the two dormitories were erected according to plan, Winthrop "will be the largest Woman's College of its kind in the Union." Tillman stressed that it was most fitting to name the boys' school after Clemson because of Clemson's help and the girls' school after Winthrop for carrying out the wishes of George Peabody, who had done so much for education in the South. It was Tillman's hope that the youth of South Carolina would emulate the examples set by Calhoun, Clemson, Peabody, and Winthrop, whose beneficence they were enjoying and would continue to enjoy for years to come.[24]

Moving rapidly in his speech to the matters of curriculum and control, Tillman made crystal clear what he expected. As Tillman viewed it, two words--Normal and industrial--would be the "lodestone which must guide our people out of the bog of poverty, ignorance, and stagnation which surrounds us." Within this context of education and work, he saw the only hope of South Carolina. Conceding the importance and need for trained teachers, Tillman was well aware that mere possession of knowledge did not carry with it "the power of imparting it, or exciting emulation, of making study interesting, of training children how to think and reason." Tillman proposed to get the best teachers and to develop the Normal training to its fullest, even though he had often thought "that teachers are born, not made."[25]

Tillman left no doubt about Winthrop's industrial feature. It would be "co-ordinated and of equal importance," he said. Since knowledge coupled with skill would always insure "any woman absolute exemption from want and poverty," Tillman was determined to change the system whereby a woman trained in a boarding school was usually left helpless by the death of a father or relative. He vowed in this college to teach "everything and have the students practice every industrial art, that will lead to independence." He specified, as an example, that music would be taught as an industrial art, "with only such proficiency in singing and playing as will insure livelihood." It would not be taught at all, he said, as an ornament: those lacking special talents in it would be excluded. Becoming more specific as to what he meant by industrial

85

education, Tillman stated that the girls would learn and practice laundering, chemistry, practical cooking, and dressmaking. They would learn by doing these things and "all distinctions of wealth will be done away with." Under his system every girl would wear a uniform, the cost of which would not exceed twenty dollars a year. Citing his own daughter who had gone off to school with a big Saratoga trunk full of clothing, he said she had been sent many more and now would need an extra trunk to return home. "We are determined," Tillman vowed, "that no girl shall ever leave Winthrop College with, or bring to it, a Saratoga Trunk."[26]

As if he had not already done so in this forthright speech, Tillman now announced that "I am going to do some very plain talking"; even though he aspired to fit women to support themselves, "I want it understood," he stressed, "that I, at least, am irrevocably opposed to anything being done or taught here that shall tend in the slightest degree to rub the bloom off the peach. God forbid that this school shall ever send forth a woman who has been unsexed." Tillman wanted the school to better fit women for the full responsibilities of motherhood. He wished to turn out well-trained, strong, modest, and lady-like women rather than "bold, brazen, self-asserting females, prating of woman's rights, man's tyranny, degradation of nursing children, and so on, ad nauseam." With parting words of platonic advice, he indicated that the young men trained at Clemson "will naturally look hither and seek amoung the students who will flock to Rock Hill their future helpmates." To the accompaniment of thundering applause, Tillman took his seat and surveyed the audience, while the Masons proceeded with the program.[27]

Much hard work took place between the laying of the cornerstone and the fall, 1895, college opening at Rock Hill. Tillman was finishing out his last year as governor and was most anxious to have the college fairly well settled before leaving office in late 1894. The college used eighty-three convicts on a twelve-month basis. This work carried over into 1895, when an average of fifty-seven were used, costing the college $7,642.80. The work had advanced well enough by fall, 1894, for the Board to consider final furnishings. Four laundry-machine makers presented their pitches. Four utensils makers displayed their wares. Classroom desks were considered. Chair manufacturers came to Rock Hill as well as mattress and bedstead companies. The New England Piano Company was there. Asking for $75,000 to completely equip and open the college until the Legislature of 1895 could make further arrangements, Tillman and the Board moved to borrow $10,000, mortgaging the property to insure the work would continue.[28]

On November 17, 1894, Mr. Tillman tele-graphed resolutions expressing deep regret and condolences on the death of Robert C. Winthrop, the friend and benefactor of the college. These were sent to Dr. Samuel A. Green of Boston on behalf of Winthrop's family and the Peabody Board. This was Tillman's last offical act for the Board before the new governor, John Gary Evans of Aiken, assumed his post on December 4, 1894.[29]

Upon assuming chairmanship of the college Board, Governor Evans reviewed progress as of December 7, 1894, and Dr. Joynes moved to refer to the Executive Committee decisions about what work to push. This was adopted. A called meeting on December 27, 1894, at the executive mansion paved the way for considering a faculty and the president. D.B. Johnson was still superintendent of the city schools of Columbia, as well as president and ex-officio chairman for the special committee in charge of the Winthrop Normal College based in Columbia.[30]

Winthrop opened in Rock Hill in 1895. In early January the Board reorganized by electing Governor Evans permanent chairman and W. D. Mayfield permanent secretary. The Board on January 9, 1895, added senator-elect B. R. Tillman to the Executive Committee. During this meeting, D. B. Johnson reported on some small expenses incurred during his trip to Rock Hill. A resolution passed asking the superintendent of education to draw on the comptroller-general in favor of D. B. Johnson for the $2,000 that had been appropriated by the Legislature to pay the increased expenses incident to establishing a two-year course at the college. The group also moved closer to selecting a faculty and a president by resolving that "the faculty shall consist of a President, who may be a professor; and of the professors or heads of departments, appointed by the Board." This was further elaborated on by the report of the Committee on Organization headed by Dr. Joynes.[31]

Dr. Joynes' committee suggested that if the college opened in September, the faculty should be elected by early June and the president even earlier. His committee recommended that the president be charged with the general responsibility of the college, "subject to the by-laws and general directions of the Board." They further recommended that while he not necessarily be assigned to teach, "he and his family should reside in the college dormitory and board at the college table, but the president should furnish his own apartment." Board, fuel, and lights would be charged to him at the same rate as to pupils. The president's salary was suggested at $2,000 a year. In light of a recent law directing Winthrop to be finished by the superintendent of the penitentiary, they recommended dropping the present superintendent as of January 12.[32]

The Board gathered again on February 19, 1895, to transact business. Chairman Tillman of the Executive Committee reported on its activities. The group resolved that Board members could file expense accounts against the $20,000 appropriated for the completion of the college buildings. Their secretary would present these accounts to Superintendent W.A. Neal, of the penitentiary, for payment. Moving to other business, the Board reviewed applications for president. The president of Mississippi Industrial Institute and College had withdrawn his application, leaving those of the superintendents of public schools in Pittsburg, Kansas; Edinburg,

Indiana; and (Mr. Johnson) Columbia, South Carolina. After Mr. Johnson's unanimous election, Mr. A. H. Patterson moved to raise his salary to $2500. The raise was defeated 12 to 2. Again Patterson moved to raise the president's salary to $2200; it was tabled by the same margin. Dr. Joynes moved that the Committee on Organization, of which Winthrop's president was an ex-officio member, act jointly with the Executive Committee to draw the plan of organization, including the courses to be taught, and to notify the public of this. Before adjourning, Senator W. A. Brown of the Committee on Education advised the group that he would offer a resolution at the next meeting to elect women teachers as far as practicable. Thus, the college moved closer to opening.[33]

By May 15, 1895, the Committee on Organization was ready with a report designed to inaugurate the first school year at Rock Hill. In essence their report helped parents make arrangements for enrolling their daughters by spelling out a simple plan for the newly located college. The committee recommended the minimum admission age of fifteen and suggested that Winthrop follow the same general requirements used by the Georgia Normal and Industrial College, to wit: the student must be "of good moral character and of sound physical health as an Industrial School is no place for weakly and sickly girls." Entrance examinations were required. No pupil would be admitted without an elementary knowledge of arithmetic, grammar, geography, and history. Mr. Johnson, who presented these recommendations for the committee, suggested that the school year be divided into three terms of three months each. There should be a summer term of at least four weeks as well. They agreed to remit tuition for those unable to pay. The Board then reviewed job applications, agreed to buy mattresses and beds, and stipulated that all teachers were not required to live in the dormitory. Those required to live in would do so rent free. Senator Brown's motion to favor women teachers carried.

The final important business concerned
teacher selection.[34] Judging by the number of
applications contained in Benjamin Ryan Tillman's
correspondence, one might conclude that the
applicants knew only of Mr. Tillman and his college,
not of the newly elected President David Bancroft
Johnson. From Anderson Mr. J. B. Martin wrote on
behalf of Verna Ayer, daughter of General Lewis M.
Ayer formerly of Barnwell. Miss Ayer sought the
stenography teacher's position as she wished to
leave her job with the Bishop of Minnesota to be
near her retired father. Congressman J. William
Stokes wrote for Professor Brent W. Andrews of
Bishopville. Georgie M. Center wrote to help her
brother get a position in English or math. There
were many more. In addition, the state superintendent of education forwarded to Tillman a list
of applicants--no doubt for Tillman to pass on.
Edward P. Moses (a friend of Johnson), writing to
Tillman from Philadelphia, made a strong pitch to
head the Department of Pedagogics, Ethics, and
Psychology; Moses listed an impressive number of
prominent South Carolinians who could vouch for him.
On May 15, 1895, the Board met and elected teachers
and other officers for Winthrop:[35]

Chair of Pedagogics, Ethics and Psychology,
salary of $1500, E.P. Moses of Anderson,
South Carolina

Chair of English Language and Literature,
History and Civics, salary $1500, James P.
Kinard of Newberry, South Carolina

Chair of Mathematics, Physics and
Astronomy, salary $1500, W. E. Breazeale
of Anderson, South Carolina.

The election of teachers and other officers
was continued May 16 with the following being
selected:

Assistant teacher of English Language and
Literature, History, and Civics, salary
$500, Miss Lee Wicker of Virginia

90

Assistant teacher of Mathematics, Physics, and Astronomy, salary $500, Miss Mary G. Pope of Greenville, South Carolina

Instructor in Chemistry and Biology, salary $800, Miss M. W. Woodrow of Columbia, South Carolina

Instructor in Free Hand and Industrial Drawing, and Art, salary $800, Miss Ella MacD. Alford of Sellers, South Carolina

Instructor in Sewing, Dressmaking, and Millinery, salary $800, Miss Lucy Dallet of Philadelphia, Pennsylvania

Instructor in Stenography and Typewriting, salary $500, Miss E. R. Hughes of Philadelphia, Pennsylvania

Instructor in Cookery and Domestic Economy, salary $800, Miss Sarah M. Wilson of Yonkers, New York

Instructor in Vocal Music, salary $700, Mrs. M. M. Souther of Quincy, Massachusetts

Instructor in Instrumental Music, salary $500, Miss Allie M. Yost of Staunton, Virginia.[36]

Later, on July 10, 1895, the first teachers of Cookery and Instrumental Music having declined, the following successors were named:

Instructor in Physical Culture, Physiology and Hygiene, salary $600, Miss Ada Wolfe of Manchester, Iowa. [The President was authorized to increase this amount by $200 if it became necessary.]

Instructor in Cookery and Domestic Economy, salary $800, Miss Laura C. Hutchinson of Philadelphia, Pennsylvania.

91

Three additional teachers were also named: assistant Instrumental Music teacher went to (salary $500) Miss Rosell Waddill of Greenville; a professor of music position (salary $1500) went to Wade R. Brown of Greenville; and a Latin instructor's position (salary $800) went to Miss Hortense Roberts of Nashville.[37]

For organizational purposes the by-laws were amended, providing that the several departments should for the present be as follows:

1. Pedagogics, Ethics, and Psychology
2. English Language and Literature, History and Civics
3. Mathematics, Physics and Astronomy
4. Chemistry and Biology
5. Latin and Modern Languages
6. Free Hand and Industrial Drawing and Art
7. Sewing and Dressmaking and Millinery
8. Cooking and Domestic Economy
9. Physical Culture, Physiology and Hygiene
10. Commercial Department
11. Department of Music
12. Practice School.[38]

With the instructional staff signed, many other problems needed tackling during the summer and early fall of 1895 before Winthrop could officially open. Trustee Tillman and his friends were waging a hot campaign to have "the proper men" elected to the state's Constitutional Convention. It became a real fight, with the Tillmanites accusing Gonzales of the State and his "Antireformers" of trying to use the Negro's vote to protest the corporations and the Bourbon-oriented class. News about Winthrop disappeared in the papers that reported anything they could get on Senator Tillman and company to cast aspersions on his cause and character. Over and over again, even the more knowledgeable News and Courier called him

"senator-elect" despite the fact that he had been
sworn in as a United States Senator from South
Carolina on March 4, 1895.[39]

The Winthrop Board held no important
meetings between July 10 and October 14, 1895.
Tillman kept busy with the hustings and the Constitutional Convention; Colonel Neal made periodic
visits to the works at Winthrop; Johnson came to
Rock Hill in late July to take care of the academic
picture; and Professor Joynes went abroad to study
women's education in Germany and France. Many
questions remained--including the uniform question,
which the Board left to President Johnson, Senator
Tillman, and Superintendent of Eduction W. D.
Mayfield. On June 25, Colonel Neal again inspected
the works at Winthrop and gave his assurance that
the plant would be ready by October 1. His certainty prompted him to take many of the convicts
back to the state farm to help "lay by" the crops
there. But he promised to send them back as soon
as possible to finish off work at the college.[40]

Winthrop's coming helped stimulate interest
and economic developments at Rock Hill. The News
and Courier tried to keep the reader abreast of all
happenings there. Interspersed between items about
Winthrop and Rock Hill's growth would be reports
like these: "A blind tiger [bootlegger] was caught
operating out of 'Brown Workman's Barber Shop.'"
Rock Hill was enjoying melons grown in Florida,
peaches grown in Georgia, and now "the local crops
are in." The paper took special note of two nice
buildings going up in Oakland, on beautiful sites,
almost in the shadow of the Winthrop College
building. By July 16, the Courier could proclaim
that "The Girl's State College" would open on
October 2, 1895. The faculty was complete and the
announcement stated that "the door of the Winthrop
Normal and Industrial College will be thrown open to
women of the state." Perhaps it was only
coincidence, but the next day the paper carried
announcements of the fall term of the Richmond
Female Seminary, Rev. M. J. Baldwin's school (the

93

Augusta Female Seminary), and the Virginia Ladies' College of Roanoke, Virginia. [41]

Finally on July 24, President Johnson arrived in Rock Hill where he joined his mother and sister who had preceded him. "This," according to the Courier, "is Rock Hill's first gain of families of the teaching force of that Institution." Two days later, Senator Tillman came through York to attend a big alliance rally at Tirzah, near Rock Hill. Tillman gave his audience of over 2,500 a replay of his famous "free silver" address delivered earlier in the year at Memphis, Tennessee. No doubt college business also took place on this journey.

The hot weather of August produced little news from Winthrop and Rock Hill except for families going to the hills and springs in search of a cooler and a more healthful climate. By early September, W. D. Mayfield's office furnished Tillman a progress report on the college following Tillman's communications with them. According to this account, the dormitory was almost finished and most of the work in the Main Building done as of September 3. The water works were in order. The grounds were being graded; the "lake" drained. Most of the furniture was in place. The Three C's Railroad wanted the college to furnish materials and do the grading for their branch line into the college. Johnson had accepted 257 applicants by this time. Colonel Neal had about exhausted his money, and Professor Moses and his family of eight would need three rooms in the dormitory. In concluding this report, Mayfield's office advised Tillman that it might "be well for you to run up to Rock Hill to act on such matters as need special attention." This is abundant proof of whom they regarded as the boss. [42]

Courier in mid-September gave a fine description of the new model women's college. The large chapel was described as seating 1200 and furnished with oak opera chairs with music rooms back of it. The Main Building had a dining room and rooms for the Training School below. The structure

94

contained an attic and three stories with beautiful wood work and all modern conveniences. Next door, connected by a covered way, was a long L-shaped dormitory with three floors and a broad piazza on each floor. The rooms were furnished with two single iron bedsteads each and other essentials, with baths on each floor. And the power-house was located about two-hundred feet to the rear of the original kitchen.[43]

This description also mentioned the academic program oriented to industrial and Normal work. The work involved four classes--the freshmen taking such subjects as Latin, French, German, botany, physical geography, math, vocal music, and physical culture. The Industrial Department offered stenography, typewriting, bookkeeping, freehand and industrial drawing, sewing, dressmaking, and hatmaking. The Domestic Science Department had schools of cooking, dressmaking, and housekeeping.[44]

The college opening had been finally set for October 15, 1895. Johnson labored to make the occasion a Roman holiday. He had asked the railroads to bring all those who wished to attend the ceremony at a reduced rate. On October 8, the Atlantic Coast Line announced its special sale of tickets. To insure the proper accommodations Superintendent Mayfield--in an article to the papers--pointed out that students coming up on the Coast Line and South Carolina-Georgia Road should get off at Camden Junction and Kingville respectively and take the Three C's Road to Rock Hill before dark. This was a most thoughtful gesture to some who had never ventured very far afield heretofore. The editor mildly rebuked Johnson, who was in charge of the opening program, because the Constitutional Convention would be in session on the sixteenth and perhaps Senator Tillman and Governor Evans could not attend. And also Buffalo Bill's Wild West Show would be playing Columbia on the same day.[45]

The paper announced three days before the celebration that two convicts had escaped at

Winthrop by crawling from the Main Building via a covered way under a dormitory. There they were out of guard limits and, after changing their clothes, they slipped away to freedom. On October 14, the Board met in the college parlor with Senator Tillman and Governor Evans. Some business was transacted before they recessed to inspect the buildings. Later President Johnson explained his organization of the executive department. He had named R. B. Cunningham as Secretary-Treasurer at $600 a year; J. L. Black, farmer at $35.00 per month; J. H. Hines, engineer at $600 a year; J. M. Daniels, laundryman at $25.00 per month; Miss Dorseth Clark, nurse at $20.00 per month and board; B. J. Barber and Frank Johnson, cook and baker at $35.00 and $20.00 respectively per month with board. The positions of fireman, pump man and librarian had not been filled. The librarian's salary was set at $12.00 per month and board. Perhaps the librarian would be compensated additionally by having first call on reading the books.[46]

Mr. Mayfield wished to carry over to November some sections of Johnson's report. Mayfield, adamant in opposing the confirmation of Mr. Cunningham's appointment, reasoned that Johnson and Cunningham were both single and that the young ladies would have to come to their rooms to transact business. In a group of young ladies there would be many kinds including truthful, untruthful, fussy, and tale-bearing tattlers. "One whisper," Mayfield warned, "of any improper conduct, or one breath of scandal, true or false, would do the college great harm. The parents might protest if they knew both men were single." Besides, Mayfield reasoned, "we are training young ladies to take jobs and be independent and there are many ladies in this State that could handle this job." Suggesting that President Johnson's sister might be a more logical choice for secretary-treasurer, he asked that the matter be given more thought. Before adjourning, the Board elected D. B. Johnson treasurer and post-poned his executive appointments until the next Board meeting, to be held November 13 in Columbia.[47]

96

CHAPTER VIII

"CAROLINA'S CROWN OF GLORY"

"We preferred to build on a large scale
rather than to have a poor cheap-John
College. But bricks and mortar don't
constitute a college, Mr. President,
ladies and gentlemen of the faculty."
B. R. Tillman

The opening exercises of the Winthrop Normal
and Industrial College--better known to South
Carolina's newspaper readers as the Girls' State
College at Rock Hill--marked a great day in the
history of York County and of South Carolina. Proclaimed as "Carolina's Crown of Glory," Winthrop
was unique as the first state college for women. The
patriotic fervor of those who loved their state
accounted for the great excitement engendered by
the dedication exercises on October 15, 1895.[1]

These exercises opened with the newly
elected music teacher, Professor Wade R. Brown,
leading the audience in singing "Praise God From
Whom All Blessings Flow." The 105th Psalm with
prayer by the Rev. Alexander Sprunt followed.
Next, Mrs. Brown, the talented wife of the music
professor, gave a rendition of the Faure's "Sonata
Maria." Since the new music faculty wished to show
off their talents, Professor Brown and Miss Rosell
Waddill played a piano duet, and finally Mrs. M. M.
Souther sang Mattel's Canta. This was followed by
the singing of the Coronation. Coming to the part
of the program that the local citizenry could better
understand, Trustee W. J. Roddey made a "happy"
introduction complimenting Rock Hill for her nerve
in borrowing $60,000 to aid in Winthrop's coming.
He was not sure, he said, "whether the college was
a monument to Senator Tillman, or to Rock Hill, or
the manhood of South Carolina"; but he left no
doubt of this school's importance to Rock Hill. "In
1880," he said, "we had a population of 812, in 1890

we had over 4,000. We predicted by 1900 Rock Hill would have between ten and fifteen thousand."[2]

Then Governor Evans came forward and delivered a fine address expressing the state's interest in nurturing its womanhood. "We are developing a new breed of women," he suggested, "but by this I do not mean bloomers and bicyclists, but such as will go from Winthrop prepared to assume woman's duties anywhere." The governor in a most dramatic gesture called Winthrop a monument to the statesmanship of Mr. Tillman. He then charged President Johnson, as he turned the institution over to him, "Guard it well, for it is the idol of a people who are jealous of its purity and success. As you succeed, in proportion will be your reward in their love. If you fail, in proportion will be your condemnation, and God pity you."[3]

Before the president spoke, Governor Evans asked Mr. J. E. Ellerbe to read a letter from Dr. J. L. M. Curry of the Peabody Board. Dr. Curry expressed his sorrow at not being able to attend. He stated that he wanted to thank the people of Rock Hill "for their generous sacrifices" and Governor Tillman "for his unwavering broad-minded and patriotic efforts to promote the highest educational advantages of the State which had honored him" and President Johnson "for his patience, tact, ability and noble devotion to his work." Dr. Curry's letter related that years before, Johnson had approached him about a training school and that Curry had arranged for Johnson's visit to the Winthrop home. In conclusion Curry reaffirmed that the Peabody trustees "regard with especial favor the Winthrop Normal and Industrial College, and we confidently expect growing usefulness."[4]

Johnson then began his speech with, as he said, "a full heart and deep sense of the great responsibility" that rested on him. Expressing his feeling that their opportunity for accomplishing good was unbounded, Johnson felt that "here [Winthrop] may be originating the most telling and far-reaching force in the society of the State."

Stressing the values of both a good Normal and industrial education, he reminded the audience that "there is no royal road to learning . . . no inventive genius will ever discover a way of dropping a nickel in a slot and taking out a complete education." He called for all parties concerned to help make Winthrop "a great and noble and enduring institution for the best education of the hand, the head, and the heart of South Carolina's young womanhood."[5]

Finally, Governor Evans called on Senator Tillman to speak. Professing to be overcome by emotion, Tillman said he was somewhat embarrassed to be singled out as "the originator of the idea whose creation you have witnessed today." But he admitted that he had begun to agitate for industrial and technical education for both sexes nine years earlier and that he wished to say a number of things to the young ladies before him. "The year 1895," he stressed, "will go in the history of the commonwealth as an epoch marked by the opening of an institution for the uplifting of South Carolina. The last five years," he continued, "witnessed a great change in things such as had not been known in the history of any state since this was taken from the Indians." South Carolina's great need, he pointed out, was education. "How are we going to get it? By using," he answered, "our representatives to raise more money for the education of the masses."[6]

Emphasizing the great positive values which would incur to the state from this school, Tillman reiterated that he wished the faculty and students to know that they were selected from a large number, that they were special, and that he expected much from them. Conceding that some mistakes had been made in the process of getting the school together, he nevertheless agreed that the "jewels of Carolina" had come for training and thought that to bring out the perfect quality of a jewel much polishing was necessary. After quoting Burns in his tribute to womanhood, Tillman concluded, "I will carry with me to my dying day the memory of your bright faces."

The exercises concluded. Thus began a great experiment--state-supported higher education for women in South Carolina. The values therefrom can never be properly measured.[7]

Tillman had insisted on the best for the Girls' State College. Like many Americans of his time, he regarded the German education system worth imitating. It required little urging to have Dr. Joynes of Carolina College, who had been schooled in Berlin, to undertake a fact-finding trip to Germany during summer, 1895, to garner the latest from the German system. Joynes loved Germany, and he suggested to the governor that if the latter would furnish him with an official commission that he (Dr. Joynes) would be happy to inspect the industrial schools in Germany and in Paris.[8] The governor agreed and Joynes set out on his mission.

Unfortunately, Joynes reached Hamburg on June 28, just three days before the summer vacation began for the industrial schools throughout the German Empire. He was able however to study the industrial schools in Hamburg, some of the country's best, while classes were being held. Moving on to Berlin, he interviewed school officials there, and eventually did the same in Dresden, the capital of Saxony; in Munich, the capital of Bavaria; and in Karlsruhe, the capital of Baden. After obtaining current ideas on the German system, Joynes moved to Paris. At each stop, he collected catalogues, programs, and valuable information to complement his summary report. The report rated the German system as superior to the French. Joynes reported that the German industrial schools for women usually contained four departments: the Review Course, the Commercial, the Professional (including fine arts), and the Domestic. Joynes summarized each. For example, the Review Course consisted of penmanship, elementary drawing, German, arithmetic, and either French or English. Students qualified in these areas could exempt this course, but those not qualified spent two years on remedial work. The most noteworthy feature on any German curriculum,

100

according to Joynes, was the drawing necessary in making patterns and designing clothing.[9]

The Commercial Course in the German industrial schools lasted, according to Joynes, from one to two years and included typewriting, stenography (French and English were optional), penmanship, mental and commercial arithmetic, commercial forms, correspondence, and single- and double-entry bookkeeping. Political economy was included in the higher courses, in addition to commercial law. A vital complement to this curriculum was the knowledge of German and of the countries Germany dealt with. This entailed knowledge of portal laws, currency, weights and measures, banking forms, exchange, and commercial forms. According to Joynes the importance of such a course was illustrated by the numerous women found in every branch of mercantile trade in Germany and France. Telegraphy, which had been proposed as a course of study at Winthrop, was not offered abroad. Joynes felt that commercial work should be extended in America, where the Victorian influence had been very strong.[10]

The third important department in the German system was the Professional. Here Joynes gave a rough description, leaving the women faculty of Winthrop who could read German to interpret further. Listed were household handiwork, clothing construction, pattern design, millinery, and ornamental work--all taught from theoretical and practical views. Listed in the more advanced fine-arts area of this department were painting, etching, art principles and history, and needlework. A new development in art--photography--had just been introduced in Dresden according to Joynes' report. It also mentioned that printing was taught at Berlin. Students enrolled in the Professional Department usually exhibited their handiwork at local, national, and international fairs, where prizes were awarded and individuals sold their arts and crafts.[11]

The climax of his report dealt with a subject of special interest to Joynes--the broad area of domestic science included in the fourth German-system department. As a connoisseur, Dr. Joynes seemed to take great delight in explaining some its facets. First, he noted the three branches--household service, washing, and cooking --were all vital but not necessarily glamorous. Noting that household service in Europe was performed by white girls who possessed much more industry, economy, and efficiency than did Negro women, the report described the training for housekeepers and maids. Joynes was further impressed by the way washing was taught and performed in a business-like manner, making use of new and improved machinery. The school in Berlin that Dr. Joynes visited specialized in labor-saving laundry machinery.[12]

In describing the German system of cooking and kitchen economy, Joynes became most lucid. According to him this department was taught "with great fullness." There were theoretical courses in chemistry--preserving, botany, and zoology--stressing knowledge of the most important sorts of vegetable and animal foods. Physiology and hygiene, dietetics, and the business side of the kitchen (marketing, bookkeeping and storage) were all stressed.[13]

Lastly but most importantly, Joynes came to the fine arts of the kitchen as he had observed from this and other trips abroad. Frugal Germans specialized in pickling, preserving, making sauces, desserts, and ornamental dishes as well as preparing food for the sick and making excellent side dishes like stews. "They save," he said, "and employ 'remnants' [leftovers] and we could learn much from their system." He heartily recommended it to Winthrop. Making a comparison with the average house in South Carolina, he said that here the wife usually provided about twice as much as the family consumed. The remnants here, except in the case of a ham or large roast, went to the kitchen and, after "extravagantly feeding the servants," were thrown to the fowl or "reserved for the friends of the colored cook"; and the next day the same waste was

102

repeated. By contrast the Germans and French saved left-overs and skillfully used them in a new and palatable form. Illustrating the art of cooking, he said that the European would use a boiled cut of beef over a period of about four days, for soup, for a roast, for a stew, and for croquettes. Joynes exclaimed: "What a benefit to our people, if we could learn this art!" If only these simple arts of culinary skill could be taught here, Joynes reasoned, "Winthrop College would save the people of the state more than enough to pay for the liberal support of itself and all other institutions of higher education."[14]

Joynes also wrote that the German schools required physical culture, gymnastics, and calisthenics, music reading, and choral singing. But he felt that in a sense, any attempt to compare the European and American school systems would be a comparison of unequals. The European schools were either city-sponsored or private. Joynes felt that the American system of state control made its schools more advanced in certain respects. Joynes also felt the system of "free" tuition gave Americans a decided advantage, but he did not want this to be abused. With his report Joynes filed documentary proof of what he had learned. He suggested that both Winthrop and Clemson might make a joint effort in sending an expert abroad to learn more.[15]

Dr. Joynes delivered his report to the Board of Trustees on November 13, 1895. It was well received. The Board agreed to preserve and widely distribute the report, ordering that it should be printed in their report to the Legislature. One may assume that the report influenced many connected with Winthrop College. Dr. Joynes, as life trustee, pushed the report and influenced his fellow trustees on this and many other phases of the college.[16]

The college opened in the fall, 1895, with 304 superior students. In the first report to the Legislature following the October 15 beginning, the college's purpose was restated as attempting "to make teachers, breadwinners, and house makers, with a separate department for the perfection of each." The work covered four levels, and a student who completed the full course was awarded a diploma, with the degree of A.B.--Artium Baccalaureate--which served as a lifetime license to teach in the state's public schools for those who graduated from the Normal Department. The curriculum included a sub-freshman class, the Industrial Department, and special arrangements for those who wished post-graduate work that could lead to the Master's Degree. The main study areas show in part the influence of Joynes' study on the industrial schools of Germany and France.[17]

Several of the Winthrop programs were more formalized than others--the Normal course, the Scientific course, and the Literary course, each of which contained industrial studies. The courses were arranged as follows:

For a   Freshman

Mathematics........................	*5
Arithmetic reviewed, Algebra through Quadratics.	
English...........................	3
Analysis, Rhetoric, Composition, Word Study.	
History...........................	3
South Carolina, Greek and Roman.	
Latin.............................	4
Caesar and Latin Composition	
Science...........................	2
Physical Geography (Second and Third Terms).	
Reading...........................	2
Hygiene (First Term)..............	2
Sight Singing.....................	2
(Second and Third Terms)	
Physical Culture..................	2
Industrial........................	2

*The figures show the number of periods per week devoted to recitations.

104

For a Sophomore

Mathematics........................ 4
  Algebra completed, Plane
  Geometry.
English............................ 3
  Rhetoric, American Literature.
History............................ 3
Latin.............................. 3
Science............................ 3
  Zoology, half year; Botany,
  half year.
Reading (First Term)............... 2
Sight Singing...................... 2
  (Second and Third Terms)
Pedagogics......................... 3
Physical Culture................... 2
Industrial......................... 2

For a Junior

Mathematics........................ 3
  Solid Geometry (First Term);
  Physics (Second and Third Terms).
English............................ 3
  Literature.
History............................ 2
  English History and Civics.
Latin.............................. 3
French or German................... 3
Science............................ 3
  Chemistry.
Pedagogics......................... 2
Work in Practice School............ 2

For a Senior

Mathematics........................ 4
  Astronomy (First Term).
English............................ 3
  Chaucer, Shakespeare, Tennyson
  and Browning, Grammar.
Latin.............................. 2
Political Economy.................. 2
French or German (continued)....... 3

For a Senior (continued)

Science.............................. 3
  Mineralogy and Geology.
Physiology (Second Term)............ 2
Sight Singing (Methods)............. 2
  (Third Term)
Pedagogics.......................... 3
Physical Culture.................... 2
Work in Practice School............. 3

       The Scientific course with Industrial
Studies required the following:

For a Freshman

Mathematics......................... 5
  Arithmetic reviewed, Algebra
  through Quadratics.
English............................. 3
  Analysis, Rhetoric, Composi-
  tion and Word Study.
History............................. 3
  South Carolina, Greek and
  Roman.
Latin............................... 4
  Caesar and Latin Composition
Science............................. 2
  Physical Geography (Second
  and Third Terms).
Reading............................. 2
Hygiene (First Term)................ 2
Sight Singing....................... 2
  (Second and Third Terms).
Physical Culture.................... 2
Industrial.......................... 2

For a Sophomore

Mathematics......................... 4
  Algebra completed, Plane
  Geometry.
English............................. 3
  Rhetoric, American Literature.
History............................. 3
Latin............................... 3

For a Sophomore (continued)

Science............................ 3
  Zoology, half year; Botany,
  half year.
Reading (First Term)............... 2
Sight Singing...................... 2
  (Second and Third Terms).
Physical Culture................... 2
Industrial......................... 2
Elective........................... 3

For a Junior

Mathematics........................ 3
Physics (Second and Third Terms)... 3
English............................ 3
German............................. 3
French............................. 3
2 Zoology.......................... 2
2 Botany
1 Chemistry........................ 3
Physical Culture................... 2
Industrial......................... 2

For a Senior

Mathematics........................ 3
Astronomy (First Term)............. 4
2 Physics.......................... 2
  (Second and Third Terms).
English............................ 3
German............................. 3
French............................. 3
Mineralogy and Geology............. 2
2 Chemistry........................ 3
Physical Culture................... 2
Industrial......................... 2

The Literary Course with Industrial Studies included:

107

For a Freshman

Mathematics........................ 5
  Arithmetic reviewed, Algebra
  through Quadratics.
English............................ 3
  Analysis, Rhetoric, Composition,
  and Word Study.
History............................ 3
  South Carolina, Greek and
  Roman.
Latin.............................. 4
  Caesar and Latin Composition.
Science............................ 2
  Physical Geography (Second
  and Third Terms).
Reading............................ 2
Hygiene (First Term)............... 2
Sight Singing...................... 2
  (Second and Third Terms).
Physical Culture................... 2
Industrial......................... 2

For a Sophomore

Mathematics........................ 4
  Algebra completed, Plane
  Geometry.
English............................ 3
  Rhetoric and American
  Literature.
History............................ 3
Latin.............................. 3
Reading (First Term)............... 2
Sight Singing...................... 2
  (Second and Third Terms).
Physical Culture................... 2
Industrial......................... 2
Electives.......................... 6 [18]

There was also a program designed for the Preparatory or Sub-Freshman Class:

108

Mathematics--Arithmetic (Wentworth's
  Grammar School) Through percentage or
  an   equivalent and Algebra to simple
  equations......................... *5
English--Including Spelling, Grammar,
  and Composition................... 5
History--United States, and
  Geography......................... 3
Latin--Collar and Daniel's
  Beginner's Latin Book............. 5
Reading............................. 2
Penmanship.......................... 2
Physical Culture.................... 2

*The figures show the number of periods
per week devoted to recitations.

    In   addition   there   were   certain   special
courses like these in stenography and typewriting:

(Nine Months)

Stenography and Typewriting....... 20
English........................... 3
Arithmetic........................ 3
Physical Culture.................. 2

Special Course in Dressmaking
(Nine Months)

Dressmaking....................... 20
Arithmetic........................ 3
English Grammar................... 3
Drawing........................... 3
Physical Culture.................. 2

Special Course in Book-keeping
(Nine Months)

Book-keeping...................... 5
Business Law (Second and
  Third Terms).................... 2
Commercial Geography............. 3
Civics........................... 2
English.......................... 3
Commercial Arithmetic............ 3
Physical Culture................. 2[19]

Vital to the success of the Normal Department was a practice school. At Winthrop, this work was partly supported by the Rock Hill City School Board. Starting with ninety-three children in the first six grades, the Practice School benefitted from the constant supervision of two skilled Winthrop professors. It was housed in the main college building until a new Winthrop Training School opened in 1912 opposite the main campus.[20]

The Industrial Department, "the pride and joy of Senator Tillman," attempted to enforce a general prerequisite for entering students. No pupil could pursue industrial studies unless she could satisfy the president that she had "a good English education." This department began teaching stenography and typewriting, bookkeeping, freehand and industrial drawing, sewing, dressmaking, millinery, horticulture, floriculture, and designing.[21]

The Domestic Science Department placed special emphasis on a cooking school modeled after one in the Drexal Institute of Philadelphia. Most important in this area was a school of sewing, dressmaking, and millinery. Girls made their clothing, hats, and uniforms. Mr. Tillman had insisted that the girls wear uniforms, and he wished to keep the cost below twenty-five dollars for each girl. Insisting that the poor not be distinguished from the rich, he wanted the uniform to be becoming and stylish. Of navy blue serge, the fatigue suit consisted of a gored skirt and a double-breasted jacket by Butterick's pattern 8441. For everyday use, the shirt waist would be of white striped or figured percale; for Sunday, a white shirt waist was required. No fancy collars or embroidery were allowed; accessories were of dark blue or black. Most interestingly, all students (except those who planned to study dress-making) were required to have the dress uniform made according to Butterick's number 1471 before leaving home. Four Rock Hill firms--the Roddey Mercantile Company, R. T. Fewell and Company,

110

A. Friedheim and Brother, and A. E. Smith and Company--were official suppliers of the uniform materials.[22]

After the school at Rock Hill had operated for a few weeks, the News and Courier favored their readers with another brief report on the "Girl's State College." Always having an eye cocked for any news about Mr. Tillman, the paper reported that Miss Addie Tillman was enrolled in the Junior Normal and that her sister, Miss Lona, was studying music. The writer pointed out that President Johnson had his office at the left just as one entered the Main Building and that Mr. Cunningham was next door. Offering as proof that the food was good, the paper revealed that Winthrop bought cattle and fattened them for the table. The college was using a barrel of flour a day and from six-hundred to seven-hundred pounds of butter a month; the boarders were eating home-grown potatoes, turnips, and peas. This article on Winthrop concluded, and appropriately so, with an account of the physical-culture program (physical fitness) that stressed the study and practice of the Ling or Swedish system.[23]

Winthrop operated under the strict Calvinistic doctrine and discipline which became a hallmark of the Johnson administration. Johnson used a straightforward approach to general behavior problems. To inform students and to prevent mis-understanding, the bachelor President Johnson published in the college catalogue a long list of rules:

> (1) Pupils will not be allowed to receive visits from men whether cousins or not, or to spend the night out of the College. This rule will not be departed from. Communications from parents or guardians concerning withdrawal, leave of absence or visiting must be made direct to the President in advance and not through the Students. No student is allowed to leave the city of Rock

111

Hill without the permission of the President. Requests not conforming to this rule will not be considered. The right is reserved to the President to refuse such requests when in his judgment it would be unwise to grant them. The college authorities do not recognize the right of parents or guardians to withdraw or detain students from any academic duty, except for reasons approved by the President. The loss of a comparatively few recitations is often fatal to a student's interest in her studies and to her advancement in her school work. Correspondence with young men unless by permission of the girl's parents is forbidden. Letters which seem to violate this rule will be forwarded to parents for investigation.

(2) A punctual attendance upon all duty is held to be essential to good discipline. All absences will be regularly noted and reported to the President.

(3) Excuses for absence must be submitted by the student to the President in writing every Monday before 4 P.M., or, in case of protracted absence, on the first Monday after the student's return to duty, and will be acted on by the President.

(4) To provide for social life and proper recreation, receptions and other such functions will be arranged for at proper times.

(5) Card playing is absolutely prohibited.

(6) Notes, bouquets or any other form of communication or marks of attention to boarding pupils from persons outside of the College are prohibited unless

authorized by consent of the President. Day pupils are forbidden, under penalty of exclusion from the school, to receive or to deliver communications of any kind whatever from or to the boarders, without the permission of the President.

(7) The young ladies are allowed to visit or receive only on Friday afternoons and Saturdays. No visitors at all are received on the Sabbath. If parents desire their daughters to visit in the city, they must write to the President designating the families they wish them to visit.

(8) Students will not be permitted to leave the college grounds oftener than once in two weeks, and then only accompanied by teachers, except to attend church on Sunday.

(9) Visitors are not admitted to the private apartments of students unless by special permission of the Matron. Calls are not allowed to interfere with College duties. Visitors are not admitted to the dining hall without permission.

(10) The College uniform must be worn as required on all occasions.

(11) Pupils will not be allowed to linger in Rock Hill after they have withdrawn from the school or after commencement exercises in the summer, unless their parents address to the President a written request to that effect.

(12) The President's authority over the conduct of students continues until their return to their homes and parents. They remain members of the school until

dismissed, honorably discharged or graduated from it.

(13) Every pupil must remain at the College through the Commencement exercises, unless called away by some providential cause, or excused by the President for some good and valid reason. Any pupil willfully violating this rule will thereby forfeit her place in the school and her right to any diploma, certificate or recommendation to which she would other- wise have been entitled.

(14) No student shall receive any degree who is in arrears for books from the College Library, or for any other College dues.

(15) Damages to College buildings or property will be charged to the one doing the damage.

(16) An unexcused absence is considered a delinquency, and will be reported as such to the parent or guardian of the student. It is also counted zero in the class mark.

(17) Cheating on examination or any dishonest practice in recitations or examinations will be visited with the severest punishments that it is in the power of the Faculty to inflict.

(18) No student or students shall be permitted to make or unite in making any party, festive entertainment or celebration, without special permission of the President.

(19) No class meeting or other meetings of the students shall be held, nor shall any society be organized without the

special permission of the President, and then only for such purposes as shall be specified.

(20) All recitations, essays, etc., to be delivered by students in public, or designed for publication, are subject to control and revision by the Faculty. All programs for celebrations or other public occasions at the College must be submitted to the President for approval before printing.

(21) Parents are requested not to send boxes of eatables, except fruit, to their daughters. They are productive of excess, sickness and loss of time, and will not be delivered if sent, except at Christmas. The fare will be of such quantity, quality and variety that it will be entirely useless to attempt to supplement it by boxes.

(22) Borrowing text-books, clothing, jewelry and other articles is forbidden.

(23) Pupils are not permitted to make account at stores. The College will not be responsible in any way for pupils' accounts.

(24) If any pupil leaves at the end of the session in arrears for College dues, she shall be debarred from entering the College as a pupil until the account is fully settled or is satisfactorily arranged with the college authorities.

(25) A part of every Saturday must be spent by pupils in regulating their wardrobes, repairing clothing and such like duties.

(26) When a pupil has selected a course of study she will be required to adhere

to it.   No dropping a subject or
changing a course will be allowed except
for most important considerations and by
consent of the President.

(27) The religious life of the institution is carefully guarded.   Attendance
upon their own churches or the churches
to which their parents or guardians
belong will be required every Sunday
morning of the students, except in the
case of sickness or for other good
reason.   They will be accompanied by
members of the Faculty belonging to the
same churches.   Attendance upon Sunday
school is allowed.

(28) Students will not be allowed to go
out to church at night in the city, but
ministers of different denominations
will preach regularly in the College
Chapel on Sunday nights, in accordance
with an arrangement made with the
Ministerial Union of the city.   All
students without exception will be
required to attend these services.

(29)   Students are required to be
present at the College the first day of
school.   Those who are not present then
will forfeit their place. [24]

The spartan requirements were viewed dif-
ferently ninety years ago than they would be today.
And "Solon" Johnson summed up the spirit of
Winthrop's government in these few words:

The whole government is conceived and
executed with a view of making the College
a pleasant, busy, and therefore happy and
well ordered home.   Its object is to
develop self-control, high character, and a
desire to do the right because it is right.

116

The students have responded to this aim with loyalty and good behavior and a fine spirit of earnestness and devotion of duty.

Courtesy and kindness are the uniform rule of the institution. The honor, pride, and interest of the students in the success of the College are appealed to.

Self government is fostered as far as possible.[25]

He forgot to add that self-government would be fostered a la Johnson.

While Johnson was busy organizing and running Winthrop in the fall, 1895, Tillman and his reform party were fighting to solidify the gains made in education and other direct-government areas over the past four years in South Carolina. As a delegate to the state Constitutional Convention, Tillman fought long and hard for a school system with adequate primary, secondary, and collegiate divisions. He held up such a system of state schools as a panacea for backwardness. In this fight he ofttimes found himself on the opposite side from his older brother, the Harvard-trained George Dionysus Tillman, a long-time Congressman. "Uncle George," as he was known in the district, considered himself a reformer until Ben's reformers "played leap frog over his head and they have gone out of sight and hearing," as George would always say.[26]

Regardless of family or other considerations, Ben Tillman was determined to enshrine his system in South Carolina because he felt he was right. Fighting to fix the constitutional school tax to three mills, he ran into serious objections from his brother as well as many others.

Winthrop now was beginning to train teachers, and Tillman wanted the public schools to

117

be worthy of good teachers. He fought hard to keep
Winthrop from being placed by the Constitutional
Convention into the university system. Winthrop
was a "beacon light" to him and he wanted it
expressly written into the new constitution, then
being drafted, that the state would provide for
Winthrop. Taking the floor, Brother Ben talked for
all the institutions of higher learning--pointing
out that of $196,000 spent a year on higher educa-
tion, Winthrop and Clemson received $25,000 each.
Referring to a little debt for buildings and
equipment at Winthrop, Tillman suggested: "We are
going to ask you members of the General Assembly
to pay us out even if you are demagogues and
whimsical." Assuring Charleston of fair treatment, he pointed out that they paid one-eighth of
the total general tax of the state, and "although,"
he said, "I may be down on military dudes and
although I have a son at Clemson, I realize that
the Citadel has a great many friends and does a good
work and has its claim."[27]

In this fight Tillman faced the proponents
of state aid for denominational schools, who were
under great pressure from the various religious
groups. Those who feared any changes also joined
against Tillman. As the Bourbon element resisted
him with all their might, he lost on several major
points but succeeded in providing for small and
compact school districts that would foster more
public education. He even won praise from the
News and Courier when it said that "Tillman has
shown a broad, liberal and genuine interest in the
schools and colleges of the state and has won many
friends by his manly fights." However, Tillman lost
the fight to give the General Assembly mandatory
rather than discretionary power to provide for the
five state institutions of higher education.[28]

In the midst of the fight over the Constitution of 1895, Governor Evans promoted a state-wide
trip of officials to visit the Southern Exposition
in Atlanta. Being educationally oriented, the
governor showed unusual interest and chartered

118

three Southern Railroad trains to take the students from Carolina, Clemson, and Winthrop over to Atlanta for the celebration. The militia and members of the Legislature went along. South Carolina was well represented. In the weeks following their return, the debate on the Constitution raged long and hard, with Tillman working diligently for his reforms and for Winthrop College, Clemson, and the free-school system, and many other things which he deemed necessary for the welfare of the state, including a more honest system of elections and the curbing of the "lynch law."[29]

Section by section the new Constitution took shape. This was the document under which Winthrop has lived most of its years, and section eight of this document provided for Winthrop as a branch of Carolina University, having the right to share in the proceeds of the federal land grant of July 2, 1862, and "subsequent funds appropriated for educational purposes by the Congress of the United States." A few days thereafter, on a more somber note, the paper reported that there were twenty-four measles cases at Winthrop College and that the afflicted students "were confined to one of the wings on a lower floor." Two days later, fearing an epidemic, the college announced that they were sending all those able to go home by special train to Columbia, Spartanburg, and points east and south. The young ladies were to have a two-week holiday, one of the longest in Winthrop's early history. Meanwhile Senator Tillman had gone to Washington to attend to his congressional duties, but he still continued to keep a close rein on Winthrop, Clemson, and South Carolina.[30]

CHAPTER IX

BUILDING ON A FIRM FOUNDATION
1896-1909

"This school is the one thing and the
only thing upon which the men of South
Carolina are at present united."
B. R. Tillman

Early in 1896 the Legislature met in
Columbia to implement the provisions of the Constitution of 1895. Among the numerous laws passed
in 1896 to this end was the "Free School Law,"
designed to give South Carolina a modern system of
public education. This law spelled out in detail
the responsibilities of a most important constitutional officer, the state superintendent of
education. One finds the leadership for the public-
school program of South Carolina revolving around
this office and the county boards of education.
The state superintendent was charged with the
"general supervision over all the schools of the
state" that were in any way supported by state
money, with visiting every county of the state, and
with "inspecting the school, awakening an interest
favorable to the cause of education, and diffusing
as widely as possible, with officials, teachers, and
parents, knowledge of existing defects and of
desirable improvements in the government and
instructions of the said schools."[1]

Since Winthrop's principal function was
to furnish teachers for the common schools, it is
easy to see the boost that the "Free School Law"
gave to the new, thriving college in Rock Hill.
Soon it was evident that Winthrop would not only
set the tone for public education in South Carolina
but would serve as a leader in many civic areas.
Early in February, the city council of Rock Hill
extended an invitation to the State Teacher's
Association to have their next meeting in Rock
Hill. President Johnson, a member of the executive committee of the Association, promised the
use of the college buildings as an added inducement

120

to the delegates. Even in the matter of getting water for Rock Hill, the city followed Winthrop by having W. S. Creighton dig deep wells to obtain an adequate supply. And the first "soirée musicale" given at Winthrop was highly advertised in Rock Hill and proved most successful. The press related that the beautiful auditorium was "tolerably well filled with an audience which gave close attention, to the fourteen selections of classic music, half vocal and half instrumental that were performed in high order by the distinguished music faculty headed by Professor Brown." [2]

Another very important factor in Winthrop's success was the interested activity of the most distinguished university scholar in South Carolina, Dr. Edward S. Joynes, a life trustee and worker for Winthrop. His ability and plain honesty brought him very close to Mr. Tillman. His influence on Winthrop, Carolina, and the state is universally accepted. While Tillman was governor, Joynes had a habit of going around to see him at odd hours to discuss problems in education. Not finding the governor at the mansion in late December, 1894, for example, Joynes wrote Tillman suggesting one of his assistants, John J. McMahan, for a job at Clemson. Joynes gave the young man a high recommendation, adding "this is not one of those 'lying testimonials' which you say professors give one another." Joynes also wanted to apprize Tillman of Dr. Curry's report in which he "alluded to Winthrop, but praised Peabody College." Joynes remembered his own problems with preachers when he was at Vanderbilt and suggested that "he [Preacher Curry] will bear watching." [3]

Joynes tried to push Winthrop fast in order to snare a greater share of the Peabody fund. His interest was underscored in March, 1896, when Dr. Curry (as he was called) made a great speech at the college. A reporter noted that the college was all lighted up for the occasion and it made a fine appearance. In his speech Curry paid tribute to Johnson as a man of ability and stressed the good work Senator Tillman had done

121

for Winthrop, complimenting him for "the zeal, sympathy, and liberality" he had shown.[4]

Later that year Curry wrote Tillman a very patronizing letter, enclosing a copy of the last Peabody report and stressing that "from no Governor of any Southern state have I received more cordial and valuable cooperation than from yourself while you were the Executive of South Carolina." Curry told Tillman that the Winthrop plant was unsurpassed in the South and that he was glad to see Tillman's picture in the halls, "as your name should be inscribed in legible characters over the portals." Finally, Curry suggested that Johnson should have more power, stressing that he was a good man for the place; "and I thank you for standing by him so effectively, when others were not so much inclined to give him the support which he needs."[5]

While Tillman wrestled with the free silver bill in the United States Senate, his partisans in the South Carolina Legislature gave Winthrop, on March 9, the largest appropriation of any state college--namely, $31,797 for back indebtedness, with the understanding that no new contracts in excess of the appropriated money would be made. In addition the Legislature gave scholarships to each county for Winthrop equal to their representatives in that body. These scholarships of forty-four dollars each were to be based on competitive examinations given by the state board of education. Thereby, Winthrop received some of the best qualified students in the state.[6]

The Legislature also passed in 1896 a joint resolution "to authorize and require the Director of the State Penitentiary to furnish to the Trustees . . . of Winthrop ten convicts." This resolution was not to the liking of President Johnson, who later took pen in hand and rewrote the statute, substituting fifteen and writing in "shall provide and pay for guards" over the statement that the college was responsible. And in a third section of the statute, Johnson revised the statement Winthrop Industrial and Normal, and placed <u>Normal</u> before <u>Industrial</u>, thereby underscoring that he (unlike Tillman) felt Normal took precedence over Industrial.[7]

Winthrop had become a full-fledged college in Rock Hill, and more and more people were attracted to it. Representative H. B. Buist of Greenville, a member of the Board and the Constitutional Convention, agreed to look after the horticultural and agricultural interests of the college. His ability as an agriculturalist was most valuable in pushing the young college forward. Expressing to Tillman that he felt that he could be of much use to Johnson, Buist undertook a variety of jobs. And Johnson reported to the Board in June, 1896, that they had laid out walks and drives around the grounds, started a lawn, built a fountain, cultivated the farm, planted fruit trees and vegetables, purchased farm implements, and put up an iron fence about the grounds.[8]

President Johnson reported other progress in June, 1896. He had been able to balance the budget and improve the library, thanks to the gifts of Dr. Joynes, Tillman, and Congressman J. W. Stokes. Also Tillman had Winthrop designated as a public depository for all books published by the United States government. Thereby, the library greatly improved. Johnson further took pride in the fact that the Young Women's Christian Association was organized and doing well. There were 332 students enrolled. Discipline was good. The faculty had increased and plans were made to hire a lady physician for an infirmary to be located at the end of the dormitory.[9]

The session of 1897 was truly an outstanding one. When the Board of Trustees met in Rock Hill on January 1, 1897, President Johnson had an impressive report ready for their approval and for the General Assembly. On Dr. Joynes's recommendation, the Board gave Johnson authority to buy lots adjacent to Winthrop from any unexpended balance. The college was now such

a going concern that it employed a full-time
bookkeeper, R. B. Cunningham, and an engineer,
George B. Green. President Johnson's report as
agreed to by the trustees was formally drafted and
presented "To the Honorable the Senate and House of
Representatives of the State of South Carolina." It
represents a synopsis of the college as of January
1, 1897.[10]

Commenting on the student body, Johnson
stressed that eight-hundred students had applied for
enrollment during the previous summer; four-hundred
and three were enrolled but only two-hundred and
forty could be housed in the existing dormitory.
Boarding in town, Johnson explained, was more
expensive and was "away from the wholesome restraint
of college discipline." Continuing to argue his
point, he gave the case for a second dormitory,
pleading mild discrimination against the girls.
Since the Main Building was large enough to instruct
approximately six hundred, all he needed was a small
expenditure of less than $30,000 together with
materials already available and the school could
reach and benefit almost twice as many girls as at
present. This was a most sensible and convincing
argument, especially when coupled with the statement
that South Carolina provided three schools for
boys.[11]

In breaking down the enrollment for the
General Assembly, Johnson showed that nearly every
county in South Carolina was represented in the
student body. York had seventy-four registered at
Winthrop, with Anderson, Chester, Orangeburg, and
Sumter having more than fifteen each. In addition
to South Carolina, there were students from North
Carolina, Georgia, Florida, and Virginia. All
these students came from families whose fathers
were merchants, doctors, ministers, lawyers, mill
owners and workers, teachers, and even a shoe-
maker and liveryman. The largest group, as
expected, were daughters of farmers. The majority
of these people were Baptists, Presbyterians, and
Methodists with a few Lutherans, Associate Reformed
Presbyterians, Catholics, Episcopalians, and one

Universalist. They represented a great cross-section of South Carolina.[12]

To facilitate his explanation to the Legislature, Johnson summarized the courses as embracing four principal areas of concentration: the Normal Department, the Industrial Department, the Commercial Department, and the Domestic Science Department. As always, Johnson stressed that one of the greatest needs of the state "is more well educated and thoroughly trained teachers--teachers with broad scholarship and culture and with thorough professional training." Sloganizing his point, he shouted, "As is the teacher so is the school."[13]

The 1897 report restated the Board's and the state's aim: to bring "the best education within the reach of the people of limited means." This had been accomplished--the regular expenses of a nine-month session amounted to $131.50 per student and for those who received free tuition the cost was reduced to $111.42. By the act that granted free tuition, one had to make a written statement of inability to pay, certified by the county auditor, except in the case of ministers' daughters and state-scholarship students. The state scholarships were competitive. Students with these scholarships, worth forty-four dollars in money plus free tuition, were well favored. This meant that the $111.42 in fees for free-tuition students would be further reduced by forty-four dollars for those with a state competitive scholarship. The correct story concerning student fees was that Senator Tillman and one other citizen were the only two paying the regular expenses of $131.50 at Winthrop in the entire state of South Carolina.[14]

Mr. Johnson displayed great pride in the 1897 report, especially regarding the new infirmary. He praised its modern facilities and noted that they had secured "a skillful, experienced female physician to take charge." She lived at the college and was constantly on call, day and night.

In addition the physician, Dr. Elizabeth K. Miller, taught physiology, hygiene, and health--all for $800 a session. With Dr. Miller, Rock Hill's pure water and fine climate, perfect ventilation, complete sewage facilities, and healthful exercise and habits, Mr. Johnson looked forward to a good health record despite state-wide measles epidemics in 1897.[15]

The farm and grounds were praised in this report to the General Assembly. The college received milk from the farm at nine cents a gallon, beef at four and one-half a pound; there was plenty of pork, and fruit from eight-hundred trees. Everything about the grounds was neat and properly secured.[16]

Every phase of the college was in good order according to Mr. Johnson. The library was thriving with eighteen-hundred volumes. The college had a lecture series and a cultural (Star) program that brought outstanding people. There were two literary societies, Winthrop and Curry; an active and loyal alumnae society; a wholesome religious life with the Young Women's Christian Association; a faculty of twenty-five; and a good system of discipline with "no friction or trouble in the discipline of the school." Before the end of the year, however, this situation had changed slightly. Some of the faculty had accused a young Winthrop girl of "attempting to incite the Senior Class to rebellion," and Mr. Johnson had dismissed the girl in question, refusing to allow her to return to school. The girl's mother--not getting any satisfaction or redress from President Johnson--decided to contact Senator Tillman, explaining that her daughter would not incite a rebellion as she was a "high toned and spirited" girl and "those are good old southern traits."[17]

President Johnson concluded his report praising his faculty and outlining college finances. According to Johnson, the Board had "spared no pains securing for the college the best teachers obtainable; twenty-five men and women of high Christian character and purpose, well trained and easy to work with."[18] On the economic side, Johnson estimated $38,303 was needed for the current year. This figure he estimated would be reduced by $5,200 from tuition fees and by $3,000 from the Peabody fund, with $29,613 needed to complete the new dormitory. Johnson projected his new budget at $59,716.[19]

In closing, Johnson invited the Senate and House of Representatives to visit Winthrop in a body and "to see for yourselves what great things have been accomplished with the money appropriated by the state to make a tardy provision for the normal, industrial and liberal education for her daughters. . . ." Johnson pledged for himself and the Board "to build up an institution, the equal of any of its kind in the country," if they were given the proper backing. This was a most laudable goal and one which the Legislature was sure to consider.[20]

The Legislature visited Winthrop during the year and left impressed by what they saw. The school year ended in June, 1897. The Board of Trustees--meeting at the president's office on June 7 and 8, 1897--reviewed the year's work and made plans for 1897-1898. The full report of the previous January needed only to be supplemented, and Johnson recommended the re-election of all teachers: "some," he said, "may not be all that could be desired in disposition and teaching ability, but they merit another try."[21]

The Board considered a summer school, for Johnson was very anxious to expand Winthrop into this field. Knowing the success of the old Teacher's Institutes, he saw a fine possibility for Winthrop in this area. However, the prospect of building another dormitory during the coming summer caused him to advise against starting a summer school then. He desired to begin the summer school on a high plane "in keeping with everything else about Winthrop College" and needed more time to formulate a proper program.[22]

127

A third important consideration that Johnson
discussed with his Board was scholarship. According
to Johnson, good teachers when complemented by
scholarship students would result in one of the
finest features of the college. Through the
scholarships' competitive examinations, the best
pupils emerged from each county. But he expressed
some concern over the state board of education's
ruling that when a scholarship could not be awarded
in the county to which it belonged, the money should
revert back to the state treasury. Urging his Board
to request a continuance of the old policy to use
the unexpended money in other counties rather than
send it back, Johnson reasoned that the old policy
would insure more teachers for the common schools.
Characterizing these scholarship girls as "a body of
earnest, conscientious, hard-working girls, who
exercise a fine influence on the student body,"
Johnson was determined to prevent the new ruling of
the board of education from applying to Winthrop.
Soon, the state board requested him to lay his
recommendation before their next meeting.[23]

Johnson and the trustees took nearly two
days in June transacting a wide range of school
matters from high policy to decisions. Some additions to the courses of study attempted to ensure
that the student received a cultural education,
thereby reaffirming that it would be "a suicidal
policy to attempt to turn out more working women
ignorant of everything except the narrow craft by
which they intend to earn their living." The Board
vowed to carry out the intended purpose of the
college to make it "good enough for the richest, and
cheap enough for the poorest"--to bring the best
education easily within the reach of people of
limited means. Before adjourning, Professor Joynes
offered a resolution to have Johnson research the
feasibility of extending the industrial and Normal
work to include telegraphy, topography, photography,
horticulture, dairying, kindergarten, and summer
school.[24]

During the summer of 1897 Johnson worked hard. There were building projects to supervise. A bowling alley took shape; a skylight brightened the laboratory; a freight elevator appeared at the back of the dormitory; two large water tanks rose; and two silos towered near the barn, each holding eighty tons of ensilage. The sewage system was extended over a mile from the college to a point below the Arcade Mill, emptying into a branch beyond the city limits. Maintenance workers graded low areas on the campus and filled land. The college buildings stood thoroughly cleaned and readied for the largest class--463 students of whom 119 were in the practice school. That September one student came from far-away Texas.[25]

Johnson had overtaxed his strength during the summer of 1897 and very soon after school started in September he was beset with more problems. Wilson and Wilson brought a complaint on behalf of Mrs. E. A. Allen against the college's sewage discharge. This and other demands forced Johnson in October, 1897, to go to Philadelphia for special treatment and rest at a hospital. Since there were no deans at Winthrop then, management of the college was entrusted to a faculty committee consisting of Professors Moses, Kinard, and Breazeale. By December, Moses (the senior member) had gained power and made the reports to the trustees. The Board on December 15, 1897, confirmed Moses as chairman of the faculty. They agreed to a recommendation of a doctors' panel to close Winthrop for a week at Christmas to check its water and sewage disposal. They also agreed to extend Johnson an expression of their confidence and best wishes for his recovery.[26]

On December 23, 1897, Winthrop closed, according to the papers, because of the risk of smallpox. The press announced that the "Girls in blue" had gone to their respective homes until January 3, 1898. Meanwhile, samples of Winthrop water shipped to Baltimore, Maryland, and Lawrence,

129

Massachusetts, for testing proved (in their reports of December 30 and 31, 1897) "very pure and fit for domestic purposes."[27]

With the fear of crisis past, the college reopened in early January, and many gladly greeted President Johnson when he returned in early February to his duties. During the crisis Tillman's watchful eye had not overlooked Winthrop. Tillman had from time to time kept up with Mr. Buist, sending plants and suggestions to him for physically improving the college. Writing to Buist in early February, he asked how the latest plants from the National Botanical Gardens were progressing and then casually inquired about Johnson. Buist replied on February 16, 1898, in straight-forward fashion, saying: "For a short time while Prof. Johnson was absent Prof. Moses had charge and to use plain language played hell generally." Moses, according to Buist, spread the word that Johnson was "dying with cancer." He also attempted to get the girls not to take the cooking course as it was "beneath them," and W. H. Stewart, his confidant and advisor, "offended nearly every member of the faculty, and by his actions and insinuations, virtually declared every one connected with the College rascals." Buist laid his feelings on the line, and recommended that there be some removals.[28]

The remainder of the 1898 academic year passed without serious incident. There can be little doubt that the communications between Buist and Tillman set the stage for Professor Moses's resignation, which was the first order of business for the Board after graduation on June 8, 1898. In this meeting, resolutions passed for establishing "the shorter English Normal Course" and for reorganizing the admissions standards. They further arranged for a system of accrediting schools whose pupils could be admitted on certificate. Steps were taken to implement a kindergarten, to establish dining-room scholarships, to set up the Department of History and Civics, and to appoint a librarian at twenty dollars a month plus board. It was most considerate of the Board that, in accepting the resignations of Professor Moses and Dr. Miller, they recognized the contributions of each and sent copies of same to both.[29]

The summer of 1898 witnessed the usual busy preparations for the new school year. Enrollees were processed, the buildings painted and cleaned, precautions taken against water contamination, and all readied to greet the new class in the fall. The summer's most distinctive feature was a summer school conducted at Winthrop from June 15 to July 13, in cooperation with the state superintendent of education. Three-hundred and seventy-five of the leading men and women teachers from South Carolina attended. Winthrop spent $500 for its summer session, plus $532.16 for extra bedding. In addition, she used her executive staff and furnished board and laundry to these teachers for twelve dollars a month. Because of its success, many persons urged that the school be held again the following summer.[30]

During the ensuing school year, Winthrop prepared to ask the Legislature for an appropriation of $35,000 to build and furnish an additional dormitory. Also during this successful year the Board adopted the motto for the college: Veritas Cum Libertate--Truth with Liberty.[31]

By 1899 Winthrop was in the forefront of higher education in South Carolina. Those jealous referred to her as "the pet institution of the state." In 1899 Winthrop and the Citadel were divested of any connections with Carolina University. The independence and respect which Winthrop had won so quickly was due to Tillman's backing, Johnson's hard work, and Joynes's expertise as the foremost collegiate scholar in the state. Winthrop's preeminence was reflected in part by the appropriations made by the General Assembly. In 1899, for example, and for many years there-following, Winthrop's appropriations were always larger than those of the South Carolina University. The figure for 1899 was $25,000 for the University and $36,598 for Winthrop. The next year the

University received $27,000 and Winthrop received a general appropriation of $38,450 and a special appropriation of $35,000 to build a dormitory.[32]

Winthrop's President, D. B. Johnson, was always able to inspire confidence. Even the most lowly freshman ever to see the distinguished-looking one-armed man who dressed like a preacher and raced from one end of the campus to the other could not help but be impressed; she knew that this man was helping her receive formal college education, something her mother had been denied. Johnson's assemblies, with his short speeches, always were designed to edify and to help. They were much appreciated. Some of the messages Johnson gave over and again, but they conveyed good sense and helpful information. Beginning always with the salutation, "Young ladies. We meet here this morning to formally begin [whatever the project or program was] of Winthrop College at Rock Hill." He always stressed at each opening session that the college had a reputation for her cordial reception of students. "The older students will help you," he entoned. Moving to his punch line, he admonished the girls "to work; don't waste time, it is sinful and will contribute to house-sickness. Time and tide wait for no man; be wise in the use of your time. You are here to learn," he would boom out; "you must prepare yourself for the long years ahead. Be thankful that a grateful state has provided this palatial home and all these advantages for her daughters. Don't neglect this great opportunity." These inspiring thoughts from a sincere man with flashing eyes was sure to impress any respectful South Carolina girl.[33]

Johnson knew how to impress people--all kinds of people including students, parents, legislators, and the man in the street. Winthrop was his great opportunity in life, and he wanted to do something for himself and for his fellow man. He conducted himself in such a way as to seem self-righteous and excellent in every respect. He

132

strove for perfection. He pushed Winthrop and Winthrop's daughters into all areas of service where their efforts would count and show. Typical of this in 1900 was the Winthrop exhibit at the state fair. The newspaper praised it as "the best educational exhibit at the fair." Continuing in its praise of the presentation of the Winthrop story, the paper stated, "like everything else which Winthrop undertakes, it has been successfully worked out, and today the thousands who will examine with interest the exhibit from this great college for women will carry away with them some idea of the thoroughness and completeness of the work done in each department."[34]

Johnson seized on any and every opportunity to push himself and Winthrop forward. He seemed to have a sense of mission and dedication found in few schoolmen. Much of his success was due to his firm tie into South Carolina's public-school system. Trained primarily in math and the classics at the University of Tennessee, Johnson later took a short course of lectures on Normal work; by his continued reading and study of school philosophy and administration, he became a leader. His life and activities brought great luster to the sleepy village in the York County boondocks. In time Johnson had magazines and newspapers in different parts of the country writing about Winthrop. The South Carolina Teacher's Journal called "Rock Hill the mecca of South Carolina teachers, and for at least one month during the year [Winthrop's pioneer academic summer school] it is the Athens of South Carolina. It is the great chautauqua of the state." Johnson was often referred to as "the great head of Winthrop" and complimented that "everything there feels the pulsations of his mighty touch." Speaking on July 12, 1900, to the National Education Association's kindergarten-department meeting, he stressed the importance of their work, saying: "there is no knowledge so high as the knowledge of how to train the little child." Johnson had established in 1898 one of the first kindergarten programs in the South. He seldom followed; he attempted to lead. But during his early career, if one judges by the minutes of the Board, he seemed to be very mindful of Tillman and Joynes.[35]

For the first several years at Winthrop there was only one professor with the final degree, the doctorate of philosophy: James Pinckney Kinard, a product of the Citadel and Johns Hopkins University in Baltimore, Maryland. Johnson was proud to list his A.B., and A.M. degrees from the University of Tennessee as well as the L.I., which no doubt Bridgewater in Massachusetts had conferred on him. His doctorate--like that of so many schoolmen of this period--was an honorary degree. In Johnson's case it was granted later by the University of South Carolina.[36] But Johnson possessed talents not easily measured by degrees.

Johnson's yearly reports to the various state superintendents of education and the General Assembly are factual and straight-forward. They show the ability and drive of this man, who was determined to help build a great college. For many years, Johnson used the same statement to the press to get more and more from the state. "South Carolina," he would stress, "has long maintained institutions for the higher education of her sons, and only recently has she begun to provide such training for her daughters in the Winthrop Normal and Industrial College at Rock Hill." But if this statement had not been a by-product of Tillmanism, the Legislature might have lowered the boom on Johnson. His second jab of his one, two, three "knock out" usually tied into a statement on enrollment: "We have admitted [appropriate number] more than last year, and this number would have been still larger if there had been dormitory accommodations for all those making applications for admission." Here Johnson was misleading in his enthusiasm because he suggested, or the Board did, that the girls had to pass the entrance exams at their county seats. Instead many would get their uniforms and come on to Winthrop. Those who failed the examination would have to return home.[37]

134

Once the General Assembly had succumbed to the pressure for more space, Johnson would write in his report:

The General Assembly, at its last session, recognizing the pressing necessity of greater accommodations at Winthrop College to provide for the great number of young women eagerly crowding to its doors to avail themselves of the opportunities there offered by the state for an education and training to fit them for life's duties as breadwinner or home makers, and that a comparatively small expenditure for additional dormitory accommodations would reach and benefit almost twice as many girls as at present--would make doubly effective this great institution established by the state for the best, broadest, and fullest education of her womanhood, than which there is no duty of the state more imperative, nor one the performance of which will be more richly rewarded in an elevated society, an intelligent citizenship, and a broad, enlightened public opinion-- made an appropriation to enlarge the college.

The Johnson-Tillman system as later perfected with the use of "Winthrop Daughters" became a classic in democratic political action in South Carolina.[38]

A closer analysis of Johnson's system reveals a preoccupation with numbers and physical improvements, even though he desired most of all to educate, to train, and to excel in so doing. For in all mortals, perfection and success breed confidence and sometimes a sense of infallibility. Johnson felt that nothing should interfere with education. For example, he had a strong feeling that long holidays were demoralizing to the academic process. Consequently he insisted on five short holidays: Thanksgiving Day, Robert E. Lee's birthday, Washington's birthday, and Founder's Day. Four of these days were devoted to special exercises, and Christmas was one "of good cheer." Johnson's insistence on the one-day Christmas holiday caused trouble during the early years. Tillman, Joynes, and many of the parents and students opposed Johnson. Pressure forced the Board in 1900 to direct Johnson to canvass the parents and guardians about their feelings on the matter. In a letter to the parents, Johnson stated that the Board had given only one day at Christmas "for reasons assigned to the catalogue"--namely, "to save parents extra railroad fare, and to prevent the serious demoralization and loss of time to the students, and the disorganization of the College work, always consequent upon the breaking up of school within three months after the opening of the session." He further claimed that students lost interest in their studies, if allowed to leave, and would return unfit for school duties. Included in this letter to the parents, Johnson enclosed a return letter, on which parents could mark with pencil if they preferred one or several days. Johnson reported to the Board later that of the two-hundred and seventy replies, two-hundred and three voted for the one day. This seems unusual despite the word of a High Presbyterian like Johnson.[39]

Johnson continued to tighten his grip on all phases of Winthrop's development. He was aided in this by his relationship with Tillman, Joynes, and others dedicated to making Winthrop a great service agency for South Carolina. Their correspondence and actions give information that at first glance is highly paradoxical. A more thorough study reveals just how Winthrop developed and shows much about the hopes and aspirations of these men.[40]

Following a Board meeting early in 1900 at which Johnson had pressed hard for his Model School concept and a new dormitory, Tillman wrote Governor Miles B. McSweeney a long letter (March 8, 1900) to acquaint the new governor with Johnson and some

136

of his backers. Trustees Joynes and Lee had talked over the meeting on the train ride back to Columbia, and they wrote Tillman to put pressure on Johnson through the executive committee to change the direction that events were taking at Winthrop.[41] Tillman expressed his views to the governor and suggested that they "may as far as practicable cooperate." But "Roddey and Crawford are pulling for Rock Hill, and to that extent the Executive Committee is handicapped in the discharge of its duty to the State and to the tax payers, and it will depend on you, McMahan, and myself to look out for the state's interest and not allow Rock Hill to get too much advantage." According to Tillman, the Rock Hillians were of the opinion that the state needed the Model School and that they would benefit greatly therefrom. Joynes, according to Tillman, was going along with Johnson on this because of "their recent antagonism." He further stated that Johnson wanted to curry favor with Rock Hill and retain his grip on controlling the college "which is now absolute as you know, to the degree that many of the teachers and professors, in fact I may say all of them, are mere nullities and dependent in a large degree upon Johnson's favor." Continuing this quiet and caustic commentary to Governor McSweeney, Tillman revealed, "we shook his [Johnson's] grip to some degree last summer and it will be necessary to give the faculty more freedom in order to lift the school to the high plane it ought to occupy." But softening his tone somewhat and showing himself to be quietly reasonable, Tillman expressed his true feelings: "I am not antagonizing Johnson because in some respects he is the best man we could get for the Presidency, but he is too narrow and too autocratic in his views and methods. We can liberalize him or liberalize his subordinates which will be the same thing to the great advantage of the college."

Continuing this long letter, without designation or paragraphs, Tillman gave his views to the governor about those on the Board and what to expect of each. Of Joynes, he said, "he knows a great deal about the interior workings of the College and is invaluable in that field, but his

137

ideas about building [buildings] are not worth much because he is not a practical man."42

Pointing out that Johnson was willing to let Rock Hillians occupy almost one-half the space in the Model School's dormitory, Tillman suggested that "we cannot expect the Legislature to respond readily in the near future [with money], and Rock Hill is in no condition to finance the extra $9,000 over and above what a plain building corresponding in almost every respect with the other dormitory . . . would cost. The idea of asking the Legislature hereafter to give us money to remodel the old dormitory so as to have it correspond with the new is as you must acknowledge chimerical. We need other things at Winthrop much more . . . especially some sandy land for horticultural uses."43

Tillman concluded by advising the governor to contact the state superintendent of education and "try to get him to understand the situation as I have outlined it, and let me know as soon as you receive this what the existing status is and if you call a meeting of the Executive Committee as you must do, consult me as to date so I can tell you when I can get off." There can be little doubt that Tillman still exercised tremendous influence over Winthrop.44

Regardless of oppressive rules and Board politics, the public saw a different side. Johnson worked hard for his girls. He sought to provide them with "the best" and to praise them for their accomplishments. And every such accomplishment was officially noted. One of Winthrop's first exhibits at the state fair was universally acclaimed. Johnson in reporting this to the Legislature included the letter of the chairman of the fair committee which read in part:

> We knew that the College was providing
> all-around education for the women of
> the state. . . . but we found upon
> examination of the exhibit, that we

138

had failed to realize the full scope of its great work. It was a revelation. It will prove a great stimulus to the attainment of the highest and best ideals in education . . . throughout the state. In conclusion we recommend that a medal be awarded Winthrop College for its full and admirable and beautiful exhibit.

Johnson also included a report of the students' attending the fair en masse, suggesting that they might wish to make another exhibit for the Charleston Interstate and West Indian Exposition to be held the next year. Johnson never passed up an opportunity, especially one of this nature.[45]

Even the catalogue which Johnson prepared to announce the 1900-1901 session managed in a highly professional manner to give special distinction to the Winthrop girl and the Winthrop facilities. The clear picture of the Main Building and the dormitory came from the Saunders Company of St. Louis. It was excellent. Photographs of the other structures were by Gatchel and Manning of Philadelphia. Pictures of the student body were also the work of Saunders. His pictures of individual students modeling the fatigue and dress uniforms--winter and summer, the cooking-school suit, and the spring uniforms-- reveal some of the most angelic faces of petite young ladies in early twentieth-century South Carolina, young ladies sure to attract attention at home and abroad. Johnson always tried to secure the finest for Winthrop and to exhibit it to the best advantage in the proper Victorian manner.[46]

A fortunate Johnson also secured the services of many good men and women who helped in Winthrop's rapid rise to prominence. One would be remiss to overlook a great public-school man, the State Superintendent of Education W. D. Mayfield of Columbia, who was so intimately asociated with Winthrop's early development in Rock Hill. Mr. Mayfield's activities as Winthrop trustee suggest he was a stabilizing influence. He was most influential in helping Johnson effect a tie into the state's school system, a tie that in time gave Winthrop ample opportunity for service in South Carolina. Mayfield's reports to the General Assembly, to the Peabody Board, and to others were of tremendous value in promoting Winthrop. One scarcely realizes how paltry state public education's financing was at the time Mayfield was struggling to improve the system. South Carolina in 1899 could boast that she led all Southern states in cotton manufacturing and ran second only to Massachusetts in the number of textile spindles, but in education she only had an average three- to four-month term in the common schools. The common schools lacked money, educated teachers, and intelligent and efficient county superintendents. Mayfield and others echoed the feeling "that the greatest blessing that could come to this State would be a first class common school opened for the full school year in every community within her borders." Thus, Mayfield's efforts to help Winthrop and the common-school system complement each other in upgrading South Carolina's education deserve more than a passing reference.[47]

Of equal importance in Winthrop's early days were the activities of Dr. Edward Joynes. Joynes--who came from a long line of political and educational leaders in Accomack County, Virginia--enjoyed showing his erudition and skill with language, of which he was a recognized master. Joynes respected Tillman and Tillman liked him. Theirs was a long friendship--a courtship over Winthrop. During his life trusteeship Joynes spread his views on nearly every page of the Winthrop record. Superior in training to any practicing South Carolina educator during Winthrop's early development, Joynes (through letters to Johnson and Tillman) showed his untiring loyalty to his favorite godchild, Winthrop College. Joynes constantly pushed to enhance Winthrop's academic life. And he frequently gave books to enlarge the library.[48]

140

Writing to the scholarly Joynes in July, 1901, Johnson indicated he did not wish to hold a committee meeting about program changes because he had other pressing college matters--namely planning for the new dormitory. Johnson said that he was anxious to simplify and reduce the study courses but that he wished to consult a faculty committee on the projected changes. Joynes finally arranged the meeting on reorganization but left unsatisfied with the results. Replying to Johnson in October, 1901, in a most complimentary and cutting manner, Joynes suggested adding a classical course to correspond to the Latin Normal class. Joynes argued such a course would necessitate little change; he wanted Greek added whether it was offered in the best women's colleges or not. Johnson, like schoolmen before and since, relied on the statement "this is done [or not done] in the best colleges," depending on what the administrator was attempting. Joynes wished to modify the program in this case to include two years of Greek and two of Latin.[49]

Joynes did not favor adding studies other than Normal and industrial. At Winthrop these two courses were offered in 1900; the faculty and Johnson sought to add four additional courses in 1901-02. Joynes made the point that these additions violated the spirit of the law that set up Winthrop. In almost all his early reports to the General Assembly, Johnson wrote that it was a "difficult and delicate task to combine in one institution this varied work (Industrial and Normal) and give to each department its due prominence." Johnson usually favored the Normal but feared going too far as Tillman liked the industrial, so Johnson would usually report that "nothing is being left undone to do this and the results must show with what success." Johnson would always report that there was "an increasing demand for _____ course" and sometimes not more than five students took a course, as in the case of kindergarten in 1900. Frequently Joynes would cooperate in a Johnson move that he disagreed with; and, quite frequently, he sent Johnson private notes

141

saying he felt that any misunderstanding could only harm the work they were all interested in, concluding with "let us have peace." Joynes always asked for documents and reports so that he might check on Johnson or compare notes with Tillman.[50]

At the turn of the century, Winthrop suffered growing pains over several important problems. For years Winthrop had maintained a Practice School to which the Rock Hill Graded School Board of Trustees contributed $360 yearly inasmuch as Rock Hill children were taught there who otherwise would have gone to the city schools. In the spring of 1900, a joint committee of the town and the college combined efforts to build a model school which would also serve as a preparatory school for the college. The "town and gown" group agreed to Mr. F. P. Milburn's plan for a new Model School outside the original plant. Finally the trustees of the public schools agreed to remit their share of the public-school taxes (county, local, and poll) to Winthrop in exchange for her building and maintaining the Model School and instructing local children. John Milady would superintend the works, erecting the dormitory portion of the Model School before the classroom portion.[51]

Another problem that one does not ordinarily associate with a college was sewerage disposal. A previous smallpox threat had alerted the community to the waste-control problem. Then as a result of a suit brought by a party living near the branch into which the college sewer emptied, the sewer was declared a nuisance and an injunction required Winthrop to abate this nuisance by April 1, 1901. Coming to Winthrop's aid, the General Assembly appropriated $3,000 to change the sewer to meet the injunction conditions. The resulting filtration system met all requirements. This, coupled with the requirement that students be vaccinated, took care of the community's health problem. The college became especially careful

142

thereafter. And the report on Winthrop's 1901 health record by resident physician Dr. Helen F. T. Cleaves showed the extreme measures taken by the college to ensure that everything was sterilized and that all the pipes stayed flushed and operable.[52]

The year 1901 witnessed other outstanding improvements at the college. South Dormitory, named for General D. W. McLaurin, added space for two-hundred extra students. The library expanded its holdings to five-thousand regular volumes plus five-thousand government publications. Among the new volumes was a copy of the school annual, The Tatler.

A most highly advertised Winthrop accomplishment was her exhibit at the South Carolina Interstate and West Indian Exposition at Charleston. The college's exhibit occupied 2,000 feet of floor space in the northwestern section of the state building and consisted of seven different exhibits that cost $1,000 to complete. The first exhibit, "Industrial Art," held nearly three-hundred works including paintings, charcoal drawings, charts, and designs. The second or "Literary" section included papers, examinations and numerous pictures representing college life as well as unusual books and portraits from the library. The third area presented the complete story of the "Practice School" with maps, art objects, and works made in that department. In the fourth area, the work of the Kindergarten appeared. In the fifth category millinery and dressmaking creations were attractively displayed, showing the great skill and accomplishments. The Domestic Science area stressed diet, food values, and food analysis; this sixth area proved most educational and attractive, especially its table set with samples of many fine foods. Finally, the horticulture exhibit held a number of flowering pots, palms, ferns, and a rubber plant, among other things.[53]

For its efforts at the South Carolina Interstate and West Indian Exposition, the college took home a gold medal and glory. A writer in Century Magazine praised Winthrop's exhibit, saying, "it seemed to me that the exhibit of Winthrop College stands first. Some 500 are being taught there and it turns out teachers for the schools of South Carolina. . . . From its kitchen exhibit to its examination papers this showing of Winthrop College is admirably presented. The institution must do great good."[54]

The highlight of the Winthrop year ending in June, 1902, was not the visit of the student body to the Exposition on April 2-5, nor the good impression the girls made in Charleston, but rather the organization in May, 1902, of the Society for the Improvement of the County Schools of the State by Mr. Johnson and the senior class. Many of these students were farmers' daughters, and they realized from their own experience the need to improve the country schools. Each society member pledged to do something to improve the school near her home and, during the next year, to try to create interest among the parents and students in the school where she was located. Thus began a movement which would help South Carolina greatly in the years to come.

Other important aspects of the year included Dr. Joynes's committee's work on college courses and by-laws, for which the Board gave Joynes and his group a deserved special vote of thanks.[55]

The college experienced its greatest growth during the seventh session at Rock Hill, with four-hundred and fifty-six pupils plus ninety in the Model School and Kindergarten. For the first time, nearly all students were under the same roof. This figure does not include the summer school at Winthrop under the direction of State Superintendent John J. McMahan, with President Johnson assisted by Miss Sara Withers. Over four-hundred teachers enrolled in the summer school. Winthrop at this session offered fourteen courses taken by students

144

from forty-two accredited schools in South Carolina.[56]

The good work and momentum continued into 1903 with eight-hundred and twenty applicants, of whom two-hundred and thirty-five failed to qualify because of strict entrance requirements' enforcement. Among the innovations this year were the nascent student government and a "most inspiring" meeting for the county superintendents of education. The latter group agreed that this meeting was the most helpful they had ever held. Johnson and his staff took a vital part in this.[57]

Early in 1903 Trustee Joynes wrote President Johnson a confidential letter which threw light on one of Winthrop's problems. Joynes told Johnson that a popular rumor attributed one teacher's death "in part and directly to extreme overwork in spite of her protest and petitions for relief reinforced" by the head of her department. Allowing for exaggerations, Joynes advised Johnson that this rumor was serious since it was accompanied by the "almost unanimous protest of the women teachers at Winthrop against dormitory and other police duty to which they are subjected." Joynes reminded Johnson that the Board had heard similar protests many times and that "the disciplinary system now existing in Winthrop is unworthy of any first class woman's college." Calling Johnson's system "unfriendly to the character of womanhood and childish" Joynes demanded an immediate change.[58]

Two weeks later Joynes fired off another letter to Johnson, suggesting immediate consideration of graduate classes at Winthrop. Joynes had submitted a report on this heretofore. He also demanded the overdue faculty report on disciplinary matters and wanted such a report to come through Johnson to the Board. He insisted, "I am clear that something must be done," since Johnson was not answering his letters. Again on March 11, Joynes wrote Johnson regarding the length of the school year and the Christmas vacation. Joynes

145

informed Johnson that Carolina, which had a lengthy Christmas vacation, taught longer during the week than Winthrop and this added about three weeks to the whole session. He intimated that if Winthrop followed Carolina, there would be no problem about losing a few days at Christmas. Joynes suggested positive thinking by concluding, "I rejoice to hear of progress toward a permanent schedule."[59]

The ever-vigilant Joynes stayed abreast of any developments in education--and he kept Johnson properly informed. Writing again on April 2, Joynes suggested that the Peabody Board sought to concentrate its efforts in establishing a "great teacher's college in the South," which would result in Winthrop's losing considerable money. Joynes requested a conference with Johnson on April 11. Johnson needed little prompting, as he always kept an ear cocked for the slightest hint of money available from funds like the Peabody and the General Education Board. These groups held open invitations to visit and see how Winthrop excelled. Dr. G. R. Glenn, the acting agent for Peabody, came in 1903 and his report called Winthrop "a noble example of the fruits of Mr. Peabody's sowing." He labeled Winthrop "the best planned and equipped normal school for whites in the South." As a result, Winthrop received $5,000 in 1904 plus $1,000 for a summer school. Not to be outdone, Dr. David E. Cloyd of the General Education Board (following his inspection the same year) wrote, "I believe that this is the best arranged plant for both academic and dormitory life that I have seen. . . . I have never spent a day in any school where there was less disturbance and less loss of time. . . . There is an atmosphere of culture and strength such as is rarely seen in a normal school. . . . this is the most wholesome place in which to educate a young lady for a life of service."[60]

Tillman, Joynes, Johnson, and others agreed with Cloyd's evaluation. On other matters they were often far apart. Tillman continued to insist that the session be extended to permit at least a week's vacation for Christmas. Joynes continued to check

146

every phase of everything, including a list of books deemed proper for the library. Replying to Johnson on April 19, Joynes was emphatic:

> I think that no book of mere current fiction--the popular novel of the day-- should be bought, by public money, for a college library. They are not literature, and are for the most part, of mere temporary popularity. If the girls want such books, they should buy them, or provide them in their society libraries. For such flimsy reading the magazines give more than enough. I think it a safe rule to buy no fiction of any living author--at least none that has not had at least ten years of life. . . . In general the list has my hearty approval.

Joynes, the liberal (as he wished to be remembered), will never be remembered as a champion of the twentieth-century novel in America.[61]

The academic side of Winthrop claimed Joynes's considerate attention. Again in 1903 he suggested to Johnson that Professor Breazeale's temporary position at Rutgers had expired and that Johnson might wish to recall him to Winthrop, if he were still acceptable to Johnson. Running through many of Joynes's letters is the feeling that Johnson was not a good judge of scholars and that he did not show proper consideration for his teachers residing in the dormitories. Addressing himself to the latter, Joynes observed that women have great imaginations and that they would tend to multiply any personal hardships. Joynes concluded: "Women are queer folks--still queerer when together. But I am glad this generation is yours, not mine, to solve."[62]

Still, Dr. Joynes continued to help solve any and all problems at Winthrop for years to come. Not one was too small or too big. In fact a cursory examination of his relation with Johnson gives one

the impression that he meddled too much. Joynes,
with his rare educational background, had suggestions and plans for every area of Winthrop's
development. Diplomas, Joynes suggested (just
before commencement in 1903), needed a different
format from the ones Bryan's printed. He suggested
dropping the words Regular Literary and instead
adding the course name in ink. This, Joynes felt,
would be more pleasing to the eye and less redundant
as regular was implied in the next line with the
word prescribed. Joynes further suggested that the
diplomas would be more dignified with the entire
border omitted. A more careful examination of
Joynes's meddling suggests his adroitness and
expertise. His veracity was never subject to
serious question. His humanity seemed unbounded. [63]

As head of the Committee on Organization,
Joynes insisted on reading the departmental reports,
on having considerable voice in the curriculum, and
on helping with faculty hirings. A new teacher from
East Orange, New Jersey, sent her thanks to Joynes
for his help in securing a position at Winthrop.
When controversy developed over the salary, Joynes
advised Johnson, "I may remind you that I am
personally responsible for the nomination of Miss C
[aspari] at $600. My reason was that she appeared
to be inexperienced as a teacher."[64]

David B. Johnson, in spite of Joynes and the
Board, managed to guide the college in his capacity
as president and treasurer. His skillful use of
money endeared him especially to the politicians.
His total 1903 budget for Winthrop was $105,623.14,
much larger (as always) than that for the University
of South Carolina. Governor Duncan Clinch Heyward,
commenting on Winthrop in 1904, praised the Board
for planning "to build up an institution for the
girls of the state the equal of any of its kind in
the country," and Heyward felt that their work would
"meet with the approval of the General Assembly and
of all broad-minded, patriotic citizens of South
Carolina."[65]

148

The 1904-05 session proved unique and most fruitful in many respects. Johnson had already started pleading Winthrop's cause to the great industrialist Andrew Carnegie. In the spring, 1904, Carnegie finally pledged $20,000 for a library. The Carnegie Library Building Committee consisted of Messrs. Tillman, Roddey, and Johnson. Mr. J. M. McMichael designed the plans. To complement South Carolina's new library law, Mr. Carnegie added $10,000 to his original pledge, thus providing room in the facility for a library-methods training program. This new library law created rural school libraries that needed servicing by trained professionals and Winthrop, with the aid of Carnegie, was able to train personnel in the selection, care, and use of books. The library plans suggested that when finished it would be the best of its kind in upper South Carolina--a beautiful and well-proportioned structure situated very close to the president's house.[66]

By 1904 Winthrop's most pressing need was a Model School building. Such a building, Johnson and others argued, would bring greater value and distinction to the Normal-school work and would relieve the pressure of maintaining practice teaching in the Main Building. The college hesitated to have visiting delegations view their work in the cramped quarters. Estimating that a new building would cost $45,000, the Board stressed its necessity, appealing to the General Assembly for the money and arguing in part that the state had made no buildings appropriations for Winthrop during the previous five years. The Board asked the Legislature for $20,000 followed by $15,000 to complete the work.[67]

During the first part of this highly successful scholastic year--July 1, 1904, to July 1, 1905--an exhausted Johnson went North for treatment by Dr. Wharton Sinkler of Philadelphia. He had planned to rest and recuperate four weeks but, unable to return before the fall term, he appointed Dr. Kinard as acting president. Assuring the Board by letter (November, 1904) of his informed following of college business, he said that he would "see Mr. Carnegie again while in the North," with the hope, no doubt, of securing a matching pledge for the proposed Model School or more for the library.

Mrs. Johnson's "Cousin," the outstanding poet and writer Archibald Rutledge, has suggested that Johnson felt no hesitation in asking friends in the North for money because the South had been ruined by the war and also because the South had helped Northern institutions before the war. He cited South Carolina's contributions to Brown and other institutions. Rutledge further suggested that "with his cheerful manner, his ringing voice, his one arm, his noble appearance as the champion of indigent and illiterate fair southern womanhood, he was a most appealing and persuasive begger." Whatever it was, Johnson's aura attracted private money for Winthrop, which in turn kept him close to the hearts of the Legislature and the populace in general. [68]

While Johnson underwent treatment in Philadelphia, college business continued as usual under the steady hands of Dr. Kinard, Joynes, and others. Writing to Kinard in October, 1904, Joynes suggested that they raise the admission age from fifteen to sixteen years and that they abolish entirely all sub-collegiate or preparatory classes. As Chairman of the Committee on Organization, Joynes felt that these matters should be taken up at the next Board meeting with or without the presence of Johnson, who he felt was long overdue in returning. Trustee Joynes was most complimentary of Kinard's stewardship. [69] But Kinard, who was hesitant to discuss such important matters in Johnson's absence, finally agreed to take up the proposals if Johnson had not returned by December. Johnson, according to Kinard, had written Mrs. Johnson that he was improving and hoped to return within a few weeks. [70]

This was not the first time and would certainly not be the last that President Johnson had left his bride home while he travelled.

Following Senator Tillman's emphatic suggestion that a bachelor was not the most appropriate male to run a women's college, Johnson had married (perhaps co-incidentally) Mai Rutledge Smith of Charleston. Miss Smith had come to Winthrop in 1897 as a student. She had worked for her future husband during a year prior to their August 6, 1902, marriage. She was twenty-three; he was forty-six. For the next seventy-seven years she would serve as Winthrop's official and unofficial (following her husband's 1928 death) first lady. Even when others ran Winthrop in Johnson's absence, Mrs. Johnson made her presence felt.

During Mr. Johnson's absence, the semester ran smoothly as the campus relaxed under the easy-going and gentlemanly Dr. Kinard. With the approach of Christmas, however, the holiday question stayed uppermost in the students' minds, and (according to Dr. Kinard) would "cause some heart burning, no doubt." Dr. Joynes, who fondly remembered his student days at Heidelberg, wanted longer vacations at Christmas but did not wish to put Kinard in an awkward position. During Johnson's protracted illness, Joynes had not only helped with problems at Winthrop, but had tried to promote Carolina College into the University of South Carolina.[71]

Trustee Joynes of Winthrop and Dr. Joynes of Carolina College had labored incessantly since 1882 to build up the teaching profession and the educational standards of South Carolina. Now in the twilight of his career, Joynes took his case to the newspapers, arguing that the term college in America meant an institution of second rank, regardless of how excellent it might be. He stressed that South Carolina needed to expand her Centennial College, to make it a university "in fact and not in name only." Now was the time. Joynes like many other South Carolinians was much impressed with Winthrop's fast growth and its state appropriations of $50,000 as compared with the $36,000 given Carolina. In addition Winthrop received more money for scholarships as well as a sizeable appropriation from the Peabody Fund, especially in 1904 and 1905. Carolina College desperately needed more help before it could become the apex of South Carolina's educational system. Joynes worked hard toward helping both Winthrop and Carolina achieve their goals.[72]

Winthrop basked in considerable publicity. For example, the account of John W. Jenkins in The Baltimore Sun on May 21, 1905, was most flattering. Mr. Jenkins summarized the school's great advantages thus: "with a dormitory system that gives girl students excellent board and service for $10.00 a month, the total cost of $104.00, but this is remitted to any student who feels that she is unable to pay it." Jenkins marveled at the arrangement.[73]

Johnson cultivated other techniques to spotlight Winthrop for the public eye. Using some phase of his annual report, Johnson would manage a nice lead story. They usually began: "President D. B. Johnson has sent to each of the trustees a copy of the annual report of Winthrop College for the semester just drawing to a close." Then the article would skip to some phase of the report, such as Manual Training at Winthrop College, emphasizing that the young women were taught to cook and to sew. A detailed program description would follow, no doubt attracting parents and girls interested in such training. A few days thereafter Johnson would follow up with a detailed summary of the weekend-long closing exercises. Always proclaiming each year as the best yet, the latter part of these articles stressed the most pressing needs for the coming year--a statement designed, no doubt, gently to inform the incoming Legislature of Winthrop's most pressing needs.[74]

Working through the office of the state superintendent of education, the Johnson-oriented and Winthrop-based Association for the Improvement of Rural Schools became a great service agency whose activities often made front-page news. The association usually met just after Christmas and

152

again in the summer; it engaged in planting trees, planning buildings, establishing libraries, and making other improvements at the rural schools. These schools were often neglected one-room buildings that served the rural sections of South Carolina even in relatively prosperous counties. The Sunday State of June 25, 1905, devoted its entire front page to improvements being made in the public rural schools of Richland County. Pictures of the schools, students, and faculties appeared with summary teachers' accounts to the superintendent. A typical picture and report from "Fairmont School - Bull Pen Section of Jacobs, that was sent to Mr. E. B. Wallace, County Superintendent, Columbia, S.C." ran

Dear Sir:

The Fairmont school is furnished with: Ten pupils' desks, one teacher's desk, one chair, one table, one stove, one blackboard, one language chart, one arithmetical chart, one globe, one map case of eight maps, South Carolina map, one United States map, map of the world, Webster's unabridged dictionary, one moulding table, four window shades, five pictures, two United States flags. We have a $10 library and a $10 bookcase. The room is ceiled and comfortable.

Sally Kelley, Teacher

The program to improve schools like Fairmont made a lasting impression on the community and its citizens. According to the editor, this program was "making for higher citizenship," thanks to the efforts of Winthrop.[75]

Despite the publicity over Johnson's accomplishments, the recurring problem of Christmas holidays hounded him. His stance remained unpopular and thus hard to get good publicity from, but he always tried. Reporting on Christmas, 1905, at Winthrop, he wrote:

153

Mrs. Cobb, the assistant housekeeper had a Christmas tree for all the
colored people in the employment of the
College. Everyone received a gift,
with candy and oranges, and many were
the blessings and thanks showered upon
the head of the benefactress.

The Winthrop girls as usual were
treated to a social at Christmas given
in the reception hall Saturday evening.
. . . Miss Inez McCullough was the
successful competitor for a Cake in the
cakewalk. . . . On Christmas morning,
at 5:30 o'clock, fifty students and
teachers, robed in white, went through
the dormitories, singing 'O, Little
Town of Bethlehem,' and 'It Came Upon
the Midnight Clear'--eventually they
went to the President's house in the
early morning light . . . later all the
girls were given a fine Christmas
dinner.[76]

Such was Johnson's program of "Christmas
cheer." A fortnight later the State suggested "the
Winthrop girls will have a holiday next Christmas if
the Legislature passes the bill to be introduced
requiring the State College to close from December
23 to January 3, each year." On January 18, 1906,
the House voted to take the privilege of granting
Christmas holidays from the Winthrop trustees and
Johnson--much to the satisfaction of the more
liberal trustees Tillman and Joynes.[77]

Whenever Johnson appeared to be checked in
one area (like the Christmas-vacation controversy),
he seemed to jump to something else that would give
him new, more positive publicity. Such was the
case in 1906 with Johnson's constant push for a
Model School. Two years before, the state Legislature had earnestly debated a Model School bill.
Johnson had "rejoiced" and reported to Tillman,

following his contact with Carnegie, that "the outlook for our Model School seems bright."[78]

Johnson was also working two other prospects in 1906. Visiting Carnegie's private secretary to seek more money for a library, Johnson assured Tillman that he could get $10,000 more if the Legislature obligated itself to give $1,000. In his reply, Tillman expressed doubt about handing the Legislature such a proposition, fearing that the legislators might become antagonistic. Tillman agreed to discuss this with Johnson. The library was later built for $30,000 (without cost to the state) and was dedicated June 4, 1906.[79]

With the Carnegie Library funds secured, Johnson began consistantly courting the Peabody Fund. In a personal letter to Tillman, Johnson confided: "I have always expected that the largest part of the fund would be given to this College," saying his efforts and those of James D. Porter, President of the Peabody Committee, were directed to this end. "I have not learned yet what has been done for Winthrop," he wrote, "but if the full program agreed upon should be carried out and the promise of leading members of the Board with whom I have been in touch for years holds good, we will be handsomely remembered." The plan was to give Peabody College (Nashville) $1,000,000 and Winthrop College $350,000. Johnson hoped that other colleges would not attempt to secure a part of the amount he believed would be Winthrop's. "It may be that definite action in regard to Winthrop will not be taken until next October," he advised, "when the final meeting of the Board will be held to wind up its affairs and dissolve. I know that Mr. Winthrop left a letter at his death for the Peabody Board requesting that Winthrop College be generously remembered at the distribution of the Peabody Fund, and that this letter is held sacred by the Board next to the Will of Mr. Peabody himself."[80]

With visions of Peabody dollars dancing in his head, Johnson early in 1906 began pushing the

155

Legislature for the Model School. Boasting the largest graduating class (sixty) ever, Johnson advertised to the Legislature that the most pressing need of the college was a Model and Practice School. "Such a building," he said, "would strengthen the normal work by providing a setting for student-teaching." It was imperative, according to Johnson, to move the model school work out of the Main building: the move would add more desperately needed teaching room, which in turn would point up the need for a new dormitory. The Model and Practice School would cost (he figured) $45,000, and with it Winthrop should at least be equal to similar institutions in the South. Since South Carolina had not made any appropriations during the past six years for buildings at Winthrop, Johnson felt that the Legislature would guarantee $20,000 on condition that he and the Board could raise $25,000.[81]

In the Legislature, Johnson's reasoning mainly fell on deaf ears. The opposition accused the state of favoring Winthrop and Clemson to the injury of other colleges while the never-satisfied duo cried for more. This view proved quite effective in a Legislature that wrestled with an austerity budget every year. The bill, as later brought out, gave Winthrop $20,000 on condition that she raise $25,000 for the Model School. A leading representative from Chester County, Paul Hemphill, ridiculed the bill's wording, which declared that the school trustees, students, and others "may see a school building that will enable them to study school architecture." The representative cried out: "they don't need to study it!" He suggested, and with some authority, that the bill's real purpose was to erect a school building for the students of Rock Hill. Others joined in the condemnation, suggesting that Winthrop had already cost the state $290,000. In the free-for-all that ensued, the Liquor Dispensary, the Immigration Bureau, and other facets of state government were castigated. One representative felt the Bureau was bringing into South Carolina "ignorant dagoes and Russian Jews" and he said, "before long some kind-hearted man will

156

bring in a bill to educate these poor people" --concluding that "money doesn't make brains."[82]

Despite politics, Winthrop emerged from the Legislature with the largest appropriation given any state school but without the Model School appropriation. The school work continued as usual during the winter and spring, with almost monthly Johnson reports of appealing news. February's announcement showcased twenty-five students who were forming a class to study mill workers' conditions in hope of organizing mill schools. No doubt many would favor this, Mr. Carnegie included. Also in February, the annual carnival featured activities at Winthrop. Simultaneously the college received an art consignment with which to decorate the halls of the Main Building. The students keenly followed the bill to provide a Christmas holiday in 1906. This bill became law despite a veto plea from President Johnson to Governor Duncan Clinch Heyward. The governor felt he could not veto and he made his position clear to the people. Prominent press releases also focus on Winthrop's model farm, Dr. Kinard's English Grammar for Beginners, Judge Alton B. Parker's visit, the new Carnegie Library's dedication, and the closing exercises--all emphasized the vitality and purpose of a rapidly expanding institution. Judge Parker's remarks on his March 16 visit to Winthrop were most welcomed by the student body; when referring to Tillman, Parker said, "Well he pushes everything he undertakes, no wonder this institution is such a success."[83]

The Carnegie Library dedication became the high point of this most successful year. Carnegie had given $25,000 in March, 1904, but completion of the building was delayed to see if Carnegie would increase his pledge to $30,000, which he did on January 16, 1906. The additional money was justified because Mr. Carnegie wished the library to serve as a library-methods training school. Finally on June 4, 1906, a thousand people assembled in the impressive new building which bore the imprint of the architect, J. M. McMichael of

157

Charlotte, and the builder, R. A. Brown of Concord. Dr. Samuel M. Smith, Edward Joynes, and others spoke. The press reported:

> It was an inspiring sight, when Dr. Johnson rapped the assembly to order and asked Dr. George B. Eager of the Southern Baptist Theological Seminary to invoke the Divine blessing. Two score of electric lights gleamed from the white paneled ceiling, twenty feet above the floor and supported by ten massive marble-like columns, surmounted by graceful capitals while from niches in the walls looked down the busts of Shakespeare, Milton, and a dozen other illustrious but dead worthies. [84]

As usual Winthrop held the state summer school in 1906. Superintendent Oscar B. Martin of the State Department conducted it; Johnson assisted him. The best talent in the state was complemented by faculty from Georgia, Ohio and New York. Two-hundred and ninety teachers attended the June 20 to July 18 session, which included the annual State Teacher's Association meeting. [85]

The summer brought a great surplus of applicants seeking fall entry. Over nine hundred applied for the four-hundred spaces available, and Johnson in August began to replay his familiar record for the press--"we need more room." Claiming that he had turned away nearly five-hundred girls, Johnson reiterated his punchline that South Carolina had provided for less than five-hundred girls. Since girls could not board in town, they were prevented from attending Winthrop. As always, Johnson asked for more money and dormitories. [86]

By 1906 definite signs of change appeared on the Winthrop campus. No detail large or small escaped President Johnson's scrutiny. Sanctioned by the Board of Trustees and guided by the watchful eye of Senator Tillman, special courses in Domestic

158

Science began, including sewing, cooking, physical culture, horticulture, and agriculture. Tillman moved late in 1905 to make all executive-branch Winthrop employees subject to the Board's approval. He was instrumental also in providing a free Winthrop education for a young lady who had lost her right hand in the school laundry. All requests to buy small blocks of land also went through the Board--this was reaffirmed in 1905. And most importantly, the Board authorized Johnson to see J. P. Morgan concerning funds for the Model School. Recognizing Winthrop's growing professionalism, the Board asked Johnson to attend all prominent educational meetings held in America, whenever possible, at the expense of the college. [87]

At each school opening, Johnson made his "blood, sweat, tears, sacrifice, and warm welcome" speech, which no doubt became more effective as years passed. The speech was a one-man orientation on how to get the most out of Winthrop. It left little doubt as to who ran Winthrop and what he expected of the students. Stressing the philosophy of "dig, dig, dig," Johnson exhorted his girls "to live nobly, to become womanly Christian women. Include in your resolution," he implored, "the determination that the end of the session shall find you with broader minds, higher ideals, stronger in faith and hope and love, sweeter in life, with much accomplished of the greatest and truest value for yourselves and others--for the great aim of your living and striving should be to become better in heart and soul, as well as in mind and body." Stressing honor, good behavior, observation of rules, care of state property, devotion to duty, and promptness, Johnson usually concluded his opening-of-school speech with the short statement: "Prayer meeting in Chapel at 7 o'clock tonight."[88]

Winthrop's visitors during the 1906-1907 session witnessed a broad scope of activities: Miss Mamie McK. Richard's free-kindergarten work at local mills; Winthrop Chapter Daughters of the Confederacy programs; a Christmas holiday; the canning and tomato clubs' meetings; a Lee's birthday celebration

159

and presentation of two large oil portraits (one of General Lee and the other of General Jackson, both paid for by the Winthrop UDC); Johnson's election as President of the National Association of State Normal Schools; financial promises from Carnegie and Morgan; and the commencement address by Governor Andrew J. Montague of Virginia, stressing "Education is a right, not a privilege." Winthrop now taught 509 students, plus 112 in the model and kindergarten programs. With 124 yearly scholarships granted by South Carolina, Winthrop could boast a program taking a child from kindergarten through college, with the total cost of attending college at $144 a year. However, this figure could be reduced to $104 for those unable to pay tuition.[89]

Taking into account Winthrop's rapid growth, the Legislature yielded and approved (February, 1907), an act providing for better training of South Carolina's future school teachers at Winthrop College. And to secure more desperately needed room, they appropriated $20,000 for building: $10,000 in 1907 and $10,000 more in 1908 for a practice school, providing the trustees would raise $25,000 additional money. The governor, comptroller, and state treasurer had to be satisfied that the trustees had raised the money before they would pay the legislative appropriation.[90]

The regular session of 1907-1908 began on September 18. Again Johnson turned away over five-hundred girls. By this time Johnson's management of Winthrop was well known in other areas. Arkansas sent a delegation of educators, at the behest of Dr. Wickliffe Rose of the Peabody Fund, to study Winthrop preparatory to setting up the Normal and Industrial College at Conway, Arkansas.[91]

During the 1907-1908 session Mr. H. P. Stuckey, a Clemson and Alabama Agriculture College graduate from Darlington, came to oversee the grounds and to teach nature study. A vital part of his work involved developing the grounds according to Harlan P. Kelsey's plan. Such work

160

had great aesthetic as well as practical and political value, since fifty members of the State House of Representatives listed their occupations as farming. These gentlemen could do much toward passing or stopping Winthrop's proposed expansion in the Legislature.[92]

Johnson, constantly attuned to politics, had the Alumnae Association sponsor a letter-writing and political-pressure campaign. In 1907 an information sheet went out to all alumnae and to the South Carolina newspapers under the signature of Mary G. Pope, President of the Alumnae Association. This letter stressed Winthrop's lack of space during the past seven years and made a strong case for providing equal educational opportunities for the state's young women. Winthrop's appropriation of $84,563.70, compared to other female colleges' in the South, was the smallest. On a per-capita basis for college students in South Carolina, Winthrop's average of one-hundred and seventy dollars lagged sadly behind the two-hundred and twenty-five dollars appropriated for each college boy. Quoting former Governor Heyward, who said, "I do not believe that the State of South Carolina is doing full justice to herself because she is not doing full justice to her daughters," Mrs. Pope urged alumnae to see their county representatives and to acquaint them with Winthrop's need for another dormitory while pointing out what Winthrop had already done for South Carolina's common schools and young women. With additional space, they argued, Winthrop could fill the greater need for more teachers and advance the state's general welfare.[93]

Winthrop, at this time, through her activities gave abundant proof of her service-oriented concern for South Carolina. From Tillman, Johnson, and others, her students learned service and dedication to the cause of advancing themselves and their state. Accounts of their public-service work appeared in the leading newspapers every month. In October, 1907, for example, Miss Catherine A. Mulligan, Head of the Department of Domestic

161

Science, published a bulletin on cookery, which proved popular. In November the State Fair Society presented Winthrop with a gold medal for her beautiful exhibit there. Later that month the YWCA sponsored a benefit for the Episcopal Church building fund. In December the Winthrop Chapter, UDC, sent Miss Sadie Goggans and others as delegates to the state convention held in Chester. (Things Confederate were very important to South Carolinians of this era.)[94]

Renewed interest in Winthrop resulted from service and polite political pressure. This interest prompted the Legislature to visit the campus early in the session. On Robert E. Lee's birthday, members of the General Assembly departed Columbia in four first-class train coaches for the pleasant trip to Rock Hill. This special train chugged into the campus' backyard on the special side track set up by Southern Railroad and Winthrop for the convenience of the college community. The gentlemen of the Legislature were met by Johnson and the Daughters of the Confederacy, many of whom were the real daughters of the legislators and their families and friends. Visiting and a campus inspection preceded a sumptuous dinner at two o'clock. The gentlemen dined; the college glee club sang "My Love Is Like A Red, Red Rose." Ten non-alcoholic toasts were drunk to Robert E. Lee, South Carolina, Winthrop, the high school--"a missing link," and others including a toast to the women, à la Tennyson: "And I would teach them all that men are taught--they are twice as quick." The contented legislators returned that night to Columbia and no doubt the extra baggage car attached to their train was well stocked with the best that Mr. Tillman's dispensary could afford.[95]

Early in the new year, Johnson was pushing the college on two fronts. Heretofore he had asked Tillman to "write two or three of your closest friends in the House, urging them to support the bill" for the practice school. Twenty-thousand dollars had been conditionally appropriated for it but more money was needed for a dormitory.

162

And since matching funds had to be raised, the practice school might take years to become a reality.[96]

In January, 1908, a committee of Winthrop trustees proposed buying the Rock Hill High School property as a site for the Winthrop Practice and Training School. At this projected site Winthrop hoped to maintain a school of not less than ten grades for boys and girls--teaching as many as three-hundred children and youth of the Rock Hill School District. In addition Winthrop offered to pay for this property what it cost the city board.

Situated diagonally across Oakland Avenue from the main campus, the high-school building stood upon the summit of a little hill reported to be the highest point of land lying near the C.C. & A. Railroad between its terminal points of Charleston and Charlotte. Operating at this site was the Boys High School of Rock Hill, which enrolled about eighty students under the guidance of Captain Gribben, a Citadel man. These boys received military training, and the school enjoyed the community patronage.[97]

Replying to Winthrop's offer for this property, Trustee W. Blackburn Wilson of the local school board emphatically stated: "the High School property must not be transferred to Winthrop." According to Wilson, "the High School property consisted of a block of eight acres and two brick buildings worth $50,000, and this is a conservative estimate of the value of the property." Wilson conceded that the school board got the property "under favorable circumstances for $12,500, for the use of the said district." Yet he viewed Winthrop's offer as "an implied threat to the effect that unless you let us have this property on our terms, we will put your High School for Boys out of business." Should Winthrop build a training school of its own on its campus, they would teach the same grades as the high school but with Normal student teachers in the presence of regular teachers from the college.[98]

163

Mr. Wilson reiterated his position in saying that it would be improper to transfer this property to the college, thereby breaking trust with those who sold it for a high school. He reinforced his argument by telling how the Rock Hill Land and Townsite Company had given this property just as they later gave the thirty-six acres for Winthrop. Nowhere in his argument did Wilson mention the increased land values that came to him and the Townsite group as a result of Winthrop's phenomenal growth in the Oakland Park area of York County.[99]

During the 1908 legislative session, Johnson pushed for money to build a new dormitory. This was forthcoming--the Legislature appropriating $48,000 to be spent on building in 1908-1909. An important factor in securing the appropriation was the Peabody Board's $12,000 gift to the college, conditional upon the state's appropriating $48,000 more. Governor Martin F. Ansel, Chairman of the Board of Trustees, reported to the Legislature that "this new dormitory has been provided for none too soon," for there were 1,162 applicants for the 432 places in the present dormitories that year. In pointing out Winthrop's virtues, the governor stressed "the uniform at Winthrop . . . as one of its best features. The richest girl in our school cannot be distinguished from the poorest by her dress." The governor also took great pride that the federal Department of Agriculture was advising Winthrop on managing her cattle and that Congressman Asbury F. Lever was having a landscape gardener sent by the Department from Washington to advise about beautification and planting. Concluding with an apology concerning the delay of the Training School, Governor Ansel said that a minority of the Rock Hill School District had brought suit for an injunction to prevent the majority from transferring the property to the college. He assured the legislators that the attorney general was looking after Winthrop's interests in this matter, that this property was necessary to future expansion, and that "as soon as

164

the matter was settled, they would proceed with the erection of the Training School."[100]

At this time especially, Johnson was very fortunate in promoting excellent publicity for his varied activities other than the local school fight. In January, 1908, The Journal of Education editorialized that, relatively speaking, education and educators were to play a larger part in the affairs of the South than of the North in the near future. Citing as a case in point the tenure of President Johnson and the great work which he was accomplishing, the editorial asked, "Where else, aside from Stanford University, has one man had such a relation to an institution from the laying of the first cornerstone?" Continuing in the same laudatory fashion, the editor questioned, "Who can estimate the influence of one man and one institution at such a time in a state? We must go back," he continued, "to the times of Horace Mann in Massachusetts, Henry Barnard in Connecticut, David P. Page in New York, Burrows and Wickersham in Pennsylvania, Newton and Bateman in Illinois, and John Swett in California to find a parallel for the achievements of Johnson in South Carolina."[101]

Johnson received further valuable publicity from the state-wide announcement that the D. B. Johnson Chapter of the School Improvement Association, composed of juniors and seniors, would offer a gold medal to the county which did the best work in improving their schools. The honor of being designated winner spurred many communities on to make valuable improvements.[102]

While the controversy raged over selling the Boys High School property to Winthrop, Johnson worked behind the scenes to have his way. Outwardly he conveyed the idea that he was working hard to help Rock Hill as well as Winthrop. Active in all civic matters, Johnson in February addressed the Chamber of Commerce on how to push Rock Hill ahead. As Johnson saw it, the two greatest needs of the town were a public library and a YMCA. In time he helped Rock Hill build both.[103]

165

But on the matter of Wymojo Mill, Johnson was defeated. The college offered to pay promoters of the cotton mill the money they had invested in land near back campus if they would build else-where. The trustees had branded such a mill a "menace and injury to the college for all time to come." Three leading citizens--J. B. Johnson, J. M. Cherry, and W. W. Moore--made a counter proposal to the college for the mill owners, offering the fifteen-acre tract to the college for $13,500. The college could not raise the money, so the mill was erected near the present location of the Grier Division of the Rock Hill Printing and Finishing Company.[104]

Again in March, 1908, President D. B. Johnson returned to the front page, basking in a shower of publicity as the new first vice-president of the National Education Association. By virtue of his office, Johnson was a member of the committee invited to meet President Theodore Roosevelt: the group conferred on agriculture as a required subject for secondary schools and colleges. Soon there-after Johnson could brag that he had been asked by a teacher's agency to supply teachers for Arizona and California at seventy dollars a month--how this helped South Carolina Johnson was unable to say. Finally, as a result of Johnson's newly acquired national educational exposure, Dr. Nicholas Murray Butler of Columbia University asked him to accompany a group of educators to Europe to study the Normal and industrial schools in England, Germany, and other countries.[105]

Sailing on October 16, 1908, Johnson was highly complimented by flowers, letters, and tele-grams sent by the students and faculty to wish him bon voyage. Doctor Kinard, the old faithful of the Winthrop faculty, served as president during Johnson's ten-week absence. Johnson returned on New Year's Day. He had missed a typhoid epidemic.[106]

The 1908 commencement illustrated in part what Johnson's newly acquired national recognition could mean to Winthrop. For the baccalaureate he

166

selected Dr. John C. Kilgo, President of Trinity College; for commencement, the Honorable Ellsworth Brown, Commissioner of Education of the United States. One-hundred seniors graduated, eighty-five receiving the A.B. Degree with a life license to teach in South Carolina. This illustrated beautifully Commissioner Brown's admonition: "inspire them [students who wished to be teachers] to try to help the community. There must be something more [for teachers] than mere mechanical perfection."107

Johnson appears as a trailblazer in certain educational programs. Speaking before the National Teacher's Association of 15,000 delegates in Cleveland, Ohio (July of 1908), Johnson pleaded eloquently for industrial education in the rural schools. "If the child is to spend his life in the country," Johnson reasoned, "he must receive the training that will fit him to be an efficient economic unit there."108

By 1908 Johnson was fast becoming an expert in American education, but his Winthrop program designed to promote public service was somewhat bogged down in the fight over the High School. The Training School's development was contingent upon this. The minority members of the Rock Hill School Board wishing to keep the High School from Winthrop --W. B. Wilson, J. M. Cherry, and Iredell Jones-- were hard fighters. But if the State can be trusted in reporting on Tillman, they made a startling announcement that this fight "provoked Tillman to write Mr. W. J. Roddey, one of the Board's Executive Committee, threatening that unless prominent Rock Hill people stopped making malignant and selfish war on President Johnson and Rock Hill, he would get his friends in the Legislature together and start a movement to remove Winthrop College from Rock Hill and use the plant there for a Colored State Insane Asylum." Mr. Roddey never made public this letter.109

A few days after this supposed letter was sent, Senator and Mrs. Tillman stopped by Winthrop

167

on their return trip to Washington from their home in Trenton. The Senator as usual inspected the plant, especially the new library and dormitory. Tillman maintained longtime interest in all things that pertained to Winthrop. So it is not surprising that on September 1, 1909, Johnson wrote Tillman that he had admitted the two young ladies that Tillman wanted admitted with free tuition. He also told Tillman that Captain Iredell Jones had put out a misleading letter on the school controversy. Johnson asked Tillman to help him persuade President William H. Taft to stop at Winthrop on the latter's southern tour. Tillman's reply suggested he could convince Taft to stop off if he came through Rock Hill. Adding some sharp words about Jones, Tillman commented: "it seems that other people besides myself consider him somewhat of a blow-hard and fraud." He added, "what you ought to do is to put out the poison all over Rock Hill in such a way as to make them get up a petition to the Legislature to get it to change the law in regard to trustees. . . . It is true that Wilson's son is a member of the Legislature and it might be difficult to get a bill through, but the way to do such things is a fight and let the licks tell. A mere quarrel with men of that type is all they want. See if you cannot get Roddey and Crawford to carry the war into Africa."[110]

The urgency to build the Training School becomes clear when one reviews the efforts that had already gone into its planning. Johnson had engaged in a lengthy correspondence with Andrew Carnegie, J. Pierpont Morgan, and the Peabody Board to secure conditional pledges for this building. Heretofore Carnegie had given Winthrop money especially for the library. Johnson had tendered the thanks of the Board for same, and he had praised Mr. Carnegie for his generous donations. Again in 1908, Johnson had asked Carnegie for $30,000 of the $100,000 he planned to raise for the Model School building. Carnegie sent $15,000. Johnson wrote in June, 1909, to Mr. James Bertram, Carnegie's Secretary at Skibo Castle, Southerland,

168

Scotland, to appeal for $5,000 more in order that the $25,000 from Morgan would be secured since it was conditional on Johnson's raising $100,000. Bertram advised Johnson in July not to ask for the increase because Carnegie had already given him special consideration. Johnson was desperately attempting to hold these pledges. Morgan threatened to withdraw his pledge on September 9, 1909, if Johnson had not raised enough to make up $100,000. But Johnson was determined to establish a superior training school, the heart of a Normal program. After pleading, begging and doing everything that he could, Johnson secured the money just prior to the deadline. Johnson advised Carnegie on January 6, 1910, "I am happy to report that with your generous and timely contribution I was able to raise the $100,000 for our Winthrop College Training School by January 1st." Notifying Johnson on January 15, 1910, Bertram wrote that Carnegie had "authorized his cashier to send you the $15,000 . . . for the school for Training Mill Children and Training Teachers." The other principal donors to this project were the Peabody Board, $5,000; Morgan, $25,000; the state, $20,000; Martin Maloney, $1,000; G. L. Winthrop, $500; and Leroy Springs, $100.[111]

Thus we see that Johnson was fighting a law suit, running a college, attempting to hold his money pledges, and striving to keep Rock Hill's good will for Winthrop. In this trying period, as always until Tillman's death in 1918, Johnson had a man in his corner who was hard to push around. In times of trouble, Johnson always was a frequent correspondent. Attempting to show why certain people opposed the college, Johnson said of Mr. Cherry that he "has had feelings against us ever since his children did so poorly in our practice school." Johnson further remarked, "he sold the land next to us for a mill without giving us any chance to buy it from him to prevent the building of a mill there." Continuing to pour out his feelings to Tillman, Johnson asserted that "W. B. Wilson, Sr., is the worst enemy we have. He and Cherry have been accustomed to having things their

169

own way here and resent our independence and resistance to their scheme for squeezing Winthrop. We have them thoroughly whipped at every point," he confirmed, and "they know it and are trying to manufacture some sentiment in their behalf." Again on September 17, 1909, Johnson told Tillman about a mass meeting directed against Cherry, Jones, and Wilson in which the participants demanded a change in the school charter so a new board could be elected. This was good news for Tillman, since he had suggested this course of action heretofore.[112]

The last-ditch fight by the dissident school trustees took place during the Christmas season of 1909. Mr. Stanyarne Wilson, their lawyer, filed thirty-eight exceptions to Mr. Glenn's report against the dissidents. Among other points, Wilson held "that the organic act creating Winthrop College gave the college no power to acquire real property and that the specific act appropriating $25,000 for the Model School didn't carry any provision allowing the college to use any of that appropriation for acquiring land upon which to erect this Model School." Finally on January 26, 1910, this long controversy was settled and the Circuit Court ordered the trustees of the Rock Hill School District to make over the title of the property in question to Winthrop within thirty days, "the considerations being $20,000." Johnson, Tillman, and Winthrop had won again. There were threats of carrying the case to the state Supreme Court. The latter did not provide the much-sought relief.[113]

The year of 1909 witnessed many improvements physical and otherwise on the Winthrop campus and farm. A new dormitory (Bancroft) rose. The dining hall, kitchen and other improvements were completed. A cold storage and ice-making plant went into operation. Roofs were fixed. Painters refreshed facades including the piazza of South Dormitory and the infirmary. Johnson listed over twenty-five improvement projects completed in 1909.[114]

Johnson's newly found local and national educational prominence is reflected in certain

170

statements now being passed on to the Board and the public. Commenting on a special committee of the NEA, Johnson noted that the Association placed character as the first qualification of a teacher, teaching ability as the second, and scholarship as the third. Johnson began to promote better salaries, especially for the women teachers, who were paid in some instances only half what the men received. Also Johnson talked more about Winthrop's standing for public service, with home and school improvements having high priorities in his thinking. He began earnestly encouraging his teachers to write more bulletins on practical subjects like gardening, sewing, and the like. His many activities make it abundantly clear that Johnson was planning to push Winthrop forward to greater service and higher educational goals. His efforts flowered and bore fruit within the next few years as Winthrop developed. [115]

CHAPTER X

1909-1913

By 1909, Dr. D.B. Johnson, with the aid of Benjamin R. Tillman, Edward S. Joynes and a host of other dedicated citizens, teachers, and trustees, had set in motion one of the greatest educational forces in South Carolina--Winthrop Normal and Industrial College. By ability, perseverance, hard work, and good fortune, Johnson and his co-workers turned South Carolina around and set her on the road to a better and fuller life for all. "What he (and others) did might have been easy," Archibald Rutledge observed, " if the people had had money, and if they had been awake." But this work was done in a period of Southern history when education was unorganized and almost unsupported. According to Rutledge, Johnson's coming to Columbia at the behest of Dr. Joynes was the beginning of "one of the great chapters in the history of American education."[1]

From 1883 to 1909 Johnson had come far in South Carolina education, with phenomenal success in route. To many, he was Doctor Success--the man to complete any task to which he set his talents. There is evidence that Johnson received great satisfaction from helping others; and if people peruse his writings, they will see that he sometimes charmed himself with his own verbosity and salesmanship. It is little wonder that most projects for civil betterment in Rock Hill from 1895 to 1928 bear Dr. Johnson's imprint. For example, in 1910 Rock Hill formed a library association. The gift of a town lot had moved town council to pledge support for a library. Johnson contacted Andrew Carnegie in March, asking for $20,000 for the downtown libary. Praising Rock Hill as "a most progressive town," Johnson said that it had grown from 2,700 to 12,000 within fifteen years: "There are eight cotton mills here

172

and one cotton seed oil mill and one buggy factory. This will give you an idea of the character of a large part of the population. These industrial classes would be very much benefited by a library and a reading room and I believe it would be a fine investment for you. . . ."2

Without the wholehearted backing of Ben Tillman and his friends, Johnson (no doubt) would have been just another high- and graded-school superintendent. Whenever Johnson and Winthrop had a problem requiring political clout, Johnson appealed to Tillman. This was especially true during Winthrop's first years at Rock Hill. In a personal letter to Tillman dated September, 1909, Johnson advised that:

The Peabody Board meets on October 8th to take action about the remainder of the Peabody Fund, which now amounts to something like $1,400,000. You know in what high esteem Dr. Curry held Winthrop College and how he always held out the hope to us that the College would be remembered, by the Peabody Board, when the Peabody Fund was finally distributed. The friendship and good opinion of the Peabody Board has been shown for many years by annual appropriations to the College (usually from five to ten thousand a year). Now, as the Peabody Fund is about to be distributed, I find that the Universities of the Southern States, have come forward with the request, that $100,000 will be given to each of them and that the remainder will be given to the Negroes. Think of that. This request is by the representatives of the Universities of Southern States. They are not content with trying to get most of the money, for themselves, but they go further and ask that the balance, if any, be given to the Negroes, thus effectually and completely shutting out Winthrop and other State Normal Schools

173

of the South, which stand for the education and training of our white women as teachers for the common schools. You will recall the attempt several years ago to take away from Winthrop for the benefit of the Universities the annual appropriation made to Winthrop by the Peabody Board. The present attempt to deprive Winthrop of a part of the Peabody Fund is much worse than that and is entirely indigestible.

The Universities have been in existence for a hundred years or more and these State Normal Schools of the South for only a few years comparatively, and they are growing very rapidly and need help in their rapid expansion to meet the great demand upon them. They are meeting the needs of the people, as shown by the great number of applications for admission to them. There were 1,254 applications for admission to Winthrop College this year and accommodations in the dormitories for only 628.

I hope you will do what you can to help me meet this new, unexpected and threatening move on the part of the Universities to help themselves at the expense of Winthrop and the other State Normal Schools of the South, which have always been understood to be the logical beneficiaries of the Peabody Fund. I do not oppose the State Universities receiving some aid from the Peabody Board, but when they ask that all of the fund, that is not given to them be given to the Negroes, I think it is time to do something for our protection.[3]

Johnson's agitation is certainly understandable if people recall that for years he had cultivated all those connected with the fund yet in 1909 he had learned that the state universities had signed a

174

statement and had sent it to the Peabody Board to exclude the Normal and industrial colleges from this money's final division.

Johnson needed no reminder that since March, 1909, Senator Tillman's blind nephew, John E. Swearingen, State Superintendent of Education, had been sitting on the Winthrop Board. Tillman—affectionately addressed as "Dear Uncle Bennie" by John—was very close to his nephew, whom he had helped get elected to the headship of the South Carolina public-school system. Mr. Swearingen, a mild-mannered and brilliant man, frequently insisted on having his own way with Johnson in public-school matters, which heretofore Johnson had attempted to dictate through Winthrop's close connection to public education. But the Tillman, Joynes, and Swearingen axis gave Johnson a greater field for service and an opportunity to extend Winthrop's influence into most of South Carolina's homes within the next ten years. Public education provided the key to his successful drive.[4]

Johnson proved himself to be an agile and excellent quarterback on the Tillman-dominated team. Despite his many activities in 1909-1910, Johnson determined to explore all possibilities for bringing the residual Peabody money to Winthrop. Pleading a two-sided case in this cause as he wrote to President E.B. Craighead of Tulane in February, 1909, Johnson suggested: "It may be that I can join you in New York during the session of the Peabody Board. Nevertheless, I am wondering what we can do." It would be better, Johnson felt, to divide the money among a few of the South's leading universities than to give it all to Peabody College in Nashville as had been suggested.[5]

Replying to President H. L. Whitfield of the Mississippi Normal School at Columbus, Johnson in April, 1909, advised him that after the experience they had with Dr. Wickliffe Rose in Atlanta, each president of the Southern states' Normal schools would be free to pursue any course of action he felt to his advantage. Johnson had

175

determined to pursue an independent course because he knew he had a chance to get more money than some of his friends did.[6]

Johnson counted on Tillman, on Governor Martin F. Ansel (now a member of the Peabody Board), and on others who had helped Winthrop many times in the past to help her again. Armed with a letter from Senator Tillman's friends--Senator Elihu Root, Governor Ansel and others--Johnson sent a long personal letter to trustee chairman Joseph H. Choate, justifying Winthrop's claim for a sizeable share of the soon-to-be-divided Peabody Fund. "I hope," he pleaded, "Winthrop College will not be forgotten in the distribution." In introducing his argument, Johnson emphatically stated:

> For over twenty years. . . we have been led to believe that this institution would be handsomely remembered when the Peabody Board distributed the funds in their banks. Mr. Winthrop confidently expected it, I know. I have scores of letters from him, many of which breathe this hope.

He quoted from Robert Winthrop's address to the Peabody Board in October, 1890: "the prosperous and most promising Training School for Young Lady Teachers at Columbia, South Carolina, bearing the name of your Chairman in grateful recognition of the inspiration and encouragement it has received from the Board over which he has the honor to preside . . . . It should receive consideration by the Board at the close of the Peabody Trust."[7] Continuing to point out that Winthrop was a child of the Peabody Board as much as any institution in the South, Johnson asserted that Winthrop had "grown as rapidly and has accomplished as much work for the time it has been in existence as any other educational institutions in this section." To Johnson and others, Winthrop was "the pioneer institution for the training of white teachers in the South Atlantic States of South Carolina, Georgia, and Florida by some six years." Therefore, in Johnson's

176

thinking, Winthrop was entitled to receive special consideration from "the Peabody Board second only to that received by the Peabody College itself."[8]

Johnson tapped other sources to illustrate his case for Trustee Joseph H. Choate of New York. He pointed out that Normal schools of the South like Winthrop trained "the rank and file especially of women who constituted eighty percent of the teachers." He further suggested that the departments of education in the state universitites were not reaching the people and that these universities were training educational leaders and high-school teachers, "the very work the George Peabody College had been established to do." This reference was most obvious--don't let the state universities have the Peabody money he was saying. He concluded that with adequate help from Peabody's money, "we can make Winthrop College what it should be and what we have always expected it to be-- second only to Peabody College." For good measure Johnson listed the college's present needs: a science hall at $80,000; a larger auditorium at $50,000; a gym with pool at $50,000; a YWCA at $50,000; facilities to teach floriculture at $20,000; a model home for teaching homemaking at $16,000; more land at $60,000; a professor's house at $50,000; a larger power house and laundry at $35,000; and astronomical observatory at $15,000; and air-cleaning equipment at $10,000--a very ambitious program.[9]

In reporting to the Legislature on Winthrop's needs, Johnson grew less grandiose but stressed inadequacies similar to those he reported to Mr. Choate: "The needs of Winthrop College, a young and rapidly growing institution, are many and urgent" but the following were imperative: the auditorium must be enlarged since the freshman class had had to be sent home just before commencement to make room for visitors. The infirmary needed enlarging. An Industrial Arts and Science Building was needed to draw together those departments' sections that were scattered from the basement to the garret of the Main Building. Other

177

minor needs included a fire-proof vault for the college books and records "now becoming voluminous."[10]

According to Dr. Johnson's impressive report, the college through its officers and teachers trained teachers for the schools of the state and also took part in many educational activities such as conferences for education, teachers associations, school-improvement work, campaigns for education, summer schools and the like. In addition to the regular activities outlined, the Legislature received the following impressive list of work and special activities of the past year:

Miss Lora B. Able, assistant in Domestic Arts, read a paper before the Rural and Home Institute of York County.

Miss Leila M. Cobb, Critic Teacher, taught in Summer School of the University of North Carolina and attended the Primary Teachers' Association of North Carolina.

E.C. Coker, Professor of Mathematics, Physics, and Astronomy, read paper before Department of Kindergarten and Primary Teachers at the South Carolina State Teachers' Association.

Miss Ida J. Dacus, Librarian, attended meeting of the South Carolina State Teachers' Association; National Education Association at Boston; visited libraries in Boston, Salem, New York, West Point, Philadelphia, and Washington.

Miss Sarah I. Grant, Critic Teacher, read paper before Department of Elementary Education at South Carolina State Teachers' Association.

178

Miss Carrie Hyde, Matron of the Practice Home, attended meeting National Education Association at Boston; went about the State last summer giving instruction, accompanied by demonstrations, in home economics, cooking, and home sanitation. Her demonstration of the making and use of the fireless cooker was a revelation to many. She organized on behalf of Winthrop College a number of homemakers' clubs in different counties of the State; conducted a cooking school in Aiken County Fair last November, for the benefit of the people of that county; conducted a cooking school during the South Atlantic States Corn Exposition at Columbia, demonstrating the different methods of cooking corn; and wrote a Bulletin 'Recipes for Tomatoes, Peppers and Cucumbers,' which was printed by Winthrop.

F. A. Hodge, Professor of Psychology and Education, gave an address at the Virginia Teachers' Association; spoke at the Rice High School in Virginia on Patron's Day; made an address at County Teachers' Association in Virginia; and taught in the Summer School at Farmville, Virginia.

Miss M. M. Isles, Head Department of Art, wrote a Bulletin, published at Winthrop College, on a Graded Art Course for Public Schools. She attended the Summer School of the Art League in New York City and read a paper before the Rural and Home Institute of York County.

C. Edward Johnson, Professor of History, Civics and Political Economy, studied three months at the University of Chicago last summer.

179

D. B. Johnson, President, made addresses
at Southern Educational Association,
Charlotte, North Carolina; to the
Conference for Education in the South,
Little Rock, Arkansas; and closing
exercises at the Fort Mill High School
and the Edgemoor High School and other
addresses were to National Council of
Education, Boston, Mass., and State
Teachers' Association of Georgia,
Atlanta, Georgia. Johnson attended the
Conference for Agricultural Education,
Clemson College; attended meeting
National Education Association, Boston,
Mass,; served on the State Educational
Commission to revise the School Laws of
the State; presided over the Interstate
Convention of the Y.M.C.A. of North and
South Carolina at Anderson, South
Carolina; and served as president of the
Normal Department of the National
Education Association.

James P. Kinard, Professor of English,
attended meeting Southern Educational
Association, Charlotte, North Carolina;
attended meeting South Carolina State
Teachers' Association, Columbia, South
Carolina; has written with Miss Withers,
two books, The English Language, for use
in the Public Schools.

T.O. Mabry, Professor of Natural
Sciences, attended meeting of Southern
Educational Association, Charlotte, North
Carolina.

Miss Minnie Macfeat, Head Kindergarten
Department, gave talk before South
Carolina State Teachers' Association,
Columbia, South Carolina; wrote paper
for Southern Educational Association,
Charlotte, N.C.; gave talk to Mothers'
Club, Fort Mill, S.C.; wrote Bulletin

180

on Elementary Agricultural and School
Gardening, published by the College;
opened a new Kindergarten at Wymojo Mill;
and made talks before Mothers' Club of
Rock Hill, which she organized.

Miss Amelia E. Mellichamp, Assistant in
English, attended meeting of South
Carolina State Teachers' Association,
Columbia, S.C.

Miss Grace L. Morrison, Head Department
of Biology, attended Summer School at
Chautauqua, New York.

Miss Alice M. Moudy, Head Department
Modern Languages, attended Harvard
University Summer School, attended
meeting National Educational Association.

L. A. Niven, Professor of Elementary
Agriculture, helped to organize the York
County Boys' Corn Club; made four
addresses to Boys' Corn Club; visited
orchards giving directions for spraying
and pruning; made many addresses at
Farmers' Institutes; attended Southern
Educational Association, Charlotte, N.C.;
and made addresses to Aiken County Tomato
Clubs.

Miss Mary L. Porter, Assistant in Modern
Languages, studied at University of
Chicago.

L. A. Robinson, Superintendent Training
School, made an address to Department of
Elementary Education at Southern Educa-
tional Association, Charlotte, North
Carolina; wrote a thesis on Practice
Schools in the United States; attended a
meeting of National Educational Associa-
tion in Boston, Mass.; attended New York
University Summer Session; and served as

181

president of Department of Elementary
Education of the Southern Educational
Association.

Miss Leila A. Russell, County Supervisor
of Rural Schools is working vigorously
supervising the rural schools of York
County. She has already secured some
good results. In her work she found that
some simple directions for rural teachers
to teach the fundamental branches were
needed and has written out such directions and Winthrop has printed them as a
Bulletin.

Miss Olga Schauweker, Assistant in Piano,
attended Summer School at Chautauqua, New
York.

Miss Mary Frances Wickliffe, Head of
Department of Manual Training, prepared a
paper for Southern Educational Associa-
tion, Charlotte, N.C.; and attended the
Summer Session of Teachers' College,
Columbia University.

Miss Sarah Withers, Principal Training
School, taught in Summer School of the
South, Knoxville, Tenn.; wrote with Dr.
James P. Kinard a book, Language and
Literature, designed for use in the
public schools of the State; and member
of the Executive Committee of the Primary
and Grammar School Department of the
State Teachers' Association.

Miss Margaret Whittemore, Head Department of Domestic Science, attended
meetings of the Home Economics section of
the National Education Association,
Boston; and read paper before the Kennedy
Library Association, Spartanburg; read
paper before the Rural and Home Institute
of York County.

As a result of the extension work at Winthrop College, our teachers meet the demand for such work that has arisen throughout the State. It is hoped that the Legislature may provide the means for Winthrop to carry on more effectively and generally its work for the betterment of the schools and homes of the rural districts.[11]

In the period of 1909, 1910, 1911 and there-following, Johnson seemed to wage constant warfare on all fronts; even Tillman and Superintendent Swearingen had disagreements with him. Late in 1909 Tillman wrote Johnson:

I hope we will be able to get the increased appropriations for salaries at Winthrop to keep us from losing the best teachers among the women. I have never been entirely satisfied that we have the best teachers among the men.

By the way, I understand from what I have heard among the drummers that there is criticism and complaint of our having so many Yankee women at Winthrop. I think it is very well to have no narrow or sectional policy in our management of the college, but this is a hint which you can consider and, if we have any Northern women who are not exceptionally good and of the right type as to manners, you could quietly eliminate them and in the meantime be looking for the homegrown product to take their place.[12]

Early in 1910 Superintendent Swearingen, Tillman's nephew, made plans to appoint a State Supervisor of Elementary Education. Peabody was helping to underwrite the office. The appointee would be based at the University in Columbia and be associated with the Department of Pedagogy there.

Johnson opposed the plan. Swearingen fired back at Johnson, saying:

> Your antagonism to my work is absolutely incomprehensible to me. I have endeavored to uphold your hand in every particular at Winthrop. I have supported every appropriation you have requested. . . . It seems to me that you should welcome, rather than oppose, the appointment of a State Supervisor of Elementary Schools to be immediately associated with the State Department.
>
> Your attitude, however, appears to indicate a desire to destroy all the work I have been able to accomplish in this particular. The geographical location of Winthrop makes the association of Professor W. K. Tate with the college an impossibility . . . . Your letter to Dr. Rose protesting against my course might have defeated my efforts had not the great need of the situation and similar appointments in other states vindicated my position without question. . . . Your record as a constructive educator at Winthrop does not seem to me in keeping with your actions in this instance.[13]

These were strong words. Few People reprimanded Johnson in this fashion. But apparently Swearingen felt no malice toward Johnson since he was attempting simultaneously to place Johnson on the newly planned Educational Commission to represent state colleges.[14]

On February 9, four days after Swearingen's first letter, Johnson wrote to Tillman, explaining that Winthrop "had been working for the elementary rural schools in many ways for years." He resented the attempts to place the elementary supervisor at Carolina because this would indicate that Winthrop was becoming secondary to "the small Department of Education at Carolina." Johnson sent a copy of his

184

letter to Rose, suggested to Tillman that the governor take a hand in the matter, and concluded: "of course everybody will say no harm to Winthrop was intended, but we would just as soon be killed intentionally as unintentionally." But when Johnson learned that Swearingen had proposed him for the Education Commission, Johnson was quick to write Swearingen, saying: "You have misunderstood me, if you think that I wish to antagonize your work. I contend if the Supervisor is connected with any State Institution, he should be connected with Winthrop." This illustrated an overriding characteristic of Johnson, who always pushed Winthrop forward, giving no quarter to Carolina College or any other school. To him Winthrop came first and foremost.[15]

Johnson and Swearingen both worked hard for educational advancement in South Carolina. Their correspondence is living proof that no detail was too small to claim their personal attentions. Writing to Swearingen On February 25, Johnson expressed concern that the Legislature had not appropriated money for the summer school and also enquired if Swearingen had any word from the Peabody Fund concerning the $5,000 grant for Winthrop Training School. Again on March 1, Johnson wanted Swearingen to recommend to the county boards of education and to the county school trustees that they give their teachers a two-day paid holiday to attend the annual spring meeting of the South Carolina Teacher's Association.[16]

In May, 1910, the Winthrop community sustained a great loss in the death of Trustee A. Markley Lee of Charleston, a man of proven ability and a specialist in law and finance, who had devotedly served Winthrop. On June 15, 1910, the trustees paid tribute to his memory, and properly inscribed their minute book with a memorial prepared by Dr. Joynes.[17]

Early in June, Johnson learned that Professor Tate had been elected Supervisor of Elementary Schools in South Carolina. Fearing that Tate would

185

join Carolina, Johnson sent a four-page personal letter to Senator Tillman, suggesting that Tate be officially connected with Winthrop because, as Johnson put it, "if the University has both the Inspector of High Schools and the Inspector [Supervisor] of Elementary Schools, then Winthrop is unjustly and unfairly shut out of all official connection with the common schools, for which it is preparing more teachers than all other educational institutions combined." To strengthen his case, Johnson added: "It would be equally as appropriate to put the Superintendent of Agriculture at the University." Noting that the Elementary Supervisor was not connected with the state universities in other southern states, Johnson reiterated how the University had harmed Winthrop when it joined the scheme to divide the Peabody Fund so that Winthrop suffered while the black schools profitted. Johnson vowed that he had not retaliated, nor had he proposed to do so, but he politely admonished Tillman that it was very plain "the friends of Winthrop must bestir themselves to guard its vital interests." Apprising Tillman that Winthrop had over six hundred enrolled in its Normal Program while the University had only sixty in its total Education Department, Johnson asked Tillman to have the supervisor based at Winthrop.[18] Such correspondence of President Johnson abundantly proves that he had already bestirred himself else- where regarding Winthrop's case for a fair share of the soon-to-be divided Peabody Fund.[19]

Johnson kept a tight, constant rein on the college's affairs. He was president, dean, business manager, guidance counselor, and public-relations man. He set the tempo for the whole school. The Charlotte Observer in extolling Johnson's abilities announced: "when Winthrop opens next September, there will be a hundred or more new girls--many of them away from home for the first time--and all of them naturally homesick and depressed." And when asked how he handled such a situation, Dr. Johnson replied, "I find, if I lay my hand on a scared shoulder and speak to the young lady by name, and if I say something about the community which she

186

comes from, it cheers her for hours. It's all a matter of habit."

There were also daughters of prominent officials who might get special attention. Senator Tillman, for example, had written to Johnson about his sixteen-year-old daughter, Sallie May, who was coming to Winthrop: "I sincerely trust that you and your good wife will take a personal interest in her. She is rather frail." Tillman wanted her to build up her body and also to study music under Miss Pawnee Jones. Johnson responded immediately that he and his wife would "look after Miss Sallie May's welfare and do all we can for her welfare and comfort."[20]

As usual Winthrop's opening exercises for Miss Sallie May's class and all other classes in 1910 proved auspicious and impressive occasions. Reporters related there were over "seven hundred blooming young women, row upon row in the auditorium, paying close attention as Johnson boomed out his great message to the girls, admonishing them 'to love God and one another.' This would bring lasting satisfaction and the only perfect joy. Be careful that your influence is always for the right, and let nothing cause you to forget the teachings of your Christian home."[21]

This fall--1910--proved to be one of the busiest and most beneficial in Winthrop's early history. At long last Johnson received the deed to the High School and Catawba Military School property. Also in September, there arrived a glowing report on Miss Carrie Hyde, who had been travelling the state to teach farmers' wives and daughters home economy, cooking, and sanitation. She demonstrated making and using the fireless cooker, which was a revelation to many. Further, Miss Hyde had organized on Winthrop's behalf a number of Homemakers' Clubs. This pioneer activity paid great dividends in time to the farm families and proved a compliment to the Tillman program of self-improvement. Under Miss Hyde's management, the on-campus Model Home trained Winthrop girls in the finer arts of practical homemaking. There the

187

girls learned how to serve nice meals at a cost as low as eight cents a meal.[22]   Meanwhile, Winthrop also sponsored annual Agriculture Institutes and the York County Boys' Corn Club.   And Professor L. A. Niven, of the Winthrop Department of Elementary Agriculture, was teaching farmers how to prune and nurture trees.   Dr. Johnson joined the program, becoming a member of the National Committee on Agricultural Education. Speaking to the First Annual Agricultural Institute on November 17, 1910, Johnson declared, "Winthrop stands for service, service to the schools and to the home."[23]

Public   speakers   proclaimed   Winthrop's phenomenal growth during its past fifteen years in Rock Hill, as well as its usefulness and influence. This was gratifying to all who loved South Carolina. More tangible proof of Winthrop's contribution can be found in the publication of five bulletins: Graded Art Course for Public Schools, Winthrop Rural School and Home Institute, Elementary Agriculture and School Gardening,   Recipes   for   Tomatoes,   Peppers,   and Cucumbers, and Suggestions for Rural Schools. These works gain even more significance when one considers that the federal government was not then actively engaged in grinding out the great mass of "betterment literature" that we associate it with today.[24]

Winthrop had touched homes throughout South Carolina society by 1910, as a list of Winthrop fathers' occupations ably illustrates. It read,

We have in the college this year the daughters of:

238 Farmers
 61 Merchants
 16 Ministers
 24 Physicians
 23 United States, State, County and
    Municipal Officers
 27 Traveling Men
 12 Insurance Men
 11 Railroad Men

```
10 Lawyers
 9 School Superintendents, Teachers,
   and College Professors
 2 Manufacturers
 6 Cotton Buyers
 4 Contractors
 5 Mill Presidents or Superintendents
 7 Bookkeepers
 3 Bankers
 1 Drover
 3 Liverymen
 5 Dentists
 4 Real Estate Agents
 1 Treasurer Telephone Company
 1 Day Laborer in Mill
 1 Marshal of Grounds
 1 Dealer in Automobiles and Wagons
 1 Superintendent of Buggy Company
 4 Brokers
 1 Brickmaker
 1 Harnessmaker
 1 Butcher
 1 Tobacco Warehouse Man
 1 Newspaper Man
 3 Hotel Proprietors
 1 Lumberman
 1 Carpenter
 1 Assistant Superintendent of
   Orphanage
 1 Photographer
 1 Druggist
 1 Laundry Man
 3 Mechanics
 1 Singer
 1 Director of Extension Work
 3 Boatmen
 1 Jeweler
 1 Plumber
 1 Superintendent Okeetee Club
 2 Clerks and Office Men
 3 Undertakers
 4 Engineers
 1 Civil Engineer
 1 Cashier
 2 Managers of Fertilizer Companies
```

1 Cotton Weigher
1 Tick Eradicator
1 Manager Gas and Water Works
1 State Lecturer Farmers Union
1 Manager of a Mine
1 Pharmacist
1 Manager of a Civil Engineering
   Company. [25]

Winthrop's success and service to this date resulted not only from the students' and their parents' labors and desires for self-improvement but also from the labors of Johnson and his faculty; from the good will, confidence, and honesty, and hearty support of the people of South Carolina; and especially from the trustees' wise direction. Life Trustee Dr. Edward S. Joynes's example cannot be overemphasized. Staying involved and enjoying the confidence of both the educators and the politicians, Joynes was invaluable in pushing Winthrop up to higher and higher pinnacles of service and excellence. On November 15, 1910, Joynes penned a lengthy letter to the Board, offering a valuable lot 190' x 200' that fronted on Oakland Avenue for a building "dedicated to the service, the comfort, the recreation and pleasure of the women teachers, the pupils, and the alumnae of Winthrop College." Joynes further stipulated that "unless within five years after my death the sum of $5,000 shall have been secured for such a building, the lot shall revert to my estate." The building was to be called the Joynes Memorial Building. As Joynes expressed it: "I shall give with it to Winthrop College what may be felt but not expressed--all the affection and benediction inspired by over twenty years of loyal service, by my gratitude for its great and good work and by my faith in its still more glorious destiny."[26]

In December, 1910, Winthrop girls starred at the Southern Corn Exposition's demonstration "cooking school" in which they presented fifty separate and individual recipes for cooking corn. This feature, under the guidance of Miss Carrie Hyde, shared equal billing with the birdman and the

190

race between an aeroplane and a Buick automobile. As usual, wherever there was action in this period, Winthrop was there.[27]

By 1911 South Carolina was beginning to see a partial shift in the political wind. Coleman Livingston Blease, an aggressive and flamboyant political leader from Newberry, had become governor after holding several local and state positions. In early January, Johnson invited Governor Blease and the Legislature to make their annual inspection tour of Winthrop. Blease was sick; the Legislature came. The Chester Lantern condemned the Legislature for the "junketing trip," suggesting that "we don't expect The Herald [Rock Hill] to do anything but 'me too' to everything concerning Winthrop College. Whenever President Johnson takes snuff The Herald sneezes."[28]

Johnson's effectiveness in dealing with the South Carolina Legislature was largely based on his successful work for the state's young ladies and on his good connections with the powerful Tillman following both in and out of South Carolina. Johnson always counted on the very active Alumnae Association, which continuously kept a program before its members and before the Legislature. Typical are the numerous letters found in the Alumnae files that present the Winthrop story. Miss Christine N. South --later affectionately known to thousands of Winthrop alumnae and friends as Mrs. Gee--sent out letters all over the state on January 1, 1911, in her capacity as President of the Alumnae Association, suggesting that "some members of the Legislature do not seem inclined to allow appropriations to Winthrop College adequate to its great work and proportionate to the amount of money appropriated to the South Carolina State Colleges for young men." Her letter stressed that Winthrop was the largest college in the state and the most efficient, with the operating cost per capita in 1910 being only $127. She emphasized Winthrop's stand for service and its pressing needs for expansion, enjoining the alumnae to ask their county delegations that Winthrop be given a fairer and more sympathetic hearing before

191

the Legislature. Winthrop daughters were encouraged to carry their case to the papers and stress that the college needed more living space for its rapidly expanding enrollment. Cited as essential were an Industrial Arts and Science Building, a larger auditorium, and a larger infirmary. But the letter's tone, designed to alert the first session of the new Legislature under Governor Blease, indicated that "we want to be given an equal showing with the men for life's duties" and that to secure this justice "we must present our case to the people."29

Soon thereafter Johnson grappled with the Legislature, attempting to wring a good appropriation from a group strapped by a tax base too weak to satisfy the demands placed upon it. Johnson worked best when he could surround his operation with a mantle of desperation or persecution. In a personal letter to Tillman in late January, he wrote: "I wish you would help Winthrop with the Ways and Means Committee of the South Carolina Legislature by writing a few personal letters to your personal friends on that Committee and in the House, making special requests that they look after Winthrop's interest. We cannot expect proper consideration and treatment from the friends of a certain institution of which I have spoken to you. . . ."30

Three days later, Johnson sent another letter to Tillman in Washington, informing him that "Mr. Andrew Carnegie is giving away his money by the millions for educational purposes and is anxious to find good uses for it." Johnson had asked Carnegie for a $12,000 pipe organ, and he remembered that Tillman had helped to secure one for the Due West Female College. Since, according to Johnson, Winthrop was behind other institutions "in only one thing"--a pipe organ--Johnson wanted Tillman to write Carnegie about the wonderful work in progress at Winthrop and "to back up this request." Getting a bit more personal, he wished Tillman "improved health and strength and that many years will be spared to you to represent South Carolina in the United States Senate."31

192

Four days later, Tillman replied to Johnson, "While I am always willing to assist you in any way I can, I dislike devilishly to beg that old Scotchman for any of his stolen money. He knows he stole it from the people through the tariff law and that is the reason why his mustard-seed conscience prompts him to give it back to them." Complimenting Johnson on managing the Legislature's visit, he informed Johnson that "some are asking how you get the money for Winthrop and whether the State at last does not pay for it." But Tillman professed to be more concerned "about your son. I may be mistaken but in looking for an explanation of his strange illness, my study of diabetes leads me to think that his ailment must be traceable to an ill-balanced ration."[32]

Despite family problems, it was back to business as usual for Johnson. In a somewhat humorous reply, Johnson confided, "I appreciate your feelings about Mr. Carnegie. My feeling is that while all the other colleges are getting some of his money I would like to get some of it for Winthrop College and purify it by putting it to the good uses to which we can put it here." Johnson likened himself to the preacher who collected from a saloon keeper, saying "he would put it to the Lord's use, that it had been used for the devil long enough." According to Johnson, "Carnegie got a lot of his money from Southern people and I would like to get it back for the benefit of Southern people." Regarding a point raised by Tillman as to who paid for the Legislature's recent Winthrop trip, Johnson stressed that "it was paid out of the interest on donations."[33]

Despite the usual criticism, Johnson and Winthrop fared well in the 1911 Legislature. Winthrop received her accustomed number of scholarships contingent on the examinations held the first Friday in July. In addition, she gained an Industrial Arts and Science Building to be erected out of a $20,000 grant from the 1911, 1912, and 1913 taxes. Winthrop's legislative appropriation for fiscal 1911 totaled $138,702.44 as compared to

193

$74,709.44 for the University (Old Carolina College), and $55,000 for the Citadel ("The Dude Factory"). Surely it would be hard for Johnson or anyone to argue that Winthrop was not on a most favored basis with the Legislature. In addition, by a joint resolution the Legislature granted a four-year scholarship to Miss Hannah Plowden of Clarenden County for producing 100 bushels of corn on an acre; to Miss Katie Gunter of Aiken they gave a similar free scholarship for producing 512 quarts of tomatoes on one-twentieth an acre.[34]

Johnson felt quite relieved at being treated so well by the Legislature in 1911. But Andrew Carnegie's secretary had stymied his efforts to extract more money from the wily Scotsman. Once again Johnson sought Tillman's help. On March 17, 1911, he wrote: "I want your aid in getting my letter to Mr. Carnegie . . . past his private secretary." Indeed, Johnson asserted, "with some such letter from you, I believe his private secretary will feel bound to submit my letter to Mr. Carnegie."[35] The letter he asked Tillman to send read:

> Dear Sir:
>
> At the request of President Johnson I give you the following facts about Winthrop Normal and Industrial College, located at Rock Hill, South Carolina.
>
> It trains young women of moderate means to be teachers, wage earners, and home-makers. All the young women in attendance are required to take cook-ing, sewing, and housekeeping. Economy in housekeeping is specially stressed in the home. A model school has been started at the College to train rural school teachers and to furnish a model course of study and model accommo-dations for the rural schools.

194

There is a great demand for this kind of
education--an education for the duties
of life and for public service furnished
by Winthrop College as shown   by   the
continuously   increasing   number   of
applicants for admission to it.

There is imperative need of enlargement
of the auditorium, the infirmary and
other departments of the College to
accommodate the present large enrollment
(of 745).

The College has succeeded in bringing
the best education down within the reach
of the people of very moderate means.
Board, furnished room, heat, light, and
laundry are all furnished for $10 a
month.   A   large   number   of   free
scholarships are provided for those
students unable to pay anything and a
number   of   students   work   their   way
through college waiting on tables and
working   in   the   kitchen.   I   do   not
believe any important institution is
doing a more important work for the
uplift of the people with an equally
small amount of money invested.[36]

Before Johnson could settle back into his
routine following the Legislature's visit, Governor
Blease publicized his opposition to out-of-state
architects such as the ones (Hook and Rogers of
Charlotte) hired for the new Industrial Arts and
Science Building. The Building Committee wrote the
governor, stressing that the contract could not be
broken. Blease shot back a letter to the Building
Committee, which clearly stated his position on
hiring local people for state jobs:

Gentlemen:

I am in receipt of your communication of
April 12th, and, in reply, beg to say
that I am absolutely opposed to this

contract with an architect outside the State. Our home architects, in my opinion, are as competent as any to be found. They are here; they pay their license; they pay their taxes; they help to keep up our institutions and they are a part of our State, and when we have work to do, I think it is our duty to give it to them.

All of our people and even our newspapers are clamoring for our boys to stay at home and ask them to remain here to help us build up our state, yet, if we want a college president, we go off to get him; if we want a professor or a teacher we oft-times go off to get them; even to our preachers, sometimes we import them from the north, and it does seem to me that with our institutions, some of them being nearly one hundred years old, and claiming to be as fine as the finest, that out of them we should be able to get men to fill any position, and if we cannot we should abolish them and quit claiming that we have extraordinary advantages to give the students and admit to the other states that we cannot compete with them. What would have been said if I had left the State and appointed a Dispensary Auditor or an Asylum Building Commissioner? In my opinion, this is the same principle.

I do not charge, or even intimate, that there is anything morally wrong, and do not for a moment believe that any member of the committee is expecting or receiving any individual favors from these architects, because I know that they are men of the highest character, and any intimation that they would be guilty of any dishonorable act, I would denounce as maliciously false. But, I am absolutely opposed to doing business in this way, for it creates suspicion in the minds of the public, while we and those who know the committee do not think so. If a party who lives in this State and is a citizen of it, (it does not make any difference where he was born or from where he came), if he is living here and is a citizen, I believe in giving him office and positions of trust or contracts the same as we would one of our home-reared men, but I do think that we should patronize citizens of our State and not those outside.

In view of your letter, I shall not call a meeting of the Board of Trustees at this time . . . .

You will please submit your contracts for the erection of the building to the full Board of Trustees for confirmation and give it to South Carolinians.

> Very respectfully,
> Cole L. Blease
> Governor and Ex-Officio Chairman 37
> Board of Trustees, Winthrop College

During part of the Blease controversy, Johnson was travelling about the North to check on the Peabody money. On May 8 he reported to Tillman that "at last the Peabody Board has finally decided to divide the Peabody Fund. Winthrop stands an excellent showing for a good part of the fund if Governor Ansel can hold his own. . . ." He added, "Before he leaves I want you to telegraph him in Greenville something like the following: 'Winthrop is expecting great things from Peabody through you. Best wishes, Ben Tillman.'"

Letters sent to other prominent South Carolina leaders asked them to telegraph similar

197

messages to Governor Ansel to "strengthen his hand with the Peabody Board." To each, Johnson sent money for the telegram, adding a postcript: "Thanking you in advance with all my heart for this service to Winthrop and the young womanhood of South Carolina." [38] Typical of the replies was a letter from Dr. Olin Sawyer of Georgetown: "I have gladly done what you requested. Wish I could do more for you and Winthrop."[39]

The other prong of Johnson's campaign for a large Peabody gift prodded the Board members to action. Seven-page personal letters with similar content went to Bishop William Lawrence of Boston and to Joseph Choate of New York. Both began, "You have always expressed an interest in Winthrop College. . . . For a quarter of a century, since its establishment in 1886, it has been understood that Winthrop College would be handsomely remembered when the Peabody Board distributed the funds in their hands. Mr. Winthrop confidently expected it, I know. . . ." Each letter made a strong case for Winthrop, stressing her unusual qualities for training teachers. While acknowledging that George Peabody College in Nashville was training educational leaders and Winthrop was training teachers, Johnson accentuated the statement in each letter that Winthrop was "a child of the Peabody Board as much as any institution in the South."[40]

The message was clear. To each Peabody Board member, Johnson added special paragraphs designed to catch the eye of the person in question. To Chief Justice Melville W. Fuller he wrote, "Mr. J. Pierpont Morgan has told me that Winthrop would be taken good care of by the Peabody Board." To Dr. Samuel A. Green of Boston, the secretary, Johnson recalled, "you have always shown such a deep interest in the welfare of Winthrop College that I feel I must write you about the College and our hope on the eve of the distribution of the Peabody Fund, of the great need to train rank and file teachers. A prominent educator, has said, 'that if millions of money were ready [for schools], where are the teachers?'"

Johnson further pointed out to Green that Grover
Cleveland had also written heretofore that Winthrop
should be "handsomely remembered" in the final
distribution of the fund.[41]

To General Secretary Wickliffe Rose,
Johnson placed his appeal more in the vein of an
educationalist. "I beg to say, "he wrote, "that I
believe that money appropriated for the strengthening and more permanent establishing of Normal
Schools in the South will accomplish, without
doubt, more for education in the South than an
expenditure for any other educational interest at
this time." Rose had already asked Johnson how he
thought $1,300,000 in funds could be best distri-
buted, assuming that a portion of it went for Negro
education.[42]

Johnson was determined that Winthrop should
receive a good share of this money. To that end,
his campaign had been designed to tie prominent
local and national leaders together in an effort to
make Winthrop appear a most deserving candidate for
Peabody funds. Statements like that of cotton
merchant and banker Leroy Springs were most welcome.
According to Springs, "I think this school
[Winthrop] is doing more to better the homes of our
state than any other institution."[43]

In September and October, Johnson's
campaign reached its apex. Writing Morgan in
September, Johnson told the financier about Winthrop's forthcoming twenty-fifth anniversary
celebration on November 15, which he wanted both
President Taft and Morgan to grace. To Morgan he
reiterated, "We consider you the oldest and best
friend of Winthrop College and the Peabody Board
since the death of Mr. Winthrop and Dr. Curry.
. . . You have a warm place in the hearts of our
people for your interest and help in strengthening
this institution . . . and now after twenty-five
years, Winthrop has a plant valued at $700,000,
with a faculty of eighty-one officers and teachers
and a student body of over seven hundred." Johnson
pointed out to Mr. Morgan in his invitation that

199

he could leave New York at one p.m. and reach Rock
Hill early the next morning "without changing cars."
Morgan, unable to come, sent his regrets and good
wishes for the occasion.[44]

Again in October, Johnson saluted the
secretary of the Peabody Board--Dr. S. A. Green--
as a staunch Winthrop patron, welcoming his promise
"to favor a goodly sum for Winthrop College when the
Peabody Fund was finally distributed." Johnson
feared that some newer board members might not know
much about Winthrop and thus implored Green to look
out for Winthrop.

On the same day Johnson wrote Morgan at 23
Wall Street, reminding him of his kind assurance
(given the previous year) that he would help Win-
throp. Johnson quoted the late chief justice to
Captain William A. Courtenay to the effect that
Winthrop should receive $500,000 from the fund. A
committee of five from the board was to meet on
November 1 to recommend the disposal of the money,
and Johnson informed Morgan that Winthrop had been
recommended for $90,000. Johnson suggested that
Morgan use his influence with Choate and Bishop
Lawrence and that he would use his with Richard
Olney and Governor Ansel. The situation was
urgent. Thus, Johnson made a special appeal to G. W.
King, Morgan's private secretary, to have Morgan
respond.[45]

When the Peabody trustees voted on the
fund's dispersal, $6,000 went to the education
departments at the universities of South Carolina
and Texas as well as at Johns Hopkins. Winthrop
received $90,000. The John F. Slater Fund acquired
the income from $350,000 "for improving the country
schools for the Negro race." Governor Ansel moved
to substitute for the latter an appropriation of
$25,000 for the state boards of education in the
eleven Southern states, the income from this to be
used to employ supervisors for black rural schools.
Ansel's move failed and the coalition of Choate,
Olney, Lawrence, Morgan, and Grenville L. Winthrop
prevailed. Johnson, no doubt, felt crushed after
counting so long on securing about a half million.

200

But Winthrop fared well. In addition, a motion carried over to the next year to give Winthrop "any balance left over after the payment of the appropriations of this meeting."[46]

Johnson was in New York when the money's disposition took place. On November 4, 1911, Johnson wrote Morgan:

I heard that you were not well and called at your Library last Thursday to make an inquiry about you.

I am thankful to the Peabody Fund for giving Winthrop $90,000. We wanted $200,000. I see that the Board has not fully wound up its affairs and I earnestly hope that at the final wind-up something more may be done for Winthrop.

If the Board could give us $10,000 more, it would have helped us out of a difficult position in which we find ourselves in the matter of some building improvements we are now carrying on. It seems that we cannot carry out the plans for the Training School because the bids of the contractors are all for more money than we have.

I hope you will soon be entirely recovered. We wish you would come to the balmy winter climate of South Carolina and let us show you how much we appreciate your great and good works.[47]

Soon thereafter Johnson wrote Richard Olney, thanking him for the $90,000 and suggesting that he had expected $400,000 of the $2,400,000 the trustees had disposed of. Johnson cited pressing needs for $200,000 and asked Olney to help him secure this. Johnson stated to ex-President Grover Cleveland's former cabinet secretary that the disposal of the

201

Peabody money was the "one chance for Winthrop College to be made the great institution we have always expected it to be. If this chance fails, Winthrop's full development will be retarded for years. You can understand my feeling in regard to this matter when you know how I have put my life into securing for Winthrop this full development." Three days later, Johnson wrote Olney for some legal advice, explaining that eight years before he had invested $1500 in the Mutual Rubber Production Company, but since this "is too small for you to bother with," Johnson thought Olney might recommend a good lawyer to see if he could get back his money. Johnson lamented: "It represents all my savings."[48]

Johnson had devoted much time to the Peabody project, yet this project was to claim his attention for several years to come. Meanwhile general administration also clamored for attention during this busiest period in Winthrop's development. In particular, two buildings claimed considerable attention from Johnson and Tillman. Writing to Johnson in October, 1911, Tillman advised that H. C. Morrison of Augusta was working at Clemson and that he had put in a bid for two buildings at Winthrop. "He is a good friend of mine," wrote Tillman, "and I have always found him a capable contractor who does good work." Tillman vouched for his work at Clemson and Augusta, adding "he built the Agriculture Building at Clemson and a three-story brick store for me in Augusta. Of course, your committee will select the lowest bid from a respectable man and if it be Morrison I shall be glad."[49]

A minor end-of-year problem involved newspaper stories in which the young ladies of the graduating class had protested against having their diplomas delivered by Governor Blease, Ex-Officio Chairman of the Board. As Johnson explained the matter to the press, Blease was absent, so Tillman had come to deliver the diplomas. However, an ill Tillman, after some remarks to the girls, had asked Johnson to pass out the diplomas for him. Reflecting on this later, Johnson wrote Tillman and thanked him for his "words of commendation at last commencement. I do not," he continued, "presume for a moment, however, to feel or claim that the success of Winthrop is due to me or my efforts alone."[50] According to Johnson, who was then displaying a more somber mood,

A number of actors have entered into the origin and development of the Institution. A loyal Board of Trustees, a devoted faculty and a liberal and appreciative State have all been necessary to Winthrop's success, but above them all I place your interest, influence, and steadfastness. I have always felt absolutely sure that your [Tillman] influence could be depended upon always without question to forward the best interest of Winthrop College without regard to person, politics, or anything else whatsoever. This knowledge has always given me the courage to stand up for the right as I saw it and has given me strength where I might otherwise have been weak. I shall always be grateful to you for the help, support, and confidence given me by you in all my work for Winthrop and for the great and vital part you have taken in the College's establishment on a broad basis and its development along right lines.

This letter leaves no doubt as to whom Johnson regarded as his mentor.[51]

Often Johnson complained to Tillman about trifling matters which seemed very important in Johnson's thinking. In early December, 1911, Johnson wrote Tillman about Mrs. Tillmans's request that her daughter be allowed to leave school early at Christmas to participate in a wedding. He complained that

203

> I have a great deal of trouble every
> year holding the girls to the Christmas
> holidays as fixed by the General
> Assembly. It will embarrass me and
> weaken my hand to hold the College
> together if Miss Sallie May should go
> home on Wednesday, the 20th, instead of
> on Friday, the 22nd, for any reason
> except a providential one, and I hope
> you will uphold my hand by not
> insisting upon it. It is one of the
> regular rules of the college that no
> student shall be absent from school
> duties to attend a wedding except of an
> immediate relative.[52]

Three days later, Tillman retorted, "you seem to
feel that your regulations, in regard to letting the
girls off, are like the laws of the Medes and Per-
sians, and will not admit of change under conditions that would warrant loosening up the rules a
little."[53] Following this were the counterpunches
of the Tillmanic treatment. "I know," he continued,
"that you are under pressure. I am not disposed to
ask you to relax your discipline, but she will only
miss one recitation." Following with his knock-out
punch, Tillman confided that his wife, "your
friend," had said, "Johnson and those old maids are
no more sympathetic with the girls than if they had
never been young themselves." Then in a more play-
ful vein Tillman cajoled, "Now try to get young
yourself. . . and see if you cannot persuade yourself to let the child go to the wedding. You
remember I had to almost coerce you into marriage."
Johnson had been bested again, but he salvaged some
of his position by letting Sallie May go on the
twentieth via the late train, at 5:53 p.m., and
admonished her father by saying, "When a student
leaves college to attend a wedding she loses just
about a week from school and is distracted before
going and after returning to such an extent that she
doesn't do much good in her studies."[54]

On the more serious side there were programs
to push forward, speeches to make, buildings to

complete, and over seven-hundred young ladies to watch over. In addition, the night school conducted by Winthrop College teachers at the Wymojo Mill, a pioneering educational effort, needed help. The teachers gave their time free to instruct the overgrown boys and girls from the mill area, and President Johnson pitched in, giving the program an added push. He promoted Winthrop's Farm Institute, a rural-life conference attended by people from all over South Carolina to learn elementary agriculture, nature study, and school gardening. The Farm Institute utilized personnel from the college, the United States Department of Agriculture, and the Forest Service and featured the Secretary of Agriculture, James Wilson. Professor Joynes always "enlivened these meetings" with his lectures on English grammar.[55]

One of Johnson's most worthwhile programs benefiting the state's general population was the Clemson-Winthrop demonstration train, which carried better living techniques to the rural areas where eighty percent of the state's population could be found. Clemson usually showed livestock, hogs, and horses, lecturing about them. Winthrop's Miss Carrie Hyde spoke on home conveniences and appliances, showing how the housewife's labors could be lessened. She demonstrated the fireless cooker, alcohol ironers, and alcohol stoves. Trustee John E. Breazeale, who was devoted to Winthrop, wrote Johnson about Miss Hyde's lectures when the train stopped at his hometown of Anderson:

> Miss Hyde made a very favorable impression here which of course is beneficial to Winthrop. I was proud of her. The Anderson Daily Mail informed its readers about the demonstrations made by Miss Hyde and her assistants, Miss Bruce Hough of Greenville, and Miss Mamie Benton of Ridgeland using a day coach for their work. The paper stressed the fact that the ladies advocated sinks in

205

the houses and they reported in more detail on the fireless cooker method that the ladies were advocating.[56]

Other items of special interest during the 1911 session included Johnson's appearance with Governor Woodrow Wilson of New Jersey when the cornerstone of the new YWCA was laid in Columbia. This began an important friendship between the men.[57] But building Winthrop Training School and the Industrial Arts and Science Building was given priority by the Johnson administration. Writing to Trustee D. W. McLaurin in October, 1911, Johnson asked permission to file the Industrial Arts and Science Building plans by Hook and Rogers in McLaurin's Columbia office so that local contractors and others might figure on them. Plans for the Training School were drawn by William A. Edwards of Atlanta. Both buildings would help Winthrop round out her program.[58]

In order to perfect the Training School and to carry out his total program, Johnson faced a tight budget. Thus, he was constantly attempting to take "in hand" the $90,000 promised Winthrop by Peabody. In December he pushed McLaurin to have the governor sign papers authorizing Ansel to obtain the money before leaving the Peabody Board. And from Ansel, and the governor, Johnson asked help in securing Winthrop some recognition by the Carnegie Trust and the General Educational Board of Mr. John D. Rockefeller. He asked the governor for a short note of introduction to the latter, who was vacationing in Augusta, Georgia.[59]

With the aforementioned programs and plans and with her largest enrollment yet, Winthrop stood on the threshold of greater service. She had expanded her program to include a course in Bible study; Professor L. A. Niven of the Elementary Agriculture Department had organized boys' corn clubs in York County. Everything was go. The Record of Rock Hill summed up the community's general feeling in announcing the $90,000 gift from Peabody and observing, "it is but another testimony

206

to the fine work of President Johnson and a fitting
reward for the high plane upon which he has placed
Winthrop." As usual the newspaper did not elaborate
on the story.[60]

Winthrop would have meant very little to
South Carolina had it not become a leader in
academics. The college constantly faced new possibilities for improving its academic and service
potential for South Carolina. Of considerable help
was the work of Tillman's nephew, Superintendent of
State Education John E. Swearingen. Swearingen had
strong ideas about how to improve public education
in South Carolina, and as ex-officio member of the
Winthrop Board, he made his influence felt. He was
the first state superintendent to insist that colleges like Winthrop furnish every teacher completing
summer courses with an official certificate or
transcript showing work done and grades attained.
Swearingen proved especially helpful in attracting
Peabody money to the Winthrop summer schools, which
were South Carolina's official summer schools for
white teachers (men and women) for several years
following the demise of the old Teacher's
Institutes.[61]

Beginning in 1911, there was a new emphasis
on rural education in South Carolina, an emphasis
Swearingen actively advanced. He knew rural South
Carolina, its problems, hopes and aspirations.
Working with Johnson, W. K. Tate (State Supervisor
of Rural Schools), and a host of leaders throughout
the state, he helped strengthen rural schools,
beginning with a new experimental rural school
backed by Peabody money. Mrs. Hetty S. Browne, a
teacher in the Spartanburg city schools, agreed to
manage the experiment, which commenced March 21,
1911, in a little building on the "railroad side" of
the Winthrop College campus. The school sought to
define the needs of a rural family and to set the
curriculum to meet these needs. This prototype,
which was later copied in many parts of the country,
attempted to provide an education that would train
the farm children for their future work in the
home, on the farm, and in society. The diary of

the school's first two weeks was later appended to the United States Bureau of Education Bulletin (Number 42, 1913). It showed how far education had come in South Carolina and the nation since 1911. Mrs. Browne's work received further national recognition when the Government Printing Office printed and distributed copies of her work, An Experimental Rural School at Winthrop College, Rock Hill, South Carolina.[62]

Winthrop was surging forward on all fronts in 1912, boasting over 900 enrolled in the college and Training School and nearly 400 enrolled in the summer school. The Winthrop program's every facet seemed well received. Johnson, despite a little earth-shaking criticism from Tillman and Swearingen, was riding the crest of a wave of popularity even through the Peabody Board still had not sent the promised $90,000. Johnson was also mapping a campaign to get the few thousands that might remain in the fund. When Martin Ansel advised Johnson that "You need hardly expect to get anything more from the Peabody Fund after you get the $90,000," Johnson stepped up his campaign to raise more from the Legislature and promptly asked help from Tillman. The latter replied that he thought the Legislature would look after "the girls college." Adding a postscript, Tillman demanded, "Why don't you make the Rock Hill people fix their streets? Mrs. Tillman bogged over her shoes in the mud at the Depot."[63]

Many things made 1912 another noteworthy year for Winthrop College. Senator Tillman, a long-time trustee, praised Winthrop's Industrial Arts training as most rewarding. In an interview with the Anderson Daily Mail, Tillman singled out the admirable way in which the young ladies of Winthrop were performing their work in the kitchen and dining room. "In former days," he observed, "labor in South Carolina was considered degrading, but this is no longer so, I am glad to say. The girls who waited on the tables and afterwards washed the dishes in the kitchen impressed me as being very valuable assets in our civilization." Tillman felt that

208

the uniforms, which he associated with democracy, would "put the Saratoga trunks out of fashion."[64]

Noteworthy also were the student body's April 11 trip in eleven railway coaches to Columbia, where they viewed the unveiling of the monument to the women of the Confederacy, and the state oratorical contest held at Winthrop on April 26. This latter event returned to Winthrop for many years.[65]

Only two qualities, however, were stressed by Johnson in his year-end report: First, "While rejoicing at the advance of the college in material and educational matters during the past year," he had "greater cause for rejoicing in the increase in the moral and spiritual earnestness and power of the students as manifested in their self-government work and in their religious and social activities." Secondly, Johnson praised Winthrop's great contributions to the homes and schools of the state, both rural and urban.[66]

Winthrop's dedication to public service is also exemplified in part by the number of outstanding men that Johnson sought to bring to Rock Hill. Johnson liked to associate with the great and near great and nearly always sought Tillman's aid in persuading these people to stop at Winthrop. In the case of President Taft, Tillman disclosed to Johnson that he had been under the treatment of an osteopath and thus did not wish to bear the invitation, because this would necessitate his (Tillman's) having to meet the president at Winthrop and to make a speech. Tillman advised that he did not have "sufficient strength to do anything of that sort." He suggested, however, that Johnson write the invitation and he would see it properly delivered to the president. Tillman later backed up the invitation by reminding Taft that he hoped "you will not allow any trivial matter [to] keep you from gratifying these seven hundred South Carolina girls, who are being taught the new education in the South, industrial and scientific . . . I am sure you will enjoy it [the

209

visit], and I know the girls would enjoy having you speak to them."[67]

Regardless of physical handicap, Tillman always felt a deep sense of obligation to Winthrop. His observations and views on education run throughout his whole correspondence. In a ten-page discourse to his daughter Sallie May, Tillman attempted to discuss the true meaning of an education and to show her that Winthrop was a good college despite her dislike of it. He reasoned, "It may not be the best school (I believe it was) and there is no reason why it should not be the very best college of its kind in the South or anywhere else. If blunders and mistakes have been made in its management, it is my duty to find them out and remedy them."[68]

Tillman's views about a college and an education differed markedly from Johnson's. He felt Johnson was too much given to show. However, even though Tillman frequently disagreed with what was happening, he was always glad to make necessary contacts for the college.

Writing to Trustee W. J. Roddey of Rock Hill, Tillman wanted to know "why Winthrop is not doing the work it ought to do." Offering a few suggestions himself, Tillman complained that "they have tried to spread out all over creation and are not knee deep anywhere." According to his prescription, "they ought to teach a few things thoroughly and quit messing up with so many 'ologies' and languages."[69]

Paradoxically, a short time thereafter, Tillman advised Clemson University President W. M. Riggs to visit Winthrop to see how Johnson did things. In concluding his letter, Tillman stated, "My ambition is to see things as well conducted and as thoroughly organized at Clemson as they are at Winthrop and I know you have only to investigate and you will adopt such things now in vogue at Winthrop as your judgment will approve."[70]

Johnson usually knew when Tillman was checking on things. Invariably Johnson would then come out with something unusual designed to placate his sponsor. For example, on April 8, 1912, Johnson wrote a patronizing letter to the senator, suggesting that he should come to Winthrop more often "to see what we are doing." As if to silence criticism that Winthrop was not up to par, Johnson honestly bragged and with some overstatement wrote:

> I do not know of a more earnest and finer student body anywhere than we have at Winthrop, and I have visited colleges all over this country and Europe. The girls who come here come almost without exception with an earnest purpose to make the most of the opportunity offered them here by the state. They are not frivilous and fashionable but have their minds on their work and are steady-going and law-abiding. They look upon it as a privilege to be admitted to Winthrop and conduct themselves accordingly. [71]

Next to the girls in 1912, Johnson seemed to take great pride in his new Training School building. But Senator Tillman wanted Winthrop "to supply the essentials of a liberal education" and expressed to Joynes in April, 1912, that "Johnson is a wonderful man in many respects, but he has some ideas which I do not like, and there is a straining after show and effect rather than an essential, liberal, education of women." And it is not surprising that Superintendent Swearingen wrote Johnson about the Training School program, suggesting that the Pedagogical Department at Winthrop seemed unsure of itself. Specifically he said, "it will be a lamentable confusion of weakness for the Training School to open without at least a tentative course of study. . . . I maintain that the subject matter of education is far more important than its methods. . . . My plea is for the Training School to stand for something."[72]

Swearingen was always effective in "defrosting" Johnson and helping to bring him around. Six days after Swearingen wrote his criticism of the Training School, Johnson responded, pledging to cooperate with Swearingen "in every way in having the Winthrop Training School serve the interest of the public schools of the state to the utmost." Reviewing the history of the Training School program at Winthrop, Johnson was careful to point out that he had "been emphasizing the importance of subject matter in the normal schools for twenty-five years" and that he was at a loss to understand Swearingen's criticism.[73]

On another matter, Swearingen proved equally adamant: he was uncertain about the Extension programs as planned by Johnson for the rural homes and small villages. Expressing his dissatisfaction about the program's slow inception, Swearingen reminded Johnson that the money had been available for six months and that "some active steps [toward initiating this work] should be taken without further delay." Swearingen felt that this work should have been placed in his Columbia office, adding that "it cannot be done satisfactorily, or effectively, without the endorsement and cooperation of the public school authorities." Seeing the logic of Swearingen's position, Johnson moved quickly to block Swearingen and was able to reply that Miss Mary Frayser would report to Winthrop by September 1 to begin her duties as Extension agent.[74]

Still not satisfied with Johnson's Training School and the Extension programs, Swearingen requested a copy of the Training School course of study. Replying to Johnson in August, he offered these criticisms: "My examination of the new Winthrop catalog shows some important defects in the college course. Algebra and arithmetic seem to have been omitted altogether. Methods in the common school branches seem to have no place in the present course, so far as the printed facts would indicate. The entrance requirements in French and German cannot be complied with in the public schools either now or within the next twenty

212

years." Continuing his criticism later, Swearingen became more dogmatic: "I have always hoped to see Winthrop College get rid of its sub-freshman classes, and to remain free from any semblance of a preparatory department or class made up of boarding students. . . . If the colleges will stand honestly for an admission age of sixteen years and for ninety months of honest preparation, they will improve their own student bodies, and at the same time will help to build up adequate schools for the ninety-two percent of the boys and girls who are never permitted to darken college doors."[75]

The State Superintendent of Education's moralistic writing tone usually offended Johnson's self-righteousness. A friendly but spirited argument always followed. On this occasion, Johnson appeared to sulk and to hold up his annual report that was usually sent to the Legislature through Mr. Swearingen's office. During this particular controversy Swearingen restated his position on the Winthrop Training School at Rock Hill, which appeared to the state superintendent as an attempt to continue a preparatory department in the college. Swearingen declared, "if the Training School was erected with this purpose in view, it was a serious blunder." Continuing to hammer away at Johnson, he reminded him that his report was due as of September 1 and that if he did not send it promptly, "I shall be compelled to omit it from the 44th annual report." Swearingen stressed to Johnson that the president, in holding up the filing of the annual report, was violating the law.[76]

In all fairness to Johnson, he was in his busiest year, with its twenty-fifth anniversary celebrations. He was attempting to complete the Training School and the Science Hall. At the same time he was pushing Extension, rural-school, and mill-school services.

Her twenty-fifth anniversary marked, in a real sense, Winthrop's coming of age. Since

213

November 15, 1911, was the twenty-fifth anniversary of the founding of Winthrop Training School for Teachers, the Board wished to take official note of this and decided on a celebration. As November 15 was so near to the opening of the fall term, they decided to postpone the celebration until the following spring. A logical date would be May 12, Mr. Winthrop's birthday, but in 1912 this date fell on Sunday, and so they finally determined to hold the celebration on May 3, 1912.[77]

Early in the year President Johnson appointed a faculty committee to make the necessary arrangements. Invitations were sent to distinguished educators throughout the United States and to Winthrop's alumnae and special friends. Johnson appealed to President Taft, who was making a southern tour, to visit. Taft expressed genuine sorrow at being unable to attend. Senator Tillman, who felt that Winthrop had more than realized his hopes and dreams, was unable to attend also, but President Johnson assured him that he would be missed and that Johnson would send him a program.[78]

On the morning of the third, the first meeting of the day-long exercises was held in the auditorium. Following the presentation of dignitaries, the procession moved to the new Training School, passing through a double column of college students. There the Reverend Alexander Martin of Rock Hill's First Presbyterian Church opened the exercises with a prayer. Dr. Johnson made a brief statement regarding this new building, and the cornerstone was laid with Masonic rites.[79]

Moving back across Oakland Avenue, the group reassembled in the Main Building auditorium (now Tillman Hall) where Dr. Edward Southey Joynes, Professor Emeritus of Modern Languages at the University of South Carolina and Life Trustee of Winthrop, delivered his notable address on the "Origin and Early History of Winthrop College." Next rose Superintendent Lawton B. Evans of

214

Augusta, Georgia, whose oration on "Education for Efficiency" was also very well received. The morning exercises closed with a benediction by Reverend E. K. Hardin of St. John's Methodist Church.[80]

The group then moved to the college dining room for a sumptuous luncheon. Trustee W. J. Roddey acted as toastmaster. Many toasts were drunk and impromptu speeches made. In the evening the Carnegie Library hosted a reception for visitors and citizens of Rock Hill.[81]

Attempting to share the publicity of this festive occasion, the Rock Hill Land and Townsite Company took a whole page in the anniversary edition of the local newspaper to promote the sale of lots around Winthrop College, which they planned for the coming month.[82] The Townsite advertisement rivaled in poor taste the biased report of the great suffrage parade held a few days before in New York City. "Ask anybody," it boldly proclaimed, "how Oakland lots have enhanced in value ever since the first sale about twenty years ago. Lots that sold then for $250 and $300 now sell for $2,000 or $3,000. Buy a lot and forget it. It will make money while you attend to your usual business." This demonstration of what Winthrop meant to the local real-estate promoters serves as a crass reminder of the way certain citizens of Rock Hill have always viewed Winthrop, while the more cultured Rock Hillians have understood that Winthrop kept Rock Hill from becoming just another mill town.[83]

Planning and overseeing construction of the Training School and the science building had required considerable effort and time. Johnson wanted the Training School to be a model. He had seen a building at Oxford whose outlines he wished to copy. And he knew that Tillman had great concern over proper accommodations for the industrial arts. Therefore, the best in thinking and planning that Winthrop could afford went into these buildings. Professors E. C. Coker and T. O. Mabry gave advice

215

concerning the physical sciences and the museum of natural history to be housed in the new science building. Professor S. A. Niven selected the first-floor location on the south side for his agriculture work. He needed a propagation house, laboratory, office and lecture room "with electric lights in all rooms." The domestic-science area under Miss Bessie W. Birdsael was to have a dressmaker and fitting and millinery rooms with a student room and a storeroom. In manual training Miss Mary Frances Wickliffe suggested large lighted rooms for hand and bench work as well as for metal jewelry. She requested a separate room for clay with an adjoining room for the kiln and a special room for demonstrations in weaving on the old colonial loom as well as the new up-to-date Jacquard loom. This work was so advertised that builders from as far away as Manhattan, New York, wanted to bid. Architects Hook and Rogers--sensing the importance of the building--agreed to station a permanent superintendent on site.[84]

In his year-end report Johnson advertised with beautiful photographs the Training School and the Tillman Science Hall as their two most significant achievements during the notewothy year of 1912. As usual, he stressed Winthrop College's stand for public service and rejoiced that it was "now equipped to render this service effectively for the most vital interests of the State, the homes and schools of the people both urban and rural."[85]

Simultaneous changes in South Carolina laws complemented Winthrop's increased capacity. Under the school-consolidation law of February 26, 1912, any rural district in South Carolina could receive three-hundred dollars per annum if it maintained "a well-housed and equipped school with three or more certified teachers and at least seventy-five pupils." The locality was empowered by this law to levy a special four-mill school tax to underwrite the six-month school term. To further guarantee the rural-school program's success in South Carolina, one or two scholarships to Winthrop College from each county would be reserved for

216

applicants from rural communities. In addition, the law stated that rural programs would be rooted in agriculture but that their purpose was not to train scientific farmers and homemakers, but rather to reach the rural children by using things they knew and were interested in. The ultimate hope was that many rural children would choose to remain in the country as better producers and more efficient homemakers.[86]

Few people in the early 1900s really understood the inner workings of Johnson's system for advancing Winthrop College. Johnson had a different sense of pride than most Southern men of his generation. Few would have constantly dinned Carnegie, Rockefeller, and other rich men as he did. With hat in hand, Johnson was always pleading for his worthy cause--the young women of Winthrop College. Writing to Carnegie's secretary (James Bertram) in 1911, Johnson casually mentioned his inspection of schools in Scotland. His real object was to ask Carnegie for an organ to benefit his young women, "who cannot afford organs in their homes, churches, or communities." He stressed to the Scotsman that every dollar invested at Winthrop, including some of Carnegie's, had yielded rich dividends. Further reminding the ex-steel magnate that he had just been elected president of the Southern Educational Association, Johnson clinched his pitch by declaring that the organ "will not only contribute to the esthetic training of the mothers and teachers of this section, but it will also furnish the incentive for others to contribute to make a much needed enlargement of the college auditorium." Adding a heart-rending afterthought, he said the organ should be given in memory of Mrs. Carnegie, "as a constant reminder to these young women of her noble, womanly character and life, which should serve as an example and inspiration to young women everywhere." Such a pitch was hard indeed even for a crusty old Carnegie to resist.[87]

Two months later Johnson was pressing another "worthy cause" on Carnegie. Informing Carnegie that he had "raised sixty-thousand to

217

erect a much needed building for the teaching of industrial arts and science," Johnson asked for $15,000 more. This tidy sum would complement the $60,000 given by the Legislature.[88]

On another front, Johnson was pushing hard for funds. With two new buildings, the high-school renovation, plus plans for a new gymnasium, he needed all the money he could get. Tillman, as always, provided both the crutch and shield that Johnson needed. Sending the senator a copy of recent Board resolutions that urged Governor Ansel to push for the remaining Peabody money, Johnson stressed that the new Industrial Arts and Science Building (a favorite of Tillman's) was a superior building in every way.[89]

Ten days later, Johnson penned another personal letter to Tillman, informing him that Governor Ansel might change his resolution to the Peabody Board, asking that the remainder of this money go not as originally suggested to Winthrop but elsewhere. Rumor had it that Ansel would try to obtain the money for the University. Johnson was determined to circumvent this. Again in June, 1912, Johnson stressed to Tillman that "we are confidently depending upon you to keep Governor Ansel steadfast by being behind his [pro-Winthrop] Peabody Board resolutions."[90]

Meanwhile Tillman scolded Johnson for not appointing one of his friends to a position at Winthrop. "I think," he wrote "you ought to give a reasonable amount of consideration to any special friends of mine . . . for I have never failed to assist you in any way you asked me to and I am somewhat hurt by the way you have treated [Eric W.] Hardy." Johnson was quick to reply, "I consider it a sacred duty to do all I can to have the Board select for every position at Winthrop the best teachers and officials that can be found for the salaries offered without any regard to friendship. It is the only way to keep up the standard of teaching for our girls and make Winthrop a success. No friend of mine has ever been elected to a

218

position here."[91]   Johnson usually made the choice
and the Board approved.   After verifying the facts,
Tillman replied, "it is entirely satisfactory to me.
I agree with you that no nepotism or favoritism of
any kind should enter our selection of teachers at
Winthrop.   I would be the last man to foist off an
incompetent teacher on Winthrop. . . ."[92]

        In   late   summer   Johnson   redoubled   his
campaign   effort   to   garner   the   remaining   Peabody
money   for   Winthrop.   To   all   South   Carolina
congressmen he wrote: "Senator Tillman joins me in
the request that you will sign the enclosed paper in
the interest of the women and the schools of South
Carolina."   These   letters   to   Congressmen   James
Byrnes, James E. Ellerbe, George S. Legare, and
others usually carried the personal touch--"a great
number of Winthrop students and graduates live in
your district."   By August 21, Johnson could report
to Tillman that he had secured the signatures of
every South Carolina congressman to the resolution
asking   for   the   remaining   Peabody   money,   thereby
placing Governor Ansel in a serious bind should he
try to divert this money to Carolina or any other
group.[93]

        Yet   again,   Johnson   solicited   individual
Peabody Board members.   To J. P. Morgan he wrote:
"Winthrop College is the youngest state institution
in South Carolina and especially needs help; therefore, for its greater and growing work."   From Dr.
Samuel A. Green, Secretary of the Peabody Board,
Johnson requested a copy of that board's minutes--
using the opportunity to remind Green of his strong
friendship for Winthrop through the years.   This
friendship, according to Johnson, had encouraged
and strengthened him in all his struggles for
Winthrop.   "May I not confidently count on your
help," he pleaded, "in this last opportunity to
make this Southern College, named after Mr. Robert
C. Winthrop, in which he was deeply interested,
the strong and helpful institution it ought to be
to serve the best educational interest of the
South. . . ." His was a very compelling plea by
any standard.[94]

219

Falling back on Tillman again to keep everyone in line, Johnson wrote on November 4 to the senator at his home in Trenton, South Carolina, informing him that Ansel would go north on November 10 to the Peabody Board meeting in New York. "I think it is vital to Winthrop's interests," he wrote, "for some members of our Board of Trustees to write him before he leaves, wishing him success with his resolution in behalf of Winthrop and telling him that we shall await with keenest interest the outcome of the Peabody Board meeting." This was a typical Johnson maneuver. Yet Tillman never seemed to object to these directions, often writing his letters verbatim as Johnson had suggested. Johnson, in this case, further suggested that the Winthrop Board members (meaning especially the senator) emphasize South Carolina stood a better chance of securing more Peabody money through Winthrop than through any other school. In concluding his letter, Johnson asked Tillman to make this point: that Winthrop was the "only institution for young women supported by the state."[95]

Simultaneously, Johnson appealed to Tillman for more help with the Lever Bill, which provided for extension work in agriculture and home economics to be carried on in the country's agricultural and mechanical (land-grant) colleges. Apprizing Tillman of this and the fact the bill was then in the United States Senate (a fact that Tillman was no doubt aware of), Johnson asked Tillman to amend the bill (when he returned to the Senate after the holidays) in order to place home-economics work in the state Normal and industrial colleges, where it was then being performed in the Southern Normal and industrial colleges for women. Knowing of Tillman's strong affection for Clemson, Johnson suggested "I am sure that Clemson College does not wish to be saddled with that work in this state and thus be brought in conflict with Winthrop College." Winthrop, he reasoned, "can certainly teach the women how to cook and sew and keep house better than . . . colleges like Clemson." Tillman fired back from Trenton the next day, agreeing with Johnson and vowing "to do some missionary work

220

when I return to Washington." Almost two years passed from the date of introduction to the final passage of the Smith-Lever Act of 1914. This important legislation bears the imprint of Johnson and Tillman and especially that of the much-beloved congressman from the South Carolina midlands, the Honorable Asbury Frank Lever, who labored in his quiet, determined way to help the farm families of his state and nation for most of his lifetime.[96]

But two years before the Smith-Lever law was effected, with his typical foresight, the president of Winthrop had contacted an unusual personality, a "blue-blooded" Virginia Baptist with unassailable credentials, who possessed a missionary zeal for developing domestic science and arts in the South. Learning of Johnson's desire to employ a head for the Domestic Arts Department through the Southern Teacher's Association, Miss Mary E. Frayser of Richmond, Virginia, wrote Johnson that his college offered "a rare opportunity for work. For I am a Virginian and I wish to serve in the South. . . . I believe I can make your Domestic Art department go forward by leaps and bounds, should you intrust it to me." Miss Frayser supported her enthusiastic application with blue-ribbon credentials which must have impressed the poor boy from Tennessee, who was now rising so fast in South Carolina education.[97] Dr. J. A. C. Chandler, head of the Richmond city schools and later president of the College of William and Mary, praised Miss Frayser. Richard Evelyn Byrd, Speaker of the Virginia House, wrote: "Miss Mary E. Frayser is a young woman of great capacity and the highest character. She will adorn any work to which she devotes her abilities." In his letter to Johnson, on May 23, President Samuel C. Mitchell of the University of South Carolina called Miss Frayser "a woman of utmost refinement." And he noted that it was largely due to Miss Frayser that the law creating the Virginia pension plan for teachers had passed. Mitchell concluded his laudatory account by stating, "I should say that she represents the finest type of Virginia culture." There were other letters of praise for Miss Frayser, but

221

the letter of Dean James E. Russell of Columbia University to Johnson on July 19, 1912, should have guaranteed any teacher a job at Winthrop. The dean wrote: "You take my word for it that you cannot find a better woman for that kind of work if you had a thousand to pick from. I speak to you as I have probably never done in behalf on any teacher." Little wonder Miss Frayser was named in August the Extension Worker in Home Economics for Winthrop at a salary of $1,200 a year with travel. Winthrop's record of public service to South Carolina--thanks to Senator Tillman, Dr. Joynes, D. B. Johnson, John Swearingen, Miss Frayser, and many others--was becoming most impressive.[98]

CHAPTER XI

"The poverty succeeding the war of the sixties and the failure to appreciate the fact that the South was too poor not to educate delayed the practical putting in operations of universal education in institutions supported by the State until Benjamin R. Tillman's administration. I could not come to South Carolina without paying tribute to that remarkable man. . . . He came to be known as a leader in national defense and the world is indebted to him no little for the naval efficiency in the World War. . . .

But in South Carolina his best monument was that he joined hands with progressive educational leaders to carry the blessings of education into the humblest homes. This was his chief work here."

Josephus Daniels

The scholastic year July 1, 1912, to July 1, 1913, was according to all physical signs "the fullest and busiest" in the history of Winthrop. It was so reported by President Johnson to the State Superintendent of Education. With 760 students in college classes and 1,643 in all departments, Johnson could boast many permanent improvements, extra public undertakings and services such as Winthrop had not witnessed before.[1]

Heading the accomplishments for this scholastic year, Johnson listed the change from the old to the new course of study--from two to three terms with a strengthened program. Students ranged from sub-collegiate to post-graduate and represented forty-four South Carolina counties. The curriculum included not only liberal arts but also industrial studies, thanks to Mr. Tillman. Of the 1,643 persons enrolled under Winthrop's banner, 346 were studying dressmaking, sewing, and millinery; 230, drawing and designing; 264, domestic arts; 177, elementary agriculture; and 188, manual training. What practical impact these students must have had on future generations of South Carolinians![2]

Looking at other Winthrop accomplishments through Johnson's eyes, one sees the following: the Training School had been organized apart from the college and a tenth grade added to the course; some departments had become more effective by adding and improving equipment; Winthrop's distinctive Extension work to improve both schools and homes, especially in mill and rural districts, was broadened and made more effective; the Student Government Association had strengthened; the Training School building and Tillman Hall were complete; the infirmary, the auditorium and the power house had been enlarged; a large heating conduit to service both new and proposed buildings was working; valuable property adjacent to campus now belonged to Winthrop; the college's helpful and well-received exhibit at the National Corn Exposition had taught better preparation of home-grown foods and had shown how to remodel a rural school at small cost to meet better the needs of a rural community; the student body had travelled by special train to Columbia to attend the Corn Exposition; the General Assembly had toured Winthrop for a day; a home institute for York County had produced the first and only alfalfa club in the state at that time; a meeting of over 1,400 school children and teachers of the county had convened at the college, as had the county organizers of girls' canning and poultry clubs and the state oratorical contest; two receptions had honored state organizations meeting in Rock Hill; the senior class had visited Washington for President Woodrow Wilson's inauguration, the trip proving most pleasant and valuable, thanks to Senator Tillman's interest and attentions; and a pageant

attended by over three-thousand people from around
the state had marked the regular spring holiday.[3]

Johnson further reported that Winthrop's
graduates were in demand as teachers and other
professionals. More and more school superintendents and others desiring teachers visited campus
each spring to interview personally the graduating
seniors. Fifty-three members of the 1913 class had
secured teaching positions prior to graduation.[4]

Johnson reported further exciting news.
During the past summer and fall, workers had
completed and furnished the new auditorium,
installing too a large $10,000 pipe organ without
cost to the state. The new infirmary--together
with the practice home, the domestic-science rooms,
and all departments requiring it--had been screened
by the State Board of Health. The old dormitory
building at the Training School had been remodeled,
painted, and furnished to accommodate fifty
students. All other dormitories had been thoroughly overhauled and sanitized in every way, with
the plastering retouched and old furniture re-
varnished and repaired. All machinery and plumbing
had been overhauled, and all roofs and gutters
repaired and painted where necessary. The grounds
of the Training School had been graded and enclosed
with a galvanized iron and wire fence; a similar
fence had been built on the north side of the
college campus. In the main building a restroom
for teachers boarding outside the college had been
fitted up. A new study room--large, well lighted
and ventilated, and properly furnished--had been
provided for day students. The equipment of every
department had been materially added to. Another
room had been assigned to the Commercial Department.
Arrangements had afforded the best teaching of
bookkeeping. The new tanks had been secured for
the farm and the waterworks there improved, thus
giving much better fire protection to all farm
property and better service in every way. The
dairy barn had been recovered and another tenant's
house built. Fifty-one sheep and 134 beef cows had

been bought to be fattened for the college dining room. A moving-picture machine had been installed in the auditorium for educational purposes. A student's exchange had begun in the old chemical laboratory through which students needing financial assistance could locate work. Some valuable bulletins had been issued. A county fair in connection with the Winthrop Home Institute had taken place on campus, selling over nine-thousand tickets. (In the school parade on school day of the fair, many of the county schools were represented.) A six-week summer school attracted 505 students. And many other college matters of minor importance had been attended to. [5]

Judging from the many other minor matters that Johnson mentioned in his 1912-1913 report, no one can doubt that Johnson was continuing his frantic drive to corner as much Peabody money as possible. In the course of these activities, Johnson showed his mastery of political flattery and upmanship. He was a truly astute operator. Before the Peabody matter was finally settled, however, Governor Blease had attempted to reap political advantage therefrom by attacking President Mitchell of the University of South Carolina for allegedly signing a statement saying that if the Peabody Fund trustees would give the South Carolina University a certain sum of money, he (Dr. Mitchell) "would agree . . . for the remainder of that money to go to the education of free negroes." This purported action implied that the white girls of Winthrop enjoyed President Mitchell's low regard and that they would be denied funds to which many felt they were entitled. "And such a man," Coley Blease bellowed, who "would rather take that money to educate negroes than give it to the white girls in South Carolina, certainly has no place during my administration in any department of the government. . . ." [6]

"Coley" had a full head of steam built up from his 1910 and 1912 campaign frustrations. Of prime concern to Blease was Tillman's preference that Judge Ira B. Jones be elected governor even

226

though Tillman had promised, Blease claimed, to keep "hands off." Among the charges Blease leveled at Tillman were hypocrisy, conspiring with W. E. Gonzales, and feeble-mindedness. Tillman--up for re-election to the Senate--was urged by his partisans to reply in kind. Both John Swearingen and Henry Tillman were quick to alert the senator about Blease's action. J. William Thurmond of Edgefield, a candidate for district attorney, wrote, "Your reply to Blease is largely expected and the people are guessing it will contain . . . dynamite. . . ." William M. Riggs advised, "The public is waiting anxiously for your reply, with a pretty good assurance that you are going to literally chew him up."[7]

Tillman struck back, answering all points thoroughly and calling Blease a past master in the art of demagoguery "who was bamboozling and deceiving the people and laying down a smoke screen of confusion to prevent the people from seeing what kind of man he was." Yet Blease managed to win a second term.[8]

Blease's second inaugural speech demanded an investigation of charges against Mitchell of Carolina in the name of fairness to Winthrop. Tillman and others felt that Blease's disdain for his alma mater was his motivating force. Then, too, rumor had it that Blease was planning an underhanded attack against Tillman's pride, Clemson College. Tillman, from his Washington vantage point, expressed concern over whether Blease was attempting to stampede the Legislature into ill-advised action. August Kohn, reporting the controversy, wired Mrs. Tillman in Washington on January 28, 1913: "Both houses today unanimously reelected Senator Tillman not a dissenting voice--tell him to rest easy."[9]

President Johnson of Winthrop, determined more than ever to capture Peabody money, reported to Trustee D. W. McLaurin in the fall, 1912, that he had worked since August to secure signatures on a petition to the Peabody Board. In a personal

227

letter to McLaurin, Johnson showed his concern about the suggested Mitchell investigation. "I hope it will be kept in mind," he wrote, "by the investigating committee that . . . I refrained from calling on the Governor to take part in it [the meeting to get money] as he had offered to do." Johnson admitted to McLaurin that Dr. Mitchell had charged him with some mean, underhanded things-- with prompting the governor to attack Mitchell, in fact. This charge had spread over the state. Johnson asked McLaurin to bring this rumor to the committee members' attention as he was concerned about Winthrop's welfare and his own good name. Johnson wished "to be exonerated from that charge by the committee." Johnson feared that the committee report would be confined to only himself.[10]

Representative Joshua W. Ashley of Anderson County introduced the resolution calling for an investigation of the Peabody Fund distribution charges. The General Assembly concurred, appointing a joint six-member committee that included Ashley and representatives W. H. Nicholson of Greenwood and R. H. Welsh of Richland. The Senate selected for its investigators senators Francis H. Weston of Richland, who served as chairman; MacBeth Young of Union; and O. P. Goodwin of Laurens. The committee began its deliberations on February 5, 1913, in the Supreme Court chamber. Over the next three weeks prominent witnesses appeared, including Governor Blease and ex-Governor Martin F. Ansel, a trustee of the Peabody Fund; Presidents Mitchell and Johnson of Carolina and Winthrop; Dr. Wickliffe Rose, the general agent of the Peabody Fund; trustees August Kohn and D. W. McLaurin of Carolina and Winthrop; and John E. Swearingen, the State Superintendent of Education.[11]

Within three weeks the committee had taken testimony and discharged its obligations on the distribution of the Peabody Funds--a project that President Johnson admitted to having worked on many years. Much of the examination centered around the activities of Mitchell, Johnson, and other principals. The legislative committee's questioning suggested that they did not have the background

228

necessary to develop a complete, factual case. (The Winthrop and Clemson files today hold hundreds of letters that, when pieced together, tell of Johnson's masterly campaign to acquire Peabody money over a twenty-year period, enlisting the support of many public figures from Chief Justice Melville W. Fuller to Representative "Josh" Ashley, a member of the investigating committee.)

Another key to the investigation was Governor M. F. Ansel's (1909-1910) close relationship with D. B. Johnson. Johnson had hailed Ansel's appointment to the Peabody Board in 1909 as "a great thing for the educational interest of South Carolina." The friendly pressure that Johnson, through Tillman and other state leaders, put on Ansel was enough to force him to divert monies available for South Carolina to Winthrop. No doubt Ansel frequently heard Johnson's most convincing argument: the state had spent many times more on Carolina than they had on Winthrop, yet Winthrop was training most of the state's teachers.[12]

Blease's outburst against Mitchell had been sparked by a conversation between Professor W. K. Tate and Insurance Commissioner FitzHugh McMaster, an alumnus of Carolina. Tate, whom Ansel had recommended for a job at Winthrop, told McMaster that Ansel had diverted $40,000 of Peabody money allotted for Carolina to Winthrop, primarily at Johnson's instigation. McMaster wrote Johnson on June 27, 1911, that he wanted the facts concerning Carolina's losing $40,000 on Governor Ansel's recommendations, a deed "which was done at your recommendation," for thereby Winthrop had received $90,000 and Carolina had received only scholarship money.[13]

Approximately two weeks later, Johnson replied to McMaster, tracing Winthrop's relationship with the Peabody Board and asserting that Winthrop had had a favored position for a large appropriation, which was cut to $90,000 due to the attack of the state universities' representatives (including Carolina's) against state Normal Schools.

229

Johnson cited a long list of correspondence to prove his case, which looked good.[14]

Johnson also forwarded copies of his reply to Winthrop's Board members. Trustee McLaurin showed copies to the governor, who congratulated Johnson on his fight and offered to assist him. Blease testified before the legislative committee that Johnson had not brought this controversy to him initially as many had charged and that he (the governor) did not bring this to public attention for some time in hopes that he could obtain a copy of the agreement that was key to the entire distribution investigation.[15]

Prior to the Peabody investigation Tillman's nephew, John Swearingen of the State Education Office, had sought stenographic notes and Board minutes bearing on the subject. Meanwhile, President Johnson attempted to elicit from Peabody Secretary Samuel Green copies of the 1909 petitions signed by the Southern universities' presidents. Green could not find them. Tillman, who fully expected Blease to entrap Johnson, wrote, "I am sorry to see by the South Carolina papers that you have been mixed up by Governor Blease in an apparent attack on President Mitchell of the State University. I hope you can show that Winthrop College is not antagonistic to the University, however badly we have been treated by some of those in authority there."[16]

The long Carolina-Winthrop fight over final disposition of the Peabody Fund in South Carolina did not help the overall cause of education. It did demonstrate Johnson's superior political clout. Fortunately, the investigation committee found that the governor "was misinformed" and that Dr. Mitchell was not guilty of signing the alleged agreement to deprive Winthrop of her funds. Later, however, when Blease got a copy of the university presidents' petition, he pointed out in a special message to the General Assembly that Mitchell's name was second on the paper which bore the words, "and the remainder [of the money] for the training of Negro teachers in same states." Blease continued to bear down on Mitchell, branding him a "nigger-lover" and "so-called president of the University."[17]

When friends in Richmond offered Mitchell the presidency of the Medical College in Virginia, he eagerly accepted, but a host of friends and well-wishers tried to keep him in Carolina. One of these --James A. Hoyt, the First Vice-President and General Manager of the Homestead Bank of Columbia--wired Tillman: "Dr. Mitchell strongly inclined to accept Richmond offer. Please wire him immediately urging stay--important." Tillman did urge Mitchell to stay, stressing South Carolina's need for men who represented progress, enlightenment, and statesmanship.[18]

While the Carolina University began reaping a harvest of indecision and trouble, Johnson and Winthrop remained leaders in South Carolina education. Much to the envy of most college students, Tillman and Johnson took one-hundred and seventy Winthrop seniors to Washington on March 3, 1913, for the inauguration. A few days before, Johnson had notified Tillman that he had shared the senator's letter with the seniors:

> and we all appreciate all you have done
> for us. . . . can you find some pam-
> phlets giving the places of interest
> about Washington to be seen by visit-
> ors? We want to be sure to arrange for
> the incoming President (Wilson) to
> receive our girls. . . . They would be
> glad to meet President Taft, if
> possible. We are depending upon you to
> arrange for the girls to see the
> parade. They are not able to pay to
> see it.

Regardless of Johnson's begging, Senator Tillman--soon to become Chairman of the Naval Committee of the Senate--provided for the Winthrop delegation in high style. Tillman arranged for President Wilson to receive the girls and the D. B. Johnsons in the East Room at 2:30. Each greeted the president; they left the White House by the front entrance. The Winthrop contingent viewed the parade from the Waltby Building and from Bland's, where they posed for photographers. Later they visited the new National Theatre to see Miss Billie Burke in "Maud the Paint Girl." On Wednesday they travelled to Mount Vernon. On Wednesday night Professor James L. Carbery of Winthrop and Washington accompanied them to the Belasco Theatre to enjoy "Bought and Paid For." This trip, one of the most thrilling that any Winthrop class ever took, was long remembered.[19]

After Washington two highly advertised events in Rock Hill's history impressed Winthrop's "well-travelled" senior class--Coca Cola was introduced and a contingent of older Yale men ended their "sentimental journey through South Carolina in a blaze of glory." These men, many of whom were Northern business leaders, took a special train through South Carolina in April to investigate prospects for Northern investment. The group, much impressed with South Carolina, noted especially their pleasant stop at Winthrop--where they were entertained at dinner by Winthrop girls cheering for Yale, Johnson, and others. The editor of the Litchfield (Connecticut) Enquirer later devoted a special edition to South Carolina, saying he had discovered among other things that "the class of girls that attended Winthrop are very much the same as one finds at Smith, Vassar, and the Wellesley"-- a great compliment justly deserved.[20]

Johnson never hesitated nor rested on his laurels. Instead, he constantly pushed on (except for the few occasions he was incapacitated). Johnson unceasingly stressed that "Winthrop College is trying to serve the state, not only through the training given to young women committed to its care, but also through its extension work carried on for the betterment of the schools and homes of the people in both the towns and the country." Before Smith-Lever ever became law, Johnson had Winthrop promoting Extension work and preparing home and farm improvement bulletins similar to those the Department of Agriculture and the land-grant colleges produce today.[21]

In 1913 Johnson proudly reported to the General Assembly that Professor Charles R. Weeks (head of the Winthrop Agriculture Department), by working through the Alfalfa Association of the Winthrop Home Institute, had aroused great interest in alfalfa growing. Winthrop had published Weeks' bulletin on alfalfa culture which attracted widespread attention. Many calls came for this bulletin. The United States Department of Agriculture pronounced it was "full of some very interesting things and we are delighted to note the work you are doing for the State and its people."[22]

Sharing equal billing with Professor Weeks was petite Miss Mary Frayser, the nattily attired Extension Worker in Home Economics. Since she was inaugurating the South Carolina program, she encountered innumerable opportunities for constructive, notable work. She was a pioneer upon whom much rested. Johnson, in hiring Miss Frayser, admonished, "I am anticipating a great and successful work for you."[23]

Miss Frayser began touring the state, meeting wives and daughters at the Farmer's Institutes. She told them about better housekeeping and cooking methods. Her well-received talks and demonstrations generated more invitations. She constantly communicated with her college base, and her letters to Johnson revealed that she often made two stops a day. From Walterboro where she was stopping at J. L. Rentz's Hotel, Miss Frayser reported demonstrating the new fireless cooker at the fair. She described her booth where--with packing box, cotton-seed hulls, buckets, and other things--"We are manufacturing a refrigerator," and mentioned that she wanted to organize a reading club in addition to her demonstrations. Typical of the testimonies drifting back to Johnson was that of the Pickens County Superintendent, who thanked the college for sending Miss Frayser and praised her splendid work: "We were

233

more than pleased with her lectures and demonstrations. . . . You are to be commended in your extension work, and I approve of your idea and effort in bringing the college nearer to the people." Miss Frayser's Homekeeper's Club Bulletin, an outgrowth of her work, for many years afterwards proved an important resource for rural schools and Extension activities.[24]

Work related to Miss Frayser's was performed by Miss Parrott, the state agent in charge of the girls' canning and poultry clubs. She represented the United States Department of Agriculture in co-operation with Winthrop, organizing sixteen counties then placing county co-ordinators in each. Some two-thousand girls enrolled in these clubs. Winthrop printed her Canning Club Bulletin, and many homes benefited--especially from the "tomato girls."[25] True to form Dr. Johnson highly praised Miss Parrott's work, saying, "we do not believe there is a more important force at work in the State for the betterment of the homes of the people than Miss Parrott's Girls' Clubs, and we rejoice that Winthrop has a part in it." A Union County agent pinpointed the significance of Parrott's work when she wrote the college that it tended "to bring the town and country closer together in addition to providing better food and a source of money to enable the girls to buy their winter clothes and still have a bank account."[26]

One of the best advertised and most unique public-service programs at Winthrop during 1912-1913 was the experimental rural school in its second year under Mrs. Hetty S. Browne. This experiment sought better programs and techniques to serve the needs of rural areas. Mrs. Browne took children from a nearby cotton mill to a home on the back Winthrop campus, teaching them gardening, cooking, homemaking, and other house-hold duties. So successful was the program that the United States Bureau of Education under Commissioner P. P. Claxton featured it in a government bulletin.[27]

234

With eighteen service manuals and handbooks to her credit, Winthrop had much to be proud of, especially since she continued to place every teacher that she trained and since she still enjoyed preferential treatment from South Carolina's officialdom.[28] Still Johnson seemed unsatisfied. Following his list of 1913's accomplishments, he included a page and a half of needs which he would ask the Legislature for at its next meeting. "There are many needs," he wrote, "which must be supplied before Winthrop can do the full work for the schools, the homes, and the young women of the State which the people expect it to do." He continued, stating:

> Besides such comparatively small needs as additional teaching force, additional furniture and equipment for many departments, Winthrop needs: a farm school building; more land for the farm; propagation house for the Agricultural Department; house for Assistant Engineer; tower clock; cement walks; coal chute; old buildings to be painted to preserve woodwork; fire escapes for new auditorium; dining-hall walls to be buttressed and strengthened; a large gymnasium; additional dormitory room; enlargement of library; old building to be connected with the new Training School, and put in condition to be used; building for manual training, Art and Music; houses for Professors; Young Women's Christian Association building; a building for teachers on lot given to the College by Dr. Joynes.
>
> To supply all of these needs would require more money than the Legislature can appropriate this year, or in several years.
>
> The question before us, then is which of these needs are the most imperative and which of them, therefore, shall we

ask the Legislature to supply at this
time. Shall we ask for $12,000 to com-
plete Johnson Hall (Bancroft) to accommodate thirty or more students or for
$30,000 as half of an appropriation to
build a new dormitory to accommodate
two hundred more students, the other
half of the appropriation to be made by
the Legislature in 1915.

We have been turning away a large
number of students every year for the
past three or four years, and should do
something to provide additional
dormitory accommodations for next
session.[29]

We have concluded that it is best at
this time to ask for $12,000 to
complete Johnson dormitory to accommodate thirty or forty more students next
session, and for $30,000 for a
Gymnasium, upon condition that the
Board of Trustees supply the remainder
of the money needed for such a
building, $30,000 or more. A compara-
tively small room in the main building
is now being used as a Gymnasium and it
has been outgrown by our growing
student body long ago. We feel that
there is nothing more important than
the health and strength and physical
development of our students, and for
that reason we are willing to postpone
the building of a large new dormitory
to accommodate the many girls seeking
admission to Winthrop and to provide a
Gymnasium for the better physical
development of the students already at
Winthrop, and to be admitted through
the years to come.[30]

It was good for Johnson and Winthrop that
his self-righteous drive and compelling publicity
did not intimidate everyone. Tillman, Joynes, and
Swearingen were often at odds with him. Each acted
from time to time as though Johnson did not know

236

what he was doing, and Johnson reacted in like manner. Swearingen, in particular, possessed all the sophistication of a modern, well-trained, professional educator. However, the straight line Swearingen walked often caused Johnson to sulk and when he did, he usually ignored his adversary. At one point Swearingen reminded Johnson that his scholarship report showed the record of a freshman from Woodruff holding a general average of 38 1/2 in four basic high-school subjects. Swearingen demanded: "Will you be good enough to write me how she was admitted to Winthrop since her examination was exceedingly low?" Johnson replied that she was admitted by a certificate from high school in accordance with Winthrop's agreement to admit graduates from this school. Yet, a month later both were cooperating again on a mutual problem.[31]

The Constitution and Statutes of South Carolina enabled Swearingen to exercise considerable power over the state's public education. As an ex-officio member of Winthrop's Board and as head of the public-school system, he dealt with Johnson on two different, and sometimes conflicting, levels. His letters--some critical, some complimentary-- covered the range of public school-college relation- ships. His versatility and brilliance made Swearingen's contributions to education outstanding as he addressed himself with vigor and clarity to a wide range of problems. He viewed, for instance, the summer term at Winthrop (the official state summer school for white teachers) as a great boon to teachers, and Johnson usually solicited his suggestions on teacher-related problems because the president said that he wanted "to serve the teachers and the schools of the state in the very best way" and he knew Swearingen could really help him. Swearingen, though handicapped by blindness, was nonetheless a careful observer of the educa- tional scene. Commenting to Johnson on a recent visit to Winthrop, Swearingen related that the industrial work at the college "was perhaps the most gratifying feature brought to my attention. . . . The finest farm demonstration I have yet observed in South Carolina was the group of young women handling hoes, rakes, and a wheelplow under the direction of the agriculture instructors."[32]

Whenever Swearingen wished to foster any new public-education program, he tapped Winthrop as its proving ground. For instance, Swearingen was concerned about the public schools' neglect of reading. He suggested to Johnson that teachers should be trained in reading to understand its practical schoolroom use. Knowing Johnson would grab almost any new program, Swearingen had already arranged for the publishers of the public-school readers to bear the course's expense. And thus, once again, Winthrop pioneered in South Carolina education.[33]

Working through the Winthrop Board and strongly backed by "Uncle Bennie," Swearingen had Winthrop agree to give credit for sewing, cooking, and manual training. His office provided $100 in state aid for schools maintaining "a successful and satisfactory course in these." This action antedated federal aid for vocational training. And Superintendent Swearingen also pushed Winthrop to give academic credit for teaching agriculture, bookkeeping, commercial arithmetic, business forms, stenography, and typewriting.

Swearingen and Johnson, despite differences, usually worked closely on certification problems. In early 1913 the State Board approved their request that any student holding a first-grade teacher's certificate--with two years' classroom experience and three years' attendance at summer school with a grade average of eighty percent and no more than one grade below fifty--was entitled to receive (by authority of the State Board) a ten-year teacher's certificate. This was a giant step forward in teacher certification. (At this time both Texas and California also honored the Winthrop diploma as acceptable for full state certification.)[34]

Swearingen used Winthrop as a summer meeting place for teachers and Johnson greeted them with open arms. Thus the satisfied teachers and schoolmen

238

channeled their students to Winthrop. Writing to Swearingen in May, 1913, Johnson suggested that he would be glad to host a conference to help implement the 1913 Kindergarten Act. Johnson also encouraged the high-school trustee's conference and the state teacher's meeting to use Winthrop during summer school, thereby serving 90.08 percent of all females then enrolled in teacher training in South Carolina. Soon, he was able to report 572 females plus 58 males enrolled at Winthrop for the summer.

During the next summer (1914) Carolina held her first summer school for high-school teachers, enrolling 33 males and 42 females.[35] Naturally, Johnson was not happy to see the university competing for the state's summer-school business. Relations between the two institutions had not been good since the Peabody Fund controversy. Relations did not grow better. Superintendent Swearingen, an alumnus of Carolina, contributed to Johnson's unhappiness in 1913 when he sent several letters requesting an account of the Peabody money. Johnson's statement returned: he had never listed the Peabody Fund in his financial report to the Legislature, and to do so would cause considerable confusion. Swearingen wrote in July that he believed "all the funds received and expended by Winthrop College should be shown, and that receipts from private sources should not be overlooked, or tucked away in a corner." Johnson, annoyed, made no mention of Peabody in his next several letters to Swearingen. Instead Johnson wrote that the college was filled "to overflowing; that the opening of the Training School Dormitory [Catawba Hall] to College students will increase enrollment" and that he was sending a copy of the Training School course for Swearingen's comments. This did not placate the tenacious Swearingen. Writing again to Johnson, he specified, "Please write me a full statement showing what use has been made of the $90,000 contributed to Winthrop College by the Peabody Fund."[36]

Compelled to reply, Johnson mailed a statement which showed a portion of this money deposited

with the People's Trust Company of the People's
National Bank and the remainder deposited on June
22, 1913, in the National Union Bank, both of Rock
Hill. This was the day that they received the
$90,000 from J. Pierpont Morgan, treasurer of the
Peabody Board. Johnson had borrowed some money from
the fund in anticipation of legislative appropriations and later had returned it. Johnson suggested
that the transaction vouchers could be verified
through Mr. D. W. McLaurin, as representative of the
Board's Financial Committee. [37]

Still dissatisfied, the inquisitive State
Superintendent of Schools wanted to know how the
Peabody money had been used. Again he wrote to
Johnson:

> I can make out from these two statements
> that part of the fund went to purchase
> the Stewart property, part to purchase
> the Wilson property, part to finish the
> Auditorium, part for work on the heating
> plant, part for work on the Training
> School, and part for work on Tillman
> Hall. The definite amounts for each
> purpose are not classified. . . . The
> balance left to the credit of the
> college from this source will barely
> suffice to build and equip the gymna-
> sium even if the Legislature grants the
> request of the trustees. At any rate,
> the use of the money has met some very
> important needs. [38]

In 1913 at least two other trustees besides
Swearingen had serious misgivings about the way
Johnson was conducting some college affairs. Earlier
in the year, Joynes had penned a confidential letter
to Tillman, suggesting all was not well at Winthrop.
As Joynes viewed it, Johnson was unhappy and the
teachers and students alike felt it. Joynes complained that the trustees always hurried through
their business without taking time to meet the
teachers and students or to ascertain actual
conditions. [39]

240

Others contacted Tillman (especially many seeking jobs at Winthrop), which no doubt irked Johnson. If Tillman thought an applicant possessed merit--personal or professional--he usually referred the application for Johnson's consideration. In the case of Mrs. Sarah Shell Martin, daughter of one of his earliest supporters, Tillman wrote, "You know enough about the Farmer's Movement and the Shell Manifesto and the Conventions of 1885, 1886, and 1887 to realize how anxious I am to do Captain Shell's daughter a kindness if I can." She sought a job as housekeeper. Since Tillman admired her mother also, he felt she merited serious consideration. He informed Johnson that the "best rule of life is that good mothers grow good daughters." Evidently, Johnson was not impressed, but Tillman seemed to be suggesting to him that without the Tillman movement, there would have been no Winthrop and no President Johnson.[40]

Three days later someone in Johnson's office sent Tillman a curt note saying they did not anticipate a vacancy for the matron's job that Mrs. Martin sought. Tillman coldly replied that he did not appreciate the note at all: "It has too much of an appearance of having been written by your stenographer without any recognition of the special claim that Mrs. Martin has on me." Asking Johnson to reconsider, he wrote, "Of course, I do not want you to turn off any good woman to make a place for her, but I am afraid you are running a machine and have become so accustomed to its smooth working that you are losing the milk of human kindness." He emphasized again that her father was one of his earliest friends "when I needed friends--and he is largely responsible, or rather is due credit for Clemson and Winthrop."[41]

At this particular time Johnson was pressuring Tillman to change the Lever Bill, which proposed to turn over to the agricultural and mechanical colleges (Clemson in South Carolina) the home-economics work already begun in the South by the Normal and industrial colleges for women. Tillman agreed "to do some missionary work" when

241

he returned to Washington, since he also wished to keep this work in the women's colleges.[42]

On the matter of employing Mrs. Martin, Johnson remained adamant, defending himself by saying that if he had lost the "milk of human kindness," as Tillman had accused, "Winthrop would be a failure." Continuing, he explained that his duties took "every ounce of vitality" he had and that he had "had no vacation for several years." Johnson reiterated his position that favoritism would ruin Winthrop and that every graduate loved Winthrop. Tillman knew better. One month later, after Johnson regained his composure and reflected on what Tillman had said, he sent a fifteen-page letter to Tillman, setting forth in a most favorable light his stewardship of the college.[43]

In essence Johnson's rebuttal is valuable not for the personal assertions he made or the defense he attempted to rationalize, but for how it expressed his own personal credo of education and general philosophy. The following gives a good sample of Johnson's system:

> The teacher who thinks his duty to these students ends with the recitations is not fit for his position. . . .Kindness and gentleness, personal interest in students does not mean laxness in discipline. I never condemn a teacher without careful investigation . . . the teacher may be doing just what is needed by the complaining student and the complaint may be evidence of it. The teacher who tries to curry favor with students . . . may be called lovely and nice by them for a time, but such a teacher usually winds up with the deserved contempt of all thoughtful, earnest students. Winthrop has been established for the benefit of the girls and not for the benefit of the officers and teachers. It takes courage and

242

character to enforce rules to require young people . . . to do that which you know is best for them.

Winthrop College differs in a good many ways from the average female college. Our students are older than those in the ordinary female college and stronger, more self-reliant, and more earnest and purposeful. They want equality of opportunity.

Winthrop cannot afford, as you yourself have often emphatically said, to pattern after the high-priced fashionable social colleges for women. All girls take their turn waiting on the table. We believe that is one of the many good lessons in democracy taught here. After all is said and done, however, a college must be judged by its graduates as a tree is judged by its fruit.

Johnson concluded this defense with impressive testimonials from satisfied parents and students and with a list of the more important alumnae among the 1,613 graduates sent out to that date--October 20, 1913.[44] Johnson, in an afterthought to Tillman, suggested that "from what I have written you must not for a moment get the idea that I think Winthrop is all that it should be. . . ."[45]

Tillman was not convinced. Two days later he advised Johnson that his use of words like him and his was improper and recommended that Johnson obtain George Meredith's Ordeal of Richard Feveral to read. Johnson agreed to do so."[46]

In the summer, 1913, the college community suffered great loss: the long-time English Department head resigned. Dr. James Kinard had been one of the best-trained teachers at Winthrop. Dr. Kinard--native of Newberry, graduate of the South Carolina Military College, and Doctor of Philosophy in English from Johns Hopkins in Baltimore--returned to his _alma_ _mater_ in Charleston to head its English Department. President Johnson wrote Joynes that the military college had offered Kinard a better salary; meanwhile, Joynes viewed Kinard's departure as "a most serious question for our consideration." Regarding Kinard's department position as the most important at Winthrop, Joynes (who for several years was listed in the university's directory as residing at No. 1 campus) could well appreciate a senior professor's role in this era. Johnson, however, did not share Joynes's high regard for the scholar.[47]

No matter what happened, few things seemed to slow Johnson's pace. He always had much to do. Writing to M. V. Richards of the Southern Railroad, Johnson suggested that Miss Frayser be allowed to join the Southern's fall special that was equipped for agriculture and home-economics demonstrations at county fairs. "She is doing good work for the people in that line," Johnson stated. He felt Miss Frayser would add much to the program.[48]

Miss Frayser's train tour was most successful, in fact. She kept Johnson properly informed: "Women are interested and the men fairly besiege me with questions concerning the cost of piping water into the house and the ways to make fireless cookers, etc. . . . I carry roast and rice in the fireless. It cooks as I travel. The people eat every bit. . . ."[49]

Meanwhile, Johnson saw greater possibilities in Miss Frayser's work. "I think," he wrote, "it very important for us to get in touch with these county fairs. It seems that the people are just beginning to wake up to the possibilities of the Extension Work of Winthrop College in Home Economics." Johnson knew that he had hired a gem for this particular work, and her services were much in demand.[50] For instance, the Pendleton Fair Association's secretary asked that Miss Frayser be sent to give "demonstrations and lectures along the line of labor saving devices for the benefit of

244

wives and daughters who live in the rural districts." Johnson obliged.[51]

By September, Miss Frayser advised Johnson in her cautious way, "I believe we did well to cooperate with the Clemson officials in the Farmer's Institute work." More and more of her bulletins on the Organization and Operation of Homemakers' Clubs found readers. Mr. W. W. Long, Director of Extension Service, praised her work on the train and asked that Winthrop furnish three home-economics workers for the following summer. Adding to her praise, Supervisor of Elementary Schools W. K. Tate spoke of "the splendid service which Miss Frayser is doing for the State of South Carolina." He wanted one-hundred copies of her bulletin, which he regarded as constituting "one of the best services which has been contributed in recent years."[52]

Against all odds, within two years Miss Frayser led the race among several important workers helping to improve rural life in South Carolina. The former Superintendent of Schools O. B. Martin had been appointed by the Agriculture Department's Dr. Knapp to spearhead development of home-demonstration work in the South. Martin seemed to favor a public-school-oriented approach rather than Miss Frayser's straight-to-the-public style. Correspondence indicates that Mr. Martin attempted to give Miss Frayser a hard time, but the dauntless petite blue-blood from Virginia possessed the breeding and stamina necessary for a long race.[53]

Meanwhile Congressman A. Frank Lever of Lexington and Senator Hoke Smith of Georgia had succeeded in passing the Smith-Lever Act, which gave federal aid to the state agriculture colleges for cooperative agricultural extension work with the USDA.[54] As Tillman, Johnson, Lever, and others worked to accommodate this law while protecting and furthering Winthrop's well-developed Extension activities, two University partisans put forward schemes that disturbed Johnson and his

245

cohorts. The insidious News and Courier carried in
its early January edition--designed for the eye of
the forthcoming Legislature--two beautiful
pictures: one of the Training School and the
other of the Tillman Science Hall. The paper
called these "monuments to the ability of Johnson.
They are part of the realization of the ideals of
the College, and they are more than half presented
to the State of South Carolina as a gift." Continuing, the Courier observed that Winthrop could no
longer be called "the spoiled child of the State,"
and the paper called special attention to the aims
of its founders: "To train girls in the domestic
and industrial arts, to train teachers for work in
the public schools of the State, to develop
homemakers and teachers of the homemakers of the
future."[55] Then, on January 11, the Courier carried
some proposals by its long-time associate August
Kohn, a trustee of the University. In essence he
proposed placing one board of trustees in charge of
all South Carolina's state educational institutions. Kohn spoke of avoiding duplication, while at
the same time people were pushing to duplicate
Winthrop's work, in another college in Columbia,
under the guise of streamlining the state system.[56]

Two days later this educational iceberg's
tip surfaced in a joint resolution that Representative Lumpkin of Richland County introduced into the
House. The resolution sought to merge the University with the College for Women in Columbia, an
institution founded in 1886 as the South Carolina
Presbyterian Institute. Under the able leadership
of Miss Euphemia Elizabeth McClintock, the school
prospered and many young ladies received valuable
training there. However, the Presbyterians had
severed their control in 1909. In 1910 it had
received a college charter. Now Lumpkin was asking
the Legislature to rescue this struggling
institution by incorporation under the aegis of the
University.[57]

Johnson saw in the resolution a veiled
threat to Winthrop: it suggested to him that
Winthrop's higher work would be transferred to

246

Columbia. Lumpkin reasoned that many young women in South Carolina desired university training, some twenty-five of them already pursuing studies in the University, in spite of the disadvantages and unpopularity that co-education held for them. Lumpkin rationalized that soon the state would have to undergo considerable expense to care for this important body of girls. Under this resolution the College for Women would turn over its property to the University, which would protect the college and in turn would provide university training for its students.[58]

At this time, Winthrop was just beginning a master's program, and Tillman stated that it was "absurd for any sensible man to assert--as had been done in the Legislature--that Winthrop graduates are not competent to teach in high schools or colleges." He suggested that Johnson ask "that Winthrop be permitted to inaugurate and provide for post graduate work along any line of teaching for which there is any demand." Tillman recommended a quiet fight and wrote "get Riggs [of Clemson] to help." His advice was designed to counter the statement made to the Ways and Means Committee that Winthrop did not prepare high-school or college teachers and that the Women's College operating in conjunction with the University could fill the void.[59]

As always when political storms were brewing, Johnson returned to Tillman, Daniel W. McLaurin, and other allies. Sending Tillman clippings and other materials on the projected merger, he reminded the senator that "I need not explain to you what a serious blow this would be to Winthrop College." A few days later a worried Johnson sent Tillman a copy of a statement by Dr. Joynes to the effect that the merger would not hurt Winthrop. In addition, he sent a statement by prominent alumna Mrs. W. L. (Mary T. Nance) Daniel, who (as Johnson said) "hit the nail on the head." Since trustees W. J. Roddey and T. A. Crawford thought it best that Johnson refrain from active involvement in the merger controversy,

247

Johnson appealed to Tillman to write a personal
letter to two or three of his "true and tried
friends in the House and Senate, requesting them to
use their influence to stop this movement." [60]

Tillman agreed. He advised Johnson: "you
know how to do these things in your own way to
accomplish results as effectively as if you fought
openly." He advised also that Johnson point out to
the Ways and Means Chairman, Dr. Dick, "what you
have been doing and what you propose to do in the
future. Work to have the law set forth what each
college should do." Tillman suggested that each
school's role should be properly specified. He
counseled against excessive clashes and extreme
jealousies, such as those which the University and
the Citadel harbored against Clemson.[61]

Tillman's counsel, Johnson's political know-
how, and a letter by Mrs. W. L. Daniel of Saluda to
the State helped to defeat the merger resolution.
Mrs. Daniel's contribution lay in calling attention
to the merger's real purpose: the demand for post-
graduate or university training, not other state
colleges' failure to provide women equipped to teach
high school successfully. "Why stress post-
graduate work for a few women students," she
argued, "when thousands of children in South
Carolina lack advantages in elementary and secondary
education?" Mrs. Daniel appealed for the masses in
the state to be "uplifted to the opportunities and
obligations of citizenship which had been Winthrop's
strong point for years."[62]

On February 13, Johnson happily reported
that the proposition to establish another women's
college had failed in the House of Representatives
by a sixty-five to thirty-six vote. Most of the
legislative leaders advocated Winthrop as a base
for building up women's education. Johnson concluded with the hope that no attempt "will be made
by anyone hereafter to cut us down and remove us
from that leadership." [63]

248

Johnson often over-played his brushes with adversity, and he ofttimes seemed to confuse destructive attacks with constructive attempts to help Winthrop. Not satisfied with the Women's College merger defeat, he immediately sought information from a friend, prominent State Land Agent D. W. McLaurin, asking for a copy of Carolina's official report in order to ascertain if the university planned "to run a summer school in competition with us. . . ."[64]

Meanwhile, the hard-working State Superintendent of Education continued to help Winthrop academically and otherwise. Writing to Johnson in early March, Mr. Swearingen (an alumnus of the University) stated without equivocation: "I opposed the Summer School to be held at the University during 1914 on the grounds that it was a duplication and a needless expense to the taxpayers." Continuing his consistent and sensible approach to South Carolina's problems, Swearingen informed Johnson again that Winthrop was operating redundant sections: "one of these sections is called the tenth grade in the Training School, and the other, sub-collegiate in the College. This policy is expensive." His prodding of Johnson brought improvements in these areas. Swearingen was glad to admit so, but he was careful to add well-deserved praise for W. D. Magginis, the Training School head.[65]

No one could deny the importance of Johnson's work. Providing education and opportunities for South Carolina's young ladies put him on the side of good, so very seldom was he subject to open attack. The public never knew then (and few know today) how Tillman, Joynes, and Swearingen evaluated Johnson. All recognized his value and his weaknesses, but all worked to make him and Winthrop the best president and college that the state could afford. Johnson held his head high, self-righteously proclaiming (and justly so) Winthrop's great public service. He always "rejoiced" in his correspondence and reports that he was better equipping Winthrop to render a greater service.

Sometimes Tillman "jerked him up short," not out of a desire to ridicule but rather to keep Johnson accountable and his verbosity harnessed.[66]

After studying Johnson's annual report in July, 1914, Tillman sent congratulations and a candid appraisal of the Winthrop President:

> While you are neither a very profound scholar or great educator in the true sense, you are a wonderful organizer, and have the best faculty to get one hundred and one cents out of the dollar of any man I ever knew. And withal you inspire the young women who are under you with your spirit and in that way are doing a great work for our State.[67]

In the next paragraph of this unusual letter, Tillman surprised Johnson by telling him that he (Johnson) was not paid enough for all his work and that he was concerned about Johnson's family as two of the three children were not well. He suggested that Johnson write which he would prefer—a raise or a paid-up life insurance policy benefiting his family. Tillman suggested that a large salary raise might be difficult to explain to the Legislature and that he felt a paid-up policy could be more easily obtained. Trustee Tillman concluded with the assurance that all true Winthrop friends did not wish to see "you spend your life in devotion to the College and leave nothing for your wife and children after you are gone."[68]

Four days later, Johnson frankly replied to Tillman. Caught by this pleasant surprise, he confessed he had been so busy doing his "best for Winthrop College and the cause of Women's education in South Carolina" that he had neglected his financial affairs and had given little thought to his salary. Stressing his love for his work, Johnson admitted that he had lost his savings in an investment and that he had only $15,000 on his life.

250

Johnson hesitated, unsure of what to say. But he did suggest he had been offered $5,000 a year at another school. Pointing out that Riggs got $5,000 from Clemson and that the presidents of the Normal colleges in Colorado, Iowa, and Illinois received $5,000 each, Johnson suggested that since Winthrop ranked with the other Normal schools, he might merit a similar amount. Expressing his desire to care for his family and his personal disregard for money, he suggested that his salary might be raised by giving him a four-percent commission on the money he attracted to Winthrop from outside sources--not to exceed $1,500 per year. This arrangement, Johnson felt, would obviate the necessity of calling on the Legislature (a very good suggestion) and would seem reasonable to those concerned.[69]

Johnson did not wish to risk throwing the state's appropriation bill one iota out of kilter, for he knew he was being treated well. As it stood then, the governor was making $3,000 and constitutional department heads, $1,900. Winthrop was receiving $152,446.08 as compared to $92,931.19 for the University. Both the Medical College and the Citadel were drawing under $40,000 each. In addition, Winthrop received state scholarships and other favors. For instance, the Legislature granted a special four-year Winthrop scholarship to Miss Lizzie Kelly. This thirteen-year-old girl from Union County--a member of the girls' canning and poultry clubs--in 1913 by her own labor produced on one-tenth acre of land 4,375 pounds of tomatoes, selling (in addition to fresh tomatoes) 700 three-pound cans. Miss Kelly won first prize in South Carolina and second in the nation; she was properly honored by the United States Department of Agriculture. The General Assembly of South Carolina further resolved to empower Winthrop to furnish this proud young lady with a free scholarship for four years, whenever she qualified and applied for study at Winthrop.[70]

One of the most beneficial arrangements affecting Winthrop in 1914-1915 was the agreement with Clemson whereby she would serve South Carolina in home-economics Extension work under the Smith-Lever Act. After the preliminaries a special meeting of the Winthrop Board took place at 8:00 p.m. on August 6. The governor, Tillman, and Joynes were absent; Swearingen arrived late. Still, the memorandum of understanding with Clemson was ratified by a quorum of the Board. It stipulated that

The following proposition submitted by Clemson College in the form on an agreement between President Riggs of Clemson College and President Johnson of Winthrop College and previously adopted by the Board of Trustees of Clemson College was unanimously accepted and the agreement approved and adopted:

MEMORANDUM OF UNDERSTANDING BETWEEN THE CLEMSON AGRICULTURAL COLLEGE AND THE WINTHROP NORMAL AND INDUSTRIAL COLLEGE OF SOUTH CAROLINA--REGARDING EXTENSION AND HOME ECONOMICS IN SOUTH CAROLINA AS PROVIDED FOR IN THE 'LEVER BILL.'

WHEREAS the Governor of the State has designated the Clemson Agricultural college to administer the funds arising under an 'Act to provide for co-operative Agricultural Extension Work between the Agricultural Colleges in the several states. . . and the U.S. Department of Agriculture,'

WHEREAS Clemson College desires to use Winthrop College as its agent in carrying out the home economics work provided for in the said Agricultural Extension Act, and Winthrop College desires to enter into this partnership:

THEREFORE the Presidents of Winthrop and Clemson College, each subject to the overruling action of his Board of Trustees, mutually agree to carry out in good faith, in spirit as well as in letter, the following understanding:

1. Clemson College agrees to devote to the home economics work to be placed under the direction of Winthrop College, twenty-five percent of the $10,000 due to and receivable by the state without appropriation, and twenty-five percent of any funds resulting from municipal, county, or state appropriations, or funds from any source (other than from Clemson College) together with the resulting federal appropriations provided for by the said Agricultural Extension Act.

2. All projects for the home economics work shall be submitted by the President of Winthrop College to the Director of Extension at Clemson College, and, if approved by him and the Secretary of Agriculture of the States, shall be executed by Winthrop College.

3. All bills for expense incurred by Winthrop College in carrying on the home economics work herein provided for shall be approved by the President of Winthrop College and sent to the Director of Extension, who shall handle them under rules prescribed by Clemson College.

4. The nomination of all agents in home economics work shall be made by the President of Winthrop College to the Director of Extension at Clemson College, whose action thereon shall be subject to the same rules as govern his appointment of agents in Demonstration and Extension work.

5. In carrying out the terms of this memorandum, the President of Winthrop

College, or his authorized representative, shall deal directly with the Director of Extension of Clemson College, but the Presidents of the two institutions reserve the right of direct intercourse regarding the work herein considered whenever deemed necessary.

6. The parties to this understanding agree to use every proper means to have the Legislature of South Carolina provide the funds necessary to a full realization of the benefits of the Agricultural Extension Act by the people of the State, and it is agreed that neither party will directly or indirectly seek to bring about Legislations out of keeping with this understanding, and, on the other hand, will use all proper means to prevent such legislation.

7. The partnership covered by this memorandum may be dissolved only by mutual consent, and then only after ample time is given for necessary re-adjustments.

Signed:

D.B. Johnson
President
Winthrop College

W.M. Riggs
President, Clemson
Agricultural College

June 26, 1914.[71]

Other important additions and changes during 1914-1915 included the inauguration of a full-scale physical-health program and the appropriation of $60,000 for building a new gymnasium. Willard-Boggs of Spartanburg erected a fine building that Johnson boasted was one of the largest and best equipped gymnasiums in the South. Believing the students' health and physical development most essential,

Johnson considered requiring all students to learn to swim before graduation, "as many institutions with gymnasiums and swimming pools now do."[72]

Winthrop continued to relate herself more closely to the people she served through helpful bulletins, the Winthrop Weekly News, and faculty addresses and through the regular Extension service, mill-village betterment work, and the newly expanded farm demonstration school at Oak Ridge. As always, each new year brought Johnson's familiar statement that "we have the largest enrollment in the history of the college. Many were turned away."[73]

It is easy to see why Winthrop was growing so quickly. The well-rounded curriculum and the attractive scholarships guaranteed a good, inexpensive education for those equipped to avail themselves of it. The state provided 124 scholarships each worth $100 and free tuition. These were competitive. Also there were thirty-one dining-room scholarships in addition to private scholarships and twelve honorary scholarships for students with the highest averages. Expenses, excluding the uniform, for tuition-paying students totaled $162; for students not paying tuition, $122; and for full-scholarship students, $22. Dr. Johnson was proud to list the Winthrop College roll with his report. Beside each girl's name there was a notation for public scrutiny. These examples seem odd for people accustomed to gaudy modern catalogs. In 1915, for example, Miss Gertrude Abrams held the Federation of Woman's Clubs scholarship; Miss Margaret Adams attended free; Miss Frances Adickes had a state scholarship; Miss Lillie Shumate Barr was on service scholarship; Miss Mildred Bowen held a UDC scholarship; Miss Kate Brandon had a dining-room scholarship; and Miss Mary Hope Crawford was designated as paying. And so it went through the whole list of 942 girls.[74]

The appealing publicity that Johnson released was enough to dazzle even the most cosmopolitan young lady. How much greater was its effect on those not far removed from the

255

boondocks. The _State_ paper in October of 1914 contained a full page showing a campus-wide view of Winthrop and carrying the caption: "Winthrop Normal and Industrial College of South Carolina-- The Only College for Women Supported By the State." On the left front, directly under Winthrop, stood the bold emblazon: "D.B. Johnson, President." Before launching into a capsuled account of the entire program, the advertisement ran a subcaption: "Buildings and Equipment Represent Highest Ideas of School Architecture and Most Approved Methods of Work." The introductory paragraph should have raised some questions in Rock Hill, because it read: "Rock Hill, South Carolina, in the foothills of the Blue Ridge. Campus large; the arrangement planned by expert landscape gardener; ample room for all games and athletic sports; fronts on main residence street; is bounded by all streets on all sides; electric street car line gives easy access to business section." Many Winthrop graduates would not recognize all these as characteristics of their _alma mater_.[75]

In his full-page ad, Johnson stressed the campus's physical features: the Training School building, infirmary, auditorium, gymnasium, practice house, rural school, and 144-acre farm. With short courses for teachers, extension work, an active Young Women's Christian Association, a lecture series, student government, the standard uniforms clothing system plus an appointment bureau, Johnson could advertise one of the best physical plants and programs available in the South.

Winthrop attracted considerable attention both inside and outside South Carolina.[76] The chief of the state board of health in Raleigh, North Carolina, wrote to Johnson in November, 1914, and observed with interest that Winthrop College and the University of Iowa were the only two colleges "thus far that have undertaken baby health work." He asked for Miss Frayser's _Bulletin_ to use in North Carolina.[77] In another area, many were interested in Winthrop's librarianship program

256

under Miss Ida J. Dacus. Winthrop required all freshmen to take a class in reference. A second course in elementary library methods for school teachers was required of every Normal-course graduate.[78]

Johnson was nearly always preoccupied with Winthrop's business and financial aspects. In the fall, 1914, he pushed to have a coal chute placed near the back-campus buildings for the college's convenience. Writing Senator Tillman, Johnson argued that Southern Railroad was violating its word and he asked Tillman to "say a word to one of the head men of the Southern Railroad in Washington insisting that the coal chute be put in for Winthrop College." Contacting President Fairfax Harrison of the Southern, Tillman received his explanation. According to Harrison the coal trestle and track would cost $5,286.27, of which the railroad would pay $1,075.17. But Johnson had only $1,500 to spend, far too little to pay for the construction. Since his total on freight delivered to Winthrop was only about $8,000 a year, Mr. Harrison felt that the $1,075.17 was all he could donate towards this service. Johnson thanked Tillman for his invaluable aid but realized that Tillman's preoccupation with naval affairs and his weakening physical condition meant that Johnson would be troubled less in the future by the senator. But Johnson still needed him.[79]

In mid-December Johnson felt compelled to draft a confidential letter to Tillman concerning an influential young lady who, not wanting to be disciplined, threatened to take her case to the Legislature. Johnson sought to counter her by appealing to Tillman. Wishing to back the student government's action against her, Johnson felt that her prominence warranted tapping Tillman's clout. A few days later (during the congressional recess), Johnson wrote Tillman's secretary, Broadus Knight, asking that his letters concerning the discipline case and those of Dr. Joynes, Mr. Swearingen, and Major W. L. Glaze be returned to him as he did not wish to bother the senator further.[80]

Johnson was nurturing several side projects in 1914-1915. Working through the national student secretary of the YWCA in New York, he secured promises for a Y building to house student activities. Using several lines of attack, Johnson affirmed that girls were more religiously inclined than boys and that girls' schools had more trouble raising money from their graduates. He appealed to every state and national Y official that could help. After a pitch from the Broadway-based, internationally famous architects of F. W. and Arthur Ware, Johnson knew what building he wanted but he had not raised enough money. Dr. W. D. Weatherford, Field Secretary for the YMCA in the South, suggested that Johnson ask John D. Rockefeller for a definite amount on the condition that he raise the remainder.[81] Soon the Wares, working on a sketch of the building, proposed visiting Rock Hill so that their plan would blend with the locale. A few days later Chicago architect Henry H. Hussey proposed travelling to Rock Hill to discuss the projected building.[82]

In the fall of 1914, Johnson stepped up his campaign to sell Mr. Rockefeller's man, Starr Murphy, on Winthrop's need. Citing figures on Winthrop's growth, Johnson praised the school, stressing how it had grown since Murphy's visit with the Ogden party. An undated memo shows Rockefeller told Senator Tillman that he wanted to help but felt his money would meet more urgent needs like those of the Belgians and some missionary groups. Johnson was sorely disappointed "that Rockefeller could not help because the girls had been working for a number of years to secure their Y, and they had their hearts set on pushing the enterprise through, but nothing can be done now without Mr. Rockefeller's help."[83]

Johnson never gave up easily. Writing to W. S. Richardson of Rockefeller's office, he told how the girls had denied themselves all Christmas gifts in order to contribute money to the Belgians: "Our girls have contributed of their slender means $553." (In this student body there were 298 farmers'

258

daughters, whose fathers "have been hit harder than any other class of people in the South.") Richardson replied that Mr. Murphy thought that this information should appear in "some Northern paper, and would Johnson object?" Johnson agreed, adding, "You could say that some of them [Winthrop girls] made money to come to college by raising tomatoes, cotton, and corn on patches of their fathers' farms."[84] Thus, the New York Evening Post (December 18, 1914) featured this story and Mr. Murphy, the Rockefeller aide, sent Johnson a copy with a nice letter. Editor O. G. Villard of the Post wrote an editorial: "What a tremendous sacrifice for girls many of whom are working their way through college. . . . Lest anyone think that giving to the Belgians is confined to the rich and prosperous in our cities. We cite a recent happening in Rock Hill, South Carolina." Johnson thanked Murphy for the editorial and said, "I shall read it to our girls to encourage them in their good work."[85]

While Johnson bargained with the architects over the next several months, other things claimed his immediate attention. Early in the year, the Legislature paid Winthrop a visit. The lieutenant governor, a bachelor named A. J. Bethea, and Speaker James A. Hoyt, one of South Carolina's youngest, headed the delegation. Their speeches were graciously received with prolonged applause for their semi-endorsement of women's suffrage. Following a tour the young ladies of the UDC, at that time one of the most prestigious groups on campus, served an elegant dinner at two o'clock. This was a festive occasion featuring music by a well-liked local band and toasts after the meal. Johnson, as always, appeared at his best when he entertained the Legislature.[86]

Winthrop dazzled the legislators: every county boasted from one up to 112 students. At least sixteen South Carolina mill presidents sent their daughters to Winthrop. Daughters of governmental officials, newspaper men, and others made Winthrop's student body interesting and varied.

259

Emphasis on physical fitness, which no doubt impressed the Legislature, reflected in part the gathering clouds of world war and the importance of all citizens' being fit and ready should America become involved. In addition to traditional school games, Winthrop advocated walking, and the elementary agriculture students got much exercise working their garden plots. After seeing so much good at Winthrop, the Legislature viewed as anti-climactic the long list of needs that Johnson brought to their attention (including cement walks, more farm land, a new barn, a propagation house, another well, a tower clock, an enlarged library, a building for music and manual training, houses for professors, a YWCA building, and a building for teachers on the lot given by Dr. Joynes). Still, this impressive list merited consideration.[87]

The ever-present State Superintendent of Education Swearingen kept Johnson out of his grandiose-buildings-and-grounds clouds and close to educational earth. Early in 1915, he wrote, "Will you be good enough to write me what results have been accomplished in mill schools and mill villages by Miss Frayser's work? I am primarily responsible," he continued, "for this experiment and this form of extension work for Winthrop College, hence I feel that you will not be unwilling to give me this information or your opinion on this point." Since Johnson and Miss Frayser had worked out a memorandum of understanding with many South Carolina mills to promote cooking, sewing, motherhood responsibilities, gardening, playground activities, night recreation, and night school, Johnson was easily able to give a good report to Swearingen.[88]

Four days later Swearingen again communicated with Johnson. This time he attempted to ascertain the calibre of student Johnson was admitting and to broaden the scholarship examination to include questions on eighth-, ninth-, and tenth-grade work. Eventually, Swearingen wanted to see state-adopted textbooks made the basis of instruction--both in matter and in method.[89]

During this period, York County benefited from Winthrop's work with the rural schools. Seniors accompanied supervisors to the country schools to observe conditions and do some teaching. The program also promoted improvements through patrons' meetings, school-improvement associations, county teachers' associations, county field days and clean-ups for the schools. This new emphasis awakened York County taxpayers to their schools' immediate needs; roughly twenty districts voted in special taxes to meet these needs. However, the Legislature disapproved of Winthrop's using state money for a county and not the whole state, so it cut slightly the avowed appropriation.[90]

Taxpayers' sensitivity to local needs might well have resulted from some educational changes taking place in South Carolina at this time. South Carolina was one of four states that passed a compulsary school-attendance law in 1915. It was a local-option law which provided that, upon petition-ing the majority of the districts' qualified electors, the county board of education had to put compulsary attendance into effect or one-fourth of the electors could petition for an election in a compulsary-attendance referendum. The law further provided that all able-bodied youths between eight and fourteen who resided within two and one-half miles of a school were required to attend at least one four-month term a year. Children between fourteen and sixteen were required to attend unless lawfully employed or unless unable to read and write simple English sentences. The South Carolina law provided that one-half the proceeds from hunters' licenses would be appropriated for schools, except in three counties where the legislative delegations felt that schools were not of primary importance.[91]

In light of these conditions, Johnson and his co-workers' accomplishments seem monumental. Accentuating his community-improvement theme, Johnson invited Congressman Asbury Frank Lever of the Midland District to make the 1915 commencement address. In introducing Lever, Johnson made a timely reference

261

to the Smith-Lever Agricultural Extension Act and to
the fact that Winthrop and Florida Normal would be
the   only   two   such   schools   administering   the
extension programs under this legislation.   In his
address Lever stressed the needs of rural women and
the importance of family--out of which grew communities, counties, states, and nations.   Making a
plea to improve the lot of the 35,000 white male
tenant farmers of voting age who were living in
three- and four-room shacks in a state that was 85
percent agricultural, Lever stressed the need for
more inside plumbing, more labor-saving devices, and
more social life.   The rural women especially, he
stressed, needed help and leadership from teachers
and   others,   and   he   appealed   to   the   Winthrop
graduates to lead in meeting these needs.[92]

Before June, 1915, Johnson had carefully
laid plans to be elected President of the National
Educational Association--the association that most
educators at that time aspired to head.   Prior to
August's national meeting in the San Francisco area,
Johnson wrote a personal letter to Senator Tillman
(who   was   planning   to   inspect   installations   in
California in his capacity as Chairman of the Senate
Naval Committee) and asked his help in becoming
President of NEA.   Johnson wrote:

The National Educational Association is
the greatest and most dignified educational association in the world.   It
would   mean   a   great   deal   for   South
Carolina for a representative from this
state to be elected President of that
organization.   In the fifty years of
the life of the N.E.A. only two Southern
men   have   been   President--one   from
Tennessee   and   the   other   from   North
Carolina.   At the annual meeting of the
N.E.A. held at St. Paul, Minnesota last
summer, I was proposed for the office
and had, without doubt, a majority of
the nominating committee and was assured
of election, but withdrew in favor of
Dr.   David   Starr   Jordan,   a   resident   of

262

California because the next annual
meeting of the Association was to be
held in California in connection with
the Panama-Pacific Exposition and the
President of the NEA was needed on the
grounds for a longer time than I could
spare from my work at Winthrop. The
California and Pacific Coast people and
all of Dr. Jordan's friends appreciated
my withdrawal in his favor to such an
extent that they said they would join
heartily with my friends at the San
Francisco meeting to make me President
for the coming year, when the
Association will meet somewhere in the
East.[93]

. . . It occurs to me that you might
know the U.S. Senators of California
well enough to write a personal letter
to them telling them that a South
Carolina educator was practically
elected President of the N.E.A. last
summer at St. Paul, Minnesota, but
generously withdrew in favor of Dr.
Jordan, in order that a Californian
might be elected unanimously; that Dr.
Jordan's friends appreciated his
generosity and voluntarily offered
this South Carolinian their support
for this meeting, to be held next
August [16-28th] at Oakland, California; and that you hoped they would
lend their influence to have California teachers carry out their generous
intentions. It might be better for
you to speak to the State Superintendent of Education. It would be a great
thing for Winthrop and South Carolina
educationally if the President of
Winthrop should be made President of
the N.E.A. I believe that a word from
you would have great weight with
California people.

I hope you and Mrs. Tillman and Miss
Sallie May will have a safe and
enjoyable trip in $_{94}$every way to
California and return.

When Johnson's letter arrived at Trenton two
days later, the Tillman party had already left for
New York to board a steamer for Balboa and San
Francisco. Young Ben apprized Johnson that "Papa
and Mother" had left and that he (Ben Tillman, Jr.)
was sending Johnson a letter of endorsement
incorporating Johnson's suggestions for Johnson's
revisions and corrections.   Young Ben agreed to
sign the jointly composed endorsement for his father
and send it on to the California senators.
President Johnson rewrote this letter, substituting
Dr. for Mr. Johnson and including a statement that
Johnson was the President of the Southern Education
Association and the head of the best Normal school
in the South.   The letter asked the senators to
advise the California superintendent of education
and the other high educational officials about
Johnson and his help for Dr. Jordan.[95]

With the groundwork well laid, Johnson won
with the aid of California and other state delegations.   Token opposition came from Grace Strachan,
but the only woman ex-president of NEA (Ella Flagg
Young of Illinois) helped with Johnson's campaign.
The victorious Johnson could doubly rejoice.   His
new national prominence did much for him.[96]

Despite Senator Tillman's intention to
leave public life after his current term, Johnson
grasped Tillman with the grip of a drowning man.
In September, 1915, Johnson made an unusual request
of Tillman--to back up Winthrop's application for
some of the statuary from the Panama-Pacific
Exposition, which Johnson understood would be
donated to institutions when the exposition dis-
banded.   Attempting, as usual, to impress the
aging senator, Johnson gave Winthrop's enrollment
as 932 and wrote that over 600 had been turned
away.   In the same letter he challenged the

264

contention of Tillman's nephew, Swearingen, that Johnson was taking sub-freshmen and weak students by categorically stating, "Our entrance requirements are the same as those of the State University and we have no sub-freshman classes." In a concluding line Johnson was emphatic: "We need more dormitory rooms badly."[97]

As the now undisputed front runner in South Carolina education, Johnson attracted jealous attacks. On September 23, he informed Tillman that the State paper was using news of Winthrop's student overflow to whip up public opinion to favor a new University dormitory while it tried to prevent Winthrop from getting one. He struck a sympathetic chord with Tillman.[98]

The aging senator was pleased with Johnson and wrote immediately to agree, adding that the State never was friendly to Winthrop or Clemson because there was too much Tillman about them. As usual Tillman suggested keeping the Legislature informed and thought the money would be forthcoming, especially if Johnson could raise some himself. Johnson knew this meant, "renew your efforts with Rockefeller on behalf of the Y, and the Legislature will look more favorably on your request for a new dormitory."[99]

Johnson, pen in hand, set himself to solicit enough money for his Y building and a dormitory. In early October, he again contacted Rockefeller's New York office. Within a week, Rev. W. S. Richardson replied, saying: "As soon as possible, the consideration of a gift on the part of Mr. Rockefeller to the Associations at Winthrop will be taken up." Writing next to Dr. Weatherford of the Southern Regional Y Office, Johnson assured him that "I do not believe that a Y.W.C.A. building would yield finer returns anywhere than at Winthrop College." He added that the Winthrop Board would request $100,000 for a dormitory accommodating 250 to 300 more girls. In December, Johnson rejoiced that Dr. Weatherford would be in New York soliciting Mr. Murphy for the Winthrop building, "if the opportunity offers." Finally, early in January, Johnson wrote Murphy that he was beginning his drive for the dormitory. Skillfully attempting to tie Mr. Rockefeller to this, he reasoned: "With Mr. Rockefeller's offer of one hundred thousand dollars for a student's social and religious building upon conditions that our Board of Trustees shall raise one hundred thousand dollars for a dormitory to accommodate two-hundred and fifty to three-hundred young women, I feel sure of success." Johnson wanted Rockefeller to understand that his pledge was "providing for a better spiritual life for the students already here" and "also making it possible for 250-300 more young women unable to go elsewhere for lack of means to come here and avail themselves of the opportunities for preparation for life's duties offered by the College." [100]   Having done all he could, Johnson awaited Rockefeller's decision. Meanwhile, he turned to pushing the Legislature, running Winthrop, and making plans to make his year as president of the NEA a smashing success.[101]

The Winthrop Board of Trustees in their closed meeting of November 23, 1915, asked for another dormitory "as an act of justice and fairness to the young women of the state." The justification that Johnson prepared to back up this statement carried great weight in South Carolina, for he told a very compelling story:

The Board of Trustees of Winthrop College, at the annual meeting held in December, decided unanimously that the time had come when dormitory accommodations should be provided at Winthrop College for those young women desiring to go to Winthrop, and prepared to go, and, in many cases unable to go elsewhere for lack of means. It is not fair to continue to turn away South Carolina young women from the only institution supported by the State for their higher education and training, especially when the State is providing

266

for the higher education of 1,700 young men at a cost of over $2,500,000 for plant and over $400,000 a year for maintenance and only 1,000 young women at a cost of $482,702 for plant and $131,000 a year for maintenance, including cost of scholarships and of all extension work for the public good; and when, further, the State has been maintaining this institution for the higher education of women for only a short time comparatively, having maintained such institutions for the young men of the State for a great number of years.

There are as many young women as young men in the State, and they are as necessary to the welfare of the State, and they need, deserve, and long for a higher education as much as the young men. There are more young women in the State ready for college each year than young men, as the records of the graduating classes of the High Schools will show.

There were 1,642 applicants for admission to Winthrop this session, and only 1,019 of these could be accommodated, and that number could be accommodated only by having a number of them board in private families.

Many of those turned away were not prepared for College, but enough of them were prepared to make another dormitory necessary. Among those turned away were some from every county of the State.

The State should make provision for accommodating more of the young women seeking admission to Winthrop College, not only as an act of justice and fairness to them but especially in the interest of the common schools of the State. The women, mainly are the teachers of the boys and girls of the State, and Winthrop College is the one institution maintained by the State to train women teachers, and the common schools of the State are in great need of more good teachers. Of 5,072 white teachers in the State, according to the report for 1915 of the State Superintendent of Education, 4,217 are women.

An appropriation to enlarge and strengthen Winthrop, where teachers for the common schools are trained, is an appropriation of the best kind for strengthening and improving common schools. It is impossible to have good schools without good teachers. In fact, a school with a poor incompetent teacher may do more harm than good. Money appropriated for the common schools is wasted in great measure unless good teachers are employed with it.

If a business corporation could increase its output 25 percent by increasing expenditure on its business for plant 10 percent and for maintenance only 5 percent, it would borrow money, if need be, to make the enlargement. This is exactly what is proposed for the State to do at Winthrop, with its business of educating her daughters and preparing teachers for the common schools. Another dormitory to accommodate 250-300 students would meet the demands upon Winthrop for some years to come. The teaching of these additional students could be provided for at Winthrop at small cost by employing a comparatively few additional assistant teachers in departments already organized under the direction of heads already

employed. The enrollment at Winthrop at
any one time with 250 to 300 students
added would not exceed 1,200 to 1,250
students, and many of our best normal
schools have enrollments much greater
than that number. The great State
Normal at Normal, Illinois, has an
enrollment of 2,253 students; that at
Cedar Falls, Iowa, 3,000, and at Greely,
Colorado, 2,350. Smith College, with a
reputation for exclusiveness and high
tuition charges, has an enrollment of
1,600. The 115 strongest institutions
of learning in the United States have
each more than one thousand students.

There is no danger of Winthrop becoming
too large, for the most satisfactory
and effective work for years to come in
our sparsely settled State of only
700,000 white people, men, women and
children, with nine other colleges for
women besides Winthrop, and with high
schools enough to prepare properly
only 400 to 450 girls for their Freshman
Classes.[102]

With Johnson holding the top honorary educational position in the United States, South Carolina
naturally emphasized education. New and interesting
demands were made on the state for more educational
opportunities. The denominational schools meanwhile
felt keen competition from the state schools, and
they were worried by the widespread rumors that most
students attended Winthrop tuition-free. Senator
Tillman's son, Henry, wrote Johnson from Greenwood,
saying he had heard that only one girl from that
county paid tuition and that the others were "exempt
because their parents have taken the pauper's oath."
Johnson countered, explaining that "all the State
Institutions have to admit free of charge, when they
have room, those students who fill out properly the
enclosed free tuition blank. . . . The fact is, I
think, that all students should be admitted free of
charge to the institutions supported by the taxes

269

of the people." He added, "the denominational colleges are trying to have all scholarships abolished and require all students in the State Institutions to pay tuition." A few days later, writing to the senator, Johnson accused the denominational schools of taking a non-Christian attitude.[103]

Criticism seemed to spur the Johnson administration to greater heights. They countered criticism with innovation. New in 1916 was the history department's agreement to furnish the Weekly News with articles on the "Great War." But the current war never prevented the News from printing a birthday issue for Robert E. Lee. To Winthrop and Rock Hill, the debut of the "Anderson Six" automobile took precedence over news of the new German submarine policy, which eventually would lead the United States to enter into World War I. The 1916 debut of the automobile--a Rock Hill product-- was described as a "brilliant affair" in which some of the Winthrop girls participated.[104]

The town and college which Tillman, Joynes, Johnson, Anderson, and others helped to build received much publicity with Anderson advertising his car in the North and Johnson flitting around the country to address sizeable educational groups. Miss Sarah R. Withers of the Training School created "Baby Ray" (a popular protagonist in a popular children's book series) and thereby became a leading woman editor for the Johnson Publishing Company, which sent her materials into many states and indirectly publicized Rock Hill.[105]

Every advancement, success, and innovation pleased the local press. They paid considerable attention to most events: the arrival of William Jennings Bryan; the latest foreign entertainment by the Winthrop Star Course; Rock Hill's eleven daily trains; Professor Butler of Columbia University's engagement for summer school; the special train taking the girls to Charlotte's Opera House to see Birth of the Nation; Winthrop's support of missionaries in India and Japan; Johnson's addresses to teachers' groups in Arkansas, Michigan, and

270

elsewhere; and the fact that "Johnson was on old #32 when she wrecked in Charlotte Tuesday morning."[106] However, the press paid less attention to Winthrop girls' favoring the minimum-wage law and to Johnson's plan to give some fifty- and hundred-dollar raises to faithful faculty. Few seem concerned that Professor Charles R. Weeks, an outstanding man affectionately dubbed "Old Hurry," was moving to direct experiment stations in western Kansas. The Record of Rock Hill listed his accomplishments and attributes: President of the South Carolina Federation of Fairs, Organizer of the York County Fair Association, the Alfalfa Growers Association, Director of the Plant Breeders Association, participant in the Chamber of Commerce, Extension work, and member of an "interesting family." (He was also being mentioned as a possible Secretary of Agriculture in the Wilson Cabinet.)[107]

The press and others virtually ignored certain problems during this "golden age." Most of the trustees accepted unquestioningly Johnson's statements and recommendations, but Tillman, Joynes, and Swearingen worked to perfect Winthrop's academic system and to harness Johnson's "New Moses" complex. Swearingen succeeded in gaining approval for a new school law in 1915 which gave considerable power to the State Board of Education. This law attempted to set standards by which local boards could prescribe and enforce a uniform system for books, certification, and scholarships--problems that Swearingen had been jousting with Johnson about for several years. Johnson was not eager to comply with certain sections of this law. A few months after its enactment, Swearingen demanded of Johnson: "Write me by what authority the words, 'Life license to teach' are used on the Winthrop diploma." Johnson replied that Section 10 of the Act of December 23, 1891, gave the Normal diploma life tenure, but that the literary diploma was not a life license. Swearingen retorted, reminding Johnson that a new law gave the state Board of Charities and Corrections authority to dictate applicants' financial eligibility for free tuition and scholarships and that the board of trustees--

271

Johnson in case of Winthrop--were relieved of
considering a student's financial status.
Swearingen wanted the Winthrop Board to know
this.[108]

Swearingen never seemed satisfied with
Johnson's financial statement. Late in 1915
when Johnson was buying 115 acres at $100 an acre
for the farm, he sent a Mr. Dunlap with the papers
to Swearingen, who agreed it was a good bargain,
but Swearingen took no part in the deal because he
was not on the Finance Committee. Instead,
Swearingen wanted to know where the money was
coming from: "You told the Board of Trustees that
this purchase would not cost the college or the
taxpayers one cent because the money was coming
from another source." Johnson replied that the
proposal had been referred to the Emergency Committee and that "we [the college] raised $26,000
more or less from fees paid by students and by
practicing strict economy in the use of fuel,
lights, in management of the farm, the dairy,
poultry plant, kitchen, and bakery."[109]

More important work called Johnson. As
President of the NEA he entreated the President of
the United States, Mr. Wilson, to address their
national meeting in July. Johnson first sent the
United States Commissioner to President Wilson; he
reported that it was unlikely that Wilson would
come. Turning as a last resort to Tillman,
Johnson wrote, "I am writing to ask that you urge
President Wilson as the Senior U.S. Senator from the
South to accept our invitation and will you get some
other Southern Senators to do the same thing?"[110]
Tillman, not feeling the urgency of this request,
replied that with the Mexican and German situations
as they were, he did not want to ask the president
because "he hasn't the time to think about anything
else but public matters." He promised that if
things improved and resumed their normal status, "I
will cheerfully cooperate with you in getting the
President. . . . "[111]

272

While other important questions were begging settlement, Johnson continued to handle most of Winthrop's petty problems until 1917, when James Kinard became dean. Even then Johnson always rendered the final decision. For example, a young lady from Georgetown County who had failed to qualify for a scholarship attested that the local school superintendent had encouraged his applicants to help each other--Johnson observed that each had received the same grade in history. Swearingen proposed that a hearing be held on this by the state Board of Education. It was his contention that the scholarship system was becoming so unsatisfactory that it should be abolished. Johnson disagreed.[112]

In any controversy involving Winthrop College, sooner or later politics would raise its ugly head. Since, for example, Governor Blease's followers were moving more to the forefront, Johnson found himself dealing with them more. Tillman cautioned Johnson to beware of the Anderson Tribune's editor, "who at the same time is paying his respects to you, he is making charges against two state officers having their daughters at Winthrop on free tuition and board." Asking for the facts behind the newspaper's allegations, Tillman opined that the newspaper was lying. Johnson answered that the report about free tuition showed Misses Marietta and Nell M. Carter, daughters of State Treasurer S. T. Carter, and Miss Louise McCown, daughter of Secretary of State Colonel R. Maxey McCown, "have complied with the law and the college had no option in granting free tuition to students whose parents or guardians have complied." The paper had addressed an open letter to McCown, asking, "Don't you think you should have saved your daughter any humiliations and paid her bills at Winthrop?" The paper also accused Carter of attempting to mismanage state bonds and characterized Tennessean D. B. Johnson as an "easy mark."[113]

To circumvent criticism over scholarships, Johnson informed the General Assembly in 1916 of the procedure he followed in this matter:

273

There were 54 vacant scholarships to be
awarded upon the scholarship and
entrance examination held at the county
court houses of the State last July 7th.
The financial eligibility of the applicants for scholarships was passed upon
by the State Board of Charities and
Corrections in accordance with the new
scholarship law passed at the last
session of the General Assembly. Our
Board of Trustees met at Columbia in the
Governor's office on September 1st to
receive the report of the State Board of
Charities and Corrections and to
recommend the award of the scholarships
to the State Board of Education upon
the results of the scholarship
examination and the report of the State
Board of Charities and Corrections.

The board did not go behind the report
of the State Board of Charities and
Corrections and did not recommend any
one for a state scholarship who was
reported by that board as financially
ineligible for a scholarship. There
was one appeal from the recommendations
of our Board of Trustees.

The 124 state scholarships provided for
at Winthrop College have been awarded
under the scholarship law to 68 young
women from towns and 56 from rural
communities.[114]

Ending an unusually successful school year
in June, Johnson had some last-minute details and
problems to dispose of before he went north to the
NEA national convention.

Miss Frayser's work with the mill people
had proved most successful, but some owners were
very difficult to deal with: they seemed only to
be trying to lay hands on Smith-Hughes money. In
a moment of open despair (a result of being stymied

274

by James P. Gossett of the Williamston, Brogan, and Calhoun Falls Mills), Miss Frayser told Johnson: "I can't help fearing what may happen if you do not look after Winthrop's mill interest in Washington. For once I believe I have lost courage. The Mill president's life," she observed, "is against anything but absolute authority and against receiving suggestions and help however tactfully received." Now after organizing seventeen mills, she feared she would lose control of the mill schools.[115]

Johnson could have saved the program, according to Miss Frayser, if he had only written to Gossett when she had asked him to--"last summer, again in the autumn, and again in February." In summation she agreed that Gossett was "a gentleman but also an irrascible aristocrat, who feels that the college has broken its agreement." Since it had taken two years to convince him to invest in mill-village improvement work, she warned Johnson that it was not easy to get the mill president to cooperate now, even with the college's offer to help pay the social worker at his mill. While Gossett claimed he had a grievance against Winthrop, Johnson advised Miss Frayser that he neither had the time nor the inclination to do more in this case, adding that so far as Winthrop's connections with Mr. Gossett were concerned, "you are it." Johnson later relented somewhat, writing Gossett that a small portion of Smith-Lever money was set aside for the mill work and that it would be some time before these funds were available to supplement the work. Attempting to meet the college half way, Gossett expressed doubts about the whole project but agreed to continue community work for the next year in his mill villages--independently and upon his own responsibility.[116]

Forward-looking owners and others could see that by improving the mill people's health the program more than paid its way several times. One of Miss Mary Frayser's prime objectives was to banish pellagra from the mills. After fighting the intense heat of the Carolina summer's day, she was off for an evening visit to a mill village.

"Sometimes   I   wonder if   you   do   realize   how
absolutely I give myself to this work--morning,
noon, and night," she wrote Johnson.   "It is a
difficult field, but with the backing for which you
are now arranging, I am counting on doing a great
work--I know it can be done."[117]

        Turning to his most exciting duty of 1916's
summer--the NEA convention--Johnson wrote Tillman
again, saying that Judge Hughes (the Republican
candidate running against Wilson) would probably
address the group. Notifying Tillman that he would
be in Washington on June 29, he asked Tillman to
lead   a   delegation   to   visit   President   Wilson.
Suggesting   that   the   South's   teachers   would   be
deeply disappointed if the president did not come,
Johnson had figured out a way to get him. "Wilson,"
he told Tillman, "could go up to New York in the
afternoon, speak to the convention, and return the
next morning.   It would really be a little outing
for him."[118]

        Before Johnson left for Washington and New
York to attend to convention business, W. S.
Richardson of Rockefeller's office wrote Johnson
that he should stop by for a few minutes while in
New York. Johnson, overjoyed, replied immediately
to Richardson, saying, "I leave today and will stop
over in Washington tomorrow to confer with President Wilson and United States Commissioner, P. P.
Claxton, relative to our meeting [note he hoped to
see the president], and will arrive in New York
Friday morning at about eight o'clock. I shall be
glad to see you sometime that day when convenient to
you.   My meetings do not begin until Saturday
morning.   I shall stop at the Waldorf and will
phone you from there as to the hour of our convenience."[119]   The   meeting   with   Richardson   was
encouraging.

        Johnson kept the   Rockefeller organization
on the line during the next several months.   In
July, Johnson stressed the mill-village program to
Richardson, calling this betterment work "one of
the important phases of Winthrop's Extension Work

for the State outside our college campus." A few days later he wrote Miss Bertha Conde of the Y program and asked her to solicit Richardson's help for the Winthrop Y.[120]

Johnson urged many people to request Rockefeller's help for a new Y. In his mid-July letter to Richardson, Johnson told of Senator Nelson Aldrich, a Rockefeller in-law, who before his death had written on Winthrop's behalf. To architect Louis E. Jallade of New York, Johnson wrote, "we expect to hear something from it [money for the Y] within the next thirty days." Writing again to Richardson, Johnson reminded him that the Peabody Fund under Joseph H. Choate had given Winthrop $90,000 five years before.[121]

On August 14, 1916, Johnson delivered his presidential address on "The Rural Home and the Women on the Farms" before the NEA in New York. (It was later abstracted for School and Society.) In this speech he suggested that President Wilson set up a national committee to investigate and report on the condition of rural homes and their women. Johnson later became chairman of this committee and told Tillman that he wanted to see the president about appointing it.[122]

Three days later, Johnson was again pouring out his troubles to Tillman. This time he grieved because Winthrop had received 1,600 applicants for 950 spaces: "It grieves me to turn away any eligible girl applying for admission to Winthrop. I earnestly hope that the next Legislature will provide for more dormitory room here."[123]

Despite the handicap of space, Johnson began the 1916 fall term in high spirits. That September when he greeted the students, they knew that they were facing the country's leading educator. He had helped to guide Winthrop through twenty-two sessions at Rock Hill, and it was largely due to his efforts that more degrees in arts and sciences were conferred in 1916 on South Carolina women than on those from any other state in the Southeast: 125 from South Carolina compared to 108 from Virginia and 33 from Florida.[124]

Winthrop's 1916 opening exercises began the morning of September 21 at ten o'clock, with Johnson booming out the Twenty-third Psalm. This was followed by the singing of <u>All Hail</u>, a prayer, and then a solo. Johnson talked, then Mayor W. G. Stevens. There were slightly over a thousand students--including Senorita Philomena Plaza of Chile, who had been recommended by the U. S. Commissioner of Education. (She was one of four the University of Chile had sent to the United States to study methods, and she was to assist in teaching Spanish at Winthrop.) "Young Ladies," Johnson began,

> we are glad to have you with us this morning for another year of work. We extend to you a cordial welcome. Many of you here this morning are away from home for the first time and feel keenly, no doubt, the separations from your loved ones. But remember nothing worth doing is done without trial and self-sacrifice. In a little while you will smile at the forlorn feeling which some of you now have. . . .
>
> We want you to feel at home and be happy in your work here and whatever we can do to make you happy we shall gladly do.
>
> I have heard nothing about Winthrop girls which gratified me more than the statement made by a lady at the dinner table of a mountain resort hotel one summer. She said that Winthrop girls are always trying to help others rather than themselves. This is a high report set for you by the Winthrop girls who have gone before you, but I feel confident that you will maintain it.

Stressing religious friendship, speaking well of others, talking less, and listening more, Johnson advised, "Look for the best in others. There is no secret of success. It is just dig, dig, dig." Quoting from Edison, who defined genius as "98 percent hard work," he appealed to his audience to perform faithfully all of their college duties.[125] These few words were simple and most effective for young people who wanted an education and the better things of life.

As soon as the session was fully underway, Johnson again contacted Mr. Rockefeller's office, writing to Richardson that he had enrolled over 1,000 students and had turned away 634. Since Rockefeller was interested in missionary work, Johnson cited the young lady from Chile, Winthrop's daughters of missionaries in China and Japan, and her many graduates working as missionaries in South America, China, Japan, and Africa. He noted that those in Mexico had had to leave because of the war.[126]

Richardson was most assuring in his answer two days later--"It should not be long now before some response will be made in the interest of a religious building at Winthrop College."[127] Johnson's interest quickened. Five days later he contacted Richardson again: "The only hope of our girls to secure the Y within the next twenty years seems to be in Mr. Rockefeller's philanthropy. One of our greatest aims," he wrote, "is to bring a thoroughly good, practical education within the reach of the poor girls who have never had a chance for an education before."[128] With a visit from Miss Harriet Taylor of the Northern Board of the YWCA, chances further improved. Writing to Johnson on her return, she said that she had talked to Richardson and had told him of Winthrop's work. She felt Richardson would recommend "granting your request."[129] To expedite matters Johnson wrote Richardson that "we shall be glad to have you and Mr. Rockefeller pass upon the plans for the building before they are finally adopted."[130]

Concurrent with these developments leading toward a Y building, Johnson was preparing to dedicate the new gymnasium on the afternoon of November 17. As usual he wanted his aging patron, Senator Tillman, to say a few words. The senator, in declining health, begged off by saying,

It would be a genuine pleasure for me to attend . . . but it will not be possible for me to come. I am very busy here (at home in Trenton), and even if I could come, my health would not permit of my making an address.

This was a far cry from the days of Tillman's youth when he was regarded as one of the ablest speakers in America.[131]

Finally, the day before the gymnasium dedication, Johnson received his long-awaited news. Richardson wrote that Mr. John D. Rockefeller's Committee on Benevolence had learned of need there and "I beg therefore to state that toward such a building [a one-hundred-thousand-dollar Y] fund Mr. Rockefeller is willing to contribute $50,000."[132]

The Winthrop Board of Trustees met at Columbia on December 23, 1916, at Governor Richard L. Manning's office. There, President Johnson submitted a letter from W. S. Richardson, dated December 16, 1916, in which Rockefeller agreed to contribute $50,000 toward the Y, provided the "Board of Trustees would provide a site, take care of heating, lighting, and janitor service, as well as aid in financing the salary of the Secretary of the Y.W.C.A." The Board passed a resolution of thanks and agreed to support raising the $50,000 by June 1, 1918, when Rockefeller's pledge had to be met.[133]

For some time prior to this, Johnson had been attempting to marshal his forces in the Legislature, the Alumnae Association, and elsewhere to push the Legislature to appropriate funds for another dormitory. His campaign literature showed

all the signs of a public-relations professional.
Letters and fact sheets about the need for another
dormitory and the need to match Mr. Rockefeller's Y
pledge tied two separate but related programs
together and used one as a pressure to get the
other. First, Johnson sent a good letter to
Legislators and others in South Carolina who could
help. It read:

WINTHROP NORMAL AND INDUSTRIAL COLLEGE
D. B. Johnson, President
Rock Hill, South Carolina

December 13, 1915.

Hon.

Dear Sir:

We have been turning away young women
applying for admission to Winthrop College for some years because of a lack of
dormitory accommodations here. Over 600
of the students applying for admission
to the college last session could not be
admitted, and among that number were
some from every county.

At a recent meeting of our Board of
Trustees, attended by Governor Manning,
Senator Tillman, State Superintendent
of Education Swearingen, Hon. J. E.
Breazeale, Major W. L. Glaze, Hon.
D. W. McLaurin, Mr. W. J. Roddey, and
Dr. T. A. Crawford, the conclusion was
reached unanimously that the time had
come when dormitory accommodations
should be provided at Winthrop College
for those young women desiring to come
here and prepared to come and unable
to go elsewhere for the lack of means;
that it was not fair or right to
continue to turn South Carolina young
women away from the only institution
supported by the State for their
higher education and training,

281

especially when the State is providing for the higher education of 1,700 young men at a cost of over $2,500,000 for plant and over $400,000 a year for maintenance and for only 950 young women at a cost of $467,702 for plant and $135,000 a year for maintenance, including scholarships.

We confidently hope that the State will make provision for accommodating more of the young women eagerly seeking admission to Winthrop College, not only as an act of justice and fairness to the young women of the State, but especially in the interest of the common schools of the State. The women, mainly, are the teachers of the boys and girls of the State, and Winthrop College is the one institution maintained by the State to train women teachers, and the common schools are in great need of more good teachers.

I am sending you herewith some extracts from the Annual Report of our Board of Trustees to the Legislature bearing upon this matter. If there are any questions that you would like to ask relative to the matter, please do not hesitate to ask them, and I will do my best to answer them.

With kind regards,

J/E   Sincerely yours,[134]

   The attack's second prong was a personal letter from the Winthrop Alumnae Association President with a fact sheet showing the need for a dormitory and with a printed invitation "to get these facts in the hands of your Legislators and before the public." A fourth form was a pledge card inviting gifts to help match Mr. Rockefeller's pledge. These forms follow in order and in toto to better show Winthrop's effective system for attracting help from the Legislature and the alumnae:

<u>PERSONAL</u>
Rock Hill, S.C., December 11, 1916.

Dear

The State Colleges for men in South Carolina are represented by their graduates on the floor of the General Assembly; Winthrop College has no graduates there and the cause of higher education and professional training of women in the State at Winthrop is in the hands of the men who have the votes.

Winthrop College must depend for fairness and justice on the part of the State, upon the loyalty and devotion of her daughters, who have never failed their Alma Mater in time of need. Although they have no voice in the acts of the representatives of the people, yet they can present the facts about Winthrop and the cause of Woman's education in South Carolina to those representatives, and thus do much to secure fairness and justice for this cause.

I am enclosing a printed statement relating to the need of another dormitory at Winthrop College to accommodate some of the South Carolina girls now being turned away for lack of room.

Can you not do something to impress the members of the Legislature from your county with the facts given in this statement in order that they may give Winthrop College a fair and sympathetic hearing in the Legislature? Call on them or write a personal letter to them

and let them know that we want to give
Winthrop a fair showing in the interest
of the women, the schools, the children,
and the homes of South Carolina. Urge
them to appropriate for Winthrop what
the Board of Trustees are asking for.
The Trustees are asking for less this
year than last, notwithstanding the
fact that the enrollment is greater.

It would be well to go into the local
papers and bring to the attention of
the people the needs of Winthrop and
the unjust discrimination being practiced in educational appropriations
against the women. Make the point
that the State was slow in beginning
to do the right thing in this matter
of higher education for women, and
ought not now to hesitate to do full
justice.

You can render Winthrop College and the
cause of woman's education great
service in this way if you will, and I
hope you will not hesitate to do it.
Let me hear what progress you make.
Whatever you do should be done at once
before the Legislators leave home for
Columbia. I enclose postage for the
correspondence I have suggested. Will
you please forward me the replies of
your representatives to your letters,
and marked copies of your county papers
when any reference is made to the matter
in the columns? I am desirous of having
this information whether favorable or
unfavorable.

Every consideration of justice, fairness, and patriotism requires that
women shall be given an equal showing
with the men for life's duties, and we
feel that all that is necessary to

secure justice in this matter is a fair presentation of it to the people.

With kind regards,

Sincerely yours,

President, Alumnae Association of Winthrop College.[135]

The following fact sheet was skillfully designed to furnish clout for this drive. It read:

Help us to get these facts in the hands of your Legislators and before the public.

ANOTHER DORMITORY NEEDED AT WINTHROP

Not Only in the Interests of the Young
Women of South Carolina and in
Fairness to Them, but Also
in the Interest of the
State and the Schools
of the State.

Dormitory accommodations should be provided at Winthrop College without further delay for those young women desiring to go to Winthrop, and prepared to go, and, in many cases unable to go elsewhere for lack of means. It is not fair to continue to turn away South Carolina young women from the only institution supported by the State for the higher education and training, especially when the State is providing for the higher education of 1,700 young men at a cost of over $2,500,000 for plant and over $400,000 a year for maintenance, and for only 1,000 young women at a cost of $485,702 for plant (less than half the value of the plant, the other half having been secured from sources other than State appropriations), and $131,000 a year

285

for maintenance, including cost of scholarships and of all extension work for the public good; and when, further, the State has been maintaining this institution for the higher education of women for only a short time, comparatively, having maintained such institutions for the young men of the State for a great number of years.

There are as many young women as young men in the State, and they are as necessary to the welfare of the State, and they need, deserve, and long for a higher education as much as the young men. There are more young women in the State ready for college each year than young men, as the records of the graduating classes of the high schools will show. It is not fair, under these circumstances, to continue to appropriate a much less amount per capita for the education and training of the young women of the State than for that of the young men. At the last session of the Legislature this already great difference in the per capita appropriation for the higher education of the men and women was made still greater against the women. The Trustees of Winthrop asked the last Legislature to provide for an additional dormitory for the young women of the State so long and so much needed, but although it provided for additional buildings at other State institutions, including two dormitories at the State Colored College, it did not do so. Not only was this most pressing need, long-felt, not supplied, but Winthrop's appropriation of the previous year was reduced by $17,000, while the appropriations for all other institutions in the State, without exception, were increased and this in face of the fact that Winthrop was the one institution which showed a decided increase in attendance, going over 1,000. It is believed that this discrimination against Winthrop was brought about by an erroneous impression, made in some way, that Winthrop College had been receiving a greater appropriation per capita than other colleges, whereas as a matter of fact it had been receiving far less per capita. Winthrop rejoices that the other institutions received the appropriations they did but cannot see the justice of making it the one exception in a cut of appropriations and in a denial of vital needs for the accommodation of the young women of South Carolina.

There were 1,617 applicants for admission to Winthrop this session, and only 1,003 of these could be accommodated, and that number could be accommodated only by cutting up the frolic hall into rooms, by crowding three girls in a room in many cases, and by having some of the students board in town.

Many of those turned away were not prepared for College, but enough of them were prepared to make another dormitory necessary. Among those turned away were some from every county in the State. Another dormitory is needed at Winthrop to make the students there now comfortable, as well as to care for some of the South Carolina girls now being turned away for lack of accommodations and also for the teachers of the State who are attending our Summer School in ever increasing numbers.

The State should make provision for accommodating more of the young women seeking admission to Winthrop College, not only as an act of justice and fairness to them but especially in the interest of the common schools of the State. The women, mainly, are the teachers of the boys and girls of the State, and Winthrop College is the one institution maintained by the State to train women teachers, and the common schools of the State are in great need of more good teachers. Of 5,289 white teachers in the State, according to the report for 1916 of the State Superintendent of Education, 4,380 are women.

An appropriation to enlarge and strengthen Winthrop, where teachers for the common schools are trained, is an appropriation of the best kind for strengthening and improving the common schools. It is impossible to have good schools without good teachers. An editorial in the Columbia State of September 12, advocating another dormitory for Winthrop College, concluded with this strong statement: 'Common sense should tell the legislators that a new problem is to be solved in the educational affairs of the State and that the building of a dormitory at Winthrop is a measure of necessary preparation. We can't have teachers without training them and we shall probably never need them so greatly again as during the next ten years.'

If a business corporation could increase its output 25 percent, by increasing expenditure for plant 10 percent, and for maintenance only 5 percent, it would borrow the money, if need be, to make the enlargement. This is what is proposed for the State to do at Winthrop, with its business of educating her daughters and preparing teachers for the common schools. Another dormitory

288

to accommodate 250 to 300 students would meet the demands upon Winthrop for some years to come. The teaching of these additional students could be provided for at Winthrop at small cost by employing a comparatively few additional assistant teachers in departments already organized under the direction of heads already employed. The enrollment at Winthrop at any one time with 250 to 300 more students would not exceed 1,250 to 1,300 students, and many of our best Normal Schools have enrollments much greater than that number. The great State Normal at Normal, Illinois, has an enrollment of 3,703 students; that at Cedar Falls, Iowa, 3,000; and at Kirksville, Missouri, 1,801. Smith College, with a reputation for exclusiveness and high tuition charges, has an enrollment of 1,877. The 100 strongest institutions of learning in the United States have each more than one thousand students.

There is no danger of Winthrop College becoming too large, for the most satisfactory and effective work for years to come in our sparsely settled State of only 700,000 white people, men, women, and children, with nine other colleges for women besides Winthrop, and with high schools enough to prepare properly only 400 to 450 girls for their Freshman classes.

The policy now generally accepted as the wisest in the matter of higher institutions of learning is that of concentration upon a few to make them strong and worthy of fullest confidence and support. There are too many so-called colleges in the South for the good of the colleges and of the cause of education. Consolidation and concentration

and consequent enlargement is the order
of the day, even in the rural school
problem. The experience of the country
pretty generally goes to prove that a
large, strong school can offer more
advantages to students than a small weak
one.

The teachers of the Summer School at
Winthrop College last summer unanimously
adopted the following resolution:

We are impressed by the excellent
opportunities offered by Winthrop College, in the regular work to the young
women of South Carolina, and have
learned with regret that many have been
denied each year, for a number of years,
admission to the one institution established and supported by the State, for
the higher education, the professional
training, and the preparation for life's
duties of the young women of the State.
We hope that the Legislature will
provide accommodations so that no
deserving South Carolina young woman,
business-woman, community worker, or
home-maker, will be denied the opportunity offered by the State at its one
State College for women.

There were about nine hundred in
attendance at this Summer School and
every part of the State was represented
in the student body.

The Alumnae Association of Winthrop
College at the regular meeting last June
adopted the following resolutions:

WHEREAS: Many South Carolina young
women have been denied each year, for
a number of years, admission to Winthrop
Normal and Industrial College, the one
institution established and supported

290

by the State for the higher education, the professional training and the preparation for life's duties of the young women of the state, over 600 have been refused admission in 1916, and

WHEREAS: The graduates and old students of an institution are the best judges of the value of the educational opportunities which it offers and of the great work which it is doing and the great work which it might do for the welfare of the State if properly equipped to do it.

THEREFORE, be it Resolved, 1st: That we, the Alumnae Association of Winthrop College, representing over 6,000 Winthrop Daughters, express our earnest and heartfelt desire and hope that the Legislature at its next session will provide another dormitory at Winthrop College in order that no deserving South Carolina young woman, prepared for and desiring to enter upon college work, to prepare herself for the duties of life, or for better service to our beloved State, as teacher, business woman, community worker, or homemaker, will be denied the advantages offered by the State, at its one State College for Women.

2nd: That a copy of this resolution be sent to the newspapers of the State and to the members of the Legislature.

The County Superintendents of Education of South Carolina in conference assembled at Winthrop College last summer adopted the following resolution:

We heartily commend the great work that is being done at this institution for the betterment of the teaching forces

of our Southern States and trust that it
will continue to grow in usefulness and
in power.

It is interesting to note in connection
with the failure of our Legislature to
provide for another dormitory at Winthrop
College what other States did for their
normal schools this past year. North
Carolina increased the appropriation for
maintenance of its normal schools and
gave its institution similar to Winthrop
$500,000 for permanent improvements.
Tennessee gave each of its normal schools
$150,000 for permanent improvements.
Georgia gave a magnificent new auditorium
and a modern new dormitory to the Normal
School at Athens. Florida gave its
State Normal School at Tallahassee
$100,000 for permanent improvements.
Arkansas gave its State Normal School
$100,000 for permanent improvements.
Great appropriations for State Normal
Schools by other States could be given
if space permitted. None of the Southern
States mentioned is better able than
South Carolina to adequately support its
normal schools, and no one of the normal
schools of these States has done a
greater work for its State than Winthrop
has done for South Carolina, and yet
South Carolina failed to make any provision last year for the enlargement of
Winthrop to meet an urgent demand for
enlargement, while these other States
made handsome appropriations for the
enlargement of session of the Legislature was inadvertent and that such
discrimination will be corrected at
the next session of the Legislature.
No one can successfully deny the fact
that Winthrop has a warm place in the
hearts of the people, and it is confidently believed that if the will of the
people is registered in the halls of

legislature that the young women of South Carolina will get the consideration due them in educational matters on account of their needs, numbers, and their value to the welfare of the commonwealth.

The State was never so financially able to make adequate provision for its educational institutions as it will be this coming year.

The Chairman of the State Council of Defense, after careful survey and estimate, says there will be from three to five times as much surplus wealth in South Carolina this coming year as at any time in its history. Business has not been as prosperous in years.

President Woodrow Wilson urges as a patriotic duty that in these distracting war-times the educational institutions similar to Winthrop shall not only be maintained in full strength but shall be strengthened if possible. The United States Commissioner of Education, P. P. Claxton, makes the same earnest call on the people. The greatest defense of any nation is the education of its people. It is not economy but the worst kind of wastefulness to limit the opportunity of the people for education and training for the duties of life. . . .

Gallant France in its time of stress and trial has not reduced its appropriations for education.

England with the terrible drain of the war upon its resources of men and money, appropriated twenty million more for education for the coming year than ever before.

Winthrop has made a large place for itself in the life of our people and is destined to occupy a much greater place.

The devotion, the unselfish spirit and public service of Winthrop daughters, and the confidence of the people secured through their good and unselfish work, has made possible the present Winthrop and makes possible the still greater Winthrop of the future--greater in achievement and in opportunity and ability to serve the dearest and best interests of the State--the children, the women, the homes, and the schools of the State.[136]

Johnson relied very heavily on his information to win the Legislature, the alumnae, and South Carolina's citizens. He waited anxiously for the Legislature to provide for the dormitory and for Winthrop's faithful to return pledge cards to help match Mr. Rockefeller's $50,000:

_____   _____191_

In consideration of the offer of FIFTY THOUSAND DOLLARS by Mr. John D. Rockefeller to Winthrop Normal and Industrial College of South Carolina, to erect a building for the students of that institution to be used by the Y.W.C.A. and other student organizations to foster and strenghthen the social and religious life of the College, upon condition that another Fifty Thousand Dollars be raised for such building, and in consideration of subscriptions by others to the same fund, for value received, I do hereby promise to pay to the Winthrop Normal and Industrial College of South Carolina by or before April 15, 1919 $_____of the amount required to meet said condition, provided the

294

whole amount needed to Meet Mr.
Rockefeller's condition shall be
subscribed.

Name_____

Address_____

(All drafts and checks should be made
payable to Winthrop Normal and Industrial College.)[137]

Winthrop made considerable progress during
1916-1917. The enrollment exceeded that of any
preceding session--reaching 1,023 for the three
regular terms and 2,235 in all departments including
the summer term. By this time the Home Demonstration Extension Department had organized all 45
counties; enrollment in Home Demonstration Clubs
had reached 20,730, of whom 13,048 were rural-based
women. In food production and conservation (as a
result of war) Winthrop was touching 250,000 additional women and girls. And Mr. F. P. Lund of
Denmark was brought to South Carolina to show the
people how to dry vegetables.[138]

Among the especially interesting activities
of the past sessions were the student body's trip to
the state fair, the dedication of the new gymnasium,
the reception for county home-demonstration agents,
a special short course for mill-village agents, the
receptions for oratorical contests and student
government groups, and the National Conference on
Rural Education and Rural Life held at Winthrop.[139]

Two days prior to the Legislature's annual
visit (on January 26, 1917), a special edition of
the Winthrop Weekly News detailed what Winthrop
students and teachers were accomplishing all over
the world. Cited for special emphasis were former
Winthrop professors teaching in China, India, New
York, Arizona, and elsewhere. In addition three
held important jobs at Alabama College, two at
Agnes Scott, one at Berry (Georgia), one at Texas
Woman's College, one at Converse, and one

295

(Christine South, head of Domestic Science) at
Greensboro Normal. Winthrop ladies held important
jobs in Extension and experiment-station work, and
Professor L. A. Nivens of the Winthrop Agriculture
Department was editing Southern Farming Magazine.
As Tillman said of this, "you know a tree by the
fruit it produces."[140]

The Legislature's visit proved most
pleasant. Governor Manning sent Lieutenant-
Governor Bethea to head the delegation. Some 350
visitors arrived, including wives, daughters, and
friends of the legislators. They detrained at
the concrete landing on back campus, where they
were met by Johnson, the marshals, and the Winthrop
Chapter of the United Daughters of the Confederacy
(UDC) who together escorted their guests to the
Main Building and then to the auditorium. There,
each student sat under the placard naming her home
county and her representatives joined the group.
Johnson gave the welcome, suggesting campus points
of interest that the legislators might wish to
visit. Much interest centered on the new gymnasium
just completed at a cost of $77,000, with the state
contributing $30,000. The Physical Training
Department held demonstrations of their work until
the warning bell for dinner brought the Assembly
to the dining hall and a sumptuous meal--which no
doubt was appreciated more by the students than by
the guests. Tables set for 1,500 were served by
the UDC girls. There were an orchestra and
after-dessert toasts to South Carolina, education,
the General Assembly, and--as always--Robert E.
Lee. In late afternoon the visitors returned to
Columbia, their praise of Johnson and Winthrop
rekindled.[141]

Johnson remained in a quandary over his
attempts to meet the Rockefeller pledge and to
persuade the Legislature to appropriate dormitory
money. A Winthrop Board member sent a letter of
introduction to James B. Duke in New York, praising
Johnson and his far-reaching work and adding:

296

Your business interests are great in South Carolina and are becoming greater, and we hope and believe that you wish to become as much identified with South Carolina as with North Carolina. Winthrop was one of the three organizations which made the first contract with the Southern Power Company for power. You could not do anything that would more endear you to the people of the State than to make a handsome donation to this institution where the daughters of the State are being educated and trained in practical ways for the duties of life.

Stressing the governor, Senator Tillman, and the state leadership's deep interest in Winthrop's success, Johnson had invited Duke to visit Winthrop when the Legislature came. Apparently meeting little success with Duke, Johnson asked the Rockefeller office for an extension in meeting the pledge.[142] Then, in early January, Johnson reported to the Southern Y leader, Dr. Weatherford in Nashville, that the girls had raised $6,600 of the $50,000, leaving $43,400 that must be begged in the North. He asked Weatherford for an introduction to Cleveland H. Dodge. To Elihu Root of the Carnegie Corporation, Johnson wrote and asked for $10,000, sending letters of recommendation from many prominent officials. Emphasizing Carnegie's early interest in Winthrop, Johnson added, "I feel confident that he would be glad to have you help us out in this emergency to the extent of $10,000."[143] And continuing to play the waiting game with the New York architects who wanted the Y contract, Johnson observed that "we would like now to make provisions in this building for some bedrooms to accommodate visiting alumnae."[144]

Johnson also hoped to parlay the fiftieth-anniversary celebration of George Peabody's gift to the South into a new device for attracting Northern money. The celebration, held on February 7, 1917, featured history professor Dr. Walmsley's

297

talk about the life and services of Peabody and
Johnson's speech on Peabody and the founding of
Winthrop. This renewed angling for Yankee money
reeled in little. In time, Johnson realized that
his salvation lay with the Palmetto State Legislature.[145]

A few days later Winthrop offered the
"Second Short Course in Social Service for Com-
munity Agents in Mill Villages in South Carolina"
--February 19-March 3, 1917--with Miss Mary E.
Frayser, State Agent and Mill Community Worker
from Winthrop, as its leader. The faculty featured
both local and out-of-state experts; the program
was timely and impressive. Fifteen of Winthrop's
best specialists joined with W. W. Long, State
Agent and Clemson's Director of Extension Work.
Outside experts included the Associate Secretary,
Social Service, of the Russell Sage Foundation,
New York; the General Secretary of the National
Consumers, New York; personnel from the Board of
Charities and Corrections, Columbia; leaders from
the Children's Bureau of Labor Statistics; and
others from related fields. All meetings occupied
the Winthrop Society Hall on the Main Building's
second floor.[146] The agenda included sessions on
dietetics; the chemistry of foods and digestion;
feeblemindedness (long associated with certain
deficiencies in mill families); delinquency,
heredity, eugenics; and (on the more practical
side) the three r's (meaning, how to deal with
mill owners and operatives, characteristics of
children, and factory conditions); mill club work
and what the social worker should do; games, story-
telling; family budgets; agriculture; textiles;
and other related programs.[147]

As an additional incentive for the Legislature to provide more space for Winthrop, Johnson
invited the South Carolina Medical Association to
study campus health. The committee praised the new
gymnasium and its contributions to student health.
They also cited favorably Dr. Belle J. Allen, an
ex-medical missionary running the infirmary. However, the medical team reported the dairy barn was

not sanitary in the modern sense and that funds were much needed there. They further found that the average freshman had gained seven pounds in two months at school; this suggested to the investigators that proper food was being served. Johnson also published a typical menu in his official report to show that the girls were getting what Tillman called a "balanced ration." Of special significance was the medical committee's statement that overcrowding made a new dormitory "an urgent necessity."[148]

The 1916-1917 session inaugurated changes in the course of study, which had remained fairly constant for many years. Since thirty-eight states had two-year Normal courses to prepare teachers for elementary and rural schools, Winthrop put in a similar course. The State Board of Education granted a five-year license, subject to renewal upon conditions fixed by the Board of Education, to those who completed the work. Other innovations included the Red Cross training program and a new Department of Rural Education. An additional department for geography and physiography strengthened the Normal offerings.[149]

In February and June, 1917. the college lost two of its most effective trustees, Major W. L. Glaze and Dr. Edward S. Joynes. Glaze, a refined Christian gentleman, was stricken on February 18. Life Trustee Joynes of the University died at an advanced age on June 19, 1917. Winthrop's Board took proper note of these two gentlemen's passings. The resolution occasioned by Dr. Joynes' death reads in part:

. . . Our Board has lost the services of one of its most distinguished and helpful members. His name and labors are inseparably connected with the inception and founding of Winthrop College, throughout his long service as a member of the Board of Trustees beginning with the organization of the College and closing with his life,

his constant interest and wise counsel
played no small part in the growth and
development of the institution. Before
his death he gave to the College a
valuable lot upon which an Edward S.
Joynes Memorial Building will be
erected, and in his will he left to the
College a part of his library. . . .[150]

Joynes's value to Winthrop is indisputable.
Mr. Tillman always paid considerable attention to
Joynes's counsel. Proof is found in almost every
letter where Joynes is mentioned. For example, on
one of Tillman's last trips to Winthrop, when he
headed the delegation from Washington to Congressman
Finley's funeral in York, Tillman wrote:

My trip to Winthrop yesterday has
aroused my interest in the College
and its history. . . . I want to get
all of these (historical and factual)
pamphlets together and have them
bound in one volume and I would be
obliged if you would send me anything
that related to the history and
development of the College that you
have on hand especially anything that
Dr. Joynes wrote or said.[151]

Regardless of affairs of state, Johnson
remained preoccupied with building and money, especially the Rockefeller pledge. Writing again to
Elihu Root, Johnson informed him that President
Cleveland was very much interested in Winthrop College during his life-time, as also were Chief
Justice Fuller and other good leaders of the
country. In his concluding words he begged Root to
ask Carnegie to donate $10,000 and suggested that
Root commend the Y project to others.[152]

Shortly thereafter, Johnson appealed to Dr.
Russell H. Conwell of the Baptist Temple in
Philadelphia, who was famous for his Acres of
Diamonds lectures that made him perhaps the richest
Baptist minister in the world. Conwell attempted

to contact people for Johnson. According to his secretary, Conwell thought of Winthrop "as one of the finest institutions in America."[153]

Johnson's next letter for help went to Judge Ben Lindsey of Denver. It asked the judge for an introductory letter to Miss Morgan, daughter of J. P. The judge advised Johnson to write her directly and to call her attention to her father's friendship with Winthrop.[154]

Later Johnson wrote Dr. John Finley, Superintendent of Public Instruction in New York, asking Finley to introduce him to members of the Carnegie Foundation. Finley helped. Johnson thanked him, writing that the Carnegie Corporation was considering giving $10,000 of the $50,000 required to meet Mr. Rockefeller's condition.[155]

Johnson now asked the state for $15,000 to help Winthrop secure the $85,000--$50,000 of which represented Rockefeller money. It was a slow process trying to raise matching funds even though the senior class helped by raising $187 toward the student building--an excellent effort on their part.[156]

By mid-1917 Johnson had his private financial campaign rolling again. Every county contained a chairwoman attempting to collect funds. Suanee Daly of Seneca wrote a typical letter, saying her county (Oconee) was "one of the smallest and poorest counties in the state, but we are going to keep working and do our best."[157] Meanwhile on the national scene, Johnson had canvassed a long list of prominent families and businesses in the more affluent parts of the country. Included were the Tafts of Ohio, the Albert Johnsons of Philadelphia, R. A. Alger of Detroit, Mrs. Cyrus McCormick of Illinois, the Cadillac Corporation, Baldwin Locomotive Company, and Proctor and Gamble. Vital to this phase of the campaign was a form letter sent under the signature of Reverend Alex Martin, pastor of the Oakland Presbyterian Church, who stated the facts about the challenge and about Winthrop's great work.[158]

301

In the midst of his campaign, Johnson fell victim to an anonymous letter-writing campaign--the origin and purpose of which has never been explained. As usual, he appealed to Tillman to put a post-office inspector on the case. "A word from you," he wrote, "to the right office in Washington would help." Tillman was glad to help, although he did not consider this problem very serious. He assured Johnson "if you don't hear anything in a few days, I will stir them up again."[159]

Of all the correspondence in the Johnson file on begging and giving, one letter stands out as most unique. Thinking Johnson a man of considerable political influence, a Bishopville entrepreneur sought his assistance in interesting the Council of National Defense in purchasing a large body of timbered land that this gentleman wanted to sell. If Johnson would agree to help with the deal, the businessman would enter an advance agreement to supply Johnson with the $50,000 he so earnestly sought. Johnson pondered the proposition. About three weeks later, he advised the man that Thomas G. McLeod of the Winthrop Board was a fellow Lee Countian, and "I would be glad for you to confer with him concerning a handsome donation to Winthrop College for our Y.W.C.A. building."[160]

Early in 1917, according to Johnson, the Agriculture Department decided against any and all special mill-village projects--such as those Miss Frayser had done so well. Writing to Miss Frayser, Johnson said that Washington had decided any work bettering the mill communities would have to be incidental to regular home-demonstration work conducted under the Smith-Lever Act. Therefore, he planned to terminate Miss Frayser's work on July 1. Johnson regretted this because, in his words, "You have done a fine piece of work for the mill communities which I am sure will be lasting and will lead in some way to still better things in the future."[161]

In approximately a week, the Auburn Extension Service was asking about Miss Frayser. Johnson wrote them that Miss Frayser "is a strong, able, well-balanced woman." On June 11, Johnson gave her a "To Whom It May Concern" testimonial, calling her "a good speaker and a good writer. She can get up a fine bulletin and her services are being terminated because of a ruling of the U.S. Department of Agriculture that the Smith-Lever Fund can no longer be used for mill village betterment work, except under regular agriculture and Home Economics programs."[162]

Immediately some of Miss Mary's unexpected friends rallied to her cause. President Emslie Nicholson of Excelsior Knitting Mills in Union, South Carolina, wrote Johnson: "It was with sincere regret that I heard that Miss Mary Frayser's connection with the Mill Community work would cease after July 1st. I really think it is a catastrophe." He wondered if the mills (which a few years before had wanted to reject her) could not each contribute $100 to maintain her work. Johnson replied to Nicholson that the USDA had decided to undertake the mill-community work as a regular part of the county home-demonstration work.[163]

Johnson was now determined to help. Writing to Dr. A. C. True of Agriculture and P. P. Claxton of the Office of Education, he told of Miss Mary's good qualities and of how the mills wanted her. He hoped that they could find her a place in the extension field somewhere in the South. O. B. Martin of Agriculture agreed to try to find her a job "as a home economics specialist in some of the regular organizations."[164]

After leaving her first love (Winthrop), Miss Mary joined the Children's Bureau of the United States Department of Labor in Washington. Over the next few years, she worked in the Department of Agriculture in Richmond as Field Director of the Virginia Tuberculosis Association, as Instructor of Sociology at Winthrop, Director of Community Activities in cotton-mill villages of Rock Hill and

303

Chester, and finally in 1926 as a home economist in the Clemson-Winthrop program.[165]

All the while, Johnson continued his push for money. He asked Bishop W. A. Guerry of Sewanee for letters of introduction to prominent New Englanders. In September, 1917, Johnson asked the Rockefeller Foundation to raise Rockefeller's pledge to $80,000 or $85,000 because "war conditions have made it impossible to raise money and I can't go to the Legislature for a religious building." The truth of the matter was that within a few weeks Johnson asked the Legislature for $15,000 to secure $85,000 in conditional gifts that included the original Rockefeller pledge.[166]

Attempting to draw Carnegie and Rockefeller into a pledge-bidding war, Johnson sent several important letters to the Carnegie Foundation from outstanding Americans like ex-President Taft, Joseph H. Choate, Edward A. Alderman of Virginia, Charles Erdman of Princeton, Charles Eliot of Harvard, and Governor Manning. These gentlemen were most complimentary of Johnson and Winthrop; their letters were designed to bring in the money needed to secure Rockefeller's pledge. Johnson told Carnegie about the canning and poultry clubs fostered by Rockefeller through Dr. Knapp. Adding information about the mill-village projects, Smith-Lever activity, and Hetty Browne's work, he suggested that "the welfare of the state is more dependent upon the right training of the women than of the men, because the woman makes the home, the very foundation of civilization and bears and rears the children, the citizens of tomorrow." Approximately two months later, Johnson's efforts paid off. Johnson wrote Dr. Charles W. Eliot at Cambridge: "I am sure that you will be interested in knowing that the Carnegie Corporation voted Winthrop College the $10,000 asked for by us. Your letter had much to do, I feel sure, in securing this favorable action, and I thank you most heartily for it." Similar thanks went to James Bertram, Secretary of the Carnegie Corporation at 576 Fifth Avenue, New York.[167]

Fresh from his success with Carnegie, Johnson wrote Rockefeller's man (Richardson) that he had raised $12,000 in a month despite the fact the girls had raised $5,100 for the war fund. Moreover, the Domestic Arts Department was sewing 1,050 garments for the soldiers, the student Red Cross was fashioning trench candles, and the Manual Training Department was making Kipling scrap-books and diaries. Richardson told his boss Murphy of this. Murphy wrote Johnson two days later that "It is this splendid spirit of self-sacrifice on the part of the women of America, with its stimulus to the men, which is going to assure us and our allies the winning of the war."[168]

Johnson's continued success caused considerable speculation that he was trying for a university. And now that Winthrop was more firmly established, Johnson was catering to the more affluent students from the towns and cities. Anything transpiring in South Carolina at this time was bound to cross the desk of Senator Tillman in Washington. Now that Joynes was dead, Tillman turned constantly to his nephew, Superintendent John Swearingen, to give him the real story on what was happening at Winthrop. Attempting to explain his position in answer to Tillman, Johnson assured the senator:

Winthrop is not trying to be a university. It is trying to prepare our young women to be teachers, business women, and homemakers. . . . I wish for our Winthrop girls that they may hold up their heads in the presence of the graduates of any college and render a service to the community and state--if not superior to that rendered by any other graduate. We are trying to train our girls for the duties of life--for service and I believe we can claim that we are succeeding in a measure at least without fear of successful contradiction.[169]

Not being satisfied with these generalities from Johnson, Tillman wrote to his nephew:

My Dear John:

Please check about charges that country girls, equally prepared with those of city in accredited schools can't get into Winthrop.

You know more about modern methods in school work than I do, and I hope you will see to it, if you can, that the claims of the country girls will be looked after and cared for. We cannot afford to make Winthrop unpopular with the very people for whom it was founded by dealing unfairly or unjustly with them or even appearing to do so.

Love to Mary,[170]

For several weeks before and after this exchange, Swearingen had been trying to discuss implementation of teacher training under the Smith-Hughes Act. As always, both Johnson and Swearingen held separate views on most matters educational. As usual, when Tillman sent any complaint to Johnson, Johnson attended to it promptly. In addition he came forward with answers to any of Swearingen's letters that he had neglected to answer. So it is not surprising that during the Christmas holidays of 1917, a tardy Johnson answered Swearingen's letters:

I am returning at once the copy of the South Carolina plan for vocational education which you so kindly sent me for inspection. I have made a copy of the plan covering the teaching of Home Economics and the training of teachers of that subject.

If Winthrop could be of any service to your office in having the plan for vocational education printed as a bulletin, crediting you and the State Board of Education with the authorship, it would be glad to render it.[171]

Before considering Johnson's Yuletide "generosity," Swearingen had looked over Winthrop's latest activity for his "Dear Uncle Bennie." This was his evaluation of Johnson's Winthrop:

In the mad race to collect an army of students at Winthrop, the college authorities have established some undesirable precedents. Under one of its precedents the faculty admits students on partial examination. This practice, in my opinion, is undesirable both from the viewpoint of the college and from the viewpoint of the public schools. But, Winthrop must have girls and they are dragged in by every sort of net that can be thrown out [citing the old argument over the prep department]. . . . Winthrop College acknowledges no control or suggestions from the outside. The faculty [under Johnson] makes its own list of accredited schools without reference to any other educational agency. The State Superintendent has begged the Board to correct this abuse. Winthrop has done good work and is doing good work, but the institution needs to learn that it was built to serve South Carolina. Winthrop should require a definite standard of entrance and should enforce this.

Love to you and Aunt Sallie.[172]

Tillman sent a copy of his recent correspondence to Johnson, and he admonished his nephew thus:

We can't afford either to let Johnson injure the College by his looseness, on

307

the one hand, or allow him to ruin the College by seeming injustice to the poor girls who are unable to attend high school. There is something wrong somewhere, and I hope you won't cease in your efforts to have it corrected. I will help you all I can.[173]

Johnson came back fast. He denied to Tillman Swearingen's inferences. He contended that the college had to be selective, that external examinations were held only in a few subjects because of the time factor, and that the students took the rest at Winthrop. He reminded Tillman that his nephew and Joynes had led the fight to abolish the preparatory department years ago. However, since this was a feeder for the college, authorities now needed a degree of latitude in their operations. Johnson denied all the discrimination charges brought by Mrs. Wilson and others. Again, he fell back on the Board in defending the requirements and admissions policy, and he piously pled that he was doing his duty "without fear or favor."[174]

While Tillman labored at his Senate post as Chairman of the Naval Committee and attempted to keep young Franklin Roosevelt (the Assistant Secretary of Navy) and countless others "in line and doing their duty for the country," Johnson pressed forward in quest of a money tree and Superintendent Swearingen worked with educational problems affecting the public schools and state colleges.[175] Tillman for the first time in his long Winthrop association was so busy and handicapped that he was unable to attend Board meetings. Concurrently in early 1918, Johnson had renewed his flirtations with the architects in New York and Chicago who wanted to design the long-overdue Y. Johnson had also broadened the base of his begging to include two whose operations had greatly benefited from the war: A. F. DuPont of Wilmington (the powder king) and Fairfax Harrison (the highly respected head of the Southern Railroad). The cagey Harrison, in answer to Johnson's self-invitation to see him, wrote, "If you will

308

indicate on what I can be of service to you, I will ask one of our people to see you about it." [176]

Addressing a new appeal to Grenville L. Winthrop of New York, Johnson wrote, "We believe with President Woodrow Wilson that it is a patriotic duty not to allow educational institutions--like Winthrop Normal and Industrial College--to suffer on account of War." Similar appeals were sent to J. B. Duke of Southern Power, to Edward S. Harkness of New York, to W. Gordon McCabe of Charleston, Dr. W. Gill Wylie and others. And in order still to keep the national Y secretary and the architects interested, Johnson suggested to Miss Conde that she suggest to the architects some alterations of their much-worked-over plans. "May I suggest," he wrote, "that for so large a college as Winthrop, a larger restroom and toilet arrangements are needed. . . . There ought also to be some toilet arrangements for men guests." [177]

Of all the answers to this latest flurry of writing, the one from Samuel Fisher (representing Harkness) is most noteworthy. Harkness expressed interest. However, since his family was then interested in building a large dormitory at Yale, the work on which had been suspended because of war conditions, Harkness was reluctant to enter any more such projects running counter to the government's desires. [178]

After all this letter writing and a confusing correspondence on pledges and contributions, no one seemed to know exactly what money was in hand and who had given what. Ira B. Dunlap of the National Union Bank of Rock Hill certified on May 15, 1918, to this information:

```
J.D. Rockefeller (pledge)------$50,000
Carnegie Corporation (pledge)-- 10,000
Individual Subscriptions------- 5,580
Cash-------------------------- 34,016
Liberty Loan Bonds------------ 300
War Savings Stamps------------ 104
                              $100,000
```

A casual observer might ask certain questions, the most logical being where was the $15,000 that the state had appropriated in 1918 to help bind the contingent pledges of Rockefeller and others? One must remember that Johnson was both president and treasurer of Winthrop and that few to this time had ever questioned Johnson's honesty or dedication to what he considered to be Winthrop's best interest.[179]

As the money trickled in over the next two years, Johnson pushed on while Swearingen clung to him, attempting to deal with the ordinary mechanics of the state's educational system. Swearingen told Johnson, "write me definitely concerning your suggestion that Winthrop College would be glad to lend to the State Vocational Board a worker to aid in the introduction of vocational classes in home economics." Time was of utmost importance so these things had to be dealt with at the earliest convenience. Once Swearingen had pinned him down, about all Johnson could say was that he had been "hunting far and near for thoroughly equipped women to take charge of the teacher-training course" at Winthrop. According to Swearingen, at least two teachers should be employed under Smith-Hughes; and since the Legislature had made no appropriations for vocational education, they looked for funding from the federal government. Johnson designated Miss Edna F. Coith, head of the Domestic Science Department, to help organize vocational classes in the schools. In late April, 1918, Swearingen advised Johnson that Winthrop must do the Smith-Hughes work in South Carolina if it was to be done at all. Johnson welcomed the chance for additional service to South Carolina. Swearingen thanked him by extending his congratulations "on the fine class just leaving the college. The schools need the service and help of this fine bunch of graduates."[180]

While Winthrop was preparing to assume her duties under Smith-Hughes, one must not assume that she was in any fashion slighting her vital work under the Smith-Lever Extension Act. In fact, Winthrop was making more organized personal

310

contacts with her extension activities than with anything that she was doing, except teacher training. A cursory look at this program for 1917-1918 reveals that twenty-four teachers and professional workers were traveling the state giving lectures, demonstrations, and professional advice to teachers' associations, superintendents' meetings, defense councils, chambers of commerce, community meetings, UDC groups, and rural and mill-school improvement associations. One of the most sought-after lecturers in this work, Mrs. Hetty S. Browne, made twenty-six appearances including the National Educational Association Superintendents Meeting in Atlantic City and the Chautauqua of the South in Macon, Georgia. Another lecturer, J. Thompson Brown, was especially effective with county teachers' associations. Miss Coith was most popular with groups interested in Smith-Hughes. W. D. Magginis of the Training School, Roy Z. Thomas, J. E. Wamsley, J. W. Thomson of the college, and other faculty and staff divided their specialties among various state groups.[181]

With the South Carolina political picture becoming more fluid in 1917-1918, Johnson--like many others who looked to Tillman for guidance and protection--grew concerned as to whether Tillman's health would allow him to run for reelection.[182] Following the announcement that Tillman would run again, Johnson wrote that he "was glad to see that you will stand for reelection." And as usual Johnson sent his yearly version of his "a tree is judged by its fruits" Winthrop analysis, which the aging senator never seemed to tire of.[183] The report nearly always inspired Tillman's reminisces about how he had fought for Winthrop. "You know," he wrote:

> the Bourbons in charge of the University at Columbia never will forgive me simply because they cannot get over the estab-lishment of Winthrop and Clemson. Over their opposition and against all the influence they could bring to bear, especially Clemson; and jealousy alone

311

of Winthrop, I think, is at the bottom
of any antagonism now. . . . Since I am
in the race for reelection, I don't
want to be beaten in my old age and
want to ask some Winthrop girls to
organize all the Winthrop girls throughout the state to get busy in my
interest. Am inclined to select Miss
Kate Wofford as the organizer and would
appreciate your giving me her present
address.[184]

In his long post-script to the letter he advised
Johnson to shun politics that summer "except in a
very quiet way. I would not for the world injure
Winthrop with the Legislature. . . ." But Tillman
left no doubt that he wanted Clemson and Winthrop
students to lend a helping hand: "It is entirely
legitimate for these young men and women to fight
my battles now that I am too old and weak to do it
on the stump; as I fought their battles a long time
ago in establishing the schools in which they have
been educated."[185]

While the politicians jockeyed for position in the summer primary, Johnson pushed his
collections for the Y and his program at Winthrop.
In late May, he attempted to collect some substantial local pledges which were not mentioned as
such in his previous accounting. A. B. Murry of
Charleston sent $1,000; W. G. McCabe, Jr., forwarded
$100; the Grahams of Greenville's Camperdown Mills
gave Johnson $500. There were others including the
merchant Julius Friedheim of Rock Hill.[186]

In early May, Tillman's declining health
induced the Wilson administration to back Congressman Lever for the Senate. B. R. Tillman, Jr., wrote
Johnson that he was anxious to reach former Winthrop
students to ask them to re-elect his father.
Johnson gladly set one of his stenographers to
work compiling a list for his old mentor's
campaign. He agreed with young Tillman that
Clemson men and Winthrop ladies "ought to rally to
your Father's standard and work for him." Johnson
volunteered his own services in a quiet fashion.[187]

The senatorial campaign heated up. N. B. Dial was running, and Cole Blease launched his own reform candidacy by suggesting that ninety percent of the people were opposed to war. Tillman denounced Blease as "a characterless traitor to God and Country." Blease described Tillman as "having betrayed reform as Judas did to his master."[188]

Tillman's death on July 3, 1918, was in a sense a great tragedy for Winthrop, but Tillman had already set her course on sound ground. His demise resulted in N. B. Dial's election to the Senate. Blease and his candidate for governor, John G. Richards, both went down in defeat.[189] Tillman's body returned home on a dignitary-laden train. Dr. Johnson got on at Rock Hill, the town to and from which Tillman had come and gone for twenty years while superintending Winthrop's development. A large assemblage paid their final respects to Tillman as he was laid to rest in the red soil of Edgefield County. As the orator proclaimed "Weep Carolina! This is the day for tears," many reflected on this man who, like Jefferson, wanted to be remembered for his role in education. The press was very generous in his memory. In the words of The Evening Herald of Rock Hill:

> Undoubtedly, several decades will pass before either the friends or enemies of the late Senator B. R. Tillman will be able to do exact justice to his record as a man in public life--such is always the case with strong, rugged characters who win firm friends and devoted followers and make bitter and unrelenting enemies.[190]

In President Johnson's report rounding out the 1917-1918 school year, he devoted considerable attention to Senator Tillman's passing. The most significant sentence in this two-page account read: "Winthrop College and its work will always be inseparably linked with Senator Tillman's name." The resolutions passed by the Board of Trustees

313

stated in part "That in the death of Senator Tillman, Winthrop College has lost one of her founders and a devoted advocate."[191]

This report was like a valedictory of Tillman's influence at Winthrop. It stressed Winthrop's raised entrance requirements, the new dormitory being built, the continued spread of home-demonstration work in South Carolina, and the increased enrollment. With 1,418 applicants for the freshman class and a total enrollment of 1,029, Winthrop could be more selective. With nearly thirty-eight percent of the students coming from farms, this training's impact on rural areas was most important. Winthrop still advertised her choice relationship with the University of Chile, under which four outstanding students from Chile came to study in the United States. The third Chilean to attend Winthrop--Senorita Mercedes Manosalva, a doctor of philosophy--came to Winthrop while two of that year's remaining three scholars enrolled at Harvard and Columbia University.[192]

Continuing his report, Johnson stressed the war's impact on education and the resultant adjustments that made college more meaningful and practical. To this end, Winthrop added more courses for training teachers under Smith-Hughes. In response to a request from the National Council on Education, Winthrop had made plans for a pre-nursing course. The college had worked with the United States Food Administration to upgrade the home-economics classes and had added more post-graduate work. The summer enrollment had jumped to 1,086--225 above the previous year. Everything at Winthrop was expanding--including the main campus, which had increased from thirty to sixty acres "without calling on the Legislature for a dollar with which to pay for" these additions.[193]

The enthusiastic Johnson concluded with a long list of needs that would have embarrassed even a most generous Santa Claus. Included in the list were these items: renovation of the Training School

314

and Main Building, enlargement of the library, a new propagation house similar to the one at Clemson, more money to employ assistant teachers, a new dairy barn (as recommended by the State Board of Health), stock for the farm, a building for the Joynes lot, houses for professors, a tower clock, and other minor things too numerous to mention. Did Johnson expect to receive all this? His answer was found at the end of the list: "We are not asking the Legislature at this time to provide all of these needs." With an overall state appropriation of $196,325.86 for 1917-1918, which was $60,000 more than the university had received, Johnson was still well provided for.[194] Now that Tillman was gone, would Johnson continue as the most-favored president of South Carolina's state-sponsored institutions? The next few years would tell the story.

Winthrop uniforms set students on an equal footing, making the
wealthy girl indistinguishable from the scholarship recipient.
Modelled here are the fall and winter fatigue and dress styles.

Above left. Edward S. Joynes--teacher, traveller, and outstanding scholar--collaborated with "Pitchfork" Ben Tillman and
D. B. Johnson in founding Winthrop College.

Above right. A consummate politician, the one-armed David B.
Johnson helped found Winthrop and served as president until his
death in 1928.

Below. Students gather in the art hall during the 1890s. Although President Johnson stressed normal (teacher) education,
a large percentage of Winthrop girls enrolled in industrial
education to study art, dressmaking, agriculture, telegraphy,
and other subjects.

Above. Modern equipment and facilities like the propagation house enhanced industrial studies.

Below left. Benjamin Ryan Tillman, a Winthrop founder and proponent of industrial studies, harnessed his tremendous popular support to provide generous funding for female education.

Below right. As Superintendent of Education, John Swearingen successfully exerted pressure to improve the Winthrop curriculum and to keep D. B. Johnson on course.

Right. As Winthrop's second president, James P. Kinard helped the college survive the Depression by retrenching.

Below. The spring outfit (left) and cooking school suit (right, _circa_ 1900) were only two of many designated styles worn on campus before uniforms were abandoned during the 1950s.

Above. In the 1940s the
student bank was popular,
as these students' smiles
attest.

Above. Shelton Phelps, a
professional educator who
became Winthrop's third
president, began his ca-
reer teaching in a rural
school.

Below. "Fort Bancroft" cadets invaded the Blue Line in
1943. Many Winthrop girls graduated early to join the
war effort.

Right. Although
accepting the
Winthrop presiden-
cy would lower his
living standard,
Henry Sims took
the job and fought
for over a decade
to win Winthrop's
reinstatement into
the professional
associations.

Below. The Daisy
Chain, an annual
event, embellished
commencement ac-
tivities.

Right. By 1958 the "Blue" Line to church boasted a rainbow of colors since Winthrop girls no longer wore uniforms.

Below. Winthrop's post-World-War-II emphasis on industrial education included a home-economics major.

Bottom. Dormitory matrons shared student joys and sorrows while maintaining order.

Above. Faculty, staff, and students relax in the popular
Canteen, located in Tillman Hall (Old Main).

Below. A budding Winthrop woman enjoys the Johnsonian during
Rat Season.

CHAPTER XII

INSTITUTIONALIZING D. B. JOHNSON

1918-1929

Schools and Colleges . . . are, always
have been, and always will be filled with
those who seek some advantage from spe-
cious adulation of those higher up. The
posed affection of those who may, by such
professions, gain something, is always to
be mistrusted. When, therefore, Winthrop
daughters have told me how they 'loved'
Dr. Johnson, I have not been impressed.
They did not know him well; and for that
reason it was idle to talk of 'love.' He
was not, indeed, a man who had many real
intimates. There was an apparent frankness about him, which was superficially
attractive. This, no doubt, was what
appealed to the girls, together with the
fact that they were pretty regularly
reminded that they were in a State College that he personally founded. The
administration did nothing to correct
this massive and pleasing piece of fiction. Governor Richardson and Tillman
were dead, together with most of the
others who had so much to do with the
establishment of Winthrop. Johnson
found himself solitarily enthroned. . . .
He was primarily, not an educator, but a
politician. This, the chief quality of
his character, has been overlooked by all
who have sketched his life.
                              Archibald Rutledge

During the late summer of 1918, Johnson was
pushing hard to insure that the next school year
would be the best ever. Taking a full-page advertisement in the State paper in late August, he
publicised Winthrop with renewed vigor. Quoting
one of the day's most popular slogans, "The school

316

room is the second line of defense," Johnson advised his readers that "it is, therefore, a patriotic duty to prepare yourselves to teach." The following four-year courses were advertised: Normal, Normal course with music, Normal kindergarten, rural-life course, and general literary leading to the Bachelor of Arts. The Bachelor of Science degree (four years) was awarded for the home-demonstration course, the home-economics course, and the Normal course with art. The B.S. was also given for the four-year music course that included piano, voice, or pipe organ. Shorter courses listed were a two-year Normal, a one-year teachers' course, and special one-year courses in commercial subjects, bookkeeping, dressmaking, and textiles. This advertisement seemed to offer something interesting to almost any young lady in South Carolina.[1]

The school year of 1918-1919 was somewhat different from any year prior because of the influenza epidemic, several teachers' resignations for war and Red Cross work, and the Alumnae Association's formalizing with Miss Leila A. Russell (formerly of the Extension force) as alumnae secretary. For the first time Johnson took official note that certain students were failing at Winthrop. This news he counterbalanced by announcing that many others were distinguished in their grades.[2]

The Extension work's success proved most gratifying to Johnson and to the state. Every county benefited. With Miss Edith L. Parrott in charge, Extension workers combed the state. As a result of their guidance, over 11,500,000 containers of fruits and vegetables were saved. The poultry clubs had made $250,000. Nearly 16,000,000 pounds of butter and 11,000 pounds of cottage cheese had been produced under demonstration methods. With their bulletins on What Shall I Eat?, Food for Mother and Baby, and other topics the Extension service brought salutary changes in the dietary habits of South Carolinians.[3]

317

Winthrop continued to excel in training teachers. Her numbers were always Johnson's best talking point with Legislature. She set up an official appointment bureau which served over 1,000 calls for college to kindergarten teachers. There were over 400 students in the Training School and kindergarten, 1,114 in the summer school, and 2,616 at Winthrop--with all counties except Jasper represented. [4]

Wartime inflation had frustrated many schools' plans. Under the circumstances Johnson found it impossible to build a 250- to 300-person dormitory with the $100,000 he had asked the Legislature to appropriate. By this session, he had built a part of the dormitory to accommodate 155 students and had laid the foundation for the remainder. He needed, according to his calculations, $87,120 to complete the job. [5]

With regard to the YWCA or student building, Johnson hit an unexpected snag. In October he, Governor Manning, and interim Senator Christie Benet visited fellow South Carolinian Bernard Baruch of the War Industries Board to seek permission to proceed with building. The state and county councils had approved this non-essential student building, but Mr. Baruch felt that Winthrop ought not to proceed with it: as he saw it, the United States needed every ounce of iron and steel and every bit of labor to win the war. This meant that Johnson had to win an extension on the Rockefeller pledge, which was finally extended to September 17, 1920. [6]

Determined to secure the building one way or another, Johnson took bids on the student building in the summer, 1918. They ran so high that the plans had to be modified, so the construction was changed to ordinary construction, not fireproof construction as originally planned. The final low was $95,667 by the Southern Ferro Concrete Company of Atlanta, Georgia. Johnson appealed again to Rockefeller's aide for extra funds to fireproof the building. Although the aide could not promise

318

any extra money, he agreed that the building should be fireproofed.[7]

With building more on his mind than education, Johnson proposed new additions at the barn and at the Training School. And fearing that he might lose Dr. Joynes's gift, Johnson reported to the Legislature that "it has been impossible for our women teachers to secure satisfactory boarding places in the city. If we could build a teacherage or teachers' dormitory," he reasoned, "we could secure and hold the best women teachers for Winthrop." He estimated that $60,000 would erect such a building on Joynes's lot.[8]

For the first time in his career, Johnson appeared to realize that good teachers were not expendable. He always proposed to seek the best teachers, but Winthrop had never furnished homes for its teachers as Carolina and Clemson had and Winthrop's salaries had been lower, with women department heads receiving only $1,500. With inflation and numerous opportunities, recent graduates sometimes earned more than long-established professors. Since the NEA had tackled "the Teachers' Problem," Johnson had begun publicizing their information in South Carolina. The NEA reported that attendance in teacher-training institutions had fallen alarmingly. To ensure the country enough trained teachers, they stated, salaries and working conditions and training should be improved. After South Carolina raised high-school teachers' salaries by forty-four percent, Johnson asked the Legislature to provide Winthrop professors with housing or to supplement their salaries with a yearly house rent of $360.[9]

During the 1918-1919 session, inflation suggested to Johnson the true value of Winthrop's plant, which was conservatively valued at slightly over $2,000,000. Of this amount, South Carolina had paid only $487,301.17 from the college's inception to June 30, 1919. Johnson had begged much of the money for the physical plant. By presenting these figures in this way, he could compare the

$500,000 in bonds that North Carolina had just voted for improving their Greensboro-based girls' college. Thus Johnson could whine that North Carolina was spending more in a single year for Greensboro than South Carolina had spent "on the permanent improvements" for Winthrop College during its thirty-three years. With this statement, Johnson was very close to the truth. However, Winthrop did not become a state college until 1891 and thus had been eligible for state improvements only 28 years, not 33.[10]

Johnson was pleading for more money to push Winthrop forward. He justified his requests, and rightly so, on the fact that the state had reaped great dividends from a very small amount of money spent on permanent improvements. This information was welcomed by the alumnae, who were just then beginning to exert pressure for Winthrop. Winthrop received $245,841.63 from the Legislature in 1919, a very substantial amount compared with the $136,800 appropriated for Carolina.[11]

Regardless of what was happening, Johnson seemed part of the action. Many think of him as dogmatic and unbending--this was especially true of his early career. Now, however, Johnson had become much more pragmatic. For example, the attack on American education during World War I tended to downgrade languages and literary subjects, and Johnson more or less identified himself with the attack. His position was that Winthrop had been established for practical training and higher education of girls and that "it has always been our endeavor to arrange the courses of study for Winthrop in accordance with the act creating it." In this statement he seemed to forget his attempts to circumvent Tillman and others. And now with Tillman, Joynes, and others gone, Johnson attempted to identify himself closely with whatever was considered a success, regardless of his earlier positions.[12]

As always, his drive and his ability to associate himself and Winthrop with that which was

320

timely and good kept Johnson ahead of the crowd. During the early fall, 1918, in "a win the war campaign," young Winthrop ladies were publicized as "unafraid of any kind of work," for they labored in neighboring fields three hours every Saturday afternoon, picking cotton. Apparently this was something more than a gimmick because they picked over five-hundred pounds on one such occasion and turned over the $5 they had earned to the Red Cross.[13]

The Y girls at Winthrop received much favorable publicity through Kate Boyd, their war-time secretary, who was helping the boys in France. Winthrop belonged to the United War Work Campaign. Her Manual Training Department made and sent beautiful scrapbooks and volumes of good literature to Mr. W. R. Carr, General Director of the Red Cross work at Fair Forest, South Carolina, for a soldiers' convalescent home at Camp Wadsworth.[14]

On the less glamorous side, Winthrop and South Carolina still wrestled with properly imple-menting the Smith-Hughes program. Johnson (like most Americans then and later) felt that if federal money were available, he should get it, spend it, be happy, then get some more. Designating Profes-sors Coith, Dodd, Welsh, R. Thomas, and Walmsley to help with this program, Johnson specified that a part of their salaries (usually one-fourth) should come directly from Smith-Hughes. Concur-rently, they would teach regular classes at Winthrop. This was not satisfactory according to Director C. A. Prosser of the Federal Vocational Education Program, who wrote Swearingen: "I think the thing that needs to be pointed out clearly to Mr. Johnson is the fact that the Federal Funds for teacher-training are intended to prepare teachers of vocational agriculture and not for the purpose of giving some instruction in agriculture to those who are to teach agriculture in connection with other school work." According to Prosser, grants were not intended for the latter, and Swearingen was not prone to agree with anything that was in the slightest contrary to what he understood the letter and spirit of the law to be. [15]

Despite problems, the 1918-1919 Winthrop session proved most productive. This year stressed quality classwork. Certain students were designated honorary scholars--although no money value was attached. "It was simply," as Johnson explained it, "a reward made on the basis of college grades, deportment, and merit," and recipients' names were printed in the catalogue. On another front, Winthrop--active in the United States School Garden Army--was cited by the regional director for its work. All the while, Winthrop strove to decrease illiteracy, which Patterson Wardlaw's special commission had branded as "the heaviest burden the people of South Carolina have to carry." Winthrop girls readily accepted the commission's challenge, "Could you not find time to teach at least one person to read?"[16]

During this school term, the cloud of influenza hovered over the educational process. Mr. Swearingen influenced the State Board of Education to adopt the view that if schools were closed by influenza quarantines, the teachers would be paid and all future holidays (except Christmas) would be omitted. Winthrop Training School was put under a quarantine, which was lifted on November 11. Since the college had lost no time to influenza and since the students had observed their own quarantine for several weeks, the Board (no doubt at Johnson's urging) decided to lengthen the Christmas holidays from December 20 to January 6. In turn, many mothers asked what had happened to "Debe" Johnson. When they were at Winthrop, they had received only one day at Christmas. [17]

Johnson no longer needed to concern himself about trivial things like holidays, for Winthrop's service was now touching every nook and corner of South Carolina. More and more Winthrop was bene-fiting the people supporting her. With her two-fold offerings of college-oriented programs and Extension work, Winthrop sought to render "full

322

and effective service to the dearest interests of the State--the homes, the schools, the women, and children." To ensure that everyone understood this, Winthrop published an elaborate <u>Extension Bulletin</u> in 1918 to supplement the college catalogue.[18]

The program advertised in the <u>Bulletin</u> encompassed two divisions. First was the Home Demonstration Division maintained co-operatively by Winthrop College, Clemson College, and the United States Department of Agriculture under the provisions of the Smith-Lever Act. Winthrop served as headquarters for this far-reaching program, which included home economics, sewing, canning, Home Betterment Club, and girls' work. Over 11,000 families profited from this in a single year.[19] The Extension Program conducted under the second division included lectures; professional talks; demonstrations; entertainments; instruction study-centers around the state; correspondence courses; judging at school, community and county fairs; and rural schools' improvement work. This division also published the <u>Winthrop Weekly News</u> and the <u>Winthrop</u> <u>Bulletins</u>. A closer look at these programs reveals a detailed picture of how Winthrop was saturating the state with her off-campus educational programs.[20]

Winthrop's state-wide lecture series was most impressive. Heading the speakers' list was D. B. Johnson, who offered twenty-one lectures, including "Education of Woman," "Southern Ideals-- Why They Should be Maintained in the Education of Women," "The Rural Home and the Farm Woman," "Training of Teachers in Library Methods," "The Efficient Country School" and others.[21] Professor J. W. Thomson of Pedagogy and Ethics listed among his specialities "The Life of John Calvin," "Stonewall Jackson," "King David," "What and How to Read," "Christian Citizenship," and "How to Get Results From a Garden." He was available for six-teen lectures.[22] Dean James P. Kinard--Professor of Psychology and expert on the history of education--included two special lectures, "There

Was a Man" and "How We Got Our English Bible."[23]
Professor J. Thompson Brown of the English Department specialized in speeches on "The Short Story," "Shakespeare," "New England," and "Southern Writers."[24]   Also included in the long list of offerings were speeches by Coker of Astronomy; Roy Thomas of Chemistry and Geology; Walmsley of History and Political Science; J. F. Thomason of Rural Life Education; T. C. Haddon of Agriculture; Henry Guelich of Music, who illustrated with the phonograph; Magginis of the Training School; Misses Meyer and Coith of Domestic Art and Science; Mrs. Beth Wetherbee of Physical Training; Miss Nettie Wysor of Latin; Miss Leila Russell on "Problems Under the Extension Service"; Miss Hughes of Office Work; Miss Marion Satterwhite of Art; and Miss Minnie Macfeat, Director of the Kindergarten, on the "Montessori Method and Other Techniques."[25]

In addition to this varied program, there were approximately two-hundred "Professional Talks" available to the public on a great variety of worthwhile topics. Forty talks in agriculture alone were available to South Carolina's communities, including vegetable gardens, swine production, clean milk, tick eradication, and others related to better agricultural practices.[26]   Thirty-six talks on education encouraged a continuing program for school improvements designed to aid the teachers, parents, and other interested persons.[27]   Sixteen other areas were covered in the professional-talk series. These reached thousands in South Carolina, many of whom had no other contact with the formal educational process.[28]

Attempting to provide something for everyone, faculty members conducted off-campus classes all over the state, usually on Friday afternoons and evenings and on Saturdays. The college attempted to organize a class wherever ten or more students indicated an interest. These classes met twice a month (or more often) for a period of five months; college credit was given to those meeting the assignments and requirements. Classes in fifteen different academic areas were offered, ranging from agriculture, art, and astronomy to household science, Latin, library methods, and manual training. Many South Carolinians had their first and only taste of college work through the study-center programs.[29]

For those who were unable to enroll at the study centers, Winthrop provided correspondence courses, individualized training under regular faculty supervision that was designed especially for those wishing to prepare at home for the county teachers' examination. Such programs enriched their participants' scholarship, and the homemakers found the courses a real complement to daily living. For most courses, the fee was $5. Nearly every Winthrop department offered four or more classes in each of their specialties for South Carolinians unable to enroll in a formal classroom situation.[30] It was no wonder so many women could count themselves alumnae of Winthrop College. And too, the rural School Improvement Association (the organized musical-entertainment clubs and programs that Winthrop sent out) and especially the Winthrop Weekly News (mailed free to all who requested it) and the official teaching and service bulletins all brought Winthrop in one way or another into the great majority of the homes in the state.[31]

Regardless of the caliber and volume of Winthrop's fine functions, staff work and problems demanded time. With the demise of Tillman and Trustee T. A. Crawford, Johnson leaned more heavily on W. J. Roddey, a longtime employee of the Equitable Insurance Company and president of the Victoria Cotton Mill in Rock Hill as well as a banker and a highly respected public-spirited citizen. He was constantly helping Winthrop with scholarships and favors of all kinds, and he was instrumental in having the president's home restored and equipped with steam heat in 1916-1917.[32]

In educational administration and in tailoring Winthrop's programs to meet state and federal laws, John Swearingen was always involved. Winthrop's fine new service programs during World War I and her highly commended teachers and workers drew such great attention that several were offered more money to work in neighboring states. Miss Coith had served as State Supervisor of Vocational Home Economics; when she wrote Swearingen that she was leaving, he asked Johnson why. Johnson explained that she had resigned for more money--a twenty-five-percent raise to do similar work in North Carolina. Attempting to shift some of the blame for losing her, Johnson asked that the State Department help pay this salary so that they might become more competitive. For the first time in his career, Johnson wanted to issue contracts early in March in order to hold the teachers.[33] Johnson also complained that the Smith-Hughes money for training teachers in home economics was always slow in coming. In 1918 Swearingen had approved four teachers under Smith-Hughes for Winthrop, with half of their salaries coming from the state and the remainder from Washington. The careful Swearingen always checked all programs and complied with governmental red tape before releasing federal money to Johnson. "I do not wish," he explained, "to be criticized by these autocratic and bureaucratic authorities from Washington." Whenever the government money finally reached Winthrop, Johnson would reply that it was "most welcomed."[34]

Late in 1918, many states including South Carolina looked toward Washington when Senator Hoke Smith of Georgia introduced a bill providing an annual $100,000,000 appropriation to be matched by the states in an all-out effort to aid education, which most vitally concerned the national welfare. Included were programs to remove illiteracy, to Americanize foreigners, to improve rural schools and teacher preparation, and to promote health education and recreation. To qualify for the much-sought-after funds, states had to require a minimum twenty-four weeks of school annually in each district, unless they had compulsory school attendance and taught basic languages. South Carolina would qualify. As the bill was then constituted, those seeking federal money had already figured out that South Carolina would get $1,754,642.45 when and if the law passed.[35]

The war period furnished other stimuli to Winthrop's educational programs and aspirations. Her summer schools concentrated more on helping with the war effort. The war emergency courses, for example, occupied most slots in the home-economics summer offerings in 1918. These courses prepared the students to teach Red Cross and sewing classes and to serve as canteen workers. More intensive courses in dietetics (for graduate students) trained those who anticipated working in war-time hospitals as dieticians. In addition, certain specialized courses readied students to enter hospitals as vocational-therapy assistants.[36]

New techniques, some born of war-time necessity, saturated short courses held at Winthrop for the county home-demonstration agents, who trained under the supervision of state agent Miss Edith Parrott and her able assistants, Miss Christine South, Mrs. Dora Dee Walker, Miss Laura Bailey, and Miss Elizabeth Forney. These were excellent programs, implementing the latest on nutrition and the best techniques for canning, pickling, preserving, butter-making, cottage-cheese-making, poultry-raising, and gardening.[37]

The faculty participating in the war effort had a stimulating effect on the Winthrop girl. Their return visits to campus always provided occasions for celebration. When Professor O. G. Brim walked unannounced into chapel and sat down in his former front-row seat, the entire student body applauded. Following the morning prayer, the senior class arose and gave fifteen rahs for the professor, and Dr. Johnson invited him to relate his experiences in France and Italy. His message was so well received that the students tried "again and again to encore him."[38]

Many war-time speakers came to Winthrop, but no one was more warmly received than Miss Anna

Ryan of Smith College, Massachusetts. Speaking to mass meetings in Rock Hill's First Presbyterian Church and Winthrop's chapel on behalf of the Red Cross, she complimented local efforts. In her address, she stated that she had visited most women's colleges in the East and several in the West and that after examining Winthrop's equipment and course of study, she believed Winthrop College would compare favorably with any she had seen. She concluded that "no Southern girl need go North or anywhere else to be educated as long as Winthrop College was here and was conducted as it is now."[39]

Not everyone was this complimentary of Winthrop. Stories of Johnson's successful fund-raising in the North and his midas touch with the Legislature alienated certain jealous and suspicious people. In spite of critical rumblings, his financial reports to the Legislature always dispelled any doubts. He was happy to inform the Legislature that the college books were now being audited by the American Audit Company, the State Bank Examiner, and the Winthrop Board's Finance Committee. To circumvent criticism of surpluses, he explained that left-over state appropriations were drawn from the state treasury as needed and that they would be accounted for in the next annual report. Assuring the world that he was obeying the law to its letter, he noted that the comptroller-general held vouchers for every bill paid from the state's Winthrop appropriation and that the superintendent of education (Mr. Swearingen) had on file an itemized account of Winthrop's expenditures from both state and current funds.[40]

All ordinary expenses were listed in Johnson's report. Salaries for the last fiscal year totalled $119,225; only $700 was listed for the trustees' and the president's expenses. Winthrop's total ordinary expenses for the fiscal year from July 1, 1918, to July 1, 1919, were $201,689.21. For the first time, Johnson elaborated upon "special expenses" and he listed an appropriation of $404,108.21 required to meet these expenses.[41]

328

The large items listed under "Special Expenses" included the following. Monies for a new dormitory approved by the 1917 Legislature amounted to $30,000 in 1918, $35,000 in 1919, and $35,000 in 1920. Completion of another new 300-student dormitory was delayed by the cost spiral; this was to receive a $40,000 appropriation in 1920 and $47,120 in 1921. For the teachers' dormitory (housing women teachers unable to secure proper places to board) and for holding valuable land Trustee Joynes had willed to the college (upon condition that such a building be erected upon it), $60,000 was projected: $20,000 in 1920 and $40,000 in 1921. Among the remaining items in the "Special Expenses" category, one finds $12,000 for an agricultural and horticultural propagation house; $12,400 for the usual state scholarships; $10,000 to acquire more land; $20,359 to increase teachers' salaries as recommended by the state's Budget Commission; $3,500 to erect four silos at the dairy barns; and $10,000 additional contribution towards completing the Y building. [42]

The activities during the later half of the 1918-1919 session were many and varied. Winthrop implemented new courses for training teachers in home economics under the Smith-Hughes Vocational Law, which included the training for welfare and home-demonstration workers. The old mill-village work that Winthrop had pioneered was not very glamorous compared to the new government programs, and Winthrop's emphasis now shifted to the latter. [43]

There were other new and exciting educational works which Winthrop jumped to cooperate with. The Director of Military Aeronautics requested that President Johnson secure the cooperation of the college community, Rock Hillians, and other South Carolinians in a national effort to assemble the personal stories of men who had served overseas with the Air Corps. Johnson, whose career shows a very scant knowledge of state and national history, was glad to oblige if for no other reason than publicity for Winthrop. [44]

Another request of some national signifi-
cance came to Johnson the same day, February 14,
1919. Ex-President William Howard Taft, who had
visited at Winthrop and in Rock Hill, was now heading the national effort of the League to Enforce the
Peace. He asked President Johnson to name five
South Carolinians as delegates to the Southern
Congress for a League of Nations to be held in
Atlanta on February 28 and March 1, 1919. Johnson
was happy to appoint Dr. S. H. Edmunds of Sumter,
W. J. Roddey of Rock Hill, Colonel Leroy Springs of
Lancaster, Superintendent Frank Evans of Spartan-
burg, and Thomas F. McDow of York.[45]

One should not assume that Johnson and
Winthrop followed or imitated every new idea and
gimmick surfacing in the educational world. Consider the publicity given to a pronouncement by
President Nicholas Murray Butler of Columbia
University. Butler contended that the popular
method of compelling students to write constantly on
assorted topics had damaged the teaching of written
English. He felt that to learn to write, students
should read good English and write only occasionally. Johnson, who was not a brilliant writer
himself, stressed hard work and good teaching
(methods contrary to Butler's) as pillars to
educational success.[46]

Johnson, as always, did his best when
begging for Winthrop or pushing a new program.
With his schoolman's zeal for eradicating illiteracy, Johnson emphasized Winthrop Training School
and the summer schools for teachers. For many
years he helped the state's Education Department
run its official summer school. In March, 1919,
he announced elaborate plans for the summer's June
17 to July 25 session. A number of nationally
prominent specialists joined Winthrop's best.
C. Alphonso Smith was coming from the Naval
Academy, Professors W. C. Bayley and W. H.
Kilpatrick from Columbia University, Dr. Edwin
Mims from Vanderbilt, and President Charles McKenny
from the State Normal of Ypsilanti, Michigan. A
month later Johnson announced one of the most

330

significant additions, courses for teachers of illiterates conducted by Miss Wil Lou Gray. Rock Hill proved fertile ground for such work: the local paper reported there were 509 persons in the community who could neither read nor write--224 whites above ten years and 285 Negroes.

In his educational drive, Johnson leaned toward a statement ascribed to John Locke, "The attainment of a sound mind in a sound body is the end of education."[47] But the erudite Archibald Rutledge proclaimed in his analysis of Johnson, "as long as I live I shall love Winthrop and I am going to try to get people to understand who made it." The keynote of Johnson's life as Rutledge saw it was "service to others, in his chosen work. He knew this, and the way to help himself was by seeming to help others." Becoming more exact, he charged that "Johnson was never a teacher. He was more aptly described as a diplomat and administrator receiving a salary equal to (or more than) that of the governor of his state, doing what he loved to do. . . . Year by year his power, his prestige, his prerequisites and his salary increased. . . . Few men have had so many desired things come their way." Few would have expressed these thoughts during the heyday of Johnson's power. He had become so much to so many. To the Rock Hillians, especially, he represented a God-sent opportunity to educate many of their children at an infinitesimal expense to themselves.[48]

Certain Rock Hillians wanted their children to attend the Training School because of its superior staff and opportunities. D. B. Johnson was amenable to almost any scheme to increase enrollment figures. Superintendent R. C. Burt of Rock Hill was eager to enroll enough students in the Training School so that Rock Hill would no longer need an additional school in its Oakland area. After some legal barriers had been removed, the Winthrop Board's proposal to make Winthrop Training School an integral part of the Rock Hill public-school system was accepted by the public-school trustees. The arrangement would be on a

331

year-to-year basis, with Winthrop providing a free
public school for not less than 350 and not more
than 500 Rock Hill school children. The program was
to begin with the 1920-1921 session. Winthrop
provided rooms, equipment, faculty, and staff; this
represented a sizeable windfall to the town's
taxpayers. The Training School's educational value
to the children of Rock Hill is hard to estimate,
but a goodly number of them attained considerable
success--due in part, no doubt, to the fine start
which the school gave to them.[49]

In the spring, 1919, the Legislature
accorded Winthrop--and related colleges and
schools--a special statutory protection against
those who would disturb its operation. It was
enacted

> that it shall be unlawful for any
> person willfully or unnecessarily to
> interfere with or to disturb in any way
> or in any place the students or
> teachers of any school or college in
> this state attended by women or girls
> or to loiter about such school or
> college premises, or to act in an
> obnoxious manner thereon, or for any
> person to enter upon any such school or
> college premises, or to loiter around
> the premises, except on business, with-
> out the permission of the principal or
> president in charge.

The Legislature deemed such persons guilty of a mis-
demeanor and subject to fine or imprisonment.[50]

Just before the end of the session, artists
from New York busily engaged in shooting activities
at Winthrop for a 2,000-foot film. This "life at
Winthrop" scenario was eventually shown in every
moving picture theater of the state and "in hundreds
of theaters all over the United States."[51]

In early June, Winthrop graduated another
outstanding class with a special sermon before the

332

YWCA. Among the honored guests was Miss Leona Thomasson, president of the 1912 class, who had just returned from a six-year sojourn in China. The baccalaureate was given by the Reverend W. W. Moore, President of the Union Theological Seminary in Richmond. The graduating address came from the United States Commissioner of Education and an old friend of Winthrop, P. P. Claxton. Their attendance indicates Winthrop had no trouble attracting the leaders in most fields. Meanwhile, Johnson was becoming even more untouchable.[52]

By this time in Winthrop's development, Johnson could boast with his ringing voice that the sun never set on Winthrop. The girls were scattered around the world, with a goodly number remaining at home and making a great contribution to education in their respective counties and cities. To maintain better contact with them, Johnson selected Miss Leila A. Russell of the Extension service as Alumnae Secretary. Part of her work (aside from the Extension service) was to follow up on the graduates and to organize Winthrop chapters around the state. With 6,000 Winthrop daughters, the task was heavy, but Miss Russell remained a hard and faithful worker for her alma mater. Eventually the alumnae became one of Winthrop's most potent and driving forces.[53]

The academic acumen instilled into Winthrop graduates and the recognition accorded them by a proud state tended to spur the girls to pioneer in many areas. Whatever the Winthrop girl did--and it was almost always worthwhile--she received abundant publicity and praise, which tended to push her towards greater achievement. Her goals and work almost always were equated to the common good. People seemed to expect the Winthrop girls to lead. For example, in the summer of 1919, a South Carolina Society of Washington was organized at the Wardman-Park Inn with Presidents Johnson and Riggs of Clemson in attendance. Senator Ed Smith was elected president; Senator Dial, vice-president. This movement had originated among Winthrop alumnae

and other South Carolinians there.   Taking a
prominent part in the movement were Misses Harriet
Godfrey, Pearl Clark, and Isla Willoughby. Winthrop
made sure that her daughters' group was properly
advertised in the local press and in the college's
Weekly News.[54]

With 1,113 students and a well-rounded
course offering the 1919 summer school was
characterized as the "most successful and best
attended summer school ever held in South Carolina."
Its students attended the Rock Hill premiere of the
newly released picture "Winthrop Day By Day"; all
agreed that it was excellent.   It provided another
means whereby the college could advertise.[55]

The fall opening on September 19, 1919,
welcomed 1,150 students. With the world-war effort
winding down and life returning to a more normal
pace, Winthrop still moved forward, not content to
rest on her laurels.   When the American Council of
Education's 1919 college list was published (ninety-
three colleges strong), Winthrop appeared along with
Harvard, Columbia, Yale and many other prestigious
colleges.   Winthrop was the only South Carolina
college listed.[56]

The new session, typically brought few
faculty changes.   However, Miss Edith Lander
Parrott, the capable State Home Demonstration Agent,
tendered her resignation in October and was succeeded by Miss Christine South. The study program with
Chile continued with Miss Merceded de la Barra
arriving to take up her work.   Shortly thereafter,
the college boasted that Mrs. Emmeline Pankhurst,
the well-known suffragette leader from London, had
delivered a well-received message.[57]

As usual, Winthrop had readied some new
bulletins for the fall, 1919.   These service
bulletins included Teaching of Hygiene in the Public
Schools, Handbook of the Results of the Rock Hill
Alfalfa Growers Association, Directions and Formulas
for Spraying, Rural Life Bulletins, Elementary Agri-

334

culture and School Gardening at Winthrop, A Physical Training Manual, The School Garden of the South, A Library Bulletin, An Extension Bulletin, Infant Feeding, The Rural Home and the Woman on the Farm, The Last Meeting of the Confederate Cabinet, and A Series on World War for Clubs.[58]

As Winthrop continued to improve in many respects, Johnson became more concerned with the students' physical well-being. Gone were the molasses-sopping days, when Johnson pinched every penny for physical improvements. Now he published Winthrop's dining fare at least once a year through-out the state. Just before the Christmas holiday, Johnson quoted Miss Helen E. Osborne, Head of Home Economics and Chairman of the Committee on Winthrop College Fare. She reported on typical meals served during the last month: for breakfast--chipped beef, grits, biscuits and sliced bread, butter, syrup, tea, coffee, and milk; for dinner--roast chicken and giblet sauce, candied yams, green peas, mixed sweet pickles, sliced bread, maple ice cream, and vanilla cakes; for supper--veal loaf, horse-radish, hot rolls, sliced bread, butter preserves, syrup, tea, fig newtons, and milk. With the abundantly yielding farm, the Winthrop larder could supply excellent meals.[59]

Since the Alumnae Society's move to power, Johnson had begun to associate himself more with it. In the fall, 1919, he announced his plan to work through the association and the Winthrop Extension Department in organizing more alumnae chapters throughout the state. Writing to Mrs. Drake, the president of the association, he said, "I rejoice that you are the President of the Alumnae Association this year." A few weeks later, Johnson explained to Mrs. Drake that Miss Russell had been organizing chapters along with her Extension work and suggested that Mrs. Drake appoint Miss Russell her associate secretary until the next association meeting (in May), with the understanding

335

that Winthrop would pay her salary and travel expenses.[60]

Early in January, Johnson sounded his clarion call and sent out "loving greetings to all my six-thousand Winthrop Daughters," assuring them that he followed their activities "with pride . . . and gratitude for the great service you are rendering for the betterment of the schools and the homes of our State."[61] Continuing his pronouncement, he informed them that there was no reward for him "for what I may have been able to accomplish for the education and training of the young women of South Carolina comparable with that of hearing constantly from all sources and directions of the fine spirit of service shown by my Winthrop daughters on all occasions and in every place where their lot may be cast." Concluding with a benediction, he asked God to continue to bless them (the Winthrop daughters) "in their life and labors and what is of still greater moment may He still continue to bless others through them." Taking the occasion to single out some who served in foreign lands, he listed six Winthrop girls in Brazil: Margaret Douglas, Carolina Kilgore, Genevieve Marchant, Ethel Sanders Dawsey, Pauline White, and Alice Rivers. Eight Winthrop daughters were then serving in China: Janie and Florence Lide, Lora Clements, Bertha Smith, Leona Thomasson, Nellie Sprunt Little, Frances Stribling, and Alice Gregg. Others were in Japan, Mexico, and elsewhere. Of those daughters married and serving in the foreign field, Johnson mentioned Claudia Brown (Mrs. Henry Reaves in Soochow), Annie Barron (Mrs. James Hopper in Korea), Mary Belle Henderson (Mrs. Hope Lumpkin in Alaska), and Annie Laurie Maynard (Mrs. George Sadler in Africa).[62]

The great red scare of the early post-war period prompted an editorial in the Weekly News which showed another side to Winthrop. It read:

Are we not preparing the teaching profession as a recruiting ground for the Bolshevist doctrine? Is it reason-

336

able to expect teachers to inculcate a healthy vigorous American point of view while living on starvation wages and so cramped as to be cut off from the usual enjoyments of the rest of the population? Is it reasonable to expect to get able and sound-minded professors to expound the economic laws of a system which makes them notable for their poverty? Or can they understand properly the world in which they live if they are too poor to move around among other people and see what is going on?

Few people, if any, seemed to be impressed with this reasoning. The South Carolina Daughters of the American Revolution did, however, send a resolution to the Legislature, requesting that Winthrop's needs should be met by that body.[63]

As was his annual custom, Johnson presented a long wish list to the General Assembly early in 1920. Most of his requests were repeats, including those for additional land and equipment, a propagation house, extra money for the Y building, the dairy barn and four silos, and increased salaries. Johnson asked for a new printing outfit, milking machines, and a dormitory for country girls attending WTS to accommodate those who wished to prepare for college but lacked adequate facilities near home.[64]

The Legislature was very good to education during its 1920 session. Laws governing public education were changed. The appropriation for public schools increased by over $200,000, and a new maximum district tax-limit of fifteen mills for the maintenance of common schools was fixed. Entrance requirements were raised in state schools to fifteen units. All these changes would help Winthrop, whose many students and alumnae welcomed the modification made in the college's name. The Act of 1920 dropped Industrial from her name since the state had established an Industrial School for

337

Girls--namely, a reformatory for girls. By the new
act, Winthrop College became the South Carolina
College for Women. Her 1920 appropriation nearly
doubled that of Carolina.[65]

Some thought Winthrop's name change indicated more emphasis on literary work and less on
vocational. However, teacher training would remain
the mainstay of Winthrop's curriculum. As a result
of the state's new school-library law, the state,
county, and community could now cooperate in
establishing and maintaining rural school libraries.
Winthrop viewed this as an opportunity to improve
her offerings. Also, by 1920 the war had
demonstrated that the schools urgently needed to
provide citizenship training, which Winthrop had
always stressed. Now educators proposed to teach
community civics in the seventh and eighth grades;
economics in the ninth; and sociology, political
science, and comparative governments in the top
grades of South Carolina's high schools. This
offered Winthrop another opportunity to prepare its
students for future service.[66]

In other developments during 1920, Winthrop
elected to join the Carnegie pension plan for
teachers--the first fringe benefit of its kind made
available to Winthrop faculty and staff. Further,
Winthrop improved its athletic program as an adjunct
to better health and made provisions to train
public-health nurses in connection with a health
unit in York County.[67]

Early in 1920, a campaign to give Johnson
some very flattering publicity surfaced in South
Carolina. The Winthrop College Daughters passed a
resolution thanking the State for its editorial
suggesting that Winthrop's name be changed to
Johnson College. Perhaps the editorial had been a
tongue-in-cheek compliment designed to suggest to
the Legislature that Carolina deserved more
attention. But most people took the editorial at
face value, including the 6,500 young ladies who had
attended Winthrop. The Winthrop Chapter of the
Winthrop Daughters further resolved that they held

themselves in readiness "to do all in our power to secure such legislation as may be necessary to substitute the name of Johnson for that of Winthrop making the name of our alma mater read: Johnson College, the South Carolina College for Women." Few college presidents have ever received such an extravagant compliment. The institutionalizing of Johnson had become a near reality.[68]

The campaign to change Winthrop's name caught on fast. People began to express themselves in person and in the press. Captain W. A. Clark of Columbia objected in his article to the State that Winthrop should bear the name of a non-South Carolinian. The publicity pleased Johnson, but he had to be careful: he had funnelled much money from the North and thus needed to be on friendly terms with both North and South. Johnson attempted to compromise public opinion by pointing out that Mr. Winthrop came very close to being a South Carolinian. The Winthrops had lived in Charleston for a time but had returned to Boston. Mr. Winthrop, he pointed out, was very sympathetic to the South. Johnson said that he would be repaid more "if those who wanted to change the name would help broaden and strengthen Winthrop's work." A few days later, the senate of New York University asked Johnson to serve as an elector for the Hall of Fame--another singular honor.[69]

With such fine publicity, one would expect the press corps to pay Johnson a visit, which they did on June 9 and 10. Johnson had announced their up-coming visit early in April. He agreed to turn over Johnson Hall (the newly completed Y or student activity building) to the editors and to provide them with reasonably priced lodging and meals.[70]

Before April ended, Johnson had scored with more unusual publicity. He invited E. C. Carr--a representative of A. G. Spalding Brothers, the great sporting goods concern--to Winthrop to observe and certify the athletic contests on April 17, 1920. According to the official record, Winthrop athletes broke four world's records. Mary Love McClure of

339

Chester ran the sixty-yard hurdle race in 9 1/2 seconds. In the hundred-yard low hurdles, Mary Alexander of York and Lucile Godbold of Wagner tied at 15 seconds. In the basketball throw, Miss Godbold established a new record of 89' 10 1/2", which exceeded the previous record of 88' 10" held by a young lady from Vassar.[71]

Every week seemed to bring some new laurel or distinction to someone at Winthrop. Dr. James Walmsley designed a new course in "citizenship" for study by club women, whose federation agreed to adopt it and publish it for state-wide distribution.[72] And from Japan in 1920 came news from Uta Saito, class of 1916, informing Miss Russell's office that she was now teaching in Miss Tsuda's English School for Girls. Miss Tsuda, sent by the empress, had studied at Bryn Mawr. Her school was not a mission school but was founded in the Christian tradition with Bible study required--most surprising for that time in Japan. It was the only school of its kind there; its work was recognized by the government. Miss Saito concluded that the four years she had spent at Winthrop "were the happiest days of my life in America."[73]

Late in the spring, the Legislature passed an act to encourage home economics. The statute carried an appropriation of $25,000--a handsome sum. It later surfaced that the money had not been included in the appropriation bill so the activity could not be supported in 1920. Mr. Swearingen gave assurances, however, that the Legislature would correct the oversight in 1921. This was a different first for Winthrop.[74]

Another successful school year closed on June 1, 1920. Just a few weeks thereafter, Johnson launched his largest summer school ever, registering 1,448 students. The six-week term offered many courses in grade- and high-school work as well as foods and cooking, sewing, and dressmaking. Two new additions on campus were ready for the students: Johnson Hall, described as the newest and "best-built and handsomest building of Winthrop's campus," and the handsome, almost-completed auditorium at the Winthrop Training School. There were Smith-Hughes and other government sponsored programs that summer. A goodly number of male school superintendents attended the Winthrop summer schools, which before 1911 were conducted by the Department of Education and after 1911 were encouraged and recommended by the Department of Education.[75]

Prospects for the fall session, which was to begin on September 10, were very good. Despite some last-minute delays involving scholarships, the new term made a grand start. All went well. During the fall, 1920, Wilson's Fourteen Points and America's possible entry into the League of Nations generated much on-campus discussion. Johnson, never to be outdone in advertising, bought a full page in the State to advertise his "Fourteen Points About Winthrop."[76] In summary, this prominently displayed advertisement read:

FIRST--In its educational and literary departments the college offers five courses leading to the degrees of Bachelor of Arts; four courses, Bachelor of Science; and one course, Bachelor of Music. There are seven short courses leading to certificates.

SECOND--There are 1,100 students enrolled in these courses, with 128 officers and teachers.

THIRD--The buildings at Winthrop cover five and one-half acres. The floor space would cover 12 3/4 acres. Five dormitories are now occupied by students. Other buildings are: Administration Building, Dining Hall, Infirmary, Gymnasium, Library, Training School, Johnson Hall, and Model Home. The Student's Building now being erected will be the center for the social and religious life of the college.[77]

341

FOURTH--The buildings are provided with fire escapes of the most approved models. Fire drills are held frequently.

FIFTH--The Infirmary is connected by covered way with the dormitories. A resident physician and a trained nurse are on duty at all times. All buildings, except the Training School, are connected by covered ways.

SIXTH--The State provides as many scholarships for each county as the county has members in the House of Representatives. These scholarships are worth $100 and free tuition, and are awarded on competitive examination held at the county court houses on the first Friday in July of each year. In addition to these there are 30 dining room scholarships offered by individuals and societies.

SEVENTH--All students, without exception, are required to wear the College uniform.

EIGHTH--The extension work of the College is far-reaching. Winthrop co-operates with the United States Department of Agriculture and with Clemson College in carrying on Home Demonstration Work throughout the State. . . .

NINTH--A summer school is held regularly at the College. It runs six weeks and offers many courses in grade and high school work.

TENTH--The students at Winthrop have an active and effective self-government association.

ELEVENTH--One of the most active organizations connected with the

College is the Young Women's Christian Association, with over 900 members. The Association meets every Wednesday night. Its members are enrolled in many Bible and mission study classes.

TWELFTH--An Appointment Bureau is maintained at the College for the purpose of aiding graduates to secure positions as teachers. Teachers who attend the summer school have the privilege of joining this bureau.

THIRTEENTH--The College owns a farm of 259 acres, maintained for the purpose of supplying vegetables, milk, butter, and eggs for the dining room. A new sanitary barn is now in process of construction.

FOURTEENTH--The entire expenses for a session of nine months are:

For students paying tuition: $234
For students not paying tuition: $194
For scholarship students: $ 94

For catalogues and other information, write to D. B. Johnson, President, Rock Hill, South Carolina.[78]

With appealing advertisements, an enviable success record, and the overwhelming good will of South Carolina, Johnson found more joy and less criticism in his position. He enjoyed having people ask what Winthrop did for a girl; his accustomed answer was "We try to make her a good citizen." By 1920 Johnson had also discovered the power that his girls could muster and, master politician that he was, he taught them to use their numbers for the continued glory of Winthrop and the state.[79] Many examples abound.

Johnson asked Mrs. John (Bessie) Drake, an early leader of Winthrop alumnae, to "accept the

343

students building on behalf of the Alumnae Association and give a five minute speech." Mrs. Drake, who was the recording secretary of the South Carolina Federation of Woman's Clubs, confided in Johnson that although she did not feel up to making the speech, she would try because the interests of her alma mater were second only to the affairs of her family--a feeling that generations of Winthrop daughters seemed to share. Wanting to do a good job, she asked Johnson for statistics and facts on her college, which she had seen grow from a main building and one dormitory to its "present magnificent proportions." Mrs. Drake concluded her letter by praising Johnson for the manner in which he had entertained the 1919 and 1920 conventions of the SCFWC at Winthrop--"My heart leaps up when I consider it."[80]

Johnson quickly replied, furnishing Mrs. Drake with his version of Winthrop's founding and development. No word of Tillman, Joynes, Swearingen, or any other of the early leaders of Winthrop came from Johnson. Instead he stressed that in thirty-four years "we have sent out some six thousand Winthrop Daughters and they are now rendering great service as teachers, homemakers, and business women to this state and country. . . . We have Winthrop Daughters on every continent, except that of Australia. . . . This past year Winthrop College enrolled 2,600 students in all departments, including the Summer School of last summer and the Training School, and we have 128 teachers and officers to care for these students."[81] Continuing his Winthrop analysis in a vein suggestive of what Mrs. Drake ought to say in her acceptance speech, Johnson stressed that according to an inventory submitted to the budget commission the past summer, "the value of the College plant at that time was over $2,000,000" and that it had been added to since then. Winthrop, he continued, had raised its standards to match those of Carolina. For long years they had been fulfilling their charter "to provide professional, practical, and a higher education to the Women of South Carolina." Finally, Johnson told of his plans to provide

344

bedrooms in the students' building for returning alumnae.[82]

Few have read the Archibald Rutledge thesis that Johnson's life was something other than a life of service and sacrifice. Rutledge attempted to research both sides of this question and readily admitted that Johnson was a first-rate "wheeler and dealer" who yearly saw "his power, his prestige, his prerequisites" grow. But it was standard knowledge at Winthrop that for several years before his death Miss Sarah Marcum (his long-time helper), Mrs. Johnson, and others of their close circle were holding a halo over Johnson's head, always collecting money for his birthdays, for example. The faculty and staff were under pressure to give time and money to support these activities. Few had the gall to imitate the old professor who-- when he walked into Johnson's office on one such occasion--threw down his dollar, growled "Here is my tax," then wheeled and stalked out. Few students in this later period knew Johnson-the-man, but they learned much about Johnson-the-founder-of-Winthrop and what he had done for them. As Rutledge viewed him, "despite the indubitably great work he accomplished, Johnson never actually thought anything; he never wrote anything in the true sense of the word, and he never spoke with any signifi-cance." [83]

Johnson was very sensitive to criticism, so he learned to manipulate events without getting involved. Writing to Mrs. Drake on Christmas Eve, 1920, he cautioned her against alumnae opposition to the University's efforts to acquire a women's building. He suggested that Winthrop alumnae opposition might be twisted by others to appear as opposition to women's education. Therefore, he recommended that the Winthrop daughters concentrate their efforts upon securing Winthrop what it needed --a new dormitory, a teachers' home, and more money to pay women department heads better salaries. Thereby, he would squelch talk of discrimination against women. [84]

345

All during his later career Johnson flirted with certain problems and programs although he never seemed to commit himself completely. He strongly supported public-school work, yet he would never agree completely to ideas that Superintendent Swearingen felt bolstered the public schools' well-being. In 1920, B. L. Parkinson, State High School Inspector, attempted to plan for better relations among South Carolina's colleges and high schools. Swearingen wrote Johnson that Winthrop College and its president should institute a practical program for advancing the public schools' interests. Swearingen wanted to know if Johnson had such a plan and, if so, he wanted to learn about it in fullest detail.[85]

As usual, Johnson did not give Swearingen what the superintendent felt was a satisfactory answer. A few weeks thereafter, the Winthrop Weekly News attacked Swearingen because he opposed the Smith-Towner Bill in Congress, which was designed to establish a National Department of Education with a secretary in the presidential cabinet and an appropriation of $100,000,000. Swearingen, who feared the centralization such legislation would bring, wrote the Weekly's editor, saying, "You have gone out of your way in the editorial columns of the Winthrop Weekly News to criticize and misrepresent me and my views concerning the Smith-Towner Bill."[86]

One is not to infer from his stance that Swearingen opposed federally sponsored programs. Quite the contrary, Swearingen attempted to push home economics and agriculture in the schools. Writing to Johnson that numerous schools planned to add home economics the next year, Swearingen asked how many teachers were being trained at Winthrop to serve this area. Johnson did not relay exactly the information asked for: he replied that Miss Lillian Hoffman would teach a six-week summer course in home economics.[87]

Swearingen faced an unexpected problem when the state changed the tax deadline from March 15 to

346

May 15. Many short-term schools had to close during the last four weeks and teachers, according to the superintendent, had been "unnerved by the delay in the payment of their salaries." What Mr. Swearingen was attempting to tell Johnson was that he had enough problems without any from the Winthrop head.[88]

Swearingen was attempting to get Winthrop to lead vocational (home-economics) training in the public schools. "Such training," he argued with Johnson, "not only aids young women, but it helps to create a new attitude toward many practical problems of life. Moreover, it will bring to Winthrop some of the finest girls South Carolina produces." Johnson replied that he had received "$5,836.56 for vocational teacher training during the scholastic year 1920-21, and Winthrop stands strong for this work and for its development." And Miss Hoffman reported to Swearingen that "21 white schools have secured teachers and are applying for Smith-Hughes funds, but eleven must be taught by teachers not qualified in this work." She felt that the girls were unaware of the state's need in this area.[89]

Johnson had other successes during 1921. These he listed in his annual report for the Legislature. In recent years the college had observed January 10, Mr. Johnson's birthday, as the founder's day. Originally, Mr. Winthrop's birthday had been celebrated, but now the faculty formally voted to make January 10 the official Founder's Day. Birthdays of Tillman, Joynes, and others who had helped to found Winthrop were lost in oblivion.[90]

In 1921 home-demonstration workers attracted much publicity by reaching many thousands of women and girls through clubs. From the surplus foods they had processed, they sold $2,186,869.88 worth, a real source of pride and profit for these people. In one special project aided by the Chamber of Commerce, Miss Juanita Neely (Home Demonstration Agent for York) put on a fruit-tree- and grape-vine-planting campaign which resulted in 900 fruit and

347

nut trees, 200 grape vines, 45 fig trees, and 1,200 strawberry plants' being set out.[91]

Many groups attended conventions and short courses on the Winthrop campus in 1921. Summer school alone drew 1,545 people. The Sunday School Convention brought many more. Home Demonstration Clubs attended short courses. The State Federation of Woman's Clubs convened on campus as did the Nurses Convention, the League of Women Voters, and the School Superintendents and Principals. But the largest single drawing card of the session was a pageant, The Making of South Carolina by James Elliott Walmsley, featuring the faculty and students with Johnson as master of ceremonies. Some 9,800 attended the performance; about 1,400 students took part. From the Training School's youngest to President Johnson and Governor and Mrs. R. A. Cooper, it was a real extravaganza à la Winthrop.[92]

During this session the Winthrop A.B. degree gained recognition from the strictest teacher-certification states like New York, California, Minnesota. and Wisconsin. (Perhaps, Johnson had forgotten in mentioning the states that California had recognized Winthrop from her beginning.) Johns Hopkins, Trinity, and Virginia recognized Winthrop's students for graduate work, and concurrently Johnson reported to the state that in the past twenty-six years he had spent $132,396.47 for lots and farmland: of this, $24,000 was from Peabody and the remainder from savings. In 1921 alone, he reported spending $407,170.90.[93]

Among Winthrop's other features, events, and accomplishments of this session, twenty-two granddaughters of Winthrop women were now enrolled. A special alumnae edition of the News celebrated the dedication of the student building--the new Johnson Hall. Miss Lucile Randle was one of three South Carolina students chosen to study at the Conservatoire Américain at Fontainebleau, France, for the summer. And other Winthrop girls--after teaching eleven lessons in a school for

348

illiterates--displayed a male pupil who could write
his name, bank checks, and a sentence.[94]

In 1921 three songs praising Winthrop
appeared. Miss Mary Frances Wickliffe wrote
"Winthrop You Are Fine" and "Winthrop's the Pride of
my Heart," with the chorus:

Here's to Winthrop Alma Mater,
May no evil her befall,
Heaven's blessings rest upon her
For we love her best of all.[95]

The official Alma Mater was published in
1921. Written by Dr. Donnis Martin, head of the
Latin Department, it was set to music by Miss Hascal
Vaughan of the music faculty. Thousands of Winthrop
daughters have expressed joy and sometimes sadness
while singing:

Fairest flower of the Southland,
Alma Mater of our youth,
Guide our minds in search of wisdom,
And our souls in search of truth.

Winthrop College! Winthrop College!
How our hearts beat high with pride!
Ever shall we stand together,
Winthrop daughters, side by side.

Fond the memories that cluster
'Round thy campus and thy halls,
Naught can ever dim the lustre
Which thy hallowed name recalls.[96]

From an unexpected corner came news of
Winthrop's influence in remote South America.
Schoolman J. K. Breedin, formerly of Manning but now
of Cajamarca, Peru, wrote Johnson that Winthrop's
influence pervaded that old Andean town where,
centuries before, the Spanish had strangled the Inca
chief after his associates had filled a room with
gold to pay his ransom. Mr. Breedin, a regional
director of education there, was using a Winthrop
catalog to guide the teacher-training classes he

was attempting to set up at a _Normalista_ located in a territory eight times the size of South Carolina. He thanked Johnson and Winthrop for helping his program.[97]

Late in December, the Legislative Committee on Economy and Consolidations employed some "experts" to handle budget problems. They asked Swearingen to budget the Smith-Hughes money spent by Johnson for Miss Hoffman's and the other home-economics teachers' services. Swearingen wrote Johnson that this money ought to be included in his budget, not in the superintendent's. "I don't know," he wrote, "what their so-called experts are trying to do." He asked Johnson, "What do you suggest? Personally and officially, I have tried to satisfy these folks and my patience has reached the breaking point."[98] This fight over home economics resulted in the committee's eliminating vocational-education appropriations. Johnson felt that the state would take a great step backward educationally if it failed to continue the vocational education so conspicuously begun with the federal government's help.[99]

The legislative Committee on Efficiency and Economy cited Winthrop for having the largest attendance of any state-supported college and the lowest _per-capita_ expenditures. Yet its educational standards were high. This praise makes it difficult to understand why the Legislature voted to eliminate vocational-education appropriations. Perhaps the Legislature was reacting to the agricultural recession beginning to affect adversely South Carolina.[100]

In the early twenties, at the behest of Johnson and Miss Russell, the Winthrop alumnae were better organized across the state. Leading ladies became district organizers. Their success was instantaneous. For example, Miss Marion Salley of Orangeburg gave particular attention to her home area and to neighboring Lexington, as well as to Manning and Bishopville. "It would be lovely," she wrote Miss Russell, "to go to those towns when the girls get together and make speeches in favor of

350

such organizations, but I realize that everyone is short of funds. . . . Send me your favorable lists and I'll make this old typewriter rattle off letters that I hope will be fruitful of results."[101]

Within a month, Miss Salley reported success, informing Miss Russell that her group had combined the Orangeburg Daughters' constitution and the Winthrop College Daughters' constitution in their work: "Susie Kortjohn Britton has organized Williamsburg, Sarah Rudd is stirring things up in Clinton," she wrote. And Miss Salley asked Miss Russell for names from Lexington, Bishopville, and Manning.[102]

The new alumnae president, Mrs. Mary T. Nance Daniel, plunged most effectively into the alumnae effort. Writing to President Johnson from the Jefferson Hotel in Columbia on November 28, she reported:

> I came to Columbia this morning as you requested and interviewed Governor Cooper relative to appointing a graduate of Winthrop College on the Board of Trustees. He evidently had his mind made up on the matter before I saw him for he said in as much as the General Assembly would so soon convene he would not appoint but leave the matter to them. He said as there was to be no board meeting between now and the meeting of the Legislature [a frequently used term for General Assembly] he would have absolutely no justification for making an appointment and should he do so, he feared the General Assembly might take it that he was only suggesting to them whom they should elect. . . . Dr. Johnson, I did all I could. . . .[103]

Johnson planned with the help of the Laurens County delegation and the neighboring Saluda delegation (Mrs. Daniel's home group) to nominate a woman from the floor to fill the Board vacancy. Mrs.

351

Daniel would be a logical choice because of her good work with the School Improvement Association of South Carolina. She confided in Johnson that "nothing would make me happier than to be able to serve Winthrop in this capacity."[104] In turn, two days before Christmas Johnson advised Mrs. Daniel, "It would be a fine thing if we could have a meeting of the Alumnae Association at Columbia to request your election as the President of the Alumnae Association, and as a member of the Board."[105] But Johnson soon remembered Tillman's frequent advice to avoid active involvement in public campaigns. Writing again to Mrs. Daniel in early January, Johnson suggested,

> It would be well for the friends of whom you wrote me to quietly see certain members of the Legislature in both the House and the Senate just as soon as the Legislature convenes and tell them that the Alumnae of Winthrop College 9,000 strong [up by about a thousand from what Johnson usually reported] wants a representative of the Association elected as a member of the Board of Trustees of Winthrop College, and that they want the President of the Association. It should be done very quietly.[106]

Mrs. Daniel entered the fight to win. She and her friends conducted an effective campaign. On January 14, the State mentioned only one trustee would be elected, not three, and Mrs. Daniel wired Johnson to suggest that he have the York delegation "Correct Resolution immediately."[107] Finally, on January 19, 1922, the General Assembly affirmed its faith in the Winthrop product when they elected Mrs. W. L. Daniel the first woman trustee. Overjoyed that she could now do even more for Winthrop in her new position, she prayed that she might "be given strength of mind and body to do all that you [Johnson] expect of me." Very soon Mrs. Daniel was in the midst of Winthrop's affairs. Her correspondence with Johnson is most revealing.[108]

352

Mrs. Daniel was an active fighter for Winthrop, and she was very much opposed to building a women's dormitory at a men's school--in this case the University--for a few women. Such a move would pass over Winthrop, her Winthrop that desperately needed one.[109]

The year 1922 brought some hot politics to South Carolina. Because of political uncertainty, Governor Robert A. Cooper resigned on May 20, 1922, to take a job with the Federal Land Bank Board. Wilson C. Harvey of Charleston served out the term. Four days earlier, Superintendent Swearingen, Ben Tillman's favorite nephew, had announced that he was planning to run for governor. On May 17, Johnson advised Mrs. Bessie Drake, whom he was urging to announce for Superintendent of Education, "You may count on me of course to go the very limits of my power. I think," Johnson continued, "you could expect about seven thousand Winthrop Daughters to back you up and also the State Federation of Women's Clubs. I believe your announcement would keep some men from announcing themselves for the position. I am not sure as to who will run for Governor. I do not think the Governor's race need affect your race."[110]

South Carolina, just beginning to experience agricultural depression, watched her political campaign heat up as her indomitable ex-governor Coley Blease raced for a third term. Blease demanded abolition of the Tax Commission and the Board of Public Welfare. Blease and Thomas G. McLeod of Lee County ran neck and neck. Charleston gave Blease its majority, but McLeod won. The News and Courier called his election "a victory for good government."[111]

Despite Johnson's interest in Mrs. Drake's campaign, he seemed timid in helping her. Writing to Mr. D. McIntyre of Blenheim, a prominent Presbyterian who supported Mrs. Drake, Johnson said he had to be "very particular about any printed or public expression of my preference for any State officer," but he would try to see Dr. Douglass of the Presbyterian College to solicit his help for

353

her. Johnson had written Mrs. Drake on May 23 that she had a good chance. Regardless of her many qualities--a good speaking manner, a good education and sound judgment--Mrs. Drake lost to Mr. James H. Hope, an experienced schoolman.[112]

Many other Winthrop friends took active parts in South Carolina's 1922 campaign. Mr. W. L. Daniel, husband of the trustee, sent his relative Carroll Nance up to Winthrop with Edgar Brown, candidate for the speakership. He wanted Johnson to help these men, since Daniel knew that the University crowd had a candidate opposing Brown. Daniel had written letters for Brown in which he indicated that Winthrop's interests would be safe in the hands of Brown and Nance. Nance favored enlarging the dormitories at Winthrop, so Daniel suggested that Johnson show his low per-capita cost to Nance and Brown. Winning them could help Johnson with the next Legislature.[113]

Mr. Daniel was later invited to speak at Winthrop. Following his visit he wrote, "again, let me caution you, Doctor Johnson, to conserve your strength, maintain an even keel, so to speak, and let the heathen rage. I am sure your place in history is secure and that its verdict will be that you wrought well."[114]

Regardless of politics and some anti-Johnson criticism, the 1922 Winthrop session accomplished much. The great Winthrop pageant rekindled interest in teaching state history. Johnson's favored publicity organ, the Weekly News, said that state history would help in rebuilding the social order: "Boys and girls of the future," the editor wrote, "must know and understand in order that the State in the future may continue its honored and prominent place among the other states of the nation."[115]

Reporting in 1922 on the Winthrop-oriented program to stamp out illiteracy in South Carolina, Miss Wil Lou Gray (field agent of the committee) listed thirty-nine schools in operation with 5,433 whites enrolled and 5,104 blacks, under a budget

354

of $27,880. Spartanburg had 800 students attending, the largest number of any county. The operation's success in the first twenty years of the century was phenomenal. In 1900, the state had 54,375 white illiterates and 293,883 black. Twenty years later, Miss Gray's report showed only 38,742 white illiterates and 181,422 black.[116]

In February, 1922, Winthrop reported the death of her first teacher, Miss Mary H. Leonard--who was born in Scotland, educated in Germany, and taught at Bridgewater Normal in Massachusetts before coming to Winthrop Training School in Columbia. Miss Leonard deserves much credit for Winthrop's early success. She also wrote fiction, serious articles for the Cotton Plant, and several books. Prior to her death she was a student of genealogy and local history.[117]

In late February, 1922, Winthrop established another first when a committee of notable women went before the Legislature's Finance Committee on behalf of Winthrop College, praising Winthrop's efforts and requesting larger appropriations. Included in this unusual group were Mrs. Bradley Morrah, Miss Christine South, Mrs. Julian Salley, and Mrs. Daniel (the trustee).[118] There was no indication that their appearance influenced the Legislature, but Winthrop was (as usual) treated handsomely with the Trustees' Note of 1920 for $17,581.06. For 1923, Winthrop was voted $427,682.11, including $20,000 for the teachers' home (the contract was awarded on June 26, 1923).[119] As had been the case for many years, Winthrop's accomplishments and publicity kept the Legislature in a friendly and somewhat generous mood.

Several significant events transpired during early 1922. For example, the Extension Department added to its service a list of reading courses appearing in bulletin form. Some of the readings were cultural; others were purely vocational. Since Winthrop benefited so from her very able Extension Department head, Professor A. P. Bourland, the college assisted him in every way possible. Later in the year, Dr. Johnson even recommended that a radio-broadcasting station be secured for the Extension Department's use.[120]

As always, whatever good was happening, Winthrop was involved. The Poetry Society of South Carolina sought to stimulate interest by offering prizes. Winthrop submitted entries to DuBose Heyward at Charleston. Even Dr. Kinard could not resist the call to literary endeavor. His play, "Mortmain," won a $50 prize in the State's playwriting contest.[121] In the state survey on preparation of high-school history teachers, Winthrop showed up very well. The sample revealed that seven percent of South Carolina's college graduates had taken no history courses in college but that twice as many college graduates teaching history in the South Carolina high schools were Winthrop graduates than graduates from any other state college. Winthrop's ratio was twelve to one over the University in the survey.[122]

In 1922 the person directing worldwide attention to Winthrop was her greatest athlete, Miss Lucile Ellerbe Godbold of Estill, South Carolina, who carried Winthrop's garnet and gold to international acclaim. Receiving her training at Winthrop under the able and efficient head of the Department of Physical Training, "Ludy" had captured most of the honors at the Winthrop athletic days--running the 50-yard dash in 6 2/5 seconds, the 75-yard dash in 9 1/5 seconds, the 100-yard hurdles in 15 3/5 seconds; leaping the hop-step and jump 33 feet, 5 inches and the running broad jump 14 feet, 10 inches; putting the shot 35 feet, 11 inches; and throwing the discus 96 feet. Following the American try-outs, she was one of eleven women chosen to go to Paris in August, 1922, to represent America in the Women's Olympic Meet.[123] In addition to these accomplishments, Ludy was pronounced by the New York Herald as one of the two outstanding stars of the Eastern try-outs.[124]

After the early summer preliminaries, the
United States team sailed on the Aquitania for
Cherbourg, then continued to Paris by rail for
more practice at Colombes. Dr. Johnson arrived in
time for the August 20 meet in Pershing Stadium.
It was there that Ludy carried Old Glory around
the track. Placing in the shot, the javelin, the
300-meter and the 1,000-meter races, Ludy had her
great moment when she stepped into the circle
before 10,000 people to battle a big French girl
in the shot-put. As Ludy later described it to the
Winthrop student body, coach Dr. Harry Stewart of
Yale shouted, "now Ol' South Carolina Mountaineer,
show 'em what the South can do! I put the pill and
broke the world's record--66 feet beating the French
girl by 6 1/2 feet. The American flag was raised;
The Star Spangled Banner was played by the band
twice and the announcer introduced me to those
thousands of people in French."[125]

The American team took second place with
Miss Godbold receiving six medals for her perform-
ances, twice as many as any other athlete there.
Results appeared in the leading newspapers of most
countries. Her achievement attracted world-wide
attention to Winthrop, South Carolina, and
especially herself.[126] Returning home on the
Saxonia, Miss Godbold met her father in New York.
She returned to her Hampton County home. There the
governor and the local citizenry held a proper
observance for this occasion--a once-in-a-lifetime
celebration.[127]

One might expect that the publicity-
craving president of Winthrop would return from
Europe in time for the local celebration, but
Johnson did the next best thing. The college sent a
special report to the State for the day after the
celebration, headlining that "Applications for
Winthrop Turned Down Since July 10. New Teachers
Added--President Johnson to Return From Europe
Within Next Day or Two." The articles stated in
good Johnsonian prose that "Everything is in
readiness for the opening of Winthrop College" on
September 20. Listing a number of new teachers

and departments, Johnson announced that Preston H. Edwards would head the separate Department of Physics and Astronomy. The separate Department of Political Science would be headed by William G. Burgin of the Mississippi State College for Women. Magginis would be promoted to secondary education, and Dr. William R. Bourne of Peabody would take charge of the Training School. The announcement affirmed that Dr. Bourland would devote all of his time to Extension work. And a new head of Music, A. Andre Schmidt, was coming from Taylor University in Indiana. Dr. Grover C. Mance, also from Indiana, would head Geography and Geology. Dr. Elizabeth Johnson from Johns Hopkins had signed for Modern Languages. New assistants in English were Louise Earle of Randolph-Macon and Margaret Finley of Winthrop. Several others came to serve other departments. This was an impressive list.[128]

Academically, the summer of 1922 was no different from others, except that it was larger--boasting 2,221 students. The student body and the faculty passed a resolution expressing their appreciation "for the unusual opportunities and advantages offered by this splendid institution in the training of teachers and others. . . ." They thanked their "honored President, D. B. Johnson" for his work and for "extending the influences of the College as to include civic organizations that are laboring for a more enlightened citizenry. . . and for his giving a close, personal attention to everything that pertains to our comfort and welfare." A copy had been sent to Johnson, who was traveling in Europe.[129]

The farm women who were also attending a Winthrop short course passed resolutions of thanks for the opportunities afforded them by Winthrop College and Dr. Johnson. In a more positive vein, the Farm Women's Council recommended that the state pass a bill requiring men to undergo a medical examination before receiving a marriage license. They also recommended federal appropriations for maternity and infant care. In addition, they sought

358

constitutional revisions and provisions for adequate support of the State Board of Health, Winthrop, and other state colleges in addition to more demonstration agents and boards of public welfare. This was a blueprint for a "great society" before the days of L.B.J. Populism was not dead in South Carolina.[130]

The 1922 fall session at Winthrop opened late, no doubt because of Johnson's trip abroad. By contrast the University got an earlier start, advertising in the State seventeen good reasons to attend the University. Winthrop began on September 20 with 1,368 students, 136 more than the previous session. With a completely renovated plant, a new well and a potato house for the farm, and an improved faculty, Johnson could expect a record year. Each one seemed better, as he told it. And imitating the English universities' system, he was now listing graduates' infant daughters on a baby-roll of admission applicants.[131]   Also arrangements in the early fall brought to campus Winthrop's Olympic star, Miss Godbold, who had signed with President J. C. Childs of Columbia College as head of the Athletic Department. (Johnson had planned a holiday for her visit in early October.)   Plans allowed Johnson to be painted by the famous artist E. Hodgson Smart, who (after finishing Johnson) was on contract to paint King Albert of Belgium, Lord Balfour, and other prominent Europeans.[132]

Because of the new women's vote and their greater awareness of government problems, Winthrop focused more attention on history and citizenship classes. In keeping with the new emphasis, Mrs. Mary C. Simms Oliphant--granddaughter of William Gilmore Simms and author of the History of South Carolina--offered a $50 prize for the best history essay. Since nine months' training at Winthrop cost $176 according to Business Manager Dr. G. T. Pugh, one can see the real monetary value of Mrs. Oliphant's gesture.[133] And special note was taken that a leading 1916 Winthrop graduate survived the second primary election on September 12, 1922, and thereby became the first woman ever elected as a

359

county superintendent of education in South Carolina. This young lady had worked for Senator Tillman in Washington. She had been a yeoman in the navy, a Red Cross and YMCA worker, and a homemaker and teacher following the death of her mother. And now she was elected superintendent. Thus, Kate Wofford became a model for Winthrop girls to emulate.[134]

By 1923, there was no question about Johnson-the-man merging with Johnson-the-institution. A second official celebration of Johnson's birthday (January 10) featured an address by the former Secretary of Navy, Josephus Daniels of Raleigh, North Carolina. Trustee J. F. Breazeale gave a short talk; Johnson, a response. Emerson's image of the length and shadow of a great man was the theme, and Mr. Daniels showed his humanity by paying his heart-felt respects to Tillman and by calling the girls in blue "shipmates."[135] The Weekly News editorialized about Johnson's second Founder's Day. Calling Johnson a builder and benefactor, they commented: "For a man in the brief space of a lifetime to build a great institution like Winthrop is a marvelous feat." Reviewing the history of Winthrop briefly, they quoted from a recent chapel address of the Hon. Cyrus L. Shealy, who said that "Winthrop is the training place for a large part of the best part of South Carolina."[136]

Mr. Daniels' scholarly speech was later included in the News. Stressing that the educational awakening of the state could be dated from the establishment of Winthrop and Clemson, Mr. Daniels continued:

> I do not by this mean to infer that South Carolina had not from its earliest days possessed an educated, indeed highly educated leadership. No State of the South ranked higher in learned men and they made themselves felt in church and state. It must not be inferred either that the State lacked excellent educational institutions in Columbia and Charleston and elsewhere. They ranked with the best in the South

and sent out men of real scholarship. But until these two institutions were made strong, the program of educating all the people lacked directness and facilities. Indeed, the truth is that in all our Southern States we were too slow in recognizing the truth that universal education was the foundation upon which our civilization must be built.

In every generation and in every community in the South there were men who saw this need and urged it, but the poverty succeeding the War of the sixties and the failure to appreciate the fact that the South was too poor not to educate delayed the practical putting in operation of universal education in institutions supported by the State until Benjamin R. Tillman's administration. I could not come to South Carolina without paying tribute to that remarkable man. He was first known in the republic as a violent and intemperate speaker, radical in his views and impatient of difference of opinion. He came to be known as a leader in national defense and the world is indebted to him for the naval efficiency in the World War. He grew to be a statesman who left his impress upon the constructive policies of the most constructive and progressive era of our century.

But in South Carolina his best monument was that he joined hands with progressive educational leaders to carry the blessings of education into the cabins of the humblest homes in the Commonwealth. That was his chief work here. He had the power to send forward the mighty impulse. The educators builded wisely and today South Carolina has an envied place in the newer educational life of the country.[137]

Turning to Winthrop's service to womanhood, the learned North Carolina statesman stressed that educated women have educated children. Mr. Daniels felt that every college graduate ought to teach at least for one year because "Nothing compels mastery of a subject so much as attempting to teach it to others." He urged Winthrop girls to study medicine, enter politics, and make politics and good government one and inseparable: "If woman would put an end to the professional politician and smash selfish machines, that alone would make her enfranchisement a blessing to the republic." He concluded with the advice that women should band together and "stand as firm as that young woman who stands ever before you [pointing to the statue of Joan of Arc]. Hear your voices and make a better world." This, Winthrop girls had been doing.[138]

Mr. Daniels' remarks about teaching must have warmed the cockles of Johnson's heart. Aside from politics, publicity, and money, Johnson's chief preoccupation was training teachers. He always favored the Winthrop Training School (WTS) and had it placed on the highest spot of land in Rock Hill. He even attempted to copy the style of architecture of an English university building for WTS. He was an educationalist. Even Tillman had chided him over the years about his undue emphasis on Normal-school work.

Some might question Archibald Rutledge's seriousness when he said of Johnson's life work: "All the training in the world will never produce a good teacher; for such a person must have been born a great human being. Those who regard teaching as a mere profession, and who therefore are advocates of special schools and colleges for the training of teachers, are probably wrong in their whole concept of education."[139] Pursuing his analysis further, Rutledge stated: "If Johnson

362

ever made a fundamental mistake in his life it was in supposing that teachers can be produced by training ordinary human beings. A teacher can no more be made that way than can an artist or a writer." The cavalier Rutledge concluded that "the most wretched waste of public funds is that cast away on poor teachers."[140]

There had always been some gossip around the state about Johnson's use of state money. During the debate on appropriations in December, 1923, a pro-University representative stated that South Carolina had appropriated $5,000,000 for Winthrop during its thirty-seven-year history and about $2,000,000 for the University in its hundred-year history. Immediately Johnson asked the comptroller-general for a statement on this. His figures showed, according to Johnson, that the state had spent $3,951,313.70 for the University, not including buildings, and $3,845,468.30 for Winthrop, including all appropriations for buildings.[141]

It was hard to beat Johnson with the Legislature (from whom he was always requesting more) or with private sources. In many of his reports to the General Assembly he mentioned enlarging the library, and he was always begging Carnegie for the same thing. "We shall need," he wrote, "$40,000 [later changed to $60,000] to make the addition to the Carnegie Library. We hope the Carnegie Corporation will give us half of this amount under conditions that we shall raise the other half."[142] And in his annual reports, Johnson nearly always listed among his needs building a new dormitory and enlarging the science hall or some other key building on the campus. He would usually conclude with the statement: "We are not asking the Legislature at this time to provide for all of these needs," but he left no doubt just what he wanted. For example, in his request for the next year, he wrote that "We shall have to provide during 1924 for the instruction and care of over 1,500 students in the College proper and for over 2,000 in our

Summer School, over 450 in our Training School, and over 2,000 in our Study Centers making a total of over 5,950 students in all departments with that asked for by similar institutions it will be seen that we are running Winthrop College on the smallest per capita cost of any similar institution in this country."[143]

The 1923-1924 session was another "best to date" one. New teachers included Gordon Worley of Cornell (succeeding Professor Haddon, who had gone to Harvard). This year witnessed changes in music and other areas, with a new resident physician arriving from the University of Pennsylvania. Winthrop had 1,400 students with 2,000 applicants from which only 575 new students were accepted. A special train brought many students up from Columbia the day before registration. Feeling better after his five-week stay at the Battle Creek Health Center in Michigan, Johnson sent good publicity to Columbia, including the faculty's worthwhile summer activities. This time he reported Professor and Mrs. Thompson Brown had spent their summer at home in Virginia; Miss Margarette Richards had returned from study at Chautauqua, New York; Dr. Elizabeth Johnson had toured Europe; Roy Thomas had conducted his annual tour, this time to the West Coast; Professor John F. Thomasón had passed the summer in the Charleston Library; and W. R. Bourne had received his doctorate at Peabody.[144] And later in the year, Johnson issued a special statewide announcement that the French government was sending twenty-five student teachers to the United States, two of whom would come to Winthrop to study and to teach their native language. Johnson viewed the arrival of Jeanne Secot of Paris and Gabrielle Demaine of Belfont as another first for Winthrop College.[145]

During the fall, Johnson seemed to favor the Music Department. He liked music and singing old hymns. In October, he brought groups from Chicago and New York. Some of the professionals sang with Miss Nancy G. Campbell's hundred-voice student choir. Some might suggest that Johnson

364

was just keeping up with the times with his emphasis on singing since nearly every issue of the State paper contained a big advertisement of Victor's Talking Machine Company of Camden, New Jersey, and the Double-Faced Red Seal Records.[146]

This year Johnson involved Winthrop in a new project just before the state fair. An announcement issued in September stated that "by special permission of President Johnson," Presbyterian and Davidson Colleges would play on the Winthrop athletic field. A week later the Blue Stockings of Presbyterian defeated the Gamecocks, giving them a game with Clemson on the Thursday of fair week. But Johnson was more concerned with his meeting of the League of Women Voters and with their discussions on economy and efficiency in county and state government than with the fair.[147]

Besides Johnson, the alumnae, and the home-demonstration leaders, there were many others working for Winthrop--some of whom had no official connection with the college. Of considerable importance was the General Federation of Woman's Clubs, many of whose members were leading South Carolinians. They felt that Winthrop was established to serve the womanhood of the state, and the News usually devoted one issue a year to the Federation. Their activities ranged widely. They worked for a better salary for the Superintendent of Education, for equalization of city and county superintendents' pay, and for a seven-month system for all state schools (a program which Winthrop had long advocated). In this period especially, the Federation was a power in the state. Some of their programs and accomplishments included an Industrial School for Boys at Florence, an Industrial School for Girls at Columbia, and an institution at Clinton for feeble-minded and retarded. They created the Commission on Illiteracy. They were a great adjunct force to education in South Carolina, where thousands of Winthrop daughters helped to fill their ranks.[148]

In 1923 Winthrop welcomed the state's new Superintendent of Schools and ex-officio member of her Board. On his first official visit for a chapel program, the Honorable James H. Hope praised Winthrop and its system. "Having been taught here," he said, "the ideal of service through work, you will go out to help in the great work of lifting our State from the low position she now occupies in the illiteracy scale." Mr. Hope (like many others) overlooked the phenomenal progress that South Carolina was making in the twentieth century.[149]

At this stage in Winthrop's development, the summer schools had become one of her strongest features. Summer school not only included those taking classes (2,135 in 1923); it also hosted the Home Demonstration Clubs, the Farm Women, the County Superintendents and others. Editorializing on this in April, 1923, the Columbia Record stated:

> South Carolinians everywhere feel a pardonable pride at the announcement that Winthrop College now is offering a summer course that gives the State College for Women a rank equal to that of the great summer schools of the South, the University of Virginia, George Peabody, and the Summer School at Knoxville. . . . Winthrop College stands second to no other State institutions now in the affection of the people. It has earned the position it holds.[150]

Several interesting and innovative things marked the final days of the 1923 class, the largest in Winthrop's history to that date. The college engaged a Mr. Montague from the Tree of Brooklyn Botanic Garden to head the Department of Horticulture and Landscape Gardening: his expertise was sorely needed. At the June graduation the chimes were dedicated to all Winthrop's daughters. A motion passed, urging President Johnson to take a two-month vacation for which a committee would raise

366

$1,000. The Board of Trustees voted to have the
Southern Railroad erect "a shed of some kind of
ample dimensions over the Railroad platform at the
rear of the campus to protect the students in case
of bad weather when they board the train at that
place." Finally, to show their appreciation, the
senior class gave Winthrop a bag full of insurance
policies amounting to $112,000, which they had
taken out on themselves to benefit the college.[151]

The old adage that men and women make the
difference can especially be seen in Winthrop
College's development. There is no doubt that
Johnson could have obtained a higher position in
American education, but one can only surmise that
elsewhere he might not have found the degree of
adulation to which he became accustomed at Winthrop
and in South Carolina. In addition, Johnson seemed
to have his pick of good personnel from all over the
United States. He obtained many of the country's
best teachers because of Winthrop's reputation, and
many found there a substantial stepping stone to
higher places. Johnson could hire department heads
for $3,000, associates for $2,000, and assistant
teachers for approximately $1,700. These people
understood the great responsibilities that were
demanded of them. They set examples, taught their
disciplines, conformed and conducted themselves in a
manner beyond reproach. Few deviated from the
accustomed pattern. Being connected with Winthrop
was a mark of distinction. The girls followed the
examples set by those in authority.[152]

Two of Johnson's favorite people (who both
did so much for Winthrop and South Carolina) were
featured during the summer, 1923, in the Weekly
News. One of these, Miss Wil Lou Gray, started
community night schools in Laurens County, her
home. Later she did similar work in Montgomery
County, Maryland, before returning to South
Carolina to work for the Illiteracy Commission "to
eliminate the cross-mark in South Carolina." When
Winthrop initiated organized courses in methods of
teaching adult illiterates, Miss Gray offered the

367

course first in 1921, then in succeeding years.
Winthrop claimed to be the first college in the
United States and possibly in the world to do this
work.[153] The other favorite, Miss Christine South,
also a graduate of Winthrop, had a most illustrious
career as a leader of the Home Demonstration Service. With her charming personality, her sympathy
and experiences, Miss South won "an everlasting
place in the hearts of the women of South Carolina."
Her name became a household word prior to her
marriage to Professor Nathaniel Gist Gee. Gee was
an advisor to the Medical Education Board in China,
sponsored by the Rockefeller Foundation with headquarters in Peking. Mrs. Gee was sorely missed by
thousands of South Carolina women when she accompanied her husband for a long stay in China. Years
later, she returned to South Carolina and took an
active part in affairs of state and was elected to
the Winthrop Board in March, 1944. There she gave
good and devoted service to her alma mater until
she was replaced on January 31, 1962, by Howard L.
Burns, her fellow townsman from Greenwood.[154]

For the 1923-1924 session, Johnson complained again that they needed more facilities at
the college--more teachers, more recitation rooms,
more auditorium space, more library and dining-
room area, and more dormitory accommodations. With
another increased enrollment, Johnson was now
placing three students in most dormitory rooms.
Every county was represented: Anderson was sending
104; Spartanburg, 99; and York, 112. With
Breazeale Dormitory in use and with the teachers'
dormitory under construction, Winthrop was becoming
a more complete plant with each passing year.[155]

In December, 1925, Johnson advised Trustee
Breazeale of his recent trip to Richmond to pursue
Winthrop's application for admission to the Association of Southern Colleges and Secondary Schools.
Johnson elatedly announced Winthrop's admission
without opposition: the result was an A-1 designation with which Winthrop thereby joined such
distinguished schools as the universities of
Virginia, North and South Carolina, Vanderbilt,

368

Johns Hopkins, and others. Now the Winthrop diploma was equal to any in the South.[156]

Despite a long series of successes--large enrollments, large gifts, winning approval of the Southern Association--there were always some minor problems demanding attention. In early February, 1924, Representative Toole of Aiken introduced a bill into the General Assembly to set up a special commission to assume many Board duties in state colleges. Disagreeing strongly with the bill, Johnson and Breazeale felt that no institution could be run by two separate boards. Included in the bill was provision for a central purchasing agency. Johnson pointed out that North Carolina had tried this arrangement and had abandoned it and that a similar bill to Mr. Toole's was killed by the South Carolina college presidents the year before.[157] Mr. Breazeale, who had mustered Tillman's technique for dealing with the Legislature, replied immediately that he would fight the Toole proposal in the committee. He asked Johnson to write others in the Legislature. Within a week Breazeale and his friends had killed the bill's central feature. Meanwhile, Mrs. Daniel advised Johnson to do the same as Breazeale had earlier suggested. She further observed that "what North Carolina does seems to be very appealing to our so-called progressives." The League of Women Voters was also cranking up to help beat the proposal. Consequently, few politicians could boast of a more effective machine backing them than Johnson's.[158]

Mrs. Daniel's association with politicians gave her an insight into how real "wheeling and dealing" was done, and she attempted to push her position via Johnson and her brother, Carroll, for the betterment of her family and Winthrop. She worked through Johnson to have the York County delegation support Edgar Brown for speaker. Brother Carroll suggested that Brown's election would help Winthrop because Brown would appoint him chairman of the Ways and Means Committee--which originated the money bills in the Legislature. Johnson obliged in trying to line up the York delegation.[159]

Regardless of what was happening at the college or in the Legislature, Johnson stayed atop the building program. For three years he had been pushing Carnegie to supply more money for the Carnegie Library. The foundation was not inclined to give more. Johnson, miffed, posted a letter asking that his aid application and his letter from Chief Justice Taft be returned: "I am enclosing postage for the service." His writing this to a company which had given one of the best libraries in the South to Winthrop would suggest that Johnson was well advanced toward his second childhood or that he was acting like a spoiled old fogy. But the unexcitable Morse Cartwright of the Carnegie Foundation replied: "It is our long established custom to retain for our records all applications made to us in good faith and we should not wish to depart from the custom without specific action by our trustees." Later the disenchanted Johnson asked again that his application be returned: "I am enclosing a self-addressed and stamped envelope in order to save you all the trouble possible in this matter."[160]

Feeling that he had ruined his chance of gaining more Carnegie money, Johnson turned again to Rockefeller, sending an article on Winthrop by Archibald Rutledge to Rockefeller's office and asking his help in enlarging the YWCA. He advised that Winthrop had enrolled 1,730 students but that they had turned away 935 that year. Johnson also publicized that eighteen women missionaries had been appointed from South Carolina by the Southern Baptist Mission Board as foreign missionaries (mainly in China and Japan) and that eleven were graduates of Winthrop, "notwithstanding the fact that there are four Baptist Colleges for Women in this State." The inference was clear. Johnson continued his appeal in a manner gauged to please the religious and frugal Mr. Rockefeller by adding: "We give board

370

here covering food, furnished room, heat, lights and laundry for $20 per month. We serve good meals at eleven cents per capita."[161]

Continuing his appeal, Johnson stated that the girls wore uniforms and that the college ran a 260-acre farm for the dining room and also for the instruction of the girls. No doubt he surprised Rockefeller with his statement that Winthrop had a Department of Agriculture and Landscape Gardening in which the girls were given instruction in farming, gardening, raising flowers, and beautifying their homes, schools, and workplaces. In conclusion, Johnson stressed the Extension Department had enrolled 11,799 country women and girls in it during the past year.[162]

Johnson focused on the public schools and Winthrop's contribution to them as a main point illustrating his work. From South Carolina's 2,980 females graduating from four-year high schools in June, 1924, Winthrop received 2,200 applications. Using the high-school inspectors' projections of 3,500 graduates the next year, Johnson concluded that Winthrop would soon be inundated with applications. In his general report he showed that of the 1,278 college graduates teaching in South Carolina high schools in 1924-1925, Winthrop had 241; Wofford, 92; Carolina, 76; and Clemson, 72. The remainder came from 20 other South Carolina colleges and related institutions or from (219 teachers) out-of-state colleges. Johnson's figures showed that Winthrop girls were then teaching a majority of South Carolina school children, especially those in the elementary grades. And Winthrop girls were teaching all over the world.[163]

Johnson had about a dozen urgent projects he commended to the Legislature in his 1925 annual report. Increasing his request for funds from $468,108.45 to $797,748.49 in 1925, he argued that Winthrop--aside from being a great educational institution--had become truly one of the biggest businesses in South Carolina.[164]

371

By this time, the new Founder's Day had become one of the most important days in the Winthrop calendar. Johnson always made a big occasion out of this celebration, inviting an outstanding speaker, the trustees, and any guest who wished to come. For January 10, 1925, Johnson had advertised that Dr. J. A. C. Chandler--president of the oldest college in the South, William and Mary in Virginia --would speak. Trustee J. S. Breazeale, a charter member of the Board, expressed his regrets in being unable to attend: "I will be present in spirit. I hope that all present will enjoy the occasion, and that you will live to see many more anniversaries of the day, and will be able to continue your wise and efficient administration of the affairs of Winthrop."[165]

Mr. Breazeale was one of the most active trustees. He was oftimes a go-between in Johnson's disputes with patrons. He was also very helpful with legislative problems. Just before Christmas, he informed Johnson that people in his area were complaining that Winthrop was charging the students more than the amount the catalogue advertised. This particular case involved the textbook fee. Breazeale wanted an explanation in order that he might inform the parents in Anderson.[166] Johnson replied that the bookkeeper, by mistake, charged no book fees the first term, postponing the charging of the book fee until the beginning of the second term. Furthermore, Johnson stated that they charged only $5 for nine months, whereas other institutions charged about $30. The confusion in this case was due to the $10 charged for matriculation and medical fees. When coupled with the text fees, they were paid in three installments.

Regarding the Legislature's tendency in 1924-1925 to slash budgets because of an agricultural depression, Mr. Breazeale felt that too much was being spent on public schools and roads. "It might not be," he wrote Johnson, "the right thing to say to the Ways and Means Committee, but I am convinced that public schools and public roads are being pressed to the detriment of the colleges while they

372

ought to be of equal importance in building up the state." But many legislators did not agree.[167]

Mrs. Daniel's brother, Representative Carroll Nance, had promised to help protect Winthrop in the Ways and Means Committee. Mrs. Daniel wrote Johnson, sending a copy of a letter which her brother had written to Senator J. Howard Moore of Abbeville. In it he said, "It is a matter of grave concern that hundreds of deserving girls must be turned away and denied admission into Winthrop College each year because of the lack of room in the dormitories. . . ." Using this verbal lever on the senator (who sought a scholarship for his daughter because he had backed Nance for Railroad Commissioner), Nance reversed the request and suggested that the senator could use his influence to help Winthrop afford more dormitories and facilities, "to accommodate all the girls who apply and are able to pass the requirements." Concluding his plea, Nance drove home his point by saying, "It occurs to me close akin to a grave reflection upon the gratitude of our people that the true and tried President should have each year to spend days before the Legislature in Columbia, pleading with our lawmakers to provide sufficient funds to keep open her doors and render a great service--not to him--but to South Carolina."[168]

John D. Rockefeller, a Winthrop benefactor, had established a General Education Board at the turn of the century to study educational problems. Johnson learned from Superintendent James H. Hope that this board contemplated establishing a bureau of research and investigation in South Carolina. Thus Johnson wrote Dr. Frank P. Bachman of the General Education Board that such a bureau would be "of inestimable value to the educational development of this State." Johnson also asked each man to help Winthrop underwrite elementary teachers' training at Winthrop College, citing Winthrop's great work on campus and in the Training Center.[169]

Hoping to tap still more Rockefeller money, Johnson wrote the Reverend Richardson (who had helped secure Rockefeller's aid for the student building), telling him about a Columbia University team who were studying Winthrop.[170] According to Johnson, they pronounced Winthrop to be strong but pointed out the student body's great need for more rooms.   Not being bashful, Johnson asked for $70,000 to complete the students' YWCA building by adding some of the features that the war-time austerity program had eliminated.   To lend more weight to his request, Johnson requested Governor Thomas G. McLeod's written support. McLeod in turn asked Johnson to supply a letter form which would serve the purpose.   The governor then wrote the Rockefeller Foundation that Winthrop College had done great work for South Carolina in its schools, homes, churches, and social betterment, both urban and rural.   Thus, he wrote, Winthrop held a warm place in the hearts of the people.[171]   Johnson followed McLeod's appeal with a full-page article from the Charleston paper, "Written," he said, "without my knowledge," telling about friends raising money for Winthrop by a "Golden Rule Dinner."   Two weeks later Johnson sent another letter telling of Winthrop's entries into the National Canning Club Program in Chicago. A South Carolina country girl had won first place at Chicago in canning fruits: Johnson was overjoyed.[172]   However, by this time in Johnson's career, he had lost his earlier ability to beg--or perhaps he had exhausted his welcome with people like Rockefeller. With absolute and friendly finality, a Rockefeller aide informed Johnson, "It is no longer wisely possible for Mr. Rockefeller to assist in building projects or with the general work of individual institutions. For this reason your request has been finally declined."[173]

Johnson's reports to the General Assembly via Superintendent of Education James H. Hope had by then become repetitious, except for a few minor changes which he usually penciled on old reports to produce the current ones. Johnson would forward Hope a report for the previous year with a statement about the new year's opening that supposedly told what had transpired up to Christmas. With the ever-alert and sometimes over-persistent John Swearingen out of the system, Johnson now seemed to do about what he wanted to do. However, receiving a flattering letter could still spur him on, as he put it, "to do more and better work than I have done."[174]

At the beginning of each of these latter-day reports to the General Assembly, Johnson meticulously stressed his enrollment, applications, and lack of space. In about the third paragraph, he usually entoned:

We have followed the law (Act of February 27, 1917) governing the admission of students to State Colleges. Daughters or wards of parents or guardians living in South Carolina have had first consideration in admission to our College dormitories. We have first admitted old students and then eligible new students in the order of their application. We have not solicited a single student to attend Winthrop College but have felt it our bounden duty to give careful, just and fair consideration to every applicant for admission. Some of those who were turned away at the beginning of the session for lack of dormitory and dining room accommodations have come here and secured boarding places in the city. . . .

It is deplorable that so many South Carolina young women prepared for College work and anxiously desiring to fit themselves for the duties of life and for service to the State should be denied the opportunity of doing so at the State College for Women on account of the lack of accommodations here. The welfare of the homes and the schools and the dearest interests of the State demand that the young womanhood of the State should receive the training . . . offered at Winthrop by the State.[175]

Apparently without any suspicion of a mental conflict, Johnson in his next paragraphs boasted that "in a nationwide Athletic Contest held last May for all the Women's Colleges of the United States, Winthrop College stood first, according to the report made by the chairman of the National Women's Track Athletic Committee." And a few pages beyond, Johnson announced that two nationally known figures had taught in the last summer school--Dr. C. H. Judd of the University of Chicago and Dr. Fred H. Hunter of Oakland, California, ex-president of the National Education Association.[176]

Johnson reported 1,730 students enrolled in college classes in 1926--158 more than in 1925. "We are teaching classes," he said, "in the garret of the Main Building and in all available places, and our sections are overcrowded." With a 23-students-to-each-teacher ratio, he felt Winthrop was doing more than her part, since similar colleges had 18-to-1 ratios. Johnson reported that Winthrop could no longer meet the demands made upon it by South Carolina, "unless we are given a larger teaching force and more accommodations of all kinds for the South Carolina young women who wish to come here to prepare themselves for the duties of life and for service to the State."[177]

Now that Joynes and Swearingen were no longer connected to Winthrop, Johnson had returned to enrolling considerable numbers of "special" (college-preparatory) students in addition to those in the Training School. Some viewed the drive for "remedials" as a step away from a college's real purpose. But the emphasis on summer school always made good sense and good headlines. With over 2,200 enrolled in 1925, Winthrop would crest with all-time high in 1926.[178]

Many of the summer-school students-- including a great number of seasoned schoolmen--felt a special appreciation for the opportunity and they usually passed resolutions conveying their senti- ments. Typical of these were the Summer School Resolutions, July 22, 1925:

376

We believe that the job of the teacher is coming to be recognized as the greatest work in all the world; that the future welfare of America lies in the hands of the teachers of America; that they are the guiding influence of the never-ending stream of unspoiled humanity, the boys and girls of our country; that teachers are and ought to be, first of all, CHARACTER BUILDERS: that

> We are blind until we see
> That in the human plan
> Nothing is worth the making
> If it does not make the man.

We believe that anyone who carefully studies the educational evolution in South Carolina in recent years will readily see that the dominating, constantly accelerating force which supplies the urge to our educational progress lies in the magic hand of Winthrop College. It continuously forges the keys that open the doors of opportunity and service in every section of our State. The Extension Department, with the assistance of County and City Superintendents, has expanded the work of the Study Center by adding the service of free libraries whose excellent collection of books carries professional reading privileges to more than two thousand teachers.

We believe that the advantages which the annual Summer School at Winthrop offers to teachers cannot be surpassed in the South. Here we have nationally recognized lecturers who bring to us inspirational messages, new and vitalized visions and conceptions of the most urgent educational needs of the hour. Here we have a library which is widely known for the variety and the abundance of its well selected books, as well as for the efficiency of its officers.

Recognizing the wonderful work and worth of Winthrop College, we, the student body and faculty of the Summer School of 1925, wish to record our high appreciation of the value of the unusual opportunities offered by the college to our teachers and to other citizens who are interested in service to our State.

THEREFORE BE IT RESOLVED: That we heartily commend the sacrifice so many classroom teachers have made in coming here to more adequately equip themselves for more effective service in the classroom and in the community.

That we are delighted to have another opportunity of extending our earnest cooperation, our grateful appreciation, and our most cordial thanks to Dr. David Bancroft Johnson, a great leader in a great work, who has made possible the assets mentioned above, who has made his vision a part of each day's work, and who, more than any one else, has given a forward look and a forward move to the Educational forces of our State.

That we wish to acknowledge our genuine indebtedness to those in office, in library, in dining-room, and in dormitory for their contributing so much toward our profit, our pleasure, and our comfort while here.

That we express our appreciation to the City of Rock Hill for its continued hospitality.

That these resolutions be published in
The Johnsonian as well as in other
papers.

J. C. Daniels
E. C. McCants
W. E. Black
O. B. Cannon

COMMITTEE[179]

This summer program was budgeted at only
$10,000, but Johnson had saved some money from the
regular session to help out although under the new
budget law, surplus money was supposed to return to
the treasury. One reason Winthrop could show the
Joint Committee on Economy and Consolidation that
her per-capita cost was the lowest of any state
institution in South Carolina was that the very
productive and efficient farming operations set up
many years before by Mr. Tillman substantially
reduced costs. The college maintained a hundred-
cow dairy and complete creamery, over four-thousand
chickens, beef and swine, an apiary, a potato curing
and storage facility, and large vegetable gardens.
Added to this was the regular 1925 state
appropriation of $419,250 and a public-service-
activities appropriation amounting to $21,800. With
requests for approximately $250,000 more in 1926,
Johnson had a good bargaining point in that Winthrop
had increased its enrollment during the past seven
years by fifty-seven percent while its appropriations had increased only fifteen percent.[180]

A few days before his annual report to the
General Assembly on December 31, 1926, Johnson
wrote Secretary Clyde Furst of the Carnegie Foundation to try his luck at begging from them, as he
had done many years before. "Winthrop recently
was placed on the approval list of the Association
of American Universities," he wrote. "We have sent
out about nine thousand young women, and they are
teaching and occupying positions of importance and
are rendering service in all good causes throughout
this country and upon every continent. We have

graduates of this institution serving as missionaries in China, Japan, South America, and Africa." Johnson told Furst that the college was planning its fortieth-anniversary celebration and that he wanted someone from the Carnegie Fund to visit on that occasion. As an added attraction, he said that they were expecting President and Mrs. Coolidge for the celebration. A few days later, Johnson reinforced his invitation, telling Furst that Winthrop was the next-to-the-largest exclusively female college in the United States, exceeded only by Smith of Northampton, Massachusetts.[181]

In early July, 1926, Johnson received distressing news from Adjutant General and Chief of Staff of the South Carolina Division of the United Confederate Veterans: Trustee John E. Breazeale, who had helped Winthrop so much, lay gravely ill. Johnson was advised to hold himself in readiness for Breazeale's pending demise. It was Breazeale who had induced the Legislature to make Winthrop a state college; it was Breazeale who had worked faithfully for the college almost until his death on July 6, 1926. As Mrs. Breazeale expressed it, "Winthrop was the joy of his life."[182] His vacancy on the Board of Trustees was filled by Colonel Leroy Springs of Lancaster and Fort Mill, South Carolina.[183]

A personnel change meant little in Johnson's running of Winthrop College. He continued to ask for more money each year, increasing the amount in 1927 by $250,000 more than his 1926 expenses. To substantiate Winthrop's increased need, he cited some compelling statistics:

> Winthrop College is by far the largest institution of learning in the State. It is the second largest exclusively woman's college in America. The enrollment in the College has increased since 1920 by 66 1/2 percent while the appropriations for operating the College have increased only 19 1/2 percent. . . . During the past year it reached

380

over 20,000 different people . . . and they in turn have taught and influenced for good over 300,000. . . . During the past year the State of Mississippi, which has suffered as much as any Southern State from deflation and the boll weevil, appropriated for its State College for Women $500,000 for permanent improvements. . . . Of the $57,032.09 spent in 1926 at Winthrop for permanent improvements, $40,000 went for the completion of the Teachers Home (Joynes Hall).[184]

With 2,264 enrolled in the 1926 summer school (not counting 163 in the Observation School) and with the college forced to turn away approximately 1,000 applicants for the fall term, Johnson was cranking up his steam roller for the next legislative session. Taking time out from his busy schedule, Johnson and his children travelled to Washington to invite President Coolidge to visit Winthrop in the spring. Writing to Mrs. Daniel, Johnson anticipated that Coolidge would come since the Coolidges made a practice of visiting colleges, "having gone to William and Mary in Virginia last year."[185]

For the fall session of 1927, Winthrop registered over 1,800 students, vastly overloading all of its facilities. Still remembering the farmer's importance in South Carolina, Johnson announced that a third of the student body came from farm homes. His listing of parents' occupations revealed over two-hundred merchants, twenty-six doctors, and two-hundred and forty widows. Nearly every other standard occupation had furnished members to this cosmopolitan student body. Johnson was especially proud to quote from an open letter about Winthrop, written by "an honored son of South Carolina," Mr. Archibald Rutledge, and printed in the State.[186]

Rutledge wrote:

Lately it was my privilege to visit
Winthrop College; and my impression was
such that I trust you may grant me the
favor of expressing it. Never, I am
sure, in all my life have I been so
favorably taken with an institution of
learning; and the thought that my own
people and my own state support Winthrop
fills me with joyous pride and deep
thankfulness.

My first impression of the College was
naturally of the physical equipment.
Of this I can only say that I fear the
people of Carolina have no conception
of the magnitude, the beauty and the
utility of this equipment. Yet,
despite the many buildings and the
manifest atmosphere of efficiency,
there is about the campus a quiet
charm, an air that is the effect of
refinement rather than the product of
expenditure. For my part, under the
spell of that splendid college, I said
in my heart, Here is a place that has a
marvelous material equipment; but it has
far more than mere physical accommodations. It has a soul as well as a
body.

Winthrop's soul or spirit is a thing I
love. Just as a mere man can never
really make a home, so he cannot make a
college. Men's Colleges—and I have
visited many—are generally clubs,
more or less amplified and glorified.
But a woman's College enjoys the
boundless home creating power of
womanhood. I know Smith, and Vassar,
Mt. Holyoke and Wilson, Radcliffe,
Barnard and Hood. With utter candor I
can say that there is a spirit at
Winthrop that none of these others
has. The charm of Winthrop is the
charm of all that is best and most

beautiful in home; for there one finds
the spirit of service, the spirit of
devotion, the spirit of consecration,
the spirit that arises from hearts
which love virture and truth. I would
that words were mine to express with
some degree of adequacy the eternal
felicity of the charm of Winthrop
College.

This great college is the realization of
the splendid dream of David Bancroft
Johnson. . . . No man whom our State
has ever produced has done more for the
womanhood of the State; and, through the
education of young women, the whole
character and morals of the state have
been elevated. Let those who question
the purpose of life take heed of what
one man has done. Let them consider
his superb achievement.[187]

Winthrop's yearly achievements received
proper publicity in the annual report. This year
the faculty house--Joynes Hall--was praised for its
sixty-four rooms, its attractive cafeteria, its
pantry and related features. It was truly a great
addition for the college. Sharing top billing with
Joynes was the report of the Sanitary Committee,
which found Winthrop's health record unusually good
during this session. Evidence included the fact
that the last session had produced thirty cases of
appendicitis compared with none in the current
session.[188]

Winthrop had all the special features and
groups in attendance in 1927 that she had become
accustomed to: the State Press Association meeting;
the home-demonstration conferences; the state
spelling, music and dramatic contests; the state
conventions of Business and Professional Women; the
superintendents' and principals' convocations; and
the summer school. But like a thunder clap,
unexpected news boomed over campus--the summer
school had to be run for the first time without an

383

appropriation.   Winthrop had to charge   tuition;
attendance decreased from 2,264 to 1,684.[189]

In early January, the Senate Finance and
Ways and Means panel hearings had reviewed Winthrop's case and had cut drastically her requested
increase, even denying money to employ a Dean of
Women (whom the Legislature viewed as unnecessary).
Despite all the support that Johnson could muster,
the cuts stayed.   Johnson wrote Mrs. Daniel,
thanking her for appearing and sending her $12.68
for her expenses.   "It is preposterous," Johnson
lamented, "for anyone to suppose that you can run an
institution four hundred students larger than
another [meaning the University] on $100,000 less
money."[190]

To bolster Dr. Johnson's spirits or to
secure advantages (it is not certain which), some
leading faculty members signed a resolution on
February 1, 1927, asking the Board of Trustees "to
sponsor through the legislature a bill changing the
name of Winthrop College so as to include the name
of President Johnson."   They asked that the name
become   "Winthrop-Johnson College, The South
Carolina College for Women."[191]   Of course, this
questionable legal action from assorted faculty
contained a justification for their request.   They
felt that Johnson's name would add strength   and
power to the college and that the college would
thereby be doubly endowed with Johnson's life and
influence.[192]   In their concluding paragraph, they
stated:

Dr. Johnson is now in his seventy-second
year of life, and his forty-first year
of service to the State as president of
its State College for Women [actually
it was thirty-sixth].   It is impossible
to calculate the value of his services
to the people.   Even if such value was
calculable, it would be impossible to
compensate   him in a material way for
his service.   We ask, therefore, for
the   higher   compensation   which   this

384

change of name would secure to him;
namely, the consciousness of the
gratitude of the generation he has
served and the assurance of remembrance by the generations that are to
come. We feel that in thus changing the
name of Winthrop College the State of
South Carolina will be using the most
appropriate means possible of expressing
the gratitude of our people toward its
most venerable and beloved educator, and
will thus record for future generations
an example of worthy recognition of a
type of success and achievement based
wholly on the principles of service to
humanity.

Most respectfully submitted,

James P. Kinard
Minnie Macfeat
Annie V. Dunn
W. D. Magginis
G. C. Nance
Gordon Worley
J. H. Hoover
Abbey V. Holmes, M.D.
E. Q. Tschudi
A. P. Bourland
Lonnie I. Landrum
J. W. Thomson
Ida J. Dacus
J. Thompson Brown
Leila A. Russell
G. T. Pugh
W. C. Mallalieu
Walter B. Roberts
W. G. Naudain
Mary Theresa Scudder
Mary E. Frayser

Dr. Kinard attested that this resolution passed by
unanimous vote of the faculty.[193]

The _State_ picked up the faculty's unusual
act, and the reactions were forthcoming. The
Johnson-Daniel correspondence is particularly
interesting. Mrs. Daniel was ecstatic, "How happy I
am that through all the generations to come _you_ are
to be so honored! I'm never too busy to respond to
any call from you."[194] Johnson was equally as
patronizing in his reply:

> I cannot tell you how much I appreciate
> your good words and your good offices
> relative to the proposed change in the
> name of Winthrop College. I have not
> asked nor expected anything for myself
> in this connection. What I earnestly
> long for is that the State of South
> Carolina shall make adequate provision
> for the education of the young women
> of South Carolina here at Winthrop
> College for the duties of life and for
> service to the State.[195]

The next day, Mrs. Daniel came down from her lofty
perch and continued with politics as usual. In her
subsequent letter to Johnson, she suggested that
her daughter Lucia be given the prestigious Chimes
Scholarship for the next year and a dining-room
scholarship for the summer, while she (Lucia)
practiced the music for the next year's appointment as a chimes scholar.[196] Three days later
Johnson replied that he would give Miss Lucia a
dining-room scholarship but not the Chimes Scholarship, since all scholarships were contingent upon
approval of the Board of Welfare in Columbia,
except the summer dining-room scholarships. Johnson
knew what bad publicity could arise should the State
Welfare Board question his giving scholarships to
a Board member's child, especially one whose father
was a member of the successful Thurmond and Daniel
law firm.[197] Seeming somewhat offended by Johnson's
refusing Lucia the Chimes Scholarship, Mrs. Daniel
replied that they would not send Lucia in the
summer. Since she could not get the chimes work,
there was no need to attend in the summer to prepare
for the fall as she originally intended to do.[198]

386

Meanwhile John Gardiner Richards of Liberty Hill, Kershaw County, became governor. He was inaugurated on January 18, 1927, the first governor under the four-year-term law. With the state witnessing economic recession, Governor Richards went on record favoring economy. In his inaugural address, he promised to administer the government upon a more economical basis and spoke out against overemphasizing college and high-school athletics. He believed, among other things, that "No person who denies the Supreme Being and man's dependence on Him should be employed in any college or public school of the State."[199]

In February, while the governor prepared to investigate the Highway Department and to cut state salaries (including his own), Winthrop proceeded with a full academic and extracurricular program. The International Relations Club and the Carnegie Foundation were co-sponsoring the visit of Dr. Ernst Jackh, head of the Institute of Politics in Berlin and a champion of internationalism. After Jackh's lectures, the Winthrop club agreed to send two students to Atlanta to the Southern Regional Conference on Internationalism. Also active in February were the French Club and the "Dramatic" Club. The latter was producing Robin Hood.[200]

In the spring, 1927, an ugly problem involving Professor William G. Burgin of Sociology reared its head. Professor Burgin was accused of making statements that mill owners employed slave labor and that the owners lacked civic responsibility. Furthermore he was accused of favoring certain girls who frequently visited with him and his wife. Then there was the interesting report of a rather weak student from a prominent Rock Hill family whom the professor called to the front of the classroom to locate Greece. She reportedly replied that it was not on the map since the map was old. Mrs. Daniel asked Johnson to have Trustee Roddey investigate these charges before the next Board meeting: "I have no idea there is anything to it beyond deep prejudice and

387

misunderstanding, and am sure you will persevere until the truth is known and right vindicated."[201]

Johnson was slow in replying. When he did reply he stated that a new Board member came to see him the night after the last meeting "and expressed himself very strongly against action passed on malicious, irresponsible whispering and gossip and he was emphatically of the opinion that if we began such action the College would suffer terribly in a very short time." This was the first publicized trouble of its kind in forty years, and Johnson wanted the matter cleared up as soon as possible to release the mounting pressure.[202] Since Professor Burgin did not wish to resign, Johnson was asked to find out "what actions he desired to take." In an executive session of the Board on May 11, 1927, Governor Richards, D. W. McLaurin, Leroy Springs, and W. J. Roddey voted against Burgin, but John Anderson, J. E. McDonald, Mrs. W. L. Daniel and Mrs. George Stuckey refused to vote Burgin out. Secrecy blanketed the whole proceedings and the documents pertaining thereto were entrusted to Johnson.[203]

Voicing her disdain of the proceedings, Mrs. Daniel wrote Johnson it was unfortunate that the fundamentalists had managed to involve themselves in it. To her, the question was "how long should those who stood for a square deal and against acting upon rumors only remain silent, while shrewd, scheming politicians distort facts for their own selfish political ends."[204]

The pressure continued not to reelect Burgin to his faculty position. The crusading editor of the Columbus Enquirer-Sun of Georgia, Julian Harris, put out a large article entitled "Shameful Educational Situation in South Carolina." The article faulted Governor Richards for leading the attack against Burgin, who had been a Baptist preacher in California before coming to South Carolina as a sociology teacher. On a tie vote Burgin was not reelected. Earlier, the campus had been saturated with anonymous cards

388

inviting the students to furnish any information regarding him prior to this vote. Generally the college community refuted the accusations against Burgin. And the stand of Mrs. Stuckey and Mrs. Daniel was commended by the press. Harris wrote:

> Is it possible that South Carolina must look to its women to maintain the ideals of liberalism and freedom of teaching in its institutions? Or is it that there are other charges against Professor Burgin based upon which he was not reelected? If so, they should be brought out in the open. If not, his constructive dismissal will inevitably raise the thought that liberal thought and the freedom of teaching within even proper bounds are in grave danger in South Carolina.[205]

Soon, Johnson complained to Mrs. Daniel that the Greenville News had changed Burgin's article on "the Challenge of Constructive Radicalism," and he continued:

> We have never had anything of this kind in connection with Winthrop for over forty years. The same malicious, secret, irresponsible, consciousless falsifier will not stop with Burgin, you may rest assured. The government of Winthrop by malicious, irresponsible, venomous falsifiers has been ushered in. There is no telling what the end will be. It cannot be for the best interest of Winthrop College.[206]

But Winthrop had become too big and great to be injured permanently by events like the Burgin case. Johnson assured Mrs. Daniel in late July that the enrollment was at its highest, and he expressed the view that "if we had the accommodations Winthrop could be the greatest exclusively woman's college of this or any country." Johnson

389

further revealed that Kinard was sick, the registrar had resigned, and he was going to take a short rest himself.[207]

The actions of Governor Richards and his cohorts suggested that only fundamentalist doctrines would be taught at Winthrop. Johnson accepted this challenge. In his next report he stressed Winthrop's concept of true education. It was not only a mastery of certain definite branches of knowledge: Winthrop sought to send out its graduates "with a thorough professional training, an erect carriage, a fine physical and mental development, a good, pleasing conversational voice, good English, good health, good manners, right ideals, and high Christian character."[208] In answering whether Winthrop had succeeded in its goals, Johnson reported first on the college's Christian atmosphere: "There are over 1,531 students of the College who have voluntarily joined the Young Women's Christian Association for active Christian work." Johnson stressed that within the student body there were 632 Baptists, 525 Methodists, 340 Presbyterians, 90 Episcopalians, 57 Associate Reformed Presbyterians, 56 Lutherans, 10 Catholics, and 12 Hebrews. Only 20 students were not affiliated with any church.[209] Stressing another area of training, Johnson listed over 2,600 Winthrop girls certified to teach in South Carolina plus many others prepared for industrial and demonstration work. In addition, he pointed out that Winthrop played host to many business clubs and professional associations that served countless thousands of South Carolina citizens. With a faculty committee working to improve the curriculum, Johnson gave convincing proof that Winthrop's performance left little ground for criticism.[210]

Winthrop soon calmed down. The Burgin affair and its attendant criticism subsided when the professor become president of the Baptist College for Girls in his home state of California. Mrs. Daniel gave up her quest for a scholarship for her daughters, declining to ask for a tuition scholarship because "Mr. Daniel refused to have his

390

private financial matters put on record in Governor Richard's office for him to ponder and pass upon." This they felt would be certainly very objectionable under the governor's present domination of the Welfare Board.[211]

The scholastic year July 1, 1927-July 1, 1928, was better than ever. With 1,748 students attending the college--544 of whom were daughters of farmers--Winthrop was still fulfilling the purpose for which it had been created. Every county was represented with from six students (in the case of Jasper and Beaufort) to 202 students (from York County). The girls continued to enroll in the industrial studies that had oftimes been considered secondary to the Normal work--320 were enrolled in stenography and typewriting; 895 in dressmaking, sewing, and millinery; 996 in fine and industrial arts; and 605 in horticulture. (Naturally one girl might take several industrial studies and would be counted in each particular class.) There were 4,411 students listed in all phases of the Winthrop operation in the fall of 1928.

Johnson apparently was beginning to feel the weight of age and declining health--at least his communications to the trustees and other associates suggest this. There was some correspondence with Mrs. Daniel, who had renewed her efforts to obtain her girls scholarships not requiring financial disclosures. Mrs. Daniel wrote Johnson in January: "My daily prayer is that all of my daughters may receive their diplomas from your noble hands."[212]

Another problem which must have troubled Johnson during his last year in office was that Governor Richards dropped trustee Colonel Leroy Springs, the highly successful local textile executive, because Springs had located his new home in Charlotte, North Carolina. Mr. R. E. Wylie was elected in January, 1928, to replace Colonel Springs. This prompted Rock Hill trustee John Anderson, builder of the famous Anderson automobile, to attempt to placate the governor while keeping Colonel Springs on the Board. Springs refused to quit his post and Anderson wrote Johnson from his winter home in Lakeland, Florida, on March 17, 1928, informing Dr. Johnson that he was sending him a copy of what he had sent the governor. He asked Johnson to "please preserve" it. "I gave him [Governor Richards], a little grudgingly, some taffy, feeling it might be well to handle him that way, because the royal road to fame and fortune lies, put not your trust in vinegar, molasses catches flies. Confidentially," Anderson continued, "Richards is a weak sister, highly prejudiced and much elated with his new job. I hope for your sake we can keep Springs--he will give you a half million if he is handled rightly."[213]

To the governor, Anderson sent his "Congratulations on the outcome of the Legislature--no freak bills, lowered appropriations and early adjournment. . . . I am always afraid when the Legislature meets lest it spill the beans. . . ." Launching into the Springs affair and suggesting that Springs did not want to embarrass the governor, Anderson advised the governor to keep him since Springs had not changed his citizenship and should continue to serve Winthrop. Stressing that Springs had promised to make it possible to add a thousand more girls to Winthrop and that he "has the means to carry out his ideas," Anderson said he was not pro-Springs or anti-Wylie, but pro-Winthrop--"We don't want any small town Lancaster politics and feuds to get into and be mixed up with Winthrop." But Richards's position about Springs' not being legally a South Carolinian prevailed. This dismissal has been conjectured many times since as the reason that the Springs organization has not favored Winthrop as it has other South Carolina schools.[214]

This school year successfully concluded during the first week of June, 1928. Mr. Angus Macaulay addressed the WTS graduating class on June 1. The YWCA sermon was delivered by Dr. Edmond Soper of Duke on June 3, and Bishop Edwin Mouzon gave the baccalaureate. The week climaxed

392

with the graduating address by Rabbi Stephen Wise of
New York on June 5 at eight o'clock.

Johnson became ill with colitis on the closing day, and went to the Charlotte Sanitarium.[215]
Miss Sarah R. Marcum, Johnson's secretary, assumed
extra responsibilities in attempting to help run the
college.   Johnson's illness proved   more severe
than expected. When it became evident that he would
be unavailable for the fall opening, he wrote the
governor and conferred with the local trustees,
making plans for the college. He arranged for Dean
Kinard to take charge as he had done on several
previous occasions--holding this time the titles of
Dean and Acting President.[216]

Johnson remained ill.   In late November he
advised the Board that the doctors told him he would
recover. Considering his sickness in relation to
the college, his letter seemed to suggest that the
Board might wish to retire him. He concluded his
letter with these telling words:

> Having been President of this institu-
> tion for forty-two years you can imagine
> how dear to my heart has been every
> brick and stone, every individual--the
> members of the Board of Trustees, the
> officers and faculty, the student body,
> in fact every thing connected with this
> institution and how it wrenches my heart
> to have to write the above. With love
> and gratitude, D. B. Johnson.[217]

The Board decided to inform Johnson that they were
"well-satisfied with the way the affairs of the
college are now being managed," and they expressed
their sympathy for him during his illness.   Their
report went on to say that they were planning to
ask the Legislature for $90,000 in permanent
improvements and had resolved to draw up suitable
resolutions concerning the death of General D. W.
McLaurin, long-time member of the Board, Commander
of the state's Confederate Veterans, and Land Commissioner of South Carolina.[218]

393

Johnson did not regain his strength and recover as he had been led to believe. Through the medium of the Rock Hill Evening Herald and his sister (Mrs. Paul Workman, Society Editor), the community and the state were given a close and hopeful view of Dr. Johnson. On December 10, the society page described the Winthrop seniors singing to President Debe Johnson. "A group of seniors assembled at late dusk outside the window of the residence of President D. B. Johnson to sing a greeting," the paper reported, "to their Debe who is still confined to bed following an illness of the summer." The article waxed eloquently:

> The 'girls in blue' assembled in solid phalanx before the lighted window, and gave round after round of familiar songs, preeminent among them the well-known 'Alma Mater.'

> Though unable to appear at the window and drop the traditional 'rosebud,' Dr. Johnson showed his appreciation by cheery waves of his handkerchief after each song, giving his girls a thrill of pleasure. [219]

While he waged a long battle against colitis with serious complications, the vitality of the 72-year-old educator took a turn for the worse on Christmas day. He died before daylight on December 26, 1928: [220]

> The newspaper reported that word of Johnson's death spread rapidly not only through the city, but through the Carolinas and press wires flashed it to every section of the country. Although his townfolk and friends throughout the state and nation had watched with dread his losing fight with the malady, news of his death fell as a heavy blow and cast a spell of sadness over thousands of hearts. Early in the day messages and tokens

394

of grief began arriving at the college 'White House' and by midday the trickle had grown to a steady stream.[221]

Most facets of Johnson's life and long educational career were elaborately set forth by the local press. The citizenry had come to regard Johnson with great respect, reverence, and awe. All local businesses closed for his funeral on Thursday, and the public was advised that his body would lie in state in the Winthrop auditorium from eleven o'clock Thursday morning until two-thirty in the afternoon when the services and interment would be held.[222]

The elaborate plans for Thursday were meticulously announced:

At the bier tomorrow as it rests in state in the college chapel and as it is borne to the hallowed spot on Winthrop campus will be many of the state's notables and not a few from more distant points. The sad duty of active pall-bearers falls upon the shoulders of the educator's own townsfolk and neighbors-- H. M. Dunlap, W. P. Goodman, C. L. Cobb, R. C. Burt, Peter Ihrie, Dr. J. R. Stokes, Dr. W. R. Sims, and J. A. Barber.

The pastor of Dr. Johnson's own church, Dr. Alexander Martin, of Oakland Avenue Presbyterian, will officiate at the last service. He will be assisted by all the other ministers of the city.

Following the casket in order as it is borne to its resting place will be:

1. Members of Board of Trustees of Winthrop College;

2. Honorary pallbearers: (a) President of the Senate, Hon. T. B. Butler (b) Speaker of the House of Representatives, Hon. J. K. Hamblin (c) Presidents of South Carolina Colleges (d) Mayor W. E. Johnson, Rock Hill, Dr. W. E. Simpson, Dr. R. F. L. Lineback, Dr. Hamilton McKay;
3. Elders of Oakland Avenue Presbyterian Church;
4. Pastors of Rock Hill churches;
5. Teachers and officers of Winthrop College;
6. The President's Council of Winthrop College;
7. Alumnae of Winthrop College.[223]

The press editorialized:

Dr. Johnson was not an individual, he was an institution. He lived not for himself but for others and especially for those who came in direct and indirect contact with the great school which he founded and for forty years or more successfully guided. He ever thought of Winthrop College and its progress in the educational world. The result is that he leaves as a monument to his name one of the greatest educational institutions of the nation and the largest woman's college. . . .[224]

Throughout the night, the body lay in the campus house surrounded by a guard of honor. At 11 o'clock, it was borne to the Administration Building to lie in State until the funeral hour of 2:30 p.m. Pallbearers were followed to the waiting hearse by trustees of the College. Winthrop girls, who have returned in such numbers that is was necessary to open Bancroft Hall to

396

accommodate them, stood at attention as the body passed by, and then with garlands and wreaths walked beside the hearse on its slow journey to the Administration Building. The college bell tolled and college flags drooped at half-mast.[225]

Soon it arrived. The casket was borne to a parlor. There it lay in state, surrounded by flowers and palms and ferns and wreaths and designs in profusion such has been equalled here a few times if any. Hundreds passed the bier in reverent tribute. As the time for the funeral hour drew near the body was borne into the college chapel, where until illness drove him from his labor, no other figure was so familiar.[226]

At the appointed hour, the sweet-toned organ throbbed and swelled in requiem for the dead. A deep silence settled. 'I am the Resurrection and the Life' came words of the burial service . . . by Reverend Dr. Alexander Martin, prayer by Reverend F. W. Gregg, and music--favorite hymns of the man who lay dead--that was the funeral service. The choir of his own college girls, the chimes of his beloved college, and the voice of Mrs. J. B. Steele, to whom he has listened often before, in the old favorite, 'One Sweetly Solemn Thought,' gave touch of sweetness to the service which the burial ritual gave in solemnity.[227]

As the service closed, the casket was borne from the chapel by neighbors and fellow townsmen. Down those flights which his foot-steps had so often trod to and from the chapel, through those halls which seemed filled with his presence and across that campus which

he had measured with prideful eye these
many years, the body was borne to a
pretty spot not far distant. There,
with the reassuring words of the burial
service, 'I am the way, the Truth and
the Light; ye believe in the Father,
believe also in Me,' still ringing in
their ears, tender hands committed all
that is mortal of the great educator and
citizen back to the dust from whence it
came. Tonight the earthly temple of a
noble soul sleeps the sleep eternal amid
those surroundings so dear to his heart;
so much a part of his life.[228]

Johnson was interred in front of Bancroft
Hall, about forty yards due east of the front porch
where he had stopped many times. No longer would
Johnson be able to brag how he "locked horns with
Tillman." He would not lead the Blue Line to
church again, nor would he accompany the capped
and gowned student body on a shopping tour downtown, nor would he preside over the chapel
exercises as he had so long loved to do. No more
would he rap the student body to order and boom out
in reverential tones the Twenty-third Psalm. D. B.
Johnson was dead! But Winthrop continued with the
memory of Debe Johnson very much alive in the minds
of countless Winthrop daughters throughout the
world.

Rock Hill soon returned to normal with the
citizenry enjoying their "Pan-Dandy, Bamby Bread,
and Temptation Cake" from the Rock Hill Baking
Company, and their radio programs that ran from six
until half past eleven every evening. There was
dinner music from Charlotte, Nashville, and Atlanta.
The Philco Hour, the Lucky Strike Dance Orchestra,
Amos and Andy, and the famous Gully Jumpers offered
something for every taste.[229]

Before the end of December, South Carolina
was in the throes of an influenza and pneumonia
epidemic which prompted the state health officer

398

to request that Winthrop's post-Christmas opening be postponed an additional week.[230]   Meanwhile, Winthrop's governing Board of Trustees met in Governor Richards's Columbia office on January 2, 1929.   In addition to his Excellency, the following attended: Mrs. Daniel, Mrs. Stuckey, Judge McDonald, Dr. Martin, Mr. Wylie, Mr. Roddey, Mr. Anderson, and Superintendent James H. Hope, who acted as secretary for Mrs. Matthews.[231]   The object of this extra meeting was stated; consequently the senior trustee (Mr. Roddey) moved that Dr. Kinard be elected to serve as president until the end of the college year.   Judge McDonald moved to amend the Roddey motion to read "that all duties of President be devolved upon Dr. Kinard for the remaining portion of the college year."   The amendment lost with Mrs. Daniel voting in favor of it. Kinard was elected with the same salary that Johnson had had.   Mr. Wylie, who had replaced Colonel Springs, moved that the General Assembly be memorialized to give Mrs. Johnson Dr. Johnson's remaining salary for the year.   A committee was selected to consider this.[232]

Other decisions affected the Johnson family and the college.   It was the sense of the Board that Mrs. Johnson continue to live at the president's home, free of charge, until September 1, 1929, and that Dr. Johnson's funeral expenses be paid by the college treasurer from funds not regulated.   Mrs. Johnson was to be offered a college job, and resolutions were drawn and inscribed to his memory.   Trustee Roddey agreed to convey the actions of the Board to Mrs. Johnson.[233]

The new president, James Pinckney Kinard, was no stranger to Winthrop and to South Carolina. A graduate of the Citadel, he had strong ties with both the Low Country and the Up Country.   He had taught from 1895 to 1913 at Winthrop.   In 1917, he had assumed duties as dean, which he faithfully discharged for the next eleven years before assuming the presidency.   Dr. Kinard had been a pillar of strength and respectability on the Winthrop campus, and he enjoyed good relations with the students.[234]

Before Kinard was in office a month, Trustee Daniel wrote him, requesting the same scholarship arrangement for the coming year that her daughters had enjoyed with Dr. Johnson--Lucia to work in the library and Mary to be doorkeeper in the dining hall. Kinard agreed. He informed Mrs. Daniel that the Legislature had treated Winthrop "pretty well this year--so far."[235]

One of the first changes Kinard instituted involved the Committee on Organization and Instruction. Dr. Johnson, according to Kinard, had advised him in April that they should prepare for a two-term college year. Now Kinard was pushing this, advising that "the large majority of standard colleges are on the two-term plan." Mrs. Daniel approved, but she wanted assurances that her daughter would be with Mrs. McBryde in the dining hall.[236]

In March, Kinard heard from Mrs. Daniel's husband, a lawyer, who enquired about parallel reading at Winthrop. He asked, "what would it profit a woman to read a whole library and lose her own health?" The subtle Kinard replied, "Students usually take care of themselves in this matter of reading, but after receiving your letter I will look into it and try to arrange the matter so that it will not be injurious to any student." For the next several months, the Daniels seemed satisfied until a third daughter was ready for a scholarship.[237]

Kinard, who knew Winthrop's needs, enjoyed a first-name relationship with Clyde Furst, Secretary of the Carnegie Foundation, and he wished to secure help from him. Also he sought assistance from the General Education Board to help develop a home-economics department to meet the growing demands for teachers in that area. The assistant director of the GEB, Jackson Davis, could give no encouragement in this matter.[238]

400

Johnson's illness and death had increased alumnae interest in Winthrop. The Alumnae Association launched a bold new program to erect an auditorium to the memory and glorification of Johnson. The alumnae secretary, who had marched so many times with Johnson in the "blue-line," had renewed her efforts on all fronts during Johnson's illness. In early May, she sent each chapter head a list of important lecturers Winthrop would host during the summer. They included Dr. Frank Bohn of the New York Times, Major Tien, Lai Huany of China, Dr. Charles Clark of Yale (speaking on the Moors), Dr. Archibald Henderson (discussing Einstein), and David Lawrence (famous for his Sunday radio programs).[239]

Kinard's 1929 session came to a fine conclusion with three nationally known speakers at the exercises. The Board in its commencement-week meeting approved on June 12 the French Club's request to join the national Beta Pi Theta. They took under further advisement alumnae efforts to raise money for the Johnson memorial, and Dr. Kinard told the Board that he wanted Mrs. Johnson to continue in the president's house during his incumbency. But the Board authorized building her a house not to exceed $25,000 and they considered buying Mrs. Johnson's lot on the corner of Oakland and Sumter for this purpose. Her letter of appreciation for their generosity was duly received and noted.[240]

Dr. Kinard's report of his first year as president was shorter, more relevant and less bombastic than the Johnson-formula report--an index of the personality of the new Winthrop president who was anything but new to the job. The generous, slow-moving Kinard did not attempt to alter Johnson's image at Winthrop. After all, this image was one of the most potent forces at Winthrop College, and it would have been senseless to attempt to change it.[241]

A look at the college catalogue suggests how Johnson had sought to dominate Winthrop's publicity and even rewrite its history. Under the heading of Historical Statement, he had had the following printed:

The act creating Winthrop College was passed by the General Assembly in December, 1891.

Liberal provision for the education of her sons had long been the settled policy of South Carolina, but at that time the only recognition of the claims of her daughters for higher education was a small annual appropriation by the Legislature for the support of one pupil from each county in the Winthrop Training School for Teachers in Columbia. By the act above referred to, this school, with its name, was adopted by the State and made the nucleus of the contemplated new institution. This school was organized November 15, 1886, under the auspices of the Board of City School Commissioners of Columbia, S.C., through the efforts of their City School Superintendent, D. B. Johnson, by the help of the Peabody Board, and for many years received an annual appropriation of $2,000 from that source for its support. The name of Winthrop, which the new institution retained, was given in honor of Robert C. Winthrop, the illustrious statesman, orator, and philanthropist, who, as President of the Board of Trustees of the Peabody Education Fund, did so much for the cause of education in the South. Mr. Winthrop was deeply interested in the success of the school from its inception, and watched its development into a great State institution with special pride and pleasure.

Hon. J. L. M. Curry, the general agent of the Trustees of the Peabody Education

Fund, was an earnest and able friend of the Winthrop School from its beginning until his death, and much of its success and development is due to his warm support.

Governor B. R. Tillman, who had advocated the normal and industrial education of women by the State in a resolution offered at a meeting of the State Agricultural Society in 1886, recommended in his inaugural in 1890 the appointment of a commission to ascertain and report the practicability of the establishment by the State of a Normal and Industrial College for Women. It was upon the report of this commission, consisting of Dr. D. B. Johnson, Mrs. M. T. Coleman, formerly Miss Hannah Hemphill, and Miss Mary L. Yeargin, that the Act was based which was passed by the earnest advocacy of the Governor.

The Management of the College is vested in a Board of Trustees, consisting of eleven members. Seven of these are elected by the Legislature, and the four--the Governor, the State Superintendent of Education, the Chairman of the Committee on Education in the House of Representatives, and in the Senate, respectively--are members ex-officio.

The value of the College plant, according to the official inventory of July 1, 1927, is $3,022,879.82, of which amount the State has appropriated $995,666.49. [242]

In Winthrop's rules and government, Johnson's personality had dominated. The "General Regulations" at the time of Johnson's death reflect much about the real D. B. Johnson. They were explicit, strict, uncompromising, and autocratic. [243]

403

The pinnacle in institutionalizing Dr. Johnson was reached with the Founder's Day celebration of January 10, 1929. On this occasion Dr. Patterson Wardlaw, Head of the Department of Education at the University of South Carolina, spoke about Johnson and their long friendship. Wardlaw stressed that the best eulogy of Johnson was all around the assembled group, "Look upon these beautiful grounds, these handsome buildings, this efficient equipment. Look and admire, Dr. Johnson in one life-time having created out of nothing a little training school, developed it into a great college, with influences section-wide and reputation nationwide." Although Johnson had developed a great student body and great corps of teachers, his most outstanding accomplishment as Wardlaw saw it was the students' remarkable loyalty: "I do not know a group that excells the Winthrop daughters in their devotion to their Alma Mater and in their love for their educational father." Estimating the beneficial influences of Winthrop to be incalculable, Wardlaw concluded that Winthrop had prepared over 9,500 teachers who in turn had taught nearly a half-million students, to say nothing of the great numbers reached in other activities. Truly Johnson's was a monumental work.[244]

Miss Bessie Harper, President of the Winthrop Alumnae Society, continued the praise this Founder's Day. To her, Dr. Johnson's monument was Winthrop College and "the Winthrop girls upon whose hearts and minds he has placed his hands." Quoting from a recent toast, she entoned:

Dr. Johnson, your daughters will ever prove true to this spirit of service implanted by you. It is natural for those whom you educate to serve gladly and well in church, home, and state. In our hearts we'll rear monuments high, and our voices in praises will soar to the sky. Our gratitude, too, will go on without end, to you, our dear 'Debe,' benefactor and friend.[245]

Trustee W. J. Roddey added his praise in the vein that "every institution is the lengthened shadow of a single man." Roddey more than anyone on this occasion should have recalled the role of others in the great enterprise called Winthrop College.[246]

The kind and genial Dr. Kinard concluded the Founder's Day celebration by expressing what Johnson had meant to him. Noting his gratitude for the privilege of having been associated with Johnson, he called the president "A builder with an almost uncanny power of succeeding where other men would have lost hope and failed."[247]

CHAPTER XIII

PRESIDENT JAMES PINCKNEY KINARD

According to Kinard, Johnson left as he would have wished to go, with much to be done. Kinard set himself to work, aiming to finish the unfinished.

James Pinckney Kinard, Winthrop College's second President, was born at Kinards, South Carolina, on July 17, 1864. He was the son of John Martin and Lavinia Rook Kinard, members of prominent families long established in the Dutch Fork and Newberry County areas of South Carolina. Young James never knew his father, a captain in the Twentieth South Carolina Volunteer Regiment, who was killed in Virginia in 1864. His mother, a gentle and learned lady, greatly influenced his later life.

Educated at Newberry Academy and Newberry College, Kinard graduated in 1886 from The Citadel. From that time until his death in 1951, he worked unceasingly to upgrade South Carolina education. A PhD in English from Johns Hopkins University enabled Kinard to appreciate further his native tongue and he shared his appreciation with students he taught at The Citadel, Anderson College, and Winthrop College. He served Winthrop for forty-eight years from the time he joined the original faculty on the new Rock Hill campus, through terms as dean, president, and president emeritus.

Remembered for his humor and his humanity, Kinard was a gentle scholar who married another Winthrop faculty member, Miss Lee Wicker of Farmville, Virginia. They and their six children enlivened campus. Generations of Winthrop students affectionately remembered him as "Jeems" Kinard.

As an adjunct to the Johnson Memorial Auditorium, Kinard wished to create an institute like the Institute of Public Affairs at the

406

University of Virginia, where intelligent men and women could meet to discuss world problems.[1] Trying his hand at begging and at promoting Winthrop programs, Dr. Kinard solicited the aid of Clyde Furst and the Carnegie Foundation in raising money for the memorial. He also wanted to approach Bernard Baruch and C.P. Huntington, both of whom had ties in South Carolina. Furst advised Kinard how to approach the General Education Board's president and promised to investigate Mr. Huntington and to advise Kinard on him later. Furst suggested that Kinard use his name--"I would be glad to have you say that you and I are old friends. Maybe," he continued, "a letter from the Governor would help you with Baruch."[2] Thus, Kinard lost no time in advising President Trevor Arnett of the General Education Board that he (Kinard) was coming to New York to see him. Governor Richards had already written, asking that Kinard be granted an interview. Mr. Arnett agreed to confer with Kinard about Winthrop's needs.[3]

Kinard was also much encouraged by the Legislature, which initially voted Winthrop $465,000 in 1929 and increased the president's salary to $9,000 for the coming year. All tuition and other undesignated fees collected by the college, according to the Legislature, should be paid into the state treasury and held in trust for permanent improvements at the college approved by the State Finance Committee.[4]

Winthrop, with over 1,700 enrolled in the regular program, made necessary adjustments. The student body was divided for chapel--freshmen and seniors attended on Monday and Thursday; juniors and sophomores, on Tuesday and Friday. With 475 in the Training School and kindergarten and with over 900 in the summer school, Winthrop was still the big school that it had been for many years past. But the stock-market crash on October 29, 1929, badly shook confidence in America's economic stability. There were repercussions throughout the land as the country slipped surely into depression.[5]

Naturally some uneasiness surfaced during the 1929-1930 session among the college community. It was a forgone conclusion that the Legislature would trim the entire state budget just at the time that Kinard was enjoying a real boost in revenue. Early in February, the House of Representatives set the pattern by cutting Winthrop's budget ten percent.[6]

Designing his plans to cushion the shock of depression, Kinard featured numerous scholarships available to Winthrop students. First and foremost, he listed the 124 state scholarships that were based on competitive examinations and open to all South Carolina girls at least sixteen years old and of good moral and physical health. In addition Winthrop offered service scholarships and the following special scholarships:

1. The A. Markley Lee Scholarship. This scholarship pays $100.00 and is awarded on the basis of the following excerpt from the minutes of the Trustees at their meeting on June 16, 1911:

"That the A. Markley Lee Scholarship shall be awarded on recommendation of the Faculty to a student who has completed without condition the full work of the Junior year of the regular normal course. In making the recommendation the Faculty shall take into consideration intellectual, moral and physical excellence during the Junior year. If, in any case, this scholarship shall fall to a student holding a State scholarship, it shall be accepted in lieu of the State scholarship. The winner of this scholarship shall be announced every year at Commencement."

2. Grace White Springs Scholarship. Provided by Col. Leroy Springs. This scholarship is awarded to graduates of the High School of Lancaster, S.C.

408

3. Dr. W. Gill Wylie, of New York City, has provided two scholarships, one to be named for his mother, Mrs. Juliet Agnes Gill Wylie, the other for his daughter, Mrs. Lucilla Damon Wylie Berg. These scholarships are to be awarded to the two applicants making the highest average in the regular examination for scholarships in this state.

4. Mr. W.J. Roddey, of Rock Hill, S.C., a member of the Board of Trustees of Winthrop College, has endowed eight scholarships in Winthrop College, of the value of $100.00 each per annum. These scholarships are awarded each year by the Trustee and the President of Winthrop College.

5. Mrs. Rachel Brawley Witsell, Memphis, Tennessee, has provided a scholarship of the value of one hundred dollars to be known as the "Judge Wm. H. Brawley Scholarship." This scholarship award will be made each year by the Trustees and the President of Winthrop College.

6. Alice Gregg-Uta Saito Scholarships, established at Winthrop College May 16, 1925, by the Winthrop College Episcopal Class as a tribute to the first missionary from the class to China and Japan, respectively. The scholarship will be awarded by a committee composed of the President of the College, the Bishops of South Carolina and the Class President. The value of the scholarship is $200.00 annually, open to Episcopalians only, and is guaranteed for twelve years by the teacher, Mrs. Alexander Long.

409

7. One Marie Cromer Scholarship is offered by the Anderson County Council of Farm Women.

8. Two Marie Cromer Scholarships are offered by the Orangeburg County Council of Farm Women.

9. One Marie Cromer Scholarship is offered by the Council of Farm Women of Darlington County.

10. One Marie Cromer Scholarship is offered by the Berkeley County Council of Farm Women.

11. One Scholarship is offered by the Anderson County Council of Farm Women.

12. One Scholarship is offered by the Aiken County Council of Farm Women to a 4-H Club girl.

SCHOLARSHIPS PROVIDED BY WINTHROP DAUGHTERS

1. Two by the Winthrop Daughters of Anderson County, to be awarded to residents of Anderson County.

2. One by the Winthrop Daughters of Charleston County, to be awarded to a resident of Charleston County, value $75.00.

3. One by the Winthrop Daughters of Clemson College, over $100.00 when possible.

4. One by the Winthrop Daughters of Columbia (Fannie McCants Scholarship) to be awarded to a resident of Richland County.

410

5. One by the Winthrop Daughters of Edgefield, Loan Scholarship of $50.00.

6. Two by the Winthrop Daughters of Laurens, to be awarded to residents of Laurens County.

7. Two by the Winthrop Daughters of Orangeburg, to be awarded to residents of Orangeburg County.

8. One of the value of $136.00 by the Winthrop Daughters of Sumter, S.C., to be awarded to a resident of Sumter County.

9. One by the Winthrop Daughters of Greenwood, S.C., to be awarded to a resident of Greenwood County.

10. One by the Winthrop Daughters of York, S.C., to be awarded to a resident of York County.

UNITED DAUGHTERS OF THE CONFEDERACY

1. One by the South Carolina Division, United Daughters of the Confederacy, of the value of the regular State scholarships. Applicants for this must stand the scholarship examination.

2. The Pee Dee District, United Daughters of the Confederacy, provides one scholarship for a student taking the business course.

3. The Ridge District, United Daughters of the Confederacy, of the value of a regular State scholarship. Applicant for this must stand the scholarship examination.

4. Piedmont District, United Daughters of the Confederacy, of the

value of a regular State scholarship. Applicant for this must stand the regular scholarship examination.

5. One by the Edisto Island Chapter, United Daughters of the Confederacy. Value $100.00.

6. One by the Ellison Capers Chapter, United Daughters of the Confederacy. Value $100.00.

7. One by the Philadelphia Chapter, United Daughters of the Confederacy. Value $100.00.

8. Two by the Pickens Chapter, United Daughters of the Confederacy. Value $100.00.

9. One by the Winnie Davis Chapter, York, United Daughters of the Confederacy. Value $100.00.

10. The Mary Bradley Reid Scholarship. This is maintained by the Lottie Greene Chapter, United Daughters of the Confederacy, to be awarded to a resident of Lee County. Value $100.00.

11. Two by the Dick Anderson Chapter, United Daughters of the Confederacy, to be awarded to residents of Sumter County. Value $100.00.

12. One by the John K. McIver Chapter, United Daughters of the Confederacy, Darlington, S.C. Value $100.00.

13. One by the United Daughters of the Confederacy, State at large. Value $100.00.

14. One by the Paul McMichael Chapter, United Daughters of the Confederacy, to a resident of Orangeburg County with Confederate lineage. Value $100.00.

15. One by the Lancaster, S.C., Chapter, United Daughters of the Confederacy. Value $100.00.

16. The Frances Sullivan McDavid Scholarship. This is offered by the Greenville Chapter, United Daughters of the Confederacy. Value $195.00.[7]

Winthrop could also boast of eighteen loan funds that helped countless numbers of South Carolina girls. In order that scholarship and fund jealousies be kept to a minimum, Dr. Kinard reverted to the old Winthrop practice of listing those students paying tuition and those receiving free tuition. The new appropriation, made in a lump sum of $375,000 to be administered by the Board, stipulated that the president's salary would be $7,500 and that the tuition fees would be used for repairs and permanent improvements.[8]

The Depression's effect on Winthrop becomes evident if one views several actions of the president's office in 1930. When Mrs. Daniel (a trustee) wrote Kinard that her daughter, Susan, would be at Winthrop the next session and that she wanted her to attend summer school and receive a scholarship "to keep one of the other dining room doors," Kinard, mustering his courage, informed Mrs. Daniel that he could not accommodate Susan as he had made other arrangements. Rationalizing his position, he told Mrs. Daniel that the Ways and Means Committee would not even give him money for a business-administration teacher "that I asked for so earnestly." Also the college's moving-picture equipment was most unsatisfactory since it was the silent type--all the good new films were talkies. New equipment, he had informed the trustees, would cost $12,000 and would pay for

413

itself within a few years; but he could not spare the funds for the purchase. Mrs. Daniel, still pursuing a scholarship for Susan, suggested to Kinard that she would approve spending the $12,000 if the others agreed. She added, "of course, I would not approve at all of the girls going up town to the theatres." A final indication of the strict financial picture can be gleaned from a young girl, a ward of the DAR School at Tamassee, who was given a dining-room scholarship. When officials learned that she had parents in North Carolina, they moved to deprive her of her appointment under Volume 3, 1922 Code, Section 2813. However, they finally agreed to let her keep the scholarship the remainder of the year.[9]

In the summer, 1930, many students wrote that they were financially unable to return to school and many approved applicants had not sent in their room-reservation money. Kinard worried over this. When Mr. Thompson asked to be relieved of his duties as dean, Kinard wrote, "This suits me because I really need for this coming year with the change of curriculum someone who can give me the same kind of help I gave Mr. Johnson so long."[10] Still worried by money pressures, Dr. Kinard selected as his Dean and Director of the Summer School Bunyan Yates Tyner.

The summer school at this time was designed to meet the needs of:

1. Teachers working for the renewal of certificates through summer school credits,
2. Teachers working toward higher certificates, or those wishing to qualify to teach specific subjects,
3. Regular college students working for degree credit, and those wishing to remove conditions,
4. Students definitely working toward the M.A. degree in either the more general academic fields or in education,

414

5. Students holding a degree from Winthrop College, secured prior to 1921, who wish to qualify for graduate standing for work leading to a higher degree here or in other accredited institutions of high learning, and
6. Supervisors, principals, and superintendents who desire further study in their respective and related fields.[11]

And Winthrop was most convenient for summer work. The college was served by the Southern Railroad and a fleet of motor coaches. The fees were most reasonable--tuition and matriculation $15.00 and board $40.00 for the five-week session. The college provided dormitory living arrangements for men students on the same terms and conditions as for women students. Couples could also be accommodated. The broad and varied curriculum included Bible and Ethics, Commercial Education, and many classes in Education--with special work in Kindergarten, Primary, Intermediate, Secondary, Administration, and Training School Practice. There were substantial offerings in English, Fine Arts, French, Health, Home Economics, Library Science, Mathematics, Music, Penmanship, Psychology, Science, Landscape Gardening, and the Social Sciences.[12]

Kinard had made a great--though not highly advertised--contribution to Winthrop as dean of the college. He had been dean in the double sense of the word--as supervisor and helper to the undergraduate and as the college's senior academic officer. He was the first, and for a long time the only, academic doctor on campus. "Dr. Johnson," one of the founders, held an A.M. degree from the University of Tennessee. But Carolina College, at Joynes's instigation, had granted Johnson an honorary LL.D. in 1905. Presbyterian College had given him another in 1924.[13]

Now that Kinard was president, one would expect him to change the curriculum and to remake the college in his own image. However, as a true South Carolina gentleman and scholar, Kinard

415

(unlike Johnson) did not take himself too seriously. He was more liberal and less given to pontification than Johnson. He loved to read, to write, to create. He enjoyed helping the girls in any way he could. From his answers to a questionnaire titled "The Inside Dope On Being A College President," we can perceive another side to Dr. Kinard:

1. How do you go about getting speakers and special entertainments for chapel?

The Presidents of colleges guard the chapel hour. Chapel hour is a President's greatest opportunity to do what he can personally for the students. It is at the chapel hour that 90% of the students learn all they ever know of the personality of their President. Many of the entertainments at chapel are seasonal, the President taking advantage of departmental activities. Generally, the President just thinks up what in his opinion would be interesting and helpful. Perhaps the students do not know how often and with what difficulty at times the President protects them from propagandists.

2. Do you ever have to soothe irate parents? If so, how do you do it?

Yes, the President has to deal with irate parents. How he soothes them, if he does, is varied, depending on the parent. To keep cool and let the parent do most of the talking often helps. A simple suggestion that the student might be better in another environment frequently has a quieting effect. If the irate parent sends a letter the President can usually settle the matter by a talk with the student, leaving it to her to settle the parent. Students know what a President can do and ought to do much better than their parents can possibly know.

3. What about the relation between townspeople and the college?

[Evidently Dr. Kinard did not care to answer that.]

4. What part of your work do you really like best?

Doing something to make living and working conditions better for students and teachers; and working with the Legislature.

5. What are some of the things you do which outsiders would not think of in connection with a college presidency?

Getting up at 4:00 A.M. to help the President of the Student Government with a hard case, and not knowing what to say. . . . finding somebody in the biology department to stuff a ring-tailed monkey, with the owner of the dead monkey calling you up every five minutes to know when you are coming for it, for obvious reasons . . . finding out the best motion pictures, and often getting caught . . . learning in the spring what are the best fall styles for women's clothes and getting them . . . removing magazines salesladies from the residence halls . . . finding a good place for the students to have lunch when they sing over WBT . . . keeping CWA workers from singing too loud in the front halls . . . keeping the peace on the campus . . . determining the comparative value of Guernseys and Holsteins . . . and other things he does not know about now but will.

417

6.   Whom do you consider the most interesting of the famous personalities who have visited Winthrop?

Dame Ellen Terry.

7.   Which is really more fun--being an English teacher or being President?

I should say both are more fun-- first one, and then the other.

8.   How does it feel to be an author and to have your play presented?

It feels fine to be an author. Whether his work is good or not an author has the joy of creation; he is doing something that no one else has done. One hears his play presented with some trepidation; he is wondering if the audience thinks it is as good as he does.   The applause, if any, has a pleasing and probably an unnaturally loud sound to the author.[14]

From Kinard's short addresses, one gleans an image of the true man that he did not wish to disguise. He always liked to share his views on reading and literature. Reading (to him) was one of the oldest and most pleasant arts, not just an escape from one's troubles. He felt a certain amount of trouble could be good for a person--"as David Harum said, a certain amount of fleas was good for a dog, it keeps him from worrying over the fact that he is a dog."[15]

Kinard liked to draw on his experiences and to relate, for example, that after the War Between the States, when everybody was poor, he was fortunate in having a few books in his home. Two impressed him greatly: Don Quixote and Lord Byron's Works. He read these many times, and he enjoyed telling audiences that Don Quixote was one of his oldest friends. Citing his classroom experience

418

with Shakespeare, he delighted generations of Winthrop girls by raising his arms as if to alight and proclaiming that his best friends in Shakespeare were women. Then he would launch into a discourse on Viola, Perdita, and a long list of others.[16] And not wishing to appear completely out of date, he would classify modern literature as different and most probably better than the old. He felt that literature, like life, was profiting from advances in science and psychology. He liked modern plays and novels, especially European ones. And he sometimes evoked curious reactions when he would state now that he had escaped from the classroom, "if I were young, today, these [the new European plays and novels] are the things I would read most; not so much of Thackeray or Scott, or even Shakespeare, though I feel like a dog in saying so."[17]

By 1931 South Carolina's financial condition had grown less stable. Evidence can be seen in Winthrop's decreased budget and her president's $2,500 salary cut. Though the Budget and Control Board slashed the overall budget by 10 percent, Kinard expressed his willingness to work for Winthrop as long as the trustees wished him to do so "for whatever salary is attached to the office of President."[18] But Kinard wanted more money to run the school.

Knowing that the Carnegie Corporation was then helping colleges buy books, Kinard asked that they send a representative to inspect the library. "I am hoping very much," he wrote, "that we shall be found worthy of receiving help for books under the Carnegie Corporation Plan." Miss Ida J. Dacus, long-time librarian, informed Kinard that since they had moved into the Carnegie Library in 1907, she had seen the library grow from 8,000 volumes to 36,000 and the student body grow from 500 to 1,750. In addition, the library had been enlarged in 1929 at a cost higher than $100,000. Years before Carnegie had agreed to give $30,000 plus 500 books when a course on "How To Use The Library"

419

was added to the college curriculum. Now freshmen were required to take this course.[19]

Within the year W. W. Bishop, Chairman of the Advisory Group on College Libraries, had recommended more aid for Winthrop. He advised Miss Dacus of two stipulations laid down by the Carnegie Corporation to secure $10,000. First, the grant would be supplementary to the regular book funds of the college library; and secondly, books would be chiefly for the use of undergraduate students. Three-thousand, five-hundred dollars of the grant would come available immediately and the remainder would arrive in two later payments.[20] Those days it was not a labor of love to buy books with Carnegie funds. With budget cuts and nearly two-thirds of the student body granted free tuition and with the constant threat that the Legislature might appropriate the tuition fees allotted for permanent improvements, Kinard had much to concern himself with.[21]

One additional problem did not seem to bother Dr. Kinard very much: Dean Theresa Scudder was not reappointed on June 2, 1931, as were the other personnel. Mrs. Daniel and others held up Dean Scudder's reappointment in the Board, charging that the dean had drunk a bottle of beer while travelling in Europe with students. The transcript of testimony against the dean shows Senator T. B. Greneker asking Kinard, "what would you say about Miss Scudder lowering or raising the Conduct of the College?" To this Kinard answered, "I think she has elevated it." The dean was re-elected.[22]

At this time Kinard submitted to the Board a revised curriculum recommended by the president and faculty. There was nothing revolutionary in it. It simply attempted to modernize and strengthen the college's offerings. For one thing, it suggested requiring freshmen to submit a doctor's certified health statement before matriculation. For another, it attempted to specify a prescribed subject list for the college's five different programs. The only curriculum not requiring two years in a foreign

420

language was home economics, which carried the B. S. degree. As one would expect of a Ph.D. in English from Johns Hopkins University, Kinard eliminated the four remaining industrial courses, courses which Tillman had loved so well.[23]

The uniform, which had become a Winthrop trade-mark, remained essentially unaltered in the new look of the Kinard administration:

> The complete uniform for the year consists of: one commencement uniform, one gymnasium uniform, one hat, one uniform coat, one coat suit, and two uniform blue silk dresses. In addition, Freshmen and new students must provide themselves with white blouses and a navy blue twill skirt as described below.
>
> All students are required to have two navy blue silk dresses; one of these dresses is to be made at home according to McCall pattern 7286 B. This dress is to be brought by the student from home upon entrance to the College in the fall. The other dress will be ordered and measurements will be taken at the college for this second dress and a deposit required for it at the college.
>
> All students are required to have one navy blue coat-suit. A deposit for this suit will be required of all Freshmen and new students upon admission to the College. Former students are advised to secure a new suit; those whose 1932-1933 suits are found in first class condition upon inspection by the Uniform Committee, may be excused from purchasing a new suit for 1933-1934. They will be required, however, to have a new uniform blouse, for which a deposit will be required.

All students must provide themselves with a small, neat, black felt hat without any ornaments; black shoes and gun-metal hose for dress. There are no regulations concerning colors of hose and shoes for campus wear. Oxfords with rubber heels are desirable.

All Freshmen and new students are to provide themselves with plain, all white cotton blouses (with short or long sleeves but not sleeveless and not made of a knitted material) and a skirt made of navy blue twill according to Butterick pattern 4016. (Color and material sample will be sent you from the college).

Any student may provide herself with plain all white cotton blouses as described above.

Students who receive a diploma, as well as any other students who are required to remain for commencement, are to provide themselves with a white uniform. The Uniform Committee will select the material and a pattern for this uniform. All the commencement uniforms will be inspected by the members of the Committee. Details concerning this will be given in ample time.

No change whatsoever may be made in regard to the requirements of the Uniform Committee without their approval and all uniforms will be carefully inspected throughout the year.

The Uniform Committee suggests that a sweater coat (not a slip-on) in some dark blue material without emblem or decoration be purchased for campus

422

wear.   They   also   advise   that   each
student   provide   herself   with   a   dark
blue   raincoat,   and   umbrella,   and
overshoes.

Requirements for uniform deposit to
be made upon admission:
  1. One uniform navy blue
        silk dress ....$ 7.75
  2. One uniform blouse ......$ 1.65
  3. One uniform coat $13.75
  4. One uniform coat-suit .. $10.75
  5. Gymnasium outfit .... $ 5.40
  6. Fee for use of bathing
        suit and gymnasium
        equipment .... $ 1.00

All   seniors,   juniors,   and   sophomores   are   required   to   make   a   deposit
for items 1, 2, and 6.

All freshmen and new students must
make a deposit for items 1, 3, 4, 5,
and 6.

The above estimates are based upon
present market prices, and are subject
to the fluctuation of the market.

Every student is required to make
the uniform deposit before she can be
admitted to the College.   In case any
part of the deposit remains unused at
the close of the session it will be
refunded to the student.

The coat, coat-suit, one silk dress
and   gymnasium   uniform   are   made
especially for Winthrop College and are
sold at a low price.[24]

Appropriately, Friedheim's (a pioneer Rock
Hill mercantile business long charged with supplying
the uniforms) gave scholarships to Winthrop College.
The college announced in 1931 that Julius Friedheim

423

had donated $12,000 "to be invested in sound security, bearing not less than five percent interest and the income there-from be used to establish and always maintain two scholarships to be known as the Friedheim Scholarships to be awarded to two eligible South Carolina girls in conformity with proper rules and regulations of the College." President Kinard and trustees Anderson and Roddey were to settle the details.[25] They determined that the Friedheim Scholarships would be awarded as follows:

> one to a member of the Junior Class who has made the highest average on the first two years of regular College work; one to the member of the Senior Class who has made the highest average on the first three years of regular College work. Each scholarship is for the period of one year but the holder of the junior scholarship may be given the senior scholarship the following year if she qualifies under the conditions. In addition to the academic excellence of the applicant for the Friedheim Scholarship the general character is taken into consideration.[26]

Fortunately for the Winthrop girl and the college during this Depression era, Winthrop--under Dr. Kinard's careful guidance--was able to improve its program and to continue providing quality education at minimum expenditure. The times lent themselves to greater emphasis on self-improvement programs through home-demonstration work.[27] Kinard reported to the Board in 1933:

> We consider the work of the Home Demonstration Department one of the most important activities carried on in connection with Winthrop College. All counties in the State are thoroughly organized and great good is being accomplished. In 1932 there were over twenty-five thousand rural

women and ten thousand rural girls enrolled in home economics extension clubs.

Through the gardening, poultry and dairy projects much food for home consumption has been produced and conserved.

Through the marketing project the farm women have been assisted in selling for cash $312,042.77 worth of surplus garden, orchard, poultry, pork, and other home produce.

In order to anticipate the food needs for the coming winter, a state-wide Production, Canning and Storage campaign was undertaken by the home agents this summer and fall. This campaign reached both white and Negro families.

Following is a summary of some of the results of the campaign. Much additional good work was done for which no reports were received. The poultry production and meat curing and canning work is just beginning and will be stressed throughout the winter and early spring months.

No. year-round gardens planted..19,697
No. containers fruits and
    vegetables put up..........2,062,923
No. lbs. fruits and
    vegetables brined and
    dried........................577,981
No. containers meat canned......43,311
No. women teaching others
    to can........................2,905
No. community canneries in
    mill villages aided by
    home agents........................8
No. Negroes helped with produc-
    tion and conservation.........7,231

In July of this year Winthrop College entertained 305 home demonstration club women and 271 4-H club girls at the State Short Course. The program for the week centered around Child Care and Parental Guidance. Never was a short course so enthusiastically received. Many women have asked that the course be repeated next year, so helpful did they find the program.

Home agents have also given assistance with relief work as follows:

1. Finding needy rural families and securing relief for them.
2. Assisting the Red Cross in distribution of garden seeds, flour and cloth.
3. Forming groups to sew for the destitute.
4. Collecting and distributing fruit jars to rural families unable to buy them.
5. Assisting in decreasing number of cases of pellagra.
6. Assisting in establishing community canneries for the unemployed.
7. Securing and distributing home canned products to the needy.
8. Planning and supervising gardens for the unemployed.
9. One home agent was responsible for establishing and supervising six unemployed families on farms. Five of these six families are now self-supporting.[28]

Kinard always listed in a prominent place (after the college's administrators) the Home Demonstration Department personnel connected with Winthrop. For example, the following appear in 1933:

426

HOME DEMONSTRATION
EXTENSION DEPARTMENT

The United States Department
of Agriculture,
Clemson College and Winthrop College,
working in cooperation

———————

Lonny I. Landrum, B.S.
  State Home Demonstration Agent
Harriette B. Layton
  Assistant State Home Demonstration
  Agent
Theodosia Dargan Plowden
  District Agent
Bessie Harper, B.A.
  District Agent
Dora Lee Walker, B.A.
  Conservation and Production Specialist
Juanita Neely, B.A.
  Extension Poultry Specialist
Harriet F. Johnson, B.A., B.S., M.A.
  State Girls' Club Agent
Minnie M. Floyd, B.S.
  Extension Nutritionist
Jane Ketchen
  Marketing Specialist
Mary Shaw Gilliam, B.S.
  Clothing Specialist
Sarah D. Carlisle
  Secretary, Home Demonstration Office
Cornelia Nelson
  Stenographer-Bookkeeper
Rita Huggins
  Stenographer
Ammie Felder
  Stenographer

COUNTY HOME DEMONSTRATION AGENTS

Name and Address   County

Elizabeth Herbert.............Abbeville
  Abbeville, S.C.

427

Elizabeth Bailey.................Aiken
  Aiken, S.C.
Lucia Porter...................Allendale
  Allendale, S.C.
Ethel M. Madden...............Anderson
  Anderson, S.C.
Margaret Martin................Bamberg
  Bamberg, S.C.
Elizabeth McNab...............Barnwell
  Barnwell, S.C.
Lula Chriesman................Beaufort
  Beaufort, S.C.
Leona Hewitt...................Berkeley
  Monks Corner, S.C.
Lottie Mae Vaughan.............Calhoun
  St. Matthews, S.C.
Caroline S. Alston..........Charleston
  Charleston, S.C.
Elizabeth Williams............Cherokee
  Gaffney, S.C.
Ethel Ayers....................Chester
  Chester, S.C.
Kerby Tyler...............Chesterfield
  Chesterfield, S.C.
Carrie Carson................Clarendon
  Manning, S.C.
Pearl Calvert.................Colleton
  Walterboro, S.C.
Emmie James Evans...........Darlington
  Darlington, S.C.
Etta Sue Sellers................Dillon
  Latta, S.C.
Ophelia Barker...............Dorchester
  St. George, S.C.
Margaret McGirt..............Edgefield
  Edgefield, S.C.
Lucile Clarke................Fairfield
  Winnsboro, S.C.
Alice Guy Courtney............Florence
  Florence, S.C.
Mildred David.................Florence
  Lake City, S.C.
Minnie E. Doar..............Georgetown
  Georgetown, S.C.

Julia W. Stebbins.............Greenville
   Greenville, S.C.
Mary Ellen Eaves..............Greenwood
   Greenwood, S.C.
Izora Miley....................Hampton
   Hampton, S.C.
Margaret Cloud...................Horry
   Conway, S.C.
Marie Lambert....................Jasper
   Ridgeland, S.C.
Sadie Craig.....................Kershaw
   Camden, S.C.
Anne M. Moore.................Lancaster
   Lancaster, S.C.
Jennie E. Coleman..............Laurens
   Laurens, S.C.
Sallie Pearce........................Lee
   Bishopville, S.C.
Winnie Belle Holden...........Lexington
   Lexington, S.C.
Nell Stallworth...............McCormick
   McCormick, S.C.
Edna McPherson..................Marion
   Mullins, S.C.
Janie McDill...................Marlboro
   Bennettsville, S.C.
Ethel Counts...................Newberry
   Newberry, S.C.
Mary C. Haynie..................Oconee
   Walhalla, S.C.
Louise C. Fleming.............Orangeburg
   Orangeburg, S.C.
Sarah G. Cureton...............Pickens
   Pickens, S.C.
Eleanor Carson.................Richland
   Columbia, S.C.
Helen D. Abernathy..............Saluda
   Saluda, S.C.
Kate M. Hooper..............Spartanburg
   Spartanburg, S.C.
Annie E. Ervin..................Sumter
   Sumter, S.C.
Mahala J. Smith..................Union
   Union, S.C.

429

Elizabeth D. Boykin.........Williamsburg
    Kingstree, S.C.
Margaret Fewell.....................York
    Rock Hill, S.C.

HOME ECONOMICS RESEARCH

Winthrop College and the South Carolina
Experiment Station, Clemson College,
cooperating

Mary E. Frayser, B.S., M.A.,............
    Home Economist
Ada M. Moser, B.S., M.S.................
Research Specialist in Home Economics.[29]

Another college position which Kinard considered very important was that of the Dean of
Women. Winthrop girls had always been chaperoned by
fine personnel including the presidents, deans, and
other trustworthy adults. Even on shopping trips
downtown, an official chaperone accompanied the
girls. For several years Mrs. Lucy Gibson--a
cultured, Virginia-reared lady--accompanied the
girls and her over-zealousness earned for her the
title of "Hawkshaw." But her work was appreciated,
and she later became Assistant Dean of Women.[30]
Thus, in line with his views Kinard sought to lure
one of his favorite former students back for this
position--Miss Kate V. Wofford, an outstanding 1916
graduate who had made a fine record as teacher,
County Superintendent of Laurens, and President of
the Alumnae Association.

Kinard had earlier obtained for "Dear Kate"
a fellowship from the General Education Board. She
had responded: "Hurrah. I got the scholarship!
Will enroll in Cornell for M.A. and will go for the
Doctors if I can finance myself."[31] Leaving for
college in the North, Miss Wofford had faced a
decision concerning her position with the Winthrop
daughters. She had expressed to Kinard her desire

430

to resign but had awaited his pleasure in the matter. Kinard had advised that she let the vice president serve but that she not resign until the following June. During the next two years, she had received her master's at Cornell and transferred to Columbia University for the doctorate.[32]

By 1930 Miss Wofford had already made her mark on American education, and she was then the National Secretary of the NEA Board of Trustees. On December 1, 1930, Kinard offered her a job but she planned to teach at Furman in the summer (1931) then continue her work at Columbia. By the summer of 1931, Kate was President of the Department of Rural Education in the NEA. She showed great promise for the future, hoping to teach at Winthrop the next summer. Early in 1932, she advised Kinard that she wanted to apply for Dean Scudder's position at Winthrop. Five days later, after winning another fellowship, she withdrew her application.[33] Meanwhile, Kinard had been thinking about offering the position to Kate, but he wanted to wait until after the Board's spring meeting. Writing to her on April 27, 1932, he said,

My Dear Kate:
I had already thought of you. One thing you would have to settle with yourself is the question of whether you would like to be a Dean of Women. Your chief duties would be to look after the morals and manners of the students, give weekend leaves of absence, control the social clubs, keep students in uniform, and supervise the matrons in the residence halls. On the higher side there would be the opportunity of helping with the Student Government, helping to mold the character of hundreds of South Carolina girls, helping in the social and personal problems of the students, and helping to make them better citizens of the state. You would be expected to teach at least one class a week. I can, of course, see many

431

other ways in which you could and would
be of tremendous help in running the
institution.

Kinard planned to nominate a successor to Dean
Scudder to the Board on June 1.[34]

Miss Wofford made a formal application on
May 10, 1932, for the position of Dean of Women at
Winthrop. Her credentials were impressive. Ten
days later Kinard informed her that he would
recommend her to the Board for approval on May 31.
The salary was to be $2,550 for nine months with
free board and room. Having high hopes for her
appointment, Kinard wrote, "I am hoping with your
help that we might develop something that has not
been fully done up to this time. I am thinking of
personnel work with the students and also with
vocational guidance as far as we can do it."[35]

Miss Wofford, who was a fine speaker and an
excellent scholar as well as an accomplished and
outstanding educator, was considered one of the
leaders of the National Education Association. Her
neighbors in Laurens of the law firm of Simpson,
Cooper, and Babb praised Miss Wofford as a "charming
personality, of impeccable character, who has the
capacity to inspire young womanhood."[36] However, Mrs.
Daniel of the Board (who was oriented toward the
legal profession) favored another candidate, Mrs.
Kate Glenn Hardin, M.A., sister of prominent federal
Judge J. L. Glenn. The Board failed to render a
decision as Kinard had expected. On June 2, he
asked Miss Wofford to have the NEA people write
since the decision was postponed until June 21. But
the influence of Mrs. Daniel and the lawyers elected
Mrs. Hardin, leaving Kinard the lonely task of
wiring Kate the decision. Informing "My dear Kate"
more fully by letter the next day, he wrote:

There were absolutely no charges of
any kind made against you by anybody.
That was studiously avoided. The whole
story is that a sufficient number to

432

defeat your elections had made up their minds before the meeting how they would vote. I read all the fine letters I had received. I tried to convince them that Winthrop had an opportunity to make a step forward in the management of all matters connected with the Dean of Women's office by electing you. All was to no avail for the reason I gave above.

I feel that I gave the Board an opportunity to do something fine for the college but they did not see it that way. I hope you will forget about it and continue your work for your Ph.D. degree and get something much better than the Dean of Women at Winthrop College. I feel quite sure that this will come about. . . .[37]

Miss Wofford continued with her work and her office in the NEA. Later she wrote Kinard:

I cannot say, truthfully, that I am greatly disappointed at the action of the Board. After all I am not interested in a political position, but in a professional one, and the action of the Board makes the place dangerously political, especially since you have lost control of it. I think my feelings are hurt, and I am much embarrassed, especially with my N.E.A. Friends. To their inquiries, I simply stated that I have decided to go on with my degree. I would like to know the tale that Mary T. Nance [Mrs. Daniel] circulated behind my back. If you ever find out, do give me the satisfaction of telling me.[38]

Dr. Kate Wofford finished her academic preparations, received a fine position in the New York state system, and became Director of Rural Education at the State Teachers' College in Buffalo.

433

She had come a long way from her happy home in
Laurens, where she had helped with her nine brothers
and sisters. During her career she held many jobs--
starting as a clerk in Senator Tillman's Washington
office, in later life helping reorganize elementary
education in Turkey and also in Korea in 1948, and
finally heading the Education Department of the
University of Florida. [39]   She represented the best
of what Winthrop had made possible in South Carolina
and the nation, but she remembered how she had been
denied the opportunity to serve her first academic
love--Winthrop College.   Years later, she wrote
Alumnae Secretary Leila A. Russell and suspended
her $200 pledge to the Memorial Auditorium fund,
stating most implicitly,

> . . . I do not intend to pay the pledge
> so long as Mary T. Nance Daniels is a
> trustee of the College.   I not only
> think that she had done the College an
> irreparable amount of harm but that she
> is also guilty of misrepresentation of
> me, an affront which I find it
> impossible to forgive or to condone.
>
> In view of these facts I shall be
> glad if you will mark my pledge can-
> celled until such a good day when she
> is defeated as a member of the Board.
> Upon that happy event, I shall be glad
> to send you a check for $200; indeed in
> my gratitude of the riddance I shall
> probably be moved to increase it. [40]

One of the most cooperative efforts of Winthrop College alumnae was the drive to collect funds
to build a Johnson memorial.   Much effort came from
Dr. Kinard's administration, which presented their
plan to the Board on June 12, 1929.   The Board
"expressed its approval and appreciation of the
efforts of the Alumnae to raise the money." [41]

The Alumnae Society, headed by President
Bessie Harper of Aiken,   printed a special edition
of their Alumnae News for January, February, and

434

March of 1929 showing the "Proposed Plans For
Memorial Auditorium In Memory of David Bancroft
Johnson." The plans, beautifully drawn and illustrated by Edwards and Sayward, showed a design which
Johnson had favored before his death--a design
projected on the same plan as New York's Radio City
that would stand between Tillman Science Building
and Joynes Hall (the new faculty home). The plans
also showed the main floor of the proposed memorial
and an aerial view illustrating how it would blend
with new buildings to be constructed near its north
and west sides. The building was designed to seat
3,500; and "out of love and gratitude, the Alumnae
of the College proposed to raise $250,000 to erect
the Auditorium as a memorial to the beloved founder
of their Alma Mater." With an appeal to the class
reunions of 1929 ('95, '96, '97, '98, '04, '14,
'15, '16, '17, and '27), this News edition also
carried special appeals from prominent alumnae
around the world and stated that a professional
solicitation firm--Browne and Browne of
Augusta--would handle the details.42 Then, the
alumnae secretary in her quest for funds cited the
great effort and results made by Harvard in its
alumni drives. In the vein of "My Debt to Winthrop
Can Never Be Paid," Miss Harper wrote:

> I wonder if we ever stop to think that
> we would not be able to hold the posi-
> tion we now hold and earn money we
> are now earning if it were not for
> Winthrop. In many instances Winthrop
> girls are given the preference over
> other girls in getting positions.
> There is a great surplus of teachers
> in the state now. Many who would like
> to be teaching can't do so, for there
> aren't enough openings. And many of
> these had to pay more for their
> training than Winthrop girls did.
> . . . If for no other reason . . .
> every Winthrop graduate should feel
> a great debt and obligation to the
> college that gave her education so

cheaply, and that gave her such a fine
standing in the educational field.[43]

Next Mrs. Daniel, not to be outdone, gave a long
discourse on alumnae affairs and college giving
and ended with a plea:

> Our great need at the college is an
> auditorium which will accommodate five
> or six thousand people. It is a need
> which President Johnson faced for
> several years and one which he longed
> to see met. The Alumnae Association
> had undertaken to meet this need,
> making the auditorium a memorial to
> him. Fellow Alumna, wherever you are,
> your Alumnae Association is presenting
> a privilege to you in that you are to
> be permitted to do honor to yourself
> by shouldering the responsibility for
> the success of the campaign from now
> on to secure the necessary fund for
> the erection of this auditorium.[44]

And from the foreign field, 32 North Compound,
P.U.M.C., Peking, came "love and best wishes" from
Christine South Gee. She had learned from her
daughter Drucilla that Debe was dead. Their long
association had caused Mrs. Gee to regard him as a
father. "He was a guide, friend, counsellor, a
strong right arm," she wrote. "Winthrop will never
be the same to me again, but his life should be a
challenge to all of us to live worthily of the great
life that has been lived so valiantly, so fruit-
fully, before us. I am sending herewith a
contribution of $100. I wish that it might have
been more nearly commensurate with my regard for the
beloved Founder of our Alma Mater."[45]

Two other comments in the News' special edition merit note. The Columbia Chapter of Winthrop Alumnae under Mary H. Swearingen was deeply
interested in the Memorial Auditorium campaign. To
her, its success would "prove the spirit and loyalty
of the Winthrop Daughters and will provide a worthy

436

addition to the college plant."[46]   And as for Eliza
T. De Saussure, she wanted the memorial because
Dr. Johnson's wish was "to have an auditorium large
enough to hold his Winthrop Daughters, without
making the Freshmen sit on the steps. . . . After
we leave our dear old college campus there are
comparatively few ways we have of showing our
appreciation of all that was done for us while
there. How we are happy of an opportunity to share
in the building of the President Johnson Memorial
Auditorium."[47]

Winthrop girls had long been famous for
community service in an era generally lacking
organized welfare activities. For years they had
led their communities in a multitude of activities:
entertaining Confederate veterans; sending games,
food, and other aid to veterans hospitals; helping
with Red Cross and federated club activities;
raising money for student loans, old ladies homes,
nursery schools, camps for underprivileged girls
(white and colored); and rendering many other
services to the community, church, and home. But
now the Daughters faced their greatest challenge in
raising a quarter of a million dollars at a time
when the Sandlapper State was thrashing in the
throes of Depression.[48]

A closer look at the financial problems
Dr. Kinard faced in running Winthrop gives a clue
to the problem the Daughters faced in funding their
memorial. With reduced budgets, no money to hire a
dean, and the room rent in Joynes reduced to
$10.00, the Board for the first time ever had to
stipulate that "owing to the depressed conditions
of affairs in the country the committee [on finance]
recommends that we do not purchase any real estate
at the present time." Prospects were also dim since
the Board anticipated a fifteen-percent appropriation reduction for the coming year.[49]

President Kinard was, at the time,
attempting to extract some financial aid from the
General Education Board to help underwrite an
expanded teacher-training plan. Having witnessed
the advantages that Johnson had reaped from his

437

unique practice (teacher-training) school, Kinard sought to make the Training School even more unique and more effective. In essence, as Kinard explained it, he had a three-year exchange plan for teachers in the field and Winthrop seniors: the senior would go to the teacher's school for a week to take her work, while the teacher came to Winthrop to observe the Training School. The program was so successful (quadrupling in three years) that Kinard wanted to establish "a big, modern, model Training School for the benefit of all the teachers in South Carolina and possibly neighboring states." The assistant director of the General Education Board promised a visit to look into this. [50]

In late 1932 and early 1933 Winthrop, like most institutions, passed through a very difficult period financially. In October the Board of Trustees passed an austerity resolution and instructed President Kinard to inform the officers and teachers. It was the sense of the Board that--from January 1 until the 1933 appropriations of the General Assembly were made--only half of each month's salary would be advanced and as much of the rest would be paid later as they could afford. During this period a statement appeared at the bottom of all college stationery: "Each ton of this paper contains a bale of cotton--another opportunity to Serve the South." But in March the college felt the financial pinch even more. The Board was forced to release twenty-one teachers and officials: Sarah Grant dropped from an English position to museum curator; the Office of Rural Education was discontinued and Professor John F. Thomason was offered work in Social Science; the Departments of Biology, Horticulture, Geography, and Geology were combined into Natural Science with members doubling up; Miss Erskine's famous college tea room was discontinued; and Professor Thomson, who had been sick, was later granted a year's leave without pay. There were others. Things became so bad that Kinard proposed buying uniforms from the manufacturers, thereby saving the students $5,000. [51]

A complicating factor in Winthrop's situation in 1933 was York Senator Walter Dunlap's attempt to pass a bill allowing local boys to attend Winthrop. Many of Dunlap's constituents could not afford to send their boys to Clemson, so he was attempting a compromise. But Kinard, who had friends in the Legislature, visited "a great many senators about this and they assured him that the bill would not pass." Mrs. Daniel and Mr. Roddey were opposed also. Mrs. Daniel replied to Kinard, "I do not think it has any chance to pass. . . ." The proposal was "decidedly unwise" as she saw it. When the appropriation bill passed, it carried the statement "That no female students be admitted to Clemson College" with its appropriation and "that no male students be admitted to Winthrop College."[52]

Winthrop's tight budget hurt many. Mrs. Daniel was "deeply concerned in regard to Dr. Thomason, because he has a family dependent upon him . . . there would be more justification for retaining him than some others." Kinard promptly replied that he would consider her request carefully but continued, "as I explained . . . he is the one teacher that we could absolutely get along without in our reorganization." From her vantage point on the Committee on Organization and Instruction, Mrs. Daniel did not hesitate to make her wishes known to Kinard about certain teachers she wished to dismiss or retain during this financial emergency.[53]

The Appropriation Act for 1934-1935 was the most restrictive that South Carolina has witnessed in the twentieth century. Only $32,845 was set aside for the governor's office--personal, mansion and law enforcement. The University was cut to $168,450; the Medical College to $65,750; and Winthrop to $176,687, "Provided that no male students be admitted to Winthrop College." And it was further "Provided that $10,000.00 of the appropriation is to be used as a payment on the purchase price of three boilers, the cost of which shall not exceed $30,000.00. The Board of Trustees of Winthrop College are hereby authorized, empowered, and

directed to execute and deliver two proper notes
for the $20,000.00 balance; one note in the sum of
$10,000.00 payable during the year 1935 and the
other note in the sum of $10,000.00 payable during
the year 1936; said notes to bear interest at a
rate not to exceed six (6%) per cent." There could
be no question about the extent of this request.[54]

The reorganization which Kinard and the
Board effected was tailored to meet this Depression-
spawned budget. Each curriculum on the campus was
streamlined and succinctly described in the catalogue. For example, these were the requirements
for the Bachelor of Arts degree with the suggested
distribution of the work:

```
                                        Semester
                                        Hours
    English...........................12
    History........................... 6
    Social Sciences................... 3
    Languages.........................12
       Ancient or Modern
    Science...........................12
       Biological.........6
       Physical...........6
    Mathematics....................... 6
    Psychology (general).............. 3
    Physical Education................ 4

    Constants...................Total 58
    Major.......................18 - 30
    Minor.......................12 - 18
    Electives...................18 - 36

       Grand Total..................124
```

Notes:

(1)   Before the beginning of the
Sophomore Year the student will decide
upon a course for concentration called
a major, and before the beginning of
the Junior Year she will decide on an
additional course for somewhat less

440

concentration called a minor. As a rule, the major and minor should be related, but in different departments.

(2) As a rule students are advised to take more than the minimum 18 hours designated as a major (24 semester hours recommended as the norm), and more than the minimum 12 hours designated as a minor, but in the general academic courses as much as 36 hours may be elective. Majors and minors include subjects taken in the Freshman and Sophomore years, but the major must include at least 12 semester hours above the required courses in Freshman and Sophomore years, and the minor must include at least 6 semester hours above the required courses in the Freshman and Sophomore years. The advice of the head of the department in which the major lies, and of the Registrar, should be sought in determining the general program for the degree.

(3) Of the 120 semester hours required for the Bachelor of Arts degree, other than physical education, which carries a credit of four semester hours, as much as 24 semester hours may be in education. For the Bachelor of Science degree in special fields, approximately 50% of the work is academic and the remainder professional. (See suggested distribution under Commercial Science, Home Economics, Music, etc.)

(4) In addition to required courses set up in any curriculum leading to the Bachelor of Arts degree students may elect and count toward the degree as much as 12 semester hours in any one, or in a combination of departments, in Fine and Practical Arts-Fine Arts, Home

Economics, Music. Not more than 6 of
the semester hours may be in Practical Music, and this shall be on a level
above that of the standards set up for
the Freshman Year.

FRESHMAN YEAR

	Semester Hours
English 1-2.....................	6
Science (Biology) 1-2...........	6
Mathematics 1-2.................	6
Language (Ancient or Modern) 1-2.	6
Library Science 1...............	1
Physical Education 1-2..........	1
Electives:......................	6

   History 1-2
   Sociology 1-2
   Geography 21
   Language (2nd) 1-2
   Astronomy 1-2
   Art 1-2
   Home Economics 1-2
   Chemistry 21-22
   Nature Study 1

$$\overline{32}$$

SOPHOMORE YEAR

	Semester Hours
English 21-22...................	6
Language (Ancient or Modern) 21-22.................	6
(1) History 1-2....................	3-6
or	
Social Sciences.................	3-6
Science (Chemistry or Physics) 21-22...............	6
Psychology 21...................	3
(2) Major or Electives..............	6
Physical Education 21-22........	1

$$\overline{31}$$

JUNIOR YEAR

	Semester Hours
Major (Cont'd)	6-12
Minor	6
Electives	12-18
Physical Education	1
	31

SENIOR YEAR

	Semester Hours
Major	6-12
Minor	6
Electives	12-18
Physical Education	1
	31

Notes:

(1) Students who did not elect History in the Freshman Year should take a full year course in History the Sophomore Year. This may be done by omitting Psychology or three hours of electives till the Junior Year.

(2) Where the major falls within one of the departments listed in this year--English, Language, History, Social Science, Science, Psychology-- the students may select six hours in electives.

(3) In order to secure credit on a foreign language the work must be pursued for two years, except that in some instances on the advice of the major professor and with the approval of the Registrar, one year of language may be counted as credit toward a degree when taken as a second or third language in the Junior or Senior Year.

443

(4) Students planning to teach are advised to consult the certificate requirements of South Carolina and neighboring states and so plan their course as to qualify for an A-Grade Certificate.[55]

With 1,573 students enrolled in the regular 1932-1933 session, with the summer-school enrollment decreasing to 276 students, and with fewer conventions, short courses, and special meetings, the Winthrop campus was less crowded than at any time in many years. The college now employed sixty-four teachers and sixteen supervisors for the Training School. The staff and related officers consisted of twenty-four people.[56] And the college's governing board, elected by the Legislature, contained certain ex-officio members as well and included several committees:

TRUSTEES

Members Ex-Officio

Hon. Ibra C. Blackwood, Governor, Chairman
of the Board................Columbia
Hon. James H. Hope, State Superintendent
of Education................Columbia
Hon. R. M. Jefferies, Chairman of the
Senate Committee of
Education.................Walterboro
Hon. M. F. Bush, Chairman of the House
Committee on Education......Ellenton

Members Elected

Mr. J. E. McDonald...........Winnsboro
(term expires 1934)
Mr. J. G. Anderson...........Rock Hill
(term expires 1936)
Mrs. W. L. Daniel............Greenwood
(term expires 1936)
Mr. W. J. Roddey.............Rock Hill
(term expires 1936)

444

Mrs. George M. Stuckey.....Bishopville
   (term expires 1938)
Mr. R. E. Wylie..............Lancaster
   (term expires 1938)
Mr. W. L. Riley...............Denmark
   (term expires 1934)

Standing Committees

Executive Committee - James P. Kinard,
   Chairman; Ibra C. Blackwood; R. E.
   Wylie; W. J. Roddey; J. G. Anderson;
   James H. Hope.

Finance Committee - J. E. McDonald,
   W. L. Riley, Mrs. George M. Stuckey.

Committee on Organization and Instruction - James P. Kinard, Chairman,
   ex-officio; Mrs. W. L. Daniel; James
   H. Hope; Mrs. George M. Stuckey; M.
   F. Bush.

Building Committee - James P. Kinard,
   Chairman, ex-officio; W. J. Roddey;
   J. G. Anderson; W. L. Riley; J. E.
   McDonald.

Library Committee - James P. Kinard,
   Chairman, ex-officio; Mrs. W. L.
   Daniel; R. E. Wylie; R. M.
   Jefferies; M. F. Rush. Faculty
   Members - Miss Ida J. Dacus,
   Librarian; J. Thompson Brown; J. W.
   Thomson; Warren G. Keith; Miss
   Elizabeth Johnson; Miss Minnie
   Snellings.[57]

   It is unfortunate that Dr. Kinard, a
scholar, served as president during the Depression
when a more practical man could have coped better
with conditions than a man given to reflection,
books, and the like. During these years Kinard
spent considerable time soliciting the Carnegie
Foundation for books to fill a special library in

445

the students' building (Johnson Hall). He reported
to the foundation that they had "about 200 undesirable books in the Johnson Hall Library, and with
some money, they could have a fine browsing room."
Also, Kinard attempted to promote alumnae reading by
patronizing the Library Extension Service of the
University of Minnesota.[58]

Winthrop appreciated Kinard's real sense of
scholarship and few would agree that Kinard's
administration was unsuccessful, regardless of what
Archibald Rutledge wrote: "Several College Presidents have had rude times at Winthrop. . . . After
such a record [as Johnson had], if the Archangel
Gabriel had been elected President of Winthrop to
succeed D. B. Johnson, the seraph would doubtless
have found the going rough."[59] Perhaps one of
Kinard's most important contributions lay in
creating a climate for learning in a rapidly
expanding institution whose first president was a
great "building and grounds man." Kinard was a
"loveable man" whom some students referred to "as
the man who was loved by more women than any other
man in the State." Perhaps this is an exaggeration,
but he enjoyed universal respect. The moving of
Kinard's classroom prompted the delightful poem:

The Moving of "Jeems"

They have moved him away from room
   fourteen
And put him in number eight
Away from the room we knew so well,
As the room of Jeems, the Great.

The walls will echo no more the names
Of Shakespeare, Bacon and Burns
Or other men that are known to fame
Whose works we have tried to learn.

The Queen of Faerie will feel dismayed
When she finds he has moved away;
Mine host of Tabord, too, will grieve,
And the Knight and Squires Gay.

446

And so it is down to number eight
They have moved our darling Jim;
And if it were to the ends of the earth,
We'd sure go after him. [60]

Kinard always deferred to the ladies, and quite frequently consulted them about college problems. On one occasion he asked an opinion from his secretary, whose answer he seemed to like. Looking a bit uncertain he replied, "let me check with Graham [Winthrop's long-time business manager]." To this the young lady retorted, "Dr. Kinard, you have little respect for a woman's opinion, don't you." Responding with a smile on his face, he said, "Oh! Shut up!"[61]

The Winthrop daughters' love for Winthrop and her fine personnel transcended any day-to-day trivia. These feelings remained with many of the girls throughout their lifetimes. Listen to the way Margaret Douglas, class of 1898, explained it from her home at the Agnes Erskine School in Pernambuco, Brazil:

Recently there came to my hands a copy of Winthrop College Alumnae News. Although it is now nearly twenty-seven years since I left the States it is surprising how many familiar names I find in the pages of this magazine.

Reading this takes me back to the remembrance of the delightful visits I made to Winthrop when I was home on my last furlough in 1931. Our wonderful Miss Russell insisted that at some time I send an article for The Alumnae News. After having enjoyed her warm hospitality there, and received many kind attentions I fully made up my mind that I would do so. However, I have been back in Brazil a little more than a year without fulfilling this obligation.

447

The lovely plan of entertaining
Winthrop daughters for a week during
the time of the Summer School is a
treat to many a one. The summer of
1931 I was one of the fortunate ones to
be invited. I never shall forget how I
felt the evening I arrived there. With
Winthrop's same remarkable systematic
management I was soon shown my
dormitory room. I did not look up
anyone. I wanted for the first hour to
be entirely alone. I wanted to walk
about that place so rich in memories
all alone. I wanted to think undis-
turbed. That place which had so much
to do with the making of my life. I
wanted again to see the room in what
was then called the North Dormitory
which I occupied when a teacher,
leaving there in June, 1906. What a
joy that the main entrance is little
changed! Also the chapel is much the
same. I wanted to walk again in those
familiar walks and remember the plans
and hopes and dreams of those days. It
was good, too, to see much that is new
and big and wonderful. That was a
great week, and rich in good things,
especially for one who lives far away
from all that is inspirational.

Also the good-bye visit a few weeks
before leaving for Brazil is a
delightful remembrance. How good it is
to find there some of the friends I
left! Miss Russell, Miss Pope, Miss
Watkins, Miss Parker, Mrs. Johnson, and
Mrs. Kinard. It is an honor to an
institute to hold its workers so long.

I cannot fail to speak of the time
when as a part of the week's program we
all in a body went to the grave of the
beloved founder of Winthrop, and placed

flowers on it. It was sad but pleasant to do this in honor of his memory.

As one looks back over the years that have past [sic] he can see which ones were the crucial ones of his life. I can know with certainty that the ones I spent at Winthrop both as pupil and as teacher was a school of preparation for my life work. Those years taught me how to train Brazilian girls.

We teachers here in the Agnes Erskine School take time about in conducting the opening chapel exercises. I based my talk the other day on the quotation given on the front page of the magazine to which I have already referred. A quotation from one of Dr. Johnson's talks to his teachers. In one of my last conversations with him he spoke of how he had become impressed with the fact that "He that loseth his life shall find it."

Perhaps another time I shall write and tell about Brazil and the Agnes Erskine School, but this time nothing comes to my pen but memories of Winthrop.[62]

Near the end of the 1933 school session, a most disturbing occurrence at Winthrop involved the late President Johnson's son. While Burgh S. Johnson of New York was in Rock Hill visiting his mother, he was accused of being in a building on campus where he should not have been. Following a meeting, the Executive Committee instructed Kinard to warn Johnson "not to trespass on the campus of Winthrop College or to enter any of its buildings." Kinard was to inform Johnson of this decision by registered letter. This decision was to remain in effect "until such time as he may appear before the Board of Trustees to justify his conduct on the campus the morning of May 24, 1933."[63] It was

449

Kinard's unpleasant task finally to instruct Burgh not to come on college property for five years except to his mother's home. Mrs. Daniel voted no on this action because there was no sworn evidence, she averred, of the girls who reported the incident.[64]

Other unpleasant duties for Kinard near the end of his presidency included attempts to retain Winthrop scholarships, to maintain faculty salaries, and to extricate Winthrop's money from unsound banks. Of course, whenever scholarships were mentioned one was sure to find Mrs. Daniel. Writing to Kinard in May, 1933, Mrs. Daniel attempted to secure scholarships for her girls as well as for daughters of her close friends. By the notes that Kinard usually made on her letters, on can judge his concern. Sometimes her affluent husband--lawyer William L. Daniel, a member of the House of Representatives--would contribute to whatever his wife was pushing. Writing to Kinard on May 30, Daniel reported on a bill to abolish free tuition and scholarships: "There has been a great hue and cry recently in favor of closing colleges, or turning them over to their Boards of Trustees, without state aid, to run as they saw fit and proper, or to cease running, if they felt unable to run them upon their income from students."[65]

The Daniels were partial to the work scholarships from which their girls had profited, and they suggested that Kinard was spending too much for salaries. Full professors then were receiving only $1,400 at the University, and Winthrop was paying much more than that. As Mr. Daniel suggested: "It would be very embarrassing to Winthrop's friends in the Legislature to explain satisfactorily to that body why salaries for teachers had been held up $1,000 above salaries paid at the University but having no money to pay tuition, board, room rent, and fees for hard working girls who only asked a chance to fit themselves for life." There were then only eighty girls on service (work) scholarships at Winthrop.[66]

450

In early June the Board decreed that no new state scholarships would be awarded and that all scholarship students would pay a sixty-dollar tuition. This would leave more money for work programs or general expenses. Still adamant on state scholarships, Mrs. Daniel wrote: "I still regard it as infinitely more worthy to allow wages sufficient to cover expenses of girls who work to pay their way through college than to award new scholarships to those who render no service in return." The Board was divided on the matter. Kinard, in a quandary, asked the governor to call another meeting. Kinard wanted Winthrop to be open to every eligible young woman in South Carolina, regardless of money.[67]

Kinard's resignation request of October 24 (to become effective the following June), which had only been privately discussed during the Board's executive session, leaked to the press. Thus, Kinard asked permission on November 18, 1933, to publish his own simple statement "of my request and the action of the Board." Mrs. Daniel replied on the back of Kinard's letter, explaining the leak by stating that she did not want him to be embarrassed--"without first having it known that you were leaving."[68]

The new legislative session had to take a very hard look at South Carolina in 1933-1934. As always the politician faced with deflation and depression invariably suggested mergers, less overhead, and the like. In January, 1934, the House Sub-Committee of the Committee on Education met to consider the governor's recommendations on merging the colleges. Kinard and others attended. He informed Mrs. Daniel that there was little enthusiasm for the plan: "I feel distinctly that it would not help Winthrop in any respect to go into such a plan at present with no knowledge of the full conditions of the plan." This plan envisioned combining the University, the Citadel, the Medical College, and Winthrop into the University of South Carolina.[69]

451

Since Winthrop had the second highest total operating costs of $634,439, twice that of Carolina and six times that of the Medical College, Kinard felt he would be in fair shape regardless of his budget cuts. At the end of January, Kinard took a group of influential girls to visit the Legislature, and in early February the search committee meeting in Columbia considered "a wealth of material" from about twenty candidates for Kinard's job. Later the college sextette was invited to sing for the Legislature. It was evident that Winthrop was subtly pushing her cause. Regardless of the state's austere finances, Winthrop felt confident of maintaining her fair share of the revenue.[70] Still, the desperateness of South Carolina's finances was made abundantly clear by nearly one-hundred qualifying amendments to the Appropriation Act of 1933-34:

> Section 53. That it shall be unlawful for any State institution or department of the State Government to enter into a contract for the services of any person, or persons, based upon an increase of salary during a subsequent year, or years, which, in effect, would be anticipating the action of the General Assembly with regard to salary increases: Provided, further, That all State institutions and departments are hereby forbidden to accept, in advance of legislative action, any gifts from the Federal Government or otherwise, which gifts, or donations are based and conditioned upon the State making an appropriation to match or supplement such fund so donated by an outside agency.

> Section 54. That all moneys can be expended only by drawing vouchers upon the Comptroller General, such vouchers to be accompanied by statements of expenditure classified according to the budget classification of objects

of expenditure (as defined in the budget for the period beginning January 1, 1933, and itemized in detail).

. . . .

Section 70. That the Board of Trustees of the various institutions of higher learning are hereby authorized and empowered to limit the number of new students to be admitted for the 1933-34 session so that the total number of students shall not exceed the number which can be adequately provided for under the available revenue in such manner that the present educational standards for graduates will not be lowered: Provided, That if necessary the said Boards shall limit the admission of students now enrolled upon a basis of scholarship standing, or upon any other basis determined upon by the respective Boards of Trustees.

Section 71. That from and after the present scholastic year of the various institutions of higher learning no student shall be granted free tuition: Provided, That tuition for the scholastic year beginning September, 1933, and thereafter, shall be Sixty ($60.00) Dollars each for residents of the State of South Carolina, and One Hundred and Fifty ($150.00) Dollars for non-residents of the State of South Carolina: Provided, further, That no fee for student activities in excess of Fifteen ($15.00) Dollars shall be compulsory: Provided, further, Except that fees at the Medical College and Law School of the University be left as now prescribed by law to be fixed by the respective Boards of Trustees.

453

Section 72. The various institutions of higher learning are authorized to retain tuition and other fees for the maintenance and operation of the several institutions but no part of such fees shall be used for the construction of new building nor shall such fees be pledged in advance to secure loans for the erection of new buildings.[71]

Talk about money and merging the state colleges prompted Mrs. Daniel to "get into the act again." She demanded of Kinard certain specific information about Winthrop's finances at the time of Dr. Johnson's death. Specifically, she wanted:

1. An itemized statement of how the money accumulated by Dr. Johnson has been spent?
2. Is it true that you had a warning of being dropped from the Association of Colleges and Secondary Schools? And
3. Did the College have to pay $600 on uniforms last fall?

Also she wanted to know what Winthrop had lost through bank failures. In turn, Kinard took her request very seriously. Three days later he forwarded a detailed reply to Mrs. Daniel's questions:

February 10, 1934

Mrs. W. L. Daniel
Greenwood, South Carolina

My dear Mrs. Daniel:

I received your letter of February 7. I am using my first opportunity to answer. It has taken us a little time to get the information needed.

In answer to question #1 these are the facts in regard to our expenditures for lands and permanent improvements since Dr. Johnson's death.

454

I. Lots and Houses
   A. Spears property including several small houses and lots..............$17,841.00
   B. Oates property..... 4,188.00
   C. J. J. Dunlap property........... 9,644.83
   D. Barber property.... 6,500.00
   E. Wyche property..... 5,283.15
   F. Mrs. D. B. Johnson's lot.................10,000.00
   G. Lot for Mrs. Johnson's residence......... 9,471.15

II. Lands
   A. 100 acres Beaty farm land.........10,000.00

III. Buildings
   A. Completion of library and Johnson Hall...............44,969.61
   B. Kinard Hall.......135,000.00
   C. Mrs. Johnson's residence......... 21,245.92
   D. Breazeale Hall.... 85,000.00
   E. Dining Room extension......... 20,007.16

IV. Miscellaneous
   A. Stokers for boiler room.............. 5,200.00
   B. Sound movie equipment........ 5,668.00

Making a grand total of $390.018.82

The total bank balance at the time of Dr. Johnson's death amounted to $412,289.20. This included a balance of $25,144.19 in the uniform account.

The securities held by the Central Union Bank were sold for $87,382.64.

Fifty thousand dollars ($50,000.00) of this is still on deposit in a savings account at the People's National Bank secured by bonds and other legal collateral.

I hope this statement of facts will give you the information you have requested in answer to question #1.

In answer to question #2, "Is it true that the college has received warning from the Association of Colleges and Secondary Schools that it is in danger of being dropped from the list?" Under date of December 22, after the meeting of the Southern Association in Nashville beginning December 3, I received a letter from the Executive Secretary of the Association from which I quote: "The Commission on Institutions of Higher Education directs me to give you its comment on your 1933 report, as follows:

1. The Commission would like to call your attention to several weaknesses in the report which you submitted this year. We do not look with favor on the policy of taking students who are not recommended by their high school principals unless they are received on a basis of examinations.

2. We note that you are giving the M.A. degree but it does not seem that your faculty and general equipment would indicate enough strength to offer graduate work. The training to the faculty seems to be below the standards which we expect for an undergraduate school.

3. We note with particular regret that the salary scale has been definitely

456

reduced below our standard for this item. We are putting all institutions on notice that we are not lowering our standards, even though temporarily we may allow an institution to fall below the requirements.

4. Please let us have, not later than September 15, through the Executive Secretary, any information which you would like to give in regard to these matters and particularly let us know the salaries actually paid for the current session and those allocated for 1934-35."

I, myself, do not consider this any warning that we are in danger in our standing in the Southern Association. In regard to comment #1 - I think Winthrop College ought to consider a long time before it would refuse admission to a graduate of a standard high school with a diploma signed by the Governor because some principal of a high school said that she was not college material. Of course, if the Southern Association and Faculty insisted on this we would give examinations to all students who are admitted.

In regard to comment #2 - we are not this year giving graduate instruction to any student. I got the permission of the Board two years ago to discontinue graduate work in our winter session. We still allow students in the summer school for special reasons to take graduate courses but I do not consider that this is the matter in which the Southern Association is interested.

In answer to comment #3 - "Did the college have to pay $600 express on

457

uniforms last fall?" I find that the
total express on all uniforms including
gymnasium shoes, coats, dresses, etc.
for this year's uniforms up to date is
$238.38.

I shall be glad to have you communicate all this information to anyone
who does not understand the facts.

I am very happy to note that the
state will probably have more revenue at
its disposal than was at first supposed.
This may help us in getting the Finance
Committee of the Senate to restore the
$67,000 now needed to bring back our
appropriation to our budget request of
$227,000 for the session of 1934-35. We
have been very much pleased with the
action of the Federal Relief Administration in regard to help for needy
students now in the college or who wish
to come for the second semester. We are
proceeding just as rapidly as we can
with this work.

We asked for a new boiler house
under the Public Works Administration.
I fear, however, that we will not get
the boiler house in that way. I am
taking up the matter with Mr. Spruill,
Mr. Bush, Mr. Jefferies, Mr. Ward, and
Mr. Bennett hoping that we can get a
supplementary appropriation covering our
needs for new boilers. These are all
matters in which you may be of help to
us and I am quite sure that you will do
all you can in this direction. I am
keeping in constant touch with the
members of the General Assembly and I am
much in hopes that we will have our full
appropriation for next session and also
what we need for new boilers.

458

Please let me hear from you at any
time in regard to matters on which I can
furnish information.

With best wishes, I am

Yours very sincerely,

President[72]

In 1934 Kinard received some extra help for
the college through the Civil Works Administration,
which approved using seventy-five extra workers at
Winthrop. These men, at federal expense, painted
the inside of the infirmary and the music and
science halls. They did a thorough job in
renovating Johnson Hall. The investigation of
charges against CWA by Congressmen Fulmer and
McMillan and by Harry Hopkins had no connection with
Winthrop. There were complaints in South Carolina
that political pull was necessary to get relief jobs
there and that the needy were often by-passed.

In 1934 at least one-hundred and twenty-six
Winthrop girls received financial aid to help them
work their ways through college. The girls were
employed in clerical positions, in the library, in
research, and in the dining room. This program
helped to save the educational career of many worthy
girls.[73]

Upon graduation the Winthrop girls of this
period experienced some difficulty in finding
regular jobs. Still, more than half the 1933
graduating class (in a very bleak year) managed to
get jobs—something of a record for that time. A
special to the local press praised Miss Sarah Rey
Marcum of Kentucky, a long-time aid at Winthrop, for
continuing her job in Washington with the Reconstruction Finance Corporation.[74]

The spring of 1934, along with a few year-
end problems, brought some excitement over the
possibilities of a new president. Mrs. Kinard was
attempting to bring the college and town closer

together with her Wednesday afternoon teas.   Dr.
Kinard, the genial Jim, was taking everything in his
low-country stride, enjoying the last months of his
presidency.   President Oliver C. Carmichael of the
Alabama   College   (Montevallo)   came   to   inspect
Winthrop,   but   he   later   went   to   Vanderbilt
University.   Mrs. Daniel attempted to push some
candidates for jobs.   Kinard asked Professor Emmett
Gore for his resignation and the professor blamed
his troubles on his department head, Dr. Walter
Roberts.[75]

        Even small matters seemed to be blown out of
proportion.   Mrs. Daniel didn't want the name of the
Northern divorcee who was to take Mr. Gore's place
brought   up   because,   she   said,   Trustee Hope had
divorced his first wife. And Mrs. Daniel threatened
to protest the divorcee's appointment because "we
must hold up before the girls the highest ideals and
it would be unfortunate to seem to put our stamp of
approval upon a divorcee." Too, she informed Kinard
that Mr. Gore's friend, Trustee Riley of Bamberg,
"would also level much criticism at this."[76]   Thus,
with these counter pressures so evident Kinard tried
peacemaking in the Roberts-Gore affair.   After both
men gave their words that they would cooperate and
work for Winthrop's good, he recommended that Mr.
Gore be kept.   This prevented the divorcee from
being hired.   Mrs. Daniel later congratulated Kinard
on the way that he had handled the matter, stating
that she regarded it as "the end of our unfortunate
disagreement."[77]

        On   April   24,   1934,   a   Board   committee
selected Dr. Shelton Phelps, Dean of the Graduate
School of Peabody College in Nashville, to be the
third president of Winthrop College.   Dr. Phelps
promptly replied on April 30, 1934, requesting that
he take office at the beginning of the fiscal year,
July 1, 1934.[78]

        The Board resolved on June 4, 1934, to keep
Dr. Kinard as President Emeritus "to perform such
duties   as   may   be   assigned   to him."   They praised

460

him as "a man of great scholarly attainment."
Kinard responded by saying: "the individual friend-
ships that I have formed in the Board will be a
blessing to me for all my remaining days." He made
his final valedictory to the graduates at half past
ten the morning of June 4, 1934.[79]

In a radio address several months before
(February 9, 1934, over WBT, Charlotte, North
Carolina, in the series of the South Carolina
Economic Association) Kinard had answered well the
question "What has Winthrop been worth to the State
of South Carolina?" He had solemnly replied:

> It has lifted the level of living in
> South Carolina, through the more than
> 11,000 young women of the State who have
> profited by instruction within its
> walls, and who have gone out to every
> corner of South Carolina as teachers, as
> business women, as church workers, as
> home makers, as wives and mothers, and
> as intelligent citizens. "What con-
> stitutes a State?" the poet asked. It
> needs no poet to answer that in these
> days, one of the chief elements in the
> constitution of a State, is the training
> of women for motherhood and citizenship.
> For no democratic State can rise above
> the level of the intelligence of its
> women.[80]

No one understood this better than Jim
Kinard. He had taught and championed the education
of women most of his adult life. Thereby, he made a
lasting contribution to uplifting the people of
South Carolina.

CHAPTER XIV

DR. SHELTON JOSEPH PHELPS TAKES THE HELM

"I know too well that the only hope of
a democratic form of government is an
enlightened citizenship and the only
way that our generation and others
before us have found how to enlighten
our citizens is through public school
and college education. Both the public
schools and the colleges are constantly
striving to give the proper kind of
education."

James P. Kinard

Dr. Phelps was perhaps the best-trained and
most properly oriented to teacher training of any
Winthrop College president. He had risen from the
one-room school to the deanship of an important
Southern college, so he knew education from the
crossroads to the big metropolitan centers. Coming
of good midwestern working people from the Missouri
heartland, Phelps taught and studied for several
years in his home state, receiving first a Bachelor
of Pedagogy from the Missouri State Normal in 1911.
This was followed by the Bachelor of Science, then
the Master of Arts and the Doctor of Philosophy at
Peabody in 1915 and 1919.[1]

In 1906 Phelps had begun teaching in rural
Missouri schools, advancing to high-school posi-
tions, principalships, and superintendency,
training-school work at Missouri Normal in
Springfield, Professor of Education at Vermont, and
Professor of School Administration and Director of
Instruction at Peabody in 1919. After nine years at
Peabody he became Dean of the Graduate School.
After six more years he assumed the presidency of
Winthrop. In addition to these professional
appointments, Phelps conducted school surveys in
several states.

A host of organizations honored Dr. Phelps
during his career.[2] Before coming to Winthrop, he
had been a member of the State Board of Education
in Tennessee, member of the Advisory Council of the

462

National Survey of Secondary Education, member of the White House Conference on Child Health and Protection, President of the Tennessee College Association, Secretary of the Southern Association of Teacher Training Institutions, member of the American Council on Education, and President of the State Teacher's Association. He was active in the NEA, Phi Delta Kappa, and Kappa Delta Pi.[3] While at Winthrop, Dr. Phelps became Secretary-Treasurer of the Southern Association of Colleges and Schools (the accrediting agency for Winthrop and other Southern schools), and Vice-chairman of the American Council of Education. Phelps also wrote extensively in his field. With such an accomplished man guiding Winthrop, her future looked very bright.[4]

Winthrop and South Carolina warmly received Phelps, who was quick to learn his new job. The new session made a fine start even as a trustee committee drew elaborate plans for installing their new president properly on November 9, 1934. Phelps, meanwhile, lost little time in seeking extra Carnegie Foundation aid. Writing to John M. Russell, Phelps angled for the famous "College Music Sets" that Carnegie had donated to some colleges. Stressing that "our music department is one of our strongest departments," that music had been emphasized there from the beginning, and that Winthrop richly deserved any help given to her, Phelps (with information furnished by music chairman Walter B. Roberts) made a good case. He later attempted to secure the new Schirmer record sets valued at several thousands of dollars.[5]

Approximately four months after Dr. Phelps assumed office, his inauguration (on November 9, 1934) presented a truly auspicious celebration. The faculty, students, trustees, and prominent state officials were joined by presidents and others representing one-hundred and five leading colleges. The main address featured Dr. David A. Robertson, President of Goucher College, Baltimore, Maryland, who discussed "Regimentation or Freedom of Individuals and Institutions."[6] His was a

463

scholarly address that balanced the complex and the simple, with comparative illustrations from the Communist and Fascist systems. From his knowledge of Winthrop, he stated that Winthrop was strong enough to compare herself with most colleges--with women's colleges, coeducational institutions, and even foreign colleges. Dr. Robertson stressed:

> Winthrop is not the Vassar or Wellesley or Smith of the South; it is Winthrop of the United States or, if you please, the universe. With its half century of honorable history Winthrop is free to pursue the truth which its motto exalts --Veritas cum Libertate, Truth with Freedom: freedom from regimentation by church or state or accrediting agencies, freedom from undue control of economic and social teaching because of the wisdom of the citizens of South Carolina, freedom to seek and know the truth.[7]

Dr. Phelps gave a straight-forward inaugural speech, pointing out what some of the non-public women's colleges were doing and what the state should do in educating its women. Dr. Phelps summarized trends in non-public women's colleges under these ten points:

> 1. The recognition of a sharp line of differentiation between the objectives, functions, and content of the first two years and of the last two years of college work.
> 2. The development of two lines of specialization in the senior college, one of which cuts across formerly recognized departmental lines to achieve its objective. In this discussion this has been referred to as functional specialization.
> 3. The return from free election to directed election and modified prescription.

464

4. Returning emphasis on comprehensive examinations instead of considering residence a measure of college achievement.

5. The recognition of two types of college achievement--Honours, or studying for distinction, and that different type of achievement which the English have recognized in the "Pass" degree of Oxford and Cambridge Universities.

6. A decentralization of library service in the interest of the use of more books by more students.

7. Encouraging a year, of the four spent in college, to be spent abroad or in another institution in this country.

8. Cooperative housing, to enable students to go to college at less cost.

9. Summer Institutes and Alumnae Colleges where more intensive work may be done on the current pressing problems.

10. Development of such things as "Playshop Laboratories" and similar projects, which together with the other nine mentioned all aim at the same ultimate purpose--the more nearly complete development of each individual student.[8]

The second part of Dr. Phelps' address was an education list's evaluation of general education as opposed to specialization by women. In this he pointed up the proper role of the women's colleges in education. He stressed new emphasis on guidance rather than on rules and suggested that classroom instruction is but a part of education. To him, a state college for women offered a most favorable field for this new emphasis.[9]

College presidents try to present attention-catching programs to focus attention on their institutions' academic areas. Shelton Phelps was typical of this. He had labored long to complete his first degree at twenty-seven years of age; during the eight years thereafter, he successfully

465

completed the master's and doctoral degrees. He was
a firm believer in well-trained personnel, and his
respect for the Doctor of Philosophy degree always
stood out. In his first comprehensive report to the
Legislature, he wrote: "There are at the present
time, seventeen members of the Winthrop faculty
holding Ph.D degrees." Hastening to point out that
the Southern Association of Colleges and Secondary
Schools had criticized the Winthrop faculty's
training a few years before, he assured the
Legislature that there was "much less basis for that
criticism at the present time." He was choosing
mostly Ph.D's for new positions.[10]

    At the end of a year and a half at Winthrop,
Phelps concluded that

> nowhere . . . is there a finer group of
> students than the 1,301 South Carolina
> girls making its student body. Nowhere
> is there a more devoted, whole-hearted,
> hard-working faculty than the group
> teaching these girls. And there has
> been built up in Winthrop during the
> past half century a most wholesome and
> praiseworthy set of beliefs with regard
> to the merits of scholarship, hard
> work, and real democracy.[11]

Then, following this complimentary introduction,
Phelps suggested to the Legislature these "Immediate
Needs and Program Needs" which became the basis of
his administration:

> Under immediate needs which we
> discuss in the next few paragraphs we
> include safety through fireproofness,
> the need of a Dean of Instruction, the
> expansion of the faculty and of course
> offerings to provide training for our
> graduates to enter more fields of work,
> and more social rooms in the
> dormitories.

Fireproofness

Winthrop College has 1200 girls housed in five non-fireproof dormitories. The fire hazard is extremely great. These several dormitories are connected by passage ways and a fire in any one of them would be very difficult to keep under control. Considering the non-fireproofness of the dormitories and their age they would burn like kindling. This is no criticism of the plan used for their construction, for had any one of us been building at the time Winthrop dormitories were built, in all probability we would have built in the same way. Building methods have improved and the idea of putting more money into a building to make it fireproof has been much more strongly developed, since the date these dormitories were built. There is only one way to make these buildings reasonably safe and to as nearly as possible eliminate this fire hazard. That way would be the installation of an automatic sprinkler system throughout the plant. The danger to girls is too great to not name this as the need of Winthrop College.

Capital investment is also maintained at Winthrop at great risk. The state has more than three and one-quarter million dollars invested at Winthrop, and it is our understanding from Mr. Robinson of the Sinking Fund Commission, that if any loss through fire should occur, that up to $25,000 the loss would be paid from the current funds of the Sinking Fund. Beyond a $25,000 loss payment must be made from the reserve of the Sinking Fund, which reserve amounts to some $360,000 accumulated from the money formerly paid for reinsurance and additional reserve approximating $900,000. There is no reinsurance of Winthrop property. There is a total risk at Winthrop College of more than twice the assets of the Sinking Fund Commission. This is not intended as criticism of the plan of insurance provided by the Sinking Fund Commission but rather presented as an argument for protecting the assets of the Sinking Fund Commission. It is mainly an argument for a sprinkler system. Such a system we estimate would cost, to install it, properly, at least $100,000.

A Dean

A Dean of Instruction is badly needed to give all of his time to the study of the curriculum offerings, the methods of classroom teaching, the needs and difficulties of students, and in general the supervision of the whole plan of college instruction. The office of dean was abolished a few years ago under the stress of the depression. The general instructional program suffers from the loss of the closer supervision this office affords. What to teach, how to teach, and a closer study of the results obtained constitute the work of this office.

An Expansion of Faculty and of Courses to Provide Training for Entering More Fields of Work is Much Needed

We need to increase the number of courses and consequently the number of teachers in order that the graduates of Winthrop may be fitted to enter more fields of work. It is half the problem of an institution to train its students. The rest of that problem consists of

planning this training to fit later uses
to be made of that training, and of
finding for students opportunities to
use that training. Winthrop College,
with its large student body of girls
from all over the state, needs to
prepare them to enter all available
avenues leading to the employment of its
girls when they have been graduated from
the college. As a specific illus-
tration, there are more than 300 high
schools in the state which employ all-
time and part-time librarians. The
standards of the American Library Association and the standards of the
Southern Association of Colleges and
Secondary Schools, being very specific
and definite in the required training of
librarians, make it necessary for these
more than 300 high schools operating
under these standards to seek other than
Winthrop graduates to fill these places.
There is no real reason why Winthrop
graduates should not be trained for
librarianships in South Carolina high
schools and in South Carolina town
libraries. No more desirable type of
work exists for one's daughter than such
a library position.

Social Rooms

To provide greater opportunities for
a more fully developed social life con-
stitutes another need. More and more we
emphasize in our national expressions
and in our local communities the fact
that all of life cannot be work. There
must be opportunity for relaxation and
for the best use of a leisure--partly
natural, partly enforced. A leisure
which calls for training, to insure its
best use. Winthrop needs very badly
additions to its dormitories somewhat
after the plan of the Woman's College

of North Carolina at Greensboro, whereby the social phases of the lives of its students can be more adequately provided for. We very much hope to be able to enlist philanthropic aid in this regard. At least we shall try.

Program Needs

Perhaps the greatest need from the standpoint of faculty happiness is some provision for retirement. The retirement of staff members who have reached the age of 65 becomes necessary for the best interest of the institution, its teaching, its students, and its general welfare. This is a principle of college and university administration which has been rather long established. Additional impetus has been given this movement, no doubt, by the discussions on a nation-wide basis which have been featured the past two or three years. Ideals have reached the point when no one is quite willing to dismiss another who has completed a period of faithful and effective work without some provision for the economic security of that one. To provide a plan for the retirement of faculty members, and of other workers at Winthrop, who have reached the age of sixty-five is something necessary to long-time planning for the institution's success and vitally necessary to the happiness of its workers.

A lecture foundation which would bring to Winthrop students at regular intervals general discussions and summaries of achievements in literary fields, scientific fields, industrial fields, throughout the whole scope of education, would be of great value to the girls sent here. We have in mind something beyond assembly speakers, and artist course numbers, and we cannot speak too highly of the last named achievement of the college. We are suggesting a plan for lectures somewhat comparable to the Cole lectures offered at Vanderbilt University, the Percy Turnbull lectures at Johns Hopkins, the Inglis lectures at Harvard, the Hibbert lectures at Oxford, and similar lectures at many other institutions.

In the longer planning for the institution it is necessary for us to determine and to establish the best policy for the state to follow in regard to tuition, attendance, summer school, institutional expansion, and many similar subjects. Some of these we have already discussed in preceding paragraphs and, as we have indicated, we hope in the next two or three years to be able to interest outside aid in helping to accomplish. The ones we are now discussing in this paragraph are strictly internal matters. We invite you most urgently to discuss with your colleagues charged with the control of this institution and with many citizens of this state what would be done with regard to the matter of tuition. Should South Carolina supply, to its daughters at Winthrop, education paid for by all of us and entirely free to the individual or should it continue to charge the tuition rate now charged? What should we do, from the standpoint of the best interests of the state, with regard to attendance? Should we invite its increase or should we select those who attend? We even invite you to consider the following carefully. Is it the more profitable to the state to raise a little bit the whole plane of the learning of its citizenship or to lift a much

greater bit a smaller portion of that
plane? Free tuition is perhaps the road
to one end. Tuition with its inevitable
economic selection the road to the other
achievement.

What shall we do about summer
school? We invite you to consider
earnestly this question. Shall we
continue to operate at Winthrop a small
summer school, successfully operated and
restricted rather largely to teachers,
particularly elementary teachers, or
shall we expand the activities of that
summer school and try to build a summer
school comparable to, let us say, the
North Carolina Summer School? May we
urge upon you that in the consideration
of this question you consider it not
only from the standpoint of Winthrop
College but from the standpoint of the
state as a whole and from the standpoint
of all institutions operating summer
schools. This is a vital question to
the state university as well as to
Winthrop College.

And finally may we invite you to
consider the whole question of the
expansion of Winthrop. A few years ago,
wisely we think, graduate work was
eliminated from the scope of the work at
Winthrop College. This was rather
definitely a trimming of our sails for
weathering the depression which was then
upon us. We need now however seriously,
not hastily, to consider the question,
is a four year under-graduate program
sufficient for the needs of the women of
South Carolina or is a five year college
program culminating in a master's degree
necessary to their needs. We have had
rather many and rather insistent calls

472

from four year college graduates, of
Winthrop and other colleges, for this
additional year. The leading colleges
for women, meaning the private colleges
such as Wellesley, Bryn Mawr, Smith and
others, seem to be going in the
direction of the five year program.

Let us all consider most carefully
both these immediate needs and the
needs which are essential to wise planning. We do not need to tell you that
all of these things are occupying our
thought rather constantly and that we
are fully sincere in inviting advice
and help at arriving at the solution of
these needs.[12]

The educationalist Phelps envisioned a good
plan for developing Winthrop, and his new administration had taken office under most favorable
conditions despite the United States' uncertain
economic position. Public-works money had already
made many long-overdue physical improvements at the
college. And Winthrop's graduates were now able, in
most instances, to find suitable employment.[13]

A strong Alumnae Association under the sure
guidance of Miss Leila A. Russell kept in close
touch with alumnae scattered about the world. The
Winthrop College Alumnae News gave unending proof of
their many accomplishments. The spring issue of
1934 recorded among other stories these items:
Mabel Montgomery was serving as a state CWA
landscape supervisor; Dorcas Calmes Cooper, first
lady of South Carolina, would accompany her husband
to Puerto Rico, where he would become a federal
judge; Sibyl Brown was heading the Newark State
Teachers College Art Department; Lena Williams
Benson wrote for Household Magazine; Ida Penney was
teaching at Farmville State Teachers College; Eliza
Macfarland McLeon (granddaughter of Dr. Joynes) had
returned via Winthrop to her home in Toronto,
Canada; Mary Tillman had married in Florida; Martha
Smith worked as a librarian in Manhattan; Frances

473

Earle headed the Geography Department at the University of Washington; and countless other items.[14]

The Winthrop which Phelps had just taken over received a larger state appropriation for higher education than any other institution. Winthrop's total operating cost of the year before Phelps' arrival was $634,439--compared to $328,451 for the University of South Carolina and $106,706 for the Medical College.[15]

Winthrop's forty-ninth session--Phelps at the helm--opened with a good student body, eight new teachers, and a promised funding increase plus more CWA projects and FERA funds to help students work to complete their educations.[16]

A self-proclaimed devotée of Jefferson, President Shelton Phelps wanted to remake Winthrop along more progressive lines. To this end he proposed reorganizing the curriculum to stress general education the first two years and to spend the latter years on more specialized work such as library science, journalism, social work, or commerce.[17] Too, Dr. Phelps wished to restore the deanship which the Depression had eliminated. And he was much concerned with teachers' improving themselves, seeking candidates with Ph.D.'s for replacements and frequently alerting the Board that people with Ph.D. degrees were replacing those with master's. He felt this would increase the college's standing. When Donnis Martin sought an unheard-of leave of absence to write a book, the overjoyed Phelps declared, "I feel that adding publications from our faculty will enhance the reputation of the institution as much as additional training for the faculty."[18] Still another side of Phelps' scholarship was his interest in bringing nationally recognized scholars to the campus for special occasions. Not only was this an inspiration to the students, but it also tended to help the entire educational picture in South Carolina.[19]

During Phelps' first two years, he made considerable progress in reorganization and in hiring personnel. His 1935-1936 budget included a ten-percent increase in most salaries except those of hostesses and of teachers who had made no attempt toward securing degrees or special training. Student fees increased slightly and house rent and board were charged to all employees living in college houses or boarding in the college. Salary adjustments took care of the latter. And finally, "no colored help was to eat in the dining room except workers in the dining room and infirmary, with wage adjustments to cover this."[20]

With rising words of thanks and appreciation ringing in his ears, President Phelps proposed more changes in the fall of 1935. The school needed a dean, a sprinkler system for fire protection, an old-age retirement for faculty and others, a summer-school reevaluation, tuition from students, a more adequate water supply, and an investment program to yield higher returns on scholarship funds. In addition, Phelps proposed buying the Blackwelder property at 926 Oakland and investigated the possibility of showing moving pictures to the students.[21]

Fortunately for Phelps, there were practical men on the Winthrop Board ready and able to help him whenever and wherever he needed it, and Dr. Kinard was always available to lend his long years of experience to the college he loved so well.[22] Just before Phelps came, Kinard had suggested to the trustees that they consider appointing a Board of Visitors, a plan that Clemson had used to advantage for years. One of the first lessons Phelps learned about South Carolina and visitor control came when Senator Richard Manning Jefferies noted that Phelps had hired two new instructors from outside the state. Writing from Walterboro to Phelps, he stated:

It has been my policy to urge the employment of South Carolinians at our State institutions when we have South

475

Carolinians who are competent. . . . When we are considering people of equal ability, South Carolina will come first. . . . Constantly, we are called upon to approve recommendations of non-residents for positions at colleges. I think the time has come for us to give qualified South Carolinians preference. Please understand that this letter shall not be construed as a reflection upon the two ladies you nominated--this is a good case for making a precedent--copies of this to all Board members.[23]

Phelps learned fast. Soon he began enlisting various committees and Board members to support his program. Working closely with trustee W. J. Roddey, the York County delegation, and others, Phelps pushed his plans for greater physical improvements and more courses. Every facet of college life felt his hand. As examples, the dry-cleaning equipment was improved, public-health nursing was instituted, and a lecture series was inaugurated.[24]

Winthrop advanced under Phelps' leadership. Her general educational climate also improved. As in most reorganizations, there were some inconsistencies, dislocations, and areas begging criticism. However, the burly, energetic mid-westerner Phelps demonstrated skill and understanding. And his gentlemanly qualities endeared him to most students, faculty, and South Carolinians with whom he had contact.[25]

Typical of the new spirit and emphasis at Winthrop, Shelton Phelps's Christmas greetings shared the front page of the Alumnae News with Johnson's "Creed for The Alumnae Association," a time-honored admonition to Winthrop daughters. Phelps wrote:

Ten thousand Winthrop Alumnae may easily become the greatest force for good in this whole region. To realize the greatest effectiveness of this

476

force will be needed: organization, clearness of vision in detecting the good, and consecration to beliefs.

My Christmas wish for Winthrop Alumnae is that they may be among those who see most clearly, in these coming days, those principles of relationship which make for the betterment of home, of state, of nation, and of the world. Never has such clearness of vision been more needed. Having seen these truths, may they have the unfaltering devotion and the courage, to go forward toward the realization of these ideals. May the name of Winthrop become, through its alumnae, more and more to mean a force for up-holding idealism in the world.

I sincerely wish for all Winthrop Alumnae a 'Merry Christmas and a Happy New Year.'[26]

What the likeable Phelps had not learned, and it was so obvious, was that the Winthrop alumnae had already become a great force in this region and that their contributions were outstanding. Winthrop was constantly touching every part of South Carolina through her cooperative services, her teaching graduates, her school contests, her club-work activity, and her Extension services.[27]

Winthrop had always publicized how the United States Department of Agriculture, Clemson College, and Winthrop College worked as a team in the Home Demonstration Extension Department. The county home-demonstration agents were based at Winthrop; and the most respected home-economics specialist, the indomitable Miss Mary E. Frayser, was still performing great service to the people of South Carolina from her Winthrop base.[28] Thus, Phelps took special note of the importance of Winthrop's home-demonstration work in his annual

477

report to the General Assembly on December 15, 1936, when he said that "There were nearly 19,782 women and 10,732 rural girls enrolled in home economics extension clubs" and that 63,763 families were influenced by some phase of this work. [29]

The president's report stressed again Winthrop's physical needs and academic standing. Winthrop belonged to the Southern Association of Colleges and Secondary Schools, the Association of American Colleges, the American Council on Education, and the American Association of University Women. It was also on the approved list of the Association of American Universities. [30] With a growing student body and a dedicated corps of workers--"no group is more faithful, more devoted, or more conscientious than they"--Winthrop's future seemed bright. Despite the slowed economy, Winthrop graduates were in great demand. The Placement Bureau was proud of its record: 96 percent of those desiring positions were placed. As Phelps saw it, the college urgently needed a home-economics building and (if the enrollment increased) a new dormitory. [31]

The successful Phelps was a bit shocked when Trustee Roddey wrote him that some Winthrop girls who often lunched with the Roddeys on Sunday had informed him of cheating in the classes. Roddey requested that a quiet investigation determine if this were true, adding, "You and I both believe that the most valuable asset of the college students individually and collectively is the possession of a high sense of honor." [32] Phelps bemoaned the Chapel Hill cheating scandal which had been publicized the year before. At Winthrop he promised to be more vigilant but noted the diffficulty in obtaining "specific charges supported by evidence" in cheating cases. [33]

With the new year, Roddey and Phelps continued discussions about building. Roddey had discovered that Clemson had secured government aid for a new building, so he suggested that Phelps investigate how Clemson had managed this. "I am

478

personally convinced," he wrote, "that there will never be again, at least for many years to come, such an opportunity for educational organizations to secure government aid. I also believe that the Government will be more favorably disposed to State institutions and, in addition, will be more ready to give support to large institutions like Winthrop.[34]

In 1936 the alumnae and Winthrop friends were glad to learn that the General Assembly had chosen State Senator James Strom Thurmond from Edgefield to complete the unexpired Winthrop Board term of the late W. J. Riley. The Alumnae News praised Thurmond--who was a lawyer, farmer, and former superintendent of education--as a prominent and influential member of the Senate and as "a statesman standing for constructive measures."[35] The senator promptly went to work. At their May meeting, for instance, the Board discussed plans for constructing new buildings. They added Mr. Thurmond to the Building Committee and to a special committee helping the president reorganize the college farm. During this first meeting, the record notes that Thurmond gave legal advice on college and scholarship investments. And in June, 1937, Mr. Thurmond was in Washington to investigate the possibility of securing federal funds for constructing two new buildings on campus.[36]

Thurmond was instrumental in pushing through the General Assembly an act providing special funds for constructing and equipping buildings at state institutions of higher learning. Winthrop was designated to receive $350,000 for an auditorium or a classroom or both. The act provided that the institutions could "accept any gifts or grants to aid in construction and equipment of said buildings." This statement was designed to enable South Carolina to supply the fifty-five percent of local funds necessary for such projects.[37]

Winthrop and the other South Carolina colleges also benefited in applying for PWA funds from the friendly expertise of Senator James Byrnes, a

479

man highly respected by the Roosevelt administration. His counsel to Phelps, Thurmond, J. L. M. Irby and others concerned with federal-state relations was invaluable in 1937 and therefollowing. From his vantage point on the Senate Appropriations Committee and from his personal friendship with many of the nation's leaders, Byrnes was able to render great service to his home state. And when in early July Phelps was attempting to expedite federal funds for the home-economics building, he wrote to Byrnes, saying: "You know that Winthrop trains all the home economics teachers of the state which are trained by state agencies." He asked if Byrnes knew how to expedite matters. Byrnes fired back the next day, writing that Phelps might communicate with Colonel H. B. Haskett, Deputy Administrator of the Public Works Administration, Washington, D.C. Byrnes had already greased the skids for the entire Winthrop project, but he never overlooked any opportunity to keep the pressure on the New Dealers. At the same time, Byrnes was attempting to help South Carolina with the Santee project and with the increased costs her entry into the social-security program had entailed.[38]

Another Winthrop project in which Byrnes proved most helpful was the gift of Winthrop's first home in Columbia and its removal with PWA funds to Rock Hill. The coachhouse (chapel) on the Ainsley Hall property, later acquired by the Columbia Theological Seminary, was given to Winthrop by the seminary of the Southern Presbyterians based in Decatur, Georgia. President J. McD. Richards and his board of directors agreed to the transfer, provided that a suitable tablet bearing the building's history be placed in the reconstructed chapel. The five-thousand dollars necessary for transferring and rebuilding came from PWA funds (Federal Emergency Administration of Public Works) secured largely through Senator Byrnes's efforts.[39]

The building schedule for Winthrop's auditorium and home-economics building was set in an early October, 1937, Board meeting. Architects Hopkins and Baker of Florence designed the home-economics building; James B. Urquhart of Columbia, the auditorium. A. D. Gilchrist of Rock Hill would serve as associate architect for both projects. The builder was Hardaway Construction Company. The Board in its October 8 meeting agreed to accept a $302,727 grant from the federal government to help with these buildings, which would be constructed using the minimum-wage scale. Before adjourning, the Board adopted a budget for the next year that included a $1,500 raise for Winthrop's president.[40]

According to the plans, the projected auditorium and the home-economics building would be two of the most impressive structures on campus. As early as 1929 the Alumnae Association had projected and adopted a most elaborate blueprint for a memorial auditorium honoring David Bancroft Johnson. They had also begun an elaborate campaign to solicit funds from Winthrop alumnae scattered around the world.[41]

The alumnae had planned a campaign to raise $250,000. Inspiring, thankful letters with contributions rolled in. Margaret Finley wanted her name placed upon that contributors' roll which would bear record of her love and admiration for D. B. Johnson. Bessie Harper pledged an all-out effort. Mrs. W. L. Daniel stressed the need for a building seating five or six thousand.[42]

Winthrop daughters' zeal in seeking a suitable Johnson memorial was tempered by life's economic realities. Winthrop graduates had long been in demand as teachers. Many were homemakers. Some were missionaries. These ladies' great contributions cannot be questioned, but their financial abilities to contribute to worthy causes were (for the most part) very limited. Thus, the cost of the auditorium and other buildings had to be borne largely by state and federal funds.[43]

The PWA building programs already underway were designated as Project A and Project B. Project A, the auditorium, was figured to cost $420,727. Project B, the home-economics classroom and laboratory building, was listed at $238,095. With adequate funding and a surplus of skilled labor available, two magnificent structures soon began to take shape next door to stately Joynes Hall.[44]

There were other important changes taking place simultaneously with the new building program. The question of out-of-state students was being carefully considered. Also, Phelps was negotiating with the Post Office Department to set up a sub-station on campus. Officials were debating a new gymnasium for the Training School to replace the old one, which had been condemned. And just when extra funds were needed to furnish the new buildings, the state had cut Winthrop's 1939 appropriations by sixteen percent.[45]

This funding cut did not prove very significant in the total Winthrop picture. The student body had increased to 1,714. Some extra teachers were hired. Mrs. Daniel was proclaiming "that the magnificent new auditorium calls for a new and thoroughly modern and adequate organ." And Winthrop had asked the Carnegie Corporation to give the college one of their famous music sets.

Phelps had initiated the music-set request in 1937, informing the secretary of the Carnegie Corporation that he had been elected secretary-treasurer of the prestigious Southern Association of Colleges and Secondary Schools. Winthrop's forceful and astute Business Manager Alexander M. Graham followed with a letter to the president of the Carnegie Corporation, which affirmed that Winthrop was properly prepared to protect the valuable music set since a new music building was under construction.[46] Then early in 1939, Phelps intensified his pitch for the Carnegie sets by re-informing Mr. Frederick Kepple of Carnegie of the new music building and auditorium financed by $20,000 from the alumnae, with fifty-five percent of the remainder furnished by the Legislature and forty-five percent by the PWA. Phelps suggested that Carnegie give $50,000 for an organ and $10,000 for practice pianos. Phelps sent along a copy of

482

the arts and lectures program, which included the National Symphony, the Marine Bands, the San Carlos Opera Company, the Monte Carlo Ballet Russe, and Mrs. Franklin D. Roosevelt.[47]

Pushing his advantage in this cause, Phelps wrote an appreciative letter to Edwin Hughes to thank him for informing Carnegie and Keppel that "there was a great awakening in art and music in the Carolinas." On the same day, Phelps wrote Keppel that the soon-to-be-finished Conservatory of Music Building and Auditorium would be "one of the finest in the entire country" and well-suited for a varied cultural program. The Music Department, he added, was planning to improve its work through its four glee clubs, band, orchestra and through private lessons for over six-hundred students, all of whom anxiously awaited a decision on the Carnegie sets.[48]

The long-awaited news brought joy to the college and especially to Walter Roberts and his music faculty when Robert Lester announced to Phelps on May 20, 1940, "that the trustees of the Corporation have allocated a music set to Winthrop College."[49] The New York music firm of Lyon and Healy handled the details. They congratulated Winthrop on her selection; with these new aids, the Music Department could rise to new heights in service to the college and the community.[50]

While it appeared that the college was absorbed in attracting Carnegie gifts, the real physical improvements of this time were the most outstanding and the most service-oriented on campus other than the Training School. These included a nursery-school project to be built in conjunction with the PWA grant.[51]

Once the new PWA buildings were completed, landscaped, and dedicated in 1939, the campus assumed a more majestic look. Many referred to a new and greater Winthrop being born. And a trustee expressed what many felt--"whether we agree with the policies of the present [FDR] administration or not, the fact remains that the Federal Government did an extraordinary service to the cause of education in South Carolina when it made the liberal contribution which enabled us to erect these great buildings."[52]

Even though some of South Carolina's leading politicians, bankers, and business people remained somewhat cool toward Roosevelt and the New Deal, the Legislature was very willing to involve itself deeply with federal public-work projects. In 1939 they passed two major acts directed toward this involvement. Act 351 authorized the construction, equipment, and operation of a Winthrop dormitory with the "Board of trustees being authorized to obtain a loan from a Federal agency and to issue revenue bonds for payment of same." The bonds' amount was not to exceed $200,000. Act 364 complemented Act 351 by validating "bonds issued to finance any work by any public body which had secured a loan or grant through the Federal Emergency Administrator of Public Works." This referred to Secretary of the Interior Harold Ickes' area of responsibility.[53]

The above arrangement held great promise for Winthrop's future physical development. But Phelps still lacked money to furnish the new buildings. Writing to Leo M. Favrot (field agent of the General Education Board) in 1939, Phelps asked for $35,000 to finish furnishing the home-economics building and the nursery school. "I believe," he wrote, "there is no phase of educational work in the State more needed in South Carolina or that will be more helpful in improving the living conditions of our people." Despite Winthrop's strong case, the General Education Board declined to help.[54]

In 1939 and 1940 the thrust of Adolph Hitler's European invasions, the United States' shorn up defense posture, and the Battle of Britain produced feelings of uncertainty and desperation among many citizens of the United States and the world. Even in the sleepy mill town of Rock Hill,

484

South Carolina, the home of Winthrop College, life began to change more rapidly. World conditions made their impact on Winthrop.

Perhaps changing world conditions had no connection with a most unusual act that took place on Founder's Day, 1940. On this special occasion, a few dissidents led by "a rather bright and disturbed local student" circulated yellow sheets of paper which attacked the most prestigious student organization, Senior Order. Calling the girls of Senior Order a special clique who did not possess the high scholarship, leadership, and character they were supposed to possess, the leaflets demanded that the Order be abolished. What might have been regarded as an exercise in poor taste by some was seriously considered since it had disturbed many in the student body.[55]

Before the Senior Order controversy had subsided, another student-oriented controversy was brewing. This time it concerned dancing--girls with boys--on campus. Dancing had been an important facet in the genteel lifestyles of many South Carolina families for generations. However, among certain fundamentalist church groups, smoking, playing cards, and dancing were considered sinful. Since three-fourths of the student body held membership in the Baptist, Methodist, and Presbyterian churches, the problem can be better understood.[56] Thus, in the best Jeffersonian tradition, Phelps canvassed the parents: do you favor dancing under faculty supervision at Winthrop? Mrs. Daniel approved of Phelps's "Dear Friends" questionnaire with the amendment "at the annual Junior-Senior," but hastened to add that "this does not mean that I approve dancing at Winthrop."[57]

Phelps uncovered sufficient sentiment for dancing. Soon, a committee consisting of Dean Hardin, Dr. Kinard, Miss M. Ellis (a hostess at Roddey), Professor Walter Roberts of Music, and Professor Frank Harrison of French were making elaborate plans to hold Winthrop's first officially sanctioned dance. Local trustees and their wives

485

would be invited, but the seniors would control the affair with no other students or faculty invited to observe. Hostesses received special assignments. Superintendent W. T. Clawson of Buildings and Grounds and Ted Blankenship (Foreman of Grounds and Marshal) would afford the necessary protection for all. From this elementary beginning, the Winthrop classes developed a reputation for sponsoring some of the best dances held at any South Carolina college.[58]

By 1940 the Winthrop Board of Trustees was beginning to consider how gathering war clouds might affect future operations. Winthrop had employed outstanding and refined aliens heretofore, but now the Board decreed that no more foreign teachers would be hired due to developing world conditions.[59] The Board directed Phelps to ascertain the citizenship of all teachers on campus. Among the group were found two Canadian ladies, Professor Lois Black and Dr. Helen MacDonald. Neither had sought American citizenship even though they had lived in the United States for many years. For the moment this did not seem to present any real problem.

Far more exciting to the Winthrop trustees was the General Assembly's permission to issue up to $200,000 in bonds to be sold to some federal agency. This money, when added to a new $160,000 request, would enable the college to build a first-class fireproof dormitory for three-hundred seniors. And trustee Charlie Cobb, president of the Peoples National Bank, apologized to Senator Byrnes on May 2, 1940, for not attending the Tillman Memorial dedication in Columbia. Using this excuse, Cobb further quizzed Byrnes about the status of PWA and begged for another federal grant similar to the one utilized in building the new auditorium and home-economics building.[60]

In mid-August, 1940, the college received a novel request from Rock Hill's non-collegiate Flying Group, seventy-five young men who wished to learn the basics of ground work in flying. They asked for a classroom and an instructor, Mr. Ralph Blakely of the Training School, so that they might complete this basic course before Winthrop's fall term began. [61] In later years, some proponents of co-education at Winthrop would point to these males, saying that they had already broken the rule about no men studying at Winthrop. However, such proponents misunderstood the rule (which sought only to provide a separate, quality education for South Carolina's women). They also misunderstood the studies of the Flying Group and Winthrop's history, for men had attended Winthrop's summer schools from the beginning.

Early in 1941 the Board recommended that Dr. Phelps be authorized to borrow $300,000 for a new dormitory instead of the $200,000 already authorized, since the Budget Commission had failed to recommend the college's request for a dormitory appropriation. [62] In other matters they took the $12,000 given from the Julius Friedheim estate for two annual scholarships to Winthrop and invested it in the Barnette property on Oakland Avenue and in the Ratterree property on Park Avenue Extension. The Board reasoned that the rental from these would bring in four percent annually for the scholarships.

Another matter concerned the Board in 1941. A leading student with three of her classmates had attended the annual Congress of the National Student Foundation held in Brunswick, New Jersey. There (as Mrs. Daniel later learned), this student had danced with a Negro attending the meeting--more precisely a Negro boy had cut in on the student in question and they had danced until a white boy had "rescued her." After a thorough investigation, the Board voted not to expel the girl. However, the Board decided that Winthrop girls should not attend any future conventions where there were mixed races and that delegations of Winthrop girls would be properly chaperoned when they attended meetings. [63]

During the summer of 1941 the Board produced some momentous decisions. The re-elections of Drs. Elizabeth Harris and Helen MacDonald to the faculty were deferred. First-year medicine and law classes were accepted as a fourth year on arts degrees. The student canteen was given an adult manager. Winthrop decreed that out-of-state students must maintain grades of C or higher to attend the college. Also Winthrop students were denied access to the Oakland Avenue bowling alley, and the new dormitory plans submitted by Mr. Hopkins were accepted.[64]

Since the Legislature had appropriated $100,000 and authorized a $300,000 loan to be amortized from the receipts of an improved student-housing plan, the way opened for greatly lessening the housing problem at Winthrop. The successful bidder on these bonds was the Satt, Horner, and Mason Syndicate with the interest rate of 2.75 percent and a premium of $1,601. By early 1942, work on the new dormitory was progressing earnestly. It opened in January, 1943, exclusively for members of the senior class.[65]

During the dormitory's construction, Phelps attempted to run the college with aid and advice from eighty-one-year-old Trustee Roddey, knowing full well that he was beginning to have vexing problems not of his making. War and American preparedness meant higher prices for food, loss of young faculty men, uncertainty over enrollment, and a tendency toward educational instability. Furthermore the MacDonald-Harris affair (the dismissal of two "troublesome" faculty members) was kindling a fire at Winthrop which threatened to burn out of control.[66]

Outwardly, all flowed smoothly at Winthrop College. The Senior Order controversy dissipated after the junior class elected four additional members to serve with the presidents of Student Government, the Y, the Athletic Association, the Senate, and the senior class. These nine members

488

would choose three additional members, thereby making this body more elective.[67]

In 1941 considerable attention focused on the Tillman Memorial Commission's gift to Winthrop of the $1,100 residue from the Tillman Monument. Former Governor John G. Richards, one of Tillman's closest friends and Chairman of the Commission, was instrumental in turning over this surplus money to Winthrop. The interest from this gift was designated to purchase a medal to be awarded each year "to the Winthrop graduate with the best general average in scholarship and deportment." In the Board's resolutions following the former governor's death on November 4, 1941, Richards was praised for his service to Winthrop "as one of the great benefactors of the institution."[68]

As the shadow of World War II crept stealthily across the nation, Winthrop attempted to contribute to the war-oriented programs. First Winthrop allowed a group in Civilian Pilot Training to use the college farm to train young men to reach the "solo stage in flying." This was followed by a request to house, train, and feed three-hundred more pilots, and the army asked permission to trespass on the farm should maneuvers make it necessary during the coming fall. Phelps felt confident that he could handle the intrusions so that they would not seriously interfere with the campus's regular work and routine. Before Phelps could properly canvass the Board on these requests, however, a committee of Winthrop daughters from Chester wrote Trustee Spruill, protesting a rumor that Johnson Hall would be offered to the government as headquarters during army maneuvers.[69]

Much more threatening to Winthrop's welfare than any influx of cadets was the forthcoming investigation of "Administrative Irregularities" at Winthrop by a Southern Association committee consisting of President B. H. Hubbard of the Texas Woman's College and President Theodore Jack of the Randolph-Macon Woman's College of Lynchburg, Virginia.[70] The investigation had grown out of the

489

dismissal of two teachers, Drs. Helen G. MacDonald and Elizabeth Lee Harris. Dr. MacDonald, Head of the Department of Political and Social Science, had been on faculty fourteen years. She was a Canadian who had never taken out United States citizenship as the Board had requested. Phelps had conveyed the Board's decision to her that she would give up teaching American government and confine herself to sociology. Dr. MacDonald, not wishing to do this, had contacted three Board members. In early June, she learned that her appointment was being held in abeyance since she had violated the by-laws by seeing these individuals.[71] Dr. MacDonald felt she was within her rights to see Board members and she submitted a written explanation to Dr. Phelps, who already knew that her appointment would not be continued. There were other details that surfaced in connection with this case including the activities of the history department head "by the name of Keith, who had absorbed one department into his own and was possibly desirous of absorbing the Department of Government and Sociology also."[72]

Then, Dr. Harris (a rather outspoken lady) had become involved by trying to help Dr. MacDonald. She was also charged for visiting a Board member, and she earned the enmity of Professor Warren Keith when she attempted to help one of his professors whom he later forced to resign.[73]

On March 5, 1942, Phelps informed the Board that the Southern Association committee was coming to Winthrop on April 6. He urged full cooperation with them. With an eye on the forthcoming meeting with Hubbard and Jack, the Board moved to appoint a committee to revise the by-laws and also one to make recommendations to the Board concerning faculty elections. Before adjourning, the Board voted to place a bronze plate on Thurmond Hall (the home-economics building) and to ask Phelps to notify the Board whenever a student was sent home for disciplinary reasons.[74]

A month later, the Board reconvened to discuss the "Administrative Irregularities" and other matters pertinent to the Southern Association investigation. After discussion with Jack and Hubbard, the Board considered withholding voluntary contributions from salaries to purchase war bonds and stamps. The Alumnae Association's recent resolution declaring itself an independent body and not responsible to any higher authority necessitated a ruling from the attorney general regarding support for this association. Before this meeting adjourned, Phelps addressed himself to recent student unrest at Winthrop. Some had complained that the long period of "waiting for grace at the table before eating" was not the heart of the problem. Rather the students wanted smoking rooms on campus, more dances, and repeal of the playing-card prohibition. [75]

While the Southern Association and the American Association of University Women studied Winthrop's problems and prepared their reports, the next few months proved decisive for Winthrop and President Phelps. Wartime conditions led to decreased enrollment, which presented additional problems for the administration and the Board. Faculty had to be dropped, and Winthrop had to face additional investigations of the AAUW and of the Association of American Universities. [76]

Looking in on the October Board meeting in 1942, one sees a problem-ridden session. Trustee Angus Macaulay reported for the special AAUW committee that he had conferred with Drs. MacDonald and Harris (who was now Mrs. Raven I. McDavid, Jr.) about a settlement which MacDonald had refused and Harris-McDavid had taken under advisement. Further action was contingent on Mrs. McDavid's response. They agreed that the governor should send letters to MacDonald and to McDavid asking them to visit the Board. [77]

During the next order of business, Phelps presented a letter from Dr. Janet Clark stating that an AAUW committee would receive a Winthrop

491

committee in New York on November 15. Phelps had agreed to send a committee, but Trustee Cobb moved that the letter be received as information and included in the minutes. At this point the governor had to leave for other engagements and Vice-chairman Spruill took over.[78]

Phelps was also authorized to cut faculty in this war-time emergency and to transfer the principal and interest of the A. Markley Lee Trust Fund from the Bank of Greenwood to Winthrop. When Governor Jefferies returned to the meeting, he requested that the Southern Association matter be considered further.[79]

Dr. Phelps read a recent letter from Dr. Goodrich White, Secretary of the Commission of Institutions of Higher Education, specifying four requirements necessary for Winthrop's continuation in good standing: one, payment of a year's salary each to Dr. MacDonald and to Dr. McDavid without any qualifications or conditions attached to acceptance of the check; two, establishment of a satisfactory tenure system; three, adequate provisions for faculty participation in Winthrop's educational policies; and four, specified improvement in the institution's spirit and tone.[80] The governor moved to accommodate the associations by paying MacDonald and McDavid a year's salary each. The Board also agreed to formulate a tenure plan and to confer with the faculty.[81]

Phelps had been feeling administrative and educational pressures for some time. On his physician's advice he asked for a leave on October 1, 1942, to enter the Vanderbilt University Hospital. There he underwent exhaustive tests. Three months later he felt compelled to resign the presidency of Winthrop. But determined to prove that his stewardship of Winthrop had been correct, he attended the December meeting of the Southern Association in Memphis to argue his position. When he returned, he wrote Vice-chairman Spruill that he "found Jack, Hubbard, and Huntley had formed adverse

492

opinions." From this meeting came the announcement that Winthrop had been placed "on probation."[82]

Phelps later informed the Board that his physical condition was "quite grave," that he suffered from "an incurable ailment" which necessitated quitting his position. Overcoming an angina attack, he requested that he be allowed to stay on until August, 1943. But on January 13, 1943, he wrote, "I am quite willing to shorten the time, if in your judgment it would be better for the college that I do so."[83]

Despite his physical handicap and the gathering clouds of uncertainty, Phelps pushed on as best he could. To bolster the college's sagging revenues, Phelps, who had unsuccessfully sought female military units for Winthrop, looked favorably on the Manpower Commission's offer to place three-hundred aviation cadets at Winthrop. Several months later, the contract terms for the cadets were made public.[84]

The cadets' invasion of Bancroft Hall in March, 1943, worked out satisfactorily. The War Department paid Winthrop approximately $180,000 a year for cadet maintenance and instruction and promised to cover any damages to the facility. In addition, five Winthrop teachers were employed in the program. There were no discipline problems and the cadets' demanding schedule plus their high honor code proved to be a salutory influence on the campus. Many Winthrop alumnae and patrons disliked the arrangement but accepted it as military necessity.[85]

A greater concern for Winthrop's welfare revolved around her difficulties with the various professional associations. Phelps attempted to give a forthright explanation of this in his 1942-1943 report to the General Assembly via Superintendent James H. Hope of the Department of Education: Winthrop was on probation. To be accredited was valuable to a college because it enabled students to go to other colleges without losing credits.

493

But he said, "it should be emphasized that this probation does not in anyway affect the value of credits which students earn at Winthrop. Those credits still retain full value in the eyes both of other colleges and of superintendents and other employers."[86]

Attempting in his candid report to explain the ramifications of probation, Phelps added "the spirit and tone of the institution has suffered . . . because of the dismissal" of teachers (the July 1941 affair), resulting in adverse publicity. He assured the state that these actions had been corrected by a new procedure whereby "faculty members are encouraged to bring in their complaints and the officials of the college have offered to discuss their policies in the open before the faculty or proper public."[87] He stressed again that "when a college is investigated by its accrediting association [the Southern in this case] it is naturally investigated also by other Associations to which it belongs." In this case the Association of American Universities and the American Association of University Women both had dropped Winthrop from membership. But neither action censured Winthrop academically. Censure was directed against the administration.[88]

These associations seemed to follow the lead of the Southern Association. Since Winthrop now had tried to comply with the Southern Association's suggestions, President Phelps and others felt that the criticisms by a few were hurting Winthrop. He frankly admitted that the college had problems, but they were being studied with a view toward taking corrective action.[89]

The record is not clear as to who brought on this gloomy state of affairs at Winthrop. Some evidence points to the actions of an uninformed and callous Board. Other evidence suggests that the highly successful Phelps became too high-handed and uncompromising. There is also the possibility that the lean, forceful, and scholarly Theodore H.

Jack over-reacted to Winthrop's case in the Southern Association's review.[90]

Rapidly declining health brought on by severe pressure forced Phelps to take a complete rest in late February, 1943. In mid-March he wrote Trustee Spruill: "I am still in the living room and we have a good fire in the fireplace." Informing Spruill that his doctor wanted him to ride a bit in the sunshine, Phelps observed: "I can't see how this is going to be arranged with reference to tires and gas." Still, Phelps continued to try to keep abreast of his correspondence.

On May 4, 1943, the Board named Dean Mowat G. Fraser and Trustees Roddey, Cobb, and Macaulay to assume the administration of Winthrop.[91] Fraser became acting president. One of his innovations was to allow radios in dormitory rooms. Since radios tended to interfere with study hours, some of the faculty led by the outstanding English Professor Hampton Jarrell fought a spirited battle against them.[92]

Outwardly, things seemed to go as usual at Winthrop. Both college and community became more involved in the war effort. Rock Hill's Evening Herald gave college news first-page billing along with war stories from all over the world. The cadets at Winthrop in the Forty-First Headquarters College Training Detachment always got good press, and the townspeople enjoyed their band, which played at formations, reviews, and retreat. Special attention was called to Dr. W. H. Kilpatrick of Columbia University, who came to campus to speak and confer with student teachers. The paper happily reported that the Legislature refused to cut Winthrop's budget for fiscal 1943-1944. Much attention focused on the fifteenth annual Grand Eastern Forensic Tourney which Winthrop was sponsoring in Charlotte. Dr. Warren Keith and his Strawberry Leaf Society girls were to have important parts in this program. Winthrop's Music Club won the coveted silver cup of the South Carolina Federation of Music Clubs. The faculty stunt night was described in the press

495

as outstanding. New student leaders and the various programs for senior week were highly advertised. There were vespers, receptions, alumnae meetings, senior chapel, senior dances, the literary socie- ties' joint celebration, the Daisy Chain, and the music concert. But the very important Board meetings caused the press to speculate who Winthrop's next president would be.[93]

As early as March 2, 1943, the Board in special meeting at the Wade Hampton Hotel in Columbia discussed several applicants for the Winthrop presidency. A special committee consisting of Chairman J. A. Spruill, Mrs. Horace L. Tilghman, Mr. W. B. Davis, and Mrs. Connie Y. Earle was given the responsibility to study the situation and make recommendations to the Board. During the session, deep concern over Dr. Phelps' illness prompted the committee to send him flowers and books with their heartfelt best wishes.[94]

The committee met again at the Wade Hampton Hotel on March 30, 1943, to consider the names of all presidential prospects. The committee agreed "that it was highly desirable to secure as presi- dent of Winthrop someone who had unquestioned standing in the educational world and who is from the southeast, if possible." In view of these considerations, a committee was to be elected and sent to Dr. Francis Gaines to offer him the posi- tion. They agreed that if Dr. Gaines rejected the offer, the committee would continue to function until a president was secured.[95]

In a special Board meeting at the governor's office on May 4, Drs. Phelps and Fraser were present part of the time. During the meeting, the Nomina- ting Committee made its report, and Senator Henry Sims of the Board moved "that the Governor be authorized to make certain investigations and that the committee be continued and bring to the Board meeting of May 29 no fewer than three recommenda- tions" for president of Winthrop. It was further agreed that Dr. Phelps be requested to take adequate rest and absence from the college.[96]

496

Many expected the anxiously awaited decision on Winthrop's presidency to come at the commencement-week Board meeting in Rock Hill. As Governor Olin Johnston emerged from this meeting, he announced to the press that the committee was not ready to make its definite report on the president. Vice-chairman Spruill added that they might be ready to report by July or August. Meanwhile the Board was subject to recall by the governor.[97]

There were other urgent matters for the Board to consider in this transition period. The governor reported at the September 1943 meeting that Winthrop's status with the associations had not changed. Mr. Roddey, representing the Emergency Committee, read a letter from the Carnegie Foundation regarding Dr. Phelps' annuity policy. His committee recommended that the college pay the premium of approximately $2,595.07. This would entitle Dr. Phelps to a monthly life annuity of $150. Roddey also informed the Board that the Emergency Committee had told Phelps he was free to occupy the president's residence until it was needed.[98]

Trustee Cobb brought to the Board's attention the fact that since Winthrop's president was also the treasurer, someone was needed to perform this task. Mr. Graham, the Business Manager, was designated Acting Treasurer. Since two parents of Winthrop girls (a Major Bethea and a Mr. Holmes) appeared before the Board to question the propriety of the college's cadet program, Mr. Graham, Acting President Fraser and Dean Hardin all were present to give a good account of the program.[99]

Before concluding the meeting, Governor Johnston welcomed Drs. Ruth Stokes of Mathematics and Vera MacNair of Home Economics. Dr. Stokes requested an additional faculty member to help with the majors and the cadets. Dr. MacNair urged the Board to specify that a properly qualified nutrition instructor be secured. Later a motion was made to release Dr. MacNair's services and Fraser told the

Board that no additional help was needed in mathematics.[100]

The 1943-1944 session at Winthrop opened for the freshmen on September 2, followed by faculty meetings and the upper classes' arrival. The following week the first chapel exercises were held, with the Reverend Francis W. Gregg speaking. Then on Sunday the long Blue Line marched down Oakland Avenue to church. With 1,525 students, the line reached almost to the railroad bridge. Monday, the students settled down to work.[101]

The usual president's reception for faculty and students was not held this year. Instead each residence hall gave one. Each church in town entertained those students and teachers who regularly attended. For the first time in Winthrop's history, the opening was different.[102]

The education curriculum was noticeably altered this year. Formerly, eight methods courses were taught with only several members enrolled in many of them. But during this session two classes were designed to take care of teaching and organizing high-school subjects in English, social studies, mathematics, science, Latin, French and fine arts. Students were given the psychology of learning, high-school materials and methods of instruction, and organization of materials, using the Training School as a laboratory. The latter would be the closest contact with actual conditions existing in the high schools of South Carolina. This new, steamlined approach in teacher training was designed fully to prepare the graduates to take their places in classrooms throughout the South.[103]

While the leadership of the alumnae chapters admonished their membership to show by their deeds the strength of their organization, the trustees earnestly sought to keep Winthrop viable and to find a suitable president for the foundering institution.[104] At their October 14 Board meeting, the Finance Committee presented the 1944-1945 budget. Governor Johnston excused himself from presiding

since later he would have to review the budget
officially as a member of the Budget Commission.
But he suggested that Winthrop be prepared and
properly represented when the Commission officially
visited the campus.[105]   Some attention was also
given to equalizing department heads' salaries:
Vice-chairman Spruill suggested that they might wish
to consider basing salary increases on experience.
Fraser's salary was increased $1,000 at this meeting
to compensate for his extra duties.[106]

    Always in Winthrop's Board meetings during
this period, the Southern Association dogged every
action.   Winthrop resolved to ask the Executive
Committee of the Southern Association again in the
Association's December meeting to remove the college
from probationary status.[107]

    In a related matter, the governor read a
letter from Dr. Payne (University of Indiana), who
had been designated to inspect Winthrop for the
American Association of Universities.   In fact, he
was on campus and was invited to confer with the
group.   They discussed liberalized curriculum,
faculty organization, promotions, administration,
teacher loads, weak spots, salary levels, and
research.[108]   However, Dr. Payne's visit was not
fruitful for Winthrop. The governor on December 4,
1943, read another letter from Dr. Payne informing
him that the AAU (like the AAUW) had dropped
Winthrop from the approved list.[109]

    Desirous to comply with some of Dr. Payne's
suggestions about an increased faculty participation
in college affairs, the Emergency Committee and the
Committee on Organization and Instruction met on
January 22, 1944, to consider mutual concerns.
Faculty members on continuous tenure were re-
elected. A twelfth grade was added to the Training
School. As a gesture to meet faculty criticisms,
the committees "resolved that to promote harmony and
loyalty," they wished to have the faculty nominate
ten of their members from whom the administration
and the Emergency Committee would appoint three as

499

a fact-finding committee to make or receive criticisms affecting the college and to ascertain the facts before appeals were sent to the administration or (if necessary) the trustees. Note was made of the many documents from Dr. Ruth Bourne of the History Department registering her personal complaints.[110]

Fraser was instructed to interview all faculty members whose attitudes and activities had tended to be detrimental to the college. Jim Kinard would be present and a stenographic record of the interviews would be made. In a more constructive way, Fraser proposed that a statement should be sent to faculty members on leave. The following was agreed on:

> All staff members on leave, of course, will be taken back on our pay roll at the beginning of the year--if possible at the beginning of the semester--following their release from the services, provided that 60 days' notice is given. This note is simply to point out the obvious fact that it may be impossible to take all faculty members back on short notice while those who are replacing them are still on the pay roll.
>
> As soon as you know when you would like to return to Winthrop, therefore, will you please let us know?[111]

Since May 4, 1943, Winthrop had continued to rock along uncertainly with Fraser as Acting President and Dr. Kinard as President Emeritus. The Board and administration wished to improve Winthrop, so they were especially troubled by the various professional associations' actions. These problems notwithstanding, students still continued to receive a good education at Winthrop with total expenses per session running $344 exclusive of the uniform.[112]

Winthrop students strictly adhered to the long-time dress standards, which were always stated in the _Bulletin_:

To conserve students' time for college activities and to aid in promoting emphasis on intellectual standards on the Winthrop College campus, the custom of wearing navy blue and white clothes was established. In recent years the students on several occasions have voted to continue the custom because they believe the spirit of democracy is promoted and because they find it convenient. Much time and thought are given to selecting materials and styles for every new session of the College.

Every student appears in navy blue for the "Blue Line" on the first Sunday after college opens; so all freshmen and new students must bring a navy blue dress to wear until the standard dress ordered at the college is secured.

Students are measured at the college for: a navy blue silk dress with long-sleeved jacket of same material, a navy blue woolen tailored coat-suit and a white blouse, an all-white dress for formal wear.

These outfits are worn for street, church, and all formal college programs according to the demands of the occasion.

In addition to the above items, all students are required to bring: a navy blue top-coat without fur trimming. Parents are requested not to ask that students wear other than navy blue coats. Merchants tell us that it is

501

possible to secure navy blue top-coats from coat manufacturers; a navy blue or black hat, navy blue or black shoes, six or more washable all-white blouses.

The following articles of clothing are recommended: a navy blue raincoat, an umbrella, a pair of galoshes, a navy blue skirt to be worn with white blouses on campus.

On the campus, students may wear: navy blue or all-white washable dresses, navy blue or all-white washable blouses, navy blue or white sweaters, navy blue coat-suits with white blouses.[113]

But the question of a president for Winthrop remained uppermost in the minds of the Winthrop community. Finally the Board, meeting at the governor's office in late May, considred Dr. E. T. McSwain, Dr. Earl Armstrong, and Senator Henry Sims for the presidency of Winthrop. Senator Sims, Chairman of the Senate Education Committee, was unanimously elected. Sims expressed his appreciation to the Board but asked to defer his decision until July.[114]

Henry Sims had grown fond of Winthrop. The Board and state leaders liked him. As he considered very carefully whether or not to assume this demanding position, two important letters and the reactions thereto pushed him into a new and precarious public position which would consume most of his life for the next fifteen years.[115]

CHAPTER XV

SENATOR HENRY RADCLIFFE SIMS ACCEPTS THE CHALLENGE

> For their outstanding service to Win-
> throp College, the Senior Class
> proudly dedicates the nineteen hundred
> and fifty-nine edition of the _Tatler_ to
> President and Mrs. Henry Radcliffe
> Sims . . . To President Sims for his
> loyal service as counselor and friend
> who has encouraged, guided and under-
> stood us . . . To Mrs. Sims for her
> ardent support and genial interest in
> all our activities. It has been our
> privilege and honor to have them here
> at Winthrop.

Before the public ever knew of Henry Sims'
decision to accept the Winthrop presidency, he was
quietly and systematically laying the groundwork for
what he hoped would be a successful administration.
At age fifty, he was a successful lawyer, a respected editor, and a distinguished public servant who
had been mentioned for the governorship of his
native state. He had made important contributions
to South Carolina's civic progress. Noted for his
interest in education, social security, good roads
and other worthwhile activities, he was better known
to South Carolinians than any previous Winthrop
presidents when they assumed office.[1]

Sims could see that Winthrop's problems were
many and varied. But the key to many of them was
the role played by Dr. T. H. Jack of Randolph-Macon
Woman's College and his associates on the Committee
of the Southern Association of Colleges and
Secondary Schools. Therefore, on June 8, 1944, Sims
sent a personal and confidential letter to Dr. Jack
designed to clear the air and chart the way for
restoring Winthrop to the associations:

Dear Dr. Jack:

I would like very much to have an

opportunity to talk with you confidentially and frankly in regard to
Winthrop College and its relationship
to the Southern Association. I will
come to Lynchburg at any date convenient to you.

In justification of this request, I
would like to advise you that the Board
of Trustees of Winthrop College at its
meeting two weeks ago elected me
President of that institution, and at
the present time I have the matter of
acceptance under consideration. This
fact has not been made public yet;
therefore, you will understand, I am
writing you in confidence.

I have been a member of the Board
of Trustees, ex-officio (as Chairman of
the Senate Education Committee), for
about eighteen months, and I am fairly
familiar with events at Winthrop during
that period. However, I was not so
associated with Winthrop when the
crisis in its relations with the
Southern Association was precipitated.

During my service on the Board, I
have taken part in the deliberations on
certain recommendations made by the
Association, such as the payment of a
year's salary in lieu of notice to two
dismissed professors, the suggestion
for more faculty participation in the
formation of educational policies, and
the adoption of a definite tenure plan
for members of the faculty. It
happened that I could very well agree
with the advisability and wisdom of
those recommendations and, I think, I
had some part in securing their
satisfactory adoption, particularly,
with regard to the last two.

504

The only other recommendation of the Association, as I recall them, was of a general nature, involving improvement in the "tone" of the College. The future relationship of Winthrop College to the Association is quite naturally a matter of some concern to me, as I feel it is essential that harmonious relations be reestablished.

The purpose for my conference is in the hope that through a frank and unrestricted conversation with you as a representative of the Association, I may be able to learn at first hand exactly what other definite steps should be taken in a mutual spirit of conciliation and adjustment so that Winthrop College might look forward to re-entering into its proper and normal relationship with your Association.

If you will excuse some personal references, I would like to assure of certain fundamental facts in relation to the offer which I have received from the Board of Trustees. Of course, you do not know me, but, I can assure you, I am stating to you, with absolute candor, my very sincere and honest attitude and thoughts regarding the presidency of Winthrop College.

I happen to know, as very good friends, Dr. Walter K. Greene, of Wofford College, and Dr. J. Rion McKissick, of the University of South Carolina, and I have taken the liberty of requesting them to write you so that their sponsorship of me may serve as some introduction to this communication.

First, I want you to know, I was not a candidate in any way for this office, nor did I solicit it. In fact,

I refused to give any encouragement whatever to the suggestion when it was made to me by some of the trustees. Except for one factor, which I shall mention subsequently, I would have flatly and emphatically prevented any such consideration of me.

Second, I am not interested in this office from the standpoint of a job. The salary it pays is less than I have been accustomed to make for some years. I have a very good law practice, I am vice-president of a fairly good national bank here, and, together with three brothers, I own a considerable interest in the corporation here which publishes a successful morning daily and another corporation which operates the picture shows in Orangeburg. From these business interests and my profession, I have had no difficulty in earning a very comfortable living, and I have no reason whatever to question a continuation of this.

Third, it happens that I have been the State Senator from my County for a period of fifteen years. I had more than reasonable expectations that I could have been re-elected this year without opposition. I will not go into my senatorial activities except to say that I believe the reputation I have over South Carolina is that of an independent and liberal, who never lined up with the politicians and who absolutely voted and acted upon his convictions. If I had any political ambitions for higher office, I think there was more than a possibility of success in that direction. (Since rumors of the Winthrop College possibility became public, I have withdrawn from the local Democratic Primary in order that a free field might be given to possible candidates for I realized the probability that I would accept the Winthrop offer.)

Further, if I accept the Winthrop presidency, I expect to abandon any future political aspirations for I would not even think of assuming the responsibility for the welfare of such an institution without making it my first and only purpose. While some people may have the idea that "politics" played some part in my election by the Board, I can assure you that this was not the case in the slightest.

Fourth, if I should go to Winthrop College, it will mean a very genuine sacrifice upon my part and will involve quite a revolutionary change in all that I had anticipated in life. In addition to the abandonment of these various business interests, I also separate myself from many close ties of friend-ship and relationship in this City, in which I have lived all my life. Only a conviction, whether presumptuous or not, that I can render a service to my State and society as President of Winthrop College could induce me to make any change whatever from a life in which I have been perfectly content and happy.

However, I sincerely believe that there is no greater service a man can render than to have a part in shaping the ideals and visions of thousands of young women of South Carolina, and this possibility is the only appeal of the Winthrop presidency which has had weight and influence upon my decision. If I go to Winthrop College, it will be with the

507

expectation that I shall give the remaining years of my life wholeheartedly and without reservation to this purpose.

I am fully conscious of the problems which I must meet as the new President of Winthrop College. I believe I have had ample executive and administrative experience; I feel that I have a sufficient knowledge of human beings and their ways; I feel that I have the patience, the tact, the ability and the determination to efficiently and satisfactorily perform the duties of this office. Believing this, I am inclined to burn my bridges here and venture upon the task to which I have been called.

I have written in great detail, but I have done so in the belief that you will appreciate my position and that you are anxious, as I am, to see Winthrop College develop into the greatest possible institution. For these reasons, I felt that a conference with you would be highly helpful to me, both because of your relationship to the Southern Association and because I was certain that out of your rich experience you could give me wise and beneficial counsel.

Therefore, I am asking that you designate a day, as early as possible, on which I may be able to have a quiet and confidential conversation with you. My only train schedule will bring me to Lynchburg at 1:40 a.m., and I would like to leave that evening at 9:30 p.m., although, if necessary, I will very gladly remain over another day if it suits your convenience better. Otherwise, I could call upon you at any time in the morning or the afternoon of the day you select. I suggest, for your consideration, any day next week, from the 12th on. I will appreciate your advising me, by telegraph collect, in regard to this, so that I can make the necessary railroad and hotel reservations.

In conclusion, I feel that it is only right that I should thank you for your time and patience in reading this long letter. I assure you, in advance, that I shall appreciate your consideration of this request of mine, as I will any cooperation and assistance you can render me.

With kind regards and best wishes, I am

Sincerely yours,

Henry R. Sims

HRS/VAB

P.S. I wonder if you knew my niece, Mary Sims, who graduated from Randolph-Macon in 1936, and who, I think, was a student there when you assumed the Presidency of the College?

H. R. S.[2]

Sims was encouraged enough by his visit with Dr. Jack that he agreed to accept Winthrop's presidency if the Board agreed with the position he outlined in the June 20, 1944, statement he read to them:

On the 23rd day of May, you elected me as the new President of Winthrop College and were considerate enough to give me a few weeks to make up my mind. I am now ready to give you a definite answer,

509

provided we agree on certain ideas about the operation of the college and my assumption of this office, which I shall outline briefly.

(1) Since the May meeting, I have held conferences with certain educators, legislators, and others whose cooperation I felt would be necessary for a successful administration of Winthrop. I am glad to advise you that in none of these contacts was there any discouraging note.

(2) The fact that I hold only an A.B. degree causes me no concern, because I find that there is a definite trend towards the selection of presidents of educational institutions who do not hold high academic degrees. A member of your Board furnished me the information that nine out of thirteen colleges in each of the States of North and South Carolina had elected presidents without such degrees.

(3) The major portion of the duties of this office is executive and administrative in nature and involves, in addition to the actual management of the College's affairs, the establishment and maintenance of proper relations with various groups, including the Board of Trustees and the General Assembly, which are the superior governing bodies of this institution; then, the student body, the faculty and alumnae of the College; and, beyond them, the public in general, and the press and other means of publicity as agencies in reaching this wider circle. I believe that my past experience with all of these groups will aid materially in the accomplishment of that necessary purpose.

(4) In connection with the office of the Presidency of Winthrop College, I think there is one very distinct need, and that is for an executive head who will face whatever problems there are and act definitely and firmly in the settlement of these problems. With all kindness, I am convinced that Winthrop's troubles have been due to a lack of firmness and decision on the part of its executive head.

(5) One phase of this indecision has been in relation to members of the Faculty. Dissention and jealousy have been reported existent in this group. Undue criticism of fellow members, attempts to override the policy of the administration, interference with the conduct of other departments, and similar acts, have been reported. I do not know how well founded these reports are or which members of the Faculty may have been guilty of them. However, Winthrop College will never perform its proper services to its students and the State if similar conditions exist in the future. I believe that the great majority of the Faculty will loyally cooperate with a fair, reasonable president, and I anticipate establishing that relationship. I shall offer every cooperation to the members of this group, recognizing the rights they have in certain matters, but, as President, I will not be willing to continue in office any member of the Faculty who does not give loyal, sincere and undivided support to the policies and purposes of the College as established by the Board of Trustees, and as carried out by the Board's representative, the President of the College.

511

(6) There has been another contributing
factor to the unrest at Winthrop
College, and, in frankness, I think it
should be mentioned here today. In the
past, the administration of college
affairs has suffered because of the
interference and improper activities of
some individual members of the Board of
Trustees. Happily, I believe this
practice will not trouble us in the
future, but in the interest of a proper
understanding, I think it might be well
for us to realize that while the Board
of Trustees is the supreme governing
body of the College, under legislative
authority, the Board acts as a unit
through the President which it has
elected, and in whom it is presumed to
have confidence. Whenever that confidence disappears, the Board should
elect a new President; until the Board
is ready to take this action, it should
give its President undivided support in
his efforts to administer the policies
which the Board decides in general
terms. No member of the Board should
go behind the back of the President in
any critical discussion of his acts
with any member of the Faculty. If
there is need for an investigation, it
should be made by a duly appointed committee of the Board, and not by individuals of the Board, self-appointed.

(7) It should be our aims to restore
Winthrop as early as possible to its
normal relationship with the Southern
Association, and other similar organizations. I have talked with several
influential members of the Southern
Association and I am satisfied that
this presents no serious difficulty
except the establishment of a proper
administration and the passage of
sufficient time for that fact to be
recognized.

(8) As, I presume, all of you know, I did not seek this position. Without going into any details, I can assure you it involves a personal sacrifice upon my part. I will withdraw from a legal practice and other business activities which have brought me a larger income than this College will pay me. In this connection, I understand that the salary of $6,000.00 a year is supplemented by an additional $1,000.00 for work in connection with the Summer School. I am satisfied that this Board will be ready and willing to make the total salary of this office $7,500.00 a year, with proper legislative authorization, which, I believe, will be shortly forthcoming.

(9) In connection with my coming to Winthrop, I will ask the following: (a) That the President's home be repainted, renovated, and altered in minor ways. I understand this work can be done by the regular College force. (b) I will also ask that the Board authorize me to employ an interior decorator and that the College furnish the draperies and one rug necessary for the two living rooms and the dining room, which will be used in entertainment on behalf of the College. (c) I will be responsible for all other necessary rugs and furniture, most of which I now have, although I will probably have to completely outfit several rooms, but I will ask that the College meet the expense of transporting these to Rock Hill.

(10) I understand, and believe your by-laws provide, that the President has

513

the right to select his own secretary and stenographic assistants.

(11) I believe your by-laws also provide that all "public announcements" shall be made by the President of the College. I think that Winthrop has suffered somewhat from an inadequate presentation of its cause in the press of this State. While I would not take part in any controversies or involve the College in any newspaper disputes, I think that proper publicity will immensely aid Winthrop College in the fulfillment of its mission and in securing support from the taxpayers of the State. If my interpretation of the by-laws is correct, I would prefer that all public announcements affecting the College be made by the President.

(12) If we are agreed on the foregoing, I am ready to accept the Winthrop Presidency. In doing so, I want you to know that I am not taking this office with any idea of using it as a stepping-stone for any other position, politically or otherwise. I am prepared to abandon my legal practice and certain business interests and to separate myself from many close ties of friendship and relationship in my native City. Only a conviction, whether presumptuous or not, that I can render a service to my State and society as President of Winthrop College, would induce me to make this change from a life in which I have been perfectly content and happy. I sincerely believe, however, that there is no greater service a man can render than to have a part in shaping the ideals of thousands of young women of South Carolina. This possibility has been the only appeal of the Winthrop Presidency which has influenced my

514

decision. I am fully conscious of many unmentioned problems which I must meet as the new President. I believe I have had ample executive and administrative experience; I feel that I have a sufficient knowledge of human beings and their ways; I feel that I have the patience, the tact, the ability and the determination to efficiently and satisfactorily perform the duties of this office. With the help of the members of this Board, both officially and personally, and many others in South Carolina who have the welfare of Winthrop College close to their hearts, I am not afraid to assume this position.

(13) There only remains the matter of determining the date upon which I will actively assume the duties of the office. From my investigation, I am satisfied that the sooner I take charge, the better it will be. Particularly, during the summer months, I will have an opportunity to become acquainted with the problems and routine of my office. I would like to assume office just as quickly as I can make arrangements to move into the President's house, say about July 15.

(14) One thing more. As I said to the Board four weeks ago, there are a few matters in my law office which I will have to wind up, including the receivership of a bank, and these matters will require me to be in Orangeburg probably two or three days out of every fortnight. However, I hope these can be all completed before the end of the present year, after which, I will not have these outside interests. I want the Board to know that I expect to give up, in addition to my law practice, any future participation in the management

of a bank in Orangeburg, although I may retain some stock I own. On the other hand, I will continue to own a considerable share in two family corporations in Orangeburg, in which I have no active participation, but in the future, I will want to attend directors' meetings of these corporations occasionally in order to keep in touch and protect my own interest.

(15) I am also glad to advise the Board that Mrs. Sims wholeheartedly agrees with me in my decision to devote the remainder of my life, if I am wanted that long, to the future of Winthrop College. She is ready and anxious to be of all possible assistance to the students and others interested in the College.

Sincerely yours,

Henry R. Sims[3]

Few people seeking a college presidency would have followed the procedure that Sims did, but then he was not seeking the job. Instead he seemed to be asking, "Do you really want me for the job?" With his newspaper (the Orangeburg Times and Democrat), his bank and theatre interests, and his Senate seat and law practice, Henry Sims' income and social position were assured for life.[4]

Those who knew Sims well appreciated his keen interest in history, law, and democratic institutions, his love of stimulating conversation, and his desire to meet and converse with learned and outstanding people. His humor, his disarming low-country accent, and his genuine smile won him a multitude of friends from the black domestics on the Winthrop campus to people in high places. He seemed to enjoy them all. But there was another side to Henry Sims. If he had cause to believe one to be an

516

impostor, a liar, or a miscreant, Sims could call forth the best of his legal background and present a compelling case employing picturesque language against the individual involved.[5]

Before Sims officially assumed his duties on July 1, 1944, the Board had already selected him as Chairman of the Executive Committee and of the Committee on Organization and Instruction. In addition, he chaired the Building and Library Committees. Entering upon his duties with great interest and vigor, Sims conducted an open-door administration. He wanted to know and to observe the Winthrop community's personnel. Confident about his ability and perception, he wanted to form his own judgments. He worked hard to discover the root of Winthrop's problems.[6]

In 1944 the General Assembly elected two new trustees, the Honorable Charlie V. Verner of Piedmont and Mrs. N. Gist Gee of Greenwood. Verner had served with distinction in the General Assembly, and Mrs. Gee had forged a distinguished career in education and public service. Sims could expect help from both trustees, especially Mrs. Gee, who had taught him English in the Orangeburg public school.[7]

The new president seemed to move with ease among the students and faculty, where his interest and concern soon won Sims the respect of many. There were some faculty who felt superior to Sims because they had earned doctoral degrees in biology, history, chemistry, math, and other disciplines, whereas Sims had one earned degree and an honorary LL.D. from Methodist-oriented Wofford College. However, the general faculty and others coming in contact with Sims soon learned that he was well-versed in many areas. His command of the English language and his ability to uncover the truth marked him as an unusual man.[8]

Writing to Vice-chairman Spruill of the Board in August, 1944, Sims reported that Dr. Warren Keith, the head of the History Department who

517

had sought the Winthrop presidency and who had been
deeply involved in several controversies there, "has
taken definite steps to eliminate the causes of dissatisfaction in which he has been involved." He
also informed Spruill that "I am going to do the
talking personally," referring to the up-coming
commencement on August 20, which would afford Sims
the opportunity to publicize his program.[9]

Sims was greatly concerned with improving
the instructional program and the physical plant,
and with increasing and adjusting faculty salaries.
To do these things he needed the support of the
trustees, the alumnae, and the General Assembly.
Working through J. A. Spruill and others, Sims
encouraged the trustees to plan their meetings in
conjunction with special college functions like
the Artist Series. Letters to these men would
often contain statements such as this: "I want to
call your attention to one of our artist numbers at
8 o'clock Monday evening--Helen Traubel will sing.
If you can stay over for this attraction, I think
you will be well repaid."[10]

At their fall meeting, Sims presented a
twenty-four item agenda to the Board, after having
them visit with the students and having Governor
Johnston address the assembly. Giving primary
consideration to salaries, Sims asked the Board to
approve increases. He wanted women department heads
to receive better treatment, and he desired to
implement salary ranges on the different levels.
Under the heading of improvements, he listed many
permanent improvements that needed to be made once
the war ended. The governor advised Sims to
document that other institutions projected similar
programs and then he would stand a better chance of
getting legislative support. Sims shared with the
Board his hope to set up stricter controls on
property, finance, and services by requiring
regularly written reports to the president from
those responsible for operating the college.[11]
Next, for information and news service, Sims
explained that he desired a good reporter, not a
public-relations official, who would publicize the

518

college by relating events and incidents that would
interest people throughout South Carolina. Moving
in a business-like manner through the long agenda,
Sims refused to approve a pacifist as YWCA secretary. He recommended more housing for faculty,
additional salary adjustments for specific members,
and a better surety-bond system for specific college
personnel. The Board took special note that Judge
(now General) Strom Thurmond, whose service in the
Normandy invasion and in the Pacific theatre
resulted in five battle stars and eighteen decorations, medals and other awards, had been wounded.
And finally, the Board voted to commend the
Johnsonian staff for its recent recognition as the
outstanding student newspaper in South Carolina.
And a compliment was directed to Governor Johnston
"for his interest in the welfare of Winthrop
College."[12]

Sims postponed his report on Winthrop's
relationship with the association until the January
Board meeting. Meanwhile he planned and hoped for
favorable news. The principal hurdle to his plan
for a successful administration would be the
attitude on Winthrop which the Southern Association
would take in its forthcoming (March, 1945)
meeting.[13] Confident that the state leadership
backed him, Sims worked hard and fast to move
Winthrop out of the impass into which it had drifted
during the last months of the Phelps administration.

Armed with a briefcase full of data and a
program requiring new expenditures, Sims visited
his old buddies on the Senate Finance Committee
before the state budget vote in 1945.[14] In visiting the General Assembly, Sims was going home. He
had chaired several Senate committees and had worked
closely with the Senate hierarchy, many of whom were
his long-time friends. In fact when Sims had
chaired the Special Committee on Social Security,
Strom Thurmond and Edgar Brown were included in
the membership. Now, Sims was asking for money,
not doling it out as he had helped to do when he
had served as vice-chairman of the Senate Finance

519

Committee.[15] Now, as Henry Sims approached the bar in the Senate committee room where his old friends were waiting to hear him explain the 1945 Winthrop budget, he began his remarks by saying: "Look here, boys, you have got to give me some more money. I can't run a first-class college on what you have allotted." A member of the committee retorted: "Henry, you helped to set this present figure before you went up to Rock Hill." Without the slightest hesitation, Sims replied, "Yeah, but that was before I learned what it takes to run a first-class college." And so Sims presented his case. During his tenure at Winthrop, the General Assembly usually took good care of Henry Sims' new love, Winthrop College.[16]

By graduation time in 1945, Sims was beginning to show that he truly controlled the most important facets of Winthrop's operation. His forthright approach continued to win him more friends. The Board seemed to appreciate his extensive planning for their quarterly meetings. Their minutes during Sims' administration showed an order and clarity not seen at Winthrop for a long time. Each of his meetings opened with general information on minor problems before they moved to the more important decisions. At the meeting of May 31, 1945, for instance, Sims reported on several minor concerns including the student nurses' from York County Hospital being housed at Winthrop, a cost-of-living conference being held at the college, the student body's general health, and the college's interest in presenting programs over the Rock Hill radio station.[17]

With a ten-page outline of important matters, Sims and the Board spent most of the day discussing such items as the new and valuable Italian paintings (given to the college by the Sassi family), the budget's status, and resolutions expressing the Board's deep appreciation for the long and valuable service of Mr. W. J. Roddey, who had died on February 15, 1945.[18]

520

In his budget review for the next fiscal year, Sims pointed out that enrollment at the University of South Carolina (including their naval cadets) was about the same as the enrollment at Winthrop. However, the General Assembly's appropriation still did not permit comparable salaries at Winthrop. After suggesting certain merit raises, Sims presented a salary scale ranging from $1,700 for an instructor to $4,000 for department heads. The entire teaching staff was given a ten-percent increase. The Board also voted that the president work out a salary scale comparable with other state institutions and present it to the Board.[19]

The Board welcomed news of the intimations several sources had made to Sims: these sources had hinted that the attitude of the American Association of Universities and the Southern Association was favorable to Winthrop. In a somewhat related move, Sims expressed the wish to employ R. Brice Waters as an executive director to help improve and control Winthrop's administrative practices. In an attempt to clear the atmosphere at Winthrop, the Board agreed with Sims not to re-elect Dr. Warren Keith of the History Department because of his connections with certain questionable practices at Winthrop. They also made plans to implement the state's retirement act at Winthrop. Before they adjourned, newly elected Governor Ransome J. Williams supported the proposal to pay the alumnae secretary an associate professor's salary.[20]

Two months later a special Board meeting implemented some of the May proposals. In this July meeting the Board voted to exchange some lots with Rock Hill. Committees were appointed to accept the Sassi paintings and to draft resolutions on the death of Trustee W. J. Roddey. The Board concurred on other matters. Mr. R. Brice Waters was elected Administrative Director; Robert M. Ward (a reporter on the Rock Hill Herald) was being secured to handle publicity. Mr. Sims reported on efforts to secure a dietitian for the dining room and on York County

521

Hospital's extended training program with Winthrop. Other items on the agenda dealt with the new retirement policy, Miss Spain and the library, enrollment projections, promotions, the improved lecture program, Sims' formal installation (planned for October 24, 1945), the Religious Education Department, and upkeep for the parkway fronting campus.[21]

Winthrop College, despite its problems and certain inept board members and administrators, struck most South Carolinians as one of the Palmetto State's greatest assets. Winthrop's presidents were regarded as very worthy people and legislative pets. Thanks to Ben Tillman and his followers a very special course had been charted for Winthrop and Clemson. Through the two colleges, Tillman's influence had touched most households in South Carolina.

Naturally, the inauguration for Winthrop's fourth president would indeed be a unique function to be publicized in every nook and cranny of the state. President-elect Sims looked forward to this occasion that would bring the state leadership, distinguished academics, and his many friends and well-wishers together for a solemn and impressive ceremony. Anyone who observed Henry Sims at close range could see that the presidency offered just what he wanted--an opportunity to have people see and hear him, to establish his forthrightness and honesty, and to impress upon his audience that he would work hard to bring about a better Winthrop.[22]

The ceremony began smoothly. Judge Arthur Gaston of the Sixth Judicial Circuit administered the oath of office to Sims. Then Governor Williams delivered the Winthrop seal to the new president, assuring the large assembly in the college auditorium that Winthrop would be in safe and trusted hands.[23]

Responding in a clear and exact fashion, Sims emphasized the opportunities and obligations attendant to his new position. He was influenced to come to Winthrop solely "by a desire to be of the greatest possible service to the people of my State." He had no misgivings about abandoning "a promising and profitable career, to devote the remainder of my life, if I am wanted and needed that long, to the all-rounded welfare and mental development of the students of Winthrop College."[24]

Then, expressing no regrets for the past and no doubts about the future, Sims referred to himself as "an unprofessional in the technical arts and methods of education." But he promised a steadfast effort to improve an already great institution whose value to South Carolina and the nation was well recognized. He noted the debt owed to many outstanding, excellent men and women who had labored and given of their lives to create and build Winthrop College.

Sims outlined five proposals for Winthrop's future growth and excellence. First, Winthrop needed to modernize its plant. Second, "We must," he said, "continue to attract and maintain on our Faculty a corps of scholars, skilled in their respective fields, dedicated to the eliminations of ignorance and prejudice, and genuinely concerned to promote intellectual honesty and achievement." Better salaries would help achieve this. Third, Sims asked for the continued support and intelligent cooperation of an active, loyal alumnae. Again he praised Winthrop's alumnae. And fourth, he cited the importance of a fine student body in creating a superior school. Last, President Sims asked for wise and intelligent leadership by the Board and administrators, with fairness to all, "always seeking to approximate the ideal vision of all that a great educational institution should be."[25]

Author and respected Birmingham columnist John Temple Graves spoke at this formal installation. His words aptly apply to Henry Sims: "South Carolina may be proud as there comes to this presidency a native son so rightly qualified by its

college, its law courts, its legislature. . . .
Henry Ratcliffe Sims has been educated in them
all."[26]

The press was quick to announce Winthrop's
rejuvenation and her fresh spirit of unity and
harmony. The new president met warmth and wholehearted accord that strengthened his determination.
"All over the campus," the press reported, "there
were heard only words of praise and commendation of
this man who, in his already brief tenure in the
office of president, had made the impact of his
personality felt in every department."[27]

The Sims administration showed great
promise. Had it not been for troubles inherited
from previous administrations, Sims would have
enjoyed a very pleasant stay at Winthrop College.
As a special Peabody College committee later
reported to the Winthrop Board of Trustees:
"Probably the most important justification for the
selection of Dr. Sims as president was the
anticipation that a person of his attainments would
be able to repair the damage done during the
administration of Dr. Phelps."[28] According to the
Peabody committee, "The Board of Trustees apparently
made the first move leading to disapproval by AAUP
by overriding the recommendations of President
Phelps and releasing two faculty members." Phelps
took the blame, and the AAUP moved to blacklist
Winthrop. Phelps refused to discuss the situation
with the AAUP. Later, Winthrop lost the AAUW's
approval, and the Southern Association of Colleges
and Secondary Schools put Winthrop on probation.[29]
This "fall from grace" was the situation that Sims
inherited along with factionalism and friction among
the faculty and in the alumnae association.

Some might question the sanity of the
middle-aged challenger who sought to bring order to
Winthrop and to lift the cloud that floated over a
vital area of South Carolina education. Sims,
however, was a successful and courageous man who
believed in himself and his ability to right wrongs.
Still, righting wrongs took time: during his
fifteen-year stay at Winthrop, Sims managed very

few vacations or trips. Usually he labored in his office six days a week and on Sunday evenings. [30]

Faculty attitudes and activities caused Sims much trouble. Several faculty members had wanted to be president of Winthrop. Dean Fraser, Warren Keith, Dr. Naudain, and others who fancied themselves as presidential timber resented the non-academic Dr. Sims and often tried to be disruptive. Dr. Naudain had announced earlier that he was seeking the presidency and that he had taken special classes to help him qualify. But according to statements from some of his students, he spent half each period in his chemistry classes discussing politics. In his class on the chemistry of food, one girl stated that they had "spent several weeks giving reports on various kinds of cows. I gave a report on the Short Horn cow." Sims always discussed problems concerning Fraser, Keith, Ruth Stokes, and various dissidents with the Board. Several were asked to resign during Sims' first few years at Winthrop. [31]

Sims refused to be distracted. He continued to work for better salaries, a tenure plan, and academic responsibility with due process. Still the associations kept Winthrop on their blacklists and the dissidents advertised that Winthrop diplomas were tainted.

One of President Sims' first big jobs was his up-hill battle to win Winthrop's restoration to good standing with the Southern Association of Colleges and Secondary Schools--the official accrediting agency for the Southern region. [32] To accomplish this, he worked unceasingly to restore dialogue. A prominent South Carolinian wrote of Sims and Winthrop early in 1946:

> Winthrop College never impressed me quite so much as it did this trip. A spirit that has been missing from Winthrop in the last few years seems to be back. I think I know why it has returned, why Winthrop is moving into

525

the fulfillment of its destiny as one of the great schools of the South.

The reason is to be found in the personality and character of Winthrop's new president, Henry R. Sims. He's a sincere, honest, plain-thinking and plain-speaking man, completely minus any affectation or hypocrisy. Everybody knows that he gave up a successful legal and political career simply because he believed that he could serve the people of his state better at Winthrop College. He has no ambition beyond doing a good job there, no expectation of being promoted to a higher post.[33]

Most students and faculty understood and appreciated what Sims was attempting. He improved the college's physical plant and the academic offerings. Many of the rundown buildings benefited from repairs and paint. A major in journalism was added. Teacher-training and education courses changed to meet the new state requirements. The Bachelor of Arts students were allowed to take more academic credits, and liberal-arts students could now elect courses in secretarial and other work-oriented fields. Home economics began to prepare students for several new vocations, including nursery school, school lunch programs, clothing design, and others. Sims had also sought advice from Peabody College on improving Winthrop.[34] Among Winthrop's strengths that Sims listed for the Peabody survey are the following:

EXHIBIT "E"

a. The student body of more than 1500 young white women, a heterogeneous group representing each social and economic level, functioning as a unit under a strong student government.
b. The reputation for success earned by Winthrop graduates.

c. Active students' clubs that advance the academic and professional work of the members.

d. An excellent weekly newspaper, The Johnsonian, edited and managed by the students.

e. Close relationship between the College and the religious organizations, an active YWCA, and numerous active religious clubs and groups.

f. The successful placement of Winthrop graduates into suitable positions.

g. The low cost at which a young woman may secure an excellent education.

h. The extensive service of textbooks and materials at a low cost to the student.

i. Exceptionally well equipped Library, Home Economics Buildings, Senior Dormitory, Infirmary, Auditorium and Music Conservatory.

j. An Artists Course and Lecture Course presenting the most able and talented artists and speakers in the nation.

k. Interest on the part of the faculty members in the academic work and progress of individual students.

l. Attention given to encouraging among students individual effort and initiative.

m. The spirit that is now at work in the faculty and student body to bring about a feeling of unity. It is fundamental, it is working, it can be felt, and it is spreading.

n. The closeness of the institution to the people of the State and the service it is rendering to the people.

Among the phases of work to which the College is giving special attention and some of which have already been greatly strengthened are:

a. Guidance of students in selecting courses of study and in other ways to equip them for the work for which they seem to be best suited.
b. Greater use of talents and special qualifications of faculty members.
c. Expansion of Public Relations Service.
d. Greater emphasis on fine arts in our program and on the campus.
e. Greater opportunity for advanced elective courses in Junior and Senior years.

EXHIBIT "F"

STATEMENT OF WAYS IN WHICH WINTHROP COLLEGE HAS RELATED ITSELF TO THE NEEDS OF SOUTH CAROLINA

Needs of the State	Ways Winthrop Has Helped
1. Educated citizenry.	1. Since its inception, Winthrop has been a four-year institution with a general education program.
2. Trained personnel for positions for women.	2. (a) Winthrop College has prepared thousands of women of the state for various occupations and positions. (b) Through a Placement Bureau the College advises employers concerning the preparation and potentialities of Winthrop students.
3. Leadership in planning and working for better education and citizenship in South Carolina.	3. Through past years and at present, members of the Winthrop faculty and administrative staff are found on practically all committees planning and furthering education in the state. For example,

528

until four years ago, a member of the College faculty had been a member of the State Board of Education for over 25 years. Four presidents of the South Carolina Teachers' Association have been members of the Winthrop faculty and staff.

4, 5, 6, 7, 8, and 9. Continuous education of teachers and adults.

4. For years Winthrop has conducted summer sessions for teachers as well as for students. Last summer Winthrop conducted a branch summer school at Parker District, Greenville.

5. For several years Winthrop has offered extension courses in the late afternoons and evenings at the College. This fall semester 1945, Winthrop is offering extension courses at the College, in Chester, and in Hartsville, South Carolina.

6. Members of the Winthrop administration and faculty hold prominent positions on practically all of the committees which are revising certification and teacher education requirements in South Carolina.

7. In the summer of 1944, a workshop of one week was held by the Nutrition Committee for South Carolina and Winthrop College for elementary school teachers and lunch room supervisors. Again in the summer of 1945 these groups sponsored a three week workshop for teachers and a one week workshop for lunch room workers contemporaneous with the workshop for teachers.

8. For thirteen years Winthrop has made an exchange of Senior students with teachers of the state for one week each semester in order that teachers may expand their ideas and improve their techniques. Approximately 1800 teachers were brought to Winthrop on these exchanges.

9. (a) For nineteen years Music Week for secondary school clubs and orchestras and their music teachers has been conducted by outstanding educators in music. These educators conducted discussions and evaluations with the music teacher. As many as sixty-five schools and 2,500 children have participated in one year. (b) For twelve

530

years during the summer a Master School of Music has been operated at Winthrop for musicians and teachers of music.

10. Entertainment and cultural development of the state.	10. Since 1897 Star Course or Artist Course Series of entertainments have been offered at Winthrop College.
11. Preparation of workers for school jobs in nursery schools and lunch rooms.	11. (a) In 1941 nursery school workers under WPA held a conference of one week at Winthrop College. (b) Likewise, in 1944-1945 workshops for lunch room workers and supervisors were held as reported in No. 7 above.
12. Adult organizations.	12. For many years Winthrop has been host to groups who wish to gather on the campus for forums and short courses. Among those club organizations were County Superintendents, 1922-1931; the Club Women's Institute, 1925-1931; 4-H Club Girls, 1915-1940; Professional Institute, 1938-1945; the Council of Farm Women and Home Demonstration Agents, continuously.
13. Changes in home and family living.	13. The Home Demonstration Department of the Extension Services is housed at and operates

from Winthrop co-ordinated
with Clemson College.

There is an organization
of Future Homemakers which
cooperates with such
organizations as the Red
Cross in the making of
layettes and other
garments. This organi-
zation works with certain
homes.

Home furnishing classes
and groups in home man-
agement work directly
cleaning and redecorating
houses in the community.

Advanced classes in foods
cooperate with mothers of
students in class and with
people in the com- munity
in preserving food and
preparing for over- seas
shipment of Christmas
packages.

Graduates in Home
Economics working in
canneries and in other
community activities
return to the campus for
refresher courses.

Seniors in Home Economics
live for at least six
weeks in one of the home
management houses and
participate in directed
home living.

Students participate in
care of children in the
Nursery School.

532

14. Social Welfare.

14. Members of the Winthrop faculty are active in the organized social agencies of the state. For example, for two summers prior to the war, a member of the Winthrop faculty promoted and conducted a camp to which under-privileged children were sent for two weeks. Students in social welfare were counsellors in the camps.

Winthrop faculty and students participated in the programs of WPA nursery schools and recreation centers in and around Rock Hill.

Winthrop students in organized groups conduct varied forms of recreation and religious programs at industrial centers in and around Rock Hill.

Winthrop in cooperation with such organized agencies as the Y.W.C.A. and Women's Land Army secures and places students for summer work in peach orchards, in tea rooms, in settlement houses, not only in South Carolina, but along the eastern seaboard.

533

15. Camps and recreation centers.	15. Winthrop conducts a Placement Bureau for camp counsellors and leaders.

EXHIBIT "G"

SPECIAL RECOMMENDATIONS ON GENERAL ADMINISTRATION THAT THE INSTITUTION DESIRES THE SURVEY STAFF TO CONSIDER

1. Equalizing teacher salary schedules of the state higher educational institutions for white students.
2. Providing through Winthrop College for more extension services to the people of the state.
3. Merging of the summer school budget and the regular term budget so that the College may operate on a twelve-month basis without special allocation of funds, etc., to the regular session and the summer school session.
4. Provision for scholarships for (a) more needy and deserving South Carolina students; (b) students of exceptional talents in special fields such as music; (c) foreign students; (d) research.
5. Plans for more individualized instruction.
6. Provision for sabbatical leave.
7. Provision for improved articulation of high schools and higher educational institutions so that their respective curricula can more satisfactorily supplement each other.
8. That a study be inaugurated looking towards raising the standards in all the state institutions by more use of comprehensive or other special examinations.

In 1946 much was happening at Winthrop College, and Henry Sims tried to keep his hand in everything that time permitted. Advising the Board in late January, 1946, of the enormous work to be done, he stated that in addition to daytime work, he had worked ninety-six evenings out of the last one-hundred and six. [35]

By June, 1946, Sims more firmly gripped Winthrop's reins as he began to distinguish foe from friend. He related to the Board in detail the activities of Dr. Ruth Stokes, head of the Department of Mathematics. He accused her of showing hostility to alumnae officers and of deliberately attempting "to prevent the Southern Association from removing the probationary status of Winthrop, both by letters and personal interviews," while professing great loyalty to Sims. She was offered a year's salary to resign: this furnished more grist for the AAUW mill. [36]

The fall session looked very promising, with more students due primarily to better admissions handling. A new Director of Teacher Education and Graduate Study, Dr. Herman Frick, was appointed. To help the freshmen, the college also instituted a new tutoring service operated by juniors and seniors (with a nominal fee of one dollar per hour). The accounting system was reorganized along the lines suggested by the Peabody Survey. Dr. Sims and trustee Christine Gee tried to secure retirement pensions for Winthrop's presidents and their wives-- the Johnson and Kinard families would especially benefit from this, while Sims (who had extra income from his publishing and other business interests) did not need it. And among the most important changes was the election of a new dean--Dr. Samuel Jesse McCoy, head of the English Department, Richmond Division, of the College of William and Mary. [37]

Sims stressed the academic, social, and cultural sides of life at Winthrop. He was a well-read, gracious host who enjoyed good food and conversation, good music, and good cigars. Each

535

year he invited prominent state and townspeople to the artist and lecture series. He and Mrs. Sims personally chaperoned the dances that the students held regularly. They loved young people, and the Winthrop girl felt that she could visit the president any day for help and comfort. He became "Uncle Henry" to thousands of Winthrop girls.

The Sims presidency held one true tragedy: he was maligned by a group of people including dissident alumnae, some politicians, professors, newsmen, and others who wished to push him and dominate Winthrop College but found they could not.[38] These people stressed Winthrop's blacklisting by AAUP, AAUW, and the Association of American Colleges and Winthrop's "tainted" diploma. The record shows, however, that the Sims administration graduated large numbers of the best-trained women in Winthrop's history. Still, many people ignored Winthrop's good standing with the Southern Association and mouthed the blacklisting line. But the National Secretary of the American Association of University Professors, Dr. Robert Himstead, stated: "Winthrop College has never been censured by the American Association of University Professors. It is the Administration of the College which has been censured by this Association." This original censure was against President Phelps, not Sims. In reality the censure was against the Board of Trustees, who had overridden Phelps and suggested the firing of Drs. MacDonald and McDavid in 1941, which in turn had initiated the blacklisting affair.[39]

In 1947 the Winthrop community welcomed a distinguished hero and friend, a former trustee, and new governor of South Carolina. The Winthrop family knew that as ex-officio Chairman of the Board, Governor James Strom Thurmond would do everything he could to help Winthrop College just as he had in the past. In his first Board meeting as governor, Thurmond expressed his pleasure at returning to the Board and demonstrated his interest in the college's welfare and development.[40]

In 1947 Sims stayed busy. He helped Winthrop join the State Retirement Act, which he had helped to shape when he was a senator. Also he requested authority and funds from the House Ways and Means Committee to acquire faculty houses. Sims had determined "to enlarge the usefulness of Winthrop" by training better teachers who would improve public instruction within the state. Citing the impressive 1946 figures, he pointed out that forty-three percent of the beginning public-school teachers that year were college graduates. Statistics from the superintendent of education revealed that in 1946 one-third of all college graduates teaching in the public schools were Winthrop graduates.[41]

In 1947 President Sims made an extra effort to involve the faculty more in making Winthrop the superior institution he envisioned. His address on the faculty's responsibilities delivered at a faculty workshop on September 5, 1947, gives ample proof that Sims was a thinker, an educator, a mover, and a leader. Sims began his address in a friendly and deliberate manner:

> I want to extend to you all a cordial welcome to Winthrop, both to the former members who are returning and, particularly, to the new members of the faculty who are beginning their association with Winthrop. I hope you will like Winthrop and its hospitality, learn its traditions, and join with us in our efforts to improve its educational service.

> I invite you to come to my office and see me at any time, as I hope to have the opportunity of knowing you, and to call on me for any service which I can render to you.

> Some of the new members have com-mented to me about the friendly

537

atmosphere on Winthrop's campus. I am glad that this is so.

There may be some excuse for lack of mental ability, because that is dependent upon opportunity, and there may be some excuse for physical imperfection, because that is dependent upon inherited characteristics, but there can be no excuse for lack of friendliness and the desire to co-operate.

To all of you, I want to express the hope that this will be the finest year in Winthrop's history. This is more than a trite expression with me. I hope you will share with me the ideal of a great college and join with me in the determination to make Winthrop exactly that.

We want vision, and we want your partnership in a great endeavor to make Winthrop College an effective educational institution. We invite you to share in the glory and satisfaction of so great an accomplishment. This is not necessarily an easy task; if it had been so, all this would have been achieved before.

In saying this, I do not mean in any way to discount the past service of this institution. Fifteen thousand of its alumnae are today reflecting the benefit of its training to them; and, I believe I can say, that Winthrop's position is established and honored in South Carolina.

Nor would I be boasting if I went further and asserted that it has an enviable reputation outside the borders of this commonwealth. This fall we are expecting students from six foreign nations, including China, Denmark, Iraq, Puerto Rico, Canada, and Hawaii. Some of them may not get here, but at least there are young women in these regions who have heard of Winthrop's reputation and aspire to become graduates of this College.

I would like to mention particularly a letter we received from a father in the romantic and mysterious city of Baghdad.

He wrote that he wanted to send his daughter to a Southern college; that her English tutor had told him that during his short stay in South Carolina he had been so impressed with the favorable comment of mothers and students on the character and work of Winthrop, that he thought it would be the college for his daughter to attend.

He stressed the fact that even in that far off country the South was honored for its hospitality and culture, and of the various institutions in this region he thought Winthrop would be ideal to complete the education of his daughter.

We are, therefore, probably justified to paraphrase the remark of St. Paul, and to assert that we are a part of 'no mean college.' We have a large and reasonably modern physical plant; we have, I think, a wonderful student body with great potentialities, but the results, in education and training, depend on you, the faculty.

This Workshop, which was begun yesterday, represents the accomplishment of a goal which we set a year ago. It has had a fine beginning. On

Thursday, the Heads of the various Departments spent the greater part of the day in a discussion and consideration of administrative procedure, just as you will largely today.

I do not think that this is time wasted, for it is vitally necessary for us to have a material foundation, a smoothly operating administrative machine, before we can accomplish the educational purpose for which we exist. We have to lay a foundation before we can build a house. (At this time the Devil is tempting me to make a side remark but I will resist the temptation.)

When I came to Winthrop, three years ago, I realized that my first task and responsibility was to organize the administrative foundations for a successful operation of the instructional tasks of this College. We have made some progress, and I wish to thank those on the administrative staff who have worked intelligently and arduously to accomplish these results.

While we have much yet to be done along this line, still, I think, we have sufficiently advanced for us to begin to consider the improvement of the educational service of Winthrop College, the activity for which everything else is preparatory and preliminary.

Here we have:

A five million dollar physical plant;

An administrative organization operating fairly efficiently, the result of long hours of heavy labor and intensive thinking by those responsible for it;

We are receiving larger State appropriations;

We are enjoying the benefit of the recommendations of our alumnae and friends, who look to us with confidence and expectation;

We have present sixteen hundred choice young women, with all their hopes and aspirations before them, and behind them all the sacrifice and dreams of their parents;

And it's up to you, the teachers. I would remind you, that all this leads up to your classrooms, to your performance there, for better or worse.

All these preparations and plans await the verdict of your usefulness and effectiveness to justify or condemn all that went before. You carry a solemn and awful responsibility. I hope and pray that you may acquit yourself creditably.

I want you to know that all of us connected with this institution are behind you, that all of us are anxious to assist you in your responsible work.

We realize that the teaching personnel of Winthrop College carries the power of veto on every hope and effort to make this College great in service to these young women who have entrusted their future into our care and control.

541

That disquieting responsibility is yours, and how can anyone, under that burden, be uninterested in the consideration and study of the topics before this Workshop, or any others, which look to the improving of our professional techniques, the planning more wisely of our educational program, or making more effective and personal our success in preparing and equipping these young students for lives of happy satisfaction, dignified self-respect, and worthwhile accomplishment.

The Workshop topics, which you will consider, will be many and varied. I would not attempt to give you advice as to their solution.

Here we have around one hundred and twenty-five individuals, trained for the art of teaching, making it their life work, and I am confident that in your ranks there are those who can point the proper solution of our problems.

I might venture to give you a few general principles upon which I think you can base your thought and action:

First, I would say, be very practical in your consideration of these problems. The only criterion by which they should be judged is how they affect Winthrop's task and Winthrop's responsibility to our girls.

Personally, I have no particular interest in educational methods in ancient Alexandria, or even in classic Athens, or in modern Heidelberg, except insofar as they furnish help to us in solving our responsibilities and performing our task in this day to the girls who come to Winthrop's campus.

Second, I would suggest, that you be critical; that you re-examine every accepted tradition, every educational formula, and every directed highway as if it had never been tried before.

I have no desire to copy the methods of any other educational institution except as these methods recommend themselves to us as being the best possible way we can fulfill our responsibility and our duty to the students who are here for training and equipment for life.

Then, I would say, that you should be courageous in exploring and proposing new ways reasonably promising greater benefits in our educational undertaking.

I think we need some pioneer spirit in education, and while I would not experiment too rashly, I would not hesitate to test and examine every new possibility which holds some promise of advancement in the art of education.

Is it, in any way, beyond the realm of contemplation that we, at Winthrop, might make a significant, definite, and original contribution to education, either in new methods and plans or greater effectiveness in employing those now in existence?

In my work at Winthrop, it is to this goal I endeavor to go, and to this possibility I devote my life; I ask you to join with me, in the vision of an ideal College and the promise of its attainment.[42]

Through Sims' hard work, honesty, and dedication, Winthrop underwent physical and educational improvements. By 1947 the loyal alumnae were exerting a more salutary influence. They prevailed on Sims to spend two weeks in New York sitting for his portrait, which they later presented to the college.[43]

In the October 1947 Board meeting, Sims summarized recent important events at Winthrop. His report noted the requirement that certain officers and personnel (including the president) employed at the college be bonded. This procedure prevented unfavorable criticism such as one previous administration had received when the president had kept his personal money and Winthrop's in the same account.[44] Sims further reported that the Lowenstein Foundation of New York, whose parent company ran mills in South Carolina that included one in Rock Hill, was giving Winthrop four scholarships. The National Cancer Foundation had agreed to give an award each year to a senior biology major for an essay on cancer, and the father of two Chinese students planned to donate a scholarship also. The Sims Publishing Company of Orangeburg, not to be outdone, had given $1,000 in trust to Winthrop, the income from which was to be used for subscriptions to its newspaper, the Times and Democrat.[45] The report's other important aspects included a new retirement policy whereby state law permitted teachers to be re-elected year by year until age seventy, although Winthrop faculty members could retire at sixty-five.[46]

During the 1947-1948 session physical improvements abounded. The lunchroom, the science laboratory, and the floors were remade at the Winthrop Training School. The thirty-four college-owned residences and apartments were being appraised for rental purposes. On June 10, 1948, Sims listed buildings needed immediately: a gymnasium for the Training School, a home-management house, and a new science building to replace the one condemned by the Peabody Commission.[47]

544

At the June Board meeting two important issues emerged. First, Dr. Sims apprized the trustees of his recent correspondence with President Poole of Clemson, who planned to introduce home economics into his curriculum: since Winthrop held the monopoly on this and on home-demonstration work, Sims wished to block Poole's plans at the trustee level, rather than through the press and in the Legislature.[48]

Second, adding the twelfth grade to state high schools had resulted in some dislocation of the South Carolina colleges' planned annual enrollment. Sims had spent a thousand dollars on an advertising campaign to combat this dislocation and consequently had attracted more out-of-state students. The Southern Association of Schools still approved admission of academically superior eleventh-grade students, but despite a smaller enrollment Sims advised prospective students to finish the twelfth grade. He was further encouraged that the number of automats--failing pupils requested to withdraw from college--had decreased each year.[49]

Despite the continued break between Winthrop and the AAUP and AAUW, there were many encouraging signs for President Sims and Winthrop's friends in South Carolina and elsewhere. Speaking to the graduates of the South Carolina College for Women (Winthrop) on May 31, 1948, the great statesman James F. Byrnes praised Winthrop College's contributions to South Carolina. "I would not minimize the work of any other group of people or of any other institution," he said, "but for years I have thought that more has been done to advance the welfare of South Carolina by Winthrop women than by any other group in our midst."[50]

Byrnes and Sims were life-long friends. They and their families had been political cohorts since Woodrow Wilson's administration, and both had given Winthrop years of special service. In fact, most prominent South Carolina leaders were personal friends of both these gentlemen. However, there were advantages and disadvantages in such

545

connections.   Sims received much criticism from
those who pretended to hate political influence even
though they longed to have it themselves.   The core
of this unhappy group included some disgruntled
professors and others determined to bring Winthrop
down.   If they succeeded, they could reclaim the
college with some professional new Moses.

The governing Board, however,   could see
that Henry Sims was beginning to turn Winthrop
around in the late forties.   They showed their
genuine appreciation through a resolution of praise
and a standing vote of confidence.   Things were
going so well at the college that the Board "ordered
and directed"   the president to take a sixty-day
vacation in the summer of 1948.   Dr. Sims thanked
the Board, saying that he planned a three-week
period of complete rest.[51]

Returning from his first Winthrop vacation
with renewed vigor, Henry Sims was even more determined to win the battle for Winthrop College.   Over
the next ten years he managed to attract more money
from the Legislature, on a per-student ratio, than
any other state college.   This meant better salaries
for the personnel, more physical improvements on
campus, and a more pleasant life for the entire
college community.[52]

In 1949-1950 Winthrop's enrollment declined
about twenty students; at the same time enrollments
at other women's colleges were declining.   The
decline, when taken with an article that the AAUP
published saying Winthrop was still on its censured
list, gave renewed breath for the warwhoops of the
"down with Sims" crowd.[53]   Viewing the AAUP article
as deceptive and unfair, Sims wrote the Executive
Secretary of AAUP, Dr. Ralph Himstead.   Sixteen days
later Himstead acknowledged Sims' letter and
promised to write again on September 15.   No letter
was forthcoming.   Mr. W. D. Workman, a newspaper
reporter trying to write an article about why the
AAUP refused to deal with the Winthrop problem and
related matters, experienced similar treatment.
Since the AAUP problem was linked to that of the

546

AAUW, Sims was attempting to work through both organizations' local chapters to remove the remaining stumbling blocks to a totally successful administration.[54]

In late 1949 and early 1950, Sims spent most of his time dealing with physical improvements, the associations, and better service for South Carolina. Sims summarized his accomplishments for the Board:

> Much money has been spent repairing the college plant in the last few years and is still being spent. Among other improvements, heating and wiring systems in most of the buildings have been reworked; bathrooms in several dormitories have been checked and reworked where necessary; floors have been checked and repaired or replaced; new draperies have been purchased for the parlors; an isolation ward has been installed in the infirmary. The physical plant is in better condition than in twenty years . . . .
>
> The Dunlap house was not purchased because of its high price.[55]

The associations matter continued to plague Sims, and as he later confided to friends it was the most time-consuming activity of his entire career. Early in 1950, he outlined his most recent information on the associations. The letter Mr. Himstead (General Secretary of the AAUP) had promised to write "on or about September 15" in reply to Sims' letter (written July 16, 1949) had not arrived. Thus, President Sims had contacted the officers, council members, and Committee on Tenure members of the AAUP to inform them of Mr. Himstead's inaccessibility. He had asked what he should do to obtain information. The Board, prompted by Mrs. Gee, approved Sims' efforts.[56]

547

Winthrop's service to the state Sims pointed
to with justifiable pride. Seventy-eight percent of
Winthrop students had taken teacher-training
programs in comparison with twenty-two percent of
the students "at the other fifteen white senior
colleges in South Carolina." A survey showed that
thirty-four percent of South Carolina's teachers
were Winthrop graduates. In turn, the Legislature
approved Winthrop's service by giving her a higher
per-capita appropriation than other state colleges.
In a related matter, the state's Board of Education,
authorized by the Legislature, began to approve
teacher-training colleges based on Southern
Association accreditation. Such colleges would not
need to file additional reports.[57]

Since the overwhelming majority of Winthrop
students came from religiously oriented families,
religious activities and problems naturally found
their way into campus life. Some of the campus
church leaders sought special privileges for their
groups, ignoring college rules involving such
things as use of the auditorium and Johnson Hall,
collections, membership drives, and the like. Just
before the 1950 session began, Sims wrote the
organizations, stating Winthrop's position that all
students would have to obey college rules. This
prompted the ministers to request a conference with
the president. After a friendly discussion, mutual
arrangements were agreed upon.[58]

Sims had always maintained good relations
with the clergy, and his background in the Methodist
Church made him more mindful of others. One of his
administration's hallmarks was the encouragement he
gave to the Winthrop Christian Association and to
the annual Religious Emphasis Week. Sims was responsible for bringing many outstanding preachers,
theologians, and lay leaders to campus. He and Mrs.
Sims seemed to enjoy such occasions as much as anyone. The WCA, with Sims' backing, gave each student
opportunities to grow into a more mature, more meaningful faith through ecumenical programs. A
student cabinet planned and carried out campus-wide

548

programs, sponsored social services, helped international students, and became involved in most
things of significance on the Winthrop campus.[59]

President Sims enjoyed great respect among
the students and among an increasing number of
faculty and staff. By 1950, had it not been for the
trouble generated from the office of the Dean of
Women, and from a few dissident professors and
alumnae, he could have coped very readily with the
problems of organizational censure.[60] Testifying
before the Winthrop Board and the AAUP and AAUW
representatives, Sims accused the dean of making
"war" on college people she disliked. He had to get
rid of her. This led to additional trouble with one
of her friends, Professor Ruth Roettinger.[61]

Before the trouble with Dean Berry,
Roettinger had appeared to be one of Sims' friends
on the faculty. Writing to Sims on September 9,
1949, Roettinger had declared: "The promotion is
greatly appreciated. I only hope I can come near
enough being worthy of it so that you will never
regret it. The salary increase is much appreciated
too and will make my old age much brighter."[62]

Because the Legislature was then being more
generous with Sims and Winthrop, he was able to
increase salaries 160 percent in eight years. Sims
felt that good teachers should be rewarded. Sims
expressed the opinion that Roettinger had a good
mind and he was appreciative of her good work and
her advice on AAUP and AAUW matters.[63]

In September, 1950, Roettinger and others
got another salary boost. This prompted Roettinger
to go to Sims' office and say to him: "I got my
contract and I thought you were a pretty good
President up to now," a comment which Sims took as
humor but which foreboded her coming hostility.
Sims countered by writing a humorous letter in which
he said:

As you know, it has been my earnest
desire since I have been at Winthrop, to have implicit confidence
of the members of the Winthrop
College faculty and staff. I had
hoped that after spending six years
working to that end, my desires had
met with some success. It is a
great disappointment to learn that
the faith I thought I had built up
on one member of our staff, is on
the verge of being shaken. Therefore, if you will return your
contract to me I will be glad to
restore your utmost confidence to
last year's level at least, and
even go beyond that year if
necessary.[64]

The influential Professor Roettinger may have been
jolted by Sims' frankness. She had been regarded as
a champion of Winthrop's cause with the AAUP to this
time, but now (1951-1952) during Sims' push to
restore Winthrop with the AAUP, he and Roettinger
drifted further apart. With Dean Berry's dismissal,
Roettinger went against the Sims administration.[65]

In his first Board meeting after Roettinger
had sent them an emotional letter on August 11,
1952, Sims gave his side of the controversy. In
regard to her statement that Sims had publically
announced Berry's dismissal, he informed the Board
that the first news account of this (on June 17)
came out after Roettinger had gone to the local
paper "with a critical statement of affairs at
Winthrop."[66]   To each accusation Sims gave his
reply, attempting to refute Roettinger's charges of
duplicity. Apparently the Board was satisfied with
what Sims had to say.[67]

Roettinger resigned her job and became a
leader of the anti-Sims group. She and her dissident alumnae friends waged a hard campaign throughout the state, as well as through the AAUP and AAUW,
demanding that Sims be fired.[68]   And the National

550

AAUP Secretary, Dr. Himstead, became a focal point for much of this activity.

This whole problem was further complicated by a case that developed during 1951-1952, involving the ranking member of the History Department, whom Sims had suspended. The controversy was precipitated in part by a student's mother, who persuaded the freshman advisor to permit her daughter to leave college for a wedding and thereby miss her history examination. Later, when the student returned to take the examination, the professor "severely reprimanded" her for missing one of his subordinate's exams, and (according to her mother) the student was too upset to do her best. Her poor showing was blamed on the professor, and her mother asked Sims to allow another examination under different circumstances.[69]

President Sims conferred with the professor about the examination and related matters. Soon thereafter differences of opinion developed between Sims and this history professor. The professor maintained that his right to freedom in the classroom had been infringed upon, and he referred to Winthrop's longstanding trouble with AAUP. Following this exchange involving several things, President Sims invited the professor to give in writing his position about an administrative officer's role in relation to a faculty member's powers and prerogatives in the classroom. A blind copy of Sims' suggestion was sent to Dean McCoy, the Academic Dean.[70]

Meanwhile Sims declined to have the professor's subordinate give the young lady another examination. He informed her mother that the student had passed only "nine and one-half hours out of fifteen and one-half" during the first semester, thereby failing to earn any quality points. This suggests that the weak student in question might have not understood what "severely reprimanded" connotated.[71]

For the next two years there were sporatic problems and pettiness between the history professor

551

and two stalwarts of the Sims administration, the academic dean and the registrar. Both were close to President Sims, and the professor continued to press his views about good and bad academic procedures. This was sure to embroil him in controversies with the administration.[72]

Sims continued to push hard to improve Winthrop physically and academically, always keeping his eye on ways to return Winthrop to the good graces of the AAUP and AAUW. In 1952 changes in the state legal code spelled out the college's internal organization, specifying the powers of the Board and the administration of Winthrop College. By this arrangement, two Winthrop graduates were to be appointed by the Winthrop College Alumnae Association to serve on the Board. Winthrop became a corporation with all powers and rights attendant thereto, including the right to sue and be sued.[73]

Sims continued to press for better-qualified students and faculty. Enrollment began to rise. He discussed tenure for department heads with the Southern Association of Colleges and Secondary Schools and was advised that these were purely administrative positions and thus were not covered by tenure plans. He also won praise by assuring those who accused Winthrop of religious discrimination that this was not the case. And A. R. Suritz of Rock Hill wrote Sims, saying: "The fine attitude of Winthrop College in not using religious affiliation as a condition for admittance is in the best tradition of our country. I hope every educational institution will follow Winthrop's example."[74]

By late 1952 a serious rift had developed between the Executive Board of the Winthrop Alumnae Association and the alumnae and others who disagreed with its policy. The Anderson Free Press featured this on August 19, 1952:

552

WINTHROP STUDENTS, ALUMNAE HERE ARE
SUPPORTING COLLEGE PRESIDENT; RESENT
TACTICS OF ALUMNAE BOARD

Assert Board Lacks Approval
of Association

There are always two sides to every
issue. This holds true in the current
controversy raging around Winthrop college, about which much has been printed
in recent weeks. Regardless of who is
right or who is wrong, the fact remains
that much damage is being done where
the good standing of the college is
concerned.

Although the Free Press takes no
stand in the matter, it has been
brought to our attention that only one
side of the issue has been presented so
far in the Anderson daily papers. A
large group of Winthrop students and
alumnae in Anderson, as well as a
Winthrop faculty member, have expressed
themselves as being distressed over the
reports which they term very unfair to
President Henry Sims.

Not only do they feel that great
damage is being done to Winthrop
college, but they also state that the
Alumnae executive board and the small
group of agitators involved in the
controversy are, in their opinion, not
representative of the Alumnae Association as a whole. That fact is borne
out by statements from alumnae not only
in Anderson but throughout the state,
who attended the annual alumnae meeting
this year.

At their request, we present the
following statement signed by five
Winthrop College Alumnae, including
Miss Sadie Goggans, retired member of

553

the Education Dept. at Winthrop, Mrs.
H. Loraine Simril, Miss Lottie Barron,
Mrs. W. D. Rice and Mrs. J. J. Rauch,
which appeared recently in the Rock
Hill Evening Herald. Claiming that
recent action of the Executive Board
seems an attempt to take over power,
these alumnae state:

"In justice to many Winthrop
Alumnae who loyally support Winthrop
college and its organized authority, we
wish to clarify some points for the
general public.

"The present Executive Board of the
Winthrop Alumnae Assn. is the same
board that failed to be supported by
the assembled association at the annual
meeting May 29, 1954. A resolution
presented by the chairman of the committee on resolutions was that the
Winthrop Alumnae Assn. assembled
endorsed the policies of the Executive
Board and the effort to carry out the
mandates of the association, and that a
rising vote of confidence be tendered
the Board. This resolution was
defeated. We believe that any action
by the Executive Board does not represent the will of the Alumnae Assn.

"Furthermore, at the regular spring
meeting of the Alumnae Assn. in March,
during the State Teachers meeting, a
decisive vote of confidence in Winthrop
college and its administration was
passed in spite of opposition by the
executive officers of the association.
This, too, is additional evidence that
the officers of the association do not
voice the intentions of the majority of
the members of the Alumnae Association of Winthrop college.

554

"We, a group of Winthrop Daughters, think that attempts to control policies of the college by any organized group of Alumnae endangers the standing of Winthrop college. The Southern Association Standards says that Alumnae should be encouraged to maintain an interest in their Alma Mater 'but care should be taken that they do not dominate the policies and programs of the institution.' The recent action of the Executive Board of the Winthrop Alumnae Assn. seems an attempt to take over power.

"We adhere to the belief that the affairs of a college are the responsibility of the Board of Trustees. We know that the Board of Trustees is and has been striving to meet the requirements of the AAUP and AAUW. We would be honored to be recognized by these two organizations but we appreciate that the accreditation of the Southern Association of Secondary Schools and Colleges is paramount. Winthrop college is accredited by the Southern Association." [75]

Despite charges and countercharges, press releases and the like, Sims was beginning to feel that he was making great progress at Winthrop. The student body, faculty, and others backed the pudgy, smiling, pleasant Orangeburger. Among the many things that Sims did was to bring national and international personalities to lecture and visit with the college community. He guarded the general welfare of the staff and workers and their families. And he constantly tried to have Winthrop's (actually the Board's) censure by the AAUW and AAUP removed.

Reporting to the Board on January 27, 1953, in Governor Byrnes' office, President Sims pointed out that

Winthrop College has been off the
approved list of AAUW since 1944. The
Winthrop College Alumnae Association,
the South Carolina Division of AAUW,
and the Board of Trustees have all
requested the AAUW to inspect Winthrop,
in spite of the fact that the college is
still on the censured list of AAUP,
with the idea of reinstating our college
on its approved list. The Association
had agreed to send a representative to
the College November 17-19, but he
explained that he delayed the action
because of previous engagements. He
further stated that Mrs. Hawkes, Chairman of the Committee on Standards and
Recognition, wrote that she was
prevented from coming later in the fall
because she was attending a National
meeting. Mrs. Hawkes later advised him
in a telegram dated October 10, 1952,
'The visit of inspection to Winthrop has
been postponed for the present.' She
stated that the committee had voted for
the inspection to be made by the
chairman of the committee, but her college schedule made it impossible for her
to come East again this year. Therefore, her letter suggested the visit of
inspection would not be made until sometime after the Minneapolis Convention of
AAUW in June, when the new chairman of
this committee had taken office.[76]

In anticipation of the forthcoming Peabody
report commissioned by the Winthrop Board, Sims
had asked the Budget and Control Board in Columbia
to recommend that the Legislature vote $500,000 for
permanent improvements at the college. At that
time Sims was holding $700,000 in reserve for a
modern science building: this was the principal
reason why the governor and the Budget and Control
Board held up the request for permanent improvements. It was Byrnes' feeling that the science

building should have been erected in 1948 since the cost would have been about one-half the 1953 cost. Byrnes further suggested, "You can draw a check today to meet any needs requested for Winthrop. Moreover, your tuition fees can be pledged for bonds for further improvements." But Sims felt that Winthrop should not be required to pledge future fees.[77]

Another item of general concern was the proposed Winthrop Foundation, which would encourage bequests in people's wills: thereby, more outstanding professors would have their salaries supplemented. Trustee Tilghman was asked to contact Mrs. Huntington of Brookgreen Gardens about donating her rare sculptures or, better still, giving a fine-arts building to the college.[78]

After being rebuffed for several years while they tried to end the AAUP censure, Sims and the Board faced an additional problem in 1953 when they felt compelled to suspend the History Department head. What had started as a purely academic misunderstanding was later magnified into a cause célèbre that seemed to warrant the suspension.

Some members of this department had taken exception to the head and his activities. Individually and collectively they wrote letters to and conferred with the administration in an effort to force this man's departure. A letter written to Sims on March 31, 1953, seemed to initiate the final phase of the controversy. This came from an apparently unhappy and disturbed woman teacher in the department who proceeded to give a year-by-year evaluation of the erratic and abnormal behavior she attributed to him. In her error-filled letter, the teacher referred to the head as "pitifully unstable and pathetically disorganized." These innuendoes apparently were designed to ingratiate herself with the move to force out her department head. There were other letters and charges. Finally Sims felt compelled to act.[79]

557

On July 2, 1953, Sims conferred with the accused department head. On July 10, Sims informed him of five charges against him and turned these over to Trustees Grier, Roddey, and Tilghman, who had agreed with his lawyer to hear these charges between July 21 and 24. Sims also asked the Tenure Committee to make a separate investigation in this case.[80]

Considerable correspondence had passed between both sides during June. It was somewhat incriminating and petty, but it would hardly stand the scrutiny of legal proceedings. There were several unsigned "verified" copies of student statements suggesting that the department head had made amorous advances toward them. One was in a "To Whom It May Concern" form. The dean, purporting shock, lamented in his letter to Sims on June 22, 1953, that he would find it "difficult to hold my head up," if the head should continue in his position.[81]

As a result of the investigation and the two committee reports, the Board's committee "unanimously recommended that Dr. Venable [the head of the Department of History] be suspended, until such time as action on the charges preferred by Dr. Sims can be considered by the full Board of Trustees."[82] And Trustee Wofford, a Harvard-trained lawyer, later moved

> That the full Board of Trustees of Winthrop College give Dr. Venable an opportunity for a full and complete hearing on all charges preferred against him as outlined to him in letter of July 10, 1953.
>
> That a competent stenographer, preferably a court reporter, not connected with Winthrop College be present to take down the testimony presented by the College to substantiate charges against Dr. Venable and any testimony Dr. Venable desires

558

to offer in his behalf either in person or by a duly appointed attorney.

The hearing date was set for November 17, 1953. Participants agreed that the hearing would be held without the press and with witnesses being heard individually, and that Dr. Venable's attorney should be notified. The charges would be heard in order as listed. Venable would not have a transcript of the testimony given before the Committee of Three.[83] Thus began a controversy that further clouded Winthrop's status with the AAUP and AAUW.

Meanwhile the Alumnae Association moved to help the Board of Trustees and Winthrop with their problems. In a report from Mrs. W. D. Workman, Jr., President of the Winthrop Alumnae Association,

she admitted the alumnae had not been as interested as they should be in Winthrop College, and she found in her travels around the State that some alumnae felt they owed Winthrop College nothing, then later asked themselves if they were getting all they paid for. Some had told her that they had been discriminated against because of their Winthrop diplomas. Mrs. Workman was asked to find what institutions had been responsible for this discrimination and what were the reasons given.

Mrs. Workman said she had been instructed by her Executive Committee to stress the following points at the District meetings.

1. Why Winthrop Alumnae should be interested in the present standing of the college.
2. The importance of AAUP and AAUW to Winthrop.
3. The necessity for a stronger financial support of the Association by the Alumnae.

        4. The academic standing of Winthrop
    as rated by the Southern Association is
    not affected.[84]

        The Board moved to have Mrs. Workman help
arrange a meeting between the Board and officials of
the AAUP and AAUW for some time in December. But
President Sims advised that he had tried to arrange
a meeting with Dr. Himstead of AAUP to discuss how
he could make the Winthrop tenure plan acceptable to
AAUP, but he had failed to get a satisfactory
answer--perhaps because of Dr. Venable's pending
case.[85]

        Dr. Himstead was invited to visit Winthrop
in December to explore the possibility of removing
Winthrop from the AAUP censured list. In a telegram
to Chairman Dinkins of the Board, Himstead stipulated that AAUP would arrange "conversations" with
the Board, provided Dr. Venable be reinstated on
faculty with pay and that the Venable hearing be
deferred until after the desired "conversations"
with the AAUP and AAUW.[86] The Board discussed the
Himstead proposals, and Trustee Wofford moved to
"notify Dr. Venable through its chairman that he is
considered a member of the faculty of Winthrop College under suspended status with pay, commencing
September 1 and continuing until further action of
the Board on charges preferred against him, of which
he has had notice." There was one dissenting vote,
that of Senator Marion Gressette.[87]

        Four days later, the Board met to hear
Venable. After reviewing the AAUP affair, a letter
was read from Venable's lawyer (Mr. Ridley) saying
that he would not appear with his client for the
scheduled hearing as he had not been officially
notified of the procedures to be followed. At this
point Senator Gressette asked to make a statement
which he felt would "shock" the Board. First he
reversed his previous vote on Venable and offered a
resolution:

                          560

That the request of Dr. Ralph E. Himstead and Charles B. Ridley, Esq., Attorney for Dr. Austin L. Venable, for continuance of the hearing set Tuesday, November 17, 1953, be granted.

Further, that Dr. Himstead be requested to designate the earliest possible date in December, next, for a conference with the Board of Trustees to consider the status of Winthrop with the AAUP, with a view of lifting the present censureship of the organization over the College; and

Further, that a copy of this resolution be mailed to Dr. Himstead and Mr. Ridley forthwith.[88]

Before adjourning the Board read and discussed a letter from the Executive Council of the SGA. The girls were concerned about Winthrop's problems with AAUP and AAUW and about improving Winthrop's esprit de corps. They were concerned with what the Board proposed to do.[89]

Someone, an insider perhaps, knew what was transpiring in the serious negotiations designed to bring together the representatives of AAUP, AAUW, and the Winthrop Board and administration in order to lay the groundwork for relieving Winthrop's censure. In order to harm the proceedings, mis-information was planted among the students in hope of having them demonstrate in November against Sims and the Board. They were fed the old line-- "Your diplomas are tainted, and Sims and the Board are running the college into the ground." Luckily Chairman Dinkins and President Sims met with the students. They calmed down. They trusted the facts as given and altered the materials that they had originally planned to print in The Johnsonian, since they did not want to hurt Winthrop and her leadership.[90]

561

Having finally met Secretary Himstead's conditions, the Board met at the Wade Hampton Hotel in Columbia on December 28 to prepare for conversations with Himstead and others involved in the censure process. The erudite Senator Gressette suggested that every courtesy be extended to Himstead and the invited guests. Sims suggested that Himstead and the AAUW start with their statements. Then the other side would ask questions. Dinkins suggested that Himstead did not wish a faculty committee to sit in on the conversations. Sims asked that the Board allow him to respond to any detrimental statements against the administration that Himstead might make. Sims further stated that he was not responsible for the publicity given in the morning edition of the State paper that was critical of Himstead. His secretary had given some of the materials therein to the faculty committee when Sims was out of town.[91]

Soon it was time for the executive conversations to begin. President Sims and the Winthrop Board exchanged greetings with Himstead and Dr. George P. Shannon of AAUP; Drs. Gillie Larew and Eleanor Dolan of AAUW; and Mrs. W. D. Workman, Jr., Mrs. P. H. Leonard, Mrs. J. L. Anderson, and Mrs. Harry L. Jones of the Winthrop Alumnae Association. Then Dr. Himstead reviewed Winthrop's problem as viewed by the AAUP. He stressed that Winthrop College had never been censured. It was the administration (Himstead meant the Board, the president, and the other policy-makers) that had been censured. He suggested that Winthrop's troubles had started during Dr. Phelps's tenure and that Winthrop "properly administered, could become a great institution."[92]

After three-hundred pages of testimony recorded by Richland County Court Recorder Joseph C. Cordell, it was evident that Himstead had Sims and the Board over the barrel and that he appeared to the administration as an unreasonable dictator, a dictator who was now adding the "mishandling" of the Venable case to his long list of complaints against the manner in which Winthrop's Board and presidents had transacted business for years. The AAUP would not change its course. The AAUW would not consider lifting their censure until the AAUP moved. The deadlock remained.[93]

At the conclusion of their December 29, 1953, meeting, the Board (at Senator Gressette's behest) moved to ask Himstead to select a one- to three-person committee to monitor the Venable hearing. Both lawyer Ridley and Dr. Venable were advised that the Board would meet on January 22 and 23, "and continue to meet as long as necessary to give Doctor Venable a fair hearing in accordance with the basic principles of democratic procedure."[94]

The Winthrop Board met on January 22 for the scheduled Venable hearing. The regular members were present. In addition to President Sims, Robert Hayes, a lawyer, also sat in. The Board decided to telephone Himstead about the Venable case and to record the dialogue.[95]

During the call Himstead estimated that the AAUP could resolve the Venable controversy in two weeks but thought that the eleven-page anti-Himstead faculty statement had certainly "muddied the waters" of the censure problem. At this point it was resolved

> that the Board take no action on the Venable case today, inasmuch as Mr. Himstead said that he thought he would be able to solve the Venable case within the next two weeks . . . the Board [should] meet on the 12th of February, 1954. . . and at that time if Mr. Himstead had not proposed in writing a solution satisfactory to the Board by that date, that on the said day the Board will immediately proceed with the hearing in the Venable case on the charges heretofore served on him.[96]

563

However, before adjourning, all members except for Senator Gressette agreed it prudent to have "an impartial, outside committee to come in and investigate the situation at Winthrop College." Peabody and the Southern States Cooperative Program in Educational Administration were to be contacted about helping Winthrop make a self-evaluation.[97]

A potential break came in the AAUP-Winthrop Board controversy early in February. Secretary Himstead of the AAUP, following a meeting in Washington with trustees Dinkins and Wofford, declared that if the Board "withdraws all charges vs Doctor Venable and pays his salary for the next academic year," the case could be closed. In a called meeting on February 3, 1954, the Board considered the implications of such a move. Both Himstead and Shannon of AAUP had stated "that Doctor Venable was innocent of the charges. . . ." There was a general consensus that if the Board would follow a sound tenure plan and meet the Venable case requirements, then the censure would be lifted. Himstead had suggested heretofore that Doctor Sims might publically apologize for information the faculty had circulated against him. The trustees concurred that the absent Sims would make no such apology.[98]

At this moment a telephone call came in from Himstead, saying "that he had agreed for Doctor Venable to resign and leave Winthrop before February 12, provided the Board pay him his salary until March 1, and that all charges vs Doctor Venable be dropped, and that Doctor Venable agree to do no talking or hold any further claims vs Winthrop." Sims wished to go through the scheduled trial; the Board thought that quietly disposing of the case in accordance with the Himstead call would resolve the trouble. A motion to this effect was made, and they recessed until February 12 (the time set for the official hearing) unless otherwise notified. A copy of this arrangement was immediately forwarded to Himstead.[99]

564

Sims continued to carry on Winthrop's business and educational programs with a confident air. On the outside everything seemed to be well-ordered. Few knew what was going on. Sims' stewardship of Winthrop usually generated favorable comments in the state's newspapers. Many of the editors knew Sims as a newspaperman and respected him. However, the Chester Reporter, a small paper, was anti-Sims. On November 10, 1954, in a scathing article, it complained about Sims' academic qualifications, his rigging the news, and his political background. And it questioned why Winthrop was receiving twice as much money from the state per student as Carolina and Clemson were. From his observations the writer concluded that "the Trustees had no choice but to dynamite him [Sims] out of his job if Winthrop is to be saved from complete disintegration."[100] At best, this view typified feelings of only a small segment of South Carolina's populace.

On June 25, 1954, Winthrop's principal administrators addressed a letter to President Sims that presented their views about the Peabody Report done for Winthrop at the insistence of trustees Grier and Tolbert. Agreeing that none of the recommendations were worthy of serious consideration, they found the survey disturbing for several reasons. These follow:

1. The basic approach to this study was only to find and to enumerate problems, difficulties, and conflicts, with no apparent effort to discover the excellencies of the institution.

2. The report contains implications and conclusions that, to us, are based on very inadequate information and that are admittedly arrived at in disregard of any quantitative assessment of points of view and of difficulties.

565

3. The report contains recommendations contrary to widely accepted college and university practices.

4. Neither in the body of the report nor in the recommendations is there any indication, or recognition of the fact, that steps have been taken to deal with the problems mentioned and to correct certain of the situations described. Some of the recommendations and concerns listed in the report were acted upon before the survey was conducted.

If it appears appropriate for you to do so, we would be glad for you to inform the Board of Trustees of our readiness and willingness to assist and participate, if they so desire, in the suggested assessment of the impressions recorded in this report.

Very sincerely yours,

Birdena E. Donaldson, Dean of
    Women
A. M. Graham, Bursar
John G. Kelly, Registrar
R. Brice Waters, Administrative
    Director
S. J. McCoy, Academic Dean [101]

After years of wrangling with the AAUP and related problems, Sims had become quite sensitive. When he reviewed Peabody's Report for the trustees, he suggested that it was one-sided, and his implication was that the Board should not consider it seriously because it was not valid in certain aspects. However parts of the Report were quite favorable to Sims and his administration. For example, the Report stated that

566

President Sims found Winthrop College on
probation in the Southern Association of
Colleges and Secondary Schools when he
began his tenure as President. One of
his first big jobs was to get the institution restored to good standing in this
organization. This he was able to do in
1946. He deserves full credit for this
accomplishment and for other steps which
he took to restore the institution to
academic standing in South Carolina and
elsewhere. [102]

It also stated in a forthright manner that

The Board of Trustees apparently made
the first move leading to disapproval by
A.A.U.P. by overriding the recommendations of President Phelps and
releasing two faculty members. For
some unannounced reason Dr. Phelps
bore the responsibility for this
action of the Board and made no
attempt to clarify his embarrassing
position. For some other unexplained
reason, he made the next move toward
the blacklisting by A.A.U.P. in his
apparently unreasonable refusal to
receive visitors from the A.A.U.P. to
discuss the situation. It is natural
and understandable that the Trustees,
in selecting a successor to Dr. Phelps
would, perhaps deliberately, perhaps
unconsciously, seek a person having
qualifications and background different
from those of the long-experienced,
highly-trained, out-of-state professional educator who had contributed to
the degrading of Winthrop's standing
with the A.A.U.P. Such a step would be
logical in groping for qualifications
and skills in human relations that
cannot be predicted. [103]

567

Perhaps the _Report_ missed the truth in certain areas because of the personnel interviewed. The anti-administration and the neutral elements of the faculty, for example, had suggested to the committee that Sims so completely controlled the college that they did "as little as possible outside the actual classroom instruction, since anything they do may get them into difficulty." Faculty who understood Sims would have given the opposite view; they fervently believed that Sims encouraged outside activity and community service.[104]

The principal objection of Sims and his administrators to the _Report_ was that it had been compiled in haste from questionable sources. And some of the _Report_ had been given orally to the chairman of the Board. This prompted Trustee Grier to observe that the "Board has invested $1300 for an objective report of the situation at Winthrop by four very capable experts and that it should be taken seriously by the Board." When he later learned that there was a private report made to Chairman Dinkins by one of the team, Grier insisted that "all of the survey team meet and submit a supplementary report concerning all the matters discussed privately . . . and the Board should meet later to discuss the Supplementary Survey."[105]

The Board meeting continued. Other matters discussed in the June 28 session included the "Biography of Dr. Johnson" by Archibald Rutledge, Poet Laureate of South Carolina; the Aeolian-Skinner organ that would cost the college $65,000; and Chairman Dinkins' program to consolidate efforts of those working to advance the college.[106] Then, trustees Roddey and Grier brought up two important matters. Roddey stated that he had heard through his town contacts that Sims was planning to release Miss Ruth Williams, Executive Secretary of the Alumnae Association, and he moved to have the Board leave the matter "in status quo" until their next meeting.[107] And Trustee Grier, boss of the Rock Hill Printing and Finishing Company, asked for an

568

investigation of the rumor that the college was losing $50,000 a year on the farm which furnished many basics for the dining hall. A committee was appointed to confer with Mr. Brice Waters, the Business Manager. Apparently Grier did not learn from his investigation that Winthrop was supplying a great public service to her young women at a very low cost to their parents. Mr. Grier's expertise was in printing cloth for the clothing industry centered in New York City.[108]

By mid-1954 most outward signs suggested that Winthrop was a happy and thriving educational institution. But inside the Board and in some alumnae groups lurked dissention and division. Director McClurkin of the Peabody Survey and Field Services apprised Chairman Dinkins in mid-July that Dr. Himstead of the AAUP had moved to lift the University of Texas censure since it had met the standard on academic tenure and freedom. This suggested that Winthrop, which was doing likewise, might hope to have her censure removed. Another hopeful sign for Winthrop was that the dissident alumnae were losing favor. As McClurkin wrote, "it does seem clear . . . that the rank and file of the alumnae want to live peacefully with the Administration."[109]

During this period the Board discussed again the "Biography of D. B. Johnson," democratic procedures in the administration, the architect for the new science building, updating the "Winthrop By-Laws," and teacher tenure regulations. Then they voted to back Sims' proposal to require entrance exams for admission to Winthrop.[110]

In his correspondence and conversations with friends, Sims stressed his feeling that certain alumnae representatives and trustees could not be trusted. But "Uncle Henry" had bigger friends including the governor, who supported him in spite of the dissidents that continued to rant and rave. With letters, gossip, and meetings, they prolonged their efforts to present Sims in an unfavorable light to any uninformed alumnae. Some became even

569

more hostile at the alumnae secretary's dismissal. But the persistence and fairness of Sims' position helped to win him greater alumnae support.[111]

Despite frequent skirmishes with dissident alumnae, Sims pursued college business with great purpose and interest. He agreed to a new tenure plan, which was drafted by the faculty and approved by the Board and the AAUP. He pushed a resolution requesting a million-dollar loan from the state's Budget and Control Board. (This loan, along with the $400,000 already on hand, would take care of renovating Tillman Hall and enlarging the physical-education facilities, while providing the extra funds needed for a new science hall.) Sims urged the purchase and installation of an Aeolian-Skinner organ for the Memorial Auditorium; alumnae funds and state appropriation money totaling $59,000 secured this project. The Departments of Chemistry and English improved. Miss Iva Bishop was named Assistant to the President, and Miss Connie Cornwell became Director of Admissions.[112]

In 1954, several Winthrop trustees proposed asking the General Assembly to consider making Winthrop coeducational. They hoped to improve the college thereby, by increasing its enrollment. Many alumnae protested this movement and shifted their opposition from Sims to the trustees. Considerable pressure was placed on the General Assembly, which was really not in the mood for such a radical change. One of the most telling attacks by an influential and distinguished alumna was that of Fanona Knox Gossett in The Greenville News on January 5, 1955.[113]

Mrs. Gossett, a professional educator, threw down the gauntlet to the Board by suggesting that they lacked the wisdom and foresight necessary to lead the college. She called for "wise, determined, vigorous and courageous leadership," and suggested that "unless the Board of Trustees can produce this soon, Winthrop--either as a woman's college or as a coeducational institution--cannot survive." Later the Education Committee of the

570

South Carolina Senate refused to vote a coeducation resolution out of committee.

During the last four years of Sims' administration, Winthrop enjoyed an increased enrollment, many academic and physical improvements, and better relations among Winthrop community and its constituency. The problems with the Alumnae Association were resolved. The college emerged from its troubles with Henry Sims basking in the glory of his hard-won, belated success.[114]

Still, there were problems in this period. Sims was seeking a Ph.D. to head the Department of Home Economics. Trustees Grier and Roddey were pushing to abolish the college farm as a food source for the dining hall, which was famous for its family-style meals and its able manager, Miss Zula Threlkeld. Sims, a newspaperman himself, sought an able scholar to head up the Department of Journalism. The question of the Home Demonstration Department's removal to Clemson still rested with the Legislature. And Winthrop met criticism that most of her graduating teachers left the state to teach with a college survey showing that seventy-two percent remained in South Carolina.[115]

In this period Winthrop progressed steadily. Trustee Gee sought assistance for Mrs. Johnson to help her record her memoirs since the more interested alumnae wished to accent the positive side of Winthrop's place in South Carolina education. Statistics compiled by the registrar noted the good showing Winthrop students made on the Graduate Record and the National Teachers exams: with but one exception, Winthrop seniors' scores climbed every year in this period, and in 1956 the Winthrop senior's GRE score exceeded the national average of women in all American colleges. As Trustee Tolbert, an educator, expressed it, "If you stack up Winthrop with Carolina, Clemson or any other college you would be surprised. Our graduates eclipse by far the graduates of other institutions."

571

The entrance exams initiated by Henry Sims were paying good dividends.[116]

With social security, health insurance and other amenities, the faculty had grown more satisfied. Contentment in the faculty ranks, coupled with the AAUP censure's lifting, reassured Sims of Winthrop's promising future. Freed from these heavy concerns, he expressed his desire to retire within two years. And he asked the Board to begin a quiet search for Winthrop's next president.[117]

Despite his pending retirement, Sims did not slacken his pace in trying to improve Winthrop. The money that he continued to pour into renovating the physical plant would have staggered Johnson's or Kinard's imagination. But the academic picture was not neglected. In 1957 Sims became the first Winthrop president to request a special appropriation ($2,000) to buy books on South Carolina history. As he told the Board, "I think Winthrop as a State institution should make an effort to have a very good library on South Carolina history and affairs. . . . We should build up a pretty good library if we are to do graduate work."[118]

There remained one great struggle that Henry Sims wanted to win--the return of the Home Demonstration Service to its original and legal home, Winthrop College. Informing the Board on October 23, 1957, of the controversy's status, Sims briefly outlined the problem, stating:

> We have not made a poll of the Legislature. Some of the members of the General Assembly have been contacted by the alumnae. Unless we press our claims vigorously we will lose. The Clemson group naturally will try to minimize it and say we are stirring up something about nothing because they are in possession and that is nine-tenths of the law. I believe the General Assembly will put it back at Winthrop provided it is handled

properly. You can't win by saying we think they did us wrong. We have to demonstrate that it is better for it to be at Winthrop, that we had a binding agreement. I have been to some of the District Alumnae meetings. There are 20 to 40 in attendance. Yesterday I took the opportunity at Assembly to talk to the students and faculty. They were enthusiastic about it. I have done some research but not all I expect to do before it goes to the Legislature. Winthrop was engaged in Home Demonstration work some years before the Smith-Lever Act was passed. The appropriations show money was spent for household economics--money was appropriated for this purpose. The Smith-Lever Act was passed in 1914. Winthrop was engaged in this work some years before, having on its payroll people who worked throughout the State. It was expanded by federal funds. Under the federal act only one agency in a State could handle the funds. Clemson had agriculture and had done some work along that line. Winthrop and Clemson got together and had an agreement. That is the basis of the 1914 Agreement. That was signed by President Riggs and President Johnson. We have a letter in our files from the President of Clemson saying the Board of Trustees had ratified the Agreement. When the Agreement was sent to President Johnson it did not have the last paragraph saying it would not be dissolved, except on mutual agreement. He suggested that that paragraph be added and it was done. He wanted the work at Winthrop protected. After Winthrop and Clemson had made the Agreement, the Department of Agriculture and Clemson and Winthrop signed the

Agreement. Winthrop's responsibility under this Agreement was recognized and approved by the Department of Agriculture when the first project was set up in 1914. This Agreement may not be changed except with the consent of Winthrop, Clemson and the Department of Agriculture. With those Agreements there was no sense in Winthrop and Clemson having a fight about who was going to be the titular agent in the State. That was passed in 1915. Nobody at that time thought the Extension Service had been entrusted to Clemson, only the agricultural part. The Director of Extension represents Clemson and to that extent he is subject to Clemson. He represents also the Department of Agriculture. When we made a recommendation we made it to the Director of Extension at Clemson, not to Clemson College. We have a letter from Dr. Long that Winthrop's work in Home Demonstration is in no wise dependent upon Clemson and that his only connection with it is to comply with the law, that his responsibility was to see that projects have been approved by the Department of Agriculture. We have a letter from Dr. Long and one from Dr. Riggs, some years after the Agreement was in effect, that Winthrop had a direct responsibility in this work.

It was logical for Clemson to be the agent because agriculture gets three-fourths of the money and home economics one-fourth. Dr. Johnson had more influence with the Legislature at that time than any other educator and could, no doubt, have had the headquarters at Winthrop if he had not felt that Winthrop was protected. We have a letter from Mr. Long in which he says he does not want questions brought to him until after they have been approved by Dr. Johnson. The Agreement gave the two Presidents the right to confer. In the appointment of agents, no agent has ever been appointed, until a few months ago, who was not nominated by the President of Winthrop. The Director of Extension had to approve before the Department of Agriculture would approve. Under the setup the Clemson Board of Trustees had no authority in the Home Demonstration Work.

To Sims' talk Mrs. Schirmer replied, "Could you get that in short form so we could have it in our hands before we talk with the legislators?" This may have suggested to the wily Sims that some Winthrop trustees would not be very effective in combatting Clemson at the Legislature.[119]

Sims never gave up on anything he considered to be right and just. However in discussions of this period, Trustee Grier (a Clemson man) seemed more concerned (along with his fellow trustees Martin and Roddey) with coeducation and the Training School, both of which could benefit Rock Hillians fortunate enough to enroll their children.[120]

Thanks to Mrs. Gee, a trustee with superior educational background and qualifications, Sims was not alone in his fight to have the Home Demonstration Service returned to its legal home at Winthrop College. Sims knew that if unchecked, Clemson would eventually move into home economics and then Winthrop would lose another valuable asset--her monopoly on training most of the state's home-economics personnel.[121] At Governor Ernest Hollings' instigation, an outside management group named Cresap, McCormick and Paget came to study state problems. One of their recommendations suggested placing the home-demonstration programs at Clemson.[122]

Undaunted by these developments, President Sims advised the Board at Winthrop, "What I can win

575

on is that an institution should observe its
honest obligations.   I have no hard feelings
towards the people at Clemson--they want to build up
their school.   They will have a hard time getting
around the 1914   Agreement plus the later project
report." [123]

      Sims' efforts continued.   He pushed hard for
a master's program in home economics since he felt
confident that Winthrop would thwart Clemson's
effort to corner the home-economics and home-
demonstration work.   In addition Sims received great
support in his renewed quest for more scholarships.
And he beefed up the departments of chemistry,
library science and music.[124]

      In early 1958, the question of Sims'
retirement came up again.   However, Sims was too
busy lobbying the Legislature in the Clemson-
Winthrop controversy to give much thought to himself.   His first concern was to win the fight for
Winthrop.   Reporting to the Board on March 28, 1958,
Sims reviewed the problems, saying:

      For a good many weeks--I found you
      cannot talk in the lobby of the Capitol
      --I arranged conferences in my room.
      There are committee meetings in the
      afternoon, et cetera, but I have been
      successful some weeks in seeing a good
      many.   My experience with the ones I
      have talked with has been encouraging.
      I talked with the ten members of the
      Spartanburg delegation.   I had them to
      breakfast and discussed the matter.
      When I got through all ten were on
      Winthrop's side.   On the other hand, I
      tried to talk with the Charleston
      delegation and they gave me about
      fifteen minutes.   I had the least
      favorable response--not that any one
      said much but you can sense certain
      things and one fellow, Mr. Ravanel,
      indicated he was against us by the
      questions he asked.   He was sitting

576

with the newspaper boys and he was an august representative of the General Assembly. Two of them told me afterwards they appreciated my coming and were glad to get the facts.

With the other delegations I had a little better luck. I had the Laurens delegation. I knew the Senator in a way and we had an alumna who had written that none of them would commit themselves. They came up to my room from 9:00 to 11:00. When they left, they were on my side. I have talked to about 40 or more. I talked with two I did not expect to get--both of them agreed with me that our case was strong and they sympathized but they were at Clemson and did not know what they could do. A Clemson graduate, who is right prominent, told me he was going to support Winthrop. Later he told me we were getting stronger. I was there a long time and I would not say today how it is going to go. The House members from York County think the House will vote with us. Some from the Senate tell me that they think the Senate will go for us. At the Senate meeting, I think I came out right well on that hearing. I was not disappointed. We wanted to get a House hearing first but it was to be secret. We wanted a public hearing. Following that I went to the Senate and arranged for a public hearing. Between arranging the hearing and the date they got an invitation to go to Lexington County to see some industrial plants and have a bird supper. It was conveyed to us that the Committee would like for us to talk 15 minutes each.

Clemson had four speakers. Bob Hayes and I talked 15 minutes. The

York people think we have a majority on the committee. The Greenville crowd is against us.

I have had some interesting experiences. I have talked with three Clemson men and they told me they were with us. I had a big business man in South Carolina come to me in Columbia. He told me who he was. He has had some daughters at Winthrop. He said: "We had an executive meeting of the Alumni Association and Edwards, the vice president of Clemson, was there. I want you to know we did not fail to tell him how we felt about the way Clemson was treating Winthrop."

Lots of them think it will be a hot potato and they will not let it come to a vote if it can be prevented. . . .

If we have the proper leadership we will get it to a vote. They asked if the Senate did not pass the Bill, would I turn the furniture back. And the same with the House. I told them only a ruling by the General Assembly. I would not stand on the constitutional ground that they have to pass this same bill.

I went by the Governor's office yesterday and I told him I did not want him to commit himself because I did not believe in that. I asked him to think about this--that the controversy should be settled this year--win or lose. I wanted him to think about the advisability of his calling to their attention that this should be settled this year.[125]

Sims' presentation to the Legislature and his review of it for the Board elicited their assessments of the controversy. The following

578

trustee reactions were noted in the Board minutes:

Mrs. Boatwright suggested that Dr. Poole made the poorest presentation it seemed possible to make. Our president certainly did much better than the President of Clemson. I thought the questions that Dr. Sims stated, the reaction was in the minds of those people hearing it that they could not properly say which was the wisest place for it to be but definitely from the information presented, it looked as if Clemson had acted in a high-handed manner.

Mrs. Gee observed that Mr. Sims made a much better presentation.

Mr. Dinkins replied that I have not had a House or a Senate member who will argue with me the question, the fact that morally under this agreement Winthrop is right and Clemson has acted in a high-handed manner. Some seem to have the idea, though you give them figures to the contrary, that it would be better under one roof.

Chairman Dinkins said that Bob Cooper wrote to let the "status quo" remain. He also reported that the Clemson men at home (Manning), seem to be just as outspoken as the men who did not go to Clemson. The husband of the President of the new Winthrop Alumnae Chapter at home went to Clemson. He said in strong language he thought Clemson was wrong.

Mr. Martin also agreed with Mrs. Boatwright and Mrs. Gee that Mr. Sims

579

did a fine job. Winthrop's President put it on the basis of living up to a contractual commitment. Clemson put its case on the need in the situation in the future. And they had a great deal to say about the changing agricultural picture in South Carolina and the need now for combining these activities under the same direction and when it came to the matters of living up to contractural commitment neither Dr. Poole nor the Clemson booster, Bob Cooper, met the issue at all and whenever questions of that kind were brought up they referred them to their lawyer, Mr. Watkins. Mr. Watkins based his answers on this notion of a moral legal situation that the Legislature which charged Clemson with the responsibility for attempting this whole program under the Congressional law that took place after the commitments. Because neither Mr. Cooper nor Mr. Poole met the issue, after the hearing was over, I (Martin) asked Mr. Cooper how a man of his Christian leadership and character would justify ignoring that contract. He said any contract can be broken--that Clemson had no record that this contract was ever approved by the Board of Trustees. I said, "why didn't you say so in the hearing?" He said: "We had no access to the Clemson Board files. All we had was the letter from the Clemson President."[126]

The reflective Sims made a few final comments to the Board. "They have a hard time explaining that their case was right," he said. "I have spent a little money entertaining some of those boys [in the Legislature]. The only money I threw away was when I fed Bob Cooper one night."

Since the home-demonstration controversy was far from settled, Sims was reluctant to think about his retirement. But as he was approaching the retirement age, he felt he should go ahead with his plans. Not wishing to leave Rock Hill, where he and Mrs. Sims had many friends, President Sims made a frank suggestion to the Board regarding this matter:

I want you to be perfectly frank about this. I will be retiring soon. I do not want Winthrop to give me anything. I want this to be profitable to Winthrop as well as to me. If I stay in Rock Hill, if possible, I would like to have a house on some of the College property where it has utilities. As I get older I do not want to mess with anything like that. We have several lots and if it meets with your approval I would like for you to authorize the chairman to appoint a committee to let me discuss this with them. If the College has a lot whereby I can make a cash payment to the College for a certain percentage of the cost, about one-third--if the house costs $30,000, I will pay $10,000. The house would belong to the College, and the Trustees would make an agreement that my wife and I could live there as long as we live. If I live ten years, it would be about even. I would like for you to authorize the chairman to appoint a committee--appoint business men. If it cannot be found to be profitable to the College as well as to me I do not want it done. Do not hesitate to state it if it is objectionable. [127]

Reactions were forth-coming. Mrs. Gee replied, "I do not know anything about that but it would be wonderful for you to be near the College."

581

Miss Tolbert felt that President Sims should move out completely when he left the college. To that, Sims retorted, "I do not want to mess in the affairs of the College."[128]

Chairman Dinkins appointed a Presidential Search Committee after President Sims expressed his desire to retire effective September 1, 1959. The Board considered in a perfunctory manner a list of possibilities. One candidate was considered too old and sick. Another was not interested. A third was not in good standing with the teachers of his college. Another's wife was "a silly little thing." Trustee Martin, who fancied himself a great business manager, professed that he was "inexperienced in hunting a president" and that he wanted the advice of his friend Donald Agnew, the former Executive Secretary of the Higher Commission of the Southern Association of Colleges and Secondary Schools.[129]

Agnew suggested to Martin--and he relayed the information to the Board--that they might wish to include the faculty in the selection process and that they might wish to employ "a person to go out and dig up information for us." And Martin suggested that the vice president of Miami University would be the man for this job. Martin, perhaps with Agnew's advice, drafted a letter setting forth suggested presidential qualifications that the Board voted on at a later meeting.[130]

Martin continued to carry the ball for his program to locate a new president, with Trustee Grier always backing him up. Martin succeeded in having Dr. James Godard, "a yankee who was in Who's Who," named to be the investigator; but the knowledgeable Sims suggested two investigators, which might have proved a great boon to the future of Winthrop College if his advice had been taken. Collectively the Board wanted a "competent, male educator, with knowledge of business, and government, a dean, a diplomat, between the age of 40 and 55."[131]

The Winthrop faculty had been asked to make suggestions to the Board. They made elaborate plans, becoming very much excited over the whole process. All kinds of "professional suggestions" were received by the faculty co-ordinator and supposedly some passed on to the Board.[132]

There were other problems to be resolved and plans to be made at this important time in Winthrop's history. Mrs. Gee sought a special retirement for Winthrop presidents over and above the state system. She also tried to nail down the executive authority of the Board because many resolutions passed but never went into effect. The governor (who seldom attended) had that responsibility, but the pro-tempore chairman who usually presided often failed to carry out resolutions. The Board planned to ask the new governor to consider the problem.[133]

President Sims was able to report several important achievements of the 1958 graduating class. These were announced at the best-attended commencement exercises of Sims' administration. Among the 243 graduates several had won scholarships for graduate work in leading universities, including Woodrow Wilson scholarships. Nearly eight percent of the students were distinguished in their work. And the college was seeking an outstanding man in music to carry on Dr. Roberts' good work. In addition, a lady with a national reputation was coming to shore up home economics, and the prospects for increased enrollments were good. The alumnae had given fifty new scholarships.[134]

On June 27, 1958, Sims wrote Mrs. Stevens of the Board that he would be retiring September 1, 1959. This specific date pushed the Board to find his replacement. Soon word of Sims' pending retirement spread. Many faculty talked with Dr. Sims, who had always kept an open door to any and all who wished to see him, about the possibility of his continuing in office. Also the Winthrop

583

alumnae of the Association's Northern District
passed a resolution to the same effect.[135]

On January 14, 1959, the Board of Trustees
met at the Hotel Wade Hampton in Columbia to
consider Sims' replacement and to secure an
academic dean. Mr. Dinkins reported on contacts he
had made with Dr. Godard and on Godard's
recommendation of Charles S. Davis of Florida State
University for president. The Board had also talked
with James Alexander Spruill, a representative of
the House of Representatives from Chesterfield
County.[136]

Mr. Spruill had graduated from the universities of North and South Carolina, as well as
Oxford and Columbia University, and he had taught
law at the universities of South Carolina and
Georgia. He had given up his professional career
because "the elder Talmadge was making it rough for
[Georgia] teachers" and Spruill declined the Winthrop offer, not "wanting to start over again."
Many felt that Winthrop could not have done better
because Spruill seemed to be the most scholarly man
considered for the job.[137]

The Winthrop Board seemed to be leaning
toward Godard's selection, Dr. Charles S. Davis.
Trustee Roddey tried to secure this choice by
suggesting that the new president of Florida State
had a brother (Ben Strozier) who lived in Rock Hill
and that Dinkins should check with President
Strozier about Davis. Dinkins felt that they had to
equal Davis's salary by working out "a $3000 fund
which he does not have to account for . . . because
we do not feel that Winthrop should lose the right
man" for a small amount of money.[138]

Davis was called in to talk with the Board,
and he gave a summary of his life and activities.
When asked about his family and religion, he told
about Mrs. Davis, their children, and his Episcopal
Church membership, adding that "All the men in our
family went to Auburn and the ladies to the

584

University [of Alabama]." Davis seemed ready to supply all the answers the Board wanted.[139]

Following Davis's meeting with the Board, there were several comments made by the trustees, to wit: "I certainly do like this man. Is anything the matter with him?" and "He is human we hope. He does not seem to take himself too seriously." One trustee quoted a prominent South Carolina lady whose son-in-law taught at Florida State, and their recommendation of him was unfavorable. Trustee Martin did not want to move too fast on this decision, and Dr. Sims counseled: "You have to wait until you can hear reactions from different groups before you can make a good decision."[140]

The Board later had Mrs. Davis visit. She and Trustee Roddey's wife had been sorority sisters at Randolph-Macon Woman's College in Virginia. Mrs. Davis was most positive with her remark, "I am a believer in a woman's college." After her visit, the Board seemed sold on the Davises. But since the faculty's suggestions on a president were not at hand, it was thought "better not to have a formal resolution because then anybody can say you have elected a president," and "If Bill Workman gets a story in the newspaper that Winthrop has elected a president," the trustee implied that then other problems would arise. Before adjourning, some of the trustees expressed their appreciation to Dr. Sims and others who contributed to Winthrop's reconciliation with the AAUW.[141] (Sims had expressed himself many times on the AAUP and AAUW censures, which had been clubs over his head, suggesting that "the main benefit will be the removal of a point of criticism which some have misrepresented as affecting Winthrop's academic standing."[142])

The Board met Dr. Davis's salary request with $12,000 and a $3,000 expense account plus various services that they could "afford him in the president's home." They agreed to have Mrs. Davis select "necessary furniture" for the home. And the necessary home repairs and decorations

585

were taken care of.[143] In addition, the eleven-year-old college automobile that Sims used occasionally would be replaced by a new one.

One sour note in Sims' last year at Winthrop was the problem with the Training School. Sims told the Board what had transpired the year before:

> We had a lady teaching there who was a nut and I had to let her go during the Christmas holidays. We brought [in] a teacher who had been a Colonel and he was a failure. One man in Rock Hill told his son, when school closes you and your gang can do anything to that teacher that you please. . . .[144]

Following discussion, the Board felt that the Training School's current year could stand improving. They concluded that the principal of the Training School was not well and that they should try to find him another job.[145]

In the interval before Charles S. Davis assumed the presidency of Winthrop, Henry Sims built a nice home in Rock Hill. He moved out in time for the president's home to be refurbished and furnished with good furniture provided by the state.[146]

Sims had invited Davis to address the graduating class on May 31, 1959. Some of the faculty were disappointed with what he had to say. One lean, grey-eyed lady professor emerged from the auditorium following graduation and snorted that she had seen traveling salesmen before--she was not impressed.[147]

On June 30, 1959, the Board voted a laudatory set of resolutions that seemed to sum up what President Sims had tried to do and what his administration had meant to Winthrop and to South Carolina:

586

WHEREAS, Dr. Henry Radcliffe Sims has reached retirement age and has expressed to this Board his desire to retire as of September 1, 1959, and whereas Dr. Sims has served Winthrop College as its President since 1944, the Board of Trustees of Winthrop College desires to express formally its appreciation of the service rendered by Dr. Sims as the President of Winthrop College, therefore be it

RESOLVED, that the Board of Trustees of Winthrop College recognizes that at the beginning of this period of fifteen years Dr. Sims faced, as the representative of the Board of Trustees, certain very difficult situations which existed at the time he became President; that Dr. Sims has dealt with these situations during his administration in a manner most acceptable to the Board of Trustees, and that these issues have now been successfully and agreeably terminated we believe to the advantage of Winthrop College and the State of South Carolina. The Board believes that for these services the Board itself, the Legislature, and the people of South Carolina, owe Dr. Sims a debt of thanks and gratitude which the Board by this expression hopes in some small measure to repay Dr. Sims for his efforts in the solution of these matters.

RESOLVED, that President Sims has encouraged and supported every effort to raise academic standards. This includes the building up of the morale and quality of the faculty. It also includes stiffening of readmission requirements, introduction of entrance

587

examinations, participation in national examination programs to secure objective measurements of achievement at Winthrop and to provide curricular insights, and support of faculty efforts to improve instruction. These actions required courage for they held down somewhat the number of students enrolled at Winthrop at a time when his critics were making effective use of the decline in enrollment.

RESOLVED, that President Sims has made Winthrop a happier place for students. Social regulations have been revised; dormitories have been renovated, making them more attractive, more comfortable and providing more social areas; a student lounge has been provided in the Administration Building; additional recreation facilities have been provided at the shack and elsewhere on college property; and in all his dealings with students he has been sympathetic and understanding.

RESOLVED, that the Board acknowledges the respect and love which the members of the Winthrop Student Body have had for Dr. Sims during these years, and that the Board acknowledges the fact that under Dr. Sims' administration the Faculty has been built up to its present state of quality and morale, and that Dr. Sims' contribution to the improvement of the physical plant at Winthrop has contributed greatly to the present fine physical plant that Dr. Sims is able to turn over to his successor, and that the Board further acknowledges its debt to Dr. Sims in his very fine and able handling of the relationships between Winthrop and the General Assembly of the State of South Carolina, and that the Board is further indebted to Dr. Sims for the very fine spirit of cooperation which he has evidenced in making the transfer from his own administration to his successor easy, efficient, and pleasant.

RESOLVED FURTHER, that all of these and many other contributions to the growth and standing of Winthrop College, the Board hereby expresses to Dr. Sims its admiration and appreciation, and that a copy of this resolution be recorded in the Minutes of the Board.[148]

Henry Sims left Winthrop a far better place than he had found it. He thoughtfully expressed to a Winthrop professor (who regretted his leaving) his true feelings about his tenure when he wrote:

While no one knows better than I the many things that should have been done, or done better, since I have been here, it's gratifying to receive such a letter as yours.

I would like for you to know, however, that it has been just as great a pleasure for me to have you on the faculty. In endeavoring to operate a college, any president would be happy and proud to have every member of the faculty possess the characteristics which you have exhibited since being at Winthrop.[149]

Sims' administration marked the end of an era at Winthrop. It soon became evident that the administration of Charles Davis had chartered a radically new approach "to education and adminis-tration" at the South Carolina College for Women. The story of this new direction will prove interesting for some future historian.[150]

INDEX

Able, Lora, 178
Abrams, Gertrude, 255
Adams, Margaret, 255
Adickes, Frances, 255
Agnes Scott College, 295
Agnew, Donald, 582
Agricultural Education, 10;
  Tillman's Agricultural and
  Mechanical College, 12-15;
  Clemson's will benefits,
  16-17; 152-53, 159, 161,
  166, 180-81, 186, 188, 205-
  06, 217, 223-24, 232-35,
  237-38, 241-42, 245, 252-
  54, 260, 299, 314, 323-25,
  329, 346-48, 366, 371, 391,
  415. See also Clemson Col-
  lege, Industrial Education,
  and Normal Education.
Aiken, William, 30
Alabama College, 295 and 460;
  Agricultural, 160
Alcohol, 3, 70; blind tiger,
  93; 420. See also S. C.
  State Dispensary.
Alderman, Edward, 304
Aldrich, Sen. Nelson, 277
Alexander, Mary, 340
Alfalfa Clubs, 224, 233, 271
Alger, R. A., 301
Allen, Dr. Belle, 298
Allen, Mrs. E. A., 129
Allford, Ella, 91
Allworden, George, 67
American Audit Co., 328
American Council of Education,
  334
Anderson, John, 270, 388, 391-
  92, 399, 424
Anderson, Mrs. J. L., 562
Anderson College, 406
Anderson Free Press, 552-55
"Anderson Six" Automobile,
  270, 391
Anderson Tribune, 273
Andrews, Brent, 90
Ansel, Gov. Martin, 164, 176,
  197-98, 200, 206, 208, 218-
  19, 220, 228
Appleton's Cyclopaedia, 76
Arkansas Normal and Industrial
  College, 160, 292; Agricul-
  tural, 76
Armstrong, Dr. Earl, 502
Arnett, Pres. Trevor, 407
Ashley, Joshua, 228-29
Auburn University, 303, 584
Augusta Female Seminary, 94
Ayer, Gen. Lewis, 90
Ayer, Verna, 90

"Baby Ray," 270
Bailey, Laura, 327
Baldwin, Rev. M. J., 93
Ballinger, Kittie, 22
Baltimore Sun, 152
Banks, A. R., 73
Barber, B. J., 96
Barber, J. A., 395
Barnard, Henry, 165
Barr, Lillie, 255
Barron, Lottie, 554

Baruch, Barnard, 318, 407
Bayley, W. C., 330
Beckham, Louise, 28, 33
Behre, Susan, 28, 33
Belasco Theatre, 232
Benet, Sen. Christie, 318
Benson, Lena, 473
Benton, Mamie, 205
Berg, Edith, 28, 33
Berry, Dean, 549
Berry College, 295
Bertram, James, 168-69, 217,
  304
Bethea, A. J., 259, 296
Bhalman, J. H., 76
Birdsael, Bessie, 216
Birth of the Nation, 270
Bishop, Iva, 447, 570
Bishop, W. W., 420
Black, J. L., 96
Black, Lois, 486
Black, W. E., 379
Blakely, Ralph, 487
Blankenship, Ted, 486
Blease, Gov. Coleman, 191-92,
  195-97, 202, 226-31, 273,
  313, 353
Boatwright, Mrs. J. E., 579
Bohn, Dr. Frank, 401
Bolton, Dr. B. M., 27
Bonham, Julia, 33; Annie, 21
Bourbons, 8, 9, 92, 118, 311-
  12
Bourland, A. P., 355-56, 358,
  385
Bourne, Dr. Ruth, 500
Bourne, Dr. William, 358, 364
Bowen, Mildred, 255
Boyd, Kate, 321
Bradford, Edward, 30
Brandon, Kate, 255
Breazeale, John, 58-62, 71,
  205, 281, 360, 369, 372, 380
Breazeale, W. E., 90, 129, 147
Breedin, J. K., 349
Bridgewater Normal School, 22,
  49, 134, 355
Brim, O. G., 327
Britton, Susie, 351
Brown, Edgar, 354, 369, 520
Brown, Ellsworth, 167
Brown, J. T., 311, 324, 364,
  385
Brown, R. A., 158
Brown, Sibyl, 473
Brown, Sen. W. A., 89
Brown, Wade, 92, 97, 121
Brown, Mrs. Wade, 97
Browne, Hetty, 207-08, 304,
  311
Browne and Browne, 435
Bruce and Morgan, 78, 79
Bryan, J. P., 33
Bryan, R. L., 21
Bryan, William Jennings, 270
Buffalo Bill, 95
Buist, H. B., 58, 60, 123, 130
Burckmyer, Charlotte, 22
Burgin, W. G., 358, 387-90
Burke, Billie, 232
Burns, Howard, 368
Burt, R. C., 331, 395

Butler, Frances, 22
Butler, Dr. N. M., 166, 330
Butler, T. B., 396
Byrd, R. E., 221
Byrnes, Sen. James F., 219
  479-80, 486, 545
C. C. & A. Railroad, 163
Cadillac Corporation, 301
Calhoun, John C., 16, 85
Camp Wadsworth, 321
Campbell, Nancy, 364
Canning Clubs, 159, 224, 234,
  251, 304, 317, 347, 374, 425
Cannon, O. B., 379
Capers, Rev. Ellison, 28
Carbery, James, 232
Carmichael, Pres. Oliver, 460
Carnegie, Andrew, 149, 155,
  157, 160, 168-69, 172-73,
  192-94, 217-18, 279, 300,
  304-05, 363, 370
Carnegie, Mrs. Andrew, 217
Carnegie Foundations, 2, 206,
  297, 301, 309, 338, 363,
  370, 379-80, 387, 400, 407,
  419-20, 445-46, 463, 482-83,
  497
Carolina College. See South
  Carolina College.
Carr, E. C., 339
Carr, W. R., 321
Carrington, Emma, 22
Carter, Marietta, 273
Carter, Nell, 273
Carter, S. T., 273
Cartwright, Morse, 370
Caspari, Miss, 148
Center, Georgie, 90
Central Union Bank, 455
Century Magazine, 144
Chandler, Dr. J. A. C., 221,
  372
Charleston, Cincinnati, and
  Chicago Railroad, 73
Charleston Interstate and West
  Indian Exposition, 139,
  143-44
Charlotte Observer, 186-87
Cherry, J. M., 71-72, 73, 166-
  67, 169-70
Chester Bulletin, 70
Chester Lantern, 191
Chester Reporter, 565
Childs, Pres. J. C., 359
Chile, University of, 278,
  314, 334
Choate, J. H., 176-77, 198,
  200, 277, 304
Citadel, The, 38, 39, 54, 82,
  83-84, 118, 131, 134, 163,
  194, 243-44, 248, 251, 399,
  406, 451
Civil War, 2, 4, 8, 30, 54,
  150, 162, 223, 361, 418
Claflin University, 54
Clark, Dr. Charles, 401
Clark, Dorseth, 96
Clark, Dr. Janet, 491
Clark, Pearl, 334
Clark, W. A., 339
Clawson, W. T., 486
Claxton, P. P., 234, 276, 293,

303, 333

Cleaves, Dr. Helen, 143
Clements, Lora, 336
Clemson, Thomas G., 16-17, 85
Clemson College (Clemson
University) 12-15, 16-17,
36, 38, 54, 69, 76, 82, 84-
85; cadets seek Winthrop
brides, 86; 103, 118-19,
121, 156, 160, 180, 202,
205, 220-21, 229, 241, 245,
247-48, 251; extension
agreement with Winthrop,
251-54; 265, 298, 304, 311-
12, 315, 319, 323, 333, 342,
365, 371, 439, 475-77, 478,
522, 532, 545, 565; seeks
Extension Service from Winthrop, 571; Sims fights "illegal" extension removal to,
572-81. See also Agricul-
tural Education.
Cleveland, Pres. Grover, 199,
201, 300
Clifford, John, 30
Cloyd, Dr. David, 146
Cobb, Mrs., 154
Cobb, C. L., 395, 486, 492,
495, 497
Cobb, Leila, 178
Coith, Edna, 310-11, 321, 324,
326
Coker, E. C., 178, 215-16, 324
College for Women (South Carolina Presbyterian Insti-
tute), 246-48
Colorado Normal College, 269
Colored People, 154, 167, 425,
475, 487, 516
Colored Schools, 6, 54, 76,
173-74, 186, 199, 200, 226,
230-31, 354-55
Columbia City Council, 65, 67
Columbia College, 359
Columbia Opera House, 23, 31,
69, 77
Columbia Public-School System,
18, 19-20, 25, 31-32, 34,
36-37, 60, 87, 402
Columbia Record, 366
Columbia Register, 69-70
Columbia Theological Seminary,
20-21, 480
Columbia University, 166, 270,
314, 330, 334, 374, 431,
495, 584
Columbus Enquirer-Sun, 388-89
Communism (Great Red Scare),
336-37, 464
Conde, Bertha, 277, 309
Conservatoire Américain, 348
Converse College, 65, 295
Convicts, 57, 68, 78, 79-80,
86-88, 93, 95-96, 122
Conwell, Dr. R. H., 300-01
Coolidge, Pres. Calvin, 380-81
Cooper, Bob, 579-80
Cooper, Dorcas, 473
Cooper, Gov. R. A., 348, 351,
353
Cordell, Joseph, 562
Corn Clubs, 181, 188, 194, 206
Cornwell, Connie, 570
Courtenay, William, 73, 200
Craighead, E. B., 76, 175
Crawford, Mary, 255
Crawford, Dr. T. A., 73, 80,
137, 168, 247, 281, 325

Creighton, W. S., 121
Cresap, McCormick and Paget,
575
Cromer, Marie, 410
Cunningham, R. B., 96, 111,
124
Curry, Florence, 22
Curry, Jabez, 3-4, 36, 60, 98,
121-22, 126, 173, 199, 403

Dacus, Ida, 178, 385, 419, 420
Daily Mail, 205, 208-09
Dallet, Lucy, 91
Daly, Suanee, 301
Daniel, Lucia, 386, 400
Daniel, Mary, 400
Daniel, Mrs. Mary, 247-48,
351-55, 369, 373, 381, 384,
386, 387-91, 399, 400, 413-
14, 420, 436, 440, 450-51,
454-59, 460, 481-82, 485,
487
Daniel, Susan, 413-14
Daniel, W. L., 354, 386, 390-
91, 400, 432-34, 450
Daniels, Josephus, 223, 360-62
Daniels, J. C., 379
Daniels, J. M., 96
Daughters of the American
Revolution, 337
Davidson College, 365
Davis, Charles S., 584-85,
586, 589
Davis, Mrs. Charles S., 585
Davis, Jackson, 400
Davis, Robert, 6-7
Davis, W. B., 496
Dawsey, Ethel, 336
de la Barra, Merceded, 334
De Saussure, Eliza, 437
Demaine, Gabrielle, 364
Democrat Party, 9, 11. See
also Politics.
Depression, 2, 407-08, 413-14,
424, 437, 440, 445, 473-74
Dial, Sen. N. B., 313, 333
Dick, Dr., 248
Dinkins, John, 560-62, 564,
568-69, 579, 584
Dodd, Prof., 321
Dodge, Cleveland, 297
Dolan, Dr. Eleanor, 562
Donaldson, Birdena, 566
Douglas, Margaret, 336, 447-49
Douglass, Dr., 353
Drake, Bessie, 335-36, 343-45,
353-54
Drexal Institute, 110
Drexel Anthony, 30
DuPont, A. F., 308
Duffie, W. J., 21
Duke, James, 296-97, 309
Dunlap, Mr., 272
Dunlap, H. M., 395
Dunlap, Ira, 309
Dunlap, Sen. Walter, 439
Dunlap, W. B., 78
Dunn, Annie, 385

Eager, Dr. George, 158
Earle, Connie, 496
Earle, Frances, 473
Earle, Louise, 358
East Tennessee University, 3,
5. See also University of
Tennessee.
Eaton, George, 30

Edmunds, Dr. S. H., 330
Edwards, Preston, 358
Edwards, Pres. R. C., 578
Edwards, W. A., 206
Edwards and Sayward, 435
Elder, W. N., 58, 59, 62, 73
Elementary Education, 153,
183-85, 207-08, 248, 324.
See also S. C. Public-
School Education.
Eliot, Charles, 304
Ellerbe, J. E., 98, 219
Ellis, Miss M., 485
English Grammar for Begin-
ners, 157
English Language, 3, 6, 7, 14,
27, 89, 90, 92, 100. See
also Winthrop Curriculum.
Erdman, Charles, 304
Erskine, Miss, 438
Erskine College, 27; Due West
Female College, 192
Europe, 2, 93, 100, 151. See
also World War I and II, and
Winthrop College Abroad.
Evans, Frank, 330
Evans, Gov. J. G., 87, 95, 98-
99, 100, 118-19
Evans, Lawton, 214
Evarts, William, 30
Evening Herald, 70, 191, 313,
394, 495, 554-55

Fairs, Winthrop at, 133, 138-
39, 162; National Corn Ex-
position, 224; Frayser at,
244-45; Panama-Pacific Ex-
position, 264; 271, 295,
323, 365
Fairmont School, 153
Farmers, in S. C., 8; in the
North, 9; Association, 10-
11, 12, 15-16; The Cotton
Plant, 16; 35; Convention,
37; 181; Institutes, 233;
241, 245; statistics, 262;
314, 353, 403
Farragut, Adm. D. G., 30
Fascism, 464
Faulk, L. B., 60
Favrot, Leo, 484
Federal Land Bank, 353
Federation of Women's Clubs,
255, 340, 344, 348, 353, 365
Fewell, Richard, 73; and Co.,
110
Finley, Cong., 300
Finley, David, 78
Finley, Dr. John, 301
Finley, Margaret, 358, 481
First National Bank of Rock
Hill, 71, 74
Fish, Hamilton, 30
Fisher, Samuel, 309
Florida State Normal College,
262, 292, 584-85
Flying Group (Cadets), 486-87
Forney, Elizabeth, 327
Fraser, Mowat, 495-96, 497-99
500, 525
Frayser, Mary, 212, 221-22,
233-34, 244-45, 256, 260,
274-76, 298, 302-04, 385,
430, 477
Free School Law, 120
French Language, 6, 15, 95,
100, 212-13, 498. See also

Winthrop College Curriculum.
Frick, Dr. Herman, 535
Friedheim and Brother, 111;
  Julius, 312; 423-24, 487
Fuller, Dr. A. C., 58-61
Fuller, M. W., 198, 229, 300
Furman University, 40, 431
Furst, Clyde, 379-80, 400, 407

Gaines, Dr. Francis, 496
Gary, Eugene, 58
Gary, Frank, 62
Gaston, Arthur, 522
Gatchel and Manning, 139
Gee, Christine, 191-92, 296,
  327, 334, 355, 368, 436,
  517, 535, 547, 571, 575,
  579, 581, 583
Gee, Drucilla, 436
Gee, N. G., 368
General Education Board, 146,
  206, 400, 406, 430, 437-38,
  484
Georgia, University of, 76,
  584
Georgia Normal and Industrial
  College, 89, 292
German Language, 2, 6, 15, 95,
  100-01, 212-13. See also
  Winthrop College Curriculum.
Gibson, Lucy, 430
Gilchrist, A. D., 481
Glaze, W. L., 257, 281, 299
Glenn, Dr. G. R., 146, 170
Glenn, J. L., 432
Godard, Dr. James, 582, 584
Godbold, Lucile, 340, 356-57,
  359
Godfrey, Harriet, 334
Goggins, Sadie, 553
Gonzales, Narciso, 64-66, 76,
  92
Gonzales, W. E., 227
Goodman, W. P., 395
Gore, Emmett, 460
Gossett, Fanona, 570
Gossett, James, 275
Goucher College, 463
Graham Family (Greenville),
  312
Graham, Alexander, 482, 497,
  566
Graham, William, 30
Grant, Sarah, 178, 438
Graves, J. T., 523-24
Gray, Will Lou, 331, 354-55,
  367-68
Greek Language, 2, 141. See
  Winthrop College Curriculum.
Green, George, 124
Green, Dr. Samuel, 35-36, 87,
  198-200, 219, 230
Greene, Dr. Walter, 505
Greensboro Normal College,
  295-96, 320, 469-70
Greenville News, 389, 570
Gregg, Alice, 336, 409
Gregg, Rev. F. W., 397, 498
Greneker, Sen. T. B., 420
Gressette, Sen. Marion, 560-
  62, 563-64
Gribben, Capt., 163
Grier, William, 558, 565, 568-
  69, 571, 575, 582
Grier, Rev. W. M., 27
Guelich, Henry, 324
Guerry, Bishop W. A., 304
Gunter, Katie, 194

Haddon, T. C., 324, 364
Hall, Ainsley, 20, 480
Hamblin, J. K., 396
Hardaway Construction Co., 481
Hardin, Rev. E. K., 215
Hardin, Kate, 432, 485, 497
Hardy, Eric, 218
Harkness, Edward, 309
Harper, Bessie, 404, 427, 434,
  435-36, 481
Harris, Dr. Elizabeth (Mrs. R.
  I. McDavid, Jr.), 486, 488,
  490-92, 536
Harris, Julian, 388-89
Harrison, Pres. Fairfax, 257,
  308-09
Harrison, Frank, 485
Harvard University, 30, 314,
  334, 364, 435, 471, 558
Harvey, Wilson, 353
Haskett, H. B., 480
Hawkes, Mrs., 556
Hayes, Robert, 563, 577
Hemphill, Hannah (Coleman), 40,
  41-55, 403
Hemphill, John, 73
Hemphill, Paul, 156
Hemphill, Sen. R. R., 36, 61,
  62, 77
Henderson, Dr. Archibald, 401
Heyward, DuBose, 356
Heyward, Gov. Duncan, 148, 157,
  161
Himstead, Dr. Robert, 536, 546,
  547, 551, 560-64, 569
Hines, J. H., 96
History of South Carolina, 359
Hodge, F. A., 179
Hoffman, Lillian, 346-47, 350
Holmes, Abbey, 385
Hollings, Gov. Ernest, 575,
  578, 583
Hollins Institute, 2
Homemakers' Clubs, 187, 323,
  347-48, 366, 383, 425-26
Hook and Rogers, 195, 206, 216
Hoover, J. H., 385
Hope, James, 354, 366, 374,
  399, 460, 493
Hopkins and Baker, 480, 488
Hopper, Annie, 336
Hough, Miss Bruce, 205
Household Magazine, 473
Hoyt, James, 231, 259
Hubbard, Pres. B. H., 489-90,
  491-92
Hughes, Miss, 324
Hughes, C. E., 276
Hughes, Edwin, 483
Hughes, E. R., 91
Hunter, Dr. F. H., 376
Huntington, C. P., 407; Mrs.
  557
Huntley, Mr., 492
Hussey, Henry, 258
Hutchinson, D., 72
Hutchinson, Laura, 91
Hutchinson, W. C., 72
Hyde, Carrie, 179, 187, 190,
  205-06

Ickes, Harold, 484
Ihrie, Peter, 395
Illinois State Normal College,
  269, 289
Industrial Education, 11, 35-
  36, 38-40; organization proposal, 41-55; experts on,

56; 65, 79, 85-86; original
  organization, 95; 99, 100-
  04; Winthrop's Industrial
  Dept., 110; 125, 141, 166-
  67, 208-09, 215, 217-18,
  223-24, 232-35, 237-38, 241-
  42, 252-54, 260, 299, 310,
  314, 316, 321, 327, 340,
  346-48, 350, 371, 390-91,
  403, 415, 421, 526. See
  also Agricultural Education
  and Normal Education.
Iowa, University of, 256; Normal College, 269, 289
Irby, J. L. M., 480
Isles, M. M., 179

Jack, Pres. Theodore, 489-92,
  494-95, 503-09
Jackh, Dr. Ernest, 387
Jackson, Gen. T. J., 160, 323
Jacques, D. H., The Rural
  South Carolinian, 9
Jallade, Louis, 277
James, Pauline, 28
James, W. A., 16-17
Jarrell, Dr. Hampton, 495
Jefferies, Richard, 475-76,
  491-92
Jefferson, Pres. Thomas, 313,
  474, 485
Jenkins, John, 152
John F. Slater Fund, 200
Johns Hopkins University, 134
  200, 243, 348, 358, 369,
  406, 421, 471
Johnson, Albert, 301
Johnson, Bancroft, 193
Johnson, Burgh, 449-50
Johnson, C. E., 179
Johnson, David Bancroft, student, 3; brief sketch, 18-
  19; 20-21, 23-25, 31; laud-
  ed, 32; financial report,
  33; 34, 35, 40; report for
  establishing model woman's
  college, 41-55; at first
  SCI and WNC board meeting,
  58; on Executive Committee,
  59; comments on seventh session, 63; 74, 77, 80; reports to Trustees, 82-83;
  offices in 1894, 87; 88; unanimous election to Winthrop
  presidency, 89; 90, 93-96;
  at Rock Hill openning, 98-
  99; strict rules, 111-17;
  120, 122; report to Legislature, 123-27; 128-31; described, 132-34; 135, 136-
  38, 140-42, 144, 145-47;
  begs money, 148-50; marriage of, 150-51; publicity,
  152-55; reports, 156; Christmas veto, 157; 158-62, 164-
  71; NEA Vice-President, 166-
  67; 168-71, 172-78, 180;
  wages war, 183-87; 190; politics, 191-202; on Tillman,
  203; Tillman on marriage,
  204; 205-11, 212-22, 223-82;
  typical Johnson reports--
  same format but differing
  statistics, 266-69 and 285-
  89; 270-82, 296-315; Rutledge on, 316; 317-25; faculty concerns, 326; 327-30;
  Rutledge on, 331; 332-34;

592

uses Alumnae Society, 335-36; 337; institutionalizing 338-39; 340-44; involuntary birthday "gifts" to, 345; 346-59; man merging with institution, 360; 361; evaluated, 362-63; 364-76, 378-80; family visits U. S. President, 381; 383-92; illness, 393-94; death, 394-98; 399-05, 406, 415-16; memorial, 434-37; 446, 448-50, 454-59, 476, 481, 535, 544; Rutledge biography, 568-69; 572, 573-75

Johnson, Dr. Elizabeth, 358, 364

Johnson, Frank, 96

Johnson, J. B., 166

Johnson, Mai (Mrs. D. B.), 150; marriage, 151; 231, 250-51, 345, 399, 401, 449-50, 455, 571

Johnson, W. E., 396

Johnson Memorial Auditorium, 401, 406, 434-37, 481, 482, 483, 527, 548, 570, 586

Johnson Publishing Co., 270

Johnston, Gov. Olin, 496-97, 498-99, 502, 518, 519

Jones, Mrs. Harry, 562

Jones, Ira, 226-27

Jones, Iredell, 72, 167-68, 170

Jones, Pawnee, 187

Jordan, Dr. David, 262-64

Joseph Payne's Science and Art of Teaching, 19

Journal of Education, 165

Joynes, Dr. Edward Southey, brief sketch, 1-3; 5-8, 19-21; addresses first WTS Memorial Day fete, 31-32; 34-37; Normal college study proposal, 40; on first trustee board, 58; 59; on Executive Committee, 59; 60-62; State praises, 70-71; 73, 80, 87, 89; abroad, 93; fact-finding Europe trip, 100-04; part in Winthrop's success, 121-22; 123, 128, 131, 136-38; early value to Winthrop, 140-42; 144, 145-48, 150-52, 154, 158, 172; Johnson's power base, 175; 185, 190, 205, 214, 222, 235-36, 240, 244, 247, 249, 252, 257, 271; death, 299-300; 305, 308, 319-20; Johnson ignores, 344; 347, 376, 415

Judd, Dr. C. H., 376

Keeley, Dr. Leslie, 65, 70

Keith, Warren, 490, 517-18, 521, 525

Kelley, Sally, 153

Kelly, John, 566

Kelly, Lizzie, 251

Kelsey, Harlan, 160

Kennedy, Mrs. J. W., 51

Keppel, Frederick, 482-83

Kilgo, Dr. J. C., 167

Kilgore, Carolina, 336

Kilpatrick, W. H,, 330, 495

Kinard, James P., English Chair, 90; 129, 134; acting

president, 149-51; 157; acting president, 166; 180, 182; resigns, 243-44; as dean, 273; 323-24, 356, 385, 393; acting president, 399-401; 405; brief sketch, 406; 407-08, 413-15; philosophy about presidency, 416-18; 419-21; 424-45; poem on, 446-47; 449-52, 454-59; retires, 460-61; 462, 475, 485, 500, 535, 572

Kinard, Mrs. James P. See Lee Wicker.

King, G. W., 200

King Co., 64

Knapp, Dr., 245, 304

Knight, Broadus, 257

Knight, Sarah, 22, 24, 60

Kohn, August, 227-28, 246

Lamar, Mrs. R. G., 33

Land and Investment Co. of Columbia, 66

Landrum, Lonnie, 385, 427

Larew, Dr. Gillie, 562

Latin Language, 6, 92, 95, 141, 498. See also Winthrop Curriculum.

Lawrence, David, 401

Lawrence, Bishop William, 198, 200

League of Nations, 330, 341

League of Women Voters, 348, 365, 369

League to Enforce the Peace, 330

Lee, A. M., 137, 185, 408, 492

Lee, Gen. Robert E., 2, 3, 5, 159, 160, 162, 270, 296

Lee, Gov. Stephen, 13, 14

Legare, Cong. G. S., 219

Leonard, Mary, 21-22, 34-35, 83, 355

Leonard, Mrs. P. H., 562

Lester, Robert, 483

Lever, Cong. Asbury, 164, 220-21, 245, 261, 312

Lever Bill, 220-21, 241, 368

Lide, Florence, 336

Lide, Janie, 336

Lindsey, Ben, 301

Lineback, Dr. R. F. L., 396

Litchfield (Conn.) Enquirer, 232

Little, Nellie, 336

Long, Mrs. Alexander, 409

Long, W. W., 245, 298, 574-75

Lumpkin, Rep., 246-47

Lumpkin, Mary Belle, 336

Lund, F. P., 295

Lyles, William, 21, 60-61

Lynch Law, 119

Lyon and Healy, 483

Mabry, T. O., 180, 216

MacAlister, Dr., 40

Macaulay, Angus, 392, 491, 495

McBryde, Mrs., 400

McBryde, Dr. John, 7

McCabe, W. G., 309, 312

McCants, E. C., 379

McClintock, Euphemia, 246

McClure, Mary, 339-40

McClurkin, Dir., 569

McCormick, Mrs. Cyrus, 301

McCown, Louise, 273

McCown, R. M., 273

McCoy, Dr. S. J., 535, 551,

558, 566

McCullough, Inez, 154

MacDonald, Dr. Helen, 486, 490-92, 536

McDonald, J. E., 388, 399

McDow, Thomas, 330

Macfeat, Mary, 28, 33

Macfeat, Minnie, 180-81, 324, 385

McIlvaine, Rev. Charles, 30

McIntyre, D., 353

McKay, Dr. Hamilton, 396

McKenny, Pres. Charles, 330

McKissick, Dr. J. R., 505

McLaurin, Gen. D. W., 58-59, 61-62, 143, 206, 227-28, 230, 240, 247, 249, 281, 388, 393

McLeod, Thomas, 302, 353, 374

McLeon, Eliza, 473

McMahan, John, 121, 137, 144

McMaster, Agnes, 22

McMaster, FitzHugh, 21, 69, 229-30

McMichael, J. M., 149, 157

MacNair, Dr. Vera, 497

McSwain, Dr. E. T., 502

McSweeney, Gov. Miles, 136-38

Magginis, W. D., 249, 311, 324, 358, 385

Making of South Carolina, 348

Mallalieu, W. C., 385

Maloney, Martin, 169

Mance, Dr. Grover, 358

Manchester, Charles, 30

Mann, Horace, 165

Manning, Gov. Richard, 280-81, 296, 318

Manosalva, Mercedes, 314

Marchant, Genevieve, 336

Marcum, Sarah, 345, 393, 459

Marks, Minnie, 22

Martin, Dr., 399

Martin, Rev. Alexander, 214, 301, 395, 397

Martin, Donnis, 349, 474

Martin, John, 575, 579-80, 582, 585

Martin, J. B., 90

Martin, Oscar, 158, 245, 303

Martin, Sarah, 241-42

Masonic Order, 1, 83, 214

Mather, Mary, 40

Matthews, Mrs., 399

Mauldin, John, 25

Mayfield, W. D., 58-59, 61-62, 68, 78, 87, 93-94, 96, 139-40

Mayo, Dr. A. D., 20, 27, 31

Medical College of S. C., 251, 439, 451-53, 474

Medical College of Virginia, 231

Mellichamp, Amelia, 181

Meredith, George, 243

Meyer, Miss, 324

Miami University, 582

Michigan State Normal College, 330

Milady, John, 142

Milburn, F. P., 142

Mill Schools, 4, 6, 157, 159, 181, 205, 224, 234, 260, 274-76, 302, 311, 329

Miller, Dr. Elizabeth, 126, 131

Miller, Esther, 22

Miller, Georgia, 33

593

Mills, Robert, 20
Mills, Textile, et al., 4, 129, 166, 181, 205, 275, 303, 325, 387, 544. See also Mill Schools.
Mims, Dr. Edwin, 330
Missionaries, 270, 298, 370, 379-80, 481
Mississippi (State College) Normal School, 175, 358, 381; Agricultural and Mechanical College, 13
Missouri Normal College, 289, 462
Mitchell, Pres. Samuel, 221, 226-31
Montague, Mr., 366
Montague, Gov. Andrew, 160
Monteith, Isabelle, 22
Montgomery, Mabel, 473
Moore, Sen. J. H., 373
Moore, W. W., 166, 333
Morgan, Miss, 301
Morgan, J. P., 30, 159-60, 168-69, 198, 199-201, 219, 240
Morrah, Mrs. Bradley, 355
Morrill Act, 10
Morrison, Grace, 181
Morrison, H. C., 202
"Mortmain," 356, 418
Moses, Edward, 90, 94, 129-31
Moudy, Alice, 181
Mouzon, Bishop Edwin, 392
Muller, Elizabeth, 22
Mulligan, Catherine, 161
Murphy, Pres., 76
Murphy, Starr, 258-59, 265-66, 305
Murry, A. B., 312
Mutual Rubber Production Co., 202

Nance, Carroll, 354, 369, 373
Nance, G. C,, 385
Nance, Mary T. See Mrs. Mary Daniel.
National Botanical Gardens, 130
National Education Association, 133, 167, 171, 179-81; Johnson's campaign, 262-64; 272, 274, 276-77, 311, 319, 376, 431-33, 463
National Theatre, 232
National Union Bank, 240, 309
Naudain, W. G., 385, 525
Neal, W. A., 88, 93-94
Neely, Juanita, 347-48, 427
New York College for the Training of Teachers, 49, 433
New York Evening Post, 259
New York Herald, 356
New York Times, 401
New York University, 339
Newell, M. A., 6
News and Courier, 10, 39, 64, 70, 74, 77, 92-93, 111, 118-19, 246, 353
Nicholson, Pres. Emslie, 303
Nicholson, W. H., 228
Niernsee and La Motte, 71
Niven, L. A., 181, 206, 216, 296
Normal Education,19; Johnson solicits money for, 20; 21-23, 25, 27, 32, 35-36, 38-

39; organization proposal, 41-55; experts' plan for, 56; 58-59, 79, 85; original organization, 95; 122-23, 125, 130, 133; kindergarten at Winthrop, 133; 141, 146-48, 160-61, 166, 169, 171, 174-77, 180, 198, 211, 220, 230-31, 235, 238-39, 241-42, 246, 248, 251, 255-57, 264, 282, 288, 291-92, 299, 310-11, 314, 317-19, 329, 330-31; leads to communism, 336-37; 338, 346, 348, 362-63, 371, 377-78, 390-91, 400, 403, 415, 437-38, 498, 526, 530, 537, 548, 571. See also Agricultural Education and Industrial Education.
North, the, 4, 9; "Yankees" at Winthrop, 183; money from, 297; 328, 339; divorcée, 460
North Carolina, University of, 76, 368, 478, 584

Oakland Avenue, 1, 163, 190, 256
Oakland Park, 71-73, 78, 93, 164, 331
Oliphant, Mary, 359
Olney, Richard, 200-01
Orangeburg Times and Democrat, 516, 544
Ordeal of Richard Feveral, 243
Osborne, Helen, 335

Page, David, 165
Panama-Pacific Exposition, 264
Parker, Col., 19
Parker, Principal, 49
Parker, Alton, 157
Parkhurst, Emmeline, 334
Parkinson, B. L., 346
Parrott, Edith, 234, 317, 327, 334-35
Patterson, A. H., 58-61, 67
Payne, Dr., 49, 499
Peabody, George, 28-31, 85, 146, 297-98
Peabody Education Board, 5, 140, 146, 155, 164, 168-69, 173-77, 197-202, 206-08, 218-20, 226-31, 240, 402
Peabody Fund, 20, 23, 28; original board, 30; 32-33, 35-37, 56, 64-65; Gonzales on, 66; 87, 98, 121-22, 155, 160, 173-74, 176-77, 185-86, 197-202, 207-08, 226-31, 239-40, 277, 348, 402-03
Peabody Normal College, 49, 121, 155, 175, 177, 198, 358, 364, 366, 460, 462, 524, 526, 535; Commission study, 544 and 556; Southern States Program, 564; Report, 565-68; 569
Penny, Ida, 473
People's National Bank, 456, 486
People's Trust Co., 240
Phelps, Dr. Shelton, elected third president, 460; brief sketch, 462-63; 464-66; lists needs, 467-73; 474-86; problems, 488; 489-91; resigns, 492; health, 493; accreditation lost, 494; 495-97,

519, 524; accreditation problem's cause, 536, 562, 567
Plaza, Philomena, 278
Plowden, Hannah, 194
Poetry Society of S. C., 356
Politics, 3, 9; 1886 campaign, 11; statewide canvass, 17; 36; 1895 campaign, 92-93 and 117-19; 95, 135, 148, 157, 160-63; a Johnson campaign, 191-203; Peabody Fund, 226-31; 246-48, 273-74, 311-15; Johnson and, 316 and 320-21; alumnae in, 333-34; 350-55, 369-70, 387-91, 451-54, 459, 479-80, 484-85; politician Sims, 506-07 and 514; 525, 536, 545-46; Sims vs Clemson in "illegal" Extension Service removal to, 572-81
Poole, Pres., 545, 579-80
Pope, Mary, 91, 161
Porter, James, 155
Porter, Mary, 181
Pratt, Mr., 50; Institute, 44
Presbyterian College, 353, 365, 415
Proctor and Gamble, 301
Prosser, C. A., 321
Prostrate State, 4
Pugh, Dr. G. T., 359, 385

Radio Programs, 355-56; current, 398; 417, 495, 520
Randle, Lucile, 348
Rauch, Mrs. J. J., 554
Ravanel, Mr., 576
Reaves, Claudia, 336
Reconstruction, 2-4, 8. See also Civil War.
Record, 206-07, 271
Reilly, John, 64
Rice, Dr. James, 31, 33
Rice, Mrs. W. D., 554
Richards, Gov. John, 313, 387-88, 390-92, 399, 489
Richards, Pres. J. McD., 480
Richards, M. V., 244
Richards, Mamie, 159
Richards, Margarette, 364
Richardson, Gov. J. P., 11, 15, 23, 25, 32, 36, 316
Richardson, Rev. W. S., 258-59, 265, 276-77, 279-80, 305, 373-74
Richmond Female Seminary, 93
Ridley, Charles, 560-61, 563
Riggs, George, 30
Riggs, Pres. W. M., 210, 227, 247, 251-52, 254, 333, 573-74
Riley, W. L., 460
Rivers, Alice, 336
Rives, William, 30
Roberts, Hortense, 92
Roberts, Walter, 385, 460, 463-64, 483, 485, 583
Robertson, Dr. David, 463
Robertson, Mrs. T. C., 21
Robinson, L. A., 181
Rockefeller, John D., 206, 21; 258-59, 265-66, 276-77, 279; 82, 294-97, 300-01, 304-05, 309-10, 318, 370-71, 373-74
Rockefeller Foundation, 304, 368, 373-74
Rock Hill, 133, 137, 156, 16!

167, 172, 208, 215, 256, 270, 331-32, 378, 395, 417, 459-60, 484-85
Rock Hill Buggy Co., 64-65
Rock Hill Town Council, 120, 172
Rock Hill School Board, 110, 142, 163, 170, 331-32
Rock Hill Construction Co., 73
Rock Hill (Boys) High School, 163-64, 167-68, 187
Rock Hill Land and Townsite Co., 72-73, 164, 215
Rock Hill Printing and Finishing Co., 166, 568
Roddey, J. T., 558, 568, 571, 575, 584-85
Roddey, W. J., 73, 80, 97, 137, 149, 167-68, 210, 215, 247, 281, 325, 330, 387-88, 399, 405, 409, 424, 439, 476, 478-79, 488, 495, 497, 520-21
Roddey Merchantile, 110
Roettinger, Ruth, 549-51
Roosevelt, Franklin, 308, 480, 483-84
Roosevelt, Mrs. Franklin, 483
Roosevelt, Pres. Theodore, 166
Root, Sen. Elihu, 176, 297, 300
Rose, Dr. Wickliffe, 160, 175, 184-85, 199, 228
Royhill, J. H., 60
Rudd, Sarah, 351
Russell, Leila, 26-27, 182, 317, 324, 333, 335-36, 340, 350-51, 385, 434, 447-48, 473
Russell, George, 30
Russell, James, 222
Russell, John, 463
Russell Sage Foundation, 298
Rutgers University, 147
Rutledge, Archibald, 150, 172, 316, 331, 345, 362-63, 381-83, 446, 568
Ryan, Anna, 327-28

Sadler, Annie Laurie, 336
St. Louis Manual Training School, 44
Saito, Uta, 340, 409
Salley, Mrs. Julian, 355
Salley, Marion, 350-51
Sassi Family, 520-21
Satterwhite, Marion, 324
Saunders Co., 139
Sawyer, Dr. Olin, 198
Schauweker, Olga, 182
Schmidt, A. A., 358
School and Society, 277
Schirmer, Mrs. A. B., 575
Scudder, Mary, 385, 420, 431-32
Sears, Dr. Barnas, 5, 28
Secot, Jeanne, 364
Selby, M. Margaret, 22
Senn, Louise, 22
Senn, Margie, 22
Shannon, Dr. George, 562, 564
Shealy, Cyrus, 360
Sheib, Dr. Edward, 27
Sheldon Axle Co., 64
Shell Manifesto, 241
Simms, W. G., 359
Simons, James, 25
Simpson, I., 72

Simpson, Dr. W. E., 396
Simril, Loraine, 554
Sims, Henry Radcliffe, 496; unanimously elected fourth president, 502; Tatler dedicated to, 503; brief sketch, 503; tackles accreditation problem, 503-09; 510-15; characteristics, 516-17; 518-21; inauguration, 522-24; portrayed, 525-26; foes, 536; faculty address, 537-43; 544-51; alumnae break from alumnae board in supporting, 552-55; 556-64; paper attacks, 565; 566-68; proposes entrance exams, 569; 570-71; AAUP censure lifted under, 572; fights to retain Extension Service, 572-81; retirement, 581; 582-86; Board lauds, 586-89; Sims to Crowson, 589
Sims, Mrs. Henry, 503, 516, 536, 548, 581
Sims, Dr. W. R., 395
Sims, Mary, 509
Sims Publishing Co., 544
Sinkler, Dr. Wharton, 149
Smart, E. H., 359
Smith, A. E., and Co., 111
Smith, Bertha, 336
Smith, C. A., 330
Smith, Sen. Ed, 333
Smith, Sen. Hoke, 245, 326
Smith, Martha, 473
Smith, Dr. Samuel, 158
Smith College, 232, 269, 289, 328, 380, 382, 464, 473
Smith-Hughes Act, 274, 306, 310-11, 314, 321-22, 326, 329, 347, 350
Smith-Lever Act, 232, 245, 251-54, 262, 302-04, 310, 323, 573
Smith-Towner Bill, 346
Soldan, Louis, 5-6
Soper, Dr. Edmond, 392
South, Christine. See Christine Gee.
South, the, educational progress, 1; 3-4; social change in, 54; 156, 161, 165, 172, 173-74, 209-10, 216-17, 223-24, 289-93, 328, 338, 360-62
South, University of the, 304
South Carolina, University of, 15, 118, 218, 221, 226-31, 239, 244, 246-47, 248-49, 265, 299, 311, 315, 319, 338, 344, 353-54, 356, 359, 363, 365, 368, 371, 384, 404, 439, 450-52, 454, 474, 506, 521, 565, 571, 584. See also South Carolina College.
South Carolina Board of Education, 122, 128, 271, 273-74, 299, 322, 548. See also South Carolina Superintendent of Education.
South Carolina College, 4, 6-7, 10, 15, 17; brief sketch, 18; 27, 31-32, 54; students expelled, 69; 76, 82-84; Dr. Joynes' fact-finding Europe trip, 100; 119, 131-32, 134, 146, 151-52, 183-86, 194, 200, 214-15. See also University of South Carolina.
South Carolina Immigration Bureau, 156
South Carolina Industrial School for Girls, 337-38
South Carolina Legislature, 10, 15, 37-41, 56, 64, 78, 81, 87, 103, 118-19, 120-22, 124-27, 131-32, 135, 141-42, 148-49, 154-57, 160, 162, 164, 167-68, 177-83, 185, 193-94, 208, 213, 218, 228-31, 235-36, 239-40, 246-48, 250-51, 257, 259-61, 265-66, 277, 282-85, 290, 292, 294, 296-99, 304, 314-15, 318-20, 328-29, 332, 337-38, 342, 347, 350, 354-55, 363, 369-75, 379-80, 384, 393, 400, 402, 407-08, 420, 444, 450-52, 458, 466, 478-79, 482, 486, 488, 493, 495, 510, 517-21, 545-46, 548-49, 556, 570, 571-73, 575-76, 578, 580, 588
South Carolina Medical Association, 298-99
South Carolina Public-School Education, 4, 117-18, 120, 133-34, 140, 144, 152-53, 165, 261-62, 266-69, 271, 273, 288-89, 308, 310, 314, 319-20, 323-27, 337-38, 346-47, 352, 354-56, 360-62, 365-66, 371, 377, 469. See also Elementary Education.
South Carolina Society of Washington, 333-34
South Carolina State Dispensary, 156, 162, 196. See also Alcohol.
South Carolina Superintendent of Education, 120, 131, 134, 138, 144, 152-53, 223, 226, 350, 353, 365, 374, 403, 537. See also John Swearingen and South Carolina Board of Education.
South Carolina Teacher's Journal, 133
Souther, M. M., 91, 97
Southern Baptist Theological Seminary, 158
Southern Exposition, 118
Southern Farming Magazine, 296
Southern Ferro Concrete Co., 318
Southern Power Co., 297, 309
Southern Railroad, 119, 162, 244, 257, 308, 367, 415
Spain, Miss, 522
Spaulding Brothers, A. G., 339
Springs, Leroy, 169, 199, 330, 380, 388, 391-92, 408
Spruill, J. A., 489, 492, 495-97, 517-18, 584
Sprunt, Rev. Alexander, 97
Stanford University, 165
State, 63-67, 69-71, 74, 76, 92, 153-54, 167, 256, 265, 288, 316-17, 339, 341-43, 352, 356-59, 365, 381-83, 562
Steele, Mrs. J. B., 397
Steele Site, 71-72
Stevens, Mrs. J. T., 583
Stevens, W. G., 278
Stewart, Dr. Harry, 357
Stewart, W. H., 73, 80, 130
Stewart Property, 79-81

Stokes, Dr. J. R., 395
Stokes, J. W., 90, 123
Stokes, Dr. Ruth, 497, 525, 535
Strachan, Grace, 264
Strait, W. F., 73
Stribling, Frances, 336
Strozier, Ben, 584
Stuckey, Mrs. George, 388-89, 399
Stuckey, H. P., 160
Suritz, A. R., 552
Swaffield, W. C., 21
Swearingen, Supt. John, brief description, 175; 183-85; improves academic standards, 207-08 and 211-13; 222, 227-28, 230; correspondence with Johnson, 236-40; 249, 252, 257; monitors extension work and academic standards, 260; 265, 271-73, 281, 305; correspondence with Tillman, 306-08; 310, 321-22, 325-26, 328, 340; Johnson omits, 344; 346-47, 350, 353, 374-76
Swearingen, Mary, 436-37
Swett, John, 165

Taft, Pres. W. H., 168, 209, 214, 231, 301, 304, 330, 370
Talmadge, Gov. Gene, 584
Tate, W. K., 184-86, 207, 229, 245
Taylor, Harriet, 279
Teacher's Institutes, 4-7, 127. See also Normal Education.
Tennessee, University of, 3, 19, 133-34, 415. See also East Tennessee University.
Terry, Ellen, 418
Texas Woman's College, 295, 489
Texas, University of, 200, 569
Thomas, J. P., Jr., 21, 67, 69-70, 77
Thomas, Roy, 311, 324, 364
Thomason, John, 324, 364, 438-39
Thomasson, Leona, 333, 336
Thompson, Dean, 414
Thompson, Hugh, 4-6
Thompson-Decker Construction Co., 79
Thomson, J. W., 311, 323, 385, 438
Three C's Railroad, 94-95
Threlkeld, Zula, 571
Thurmond, J. William, 227, 386
Thurmond, Sen. Strom, 479-80, 519, 536
Tien, L. H., 401
Tilghman, Mrs. H. L., 496, 557-58
Tillman, Addie, 111
Tillman, Benjamin Ryan, 3, 8-12, 15-17; "Gives a Big Push," 34-41; 56, 58, 60-64; State articles on, 65; works to find Winthrop site, 67-68; 71, 73; aids WC in Legislature, 78-79; 80-82; cornerstone speaker, 83-86; last official act as governor, 87; on Executive Committee, 87; faculty prospects,

90; 1895 campaign, 92-93; 94-95; WC Rock Hill opening, 97-100; 111, 117-19; works to curb "lynch law," 119; 120-23; among few paying full WC fees, 125; 130-31, 134, 136-38; relationship with Joynes, 140; 141-42, 146, 149, 154-55, 157-58, 161-62, 167-70; force behind Johnson, 172-73; 175-76, 183-86; daughter, 187; 191-92; on Carnegie, 193; 197, 202-04, 207; on industrial education, 208; 209-11, 214-15, 218-22; tribute to, 223; 226-27, 230-31; arranges senior trip to Wilson inauguration, 231; 236, 238, 240-42; corrects Johnson's English, 243; 247-49; evaluates Johnson, 250-51; 252, 257-58; helps Johnson gain NEA presidency, 262-64; 265, 270-72, 276-77; declining health, 280; 281, 296-97, 299; Joynes' value to, 300; 302, 305-08, 311-12; death, 313-14; 315-16, 320, 325, 344, 347, 353, 359-60; Daniels' tribute to, 361-62; 369, 379, 398; Johnson mentions Tillman's Winthrop role, 403; 434, 486; Tillman Memorial Commission gift, 489; 522
Tillman, Mrs. B. R., 168, 203-04, 208, 227, 264, 307
Tillman, B. R., Jr., 264, 312
Tillman, G. D., 117
Tillman, Henry, 227, 269
Tillman, Lona, 111
Tillman, Mary, 473
Tillman, Sallie May, 187, 203-04, 210, 264
Tolbert, Marguerite, 565, 571, 582
Tomato Clubs, 159, 181, 194, 234, 347
Tompkins, D. A., 80
Tompkins, Stonewall, 76
Toole, Rep., 369
Traubel, Helen, 518
Treadwell, Nina, 77
Trinity College, 40, 348
True, Dr. A. C., 303
Tschudi, E. Q., 385
Tsuda, Miss, English School for Girls, 340
Tulane University, 175
Tyner, B. Y., 414

Union Theological Seminary, 333
United Confederate Veterans, 380, 393
United Daughters of the Confederacy, 159-60, 162, 255, 259, 296, 311, 411-13
United States Air Corps, 329
United States Naval Academy, 330
Urquhart, J. B., 481

Vanderbilt University, 3, 121, 330, 368, 460, 471, 492
Vassar College, 232, 340, 382, 464
Vaughn, Hascal, 349
Venable, Dr. Austin, 557-62, 564

Verner, Charlie, 517
Vest, Eliza, 2
Villard, O. G., 259
Virginia, University of, 2, 76, 348, 366, 368, 407
Virginia Ladies College, 94
Vocational Education. See Industrial Education.

Waddill, Rosell, 92, 97
Walker, Dora, 327
Walmsley, Dr. James, 297-98, 311, 321, 324, 340, 348
Ward, Robert, 521
Wardlaw, Patterson, 322, 404
Ware, W. F. and Arthur, 258
Washington College, 3, 5
Waters, R. B., 521, 566, 569
Watkins, Mr., 580
Weatherford, Dr. W. D., 258, 265, 297
Weeks, C. R., 233, 271
Wellesley College, 232
Welsh, R. H., 228, 321
Weston, Sen. Francis, 228
Wetherbee, Beth, 324
Wetmore, Samuel, 30
White, A. B., 72
White, Dr. Coodrich, 492
White, Pauline, 336
White, William, 72
Whitfield, Pres. H. L., 175
Whittemore, Margaret, 182
Wicker, Lee (Mrs. James P. Kinard), 90, 406, 448, 459-60
Wickliffe, Mary, 182, 216, 349
Willard-Boggs, 254
William and Mary, College of, 2, 76, 221, 372, 381
Williams, Gov. Ransome, 521-22
Williams, Ruth, 568
Willoughby, Isla, 334
Wilson, Mrs., 308
Wilson, James, 205
Wilson, Dr. Joseph, 21
Wilson Stanyarne, 170
Wilson, S. W., 91
Wilson, Pres. Woodrow, recalls WC chapel, 21; 206, 224, 231, 271-72, 276-77, 293, 309, 312, 341, 545; scholarships, 583
Wilson, W. Blackburn, Sr. or Jr., 72-73, 163-64, 167-70
Wilson and Wilson, 129
Winthrop, G. L., 169, 200, 309
Winthrop, Robert, meets Johnson, 20; 23-24, 28-29; brief sketch, 30-31; usual gift, 60; 63, 77; honored at Founder's Day, 83; 85; dies, 87; remembered, 98; literary society, 126; 155, 176, 199, 214, 219, 339; birthday no longer Founder's Day, 347; 402
Winthrop, Thomas, 30

WINTHROP COLLEGE:
Winthrop Training School, founded, 20-23; first graduates in demand, 24; benefactors, 31; first Memorial Day fete, 31-33; early years in Columbia, 34-40 and 56-58; 59; rules for Winthrop Normal College, 60; 63; name change, 80; 176, 214, 355, 402. See

also South Carolina Normal and Winthrop Industrial College, Winthrop Normal and Industrial College, and Winthrop College.

South Carolina Industrial and Winthrop Normal College, new name, 56; 58-60; bidding for, 61-62; original trustees, 58; 63; State urges Columbia to keep, 65-67 and 69-71; Rock Hill wins, 70; organization, 74; 1893 diplomas, 76; governor checks Rock Hill bid, 78; name revised, 122-23; 403. See also Winthrop Training School, Winthrop Normal and Industrial College, and Winthrop College.

Winthrop Normal and Industrial College, new name, 80; furnishings, 87; Courier article, 93; Rock Hill opening, 95; 103, 119; "soirée musicale," 121; name affirmed, 122-23; Johnson's 1897 report, 123-27; purpose, 128; motto, 131; Johnson at assembly, 132; kindergarten pioneers, 133; 134; fair exhibit, 138-39; 1900-01 catalog, 139; 1902-03 enrollment, 144-45; praised, 146; diploma format, 148; library methods course, 149; publicity, 152-55; typical opening, 159; 1906 enrollment and fees, 160; public service, 161-62; virtues, 164; graduates in demand, 166; improvements and service, 170-71; in 1909, 172; new girls' treatment, 186-87; 194-95, 209; twenty-fifth anniversary, 213-15; Winthrop Home Institute, 226; compared to Northern colleges, 232; pioneer reading program, 238; course-duplication controversy, 246-49; extension agreement with Clemson, 251-54; WWI student effort, 258-59; Legislature's visit, 259-60; denominational schools' jealousy, 269-70; 1916 opening, 277-79; 294-95; university speculations, 305-06; 309; jealousy over, 311-12; Tillman's influence, 314; Rutledge states Johnson's influence on, 316; demographics, 318; literacy drive, 322; Legislature protects, 332; alumnae impact, 333; publications, 334-35; name changed, 337-38. See also Winthrop Training School, South Carolina Industrial and Winthrop Normal College, and Winthrop College.

Winthrop College, the South Carolina College for Women, named, 337-38; "Johnson College," 338-39; Founder's Day date changed, 347; 22 granddaughters enrolled, 348;

Alma Mater, 349; colors in Olympics, 356-57; "blueprint for a 'great society,'" Kate Wofford as role model, 358-60; pioneers in adult-illiteracy classes, 367-68; diploma's value, 369; "Winthrop-Johnson College," 384-86; two-semester year, 400; uniform, 421-23; contribution to state, 461; Phelps' wanted list, 467-73; original building moved, 480; Senior Order attacked, 485; dancing controversy, 485-86; Flying Group incorrectly cited in co-education fight, 486-87; segregation, 487; Phelps informed of accreditation probation, 493; 1949 Blue Line, 498; rejuvenated spirit under Sims, 524; in 1946, 525-26; known in Baghdad, 539; turning in better direction, 546; incorporated, 552; co-education defeated, 570-71; entrance exams, 572; See also Winthrop Training School, South Carolina Industrial and Winthrop Normal College, and Winthrop Normal and Industrial College.

Abroad, Alumnae, Programs, and Faculty Working, 270, 278, 295, 333, 336, 344, 348-50, 364, 368, 370-71, 380, 420, 434, 436, 447-49, 465, 473, 481, 538-39, 544

Accreditation, 307, 348, 368-69, 379, 454-59, 463, 466, 478, 489-92; Winthrop "on probation," Phelps informed, 493; 494-95, 497, 499-500; Sims tackles probation problem, 503-09; 512, 519, 521; problem analyzed, 524; 525, 535; cause of blacklisting, 536; 545-52; alumnae interference, 555; 1953 status report, 555-56; 557, 559-70; Himstead explains censure, 562; Peabody Report explains censure, 567; AAUP censure lifted, 572; 585, 587

Admissions, 89, 94, 130, 134, 145, 150, 158, 174, 195, 212-13, 237, 260, 265, 267, 269, 271, 277, 287-91, 305-08, 314, 357; baby applications, 359; costs, 359; 373, 375, 379-81, 453, 456-57, 471-72, 500, 533, 545

Alma Mater, 349, 394

Alumnae, 1, 27; first completing two-year course, 82; 214, 219, 225, 242-43, 282, 291, 294, 297, 310-11, 316, 318, 320, 325, 333, 337, 343-45, 365, 379-80, 396-97, 398, 401, 404, 410-11, 434-37, 446-49, 459, 473-74, 476-79, 481-82, 489, 496, 510, 518, 523, 526-28, 536-38, 541, 544; praised, 545; 548-50; rift with Association Board, 552-55; 559-60, 569-72, 583; ask Sims to postpone retire-

ment, 583-84

Alumnae Association (Winthrop Daughters), 77, 83, 126, 135, 144, 161, 191-92, 280, 282, 285, 290-94; formalized, 317; secretary, 333; 335-36, 338-39, 343-45, 350-55, 404, 430-31, 434-37, 476, 481, 491, 498, 520, 524, 552; Board rift with alumnae, 552-55; 556, 559-60, 562, 570-71, 573, 578, 579

Alumnae News, 434-37, 447, 473-74, 476-77

Athletics, 6, 21-22, 95, 103, 111, 126, 129, 159, 254, 256, 260, 296, 298, 338-40; Olympics, 356-57; 376, 387. See also WC Gymnasium.

Auditorium (eventually Johnson Memorial erected, later named Byrnes), 1, 48, 177, 192, 195, 214, 224-26, 235, 256, 296, 327-28, 395

Board of Trustees, 1, 22, 25-26, 28, 36, 53, 56-58, 60-62, 67-69, 71-73, 77-80, 82-83, 87-93, 96, 103, 122-24, 127-30, 134, 136-38, 144-45, 148, 154, 156, 158-64, 166-67, 170-71, 203, 207, 214, 219-20, 230, 240, 246-47, 252, 265-69, 271-72, 274, 280-82, 284-86, 299-300, 308, 313-14, 325, 328, 351-55, 566-70, 372, 380, 384, 387-89, 391-93, 395, 399, 401, 403, 419-20, 424, 432-34, 438-40, 444-45, 449-51, 453, 460-61, 463, 475-76, 479-80, 483-87, 489-91, 493; role in accredidation loss, 494; 496-500, 502, 504-07; Sims address to, 509-16; "inappropriate" interference of, 512; 517-25, 535; cause of accredidation blacklisting, 536; 544-46, 550, 552, 555-70, 572, 575, 578-89

Budget, 80, 82, 118, 123, 126-27, 140, 240, 251, 257-58, 266-67, 271-72, 282, 285-87; President and Treasurer Johnson, 309-10; 312; 315, 318-19, 320, 328-29, 343, 347-48, 350, 355, 363-64, 369-72, 379-81, 384, 387, 393, 407-08, 413-15, 419-20, 437-40, 452, 454-59, 474-75, 481-82, 486-88, 493, 495, 498-500, 513, 518-22, 527, 534, 537, 541, 546, 549, 556-57, 570, 585-86

Bulletins, 234, 245, 256, 322-23, 501

Co-education, Flying Group incorrectly cited as Winthrop students, 486-87; 570, 575

Curriculum, in 1895, 104-10; in 1897, 125; 128, 130, 139, 141; exhibits, 143; 146-48, 158-59, 194-95, 207-14, 216, 223-24; Swearingen comments on, 249; librarianship program, 256-57; 260, 271-72, 299, 306-08, 317, 320; "honorary scholars," 322; 338, 341-43, 387, 415, 420-21; Depression influenced, 440-44; 468-69, 474-75, 488, 498-99, 518, 526; Sims implements

entrance exams, 569; 587-88
Dining Halls, 126, 215, 225-
26, 235, 255, 296; typical
fare, 335; 341, 343, 368,
371, 378, 400, 455, 459,
475, 521, 569, 571
Discipline, proposed student
duties, 47; possibility of
rumors, 96; Johnson's rules,
111-17; 123, 126, 145-46;
graduates protest, 202; 203-
04, 257, 278-79, 490-91
Dormitories, 82, 89, 95-96,
124, 129, 131-32, 134-39,
141, 143, 146, 156, 161-62,
164, 170, 225, 235-36, 265-
69, 277; angling for, 280-
95; 299, 314, 318-19, 329,
337, 341, 344-45, 353, 363,
368, 373, 375, 378, 396-98,
448, 455, 466-67, 469-70,
478, 484, 486-88; male cadets in Bancroft; 493; 498,
527, 547, 588
Extension Work, 173, 178-83,
187-88, 190, 205-09, 212-13,
216-17, 220-23, 232-35, 244-
46, 252-57, 260-62, 271,
274-77, 294-96, 298, 302-04,
310-11, 314, 317; Extension
Bulletin, 322-23; 324-27,
333-36, 342, 344; radio station advised, 355-56; 358,
365-66, 368, 371, 377-78,
390, 424-26; Service--Coun-
ties and Agents, 427-30;
477-78, 531-34; Clemson
threatens to duplicate, 545;
Sims fights Extension Service's "illegal" removal to
Clemson, 572-81
Faculty, 1; proposed ratio to
students, 47; 57; changes,
60; defined, 88; 110, 114-
16, 123, 126, 130; death
rumors, 145; 147-48, 177,
183; publications, 188; 199,
203, 214; hiring, 218-19;
235, 239-43; Johnson on,
242-43; Dr. Kinard resigns,
243-44; 271, 298, 307, 310-
11, 315, 317, 319, 322-29,
334, 338, 341; involuntary
"gifts" to Johnson, 345;
347-48, 357-59; 1924 summer
activities, 364; 367-68;
student-faculty ratio, 376;
384-86, 404, 438-39, 444,
450, 456, 466, 468-70, 474-
75, 482; Board prohibits
foreign teachers, 486; 491-
92, 494, 499-500, 510-11,
517-18; salaries up, 521;
522-34, 536; Sims' address
to, 537-43; 544, 549-52,
555, 557-58, 562-70, 572,
573, 582-83, 585, 587-88
Farm, 79, 81, 96, 111, 123,
129, 225-26, 235, 256, 260,
272, 298-99, 315, 319, 329,
335, 337, 343, 359, 379,
417, 455, 479, 489, 569, 588
Founder's Day 28, 36, 136,
347, 360, 372, 404-05, 485
Graduate Program, 145, 246-
48, 314, 327, 348, 414-15,
456-57, 472-73, 572, 576
Gymnasium of 1916, 79, 177,

218, 235-36, 254-55, 280,
295-96, 298, 341. See also
Athletics.
Health. See Infirmary.
Holidays, 113, 119, 145-47,
151, 153-54, 157, 159, 203-
04, 306, 322, 399, 135-36
Home Economics Building (later
Thurmond Hall), 479-82, 486,
490, 527
Infirmary, 81; measles, 119;
lady physician, 123; 125-26;
smallpox threat, 129-30;
142-43, 166, 170, 177, 192,
195, 224-25, 256, 317, 322,
341-42, 364, 383, 420, 475,
520, 527, 547
Johnson Hall (YWCA and student
building) 339-41, 348, 381,
446, 455, 489, 548
Johnsonian, 379, 519, 527, 561
Joynes (Edward S. Memorial)
Hall, 190, 235, 260, 300,
319, 329, 383, 437, 482
Library, 60, 79, 96, 114; government depository, 123;
126, 130, 140, 143; book
guidelines, 147. Carnegie
Library, Building Committee,
149; funding, 155; dedicated,
157-58; 168-69, 215, 235,
256-57, 260, 300, 315, 323,
341, 363, 370, 377-78, 400,
419-20, 455, 459, 465, 517,
522, 527, 572
Model (or Practice) School,
136-38, 142, 144-45, 149,
154-57, 160, 162-64, 168-70,
185, 194. See also Winthrop
(Practice) and Training
School.
Organ, 192, 217, 225, 568, 570
Physical Plant, proposed cost,
47-48; water source, 82; progress, 94-95; laid out, 123;
129-32, 135, 139; praised,
146; 160-61, 164; unsuccessful addition, 166; 177, 195-
97, 199, 202, 218, 224-26,
235-36, 256-58, 267, 282,
285-86, 314-15, 319-20, 328,
337, 341-43; 1920 value, 344;
359, 363, 382, 403-05, 459,
467-68, 473, 518, 521-23,
526, 540, 547, 572, 588
President's Home, 79-80, 88-
89, 149, 154, 325, 395, 401,
513, 516, 585-86
Relocating Campus, 50-52, 58-
59, 61-62, 67-69, 71-73, 77-
78
Scholarships, established, 26;
typical recipient, 26-27;
move to abolish, 36; work
for proposal, 47; 53; put into law, 57-58; important for
growth, 63-64; advertised,
76-77; 89, 122, 125, 128,
130, 151-52; awarded to maim-
ed student, 159; 160, 168,
193, 195, 216-17, 226, 237-
38, 251, 255, 267; criticism,
269-70; 271-74, 286, 325,
329, 341-42, 373, 386, 400,
408-14, 420, 423-24, 450-51,
453-54, 459, 471-72, 475,
479, 487, 534, 544, 583
Senior Order, 485, 488

Special Programs, 1, 95, 97,
111, 113, 116, 126, 136, 145,
152-53, 157, 162, 166, 178-83,
187, 199-200, 202, 209, 213-
15, 224-26, 231-32, 256-57,
261-62, 270-71, 277-79, 295-
96, 323-25, 332-33, 348-49,
358-59, 364-67, 372, 383, 387,
390, 401, 444, 461, 463-65,
470-71, 474, 476, 482-83, 495-
96, 518-19, 520-24, 527-28,
530-31, 534-36, 545, 555, 583,
586
Student Body, 123-25, 129, 139;
1910 demographics, 188-90;
199, 208; trip, 209; 211, 223-
25; at Pres. Wilson's inauguration, 231-32; 236, 240, 255-
57; war efforts, 258-59; 260,
264-65, 267, 269; favors minimum-wage law, 271; 277-79,
289, 295; fatter freshmen,
299; 301, 305-06; ill Tillman
counts on, 312; 314, 316-18;
war efforts, 321; 322, 327-28,
334, 337, 341-45, 348-49, 359,
363-64; insurence benefiting
Winthrop, 367; 368, 370-71,
376; demographics, 381,390,
and 391; 394, 398, 404, 407,
416-17, 419-20, 444; example
to, 460; 466, 468-69, 482;
first dance, 485-86; unrest,
491; 498; dedicates Tatler to
Sims, 503; 507-08, 510, 516-
21, 523, 526-27, 536, 539,
541; smaller but better, 545
and 546; 548; religious activities of, 548-49; 552, 555;
accreditation misinformation
spread among, 561; 571; high
test scores, 571; 573, 583, 588
Student Government, 145, 209,
224, 295, 342, 376, 417, 431,
488, 526, 561
Summer School, 127, 131, 133,
144, 146, 158, 178, 181-82,
208, 237-39, 249, 290, 295,
318, 327, 330-31, 334, 340-
42, 344, 348, 358-59, 363-64,
366; resolutions, 376-79; 381,
383-84, 407, 414-15, 448, 465,
472, 475, 513, 529, 534
Tatler, 143, 503
Tillman Hall (Old Main), 1, 79,
82-86, 94-96, 110-11, 139,
149, 156-57, 290, 298, 341,
344, 376, 396-97, 570, 588
Tillman Science Hall (Old Till-
man--later razed) 177, 213,
215-16, 224, 246, 363, 544
Uniform, 47, 86, 93, 110-11,
113, 115, 134, 139, 164, 208-
09, 255-56, 342, 360, 371,
421-23, 438, 454-55, 457-58,
500-02
Weekly News, 255, 270, 295, 323,
325, 334, 336-37, 348, 354,
360, 365, 367-68
Winthrop (Practice and) Training School--WTS 110, 163-65,
167-70, 201, 206, 211-12, 214-
16, 224-25, 235, 239, 246,
249, 256, 271, 311, 314-15,
318-19, 322, 324, 330-32; WTS,
337; 341, 344, 346, 348, 358,
362, 364, 376, 392, 407, 444,
482-83, 487, 498-99, 544, 575,

586. See also Model (or Practice) School.

Young Woman's Christian Association, 123, 126, 162, 206, 209, 235, 256, 258, 260, 265-66, 276-77, 279-80, 297, 300-02, 304-05, 308, 312, 318-19, 321, 329, 337; named Johnson Hall, 339; 342-45, 370-71, 374, 390, 392, 488, 519, 527, 533

"Winthrop Day By Day," 332, 334

"Winthrop's the Pride of my Heart," 349

"Winthrop You Are Fine," 349

Wise, Rabbi Stephen, 393

Withers, Sara, 144, 180, 182, 270

Witsell, Rachel, 409

Wofford, Kate, 312, 359-60, 430-34

Wofford, Tom, 558, 560, 564

Wofford College, 6, 76, 371, 505, 517

Wolfe, Ada, 91

Women's Liberation, "rubbing the bloom off the peach," 86; "bloomers and bicyclists," 98; 135, 145-46, 159, 161, 190, 192, 259, 266-69, 282-85, 290-91, 332, 334, 345, 348; premarital exams for men, 358; 362, 365, 518

Women's Olympic Meet, 356-57

Woodrow, Marion, 28, 33, 60, 91

Woodward, F. C., 27, 50

Workman, Brown, 93

Workman, Mrs. Paul, 394

Workman, W. D., 546, 585

Workman, Mrs. W. D., Jr., 559-60, 562

World War I, 258-60, 270, 272, 293, 295, 304-05, 308-09, 313-14, 316-18, 320-21, 326-27, 329, 334, 338, 361, 374

World War II, 484-89, 491, 493, 495, 518-19, 533

Worley, Gordon, 364, 385

Wylie, R. E., 391-92, 399

Wylie, Dr. W. G., 309, 409

Wylie, W. H., 73

Wymojo Mill, 166, 181, 205

Wysor, Nettie, 324

Yale University, 232, 334, 357, 401

Yeargin, Mary, 40-55, 403

Young, Ella, 264

Young, MacBeth, 228

EPILOGUE

The editor surprised me today by requesting an epilogue to this history. Of the several books and hundred-odd articles I have published, this is the first to incorporate personal reminisces. Perhaps such an ending will explain how The Winthrop Story came about.

Mrs. Crowson and I came to Winthrop College early during its "Fabulous Fifties." I retired over thirty years later. Compared to the nation's capital, from whence I had come, everything and everyone on campus from the janitor to the president seemed unhurried, friendly, and helpful. Each uniformly blue and white class proved to be populated by a diverse mix of up-country, sand-hill, and low-country ladies. Their charm, talent, and purpose struck me early on. Our accents were different but our desires were the same--to teach, to learn, to enjoy the educational process. Classes met six days a week. Everyone went to town on Saturday afternoons, and Sundays saw a great influx of faculty and students into the local churches. Life was full.

Our children practically grew up on campus. They knew the buildings, grounds, and personnel. Tommy enjoyed keeping tabs on the watchmen and spent every Faculty Family Night in the swimming pool. Susan accompanied me to the archives almost daily for her chats with Miss Iva Bishop and for the fun of helping me research. Richard enjoyed ice cream in Old Main's canteen and began summer class at age fourteen. All three would stroll across campus on registration afternoons "just in case" an incoming freshman needed help. I remember Susan proudly reporting that she had guided a lost "rat" from the library to the greenhouse in time for an appointment. All three delighted in overhearing a student talk about their father, especially if the student indicated he was a demanding professor.

By 1959 I was happily submerged in teaching, writing, and public-service work. South Carolina history, colonial American research, Latin American studies, and American government took up my time. One day President Henry Sims called me in for a chat. Talk turned serious. Before leaving, I agreed to prepare a Winthrop College history by the 1986 centennial. Dr. Sims stipulated one point: that the work be straightforward with no Winthrop warts or beauty spots hidden. Towards that end he eventually gathered boxes of documents from his personal papers, to Board transcripts, to Archibald Rutledge's Johnson report (which he explained Mrs. Johnson had tried to suppress). Sims believed that Winthrop was a triumph of South Carolina's citizens, citizens who so strongly cared about their daughters' welfare that they sacrificed endlessly. He indicated that although some self-serving men had tried to use the college for their own political or economic gain, most connected with Winthrop had repeatedly given themselves to improve woman's lot. I came to understand Sims through research. Winthrop had indeed liberated women from ignorance and dependence.

Dr. Sims retired and later died childless. My research began. It lasted twenty-five years. I haunted various archives, libraries, and newspapers. There was more, always more information. I learned Winthrop's history could not be separated from the economics, politics, demographics, and presidencies of each year. Her progress hinged on the ethics and morals of her leaders. This book incorporates such aspects.

The Winthrop Story ends in 1960. Records are not yet available to make an objective assessment of the college since then. Pop historians may seize on fun facts to illustrate the sixties and thereafter, but that method is not for me. I only regret that space does not allow us to include this book's hundred-and-twenty-odd pages of footnotes.

Winthrop College has meant much to me, especially my seven-thousand students, who still invite their old professor to join them at reunions. They are my joy. They are part of that better life Winthrop has built for future generations. It is my hope that you, the reader, will share some of the joy and concern I felt in compiling this compelling story.

E. Thomas Crowson